WITHDRAWAL

The Consumer Protection Manual

The Consumer Protection Manual

Andrew Eiler

Facts On File Publications
New York, New York ● Bicester, England

The Consumer Protection Manual
Edited by Valerie Pitt

Library of Congress Cataloging in Publication Data

Eiler, Andrew.
  Consumer protection manual.

  Includes index.
  1. Consumer protection—United States—
Handbooks, manuals, etc.   I. Title.
HC110.C63E38   381′.34′0973   82-1464
ISBN 0-87196-310-8   AACR2

Printed in the United States of America

10 9 8 7 6 5 4 3

To my mother,
who always loved books

Acknowledgments

This book is a product of my years of experience as a consumer advocate in Michigan. When I first joined the newly established Michigan Consumers Council as its only staff member, my first project was to prepare a summary of Michigan consumer protection laws in order to inform consumers of the protection they were entitled to and how to avail themselves of it. It was then that I first learned about laws affecting consumers. My subsequent experience, however, as a legislative advocate made it clear that none of the laws that were meant to help consumers would do them much good unless they had practical information about putting those laws to use. I have tried to include such information in this book.

To the extent I have succeeded, I owe much to many who have aided me along the way; I can never thank them as fully as they deserve.

First and foremost, I could not have succeeded at all without the love, understanding, and assistance of my wife, Trudy Lieberman, who was, throughout the time it took to complete the book, my constant and most helpful critic. She was my full partner in this effort, and with selfless dedication helped shape my drafts into a presentable manuscript. Her own experience and expertise as a consumer reporter and writer on economics added an extra measure of substantive knowledge to the editorial skills she used on the manuscript.

I also could not have done without the skillful editing of the manuscript done by Valerie Pitt. Only those who see the edited manuscript will ever know what she accomplished, yet the words still seem to be mine. It would be impossible for anyone to have done more.

I must also express my very special thanks to Eleanora Schoenebaum, Editorial Director at Facts On File. It was her confidence in me that helped get this project off the ground, and it was her constant encouragement and good humor that kept me going. It is a pleasure to have worked with her.

There are many others who directly contributed their time and knowledge. Among them are the many staff attorneys of the Federal Trade Commission who reviewed the portions of the manuscript that cover the laws their agency enforces, and staff attorneys from the National Consumer Law Center who made numerous helpful suggestions.

I was indeed fortunate to have so many willing to give me so much.

Andrew Eiler
New York City, June 1984

CONTENTS

PREFACE: How to Use this Book

During the four years I was assistant director of the Michigan Consumers Council, we handled countless consumer complaints. One in particular stands out in my mind.

A woman bought a used car from a dealer for $1,600 and was given a warranty. Soon afterward the car broke down and the dealer told her it would need $300 worth of repairs; repairs, he said, which would not be covered by the warranty. The woman came to us for help.

The council first asked the dealer to honor the warranty. He refused. Since the council had no legal power to settle disputes, we could not force the dealer to make the repairs. But then we discovered a solution to the problem. The woman had financed the car with an automobile installment contract which the dealer had sold to a bank. A Michigan law regulating such contracts made it possible for her to hold the bank legally responsible for the dealer's promises. And that meant she could refuse to pay the bank if the dealer didn't make the repairs. The fact that the woman's contract contained a clause saying, in effect, she still had to pay the bank even if the dealer didn't honor the warranty gave us additional leverage—such a clause was illegal under the law.

We drafted a letter for the woman to send to the bank stating that the dealer refused to honor the warranty, that the contract contained an illegal clause, and that she would be entitled to deduct the cost of the repairs from the amount she owed the bank if the repairs weren't made. We told the woman to copy the letter, sign it, and mail it.

A week later the dealer fixed the car.

The woman couldn't believe how just one letter had changed the dealer's attitude. In fact, the letter worked because a specific law applied to the situation. The woman could refuse to pay the bank. The bank, in turn, could put pressure on the car dealer. And the car dealer, in his turn, could not afford to alienate his banker. All we did was help the woman assert her rights under the law.

That is what this book is all about—asserting your rights under consumer protection laws. Over the last fifteen years Congress and state legislatures have passed many such laws; one or more applies to just about every consumer purchase you make. Usually you can enforce these laws on your own, too, without depending on government agencies. Yet few consumers know about these laws, and even fewer know how to use them to settle disputes.

This book aims to change all that. It does four main things.

- It tells you how to plan an effective negotiating strategy and make a convincing case.
- It tells you what you need to know about the legal system to make it work for you.
- It tells you about rights under a specific law (or laws) that could apply to your particular dispute and thus puts the backbone into your strategy.
- And, finally, it provides sample letters that you can adapt to put your strategy into action and settle a dispute.

How, first of all, do you find the laws that actually apply to your case? There are four ways the book helps you to do this.

First, check the table of contents. The sections follow the purchasing sequence. Section III, for instance, covers laws that apply to advertising and sales practices—inducements made *before* you buy. Section IV covers laws that apply to a contract you make *as* you buy. Section V covers warranty and product liability laws that apply when products turn out to be defective *after* you buy. Section VI covers laws that apply to different payment methods, such as checks, electronic fund transfers, debit cards and credit cards.

Chapter headings and sub-headings also specifically identify the topics covered to help you find the requirements that could apply and the negotiating steps you could use as part of your strategy for resolving a dispute.

Sometimes, several laws can apply to one purchase. Say you're considering buying some knives from a mail order company, for instance. First you might consult Chapter 26 which discusses your legal rights when buying through the mail. If the knives turn out to be defective—let's say they don't cut food the way they are supposed to—you might then find the federal Magnuson-Moss Warranty Act applies. If you charged the knives to a credit card account, and want to stop payment, you might find the federal Fair Credit Billing Act also applies. The more laws that apply, the better your negotiating leverage, of course.

The second way to find applicable laws is to use the book's cross references. They refer to possible laws that could apply to a dispute.

The third way is to use the subject index. This lists the kinds of consumer problems that might arise. Say the handles of the knives you purchase crack in your dishwasher, for instance. You would check the index under "defective products"; this listing would refer you to federal and state warranty laws. The subject index also lists specific types of purchases, such as mail orders, for example.

The fourth way to find applicable laws is to consult the laws index: it describes all the laws discussed in this book. A law is identified by its official name, if it has one, such as the Equal Credit Opportunity Act. Otherwise the descriptive name is used: the Door-to-Door Sales Law, for instance.

When you have located the laws that will work for you, use the sample letters to put your strategy into action. Each letter describes the type of dispute covered by a particular law (or laws), and notes the pressure points the law provides for settling the dispute. Each letter shows the important details to include, such as names, dates, account numbers, and so on. Of course, you must supply the correct details for your particular situation. But be careful not to change the parts that refer to your rights under the law. Copy these exactly.

On pages 639–645 there is a directory of major federal and state agencies that enforce the laws described in this book. There are also appendices that show how you can obtain the legal name of a local business you may want to sue, and the names, addresses, and titles of officers in corporations you want to contact.

This book is *not* designed to turn you into a lawyer or enable you to argue fine points of law. Instead, it is designed to help you understand the basic rules that apply to consumer transactions. By following these basic rules, you can take initial and vital steps to protect and use your rights under the law.

Knowing the basics should also help you identify when it is time to consult an attorney. And if you do need a lawyer, he or she will be in a better position to help you if you have already assembled the important documents and facts needed to build a strong case, and followed the steps that protect your rights. Remember, it is tough for someone to help you unless you are ready to help yourself, and the toughest thing of all is to try to *undo* mistakes that you could have avoided.

It is important to keep in mind that there are two ways you can protect yourself from abuses in consumer transactions.

One way is by arranging purchase terms and conditions in advance. This helps you hold a seller legally accountable for his service or product, and gives you a concrete legal base on which to seek redress if the terms and conditions are not satisfied. This book shows you how to give yourself fuller protection than the seller might want to provide and shows you how to arrange such transactions.

The other way you can use your rights is retrospectively. You do this by holding the seller accountable according to the terms and conditions of your contract and according to additional rights and remedies you could have under laws that apply to the purchase. Your main bargaining leverage at this point is what you can make the seller pay and/or what you could be entitled to avoid having to pay because he has failed to live up to the contract or failed to comply with a law that applies. Using this leverage almost always involves a legal dispute.

This book describes rights you could have under key federal laws and fairly uniform state laws that apply to consumer transactions. There are, however, some points to bear in mind when using the negotiating strategies included in this book.

Generally, the book describes rights you could have as of mid-1983. Although the particular laws involved are unlikely to change drastically, it could happen. While the book does not discuss many of the fine points that could apply to particular situations, it does cover key rules as they have been interpreted by courts in order to point out the strongest arguments you could bring to bear.

Since laws change, however, courts and lawyers often differ about what a law really means, and your particular situation can be affected by how the law is interpreted in your specific dispute. This book is not, therefore, meant to provide personalized legal advice.

Whenever you are involved in a dispute in which more is at stake than you can afford to lose—or it is clear you would be getting in over your head by pursuing a dispute on your own—promptly seek legal advice before taking any key steps to assert rights you could have, and especially before taking any measures which could provide your adversary with an opportunity to sue you. The negotiating strategies in this book identify the principal steps you can take and what may happen if you take them. This enables you to plan ahead, recognize the risks involved, and utilize any necessary legal assistance effectively.

If a dispute does not involve enough money to make it worth seeking legal advice, your practical options are to assert any rights and remedies you may be entitled to on your own, or give in to the seller and take your losses. If doing nothing means you would be out money you could otherwise recoup by using leverage available to you, you might just as well assert your rights. And you may just as well assert your rights as forcefully as a lawyer might assert them for you.

My hope is that this book will save you time, trouble, and expense by helping you protect yourself more effectively when you buy goods, and by helping you deal more effectively with problems if they should arise.

SECTION I
EFFECTIVE NEGOTIATING: COMBINING LEGAL AND PSYCHOLOGICAL WEAPONS

1 · The Wrong Way: How to Make an Unconvincing Case

A survey that Louis Harris and Associates made in 1976 for the Sentry Insurance Company found that sixty-five percent of the public believed it was very difficult for consumers to correct problems they had with purchases. The survey also found that sixty percent of consumers were worried because they felt it was worthless to complain about problems and believed companies would not handle their complaints properly. Even larger numbers of consumers were worried about the poor quality of products (81%), the failure of companies to live up to advertising claims (76%), the poor quality of post-sales service (69%), manufacturers not caring about consumers (69%), too many products breaking down (64%), and misleading packaging or labeling (63%).

When I was on the staff of the then newly formed Michigan Consumers Council, we received thousands of complaints about purchases from consumers who had tried unsuccessfully to resolve them. We helped about seventy to eighty percent of those who contacted us even though the Council had no enforcement powers to make a business settle a problem.

Most of the complaints we received could have been just as successfully handled by the consumers themselves if they had been more knowledgeable about asserting their rights. This does not, of course, mean that consumers would have succeeded instantly—success sometimes requires a lot of effort and patience. Nor does it mean consumers can successfully settle every problem on their own. But consumers have a lot more going for them when it comes to successfully resolving consumer problems than the poor chances indicated by the Harris survey.

Why do consumers fail so often? The reasons are usually very simple. They don't organize what they say effectively. And they don't bring the right legal pressure to bear. The messages consumers use are often counterproductive because they either pressure the other side the wrong way, or—unintentionally—they reveal an important weakness in their own position. Thus, a business is likely to know right away that it can safely ignore whatever pressure the consumer tries to apply.

There are four main kinds of ineffective messages many consumers send:

1. The panic letter (or the strike-out-at-everything approach).
2. The pleading letter (or the please-be-nice-and-take-care-of-my-problem approach).
3. The mayday letter (or the somebody-out-there-help-me approach).
4. The ESP letter (or the you-must-know-what-I-am-talking-about approach).

Here's how these messages read and why they won't work for you.

THE PANIC LETTER
(or the strike-out-at-everything approach)

This is the worst kind of letter anyone could send. It has also been described as the "crackpot" or "crank" letter, but it is really the product of panic. You may laugh when you read it, and not believe anyone could write it. Unfortunately, I have read more letters like this than I'd care to name.

The panic letter usually goes something like this:

28 Roseview Lane
Anytown, USA 00000

March 27, 19___

President
Honesty Department Stores
Grandplace Mall
Anytown, USA 00000

Sir:

You people must want to lose customers because you got too many of them. I've noticed how your store is getting more and more crowded, and the service is getting LOUSIER AND LOUSIER. It's getting practically impossible to get anybody to wait on you in your lousy store. And the clerks are so RUDE and act like they are doing you a FAVOR just taking your money. I guess you don't care any more about faithful customers, since people don't count for you any more, JUST MONEY!! You used to have good merchandise. That's why our family has been shopping in your store for twenty years. But now the merchandise has been getting CRUMMIER AND CRUMMIER, so I should have known better than to keep coming back to you.

That's what happens to customers when they buy the JUNK you got in your store. I bought this dress in December for $169.95 so that I would have something new to wear for a New Year's Eve party. You almost loused that up because it didn't get delivered until December 30. I had to call your store THREE TIMES even though your clerk promised delivery in five days. Some delivery service you got.

But that's not the worst part. When I got the dress cleaned after wearing it just ONE TIME, the colors ran. If you think I am going to pay $169.95 for rags, you had better THINK AGAIN. I charged the dress to your Easy Budget Account we had for years. If you think you are going to collect this money, JUST TRY ME. And that's another thing—the twenty-four percent interest you're charging is a crime. Naturally, I took this junk back to your customer service department in January. I had to wait an hour before somebody finally had the time to look at the dress. But that's not surprising. There were a lot of other people in the same boat. I had to talk to three people before somebody finally promised that everything would be taken care of. That's when I left those rags with the person at the customer service desk.

But I should have known better than to trust you people after the way you treat your customers. I got my February charge account bill and you were still charging me for the crummy dress. Of course I didn't pay for it—WHY SHOULD I? Your customer service people told me I should get a credit for returning it. So I called your credit people and they told me it would be taken care of—credit slips are sometimes lost, but they would track it down. So I believed them again. Now I got my March bill and I am still being charged for that lousy dress. And on top of that, you're charging me outrageous finance charges for something I don't even owe. And now your credit people are telling me they can't find the credit slip. That doesn't surprise me in view of the slipshod operation you people are running down there. But you're crazy if you people think I am going to pay for that crummy dress just because you can't keep your books straight. The people at the service desk never gave me a credit slip like they claim now. THEY WERE TOO BUSY. And even if they handed me some crummy piece of paper, they didn't tell me to keep it. Why should I? They promised everything would be taken care of. That's what I get for believing people like you.

And believe me, after this rotten experience with your store, I am TELLING ALL MY FRIENDS TO STAY AWAY from your CLIP JOINT. Wouldn't you?

ENOUGH IS ENOUGH, SO THIS HAD BETTER BE TAKEN CARE OF RIGHT AWAY, OR ELSE!!!!! Just remember, there are LAWS to take care of people like you!!!!!!!

Disgustedly yours,

/s/ E. Z. Mark

This letter violates every rule. It is disorganized and practically endless and therefore guaranteed to try the patience of someone who may be trying to help. It is insulting; it harps on trivial issues that have nothing to do with the real dispute; and it omits details that might help resolve it, such as when the dress was returned and the name of the person who took it back.

E. Z. Mark doesn't clearly say what she wants the store to do. Instead, she makes vague and impractical threats which show she doesn't really know how she could effectively back up her demands or what kind of leverage she could use if the store refused to help her. The letter is cluttered with punctuation and capitalization that is meant to strengthen her words and so convince the other side she means business, but which, in fact, merely reveal her doubts about her ability to convince the store with the facts she has.

A letter like this is certain to be ignored no matter who gets it. A reasonable business is likely to think: If we are really as bad as you say, why are you our customer? And if you are going to be as nasty as this, who needs you as a customer?

Someone at a "ripoff" business won't even finish reading the letter before he thinks: Even if we are as bad as you say we are, you are the one dumb enough to get into this mess. Everything in the panic letter tells him E. Z. Mark doesn't know how she can back up her demands. It's easy to ignore her.

A panic letter like this is obviously self-defeating. Why then do consumers send them? Not because they are stupid, but because they panic and don't know where to turn.

But why should E. Z. Mark have panicked?

The store wants her to pay for a defective dress that she doesn't even have any more. She returned it, and the store took it back. But neither the store nor E. Z. Mark have any record of the return. She has no record that her account should be credited for the purchase price. The store wants proof she is entitled to the credit. She doesn't know where to get this proof or what her legal rights are. She has already tried everything she can think of to convince the store it has made a mistake. She suddenly feels powerless and is afraid she must pay for an expensive dress she doesn't own. So she strikes out at everything and everyone hoping that one of her strikes will hit home.

Panic will never help you settle a dispute: If you are at a loss about what to do next, thinking through the problem is the only thing that will help. This way you may be able to come up with needed proof to back up your claim and find out what law you can use to assert your rights.

For instance, in the case of E. Z. Mark, since the dress was ruined when it was cleaned, the cleaner must know about it, and might be willing to back up her claim that the dress was, indeed, ruined. And the store itself didn't just throw the ruined dress into the trash can. It probably returned it to its supplier for a credit, so it must have some other record that the dress was really returned.

The important point is that instead of panicking, E. Z. Mark would have been better off thinking of ways to make her case convincing.

THE PLEADING LETTER
(or the please-be-nice-and-take-care-of-my-problem approach)

While it is ineffective, the pleading message does avoid the deadly sins of the panic letter. It gets to the point; describes the problem; provides the relevant facts; and is well organized. It demands that the business take some specific action to solve the problem. And it seems to back up the demand with some real leverage.

> *200 Pleasant View Road*
> *Anytown, USA 00000*
>
> *March 27, 19___*

> *Ms. I. C. Golden*
> *Credit Manager*
> *Honesty Department Stores*
> *Grandplace Mall*
> *Anytown, USA 00000*

> *Dear Ms. Golden:*
>
> *A credit for $169.95 that is due me has still not been applied to my Easy Budget Charge Account (000-0000-000) as of the billing period ending March 15, 19___.*
>
> *The amount is for a dress I purchased and charged to my account on December 8, 19___. However, the dress was badly damaged when it was cleaned for the first time on January 5, 19___. The colors ran even though Mr. Walker at the Fast Service Cleaners assured me they had followed the care instructions on the garment label.*
>
> *I therefore returned the dress to your Customer Service Department on January 10. Mr. Smiley accepted the return of the dress. Since the amount had already been billed to me during the January billing, he assured me the purchase price would be credited to my account by the February billing period.*
>
> *There was a billing error on the statement for the billing period ending February 15 since the amount was not credited to my account. I therefore called the Credit Department on February 24 and explained the situation to Mr. Caseman, who assured me that the problem would be straightened out by the next billing period. However, the amount still has not been*

credited to my account. Moreover, since I have not paid this amount, I am also being billed for finance charges that I shouldn't have to pay.

I feel I have been very patient about a simple matter that should have been cleared up long ago. Please make sure that my account is properly credited with the amount due me and that all finance charges imposed on this amount are deducted from my account by the April billing period. If you need more information about this, you may call me at 111-2222 from 9:00 A.M. to 5:00 P.M.

If this matter is not taken care of by the next billing period, I shall bring it to the attention of the company's president, Mr. Grant Good.

Sincerely,

E. Z. Mark

As you can see, this message doesn't resemble the panic message at all. This time, E. Z. Mark supplies her account number and identifies and focuses on the main problem—the store's failure to credit her account for a refund and the finance charges that were imposed on that amount. Related points are grouped into separate paragraphs, the letter is neatly typed, without underlining or extra emphasis, and the words speak for themselves. She tells how the dress was ruined to help convince the store that there really was something wrong with the dress; remember, she doesn't have the credit memo that would clinch her case.

This is the kind of letter that some consumer advisers recommend as a basic model for consumers to copy. It's handy since the form can be used in many situations, from asking an appliance store's service department to look at a defective washing machine to demanding that a billing error be corrected.

But this is really an example of an ineffective pleading letter. Why? Because nowhere does E. Z. Mark mention what law might back her up if the store fails to credit her account. She is really depending on Ms. Golden's goodwill to solve her problem. E. Z. Mark actually doesn't know what more she can do to make the store correct the billing error. She has followed the model letter, pushed by some consumer advisers, which suggests that she apply some additional pressure to convince the store to take care of the problem by threatening to write to the company president.

Such pressure in this situation makes the letter self-defeating. E. Z. Mark is threatening to tell Ms. Golden's boss if Ms. Golden doesn't take care of the problem right away even though E. Z. Mark needs her goodwill and assistance to get the problem solved. Threatening to tell the boss provokes resistance rather than help in solving the problem. And it doesn't put any pressure on Ms. Golden because even if the president later asks about the problem, she could say she has not settled it because E. Z. Mark is unable to verify her claim. Thus, E. Z. Mark has not, in fact, any leverage for taking follow-up action.

If a pleading message works, it is not because of the message itself. It's because the business is willing to settle the matter on its own.

THE MAYDAY LETTER
(or the somebody-out-there-help-me approach)

The "mayday" message is just as ineffective as the pleading letter. Like a message sent by a person in distress, it is directed at anyone who might help.

E. Z. Mark might have heard that the mayday message produces some real clout. It certainly sounds tough, and many consumer advisers tell her it's just what she needs when politeness fails to work.

200 Pleasant View Road
Anytown, USA 00000

April 30, 19__

Mr. Grant Good
President
Honesty Department Stores
Grandplace Mall
Anytown, USA 00000

Dear Mr. Good,

The $169.95 credit due me has still not been applied to my Easy Budget Charge Account (000-0000-000) as of the billing period ending April 15, 19__.

I have tried to get this error corrected since February 24 and have explained it completely in my letter of March 27, 19__, to Ms. Golden, a copy of which is enclosed.

Now Ms. Golden informs me that she needs additional information to verify my claim for a refund and credit for the dress that I returned. But I have already furnished her all the details to show why I am entitled to this credit and I am at a loss to know what more I can tell her.

I simply cannot believe that Ms. Golden and the credit department are doing all they can to resolve this matter. I am still hoping that your company will take care of this matter by having the credit due me applied to my account and by deducting from my account the finance charges that have been applied to the amount I do not owe. But since it has already taken this long to resolve what I consider a serious problem, I feel it is appropriate to have an outside agency investigate this matter. I am therefore sending a copy of this letter to the agencies listed below.

Sincerely,

E. Z. Mark

cc: Federal Trade Commission
Attorney General
Local County Prosecutor's Consumer Action Office
Better Business Bureau
U.S. Office of Consumer Affairs
State Consumer Agency
Local Newspaper or TV Hotline

If nothing else, the letter shows she is persistent. Such persistence may be enough to get her problem solved. Or maybe one of the agencies will respond. And maybe one of the agencies has a law it could use to pressure the company to act. That's the main problem with the letter—E. Z. Mark has a lot of "maybes" working for her, but no real leverage.

There are many reasons why the maybes probably won't work at all. As in the case of the pleading letter, the message either creates too much pressure or not enough. Threatening to call in a government agency might cause resentment if the message reached a Mr. Good who really valued customer relations and who might have been willing to tell the Credit Department to give E. Z. Mark the credit to maintain goodwill. But such a message is not likely to scare a Mr. Ripoff.

Listing all the agencies tells Ripoff that her threat is really a bluff since, like a real mayday message, it is being sent out in all directions by someone desperately crying for help. He also knows how effective her cry for help is likely to be because he is aware that most of the agencies listed in her letter can't solve individual grievances. Ripoff knows he has nothing to lose by waiting. If none of the agencies respond, he has successfully called her bluff. If an agency does respond and it pushes hard, Ripoff can always agree to settle, so he risks nothing by waiting.

The mayday message can also backfire. If they think the dispute can be solved quickly and easily, all the agencies might decide to help and E. Z. Mark will have more rescuers than she can use. But if they consider it a tough problem, they might all decide to pass the buck to one of the others on the list. Consequently, no one will try to rescue E. Z. Mark.

There are times when it is important to contact a government agency for help. But the mayday message is not the way to do it. It simply is not potent. It is backed up by nothing more than a list of names, and because there are so many that backing may amount to nothing.

THE ESP LETTER
(or the you-must-know-what-I-am-talking-about approach)

A final ineffective type of letter sent by some consumers is the ESP message. So named for obvious reasons, it is guaranteed to fail to solve the problem. The examples below are the complete texts of actual letters sent to a government agency; however, to preserve anonymity all identifying information has been blacked out by the agency. So I have supplied hypothetical names.

200 Pleasantview Road
Anytown, USA 00000

March 3, 19—

Urgent

The Director
The Federal Reserve Bank
New York

Dear Sir:

I am in desperate (sic) needy (sic) help. I have an account at (The Riverside Financial Institution). Money is paid into that bank for me every month. The bank failed to let me know if payments in were made in February and March and does not reply to letters. In the last year it has failed to let me know about payments.
Can you help?

Yours truly,

E. Z. Mark

P.S. Are you the regulatory agency for banks? (sic) If not, please give me the name and address of that agency.

The consumer marked it *urgent,* but thoughtfully left out such details as the type of account, account number, and type of payments involved, such as automatic deposits of government checks or regular payments received from someone else. And if it was really urgent, the person could have made a phone call to find out what agency to contact.

It's an ESP message because the receiver must read the sender's mind. Another version of the ESP letter goes like this.

200 Pleasantview Road
Anytown USA 00000

Master Charge
XXXXXXXXXXXX
XXXXXXXX, XXXXXX XXXXX

Re: Notice of Adverse Action Taken Applicant: XXXXXXXXXXXXX

Dear Sir:

I wish to take exception to the reasons given for rejection of my recent application for a Master Charge. The reasons stated for such "adverse action" were: 1) lack of credit references; and 2) not living at present address long enough.

In view of the above stated reasons, which are due to my sex (all credit purchases have been made in my husband's name) and my marital status (have been separated from my husband since October, 1976) I suggest you review the Federal Equal Credit Opportunity Act, which prohibits such discrimination.

Very truly yours,

E. Z. Mark

cc: Federal Reserve Bank of New York
Bank Regulations Dept.

This time, the consumer conveniently left out the name of the bank that rejected her application. Neither Master Charge nor the Federal Reserve Bank would know who to contact about this problem without that detail.

The letter also illustrates the worst possible way to use a law that might actually apply to the situation. The Equal Credit Opportunity Act does prohibit certain types of credit discrimination; and it gives consumers definite pressure points they can use to force creditors to take corrective action.

But the consumer neither spells out what she specifically wants done to correct the problem, nor how the law backs up her demand. In effect, her threat (mentioning the law) amounts to little more than a hope that someone at Master Charge is bright enough to read between the lines and realize what she wants and how the law might help her. And, of course, her letter does not strengthen her position for taking any follow-up action.

You won't ever send the kind of ineffective messages E. Z. Mark and others sent when you use the negotiating strategy and the laws described in this book. And there won't be any doubt in your adversary's mind that you are a tough customer who knows how to use the real leverage created by laws that could apply.

2 · The Right Way: Preparing For Action

While I was at the Michigan Consumers Council, I had worked for the passage of a law that requires landlords to refund security deposits to tenants when they vacate their apartments. Under this law, the landlord must send the tenant an itemized list of damages and refund the balance of the deposit within thirty days. If he fails to send the list, he must return the entire deposit. If a tenant disputes the amount claimed, the landlord must file suit to collect the money or refund the rest of the deposit within forty-five days. If a tenant leaves his forwarding address but the landlord does not comply with the law, the tenant can sue for twice the amount of the deposit.

When my wife and I moved from Michigan to New York we had a chance to see how well the law worked. Our landlord didn't send us a claim for damages; but neither did he return our $285 security deposit. After the forty-five days had passed, we began asserting our rights under the law.

We called the landlord who promised to return the deposit. It didn't come. Three weeks later we called again. This time we reminded the landlord he was violating the law. In a few days a refund check for $240 arrived. The landlord now claimed we owed him $45 for a lost broiler pan and for three days' rent; we had left the apartment three days after the expiration of our monthly lease, but the landlord had given us permission to stay on a daily basis.

However, under the law the landlord was no longer entitled to the money. For one thing, the broiler pan was next to the stove; and for another he had not returned our deposit within forty-five days, and so was not entitled to keep the three-days' rent.

We sent the landlord a letter outlining these facts. We also mentioned another fact. Because he had not complied with the law, we were entitled to sue him and collect an amount equal to twice the security deposit, or $570. We threatened to do this unless he refunded the $45 immediately.

Our landlord returned our deposit by the next mail.

My former landlord in Detroit didn't refund my security deposit just because Michigan has an effective security deposit law. Nor did he refund the deposit just because I wrote a letter that showed I knew about the law. These things helped, of course, but what made them work was the negotiating strategy I used to get my money back.

My strategy was to call the landlord twice, then write a letter spelling out what it could cost him if he still refused to refund the deposit.

A negotiating strategy is a coordinated plan for using the law to negotiate a settlement. When you learn about various laws and study the art of negotiating, you won't feel powerless in the marketplace. You really will be able to fight city hall.

A strategy consists of all the steps you plan to take to negotiate a settlement based on the legal recourse that could be available in that situation. It helps you get the most leverage from the pressure points particular laws create for you. It may include making telephone calls, personal visits, or writing letters. It may include seeing an attorney, threatening a lawsuit or even filing one. In rare cases, it may include going to court.

A strategy might succeed after one step. Sometimes it won't succeed until you have taken several steps. It's hard to tell in advance, so planning and timing are important. For example, if I had sent the letter and threatened to sue my landlord after he missed the first deadline, he might have refunded the entire deposit there and then. On the other hand, he might also have kept the $45. How could I then have pressured him to refund the rest? I couldn't threaten to sue him again; I would have used up that bargaining chip already.

If I had sued him right away I would also have been in a much weaker position. The landlord's attorney might have had no trouble in convincing a judge that I was only out to make some extra money: I was taking advantage of a landlord who had simply missed some obscure deadline by a few days, the argument could have run.

But my phone calls to the landlord invalidated this argument. If the case had gone to court, I could have used the phone calls to show that I had given the landlord every chance to comply with the law. When the landlord ignored these chances, he showed he really was disregarding the law. Thus, instead of being reasonable, he bought the rope to hang himself: my threat to sue him then became very convincing.

WHAT A NEGOTIATING STRATEGY WILL DO FOR YOU

Having a negotiating strategy is vital to success, no matter what consumer battle you are fighting. A strategy will:

1. *Guide your actions so that each step will be directed toward reaching the goal you have set yourself.* A plan keeps you from getting sidetracked. If you want a department store to correct a billing error, for example, you don't want to confuse the issue by also throwing in a complaint that the store is dirty. You focus instead on the issue, the recourse available to you and plan ahead for follow up steps you may have to take and counter-measures for which you should be prepared in case a step fails to work.

2. *Allow you to react quickly and appropriately to the other side's responses.* For instance, success sometimes depends on how quickly you react to what the other side does. A quick reaction might catch them unprepared and if they are unprepared they might be more willing to do what you want. Quick reactions will also help convince them that your case has been thoroughly prepared. Being prepared for follow-up steps you may have to take and countermeasures the other side might take can help you fend them off, tell you when to stop to avoid trouble you may not want to face, or tell you when you should seek legal advice before going further.

3. *Help you evaluate your actions so that you can learn from each step as you proceed.* If you know what you are trying to accomplish, then you can more easily tell what is working, what isn't working, and how you can improve as you go along.

4. *Allow you to link each step together.* In this way you can use the results of each step to improve your negotiating position later. That's how my phone calls strengthened my position when I threatened my landlord with legal action.

COMBINING LEGAL AND PSYCHOLOGICAL WEAPONS

To use a negotiating strategy effectively, remember that negotiating means *convincing* the other side to settle on terms that are acceptable to you. You will be most convincing when you leave no doubt in your adversary's mind that you not only *can,* but *will* make it very costly if he refuses to negotiate a reasonable settlement.

Your negotiating strategy should have two sides—a legal side and a psychological side. The two will reinforce each other.

The legal strategy tells your adversary what legal weapons you have and how you could use them in a court battle if he refuses to settle the matter. The more prepared you are to win such a battle, the more pressure you can put on the other side.

This is where the psychological strategy comes in. What you are really trying to do is convince the other side that it is *better* to settle than fight. What you say and the way you say it are your psychological weapons. They put pressure on the other side by demonstrating your determination to succeed.

How can you combine the two sides of your negotiating strategy? It helps to keep the following objectives in mind:

GET THE OTHER SIDE'S ATTENTION

You must convey the message: Here is somebody I had better listen to because I cannot afford to ignore what he is telling me.

You transmit this message by being cool, calm, clear, precise, organized and deliberate. Try to keep your manner impersonal and businesslike so you avoid making the other person feel personally responsible for your problem. While it often helps to make the person feel responsible for *not* taking care of your problem, it won't help to hold him personally responsible *for* the problem.

IMPRESS WITH YOUR DETERMINATION TO SUCCEED

Your adversary will take you seriously when it becomes obvious that each step you take is directed toward reaching the final goal of settling the dispute. You make it clear that you have a plan by what you say and how you organize it. This immediately impresses upon the other side the fact that you know what you are doing. And when your adversary knows that, he cannot afford to ignore you when you tell him you will make it costly for him if he ignores your rights and refuses to settle the dispute fairly.

MOVE FROM LOW TO HIGH PRESSURE

You must keep the pressure on until you reach a settlement. You do this by following a low to high-pressure sequence. At first, always use relatively little or no direct pressure; then quickly increase the pressure if the other side refuses to settle. You increase the pressure as the cost of each action goes up for the other side, and the dispute moves closer to going into court.

Moving from low to high pressure-tactics, rather than starting off strongly, is important. Because it is impossible to tell in advance exactly how the other side will react, it can be inadvisable to apply unnecessary pressure at first. For one thing you may not need pressure to force a settlement, for another unnecessary pressure might make the other side hostile and perhaps unwilling to settle. That doesn't mean you avoid all pressure, of course; it just means that at first you keep the pressure to a minimum by being indirect or vague about what further action you will take. Say for example, you first talk to a store about a defective pop-up toaster. Instead of saying that unless they fix it within two weeks you will sue them under the Magnuson-Moss Warranty Act, say something like: "Thank you for repairing the toaster as you promised so I won't have to pursue the matter further." That's a gentle way of letting them know you expect them to keep their promise and that you are also ready to do "something" more if they don't.

If your adversary is unwilling or refuses to settle the dispute, you then increase the pressure by being more specific about what further action you will take and what it could cost them. And remember it is their refusal to be reasonable that is forcing you to go further and put additional pressure on them, so don't feel guilty.

FORCE THE OTHER SIDE TO ACT

The key to a successful strategy is to give the other side a choice between two unequal alternatives, then make them choose one.

One alternative should be the reasonable solution to your problem based on the recourse you have. The other should be the more costly solution a particular law provides for if they don't settle . The inequality between the two choices creates the leverage that forces the other side to act. In my own case, I gave the landlord the choice of returning the $45 or facing the possibility of having to pay $570 if I sued and won.

The costlier solution pinpoints the other side's weakness: you should always look for it and use it when it is available.

But always be reasonable. It is never worthwhile to hold out for the last penny because you can never tell what the last penny is for the other side. It may be the final demand you make, for instance, that pushes your adversary into fighting back. Of course, the harder he makes you work, the more you can reasonably demand based on the recourse you have.

USE THE LAW TO BACK YOU UP

When you present the two alternatives, always refer to the specific law that entitles you to carry out the specific action you threaten. Show how the law applies to the dispute. If your adversary ignores you, he will then be faced with arguing with the law, not you.

MAKE IT COSTLY TO REFUSE YOUR OFFER

Make it tough for the other side to argue with you so that it will cost them something just to say no to you.

By showing why you are entitled to the settlement you seek, and by backing up your demands with a specific law, you make it harder for the other side to argue with you. You could be right about the law; and you could go through with your threat to sue them. If they ignore you, they will—at the very least—have to worry about what more might happen. Alternatively, they might decide to seek their lawyer's advice or find out the facts to see if they can beat your case should you go to court. It might be easier for them to say yes than to go through all that trouble to say no.

GIVE THEM AN ESCAPE ROUTE

Always give the other side an easy way out to avoid the costly action you threaten to take. Never back your opponent into a corner with an ultimatum that leaves him no choice but to cave in completely or to fight you. The easy way out should be the reasonable alternative you offer. And if he agrees to it, you then promise not to take the step that will cost him more. This sometimes means giving up what a law might entitle you to make the other side pay but which you may be unable to get without a full scale fight.

Remember that the more pressure you apply by showing how much more costly it could be for the other side to refuse and the easier you make it for the other side to escape a more costly solution, the more likely it is that your complaint will be settled. When I threatened to sue the landlord for the $570 unless he returned the $45, for example, I also told him I would not sue if he returned the money.

When the settlement you want is also the easiest and safest way out for your opponent, use this pressure to help you negotiate a settlement. If the other side finds another escape route, of course, the pressure won't work.

3 · The Strategy

There are six main stages to any good negotiating strategy. The first begins when you notify the company, or other party involved, of the problem and the last occasionally ends in a court decision. At each stage, you build the pressure on your adversary. During the first three stages, you put the pressure on by telling the other side what more you *will* do. During the last three stages, you put the pressure on by *carrying out* what you said you would do.

Calling on the telephone, discussing the dispute in person, and writing letters are ways of implementing your negotiating strategy. What you do depends on what stage of the dispute settlement process you have reached.

First, let's look at each of these stages in general to get an overall picture.

STAGE ONE: OPENING SKIRMISHES

The first stage consists of what I have called the opening skirmishes when you initially notify a business about a problem and explore how willing it appears to be to correct it. The corrective action you request would, of course, depend on the problem, what you were entitled to have as part of the deal and what recourse could be available under the agreement and laws that could apply to the transaction.

You can conduct these initial negotiations by telephone, in person or in writing. Conducting these initial negotiations verbally keeps them more informal and gives both you and the other person more flexibility in dealing with the problem. Always keep in mind, however, that stating the problem in writing even at this stage can be very important for putting on the record what happened and when it occurred in case things don't get corrected.

At this point, you assume the company is ready to settle the problem and you apply very little or no pressure. Many complaints are resolved at this stage, especially when they involve businesses which value customer relations and which stand ready to back their promises without having to be pressured. How a company responds initially will tell you what further steps you should be prepared to take.

You start stage one by contacting the person at the *lowest* level of an organization who is authorized to deal with the problem. For instance, if an organization has a Customer Service or Customer Relations Department, you go there first.

While you start by contacting the person at the lowest level, you should be prepared to increase the pressure immediately by going on to seek a person at the next highest level of authority. For example, suppose the person in the Customer Service Department refuses to do anything about a defective washing machine you have recently purchased. You increase the pressure by asking to see the person's supervisor, or the person in charge of the Customer Service Department. You can do this nicely by simply asking for the name and title of the person's supervisor, and by saying that you would like to see the supervisor about this matter right away. If the person seems unwilling or unreasonable, don't argue or get nasty; instead, politely and firmly increase the pressure by insisting that you would like to see someone with more authority.

If that someone agrees to handle the problem, pin down his or her commitment as specifically as possible. Never be satisfied with an evasive answer like: "We will try to send somebody over to look at what is wrong with your washing machine sometime next week." That promise is much too vague and too easy for a store to break. Find out exactly who will do what, when, where, and how.

If you make your complaint on the telephone, take notes that give the relevant details, such as the name of the person you talked to, the extension number, the time, date, what you talked about, and what you agreed upon. Always end your conversation by restating the agreed-upon solution. For example, "Thank you Mr. Smith. Then I can expect your serviceman to be at my house at 1122 Roseview Drive between 1 and 5 P.M. on Tuesday, October 5, to look at my defective General Watts washing machine."

Restating the solution helps verify all the crucial details and helps ensure that there are no "misunderstandings." By mentioning the other person's name, you are telling him or her that you know who to hold accountable if the promise is not kept.

It sometimes helps to write a confirming letter that sums up the results of your conversation. A confirming letter is also an effective way to restate when and how you notified the company about the defect or problem.

Here is an example of such a letter. All names, addresses, dates, and details are only for illustrative purposes, of course.

2211 Roseview Drive
Anytown, USA 00000

September 26, 19___

Mr. John H. Smith
Manager
Customer Service Department
Honest Sam's Department Store
Futura Mall
Anytown, USA 00000

Dear Mr. Smith:

I am writing to confirm our telephone conversation of September 25, 19___, when we discussed the matter described below:

I informed you that the Super X General Watts automatic washer, serial number 11335XB12, that we purchased on September 12 and which was installed in our home on September 19, 19___, was defective because it fails to empty the water at the end of the rinse cycle. I have been unable to use the machine since I discovered the defect the first time I used it on September 23.

You agreed to have a serviceman look at the machine between 1 and 5 P.M. on October 15 and to have it picked up for warranty servicing if repairs cannot be completed at my home. You also agreed to have the serviceman reattach the water hookups for my old machine if the new one needs to be picked up for servicing.

I will appreciate your servicing the machine according to my warranty.

Sincerely,

In some cases you will find you *must* notify the business in writing at this very early stage because the law on which you will be basing your strategy requires it. If you are complaining about a billing error, for example, in order to preserve your rights under the Fair Credit Billing Act, the law requires that you notify the business in writing within a very short time. Obviously, then, you won't be able to start out with an informal step in a situation like this because you might miss the deadline for officially notifying the company in writing, and lose your rights under the law.

STAGE TWO: THE LOW-KEYED WARNING

The next stage is what I call the low-keyed warning you give after a business has failed to take appropriate corrective actions. It consists of a low-keyed warning letter that describes the problem, the company's failure to take care of it and proposes how it should now be settled. But you now increase the pressure by spelling out more clearly what more you could do if the company still fails to be reasonable.

If this step is a follow-up to more informal verbal negotiations, it now also puts the dispute on the record.

This interim low-keyed warning shows that you are prepared to be tough if you have to be, but it also shows that you are willing to settle peacefully and to give the company another chance to solve the problem. By accelerating the pressure this way, you automatically make the company or store more accountable to you because you force them to make a commitment one way or the other. The way the company responds will give you an idea whether it will make a reasonable settlement without having to be pressured further.

This letter is always addressed to someone in a position of authority. If you are dealing with a small business, the person's identify may be obvious. With a larger company, the letter should usually be addressed to the person in charge of the department that's responsible for handling your kind of problem; perhaps the head of the Customer Service Department or the Credit Department. At this point, don't go all the way to the top of a large company.

You can either mail the letter or memo or hand it to the store representative in person.

STAGE THREE: THE ULTIMATUM

This stage gives the company a last chance to cooperate. Up to now, you have tried to negotiate by keeping the pressure down. But a refusal to reach the reasonable settlement proposed in your low-keyed warning letter tells you the company is unwilling to settle the matter on its own. Now you send an ultimatum. It tells exactly how the *law* provides for a settlement if the company again refuses to cooperate.

This step also consists of a written demand, but now there is a big change in emphasis. In your first letter you described the problem and how it should be settled. Now you increase the pressure by focusing on what it will cost the store if it still refuses to accept your proposed settlement.

In this letter, you summarize the dispute, then refer to your previous letter, in which you described the matter in detail, and enclose a copy.

The ultimatum letter is sent to the top person in the company. It is unlikely that he or she will actually see the letter, but a decision on a settlement will be made by a person close to the top.

Your ultimatum tells exactly what risks the store runs if it continues to be unreasonable. It forces the issue. Unfortunately, though, the ultimatum is not a magic wand that can wave your dispute away. There will always be companies or stores so foolish, or so obstinate, or so convinced that they are in the right, that no ultimatum will do any good. Then, enforcing the law is the only answer.

When you send your ultimatum, decide which of the two available legal sources (see below) will help you back it up most effectively. The choice depends on what weapons the law makes available to you.

STAGE FOUR: GETTING LEGAL HELP

If the company involved still refuses to settle the dispute after you send your ultimatum, you need outside help to keep the pressure on.

There are two main sources of outside help you can use to back up your ultimatum. One is a government agency—a local prosecutor or a state or federal agency that enforces some consumer protection law. Such an agency might help you by enforcing the law against the business you are dealing with. The other source of outside help is an attorney who can help you enforce the law.

GETTING HELP FROM A GOVERNMENT AGENCY

Using a government agency won't cost you anything. If the other side is disobeying a law that the agency enforces, a word from the agency might be the additional push needed to settle your dispute. But government agencies are seldom authorized to negotiate settlements for individual consumers, so you cannot count on them to enforce the law for your direct benefit. Nevertheless, an agency might intervene informally by contacting the company about your problem and by trying to mediate a settlement.

When you ask a government agency for help, always ask in writing. Since you have already described what the dispute is about in the ultimatum and warning letters you sent to the company, forward copies to the agency with a short covering letter along with *copies* of relevant documents. Identify the law that you think has been violated and tell the agency what action you want it to take.

If you have told the company or store involved that you are calling in a government agency to help back up your ultimatum, there is no point in sending the business a copy of your letter to the agency. If your ultimatum didn't work, a copy of your letter to a government agency won't help either.

GETTING HELP FROM AN ATTORNEY

The other way to back up your ultimatum is to contact an attorney. He or she can take legal action to enforce the law for your direct benefit. In contrast to calling on a government agency for help, using an attorney will, of course, cost you money.

When you first seek the help of an attorney, don't do it with the idea of starting a law suit right away. He or she may be able to help you settle your dispute simply by writing to the company involved and *threatening* legal action.

Why should a lawyer's letter work any better than yours did? Because it puts more pressure on the business. First, the company knows it costs money to hire an attorney, so just the fact that you have a lawyer on your side indicates you are serious about pursuing your complaint. Second, what counts now is not so much what the letter says, but *who* says it. The company could ignore what you said you *could* do to enforce your rights, but it might not easily ignore what an attorney says he or she *will* do; after all an attorney knows the law and how to take a business straight to court. That's why a lawyer's letter that reinforces what you have already said may be all the extra push the company needs to settle.

Always try to find a lawyer who specifically handles your type of case. Obviously, there's no point in going to a tax specialist when you are involved in a warranty dispute, for instance. If you need help in finding an attorney, telephone the Bar Association and ask for the lawyer referral service.

When you first contact an attorney for an appointment, find out exactly what he or she charges. Is there a charge for an initial consultation? If so, are you allowed any free time before the charges start? What does the initial consultation cover? Does the attorney charge even if you decide not to use his services? If he takes the case, what services might be needed and what will they cost you?

Prepare for the initial consultation. Identify in advance what you want to find out and what you want to discuss. Stick to the main points of your dispute. Organize the backup material that explains what the issues are and that substantiates your claims. This includes copies of letters you have sent, copies of contracts, and any other written documents. Arrange the material in order so it helps explain the dispute as quickly and completely as possible. Don't leave this until you get to the lawyer's office—unless you want to pay for him to watch you organize your case.

Before you let the lawyer take the case, find out how he thinks it can be settled and what he is willing to do to help you settle it.

If the law that applies entitles you to recover your attorney's fees if you sue and win, be sure to ask the attorney if he or she will take the case based on the fees you could recover upon winning.

WHICH SOURCE SHOULD YOU TRY FIRST?

Suppose you try either a government agency or a lawyer and their efforts to settle don't work. Can you still call in the other to help you back up your ultimatum before you actually file a law suit? Sometimes you can, but the strategy will only help if you go to a government agency first. A lawyer is really the person of last resort.

When I was at the Michigan Consumers Council, there were consumers who sent us their complaints after attorneys' efforts to settle had failed to work. When we tried to help, the business invariably told us: "An attorney has already contacted us about this. We told him we are not going to do what the consumer wants, and he can go ahead and sue us. And we are telling you the same thing."

As a practical matter, then, you will usually use one *or* the other. If the company involved doesn't listen to the first, it isn't likely to pay much more attention to what the second has to say. At this point you have to choose between increasing the pressure by filing a lawsuit, or dropping the matter.

STAGE FIVE: STARTING LEGAL ACTION

If none of the previous steps produce a settlement, the only way to keep the pressure on is by going to court.

Starting a lawsuit doesn't mean the dispute will go before a judge; most legal actions never do. They are settled "out of court." Often judges encourage people to settle even after a dispute gets into court. So, if you start a suit, there will usually be a further opportunity to negotiate a settlement.

While a lawsuit is a serious step, you should not be afraid to start one if necessary. Such an action demonstrates very clearly to the other side that you really are determined to make them settle.

There are two ways to get a dispute into court. One is for you to sue the company; the other is to do something that forces the company to sue you. You can, for example, force a suit by withholding payments on *some* types of consumer credit contracts if a seller refuses to live up to his side of the bargain. If the seller then sues you, you can tell the court why he is not entitled to the money.

Forcing legal action in this way is cheaper because the other side has to pay the cost of starting the suit. It is also easier to defend than it is to attack, especially if you have a strong case. On the other hand, forcing a suit can be risky. If you lose, you pay and the seller/creditor may be able to use other collection remedies.

When you are considering forcing a business to sue you, remember two key points. First, make sure that the law you are using allows you to defend yourself legally when a business claims you didn't live up to your contract. (Later in this book you will find descriptions of laws that will allow you to do this in common types of consumer disputes.) Second, always see an attorney—at least for an initial consultation—*before* you force a suit.

If you start a suit and find the other side is ready to settle before you get to court, then you should up the ante at least enough to cover what it cost you to start the suit especially if a court would probably find in your favor and require them to pay a lot more.

And make sure any settlement is in writing.

STAGE SIX: THE TRIAL

The final stage of a negotiating strategy is the trial stage, and at this point the dispute is really in the hands of your lawyer unless you are using a small claims court.

After you file a suit, the other side receives a formal notice of the fact which they must answer. (If they do not answer the notice, you automatically win the case.) The court then sets a trial date and, unless the dispute is settled out of court, action begins. The same applies to you if you are being sued.

If the dispute gets this far, a judge or a jury will decide how it should be settled. The decision will be final unless someone appeals it.

If you win, you will have to collect from the other side. Sometimes it can be difficult to make an adversary pay and you may have to use the courts to force payment.

SEEKING LEGAL ADVICE.

Whatever steps you take as part of a negotiating strategy for asserting your rights involve some legal consequences. There are rights you thereby acquire and rights you may be giving up. And the steps you take could sometimes give the other person a chance to take action against you.

Taking steps to assert your rights can get tricky. Doing it properly can depend on technicalities that are beyond the scope of this book. Whether a particular remedy actually applies in a particular situation could be hard for you to evaluate. If the stakes involved in a dispute are more than you can afford to lose because of a mistake you might make by trying to handle it yourself, seek legal advice rather than taking the step on your own.

The negotiating strategies included in this book should help you identify in advance when you might be forced to take the important steps that I have described as the first three stages of a strategy. By now you should be alerted to whether you may have to take steps that could get you in over your head. Before you reach deep water you can get timely legal advice while pursuing your claim. Knowing the kind of legal recourse you may have, and what you may have to do to use it, will give you a better idea whether it is worthwhile to get legal advice for pursuing your claim.

Using a sample letter after you have sought legal advice seems, at first glance, to be putting everything into a lawyer's hands so why not simply let the lawyer handle everything?

Drafting a letter will force you to think everything through and spell out what could be involved so as to make it easier for a lawyer to advise you whether to send the letter as is, or make some changes in it. After you see a lawyer you can then still write and send your own letter rather than having your attorney do it for you (and charging you for it), but now your action is based on advice that takes your situation into account.

Writing and using your own letter could also be cheaper. And finally, if you, instead of a lawyer, send the letter spelling out the legal demands you are making, the other side may be more willing to settle rather than turn the matter over to its attorney (which it is more likely to do once an attorney is formally involved on your side). You then still retain the option of having a lawyer formally step in on your side later as a way of keeping the pressure on if the other side still refuses to resolve the problem.

Remember, this book is not meant as a substitute for legal advice about specific legal problems. But knowing what could be involved can help you use legal advice more effectively and alert you to when it might be timely for you to get such advice. An attorney can then most easily and cheaply help you assert your rights rather than having to undo mistakes you might have made while trying to assert them on your own.

4 · Making a Convincing Case

Since your objective is to actually reach a settlement, let's consider how you can negotiate convincingly at each stage.

Of course, you will always have to use common sense to decide how far you will take any dispute. But during each step of your negotiating strategy, you will be able to proceed convincingly if you follow this rule: Always give the other side information that answers the following five basic questions:

1. What is this dispute about?
2. Why are you coming to me about it?
3. What do you want me to do about it?
4. How much time do I have to do what you want?
5. What if I don't do it?

If you organize the information in this order in your letter you will automatically make a convincing case. You will impress upon the other side the fact that you know what you are doing because you will be answering the questions that will be upper-most in their minds as they try to understand the dispute. And you will be presenting the information in a way that puts the maximum pressure on them.

This is what you should include in your letter when you answer each point:

WHAT IS THIS DISPUTE ABOUT?

Here you should describe the what, when, where or how of the purchase. Identify what is wrong with the product and say when you discovered the problem.

If the problem is a pop-up toaster that doesn't pop up the toast, for example, start off your letter something like this:

"I am notifying you that the Sunray pop-up toaster, Model #101 XL, serial number 3352189, that I purchased from your company on April 15, 19__, for $34, is defective because it fails to pop up the toast. I used the toaster according to the manufacturer's directions about five times before I discovered, on April 25, that the pop-up mechanism remains stuck in the "toast" position no matter how the appliance is used."

By specifically spelling out the problem, you will leave the store with no doubt about what the issue is. This way, it cannot dismiss your complaint by wondering whether you plugged in the appliance or properly followed the manufacturer's instructions. Including the date when you discovered the problem tells the store you are notifying them without delay. The store cannot then blame the malfunction on normal wear or claim that you waited too long to notify them.

WHY ARE YOU COMING TO ME ABOUT IT?

Give this information by telling the store exactly why it is up to them to take care of the problem. In the case of the pop-up toaster, you could point out that the store had sold it as a pop-up model, thus it is the store's responsibility to see that it works as such.

What you expect a store to do might depend on what it promised when you made the purchase or whether you can hold it to a promise because of a contract you have or because there is a law on your side.

The reason for going to the store might be obvious. But spelling it out specifically makes it harder for them to evade their responsibility by shifting the blame to you.

This is also the point where you would describe what steps, if any, you had already taken to solve the problem and what happened as a result. If you have already talked to the store about the problem but nothing happened, for instance, or if the store promised to fix the toaster but didn't, these are additional reasons to explain why you are coming to them again.

WHAT DO YOU WANT ME TO DO ABOUT IT?

Provide this information by stating how you want the problem to be solved. Do you want the toaster fixed? Do you want your money back? Do you want to exchange the toaster for another model? Did you suffer any other losses that may not be obvious but which you want the other side to take care of? You must tell the store what you want done about the problem, or it will be too easy for them to think you'll be satisfied if they do nothing.

When you answer this question, your request must be reasonable and based on the recourse you could have. What is reasonable may depend on several things. It could depend on whether the defect can be repaired, how costly the repair will be, or whether you suffered other losses. For instance, if a dealer doesn't fix your car correctly and you must return it again and again, it may be reasonable to ask the dealer to give you a loaner while your car is repaired. Or maybe you will want the dealer to reimburse you if you have to rent a car.

Sometimes consumers may be tempted to make unreasonable demands. You can't really expect a store to let you exchange a $34 toaster for a fancy $60 model, for example. It might also be unreasonable to expect a store to exchange the toaster for a new model if the pop-up mechanism can be easily fixed. And if the store is willing to exchange the toaster, asking for your money back might be unreasonable.

It is important to remember, though, that what might be considered unreasonable when you first complain, could become reasonable later on if the store fails to solve the problem. If the store says it will fix the toaster and then doesn't keep its promise, for instance, it might be reasonable to demand your money back.

The recourse laws make available to you help you spell out what could be reasonable in a given situation.

HOW MUCH TIME DO I HAVE TO DO WHAT YOU WANT?

Always provide the answer to this question by setting a deadline for doing what you ask. Again, be reasonable. A week might be enough time to fix a toaster; but it might take a month to solve a complicated credit dispute.

Sometimes the law is very helpful on this point because it spells out how much time is allowed for complying with certain legal requirements. The Michigan security deposit law, for example, sets specific deadlines for the refunding of deposits.

When you give a deadline, it may not always be desirable to set a specific date or a given number of days in which you want the problem solved. Also, since you can't always be sure about the speed of the mails, a letter with a specific deadline might be outdated before it arrives. When you can't be sure exactly how much time you should allow, a word like "immediately" will often get the message across effectively. Although it does not tell the store exactly how much time it has to solve the problem, it does tell them you want it solved quickly.

Setting a deadline is important because it triggers the answer to the next question.

WHAT IF I DON'T DO IT?

The answers to all the previous questions are designed to convince the other side that it *should* do what you ask. But no matter how convincing these answers might be, the other person will always be thinking of what will happen if he doesn't do what you ask.

You provide the answer by spelling out what follow-up action you will take and how costly it might prove for the store. Your answer will be an increasingly tougher ultimatum that says: Either do the reasonable thing I ask, or be prepared to take the consequences.

By giving this information last in your letter, you make the consequences appear very unattractive at the very moment the other person begins to think about them. A final mention of the deadline will also reemphasize the importance of getting the problem solved and make it uncomfortable for the other person to think about avoiding the solution.

ORGANIZING YOUR CASE

You need to be organized to put your negotiating strategy to work.

COLLECT THE FACTS

Get together all the facts you need to resolve your dispute. Do you have records, bills, canceled checks or receipts? Who else knows about the problem who might be able to verify what you say? Do you have the advertisement which induced you to buy the merchandise in question?

Double check and make sure the facts are accurate. Nothing will destroy your credibility faster than a false claim. Be sure you have some way to back up your facts. Remember, if some important information is missing, the other side can easily undermine your position.

ORGANIZE THE FACTS

Group together the facts you need to answer each of the five main questions on page 24. Put the different facts in sequence so that each point you make leads logically to the next and you build up an effective case. Use the sample letters printed later in this book as a guide for supplying the facts that apply to your problem.

IDENTIFY THE COMPANY RESPONSIBLE

In order to correct the problem, make sure you have identified the company really responsible. It may be the firm that sold the merchandise or the service you are complaining about, or it may be the manufacturer. If you bought something on credit, you may have to complain to the creditor who holds the contract as well as to the company that sold you the merchandise or service.

FIND THE PERSON AUTHORIZED TO SOLVE THE PROBLEM

Get the name and title of the person who has the authority to act for the company, and take the case directly to him or her. Addressing the person by name shows that you consider the problem serious enough to have gone to the trouble of identifying him—and that tells the person you are determined to pursue your complaint. It also tells him you know who to hold accountable if something goes wrong.

To find the right person's name, you may have to make a couple of phone calls or a personal visit to the store. Ask: "What department handles complaints about . . .? Could you give me the full name and title of the person in charge?" Appendix II of this book identifies directories you can use to locate names and addresses of companies and their officers.

IDENTIFY THE OTHER SIDE'S WEAKEST POINT

You can identify an adversary's weak point by figuring out which law hits him in the pocket book the hardest. The weak point will almost always involve money in one of three ways. First, how much can the law make the company pay if it does not do as you ask? Second, how costly can you make it for the company to fight you? And third, if it refuses to do as you ask, can you withhold money the company wants from you?

REHEARSE WHAT YOU PLAN TO SAY

If you make your complaint in person or by phone, always rehearse first. Write down the answers to the five questions on page 24 even though you will give them verbally. This helps you present the facts in an organized way. Rehearse the answers by having someone else play the part of your adversary. A good rehearsal helps you spot weak points in your story. It also lets you know whether you are making your points effectively.

Anticipate questions but try to be flexible and allow for the unexpected, too. Nobody can think of *everything* that might be said in a conversation. If some question comes up that you haven't thought about, don't panic. Instead, say something like: "Let me make a note of the point you are making. I'll check into it and get back to you. Meanwhile, let's go on to the next point." A cool head will impress the other side.

MAKE COPIES

Make at least one, but preferably *two,* good copies of *any* letter you send. Always keep at least one good copy in your files so you can make additional ones if you need them later. If you have to take follow-up action, you can then send along copies of the previous letters to provide background.

Make a *written* record of any conversations you have. Memory is fine, but writing is better. So take notes as you talk. Write down the full name and title of the person, the date, the phone number, and any other identifying information.

GET PROOF OF MAILING OR DELIVERY OF LETTERS

You should get such proof for any letters you send. There are two ways to obtain proof from the post office. First, you can simply get a mailing receipt for a small fee. This receipt gives you written proof that you *mailed* something to a specific person on a certain date. This kind of receipt doesn't prove the letter was delivered; it only proves when you sent it. If a particular law requires that you show when you sent a notice to someone, a mailing receipt will be enough.

The second way to obtain proof you sent a letter is to send it by certified mail, return receipt requested. This is more expensive than a mailing receipt, but well worth the cost. Each letter is assigned a specific number, and the post office keeps track of when the letter was delivered and who received it. You can also ask the post office to tell you when the letter was delivered by requesting return receipt. Sending a letter this way gives you proof not only of when you mailed it but when the letter was received, and who received it.

Always use this kind of certified mail if a law requires you to show when the other side *received* something. This kind of proof can be very important in preserving your rights when a pertinent law has a short deadline for filing complaints.

If the law gives you plenty of time to act, and if you can afford to wait, then you might use ordinary mail the first time you write. If the company fails to respond, you might follow up by sending an almost identical version of the original letter. This time, however, use certified mail. You could, for example, simply add the following phrase to the first sentence of your original letter:

"Since you may not have received my original letter of April 27, 19__, I am again notifying you that . . ." and then continue the rest of the first sentence describing the dispute. Everything else in the second letter would be the same, except that obviously you would change the deadlines you set.

A follow-up letter sent by certified mail keeps the pressure on the other side and gives you a little extra time to take the action mentioned in the first letter. The second letter tells the other side: Maybe you failed to reply to my first letter because you never received it, but we both know that you received *this* letter. If you don't reply this time, you can't expect me just to sit still.

To reinforce the impact of certified mail, record the certified mail number at the top of your letter.

A letter like this may be the only additional push you need to get your adversary to respond positively.

It is possible someone may refuse to accept a certified letter. The post office will then return it and note that the addressee has refused to accept and sign for the letter. If that happens, do *not* unseal the envelope. Keeping the contents in the sealed envelope, showing that it had been delivered but refused by the addressee, could later help you prove you had, in fact, notified the person.

Take whatever follow-up steps are then appropriate. If the dispute gets to court and your opponent claims you failed to give timely notice, the sealed envelope can then be opened in court to show exactly what you told the person in the letter he or she refused to accept.

MAKE CLEAR HOW OR WHERE A BUSINESS CAN CONTACT YOU.

State in any letter you send how or where a business can contact you or where you want a business to pick something up from you when that's appropriate. For example, if you want a business to contact you to arrange something, then include in a letter something like: "You can call me at 333-4444 between 9:30 A.M. and 5:00 P.M. or at 222-3333 after 6:30 P.M." Whenever you want a business to pick up something from you, be sure to identify the address either by referring to the address you give in your letter heading or by giving the address when it differs from the letter heading. Some sample letters include such wording, but don't forget to add this information when appropriate.

Section II
WHAT YOU NEED TO KNOW ABOUT CONSUMER PROTECTION

5 · How Disputes Arise: The Purchasing Sequence

When Francis Bacon said "Knowledge is power" he wasn't talking about consumer battles, of course, but the advice holds good. The more background knowledge you have, the easier it is to avoid pitfalls, and the easier it is to build a convincing case when you have to.

How do disputes generally arise in the first place? How can you learn to avoid trouble? And what can you do when it happens?

A dispute arises when something goes wrong with a purchase. But a purchase doesn't just involve a single step. Every purchase is made up of a number of separate steps that are linked together in what I'll call a purchasing sequence. Various laws cover different things that can go wrong during each step and the recourse you have for setting things right.

By becoming aware of what happens during each step of the sequence as you buy, you'll be able to spot potential trouble more easily.

INDUCEMENT TO BUY

During this initial step, the seller, often with the help of the manufacturer, tries to convince you to buy. Information on a label, pictures on a package, or even the color or shape of a product might induce you to buy. Sometimes the way things are displayed will tempt you into buying. At this point, promises or information given by sales people will often clinch the sale.

Your commitment to buy is the most important thing you have to give to get the sequence started. Without it, a business can't *make* you take any of the other steps in the purchasing sequence. Once you commit yourself, however, it is possible to be rushed through all the other steps so that you are not consciously thinking about what you're doing. There is a reason for this.

Before making a commitment, you look for and evaluate information that helps you decide whether to buy. But once you've made the commitment, your mind tends to block out information that might make you change your mind. Sales pitches help secure your commitment and make it as hard as possible for you to have any second thoughts about your buying decision. At this point, of course, the salesperson has you hooked.

Since this commitment affects what happens during the rest of the purchasing sequence, DON'T GIVE IT CHEAPLY. This means asking questions that will force the salesperson to spell out and substantiate his or her claims with details, facts, and figures. Ask about alternatives and how they specifically compare with what the store is offering. If a store claims that its super-deluxe model dishwasher is better than anything else on the market, for instance, ask exactly how it is better, what features it has that some other model doesn't have, and how it compares in price. Have the salesperson write down the answers. Keep the information until you are sure the purchase is satisfactory.

MAKING THE AGREEMENT

When you make an agreement to buy, you formally and legally commit yourself to a purchase.

During this step, you spell out the terms under which you will buy. It is at this point that you get the chance to see whether the seller is willing to put his promises and claims in writing. If he refuses to do so, it is time to revoke your psychological commitment to buy.

Although it is often tough to change the preprinted form contracts stores use, there are things you can do to make an agreement more favorable to you. But you have to be willing to say no if the seller doesn't accept your terms. Further details on how to pin down specific terms that could be important are included where the relevant requirements are described.

Each agreement spells out the sales terms—what you are buying, the warranty, and the delivery conditions. These terms state what the seller is obligated to provide and what you are entitled to receive. An agreement also spells out the payment terms. These concern your obligations—how and when you will pay for the purchase.

It is wise to try to fix the payment terms so that you don't have to pay until the sales terms have been fulfilled. This way you retain your economic leverage to make the seller honor his bargain if necessary. Otherwise, these two parts of your agreement can easily become separated. Let's say you contract with a home improvement contractor to re-side your house, for example. If you pay for the job in advance, what leverage will you have if he fails to complete the work? You've already carried out your part of the bargain.

On page 526 I show how you can keep sales terms and payment conditions locked together when I describe the laws governing the purchases you make with credit and other non-cash payment systems.

DELIVERY AND INSPECTION OF GOODS

Always *inspect* what you buy to make sure the seller is delivering what you agreed to purchase. If he isn't delivering what he is supposed to, usually you don't have to complete your part of the bargain either and pay for the goods. If the goods are defective when the seller delivers them, you can usually reject them, but your right to do so sometimes depends on whether the goods are custom-made and also on the extent to which the seller has failed to live up to the agreement.

What happens if you don't inspect and later find something wrong? It depends on the circumstances. A sign in a New York City fabrics store, for instance, told its customers: "No goods on approval. We ask you to inspect the goods and reserve the right not to give cash refunds except for goods with latent defects which reasonable inspection would not have revealed." If you ignored that sign and found a rip in your fabric after you got home, you wouldn't get a cash refund. If, on the other hand, you washed the fabric and the colors ran, you would have a latent, or hidden, defect you could not have discovered by inspection, which could entitle you to a cash refund.

ACCEPTANCE AND PAYMENT

If the goods pass inspection, then you must accept them. A clear example of how inspection and acceptance works occurs when you order a bottle of wine in a restaurant. First, the waiter shows you the bottle to make sure it is what you ordered, then he opens it and pours a sample for you to taste. You can refuse the bottle at this point if something is wrong with the wine, but if you tell the waiter it is okay, you will be considered to have accepted it and must pay for it. You can't change your mind after drinking a couple of glasses.

Your acceptance will almost always be considered "final and complete" when you start to *use* a product. The only exception is a "sale on approval," a specific kind of trial offer, which is described in Chapter 26. In this case, the seller says you can try out something before accepting it.

Once you have accepted a purchase, you must usually find something seriously wrong before you can *make* the seller take it back; sometimes he may only be obligated to repair a defect.

USING THE GOODS AND COMPLETING PAYMENTS

At this point, you usually find out whether the product is as good as the claims made for it.

How long this step takes depends, of course, on what you buy and how long the seller must stand behind his sale. At this stage you will depend on warranty or product liability laws to enforce any rights you have if the purchase turns out to be defective. But you might also be able to depend on laws that regulate other steps in the sequence, such as deceptive sales practices laws you can use to enforce any rights you have when the seller's claims turn out to be false.

6 · Consumers and the Law

Three kinds of law apply to consumer purchases: common, or case, law based on court decisions; statutory law passed by legislative bodies such as the United States Congress and state legislatures; and administrative law adopted by an administrative agency, such as a state banking department, or by a federal agency, such as the Federal Trade Commission (FTC).

COMMON LAW

Common, or case, law is based on major legal decisions made by judges. Lawyers refer to such a case as a "landmark decision," or a "leading case" (hence the name case law). In such instances, judges state the legal basis for deciding a case in a certain way; they set precedents that later courts follow to decide similar cases.

Let's look at an example of case law. At one time it was hard for a consumer to sue the manufacturer of a product that had caused him injury. U.S. courts followed a rule adopted by an English court in 1842, which said, in effect, that a consumer couldn't sue a manufacturer for injuries caused by a defective product unless he or she had bought the product directly from the manufacturer. When manufacturers began selling through middlemen, it meant that consumers had little recourse if they were injured.

Things began to change in 1916 when the U.S. Supreme Court decided that the Buick Motor Company was responsible for the injuries a consumer had suffered when a defective car wheel collapsed. By the late 1960s, further court decisions had completely reversed the old English rule. Today, manufacturers are liable for injuries resulting from defective products.

Since common law is spelled out in many court decisions, unfortunately it isn't written down in any one place where you can look it up. Other chapters will refer to important rights created by case law.

This book primarily focuses on protections created for you by statutory law and on some important rules adopted by Federal agencies. The requirements of statutory law are also, however, interpreted and affected by court decisions which often spell out how the statutory law applies to specific factual situations. So court decisions usually do have a bearing on how statutory laws apply to a dispute. This can sometimes create uncertainty about how a law could apply to a particular situation. At the same time, specific situations also affect court decisions about how the law applies.

How courts interpret and apply the law always creates at least some uncertainty about how a statutory law or previous decision applies to a particular dispute, especially one involving unusual problems. That's how case law changes as decisions are made to make the law fit new problems. Courts, however, also try to be consistent. They try to follow important precedents and strictly apply requirements spelled out by statutory law in the usual situation. That's how law promotes certainty.

No one, however, can ever really be sure how a court will decide a dispute even when following important precedents and statutory laws. That's what makes lawyers a cautious lot when it comes to telling someone what their rights could be and how a case might turn out. That's why lawyers often say that taking a case to court is like gambling, especially when both sides have reasonable justifications for their claims.

It can work to your advantage when you have a reasonable basis for asserting that protections available under a law apply to your situation. You may be unsure about whether you are right and there may well be technicalities this book doesn't cover which can beat you, but if you at least have a reasonable basis for your claim, your adversary can't really be sure that you are wrong, especially if their loss could be costly. That's why telling the other side why a specific law applies to your case strengthens your argument. They may not be willing to chance testing the law, so they solve the dispute instead.

STATUTORY LAW

Statutory law is enacted by legislative bodies and is written down in statute books. Statutory law usually covers a subject more comprehensively than case law which usually deals with a specific legal issue that comes up in a case.

The Federal laws (or acts of Congress) covered in this book apply in every state. Laws passed by a state legislature, on the other hand, apply only in the state that enacted them. This book only covers state consumer protection laws that have been more or less uniformly adopted by a majority of states. The Uniform Commercial Code, which covers contracts for the sale of products, is one such law.

ADMINISTRATIVE LAW

Administrative law covers regulations adopted by federal or state administrative agencies. These agencies are responsible for enforcing specific federal or state statutory laws and number in the thousands. Among them are federal agencies, such as the Federal Trade Commission (FTC), and state agencies, such as insurance departments and utility commissions.

Such agencies adopt rules and regulations that spell out in detail what a statutory law means, what it covers, and how it is to be enforced. These regulations have the *force of law,* just as the laws adopted by legislative bodies do. For instance, the Federal Trade Commission Act prohibits the use of unfair or deceptive acts or practices. Congress has now authorized the FTC, which enforces this law, to adopt regulations that define specific acts or practices that are prohibited by that act.

Administrative law has become more important in the last few years as legislatures have delegated the job of spelling out what various laws cover to administrative agencies. This has happened because the topics covered by statutory law have become more technical and complicated, making it difficult for legislatures to write laws covering subjects in every detail.

This book covers a few very important federal regulations, such as the Federal Trade Commission rule on mail order purchases, which you can use to protect yourself.

PUBLIC AND PRIVATE LAW

Public law is enforced on behalf of the public by a government official, such as a state attorney general, or by a government agency, such as the FTC. The government enforces this kind of law because it regulates practices considered harmful to everyone in a community, or the public at large. Laws with criminal penalties or laws that can be enforced solely by administrative agencies are examples of public law. Although you usually can't personally enforce such a law, if you believe one has been violated, you can complain to the appropriate agency or official who does enforce it.

Private law, also called civil law, on the other hand, is enforced by an individual to settle a dispute. This kind of law regulates relationships between individuals to help them protect their own person or property. Laws regulating the terms and conditions of contracts are examples of private law. These laws are, of course, also adopted by legislatures or established by court decisions. But government or other officials do not enforce this kind of law.

Most of the consumer protection laws enacted during and after the 1960s allow both consumers and government agencies to enforce them. These laws create rights that you can enforce on your own without waiting for a government agency to help you. And these laws often make it costly for the business that violates them. My landlord, for example, found out how costly it could have been when he violated the Michigan security deposit law.

ENFORCING LEGAL RIGHTS

The rules that laws create would be useless if there were no way to enforce them. Courts and administrative agencies are the main governmental institutions that enforce legal rights. Courts, however, have the final say since decisions by administrative agencies can almost always be appealed to them.

FEDERAL AND STATE COURTS

There are two separate court systems in the United States—the federal court system and the state court system.

Basically, the federal court system consists of three judicial layers stacked like a pyramid. The U.S. Supreme Court lies at the top; below come eleven U.S. Courts of Appeals; and below them come many U.S. District Courts.

When you take a dispute to the federal court, the district court is the first court you would use. The district court would try the case and render a decision. Its decision could be appealed to the court of appeals, and that decision might be appealed to the Supreme Court. But, in practice, few district court decisions are ever appealed, and very few cases ever reach the Supreme Court. Decisions by state courts can sometimes be appealed to federal courts.

The state court system works very much like the federal court system except that usually there is an additional fourth layer of courts. These courts enforce state laws along with federal laws. At the top of the pyramid is the state's supreme court. It has the final say about state laws. Below it are appeals courts, and below them are trial courts which are similar to federal district courts. State trial courts are known by different names, such as county courts, district courts, circuit courts, common pleas courts, and superior courts. Each county in a state usually has at least one of these courts. It is in this court that you would usually begin to enforce any state consumer protection law. But sometimes disputes based on state laws must be started in federal courts.

The fourth layer of state courts is local, or inferior, courts that have been specifically set up to hear minor cases. They may be called municipal courts, justice of the peace or magistrates' courts, or small claims courts.

Many consumer disputes—but not all—can be settled in these local courts, rather than the state trial courts. They operate more informally and are less costly to use. You don't need a lawyer to use them, either. For more information about these courts see Chapter 75.

ADMINISTRATIVE AGENCIES

Federal and state administrative agencies vary in size, organization, and responsibility. Some are headed by a board or commission composed of several people; others are headed by only one person. Some are large organizations with a staff of thousands and many responsibilities; others, such as state occupational licensing boards, may have a staff of one or two and limited responsibilities.

Some agencies closely monitor the economic activities of the businesses they regulate to protect the public: federal or state banking regulators, for instance, periodically audit and inspect banks. Other agencies may check on businesses only when they receive consumer complaints. State occupational boards often work this way.

Some agencies, such as a public utilities commission, regulate all aspects of a firm's business including the rates it can charge, where it can operate and what services it can or must offer. Other agencies, such as the National Highway Traffic Safety Administration, regulate only one aspect of a company's business. In this case, the agency is primarily concerned with the safety of automobiles.

An agency usually has three governmental powers that are normally divided among separate branches of government. It has legislative powers to adopt rules and regulations that set standards. It has executive powers to discover and investigate violations, prosecute violators, and gather information to establish the need for adopting rules and regulations. It also has judicial powers to decide whether its laws and rules have been violated and impose punishment.

Many agencies can now impose specific penalties or issue orders to enforce their decisions. Agencies never impose criminal penalties, but they can assess monetary fines, revoke licenses, or spell out "corrective actions," such as ordering recalls for cars with safety defects.

When an administrative agency enforces a law, it acts like a court. Administrative law judges, or hearing officers appointed by the agency, hold the hearings, take testimony, and render decisions based on the evidence presented. While their decisions can almost always be appealed to the courts and overturned, in practice they are often final because courts usually don't overturn them unless the agency has stepped beyond its authority under the law it enforces.

Agencies often have the flexibility to enforce the law by informally negotiating voluntary settlements with businesses. An agency often makes these settlements based on complaints from consumers. However, agencies usually lack the formal power to make a business settle a consumer complaint. Sometimes, though, a business would rather settle a complaint informally by negotiating a settlement with the agency than risk a formal administrative hearing. Losing such a hearing may be more costly than settling the complaint.

While the help consumers can get from most agencies depends on the skill and willingness of those who run them, in the last few years some administrative agencies have been specifically authorized to help consumers who have been injured or damaged by a business which has violated the laws they administer.

7 · Protecting the Consumer

A FAIR BARGAIN

Laws evolve over time and reflect the public policies a community believes are important.

During feudal times, for instance, the marketplace was regulated by laws very different from today's. A merchant couldn't simply charge what he wanted for a loaf of bread, say: he could only charge what the law said was a "just price." And in return for his "just price," the law required a merchant to deliver a "sound product." In effect, the law set quality standards for products. If a merchant charged a higher price, it automatically meant the product had to be better. In turn, if consumers paid more, the law entitled them to expect more for their money.

These and other legal rules regulated all aspects of sales. When a dispute arose, a court would first evaluate whether a merchant had delivered a sound product for a fair price before ordering a buyer to pay. The courts made people live up to the principle of a "fair" bargain.

In fact, it wasn't hard for people or the courts to decide whether a merchant had delivered a sound product for a just price. In those days, people bought few goods in the marketplace and the goods they did buy were usually made locally. Products seldom changed; not just from one year to the next, but often for hundreds of years.

But as commercial and manufacturing activities became more and more important, legal doctrines slowly began to change. During the eighteenth and nineteenth centuries both English and American courts replaced the "sound goods for a just price" doctrine with new rules that largely regulated the marketplace right up until the 1960s, and in some instances still do.

These new rules have been called the *caveat emptor* and the "sanctity of contracts" doctrines. (These doctrines refer not to one law, but to many laws courts used when they decided consumer disputes.)

"LET THE BUYER BEWARE"

Caveat emptor is Latin for "let the buyer beware." The doctrine meant just that, and it became the new law of the marketplace.

Now courts seldom looked at *how* people arrived at a bargain. Instead, the law assumed that buyers would automatically distrust what sellers said about their goods or services, and that they would base purchasing decisions on their own knowledge and experience.

Caveat emptor generally meant that sellers were relieved of the obligation to tell a buyer something about the product; they could even withhold important information such as that a house was infested with termites. They could also state their opinions about their products without having to stand behind them. This practice became and is known as "puffing," and "puffed" statements could obviously mislead consumers. The law sanctioned them, however, because—as one judge saw it—the law takes into account that people naturally exaggerate the worth and qualities of the products they sell. Or as another judge saw it, neither party really believes the opinions the seller expresses about his products, and they both know it. But why would a seller make false claims if nobody believed them? Because, said the judge, buyers would get suspicious if a seller didn't make them.

Thus, the doctrine allowed sellers to make such claims as "This is the best car on the American market," or "This is the most economical car you can buy," without worrying about whether their statements were really true. If challenged, sellers could say they were merely expressing an "opinion" on the subject.

Caveat emptor meant that most of the time buyers could not hold sellers legally responsible for the claims they made about their products or services. In 1794, for instance, a buyer paid 25 cents an acre for 32,000 acres of what he was told was rich Virginia farmland. When he found out he had actually bought Virginia mountain country, he sued to get his money back. The court, basing its decision on the *caveat emptor* doctrine, found for the seller. The consumer could have traveled to Virginia before he bought the land, the court apparently reasoned, and found out for himself whether he was being conned.

This doctrine could effectively regulate the marketplace it is true—but only if buyers treated all sellers as though they were crooks. Of course, buyers didn't do that, which is why the *caveat emptor* doctrine was able to encourage the growth of commercial activity. If people had really acted the way the law expected them to act, few people would ever have dared to buy anything. Who, after all, would buy anything from a crook?

THE "SANCTITY OF CONTRACTS"

The other doctrine the courts established—the sanctity of contracts—made it possible for a seller to finish the job of fleecing the consumer. In effect, it meant that once a buyer and seller had struck a bargain, the courts would force them to live with it without looking to see whether the bargain was fair or honorable to both sides. Even if a contract was ridiculously one-sided, a court generally decided that the buyer was stuck with it because he had "agreed" to the contract in the first place.

A piano manufacturer, for example, might give a lifetime warranty on a piano, but require the consumer to ship it back to the factory at his own expense before the manufacturer would repair it. And the warranty might further state that it was up to the manufacturer to decide if the defect was his fault. If it wasn't his fault, it wouldn't get fixed and the consumer might have to pay for return shipping costs as well. Courts made consumers live with whatever a seller managed to sneak into the fine print of a contract. So it was easy to offer "lifetime" warranties on practically anything.

The sanctity of contracts doctrine was probably not an important factor in most consumers' lives when the courts first established it during the nineteenth century. Ordinary purchases seldom involved complicated contracts, and anyway people generally bought things for cash, dealt with small, local merchants that they knew, and could make most repairs themselves.

But as the marketplace became more complicated and impersonal, products and services more technical, and the use of credit more widespread, formal contracts and legal technicalities became an important part of everyday consumer transactions. Changes in the marketplace made it harder and harder for individual consumers to protect themselves as long as consumer transactions were regulated by the *caveat emptor* and the sanctity of contracts doctrines.

Until the 1960s, the laws that were passed to protect consumers didn't really change these doctrines. Instead, they relied on criminal laws or licensing laws to ban goods or business conduct considered harmful to consumers. As long as everyone complied with them, these laws effectively protected consumers. But if the laws weren't obeyed, or if it was so tough to enforce them that they could easily be evaded, the consumer had no more protection than he had under the earlier doctrines.

Then in the 1960s, Congress and state legislatures passed laws that meant consumers would no longer have to play only by the rules based on those doctrines; the doctrines were not, however, completely replaced by the consumer protection laws that were passed so that these laws only protect you from some of the nastier things that were formerly justified by those doctrines.

8 · New Legal Tools

Gradually, the new laws have begun to shift the balance of protection toward the consumer, and the balance of risk toward the seller. They give individuals new legal tools to protect themselves.

In general, consumer protection laws help you by:

- Requiring businesses to disclose important information about products, services, agreements, and credit terms.
- Prohibiting businesses from using misleading or deceptive information or practices.
- Establishing health, safety, and performance standards that spell out how safe products or services must be, or how well they must perform.

For example, a law now requires that drug companies market drugs in "child-proof" containers to prevent accidental poisonings. Before the 1960s, health and safety laws generally banned the sale of products that were considered particularly harmful, but normally the marketplace regulated safety practices. In other words, it was up to parents to keep medicine bottles out of their children's reach.

- Regulating some of the terms and conditions included in consumer contracts.

The sanctity of contracts doctrine let the buyer and seller agree on the contract terms, but since sellers or creditors normally actually wrote the contracts used in most transactions, the provisions were rarely favorable to consumers. Consumer protection laws now prohibit some unfair contract clauses.

Until states began regulating consumer credit contracts, for instance, they might contain clauses that required a consumer who was being sued for non-payment to pay his creditor's attorney's fees. No contract ever said that a consumer would be allowed to collect his attorney's fee if he was forced to sue the seller to honor a contract.

- Providing extra protection against sellers who are especially likely to use abusive or misleading practices.

Laws regulating door-to-door sales, for example, allow customers to cancel contracts for any reason within a certain number of days. They make it possible for you to re-think a purchase that might have been made because of high-pressure tactics which you would be unable to do under contract law once a binding agreement has been made.

- Authorizing consumers to enforce regulatory laws that protect them.

It used to be that consumers had to depend on regulatory agencies to enforce consumer protection laws, but now many of the laws can be enforced by consumers themselves.

- Making it practical for consumers to use the courts to enforce consumer protection laws.

Many laws now allow consumers to collect their attorney's fees when they win; and some require businesses to pay consumers a minimum amount or punitive damages in addition to the consumer's actual damages.

- Authorizing government agencies to sue businesses on behalf of consumers, or authorizing agencies to order a business to take corrective action that directly benefits consumers.

For example, when the Federal Trade Commission Act was amended by Congress in 1975 to allow the FTC to adopt rules spelling out specific practices prohibited by the Act, the agency was authorized to take action on behalf of many consumers injured by prohibited practices.

Newer consumer protection laws like this one have begun to shift the legal balance more in the consumer's favor. The *caveat emptor* and the sanctity of contracts doctrines still live on, but they don't disarm consumers as completely as they once did. And some judges have begun to interpret the old doctrines in a more favorable light for consumers.

Interpretation of the law often depends, of course, on how forcefully consumers assert their rights.

CONTRACT AND TORT LAW

You derive your basic legal rights in consumer transactions from two main sources.

One source is contract law. It spells out the legal principles that govern a contract or agreement you make with someone. The other source is tort law which makes individuals or firms responsible for injuries or damages they cause to other people. Consumer protection laws usually strengthen the basic legal rights provided by these two sources.

(Note: The general rules discussed here are based on common or case law which does *not* apply in Louisiana. Laws in that state are based on the French rather than the English legal system.)

CONTRACT LAW

Contract law requires people to hold up their end of an agreement. It covers what kinds of commitments parties can make, when these commitments are binding, and what can be done when they are broken.

A valid contract or agreement is court-enforceable. Broadly speaking, an enforceable agreement is struck by the making and accepting of offers. But once that happens, there can be an agreement that is enforceable in court. Courts in turn make people live up to valid agreements because people have voluntarily committed themselves to do what their agreements call for. In order to be legally valid a contract or agreement must satisfy the following important requirements:

Offer

Either a buyer makes an offer to buy or a seller makes an offer to sell. The offer states the conditions under which a sale will be completed. For example, "I will sell you this 1980 deluxe model Freecare refrigerator if you pay me $499." The person making the offer leaves it up to the other person to accept or reject the offer.

It seems straightforward enough, but sometimes an offer isn't quite as simple as it seems. Most advertising, for instance, is not considered an offer to sell. Instead, it is considered merely an "offer to negotiate" with the store about the purchase. This enables some stores to advertise an item for one price, say it isn't available and then try to persuade you to buy a higher priced item. What the store advertises usually isn't really an offer that a customer could accept so as to hold the seller to the offer.

In some sales situations, what looks like the written sales terms you negotiated actually turns out to be an offer to buy. This happens most often with car sales. The salesperson fills out what looks like an agreement you're happy with. You sign it, and the salesperson signs, but it turns out that you're really signing an offer to buy that still has to be accepted by the manager. The manager then rejects it because the deal is too favorable to you. Sound familiar? It's a way of using legal technicalities as part of a sales pitch to catch unwary consumers.

Intent

The offer must be meant as a serious effort to make a sale or a purchase. The person making the offer must clearly indicate his intention to sell. A casual comment or a joke can't be treated as an offer that someone can legally enforce by accepting it. For example, if you got mad at your car and screamed, "I would sell this clunker for a dime," that's not an offer anyone could accept.

Certainty

The offer must be definite and specific and must clearly identify what is to be bought or sold. For example, if a used car dealer says: "I'll sell you a 1974 Ford two-door sedan for $2,000," it is not an offer you could accept. It doesn't specifically identify the car he is offering.

If, on the other hand, he says "I will sell you *this* 1974 Ford two-door sedan for $2,000," it is an offer you could accept.

If an offer does not clearly identify what is to be bought or sold, you can't make a seller complete the sale.

Communication

An offer can only be communicated to and accepted by the person to whom it is directed. If a company offers to open a charge account for you with a $1,000 credit limit, it is an offer that only *you* can accept. If you don't want to accept it, you cannot, for example, pass the offer along to a friend.

Acceptance of the Offer

A contract or agreement is created when the offer is accepted by the person to whom it was made. For example, when you agree to pay $499 for the Carefree refrigerator the dealer offers to sell, you have *accepted* the offer. Once you accept, both sides are committed to complete the sale.

Making and accepting an offer can be tricky. Be sure you know the terms of the offer, *who* is making it, and *who* is free to accept or reject it. If you don't understand the terms and you accept, you might be stuck with a bad deal. And if you are making an offer, don't omit anything that makes the deal favorable to you.

Rejected Offers and Counter-Offers

Once you have rejected an offer, it is dead. You can no longer make the other person buy or sell under the conditions set forth in the offer. In other words, you can't reject an offer and later say, "I'll take it after all." Once you reject an offer, the other side can change the terms, though, by increasing the price, for instance.

And usually you can't accept another person's offer by changing any of his conditions or adding your own. For example, you can't tell the appliance dealer: "I'll take your offer to sell the Carefree refrigerator, but I will pay only $459." That would be changing the other person's offer by adding your own conditions. It is the same thing as rejecting the offer. What you are now doing, in effect, is making a new offer (or counter-offer) the other person can refuse—but if *he* accepts, he is bound to the terms *you* stated.

You are always free to change the terms of an offer that someone makes to you, but remember that if you do, you cannot then still hold the other person to the original offer and the other person does not have to sell to you under the conditions you set. This may be a blessing since it may mean you will be avoiding what could turn out to be a very bad purchase.

Mutual Consent

Since a contract involves obligations that people assume voluntarily, both parties must agree to the same set of conditions. This mutual assent has been called "the meeting of the minds." If one party misrepresents, deceives or misleads the other, the contract may not be valid because it can be said that the two sides never reached a genuine agreement. But a deception or misrepresentation must be something important before you will be able to claim a contract doesn't exist, especially after both sides have carried out parts of the deal, such as taking delivery of the goods.

Suppose for example, you go into a store that sells antique wicker furniture and buy what you think is a Victorian wicker chair, but which the store never actually describes as such. If you later learn that the chair was recently made in Hong Kong, it would be very hard for you to claim the store had deceived you. But if the store *tells* you the wicker chair was made in England around 1890, and you later learn it was made in Hong Kong, you would have a strong argument for getting out of the contract since you had not agreed to buy an imitation Victorian wicker chair made in Hong Kong.

Having all the details of the purchase in writing would help you show a lack of mutual assent to avoid being bound by the supposed agreement.

Consideration

Before a contract becomes binding, both sides must exchange something of value. To lawyers, this value is known as "consideration." Consideration can be what somebody either does or promises to do, such as *paying,* or *promising to pay,* $499 in exchange for what someone else does or promises to do, such as *selling,* or *promising to sell,* the refrigerator.

The exchange does not have to be something of equal value, or anything very close to it, but just something of value. That's why courts will seldom look at whether you got *enough* for your money, as long as you got something for it.

Competent Parties

A contract is valid only when it is made between people who are legally competent to enter into contracts. Minors, for instance, are not considered legally competent and can't be held to any agreement unless they have bought necessities such as food, clothing, shelter or some services—like health care and education.

Parents are not responsible for contracts their children sign because contracts bind only those who actually agree to them.

Lawful Purpose

A contract must be for a lawful purpose. If a contract is written for an illegal purpose, such as murder, a court obviously won't enforce it if someone defaults.

Often courts will not enforce contracts made by unlicensed doctors, plumbers, real-estate brokers, dentists and so on, who are required to have a state license. If you have a contract with such an unlicensed practitioner, and a dispute arises, you may be able to get out of the contract.

Legal Form of Contracts

Except in a very few instances, such as fire insurance policies, contracts or agreements do not have to follow any specific format. And for practical purposes, the terms contracts and agreements refer to the same thing—the terms and conditions of a purchase and the legal rights and obligations that go with it.

Oral contracts may be just as valid as written ones, but it is a lot easier to enforce an agreement when it is in writing. And certain contracts *must* be in writing to show that there is an enforceable agreement. Contracts must be in writing when:

1. You buy real estate.
2. You buy items usually costing more than $500 (the limit varies from state to state).
3. The terms of a contract *cannot* be completed within one year: for instance, a lease that runs for more than a year.
4. You sign for someone else's debts.
5. You use most types of consumer credit (state and federal consumer credit laws usually require that consumer credit contracts be in writing).

In these cases, the contract must clearly identify the purchase; include important terms and conditions; and include the signature, initial, stamp, or mark of the person you want to hold to the contract. There must be tangible evidence that there was a sale, what was sold, and who was bound by the agreement. If a contract is supposed to be in writing but isn't, it usually can't be enforced.

Performance of Contracts

When each side has completed its part of an agreement, the contract has been performed and neither side is entitled to anything more.

Breach and Remedies

A contract is breached when someone fails to honor his part of the agreement. Your remedies depend on the rights you have under the contract and the law, and what the failure to perform was. Remedies refers to the legal recourse for correcting a wrong.

TORT LAW

The rights and remedies you could have for holding someone accountable under tort law do not depend on your having an agreement, but depend instead on duties the law imposes on how careful people have to be when they do things that affect others. Anyone who fails to observe those legal duties commits a legal wrong.

If someone is harmed as a direct result of a legal wrong that a person commits, tort law makes the person liable for the losses suffered by the injured person.

These are the important criteria that describe the legal wrongs people can commit.

Intentional Harm

If a person deliberately intends to harm someone and does so, tort law will hold him liable. Consumer fraud, slander, assault and battery, and invasion of privacy are examples of torts involving intentional harm.

Absolute Liability

A person becomes absolutely liable when the law holds him responsible, regardless of whether he or she intended to harm anyone. For example, tort law now makes manufacturers absolutely liable for harm caused by defective or unsafe products. It doesn't matter whether the manufacturer meant his product to harm someone or whether he was careless in designing the product; if a defective product injures someone, courts will usually hold the manufacturer liable.

Negligence

In most cases, tort law holds individuals liable when they act carelessly or negligently and someone is harmed as a result. This criterion covers many situations and is purposely flexible so courts can adapt the law to new situations. It is intended to make people err on the side of caution.

Violation of a Statute

A person can also be held liable for the harm that may result when his conduct violates a statute. Courts have held that such violations amount to negligence since people are expected to obey the law.

On the other hand, courts have also held that liability results only when the statute was specifically meant for the protection of those harmed. You might be able to use this interpretation to take action against a business that violates a law meant to protect consumers.

SECTION III
FIGHTING DECEPTIONS AND FRAUDS

9 · Recognizing What Makes You Vulnerable

Deceptions and frauds wear many faces, but they all mask one or more unpleasant truths about the real characteristics, quality, value, usefulness or capabilities of various products or services you may buy.

The deception may be quite elaborate. There is a phony "building inspector" routine, for instance, that is meant to scare you into having expensive—and useless—furnace repairs made, or even into ordering a new furnace, when the "inspector" discovers that yours is "ready to explode."

Or the deception may be a simple affair, such as the case of a company that used the name "Greenland halibut" to describe a fish that was similar to a variety known as Pacific or Atlantic halibut which is more commonly known simply as halibut. Greenland halibut, however, contained seven times more fat and twenty-five percent less protein than the other type of fish. Were consumers deceived? A U.S. District Court in Oregon thought so when it noted that sales of the fish declined sharply after the state of Oregon banned the use of the name Greenland halibut under its deceptive sales practices law.

TODAY'S MARKETPLACE EQUALS VULNERABLE CONSUMERS

You might encounter examples of deception or fraud when a salesperson pressures you to buy; or when you read a label, or sales literature, or the warranty on a product. Some of these representations may just be incomplete or inaccurate claims, of course. The name Greenland halibut, for example, wasn't a complete falsehood: some scientific articles and several editions of Webster's New International Dictionary had used the name to describe that particular fish. But how many consumers knew the name actually referred to a different kind of fish than the one normally sold as plain halibut?

This example shows why efforts to warn consumers to be wary of certain frauds and deceptions seldom succeed unless backed up by tough laws. This is not because we refuse to listen to warnings, or because we are too gullible, but because we are extremely vulnerable in today's marketplace.

Why are we so vulnerable? For a start, we depend on the marketplace to supply almost everything we need: in the past people made many more things and did many more jobs for themselves. This dependence makes us vulnerable in at least two important ways.

First, it requires us to make thousands of purchasing decisions instead of just a few important ones. Making all these decisions takes time and cuts down on what we can find out about purchases we make.

Second, dependence on the marketplace makes it hard for us to say no when we consider a purchase. When people could do many things for themselves, a seller had to overcome a consumer's strong, built-in resistance in order to make a sale, because when a consumer said no it didn't necessarily mean he had to do without. But today, since we have to buy almost everything we need, we are already halfway committed to buy before we meet a seller. That makes his job of closing a sale a lot easier. It also makes it harder for us to walk away from a sale if the seller refuses to agree to certain terms we may want to include in an agreement.

Increased dependence on the marketplace really means that consumers have lost leverage in the bargaining process, something we had almost automatically before. Now, we must make a conscious effort to create bargaining leverage for ourselves.

CREDIT: INSTANT BUYERS

Consumers are also vulnerable in other ways. The modern marketplace makes "instant purchases" possible with the use of credit. Before the use of credit became widespread in the mid-1950s, buyers used cash—and spending cash generally forced them to be careful shoppers. It also helped immunize people against many frauds and deceptions because they had to save for costly purchases. Having to save gave people time to shop around for the best buy before they were ready to buy. When it was time to buy, the serious shopper was likely to investigate claims and come back to the seller who was the most informative and helpful. This gave sellers an incentive to tell the truth.

With the advent of credit, however, serious shoppers could be turned into instant buyers if they could be convinced to buy then and there. And the store that failed to convince when the consumer came in for the first time might well lose the sale to the store that did. So the watchword for salespeople became "close the sale now" before the consumer had a chance to see anything else or to change his or her mind. The pressure to make a sale became heavier and heavier, and consumers got hooked with many schemes.

When consumers bought on credit, it also became possible for sellers to persuade customers not only to part with the money they currently had on hand, but with money they would earn in the future, too. With consumers committing themselves to costly purchases, frauds and deceptions became lucrative areas.

BELIEVING A SELLER'S CLAIMS

Every buyer/seller relationship depends on mutual trust. The *caveat emptor* doctrine assumes that buyer and seller deal with each other on the basis of mutual distrust, but in reality few people ever deal with sellers they really distrust. That, of course, is why businesses go to a lot of trouble to convince customers that their products and services are reliable and can be trusted. Have you ever heard of a store that called itself Frank's *Dishonest* Discount Shop, or advertised that it was selling services you could *not* depend on?

While people need to trust the merchants they buy from, today's impersonal marketplace means we are often forced to deal with strangers and put our faith in trust alone. Deceptions and frauds play on this trust, of course.

Besides trust, consumers also need reliable information when they make purchasing decisions. Of course, advertising, sales pitches, and the actual product supply a good deal of information, but it is often hard for consumers to evaluate its usefulness, accuracy, and reliability. How many people, after all, really know enough about microwave ovens, say, to decide whether a particular model is actually safe to use? How many of us can tell if a sweater really is made of eighty percent cotton and twenty percent polyester fibers? The lack of knowledge, not to mention the lack of means needed to evaluate such claims, makes us vulnerable to deceptions and frauds.

There is a psychological aspect to all this, too: people usually hesitate to question another person's honesty, unless they are *sure* his claims are untrue. Confrontations are unpleasant and most people want to avoid them. They also want to avoid looking foolish if it should turn out they are wrong.

Finally, there is a strong tendency for a consumer to believe a seller's claims if he or she is to make the purchase at all. This is simply because a seller is usually the major source of information: the buyer *wants* to believe his claims because he depends on the information so much.

When you recognize the kind of things that make you vulnerable, you can defend yourself in two ways. First, you can avoid trouble by testing the seller's sincerity before you buy. And second, you can use the law to fight those who do manage to deceive or defraud you.

10 · How To Test the Accuracy of Claims

You can protect yourself against frauds and deceptions, if you are prepared to test a seller's sincerity and the accuracy of his or her claims before you make your commitment to buy.

How do you go about it? The questions you ask yourself, and the questions you ask the seller, are your most important tools for testing the reliability of what you are told.

QUESTIONING CLAIMS

The most important questions to ask yourself before making a purchase are these: Why do I want this product? Will it be adequate for the purpose I have in mind? Will I be able to depend on it? Is it as good or better than something else that might do the job? Is it worth what I have to pay for it?

Some advertising and sales pitches make you believe they are providing answers to such questions. The claims work most effectively when you accept the answers without thinking much about the questions. Then it's easy to jump to the conclusion -that you have the important facts. But such ready-made answers actually dull your curiosity: it's almost as though they put your brain to sleep.

Say you are concerned about getting enough nutrients. An ad for a cereal company, for example, may tell you about its fortified breakfast cereal that supplies one hundred percent of the minimum daily allowances of certain nutrients. That seems like an easy answer to your concern about nutrients, and you forget to ask yourself other important questions, such as: Do I really need to get all these nutrients out of one serving of fortified breakfast cereal when I usually eat two other meals during the day? How much am I paying for all this fortification I might not need?

While it's impossible to question every claim you hear, try to pinpoint answers to at least the following questions. The answers will quickly show you the tactics a seller is using to try to convince you. For instance:

1. *What does the claim tell me?* Does it tell me how useful or effective a product is?

If, for example, an ad says: "Four out of five doctors recommend *this* pain reliever," it seems to be answering a question about the product's effectiveness. But has the seller really given you a convincing or important reason for buying? Test it by asking yourself: Did the answer say the four doctors recommend that it is more effective or better than others I could use? No, it simply said four out of five doctors *recommend* it, not that it was *more effective* than another pain reliever. Did the answer say that the product would effectively relieve *any* pain? It didn't specifically say that either. The claim didn't say what ailments the doctors were recommending it for.

By asking questions like these, you can test how substantial a claim really is. Vague claims like "Four out of five doctors recommend this pain reliever" are meant to make you think you have convincing answers.

2. *Is the claim reliable?* In the case of the pain reliever for instance, ask yourself: How many doctors actually made the recommendation and who were they?

Who knows? The claim doesn't tell you. It might have been no more than the four mentioned in the ad. Nevertheless, the ad can make you think hundreds, or even thousands, of doctors recommend the pain reliever. The claim appears reliable but you can't tell how reliable because the number of doctors surveyed isn't mentioned. Nor do you know which particular doctors were asked. Was the survey made only among doctors who worked for the drug company, for instance? The ad forgot to say.

These questions help you test the believability of a claim. If you haven't been given convincing answers, don't believe the claim.

3. *How firmly does the seller stand behind his claim?* What does it commit him to if the claim proves false? Can I get my money back, for instance, or will he repair the product to my satisfaction? How long will he stand behind his claim? Answers to these questions test how reliable the answers to other questions are.

There is no way you can possibly test every answer, of course. But if a seller believes his own claims, then he should be willing to back them up. If he is unwilling to stand behind them, you may be taking the entire risk if the deal turns sour. Suppose, for instance, you bought those pain relieving tablets and they didn't work for you. What good are the doctors' recommendations now?

4. *How can I hold the seller to his claims if things go wrong and he refuses to help me?* You can determine this by checking the laws discussed in this book and finding out what it would take to get your money back.

These are the questions to ask when you make a purchase. But obviously it's not sensible to ask them in a way that directly challenges the seller's honesty. Just ask for the facts. No honest business should object to your finding out facts that will show just how good the purchase will be.

THE IMPORTANCE OF WRITTEN EVIDENCE

Getting the seller's claims and promises written into your agreement is the best way to protect yourself if something goes wrong later. If you don't do this, at least keep *something* that shows *when* a purchase was made, *who* sold it to you, and *what* was promised. Written materials, documents, brochures, advertising, and even notes that show what was promised, can be important evidence.

So, get in the habit of collecting documentation that shows proof of a purchase and a seller's claims. You never know when you might need it. If you send away for a product, keep the ad that induced you to buy, and keep a copy of your order form. If you saw the product demonstrated on television, note down when you saw the commercial or program and what it demonstrated. If you buy the item at a store, ask if the product works as effectively as shown on television. Write down the answers. If you don't, and the product doesn't prove to work like the TV demonstration, how can you show you were misled?

Here is a form you can make up to pin down a seller's verbal representations. Take a copy with you if you plan to buy an important item you expect to discuss with the seller.

"As agent for _____ I made the fol-
(insert name of company, as shown in agreement)
lowing   representation(s)   on   _____   to   induce   the   purchase
(insert date)

of _____ for $_____ by _____

     (identify purchase, as in agreement)   *(insert your name)*

and I knew that the buyer relied upon the representation(s) I made which is/are

the basis for this bargain that is described in more detail on the seller's printed agree-

ment/bill of sale dated _____:"

                    (insert date, as in agreement)

(Write down the specific representations or promises that convinced you to buy.)

Before you sign anything, make sure the salesperson prints and signs his or her name below the representations.

Make sure the purchase and the company are identified on this form in exactly the same way they are identified on the printed agreement. If the agreement or bill of sale, says "1 GE dishwasher," for example, then that's how you identify the purchase on this form. Include the serial number and the purchase price, and make sure you correctly state the date of the agreement.

DANGER SIGNALS TO WATCH OUT FOR

There are certain danger signals that should alert you to the possibility of fraud and deception. When you hear any of the following think carefully about what you are doing:

1. *A seller describes a fantastic deal that sounds too good to be true.* If it sounds too good to be true, it probably is. Ask yourself: If it's really that good, why am I the lucky one?

One way to tell if a deal is as good as the seller says it is, is to price the market. If you shop regularly, you will have a fair idea of this.

2. *A seller promises something for nothing.* You may get gifts from relatives and friends, but *never* from people who are in business to sell. How can the seller stay in business if he doesn't charge you?

3. *A seller says a deal is only good for today.* Why? Is he going out of business? Is the item the only thing of its kind on earth?

4. *A seller says he can do the job for less because he just finished another job in your area.* Ask yourself what reputable contractor or repair company can stay in business when he is paying work-crews to stand around while he drums up work?

5. *A repairman "discovers" a dangerous defect in something you own that must be repaired immediately.* Ask yourself: How could he suddenly discover a grave defect when I had no inkling anything was wrong? What tests did he do and how could he find the defect so quickly? Remember, catastrophies seldom just happen; there is usually a previous indication of a malfunction, and thorough tests are generally needed to find hidden defects.

6. *A contractor has no references you can check.* What's the matter, doesn't he want you to find out how honest he is?

7. *A sale item isn't available shortly after a sale starts,* or the store disparages the advertised item in an attempt to make you buy a higher priced product. What honest business advertises goods it doesn't have in stock or it doesn't think are worth selling?

8. *A seller asks you to sign a contract with blanks in it or he doesn't give you a chance to read it before signing.* Ask if he would be willing to sign the contract and let you fill it in later. If he doesn't like your suggestion, why should you like his?

9. *A seller emphasizes the cost of each payment rather than the total cost of the sale.* What honest person wants to hide what you really owe him?

10. *A seller says you must pay in advance,* before the merchandise is delivered or before any work is done. Ask yourself if the business can be in good financial shape if it has to be paid before it has *earned* its money.

11. *A seller tries to make you feel guilty for asking legitimate questions about his claims or products.* What business tries to keep you from learning about what it's selling if something is worth buying? Won't the truth sell? Only a dishonest person uses this technique.

12. *A seller asks, "Don't you trust me?"* A seller throws this one at you to put you on the defensive. If you say no, you are directly accusing him of dishonesty; if you say yes, you are forced to believe him. If a seller has really earned your trust, he doesn't have to ask you about it. And if he hasn't done anything to earn your trust, don't trust him simply because he puts you on the spot with this sort of question.

PUTTING THE SELLER ON THE DEFENSIVE

A seller's "Don't you trust me?" ploy, or a variation on the theme, is designed to put you on the defensive. It forces you to challenge his honesty when you are least prepared to do so, and stops you cold as you question his claims.

What can you do to beat the ploy? Throw the challenge back at him. Since the seller has asked whether *you* trust *him,* force him to say whether *he* is ready to trust *you.*

Suppose, for example, you are ready to leave your TV at a repair shop, but you want to include on the repair record that repairs are not to exceed $50. Instead of simply agreeing to the suggestion, the salesperson says: "That's not necessary. Don't you trust us?"

You could say something like this: "Of course I trust you. And since we trust each other, let's forget about signing the repair order. Just give me a signed receipt for the TV set, and I will promise to pay you not more than $50 for the necessary repairs we agreed upon."

When the salesperson says he needs a signed repair order, simply say: "I agreed to pay you for the necessary repairs. What's the matter, don't you trust me?"

Now you have turned the challenge around and put him on the spot. And you can keep on doing so simply by matching him. If, for example, he says he needs the order in writing because the law requires it, then that's why you need your demand in writing. This sort of tactic forces the other side to recognize just how unfair it is being. If, in the end, he still refuses to be fair, it is time to go elsewhere.

Avoiding traps by spotting them before they catch you is always your best protection. But you also need a tough second line of defense: laws that can help you make it very costly for those who manage to slip through the first line.

11 · Legal Weapon No. 1:
The Federal Trade Commission Act

You have three major legal weapons to fight a seller who misleads or deceives you. They are the Federal Trade Commission (FTC) Act; state deceptive sales practices laws; and state fraud laws. Sometimes, as I'll show you later in this section, you can combine these different laws for maximum effect.

This chapter tells what the FTC Act is and what it prohibits, and when a complaint to the FTC is a worthwhile step in your negotiating strategy if someone has violated the FTC Act.

What is the FTC Act? It is the broadest federal law dealing with consumer deception in the marketplace. Congress created the Federal Trade Commission in 1914 to enforce it, but today the FTC also enforces a number of other consumer protection laws.

WHAT THE FTC ACT PROHIBITS

Not everything in the FTC Act applies directly to consumer transactions. The part that does, however, makes it illegal for a business to use "unfair or deceptive acts or practices" that affect interstate commerce which, as a practical matter, covers almost any business practice in today's marketplace. Broad and flexible standards are used to define the words "unfair" and "deceptive," in order to make it hard for businesses to evade the law by coming up with some new practice not yet precisely defined. These guidelines have been established over the years via FTC and court decisions.

The act applies to almost every kind of business and industry except banks, common carriers such as railroads and bus lines, air carriers, meat packers, insurance companies and communications businesses such as TV stations and telephone companies.

DECEPTIVE PRACTICES

"Acts and practices" covers what a seller does to induce you to buy. Such acts are considered deceptive when they mislead you in some way about the characteristics, quality, price, benefits, usefulness or other features of the product or service you are buying. A selling practice can be deceptive in one of two ways: either because it misleads by what it tells you, or because it misleads by what it doesn't tell you about a product.

However, when a salesperson engages in "puffing," that is, when he only praises his own product or service or when he makes purely fanciful claims, the law may not consider these practices to be deceptive. For example, a puffing claim might occur when a car salesman says: "You'll really be happy with this car." Though you may later find out the car is defective, to be considered deceptive, the salesman's claim would have to have been much more specific, such as: "We have inspected the car and found it to be in good mechanical condition and free of defects that would impair its performance." A fanciful claim is one like the TV commercial for a cleaning product where a white knight charged into the kitchen to help clean it, which obviously would not really happen.

UNFAIR PRACTICES

The FTC Act also prohibits unfair practices. A 1972 Supreme Court decision gave the word "unfair" a broader meaning than deception. It said a practice is considered unfair when it offends public policy; that is, some firmly established community standard of right and wrong. A practice is also considered unfair when it violates some standard of fairness established by another law, or when it is immoral, unethical or unscrupulous, or when it causes substantial harm to consumers.

These guidelines are vague, it is true, but they show that unfair practices cover more ground than deceptive practices, so the seller takes a bigger risk when he acts unethically.

WHAT THE FTC ACT CAN DO FOR YOU

You may well ask why, if the FTC Act prohibits acts or practices sellers might use to gyp consumers, hasn't the law worked more effectively to keep consumers from being gypped? The main reason is that the act still lacks some of the teeth necessary for really effective consumer protection. While it was strengthened by congressional amendments made in 1975, it still needs improvements before consumers can really use it to protect themselves.

There are at least three reasons why the FTC Act lacks sting. One reason is that consumers cannot take legal action on their own against someone who has gypped them by acts or practices prohibited by the act. The FTC Act can be enforced only by the FTC. Another reason is that the FTC still has only very limited authority to enforce the act, such as getting money back for consumers who have been victimized by an illegal act or practice. And finally, the FTC simply lacks the resources needed to take action against everyone who might violate the act. So even though the FTC has been set up as the federal agency primarily responsible for policing the fairness of marketplace practices, it lacks the resources for constantly patrolling its beat.

There are, however, some important ways the FTC Act and the FTC can be of help to you. In 1975 Congress authorized the FTC to adopt what are called trade regulation rules that specifically describe unfair or deceptive acts or practices. These regulations spell out what steps businesses must take to avoid violating the act. This and other sections cover important rules the FTC has adopted that can help protect you (the rules are identified in the chapters where they are described). Although you cannot take action on your own to enforce these rules, the rules sometimes require businesses to do things which become part of your agreement so that you can then enforce those requirements as rights you have under your agreement.

While the act can only be enforced by the FTC and you cannot personally sue someone who violates it, the 1975 amendments permit the FTC to take legal action on behalf of consumers who have been the victims of an act or practice prohibited by the trade regulation rules adopted by the FTC. The FTC can also take action on behalf of individual consumers if a business continues to use a practice after the FTC has ordered it to stop by issuing what is called a cease and desist order. In these two situations, the FTC can, for example, go to court to recover money consumers might have lost as a result of a company's violation of the act. It can also collect a fine of up to $10,000 per violation if a business violates a trade regulation rule. So it is now riskier for a company to use any practice which has been specifically declared as unfair or deceptive over a long period of time because then each day could count as a separate violation.

The FTC has not used these powers very often; and because they are so new, it still isn't clear how effective they'll be. But what business wants to be the first to learn how the FTC powers can sting?

In 1980, for example, the FTC charged that the Chrysler Corporation had failed to disclose to consumers a design defect in its 1976 and 1977 Dodge Aspen and Plymouth Volare models that caused the top front fenders to rust prematurely. In effect, the FTC claimed that consumers had been misled by the company's failure to disclose pertinent information.

The FTC also charged that Chrysler had failed to tell all the affected car owners that it would repair the defect at its expense, and in fact only did so for those consumers who persistently complained about it.

Instead of fighting the FTC over the issue, the company agreed to settle it by replacing or repairing the rusted fenders without charge, and by reimbursing those owners who had already replaced them. The $45 million settlement affected about one million cars.

When the FTC began to use its new powers to adopt trade regulation rules prohibiting unfair or deceptive practices, and to implement them over such problems as the rusted car fenders, business began to complain to Congress. During the 1979–1980 session, Congress threatened to cut off the FTC's budget and tried to curb its powers.

HOW TO USE THE FTC ACT

Because you cannot personally take legal action to enforce it, the act is not always your most effective weapon. Usually, you will find your state's deceptive sales practices law is the more useful because these laws usually allow consumers to take personal legal action against a business. (See chapter 18). Most state deceptive sales practices laws are also closely patterned after the FTC Act. And state courts usually follow the FTC Act guidelines when deciding what business practices the state law will prohibit, so that you may be able to use your state's deceptive sales practices law to take action against someone who violates the FTC Act.

In many instances the FTC Act and FTC trade regulation rules will also be important to your negotiating strategy even though you can't enforce them. Some of the trade regulation rules covered in this book require businesses to include important clauses in your agreement that will create rights for you which you can enforce or which prohibit a business from doing certain things. When you make a purchase from a door-to-door salesman, for instance, the FTC "Cooling-off Period for Door-to-Door Sales" rule entitles you to cancel most agreements within three business days after the purchase. This rule is covered in the next two chapters.

You gain your right to cancel because the rule requires the business to include it as part of your agreement. You can then enforce that right not because of what the rule says, but because of what your agreement says. To be sure of acquiring the rights, you must, however, make sure that the business complies with the rule. Other important rules work in a similar way.

There are times when a seller might claim that an FTC trade regulation rule does not apply to your specific purchase. Most of the rules have some exceptions, and I will tell you about the important ones to prevent you from being fooled by this tactic. If you are not sure whether a rule applies to your situation, simply tell the seller: "If this purchase isn't covered by this rule for the reasons you give, then I can't buy it because the rights I have under that rule are important to me." If the seller doesn't want you to have the rights to enforce your agreement, what makes you think you can trust him to live up to any promises he makes?

CALLING IN THE FTC TO HELP SETTLE A DISPUTE

Sometimes your negotiating strategy might require you to ask the FTC for help. When a business violates a trade regulation rule, it is certainly worth notifying the FTC if the business refuses to settle your dispute.

In the next few chapters of this section I will show you how to use this leverage as part of your negotiating strategy for each of the trade regulation rules.

Here is a sample letter you can adapt for notifying the FTC about violations of the FTC Act or trade regulation rules.

Always address such a letter to the FTC's Washington office. Use the basic format that follows, but obviously you must describe your specific complaint, and refer to the specific rule the company in question is violating.

200 Forest Lane
Anytown, New York 00000

March 11, 19___

Regional Director
Federal Trade Commission
26 Federal Plaza
New York, NY 10007

Dear Sir,

I am hereby notifying you that the _____,
(name of company)
may have committed an unfair or deceptive practice by its failure to comply with the cooling-off period for door-to-door sales trade regulation rule.

The details about the transaction and my efforts to make the company comply with the rule are described in the letter I wrote the company on February 10, 19___, a copy of which is attached.

To date, the company has refused to refund my down payment after I canceled the contract according to the requirements stated in the FTC rule.

I am requesting that the FTC investigate the practices of the company and use its authority under the FTC Act to seek redress for injuries suffered by consumers as a result of any violations of this rule and to collect from the company the maximum civil penalty allowed by the act.

Thank you for your prompt action in this matter.

Sincerely,

12 · The FTC's and State Rules on Door-to-Door Sales

Door-to-door selling is an ancient practice that has been expertly refined to fit the modern marketplace. While door-to-door salespersons can certainly make it easy for us to buy, they can also spring traps on the unwary.

The fact is that buying in the comfort of your home puts you at a tremendous disadvantage psychologically. This is the place where you normally entertain and try to make guests feel welcome, and salespersons often take advantage of that fact. They have carefully worked-out ploys to get inside your home in the first place, and, once inside, they have well-rehearsed sales pitches to try to convince you to buy. You may not know a thing about the product or service a seller is pushing and be completely unprepared to counter his pitch. You can't just walk away from him, though, as you might in a store, and it isn't easy to throw someone out of your home. Seldom are you placed in a more vulnerable position; tailored to make you fall for high-pressure tactics, deceptions, and frauds.

Until consumers acquired the right to cancel a home-solicitation sale for any reason, they were usually stuck with an agreement they had signed; unless they had legal justification for getting out of the deal, such as fraud committed by the seller. If they bought on credit, but the seller broke the agreement, they often had to continue paying anyway—in this case to a third party, such as a bank, that bought their contract.

The FTC's trade regulation rule governing door-to-door sales now gives consumers the right to cancel a door-to-door sale during a "cooling-off" period. This period usually runs for three business days after a sale is made in your home. The FTC's rule applies in every state and gives you basic protection. In addition, almost every state has a home solicitation sales law which may provide you with extra rights.

This chapter describes the rights you have under the FTC's rule and tells you how to find and use any additional rights created by state law.

HOW TO AVOID TROUBLE

Since a home-solicitation sale puts you in such a vulnerable position, the surest way to avoid trouble is never to buy from a door-to-door salesperson in the first place. An exception might be when you have specifically invited the person to your home and are prepared to discuss the purchase you want to make and have familiarized yourself with the law beforehand.

If you are unwilling to follow that dictum (and many consumers are, or else they forget it), then here are a few suggestions you can follow to protect yourself.

Before you let anyone inside your home, question the story a salesperson tells you in the hope of getting inside the door. Salespeople call this pitch the "door-opener" story: it is a ploy to gain your confidence and make you lower your guard.

Ask for positive written identification, such as a business card. It should include the person's name, the organization he or she represents, its local address, and telephone number. Make sure you identify the *complete* name of the organization (especially if the person claims to represent a government agency, a non-profit organization, or an established business). *Never* let anyone inside until the person has given you this information and you have verified his identity and the purpose of the visit. Close the door and let the person wait outside while you check.

Don't be fooled into ignoring this rule. Suppose, for example, you don't get the information needed to verify the salesperson's mission because he starts out by asking you to complete a questionnaire at the door. Then after you get started, he suggests it might be easier to finish the interview inside the house. Don't let the person in until you get the identification and check it out. If you do, you will be falling for a "door-opener." Say something like: "That would be fine, but first I would like some written identification I can verify before we go inside."

When you are verifying the information, don't immediately call the telephone number the salesperson has given you. It's easy to make up identification and business cards, and the salesperson's accomplice could be answering the phone number given on a phony business card. Instead, test the reliability of the information by looking up the organization in the telephone book. If the organization is listed and the numbers match, then place your call. Now you can verify the salesperson's identity and the story he told you. Of course, if the numbers don't match or if the organization isn't listed in the phone book, don't proceed any further with the purchase.

You can also check an organization by calling a city or county consumer protection department or agency. Ask if the office has heard of, or has any complaints about, the organization. If there have been complaints, don't go ahead with the purchase.

A further word of caution. If the seller gives a post office box number as an address, don't buy. And if he gives an out-of-state address and there is no local address and phone number you can check, don't buy. In either case, if trouble arises, it will be hard to *locate* the seller, let alone get him to remedy the situation.

TAPE-RECORD THE CONVERSATION

Once a salesperson is inside your home there is a simple way to check on his or her honesty: tape-record the conversation. Because your conversation will be "on the record," the salesperson will either tone down his pitch or else he will decide to leave before launching into it. Someone intent on deceiving you is likely to decide to move on rather than allow himself to be recorded.

If you decide to use a tape recorder, don't let the person get started until the recorder is switched on. Here are the important questions and facts to get on record:

1. Are you aware that I am recording our conversation?"
2. Could you tell me your name and would you spell it for me?
3. What is the name, local address, and phone number of the organization you represent?
4. What is today's date?
5. Could you describe the purpose of your visit?
6. Is that the *sole* purpose of your visit? (Ask this as a follow-up question to spot any deceptive "lead-in" pitch meant to disguise the real purpose of the visit.)

WHEN DOES THE COOLING-OFF PERIOD APPLY?

The FTC's rule giving consumers the right to cancel a door-to-door sale during a cooling-off period applies in the following instances:

● When the purchase involves the sale, lease, or rental of consumer goods or services (that is, those intended primarily for personal, family, or household use) costing $25 or more.

• When the seller contacts you in person and you make the purchase; that is, you agree to buy or sign an agreement somewhere other than the seller's permanent place of business or permanent local address. The rule also covers purchases made at a friend's house, at your office, or at a temporary sales location such as an hotel meeting room used by the seller.

Thus, in short, the rule applies when the purchase price is $25 or more; the sale involves personal contact by the seller; and the sales contact occurs and the purchase is made some place other than the seller's place of business.

WHEN THE RULE DOES NOT APPLY

There are some important exceptions to the FTC rule, however. It does *not* apply to purchases:

1. When you initially discuss the purchase at the permanent location of a retail business establishment where goods are exhibited or services offered for sale. This means, for example, that the rule does not apply if you first visit a retail store, discuss a purchase, then ask the store to send someone to your home to complete the purchase. (The rule would apply, though, if you simply ask a store to send a salesperson to your home and you make a purchase there.)

2. When you are entitled to cancel an agreement because of rights you have under the Truth-in-Lending Act. This law creates a cooling-off period which applies in many credit sales situations. See Chapter 54 for details.

3. When you call a seller and ask him to provide goods or services during an emergency. An example would be if a pipe bursts, your basement gets flooded and you call a plumber to fix it right away. But this exception applies if *you* initiate the contact with, say, the plumber *and* you also write out and sign a statement describing the emergency and give up your right to cancel the agreement. A seller might ask you to sign such a statement even though this exception may not apply. Don't write out and sign a statement like this unless it is a real emergency.

4. When you make a purchase by mail or telephone and there is no contact between you and the seller until the goods are delivered or the services performed. This exception applies even if a seller calls you first and you agree to buy while you discuss the purchase over the phone. Obviously, it pays to be careful when you buy something over the phone.

5. When you initiate the contact and specifically ask a seller to visit your home to repair or perform maintenance work on your personal property. If you call a TV repair shop and ask them to send someone to your home to fix your TV set, for instance, the repairs would not be covered by the rule. But if the repairman tries to sell you a new TV set and you buy it, the purchase would be covered.

6. When you purchase or rent real property, buy insurance, or buy securities or commodities from a broker-dealer registered with the Securities and Exchange Commission.

YOUR RIGHTS UNDER THE RULE

The FTC trade regulation rule governing door-to-door sales gives you these rights:

1. The seller must give you a written receipt that describes the purchase, or a copy of any written contract you sign. The contract or receipt must include the date of the sale and the name and address of the seller. It is vital that your receipt or contract be dated accurately because your cooling-off period begins on the date stated on your receipt or contract.

2. The seller must allow you three business days during which you can cancel the purchase. You do not have to give any reason for canceling.

3. The seller must include a statement of this right on your receipt or in your contract. When he does this, your right to cancel becomes a contract condition you can enforce in court. To describe your right to cancel, the seller must include the following statement (or something very similar) on the front page of the receipt or near the space where you sign a contract:

"You, the buyer, may cancel this transaction at any time prior to midnight of the third business day after the date of this transaction. See the attached notice of cancellation form for an explanation of this right."

4. The seller must also give you a separate notice of your right to cancel when you sign. The notice must be in duplicate, it must be identified by the words "Notice Of Cancellation," and it must be attached to the receipt or the contract in such a way that you can easily remove it. Here is what the notice must say in at least the following size type:

NOTICE OF CANCELLATION

[make sure the date given is accurate]

_____

(date)

You may cancel this transaction, without any penalty or obligation, within three business days from the above date.

If you cancel, any property traded in, any payment made by you under the contract or sale, and any negotiable instrument executed by you will be returned within ten business days following receipt by the seller of your cancellation notice, and any security interest arising out of this transaction will be canceled.

If you cancel, you must make available to the seller at your residence, in substantially as good condition as when received, any goods delivered to you under this contract or sale; or you may if you wish, comply with the instructions of the seller regarding the return shipment of the goods at the seller's expense and risk.

If you do make the goods available to the seller and the seller does not pick them up within twenty days of the date of your notice of cancellation, you may retain or dispose of the goods without any further obligation. If you fail to make the goods available to the seller, or if you agree to return the goods to the seller and fail to do so, then you may remain liable for performance of all obligations under the contract.

To cancel this transaction, mail or deliver a signed and dated copy of this cancel-

lation notice or any other written notice, or send a telegram to [name of seller] _____

at [the seller must insert the address where you can mail the notice] _____ not later

than midnight of _____ . [Seller must insert the date by which you can cancel.]

I hereby cancel this transaction.

(Date) [write in the date on which you cancel.] _____

(Note: We have added the words contained within the brackets, which are _not_ part of the notice. Sundays and the following holidays do _not_ count as business days:

New Year's Day, Washington's Birthday, Memorial Day, Independence Day, Labor Day, Veterans' Day, Thanksgiving Day, and Christmas Day.)

If the seller fails to include the required clause in your agreement, it may be hard for you to argue you are still entitled to cancel the contract because of what the FTC rule says. (You might, of course, still be entitled to cancel it because of a state law.) So, always check to make sure the clause is included. And always insist that it is followed. If a seller balks, point out, for example, that the FTC cooling-off-period rule requires that your cancellation rights be included in an agreement made by a door-to-door seller, and that the failure to include it is an unfair or deceptive sales practice. If the seller insists on ignoring the rule, don't buy from him.

The notice describes these rights:

• If you cancel, within the specified time, you no longer owe the seller for the purchase.

• If you cancel, the seller must refund any payments you made, and return anything you traded in, within ten business days. If you made a purchase on credit and signed any paper (negotiable instrument) which was a promise to pay for what you owed (a postdated check, for example), the seller must return it to you.

• If the seller acquired the right to repossess any collateral, in case you failed to pay (that is, a security interest), he must cancel his right to do so.

• If you cancel, you must return any goods you received, and they must be in substantially the same condition as when you received them. You must also allow the seller to pick up the goods at your residence; you do not have to ship them back, even if the seller asks you to. You can, however, send the merchandise back if the seller pays the return postage and is willing to assume the risk of damage in shipment.

Remember, *do not* use the goods and *do not* throw away any packing materials or anything else that came with the merchandise so you can return the goods in almost exactly the same condition as they arrived. This way you will preserve your right to cancel the purchase.

• Within twenty calendar days (not business days) after you send your notice of cancellation, the seller must pick up the goods. If he does not do so, he loses his right to them. You don't have to pay for them and you can keep them or dispose of them as you wish. If you don't make the goods available to the seller during that period, however, or if you fail to ship them back once you agree to do so, then you may have to honor your agreement and pay for the goods.

Unfortunately, the rule does not spell out what you have to do to make the goods available to the seller during the twenty-day period. For this reason it might be easier to send the goods back if the seller asks you to, otherwise you may have to arrange for someone to be at your home during this period. Alternatively, try to arrange a pick-up date with the seller.

• Your notice to cancel must be in writing. You can do this by simply signing, dating and returning one copy of the Notice of Cancellation form to the address shown. Keep the other copy for your records. To be on the safe side, however, I suggest that you send the notice along with a separate cancellation letter.

WHAT A FIRM CANNOT DO

If a business ignores the rights the FTC rule creates for you, it is guilty of an unfair practice under the FTC Act. A business is also guilty of such a practice if:

• It fails to inform you orally about your right to cancel when you make a purchase.

• It misrepresents your right to cancel. A salesperson might tell you, for instance, that the purchase can be canceled up to one week after the merchandise is delivered. If you did cancel in a week, of course, you would be too late to preserve your rights under the door-to-door sales rule.

Or the salesperson might tell you that you can still cancel after trying out the product. But remember the rule does not require a business to honor your cancellation if you do not return the product in substantially the same condition as you received it.

Always follow the instructions on your Notice of Cancellation, and ignore a salesperson's promises about cancellations unless he puts them in writing.

• It fails to notify you whether it will pick up or abandon any goods shipped to you. The seller is supposed to send a notice telling what he will do within ten business days after receiving your notice to cancel. But your obligation to return the goods does not hinge on the seller sending this notice; you still have to make the goods available during the twenty-day period. However, if the seller does not notify you and then claims he won't honor the cancellation because the goods weren't available when he wanted to pick them up, you could argue that because he failed to notify you, you were obviously unaware of when he wanted to pick up the goods.

WHAT REMEDIES DO CONSUMERS HAVE?

Assuming the rule is part of your agreement, the most likely disputes to arise will concern either a seller who fails to refund your money, or a creditor who tries to collect on a contract when you made the purchase on credit.

While you cannot sue the seller for violating the rule (only the FTC can do that), you can enforce your rights in other ways.

• First, if a business ignores your rights or commits any of the unfair or deceptive practices described on page 60, it can be penalized by the FTC for up to $10,000 per violation. The FTC can also recover money lost by consumers.

• Second, if the company includes the cancellation clause in your agreement, these rights become part of your agreement and you can sue if the agreement is broken.

The cancellation clause also gives you leverage if you use certain types of credit to pay for the purchase. In some cases, a creditor would be unable to collect when you canceled. Page 523 tells how you acquire these rights under the FTC's "Preservation of Consumers' Claims and Defenses" rule when you make a credit purchase, and page 482 describes how you acquire these rights under the Fair Credit Billing Act when you charge a purchase to a credit card account.

• Third, almost every state has adopted a home solicitation sales law that creates a cooling-off period for door-to-door sales similar to the one created by the FTC rule. These laws often allow you to sue a seller. Sometimes you can also recover your attorney's fees. State laws do differ, of course. Some state laws may only apply to credit purchases. Others may only cover purchases costing more than $25. Still others may not cover purchases charged to an existing charge account.

But even if your state law creates fewer rights, remember the seller must still comply with the FTC rule.

To find out what your rights are under your state law, write to your attorney general's office—listed in the Directory of State Agencies—and ask for their brochure on the law. Ask specifically if the law allows you to recover your attorney's fees in case the brochure does not tell you this.

• Finally, a seller's refusal to honor a cancellation or to refund your money might be an unfair or deceptive practice under your state's deceptive sales practices law. (See Chapter 18.) State courts often follow the guidelines established under the FTC

Act when they interpret their own deceptive sales practices law. Your damages would be the money the seller failed to refund. And if a seller ignores your contractual right to cancel the agreement by failing to respond to repeated requests for a refund, he may be committing a fraud. (See Chapter 21.)

Remember, none of the laws will help you if you can't locate the seller to sue him, or if the seller's office is so far from your home that it is difficult to start a suit. So if the seller tells you to mail the cancellation notice to a post office box, or does not have a local address *don't buy*. Just imagine the difficulties involved in suing a post office box, for instance.

13 · Negotiating Strategy for Door-to-Door Sales Disputes

First, quickly decide if you really want the product. The cooling-off period is not a trial period to enable you to find out if the product works; it just gives you a chance to decide whether you still want to buy after the salesperson has left.

As an example of how to use your rights, let's suppose you purchase a complete home security system, including fire and burglar alarms, from the Supersafe Security Company on May 10 for $400. The salesperson leaves the set with you since you are going to install it yourself. You pay $100 down and charge the rest to your Master Money credit account.

Before you install the system, call the local fire or police department, or a store that sells alarms, to find out if they have heard of the system and what they think of it. Ask what kind of system they recommend and how much it costs. Experts like these can sometimes suggest alternatives that will help you evaluate whether you are really getting a good deal. If the fire department, for instance, tells you about an adequate system that costs only half what you are paying, then naturally you should cancel.

CANCELING A PURCHASE

Here is a sample letter you can adapt for canceling a purchase.

2101 Culver Street
Anytown, USA 00000

May 12, 19___

Supersafe Security Company
500 Burglary Road
Anytown, USA 00000

Dear Sir:

I am enclosing my signed Notice of Cancellation dated May 12, 19___, to inform you that, as provided in our agreement and the FTC trade regulation on door-to-door sales, I am canceling the transaction for the fire and burglar alarm system I purchased from you for $400 on May 10, 19___. The purchase is identified on your sales receipt number 100-2001. I paid $100 by check on May 10, and charged the $300 balance to my Master Money credit account, number 000-0000-00.

Please refund the $100 down payment and take whatever steps are necessary to ensure that my Master Money credit card account is not billed for the charges I no longer owe, as called for by our agreement and the FTC trade regulation rule.

I am prepared to return the fire and burglar alarm system to you at your convenience if you will give me two days' notice so I can arrange for someone to be home when you call. Or if you request, I am prepared to ship the goods back to you, at your expense and risk, upon receipt of the refund and a credit to my Master Money account. In the meantime, I am storing the alarm system in its original packing carton.

    You may contact me at 555-7777 between 9:00 A.M. and 5:00 P.M. and at 111-9999 between 6:00 P.M. and 10:00 P.M. so we can arrange for the return of the merchandise.

    Thank you for settling this matter promptly.

Sincerely,

If the merchandise has not yet arrived by the time you cancel, substitute the following sentence for the first sentence of paragraph four.

    "I am prepared to hold the fire and burglar alarm system when it arrives and to return it at your convenience if you will give me two days' notice so I can arrange for someone to be home when you call."

If the purchase involves a service, such as dancing lessons, simply delete the fourth paragraph.

You must get proof of mailing when you send this letter, so you can show it was mailed in time. Since the rule only requires you to *send* the cancellation within the cooling-off period, a receipt of mailing from the post office will be enough to support your case. Some state laws may require you to use certified or registered mail. Follow any instructions in any cancellation notice required by state law to preserve your rights under the state law.

Please note that neither the FTC rule nor the state laws *require* you to use the kind of sample cancellation letter shown. You could simply send the signed and dated copy of the Notice of Cancellation, or just write "I am canceling the purchase I made on May 10." I recommend, however, that you use the more detailed sample letter for two reasons. First, it shows that you know about your rights. A company is less likely to ignore a letter like this than if it is a simple cancellation statement. Second, the letter puts the company on notice that you expect it to perform its obligations, and it indicates your willingness to be reasonable about returning the merchandise. If the company ignores the letter, it will be hard for it to claim that *you* failed to do what the rule required.

I also recommend that you detach only one of the two copies of the Notice of Cancellation from your receipt or contract. Leave the other copy attached so there won't be any question that the notice was part of your agreement.

PRESERVING YOUR RIGHTS WHEN YOU BUY ON CREDIT

If you charge a purchase costing at least $50 with a credit card and are billed for a purchase you have cancelled, immediately tell the credit card issuer about the cancellation and that you no longer owe the money. The Fair Credit Billing Act gives you some protections here. (See Chapter 58.) The $50 limit is important so *never* let a seller talk you into signing several charge slips for less than $50. The cancellation and your refusal to accept the product could also be a "billing error" as provided by the Fair Credit Billing Act that can trigger other protections you can use to avoid having to pay the card issuer. (See Chapter 56.)

If you used any other kind of credit such as an installment sales contract and the seller complied with the FTC's "Preserving Consumers' Claims and Defenses" Rule at the time of purchase, the rule will probably help you stop the creditor cold if he tries to collect after cancellation. But, again, you will have to notify the creditor immediately that you have cancelled the agreement. (See Chapter 64) for an explanation of how to use these rights.)

STAGE ONE: OPENING SKIRMISHES

Wait at least twenty days to see if the seller responds to your cancellation letter. If he makes no effort to contact you about returning the merchandise, you are almost certainly entitled to keep it without having to pay for it.

Getting back the money you have paid, though, may be difficult.

Your opening skirmish in these situations would usually be trying to get your money back. You should put your request in writing. Here is a sample letter you can adapt for requesting a refund. The wording assumes the May 12 cancellation letter was mailed on May 13.

2101 Culver Street
Anytown, USA 00000

June 3, 19—

Supersafe Security Company
500 Burglary Street
Anytown, USA 00000

Dear Sir:

I am notifying you that I have not received the refund due for the down payment of $100 I made on the door-to-door sales transaction for the fire and burglar alarm system I purchased from you on May 10, 19—. I canceled the purchase by mailing my letter of cancellation on May 13, as shown on the copy of the enclosed mailing receipt.

As called for by our agreement and the FTC trade regulation rule on door-to-door sales, the refund was to have been mailed to me within ten business days after you received my cancellation notice. You were also supposed to notify me about what you intended to do with the merchandise that was delivered, but I have received no notification. And although I have been prepared to return the merchandise during the twenty-day period stated in the FTC rule, you have apparently made no effort to arrange for the return of the merchandise as I suggested in my cancellation letter.

If the refund is not already in the mail, please mail it to me immediately and also take the necessary steps to credit my Master Money account, number 000-0000-00, for the $300 purchase balance I charged to that account but which is no longer due or owing upon cancellation. I am also still prepared to return the merchandise if you make prior arrangements for picking it up or furnish me instructions for returning it at your expense and risk.

I will appreciate your mailing the refund and crediting my account promptly so I will not have to pursue this matter further.

Sincerely,

Include a *copy* of your proof of mailing to show that you have a solid cancellation.

This letter gives the company a chance to correct a mistake, and it also shows your continued willingness to return the merchandise even though you may no longer be required to do so. Give the company at least fifteen days to respond.

If it does not, send the same letter, but this time by certified mail, return receipt requested. Type or write the certified letter no. at the top, and add the following words to the beginning of the first sentence:

> *"Since you may not have received my letter of June 3, 19___, I am again notifying you . . ."*

then continue with the rest of the letter.

Give the company at least another fifteen days to respond from the date that they receiyed your letter. The return receipt will give you this information.

STAGE TWO: THE LOW-KEYED WARNING

If you still do not receive a response, it's time for the low-keyed warning. The sample letter below assumes the purchase was made in Rhode Island and that a violation of the state's deceptive sales practices law occurred. (See Chapter 18.)

Certified Letter No. 03948572

> *2101 Culver Street*
> *Anytown, USA 00000*
>
> *July 10,19___*

> *Supersafe Security Company*
> *500 Burglary Street*
> *Anytown, USA 00000*

> *Dear Sir:*
>
> *I am notifying you of the unfair or deceptive practice that occurred when you failed to refund my $100 down payment, or to credit my Master Money credit account, number 000-0000-00, for the $300 purchase balance as you were required to do by our agreement and the FTC trade regulation rule on door-to-door sales. (Your failure to refund the down payment also disregards the requirements of the Rhode Island home solicitation sales law.)**
>
> *I was entitled to the refund and the credit when I canceled the May 10 door-to-door transaction for a fire and burglar alarm system, as I have more fully explained in previous letters.*
>
> *I have received no response from you although I have repeatedly notified you that I have not received my refund. The last letter was sent by certified mail dated June 19 which the post office said was delivered to you on June 25, 19___, a copy of which is enclosed. Nor have you responded to my letter of June 3 or the cancellation letter I mailed on May 13.*
>
> *You are immediately to refund the $100 down payment, and when you do, I would still be prepared to return the goods to you at your expense and risk.*
>
> *I hope that your immediate refund will finally resolve this matter so I will not have to pursue it further.*
>
> *Sincerely,*

*NOTE: You would include this sentence only if you know what a seller is required to do to comply with your state law.

If you were going to base your negotiating strategy on the fraud law (see Chapter 21) instead of the deceptive sales practices law, then substitute the following sentence at the beginning of the letter.

> *"I am notifying you that you may be liable for intentional fraud because of your continuing refusal to refund my $100 down payment, or to credit my Master Money credit account, number 000-0000-00, for the $300 purchase balance as you were required to do by our agreement and the FTC trade regulation rule on door-to-door sales."*

Leave the rest of the sample letter the same.

Remember, however, that if you have been billed for the purchase by the creditor, you should already have notified him about the cancellation in order to preserve the rights available to you under consumer credit laws.

STAGE THREE: THE ULTIMATUM

Allow the company another fifteen days from the date you send the low-keyed warning letter; if there is still no response, then write your ultimatum. The company's failure to respond to all the past chances you have given it demonstrates a determination to ignore the law that should make it vulnerable to all the penalties the law imposes.

Certified Letter No. 02938475

> *2101 Culver Street*
> *Anytown, Rhode Island 00000*
>
> *July 26, 19___*

> *Supersafe Security Company*
> *500 Burglary Street*
> *Anytown, USA 00000*

> *Dear Sir:*

> *I am notifying you of the violation of the Rhode Island deceptive sales practices law which occurred when, upon proper cancellation of my purchase, the Supersafe Security Company failed to refund my $100 down payment, or to credit my Master Money account, for the $300 purchase price balance as required under both the agreement of May 10, 19___, and the FTC trade regulation rule on door-to-door sales transactions. (The failure to refund the down payment is also a violation of the Rhode Island home solicitation sales law.)**
>
> *I canceled this transaction for a fire and burglar alarm system, as I was entitled to do under our agreement, the FTC trade regulation rule and the Rhode Island home solicitation sales law, as shown by the proof of mailing receipt I have for the cancellation letter I sent on May 13 (a copy of the receipt is enclosed).*
>
> *But contrary to the requirements of our agreement, the FTC rule, and the Rhode Island home solicitation sales law, the Superior Security Company has refused to refund the down payment despite my repeated requests that it be returned. These requests were described in my letter of July 26 (copy attached). This failure to refund the down payment or to credit the balance due on my credit account as required by the FTC rule*

has been declared an unfair or deceptive practice under the FTC Act, which can also make you liable under state law.

The company is to refund the $100 down payment and to credit my Master Money account for the $300 balance no longer due or owing within three days of the receipt of this letter. I am also no longer holding for you any of the merchandise which was left with me.

If the company fails to send a full refund and to credit my account within the time specified, I shall seek to hold you liable at least for a deliberate violation of the Rhode Island deceptive sales practices law and the home solicitation sales law. Under the Rhode Island deceptive sales practices law, you may be liable for my attorney's fees and court costs, my damages or $200, and punitive damages. (You may be subject to other liability under the home solicitation sales law.)*

Sincerely,

John Consumer

*NOTE: Include these references—and the other references to the state law—only if you know what your state's home solicitation law requires and that the seller has violated it.

Since this ultimatum is based on the leverage created for you by your state's deceptive practices law, please refer to Chapter 18 where your rights under these laws are described, and be sure to review the "ultimatum" section for deceptive sales practices disputes on page 99.

If you base your negotiating strategy on the fraud law, then you should change the first and last paragraphs of the ultimatum letter as follows.

Paragraph 1—substitute the following sentence for the first sentence in the paragraph:

"I am notifying you of the intentional fraud which occurred when, upon proper cancellation of my purchase, the Supersafe Security Company refused to refund my $100 down payment, or to credit my Master Money account, for the $300 purchase balance as required under both the door-to-door sales agreement of May 10, 19__ for the purchase of a fire and burglar alarm system and the FTC trade regulation rule on door-to-door sales."

Paragraph 5—substitute the following paragraph:

"If the company does not make the refund within the time specified, I shall seek to hold you liable at least for tortious fraud, and I shall seek a jury verdict to recover all my losses. I shall also seek punitive damages for your company's reckless, deliberate and wantonly fraudulent conduct. I will also inform the state attorney general about this matter and seek information about the number and nature of other consumer complaints that may be in the attorney general's files in order to strengthen my claim for punitive damages."

Instead of threatening your own legal action, you may sometimes want to rely on whatever leverage the FTC might create for you. That could be your most effective tool if you are dealing with an out-of-state company. In this case, you should adapt the ultimatum in the way described on page 100, in the section "Calling in a government agency instead of threatening to sue."

14 · The FTC Rule on Items Advertised by Food Stores

At some time nearly all of us have been lured to a store by an advertised special—only to find it was not available when we walked in to buy it.

While many types of retailers may use phony advertising claims, the FTC found that food stores were the most likely to do so. As a result it adopted a trade regulation rule covering "Retail Food Store Advertising and Marketing Practices."

The rule imposes two requirements on retail food stores.

1. A store cannot advertise items for sale at a stated price if the items are not in stock and readily available during the sales period stated in the advertising. If the items are not displayed, then the store must post a sign that clearly tells consumers the items are in stock and available on request.

In the case of a chain store, advertised items have to be available in all the branches in the area reached by the advertising, unless otherwise noted. All exceptions must be clearly stated. A store cannot advertise several specials and then say something like: "Not all items available at all stores," or "Available at most stores," for instance. Instead, the advertising must either identify the stores where the items will be available, or identify the stores where the items will not be available.

If it runs out of an advertised item, a store might not be guilty of violating the trade regulation if it can show that it ordered sufficient quantities to meet the demand reasonably expected for the item. A store also might not violate the rule if items were ordered but not delivered on time.

2. Second, a store must sell the advertised items at or below the advertised price. All limitations or restrictions, such as only one item allowed per customer, must be clearly and conspicuously disclosed.

A store that does not comply with these two major requirements can be fined up to $10,000 per violation by the FTC.

HOW TO USE YOUR RIGHTS

The best way to use your rights is to insist that retail food stores sell items at the prices they advertise. Sometimes a store will offer a rain check for an item, or perhaps a comparable item for the same price. If a store manager is completely unreasonable and doesn't offer any alternative, mention the possible penalties for violating the trade regulation rule.

If you still need to inform the FTC about a possible violation, use the sample letter on page 55 as a guide. Describe what happened, and be sure to send a copy of the advertisement involved.

15 · Federal and State Rules on Unordered Merchandise

Receiving and being billed for unordered merchandise is an especially vexing problem. Consumers seldom want the merchandise and in the past they were often the targets of unpleasant collection practices aimed at forcing them to pay.

Congress, and most states, have now enacted laws protecting consumers from the unordered-merchandise sales gimmick. The federal law prohibits the mailing of unordered merchandise, for instance. Even so the FTC has found that some companies are still illegally mailing unordered merchandise to consumers and trying to collect for it. In 1980, the FTC began to investigate some one hundred companies involved in these practices. Consumers complained particularly about companies sending goods "on approval," and of book clubs and record clubs continuing to send merchandise after they had properly canceled their membership.

WHAT THE FEDERAL LAW REQUIRES

The Postal Reorganization Act, which is jointly enforced by the U.S. Postal Service and the FTC, makes it illegal for anyone to mail unordered merchandise or to send bills or dunning notices to collect for it. Unordered merchandise is defined as anything mailed to you without your prior expressed request or consent.

There are two exceptions which allow someone to mail you unordered merchandise. One is when a company sends out a free sample; but the merchandise must be clearly marked as such. The other is when merchandise is mailed by a charitable organization seeking a contribution.

Please note that the act applies only to merchandise sent via the U.S. Postal Service. It does not cover merchandise sent by other delivery methods; a private delivery service such as the United Parcel Service (UPS), for instance.

However, a violation of the unordered merchandise provisions of the Postal Reorganization Act is also considered a violation of the FTC Act. And the FTC has determined that sending unordered merchandise by *any* means of delivery is an unfair or deceptive practice. Although this action by the FTC covers the sending of unordered merchandise not covered by the Postal Reorganization Act, this ruling does not directly protect you since only the FTC can take action against violations.

CONSUMER RIGHTS

The Postal Reorganization Act entitles you to treat as a gift any unordered merchandise that is mailed to you. You can keep, use, or throw away such products without having to pay for them. Even a company that *is* allowed to mail unordered merchandise must include a statement informing you that the merchandise is a gift you are not obligated to pay for.

You are also entitled to sue a seller who violates the law to recover any losses.

Forty-five states have enacted their own laws to protect consumers. They do not prohibit the sending of unordered merchandise, as the federal law does. Instead, they simply classify such merchandise as free gift material. Many of the state laws include not only merchandise sent by mail but merchandise sent by all other delivery methods as well.

To find out the specific provisions of your state law, call or write a consumer protection office, or the state attorney general's office, and ask for a brochure describing the law.

The following states have *not* enacted laws to protect consumers in this way: Alabama, Colorado, New Mexico, North Dakota and Utah.

HOW TO USE YOUR RIGHTS

If you receive unordered merchandise through the mails, you are never obligated to pay for it. Nevertheless be careful when responding to any offers or advertisements.

The FTC found that companies sometimes use ambiguous advertising that misrepresents or fails to disclose the terms of an offer. And when consumers respond to the ads, they may end up ordering or consenting to the shipment of goods without realizing it.

Here's how to make sure this does not happen to you. When you reply to an advertisement asking you to write in for more details, say, write the following: "This is not an order, request, or my consent for the shipment of any merchandise for which you may bill me."

Although the FTC has ruled that sending unordered merchandise by *any* method is an unfair practice, and can take action against a company, if you receive unordered merchandise via a delivery method not covered by either federal or state law, then to protect yourself you should either refuse the merchandise on delivery or—if you have taken delivery—immediately send the company an ultimatum saying you do not want the merchandise.

An immediate ultimatum is the only way to deal with a problem like this because a company sending unordered merchandise is not doing it by mistake. It is deliberately using an illegal or a deceptive practice, and it is therefore not likely to pay much attention to anything other than an ultimatum.

ULTIMATUM FOR REFUSING UNORDERED MERCHANDISE

When you cannot treat unordered merchandise as a gift under either federal or state law, here is a sample ultimatum you can adapt and send immediately to make clear you are refusing the merchandise.

800 Elm Grove
Anytown, USA 00000

April 1, 19___

Innovative Merchandisers, Inc.
Post Office Box 100
Anytown, USA 00000

Dear Sir:

This is to notify you of the unfair or deceptive practice that occurred in violation of the FTC Act when Innovative Merchandisers, Inc. sent me by Speedy Parcel Service a set of four six-ounce bottles of hand lotion without my prior request or consent. The company also billed me $15.95 for the merchandise.

The set was delivered to my address on March 31, 19___. I am hereby notifying you that I refuse to accept this merchandise and that you are either to pick it up at my residence not later than May 1, 19___, or make other arrangements by that date for the return shipment of the goods at your expense and risk. And you are not to bill me for these goods nor make any efforts to collect any payment from me for this merchandise.

If you fail to pick up the goods or make arrangements for their return shipment by that date, I reserve the right to dispose of the merchandise as I see fit without further obligation to you. I am also reserving the right to charge you a storage fee while I store the merchandise for you.

I am notifying the FTC of this violation of the FTC Act.

Sincerely,

Keep a copy of the letter and get a mailing receipt when you send it. This letter protects you in case the company doesn't retrieve the goods and still tries to collect for them. Keep the goods without using them until the deadline you set for the company to pick them up. The deadline should be a reasonable one; thirty days, for instance.

Use the sample letter on page 55 to notify the FTC of this kind of violation.

ULTIMATUM: IF THE COMPANY STILL TRIES TO COLLECT

If the company still tries to collect after you send your letter refusing the merchandise, you can adapt the following sample ultimatum to make clear you don't owe the money. (See Chapter 18 on the deceptive sales practices law.)

Certified Letter No. 11112222

800 Elm Grove
Anytown, USA 00000

May 10, 19___

Innovative Merchandisers, Inc.
Post Office Box 100
Anytown, USA 00000

Dear Sir:

This is to notify you of the continuing violation of the FTC Act which occurred when you billed me for $15.95 for the set of four six-ounce bottles of hand lotion sent to me by Speedy Parcel Service without my prior request or consent. I received the merchandise on March 31, 19___, but in my letter of April 1, 19___, I refused to accept the hand lotion and ordered you to retrieve the merchandise by May 1, 19___.

But on May 8, I received your bill dated May 2, demanding payment for this merchandise despite the fact that I ordered you to retrieve and not to bill me for it. Nor did you make any effort to retrieve the merchandise as I directed you to do. I informed you that I reserved the right to dispose of the merchandise without further obligation to you if you failed to follow my instructions. Since you failed to do so, I am under no further obligation to you.

You are therefore immediately ordered to stop further efforts to bill me or to collect for amounts I do not owe.

If you fail to stop, or if I find that you informed a credit reporting agency that I have not paid for this merchandise, I shall seek to hold you liable at least for the cost of storing your merchandise for thirty days and *for a deliberate and reckless violation of the state's deceptive sales practices law. I shall also seek to hold you liable in tort to the fullest extent provided by law for deliberately and maliciously making false statements about my credit standing. (Under the Rhode Island deceptive sales practices law, you may be liable for my attorney's fees and court costs, my damages or $200, and punitive damages.)**

I will not respond to any further communications from you on this matter, and I shall inform the FTC of this unlawful attempt to collect for unordered merchandise.

Sincerely,

*If you refer to your state's deceptive sales practices law, see Appendix I for a description of the specific rights available under your state law.

Since the FTC says that sending unordered merchandise is an unfair or deceptive practice under the FTC Act, we suggest that you refer to your state's deceptive sales practices law if a company tries to collect for unordered merchandise in any situation that is not covered by the Postal Reorganization Act or state law governing unordered merchandise.

If a company sends you more bills for unordered merchandise after you send your ultimatum you could ignore them. But be sure to notify the FTC of the continuing violation of the law or of the FTC Act. Wait to see if the company sends you several letters, and then forward copies of all of them to the FTC.

If you receive any dunning notices from a collection agency, assert your rights under the Fair Debt Collection Practices Act described in Chapter 72.

ULTIMATUM TO STOP COLLECTION EFFORTS ON MERCHANDISE CONSIDERED A GIFT

If a company tries to collect for unordered merchandise which you *can* treat as a gift, immediately adapt and send the following ultimatum.

100 Elm Street
Anytown, USA 00000

September 1, 19___

Alert Sales Promotions, Inc.
100 Newstone Lane
Anytown, USA 00000

Dear Sir:

I am notifying you of the unlawful attempt to bill me for $13.95 for the eight-ounce bottle of Aromatic Perfume which you sent me without my prior request or consent.

I received your bill for this perfume on August 28, 19___. You claim I owe this money for merchandise received during the week of August 4. I never ordered the perfume. Nor was the perfume labeled as a gift as required by the Postal Reorganization Act when unordered merchandise is sent to a consumer.

Since the Postal Reorganization Act and state law declares that unordered merchandise is a gift and makes it unlawful for the sender to bill for the merchandise or to send dunning notices, you are immediately to cease any further efforts to bill me or to collect money I do not owe for unordered merchandise.

If you don't immediately stop sending me bills, or if I find that you informed any credit reporting agency that I am delinquent in paying for or have failed to pay for this merchandise, I shall at least seek to hold you liable in tort for deliberately and maliciously injuring my reputation by making false statements about my credit standing.

I will not respond to any further communications from you about this matter, and I shall inform the FTC about this unlawful attempt to collect for unordered merchandise.

Sincerely,

NOTE: If the merchandise was not *mailed* to you, delete the references to the Postal Reorganization Act. In this case, you would refer only to the state law, but check first to see your state law covers unordered merchandise sent by the method used by the company.

At the minimum, you should get a mailing receipt for this letter to prove you sent it. But if you send the letter by certified mail, return receipt requested, it will help you prove, if necessary, that the company received your warning not to report you to a credit bureau. That could help you hold the company liable if they continue to harass you.

Referring to the company's potential tort liability strengthens your claim that the company made a deliberate and malicious false statement to injure you since it had been clearly warned you did not owe the money.

The sample letter on page 55 shows how to inform the FTC about a violation of an FTC trade regulation rule. In this case, refer to a violation of the Postal Reorganization Act provision on unordered merchandise rather than to an FTC rule.

Always notify the FTC if a company tries to collect for unordered merchandise.

If you receive a dunning notice from a collection agency, assert your rights under the Fair Debt Collection Practices Act. (See Chapter 72.)

16 · The FTC Rule on Book and Record Clubs and Other Negative Option Plans

The negative option sales plan is an effective and convenient way to promote repeat sales by mail. It has been used successfully to sell books, records, tapes, and collectibles.

The idea is simple. Once you sign up for such a plan, the company regularly sends you an announcement describing the next item to be shipped. The item is shipped automatically—and you are billed for it—unless you tell the company by a certain date that you do *not* want the item. Instead of being obligated to buy only when you specifically order something, you become obligated to buy whenever you do not specifically say you do not want to order an item. Hence the name "negative option" plan.

Companies usually give subscribers an introductory or bonus offer of free, or very low-priced, merchandise to make it as attractive as possible to join the plan. Generally, you have to buy a minimum number of items before you can terminate membership. If you don't buy the minimum number, you may receive and be billed for items you don't want.

In the past, membership terms and requirements were not always clearly disclosed to consumers. Often you had to buy a lot of unwanted merchandise, and it was sometimes difficult to cancel a membership even after buying the minimum number of items. All too often consumers received unwanted merchandise because they weren't given enough time to notify the seller not to ship an item. Sometimes companies would send a substitute selection for the one chosen, and the subscriber would then either have to pay for it or argue with the company to take it back.

Now consumers have protection under the FTC trade regulation called "Use of Negative Option Plans by Sellers in Commerce."

WHAT THE FTC RULE REQUIRES

The FTC rule applies only to the type of plan already described. It does not, for example, apply to a plan where the seller regularly ships merchandise you can return. To protect yourself, don't sign up for such a plan unless the seller fully discloses the terms.

The FTC regulation requires sellers of a negative option plan to follow these rules:

1. Before shipping a selection, the seller must send you an announcement identifying the selection to be shipped and a form telling you the selection will be shipped unless you say *no*. The form must give either a mailing date by which you must mail back the form, or a return date, by which the form must be received by the seller, to avoid receiving the selection.

2. The seller must give you at least ten days to mail back the form.

3. The seller must allow you to return, at his expense and for a full credit, any shipment you receive after you notify him by the mailing date, or the return date, that you do not want the selection. If the seller specifies a return date, the form must be postmarked at least three days beforehand. If it is, then you have notified the seller in time regardless of when he actually receives the form.

4. The seller must promptly terminate your membership in a plan when you cancel after purchasing the minimum number of selections. If the seller sends you another selection after receiving your written cancellation, you can return it at his expense for a full credit. If the seller sends you further announcements, you can ignore them after you have sent back the first shipment. Any additional merchandise sent by the seller is considered unordered merchandise which you can keep. (See page 70 for information about unordered merchandise and rules that apply.)

5. The seller must ship your bonus or introductory merchandise within four weeks. If he is unable to provide the selections you requested, he may make an alternative offer. You are entitled to refuse the alternative offer and cancel your membership if you wish to. You must, however, return any introductory or bonus merchandise you did receive.

7. The seller cannot ship any substitute merchandise for a selection you make, unless you specifically allow it. In the past, some book clubs, for example, often sent substitutes when a particular selection wasn't in stock.

8. The seller must clearly spell out important terms of the plan in any promotional material or advertising. The seller must disclose:

- How you notify the seller when you don't want a selection.
- The minimum number of items you must purchase to complete the plan.
- Your right to cancel at any time after you have completed the plan and have purchased the minimum number of items.
- Whether you will be billed for shipping and handling charges.
- The fact that you have at least ten days to mail back the form the seller furnishes, saying that you do not want a selection.
- Your right to return, for full credit and at the seller's expense, any selection sent to you when the seller fails to send the announcement and the form in time to give you at least ten days to notify him you do not want the selection.
- How often the announcements and forms will be sent to you and the maximum number sent during a twelve-month period.

While companies do generally make the required disclosures in their promotional material, you often have to read carefully to discover each point.

To illustrate how these items might be disclosed, here is how one book club did it (though I have slightly changed the wording to avoid identifying the club).

The following sentence disclosing the minimum number of items to be purchased—"You simply agree to buy four books within the next two years"—appeared in small print next to some very large print identifying an extraordinary introductory offer.

The order form contained the following sentence describing a buyer's obligation: "I agree to buy four books during the next two years. A shipping and handling charge is added to each shipment."

The company then disclosed all the other items in the following paragraph.

"*Facts about Membership:* You receive the [club's announcement] 15 times a year (about every 3½ weeks). Each issue reviews a main choice plus scores of Alternates. If you want the main choice do nothing. It will be shipped to you automatically. If you want one or more Alternate books—or no books at all—indicate your decision on the reply form always enclosed and return it by the date specified. *Return privileges:* If the [announcement] is delayed and you receive the main choice without having 10 days to notify us, you may return it for credit at our expense. *Cancellations:* Membership may be discontinued, by either you or the club, at any time after you have purchased four additional books."

Described simply as "Facts about membership," the company uses this paragraph to disclose other required terms of the plan, including your right—not privilege—to return selections.

Disclosures about the terms of a plan and your rights under the FTC rule might be identified in other ways. One club, for example, identified its disclosures as "Membership benefits." Another used the description "Here's how the plan works," and still another "How membership works."

A seller who ignores the FTC trade regulation rule is committing an unfair or deceptive practice.

HOW TO PROTECT YOUR RIGHTS

Don't join any plan unless the seller clearly discloses in his promotional material all the important terms of the plan as required by the FTC rule. The rule works best if a seller is willing to comply with it. If his promotional material violates the rule, how can you expect him to live up to the other requirements?

When a seller states the terms of the plan in promotional materials, the terms become part of the conditions of the plan that you can hold the seller to under your agreement. In such a case, you would not have to rely solely on the FTC to enforce the rule. Say, for example, the seller tries to collect for unwanted merchandise sent in violation of the rule and the terms of your agreement. You could then say you did not owe the money because you were entitled to return the merchandise under the terms of the plan the seller described in the promotional material.

If you join a plan, keep the promotional material describing the terms. Also make a copy of the application form you return, and note when you mail it. The application form may be the only place where the seller discloses some terms of the plan. If you have a copy you will know what obligations you are assuming, and what you ordered as part of your introductory offer, in case the seller sends you a selection you didn't ask for.

17 · Negotiating Strategy
for Disputes Involving
Negative Option Plans

If the seller fails to follow the FTC rule, then put your negotiating strategy into gear.

STAGE ONE: OPENING SKIRMISHES FOR UNWANTED MERCHANDISE

When you receive the announcement for the next selection, check whether the seller has given you at least ten days to return the form. If you haven't been given enough time, write something like this on the form:

"Received form on June 2 and did not have the required ten days to return it by the June 10 return date."

If the announcement does not reach you in time to return the form, keep the mailing envelope and note on it the date you received it. If there isn't a long gap between the postmark date on the envelope and the date you say you received it, say five days or less, you won't have any trouble supporting your claim that the seller must take back the shipment.

Keep a record of the date you mail back a form to refuse a shipment. Also keep a record of the selections you order. If you know exactly what you ordered and when you mailed the form, you will be able to back up a claim with specific details if the seller ignores your instructions.

You can, of course, get definite proof of mailing by obtaining a mailing receipt from the post office, and you can make a definite record of what you order by making a copy of the return form. If you are dealing with a reliable company, these steps are not necessary. If, on the other hand, the company appears not to be reliable, and you have trouble with them, start obtaining mailing receipts to support your claim in case of further disputes. If you have made the minimum purchases, cancel the plan immediately to avoid future hassles.

If you receive any shipment you are entitled to return, don't open the carton. If there is an invoice, or bill, attached to the outside, take it out to identify the contents and write on the part you would return with your payment: "Shipment refused on (give date). Return to sender." Make a copy of the invoice, then put it back in the envelope.

If you ordered one selection but find the seller has sent you something else, write: "Shipment identified on invoice refused on (give date). Merchandise received is not the selection identified in the (give date) announcement which I ordered."

Send the item back in its original shipping carton. This will usually have a return postage guarantee label on it so you should not have to pay postage. On the outside write, "Shipment refused on (give date). Return to sender." Get a mailing receipt to show when you returned the shipment.

Since you would have to conduct all negotiations by letter, here is an initial sample letter you would adapt if, for example, a company tried to bill you for a shipment you were entitled to—and had—returned. Supply your own wording to describe other reasons that entitle you to return the merchandise, such as the seller's failure to give you enough time to return the form.

> *100 Reading Court*
> *Anytown, USA 00000*
>
> *December 15, 19__*

> *Volume of the Month Club*
> *300 Publisher Plaza*
> *Anytown, USA*

> *Dear Sir:*
>
> *I am notifying you that I do not owe the $15.99 you are billing me for the shipment identified on your statement dated December 5, 19__. I refused to accept the merchandise and returned the shipment to you on November 6, 19__, as shown on the enclosed copy of the mailing receipt. My membership number is 123456.*
>
> *As I indicated on the invoice enclosed with the shipment I returned, I refused to accept the merchandise because you failed to send what I ordered. I ordered (describe item) which was identified as the main selection in the (give date) announcement, but as shown on your invoice, you shipped (describe item) which I did not order and do not want. I would, however, still be willing to accept the merchandise I ordered if you send it promptly.*
>
> *Please correct and promptly credit my account for this item.*
>
> *Sincerely,*
>
> *J. Consumer*

STAGE TWO: THE LOW-KEYED WARNING

If the company fails to settle the dispute after your initial letter, follow it up with the low-keyed warning. If any dispute reaches this stage and you are entitled to cancel the plan, quit immediately. (See page 8)

> *100 Reading Court*
> *Anytown, USA*
>
> *January 17, 19__*

> *Volume of the Month Club*
> *300 Publisher Plaza*
> *Anytown, USA 00000*

> *Dear Sir:*
>
> *I am notifying you of the unfair or deceptive practice which occurred when the club continued to bill me on January 11, 19__, for $15.99 for the shipment I refused to accept and returned to you on November 6, 19__. My membership number is 123456.*
>
> *Since the FTC trade regulation rule on negative option plans prohibits the shipping of substitute merchandise, I refused to accept and returned to you on November 6, 19__ the merchandise for which you are billing*

me but which I did not order as I explained in my letter of December 15, 19___. A copy of the letter is enclosed. I also agreed to accept the shipment that I originally ordered, which you have still failed to send.

The $15.99 is, therefore neither due now owing for this merchandise which I did not order and returned to you, as I am entitled to do under the FTC trade regulation rule, and our agreement and you are to credit my account promptly and to stop further efforts to bill me for merchandise sent contrary to the requirements of the FTC rule, and our agreement. Nor am I still willing to accept the main selection identified in your October 10 announcement that I ordered but which you failed to ship promptly.

I will appreciate your resolving this matter promptly so I will not have to pursue it further.

Sincerely,

STAGE THREE: THE ULTIMATUM

If the company still refuses to settle the matter after the low-keyed warning, here is a sample ultimatum you can adapt for telling the club that you will notify the FTC about the violation. Refer to the penalties the FTC might make the company pay for violating the rule. If you find the name of the president of the club, address the letter directly to that person.

Certified letter No. 111222333

100 Reading Court
Anytown, USA 00000

February 20, 19___

Volume of the Month Club
300 Publisher Plaza
Anytown, USA 00000

Dear Sir:

I am notifying you of the violation of the FTC trade regulation rule on negative option plans which occurred when the Volume of the Month Club refused to stop billing me for a shipment that I did not accept and returned to you on November 6, 19___. The shipment consisted of substitute merchandise sent in violation of the rule. My membership number is 123456.

I have already explained why I refused the shipment and requested you to stop billing me for it in my letters of December 15, 19___, and of January 17, 19___. Copies of these letters are enclosed.

Despite my efforts to explain the matter, I again received a bill dated February 10, 19___, for $15.99 for a shipment that was sent in violation of the FTC trade regulation rule and our agreement and which I returned on November 6, 19___, for a full credit as I am entitled to do under the FTC rule and the terms of our membership agreement. The Club also made no effort to send the merchandise I ordered even at a time when I was still willing to accept it.

You are to credit my account promptly for the $15.99 I do not owe, and to cease immediately any further collection efforts.

*If the club fails to comply immediately with my request, I shall notify
the FTC of the club's deliberate and continuing refusal to comply with
the FTC trade regulation rule on negative option plans, and request that
the FTC take action under the FTC Act to protect consumers from such
violations. A violation of a trade regulation rule may make the club liable
for a civil penalty of up to $10,000 and entitle the FTC to seek restitution
on behalf of consumers damaged by such violations.*

Sincerely,

The sample letter on page 55 shows how to notify the FTC about a violation of a
trade regulation rule.

If you receive a dunning notice from a collection agency for a bill you do not owe,
use your rights under the Fair Debt Collection Practices Act described in Chapter
72.

OPENING SKIRMISHES FOR CANCELLING A PLAN.

You must cancel the plan in writing to be protected under the FTC rule. If you have
had any previous trouble with the seller, send your cancellation by certified mail,
return receipt requested, and make sure you keep a copy of the letter and certified
mail receipt. It proves when the seller received your cancellation letter, so you will
know when you acquire the cancellation rights the rule creates for you. If the seller
fails to acknowledge a cancellation letter sent by ordinary mail, then send one by
certified mail, return receipt requested.

When you are ready to quit the plan, here is a sample cancellation letter to write.

Certified Letter No. 111222333

*100 Reading Court
Anytown, USA 00000*

March 1, 19___

*Volume of the Month Club
300 Publisher Plaza
Anytown, USA 00000*

Dear Sir:

*Since I have purchased the minimum number of items required by the
Club's plan, I am hereby canceling my membership in the Volume of
the Month Club, effective immediately. My membership number is
123456.*

Sincerely,

The return receipt will tell you when the company receives your cancellation. Say
it's March 10. You would have to return the first selection the company ships after
March 10, and the company is obligated to take it back. But if the company ships
you additional selections, the merchandise is yours to keep as a gift. It is considered
unordered merchandise under the Postal Reorganization Act.

Here is a sample letter you can adapt if the company tries to bill you for anything
that is unordered merchandise.

100 Reading Court
Anytown, USA

June 10, 19___

Volume of the Month Club
300 Publisher Plaza
Anytown, USA 00000

Dear Sir:

I am notifying you that I do not owe the $17.99 for the shipment of (describe item) identified on your bill dated June 2, 19___. The amount is for unordered merchandise I received after canceling my membership in writing on March 1, 19___. A copy of my cancellation letter is attached.

You received my cancellation letter on March 10 as shown on the attached copy of the post office return receipt for the letter. The shipment identified on the June 2 bill was sent on April 20, 19___. It was the second selection shipped to me after you received my cancelation letter.

The amount is not due or owing since I did not order the shipment and the FTC trade regulation rule on negative option sales plans declares that such shipments are unordered merchandise as described by the Postal Reorganization Act. That Act declares that such merchandise is a gift and prohibits the sender from trying to collect for it.

You are immediately to cease trying to collect for this merchandise. You are also to cease sending me further selections, which are being shipped without my prior request or consent, since I have canceled my membership.

I will appreciate your settling this matter promptly so that I will not have to pursue it further.

Sincerely,

If a company continues to bill you for unordered merchandise, you would adapt the ultimatum letter on page 72, used to illustrate your rights under the Postal Reorganization Act.

In this case, however, replace the first paragraph in that sample letter with the following paragraph:

"I am notifying you of the unlawful attempt to bill me for $17.99 for a shipment of (describe item) identified on your bill dated June 2, 19___. The shipment was sent without my prior request or consent after I cancelled my membership in your club as I described in my letter of June 10, 19___."

Use the remaining paragraphs of that sample letter, but change the wording to describe what happened, and delete the references to state law.

18 · Legal Weapon No. 2: State Deceptive Sales Practices Laws

The District of Columbia and every state have now adopted a deceptive sales practices law that is similar to the FTC Act. Each one makes it illegal for a seller to use a broad range of practices that could mislead consumers.

The laws are not equally tough in every state, though. For example, in forty-five states and the District of Columbia consumers are allowed to sue a seller to recover damages if he is in violation of the law. Arkansas, Iowa, Nevada, New York, North Dakota, and Oklahoma, on the other hand, do not allow consumers to sue. The important differences among these state laws are listed in Appendix I.

In most states, the deceptive sales practices laws are enforced by the state's attorney general. Nineteen states allow a local agency, such as a county prosecutor, to enforce them. In a few states, the laws can also be enforced by a specialized agency. Except in Indiana and West Virginia, the enforcing agency is allowed to recover losses on behalf of consumers when a business violates the law. (Enforcing agencies are identified in the Directory of State Agencies.)

WHAT THE LAWS PROHIBIT

State deceptive sales practices laws may prohibit practices in one of three ways.

1. A state law may prohibit a wide range of practices without spelling them out specifically. Instead, it uses a broad standard which may be stated in one of two ways. Sellers are either prohibited from using *misleading* or *deceptive* practices, or from using *unfair* or *deceptive* practices. In both cases the practices are generally defined in the same way as the FTC Act. The importance of the unfairness standard, which is broader in sweep than the deceptive standard, is that it may allow you to base your claim on some *other* law the seller ignored, but which cannot be enforced as effectively as the deceptive sales practices law.

2. A state deceptive sales practices law may prohibit a wide range of practices which it does spell out specifically. The itemized practices are usually known as a "laundry list." Some state laws prohibit only the practices included on its list; even so they are generally described very broadly so the law can be used to cover many situations.

3. Some state laws may combine a laundry list with a broad "catchall" standard that covers misleading or deceptive practices, and unfair or deceptive practices. This kind of law creates definite standards which make clear exactly what the law covers but also includes a very broad standard to cover practices that are not listed specifically.

Here are some examples of specific practices included in almost every laundry list. But remember, these are not the only ones covered by these laws. If you are concerned about a practice that isn't illustrated, don't assume the law won't apply. If the practice even slightly resembles one of these examples, assume the law *does* cover it, especially if your state law includes a general standard or a catchall clause.

DECEPTIVE PRICING

Stores are not allowed to mislead you about price reductions, to try to make you think you are getting a bargain when you are not. They cannot, for example, raise the price of an item—or claim they have previously sold the item at a higher price— just to make you think you are getting a bargain when they cut the price.

Similarly, they cannot offer a "two-for-one" sale or a "buy one, get-one-free" sale when the price for one is really the price for both. A store that regularly sells tires for $40, for instance, cannot suddenly decide to double the price, then give away a "free" one when you buy a tire for $80. This would be a deceptive practice.

USED PRODUCTS

If a seller says something is brand new or never used, it really must be new. Selling a repossessed freezer, say, as a brand new model is not an acceptable sales practice under these laws.

DESCRIPTIONS AND MISREPRESENTATIONS OF PRODUCTS

Businesses cannot misrepresent the grade, model, usefulness, durability, reliability, or benefits a consumer can expect from a product.

For example, a product which the seller claims is "rust proof," or "shrinkproof," or "unbreakable," or "fire-proof," or "water resistant," or "lifetime durable," or "dishwasher-proof," must live up to the claim. If your set of "dishwasher-proof" dishes melt when you wash them in your dishwasher, the seller is in violation of the law.

BAIT ADVERTISING

A store cannot advertise an item and then say it isn't available. Some stores use this trick to lure customers: they advertise a very special item, then say it has been sold out. Or they may try to get a customer to buy a higher priced model. If a store advertises an item and then doesn't sell it under the conditions advertised, it is probably violating the law.

SPONSORSHIP, APPROVAL, OR AFFILIATION CLAIMS

Businesses that make claims associating them with other companies, must have the proper authorization to do so.

A business that claims to be an authorized "Whirlwind" repair facility, for example, must have obtained its authorization from the "Whirlwind" company.

DISPARAGING A COMPETITOR

A store that makes false or misleading statements about what a competitor is doing or selling is using a prohibited practice. If a business tells you that a competitor down the road is selling higher priced goods or shoddy merchandise when it is really selling the same kind of goods, for example, it is not complying with the law.

SERVICE ESTIMATES AND REPAIR WORK

If a repair shop gives you an estimate that is far different from what it actually costs to fix something, performs repairs you have not agreed to, or charges you for repairs it hasn't made, it is almost certainly engaging in deceptive practices.

Almost every state attorney general's office provides a publication that describes what its state deceptive practices law covers. Just write to your local office, listed in the Directory of State Agencies, and ask for it.

WHICH BUSINESSES ARE COVERED BY THESE LAWS?

The sales and advertising practices of businesses that sell or lease consumer products, such as cars, appliances, clothes, and food, are always covered. The laws also cover the sale of most services, such as repair work, dry cleaning, home improvements, driving schools, and vocational schools.

Some state laws may exempt certain businesses, industries, or professions already regulated by other laws. These may include public utilities, banks, lawyers and doctors.

Three types of consumer transactions may also be exempted. They are the *extension* of credit (though the sale of what you bought *on* credit would always be covered); the sale of insurance; and the sale or leasing of real property, such as your home.

WHAT CONSUMER RIGHTS AND REMEDIES DO THESE LAWS CREATE?

All but a few of the state laws provide a combination of rights and remedies (the legal term for what the other side has to do to make good a failure) you can use to create the leverage you need to negotiate a settlement. (NOTE: The deceptive sales practices laws in Arkansas, Iowa, Nevada, New York, North Dakota, and Oklahoma do *not* create *any* of the following rights or remedies.)

CONSUMER'S RIGHT TO SUE

Forty-five states and the District of Columbia allow consumers to sue a business for violating the law.

If you sue, you will usually have to show only that a business practiced something that the law prohibits. This makes it possible to win a deceptive practices case without having to prove a lot of other tricky things that you would have to prove under the fraud laws, for instance. To hold someone liable for fraud, you may have to prove, for example, that a seller intentionally lied to you. The deceptive sales practices laws make it easier for you to win your case.

Your right to sue and hold the seller accountable also depends only on the seller having violated the deceptive sales practices law rather than the seller having failed to live up to terms and conditions of a contract that applies to the transaction. This can help you hold a seller accountable for violations involving false or deceptive claims or promises made about a purchase which were not spelled out in a written agreement.

CONSUMER REMEDIES

Under state deceptive sales practices laws, consumers who win a suit can recover any damages they suffered. Damages covers a tangible, usually monetary, loss. Generally, this is taken to mean the difference between the value you should have received and the value you actually got.

Suppose, for example, a store sells you a waterproof watch for $99, but as soon as the watch gets wet the mechanism rusts. Since the watch is now worthless, the damages you could claim are what you paid for the watch.

Sometimes, a store is also liable for other monetary losses, such as those incurred by a personal injury, damage to other property, or special expenses you had as a direct result of the violation. In this case, for example, if you had to pay a jeweler to examine the watch, the law might allow you to collect those expenses from the store.

Most of the states that allow you to sue a business for violating the law, also specifically allow you to recover your attorney's fees and court costs if you win your case. This creates an incentive for an attorney to take your case, as well as an incentive for a business to negotiate a reasonable settlement with you. (NOTE: These states do *not* specifically allow you to recover for attorney's fees and court costs: Arizona, Maryland, South Dakota, West Virginia and Wyoming.)

Many state laws specifically allow a consumer to recover "something extra," above his damages, attorney's fees and court costs. (Appendix I describes the conditions that apply in your state.)

In fourteen states, the law sets the minimum damages a consumer can recover. This means you can either recover your actual damages or the minimum amount set by the law, whichever is the *larger* amount. The minimum amount varies from as little as $25 in Massachusetts to $1,000 in Hawaii; but the usual amount is around $100–$200. This makes it practical for a consumer to assert his rights under the law even when the actual damages might be very low or hard to calculate. Minimum damages are intended to penalize a business for violating the law.

In seventeen states, the law allows a consumer to recover some multiple of his actual loss; that is, two or three times the loss. If, for example, you bought the $99 "waterproof" watch in one of these states, you might recover up to $297, or three times its cost.

In some cases, a consumer can recover multiple damages when a business uses a prohibited practice; in other cases, the rule applies only when a business *deliberately* uses such a practice. You can get an idea whether a store deliberately deceived you if it refuses to be reasonable about correcting a problem. This is usually a tip-off that the behavior in question didn't occur by accident. After all, if a store makes an "honest mistake," it should be willing to correct it. If a business refuses to be reasonable, *always* mention the "something extra" it might have to pay if this applies under your state deceptive practices law. Let the business decide whether it wants to take a chance a court will agree with you.

Finally, in ten states the law specifically allows consumers to recover punitive damages in cases involving serious violations. These damages are recoverable only when a business deliberately violates the law, and it is left up to a judge or jury to decide exactly what they should be. If you live in one of these states always use this rule as part of your negotiating strategy when a business refuses to be reasonable.

HOW TO USE YOUR RIGHTS BEFORE A SALE

One way to use your rights under your state deceptive sales practices law is to insist a business live up to its advertising. Say, for example, a seller advertises an inexpensive TV set but when you get to the store the set isn't available. In a case like this, the store has gypped you or, at the very least, inconvenienced you by luring you with a deceptive practice.

Deceptive sales practices laws entitle you to expect sellers to honor any sales conditions they set out in their advertising.

So, if the set is in stock, insist the store sell it to you for the advertised price. If the set is not in stock, ask them to sell you a comparable model or brand at the advertised price. Let's say the store advertised a twenty-five percent reduction on the price of a brand X TV set and the set isn't on hand. The store does have brand Y, however, which sells for the same or only a slightly higher price than the advertised model. Insist the store sell you brand Y with a twenty-five percent price reduction.

If the salesperson will not agree, insist on seeing the manager. Be polite and firm and if the manager refuses your alternatives, mention that the failure to sell the set under the conditions advertised could be a prohibited practice under your state's deceptive sales practices law. Remind the manager the store may have to pay you damages for engaging in a deceptive advertising practice.

A little pressure and bargaining at this point might get you the advertised set or a comparable model. But if it doesn't, do not get nasty. Simply tell the store you are going to contact your state attorney general, and then follow through on your threat. Adapt the sample letter included on page 55 for notifying the FTC about a possible violation of a law it enforces.

In some cases, a store might be willing to give you a rain check if the advertised item is not in stock. This might be reasonable if you buy regularly at the store. But if you have made a special trip because of an advertisement, insist the store sell the item, or a comparable model.

When you assert your right to make a business sell you something, keep three points in mind. First, be sure to take along the advertising or promotional material that lured you to the store. It will be tough for you to insist that a store honor conditions it sets unless you can point out exactly what these are.

Second, be *absolutely sure* the advertised item is really worth having. If there is a question in your mind, or if the store must perform some work after the sale, such as an installation, don't insist on getting the item. If a company misleads you in its advertising, how can you be sure it will perform after a sale?

Third, if the advertised item isn't in stock, you must be reasonable if you ask for an alternative. If the store advertised a twenty-five percent reduction on brand X that regularly sells for $299.99, you can't expect a reduction on brand Z that regularly sells for a lot more, say $499.99.

ASSERTING YOUR RIGHTS AFTER A SALE

Most often you will use your rights under your state law after you have made a purchase.

As soon as you discover that the product doesn't measure up to the claims made for it, you *must* notify the seller. Acting quickly shows that the failure is important and unacceptable to you; it makes it harder for the seller to claim that you caused the problem; and it gives him a chance to fix the defect right away, before the product deteriorates or loses any more of its value. Resist the temptation to try things out when there is obviously something wrong: if you buy a four-speed mixer and find it has only a one-speed setting, take it back straight away and don't try it out first.

The law does not state exactly how quickly you must act once you know a product or service doesn't measure up, and you have more leeway when a delay in telling the seller doesn't affect the product or hurt the seller. But it is not wise to test how much time you have: instead, act right away.

If you wait too long, the seller is likely to say: "If the product wasn't any good, why did you wait so long to tell us? We would have made the product good if you had brought it right back, but there isn't anything we can do for you now." It is easy for a seller to say this, of course, because he knows you are in a poor position to test him.

Some state deceptive sales practices laws require that you first notify a business about a violation before you become entitled to sue. This requirement gives a business a chance to take care of the problem first. But many state laws do not specifically require this initial notification before you can sue. Eliminating this requirement is simply meant to minimize legal roadblocks that could get in the way of consumers taking legal action. However, doing away with the formal notification requirement doesn't really give you a chance to ignore a violation and go on with a transaction as though nothing was wrong, but then still try to hold a seller accountable for it much later.

Waiting too long to notify a seller is one of the most frequent mistakes consumers make. It is a tough mistake to undo, too, because the law assumes that if you keep using a product after learning it doesn't live up to the seller's claims, the misrepresentations can't really be that important. Using a product also means you are getting a benefit out of it. The law makes it much harder to get your money back in such circumstances. You can end up losing your rights and waiving your claim.

COMBINING RIGHTS

Keep in mind that the rights and remedies created by deceptive sales practices laws supplement rights you may have under other laws that regulate contracts. Your leverage for settling disputes increases when you combine rights. You can, for example, use the Uniform Commercial Code in combination with the deceptive sales practices laws. The Code governs the rights and remedies available under contracts for the sale of products. (Section IV of this book covers the Code in detail.) Here is how the two can work together:

Deceptive practices laws usually allow you to recover only the damages you suffer as a result of a violation (plus any additional amounts the seller may be required to pay), rather than entitling you to get out of the contract completely.

The Code, on the other hand, makes available remedies that allow you to get out of an agreement completely and recover your payments, if a seller makes important misrepresentations, but it does not specifically allow you to collect your attorney's fees or other legal costs if you have to sue.

You can increase your leverage by using both of these laws as part of your negotiating strategy. Together they give you more grounds for taking legal action; this, in turn, puts more pressure on the seller to settle.

The next chapter outlines a suggested negotiating strategy that shows you how to combine these rights to settle disputes involving products. Chapter 20 provides a strategy for disputes involving services.

PRODUCT CLAIMS AND WARRANTIES.

As more fully explained in Section V, factual claims or promises made about a product can count as express warranties a product must conform to. You then have various remedies under your contract or warranty if the product doesn't measure up to warranties that were given to you.

A product can, of course, fail to conform to claims or promises made about it because it turns out to be faulty rather than because the claims or promises made were, in effect, false to begin with.

Broadly speaking, if a product fails to conform to claims or promises made which would count as warranties because the product simply turned out to be defective or faulty, your main recourse may be the remedies for holding a seller or other warrantor accountable under the contract or warranty. But if the claims or promises made were, in effect, false or untrue to begin with, or it becomes clear someone made claims or promises the person never really meant to keep, such acts or practices then increasingly count as violations of a state's deceptive sales practices law, especially those laws which broadly define what acts or practices they prohibit. You could then use the recourse available under these laws even though the claims or promises made might also have counted as warranties.

Keep in mind, therefore, that when you first discover that a product does not measure up to claims or promises made, it is sometimes difficult to tell whether you are dealing with someone engaging in a deceptive practice or whether the product involved is simply defective.

You have to decide which of these two possibilities is most likely to apply and plan your negotiating strategy accordingly. If you are in doubt, it is usually better to assume at the outset that the seller will live up to claims or promises made which could count as warranties and use the recourse available for holding someone accountable under your contract and warranty. If the seller, however, actually violated the deceptive sales practices law by making false claims or promises, switch to the negotiating strategy for holding him accountable under that law in addition to using the remedies for holding a seller accountable under your contract.

WHAT IF YOU MADE A PURCHASE ON CREDIT?

The sample letters included in this section assume you have paid cash for a purchase. In situations like this, you would, of course, be trying to get your money back.

The situation is different when you make a purchase on credit. In these situations, you may have to try to get back what you have paid and also withhold further payment and settle up with a creditor for the outstanding balance. Withholding payments called for by an agreement does, however, mean the other side could take action against you. If you are wrong about not owing the money, you may face nasty collection actions by the seller/creditor.

If you are trying to hold a seller/creditor accountable for violations of a deceptive sales practices law, it's important to invoke the remedies available from the Uniform Commercial Code.

Steps for holding a seller accountable are covered in Section IV—for situations in which you could get out of an agreement completely; and in Section V—for situations in which you could only hold a seller accountable for damages.

If a separate creditor was involved, you would then usually have to take steps in addition to those you would use for holding a seller accountable. These additional steps are explained in Section VII.

19 · Negotiating Strategy for Disputes Involving Products

Suppose you buy a set of "dishwasher proof" plastic dishes for $89.95 from, say, the Meadowlark Plaza branch of Reliable Discount Shops, Inc., then find that, once in the dishwasher, the dishes are warped by the high temperatures.

Since the dishwasher does not damage other plastic dishes you own, you know the machine itself is not faulty. So you will have to decide what you want a store to do about the problem. Depending on what's wrong, that could be getting some money back (damages) while still keeping the product, requesting the seller take it back and refund the full purchase price, or getting a credit or a replacement.

If you insist that the seller take the product back, a key point to remember is to stop using it and treat it as the seller's rather than your property. This is important so you can keep open your options for using additional key remedies of the Uniform Commercial Code.

One thing to keep in mind about the initial request you make: if a possible violation makes it reasonable to insist a store take the product back, your most reasonable request would usually be asking for a credit or a replacement. The store is more likely to accomodate this request.

Important from both a bargaining and even a legal standpoint, is that asking a store to furnish a replacement helps substantiate that you really want to go through with the sale rather than simply looking for excuses to get out of it. A store's refusal to make things right can help demonstrate the store acted deliberately. And that almost automatically strengthens your position to demand your money back later and possibly hold the store accountable for violating your state's deceptive sales practices law.

To illustrate how you could refer to remedies available under deceptive sales practices laws, the sample letters assume the transaction occurred in Rhode Island and refer to that state's law. You must, however, adapt the wording to fit your state's law. (See Appendix I.)

Naturally, all the names, dates, and other details in the sample letters are hypothetical and are used for illustrative purposes only. You have to adapt the wording to fit your factual situation.

STAGE ONE: OPENING SKIRMISHES

Your first move in such situations should always be to return to the store and try to resolve the problem by verbal negotiations (but you could put the matter in writing). If practical, take the merchandise with you, explain the problem by noting the difference between the representations made and what actually happened, and propose your reasonable solution. Don't immediately accuse the store of violating the deceptive sales practices law. Be friendly but firm, and assume the store has made a mistake which it will correct.

If you are willing to accept a solution other than a full cash refund, make sure you get a written statement spelling out what the store will do. Ask for a written credit memo made out in your name, for instance. The memo should identify what you returned, why you returned it, and the amount of the credit. Make sure an authorized person signs the memo and that it is dated.

If you are unable to return the product yourself, insist the seller pick it up. And try to get in writing the seller's commitment for resolving the problem before or at the time the product is returned.

Following is a sample letter you could adapt for initially telling the seller about a possible violation of a deceptive sales practices law. If you give it to someone at the store in person, ask him or her to sign showing receipt of the letter.

1358 Clearview Terrace
Anytown, Rhode Island 00000

June 7, 19___

Mr. Wheeler Dealer
Manager
Reliable Discount Shops, Inc.
Meadowlark Plaza
Anytown, Rhode Island

Dear Mr. Dealer:

This is to inform you that the 30-piece set of Plasticware dishes I purchased and received on May 29, 19___ does not conform to the representations that were made to me when I bought it. The purchase is identified on your sales receipt dated May 29, 19___.

The dishes were represented as being "dishwasher proof" by the salesclerk in the housewares department and by the label on the package. This feature was important to me because I intended to wash them in my dishwasher and had specifically asked the sales clerk about this feature and was told the dishes were suitable for this purpose.

But by June 5 after I had washed them in the dishwasher for only the third time, four dinner plates and three salad plates were badly warped. As indicated by the dishes I am returning, they are no longer usable. None of the other plastic dishes that I own and which I washed at the same time were similarly warped. The representation that the Plasticmade dishes were "dishwasher proof" was not, in fact, true.

Since the Plasticware dishes do not have the "dishwasher proof" characteristic that was represented to me, I have been denied an important feature I was told they had. Their failure to conform to this representation also resulted in the dishes being ruined when I used them in a manner that should have been suitable had they conformed to the representation made about them. The damaged dishes now substantially impair the value of the entire set.

For the purpose of promptly resolving this matter, I am returning the entire set and request a refund of its $89.95 purchase price plus sales tax (OR) a credit for its $89.95 purchase price plus sales tax toward the price of (OR) that you replace it with a comparable set that is, in fact, "dishwasher proof" (OR) describe other solution.

I will appreciate your promptly resolving this matter as I have proposed so that we can still successfully complete the transaction we made for the sale of "dishwasher proof" dishes.

Sincerely,

You will have to adapt the wording to fit your situation, of course, but be sure to include the same kinds of details. Specifically describe the representations a store made to you, or important information it withheld from you, and explain how the purchase fails to measure up to those representations. Make clear why the representation was important, but don't lie. If you did not, for example, tell the clerk that the feature was important to you, don't say you did. (Remember, an alert consumer will tell the clerk what's important in order to start building a case right from the beginning.) And if you did not, for example, wash any other plastic dishes, don't say you did. But details like these show what's wrong and can help you demonstrate the product failed to measure up.

ILLUSTRATIONS FOR ALTERING THE LETTER TO FIT OTHER SITUATIONS

If the merchandise is so bulky that it will be hard for you to return it (say, for example, a freezer which has been sold as new but is, in fact, a repossessed model), ask the store to pick it up at your home, and change the fifth paragraph as follows:

> *For the purpose of promptly settling this matter, I request a refund of the $349 purchase price plus sales tax for the General Watts freezer [(OR) a credit for the $349 purchase price plus sales tax for the General Watts freezer toward the price of the same model that is, in fact, new (OR) that you replace the model that was delivered with one that is, in fact, new and that you then pick the appliance up at my home at the above address]. You can call me at 333-4444 between 9:30 A.M. and 5:00 P.M. or at 222-5555 after 6:30 P.M."*

It is also possible a seller's violation could cause monetary losses (damages) which you could recover in addition to the price. If you have such additional losses, it would usually be worthwhile for you to make clear to the seller what they were and to claim them. (See Section IV where these types of damages are more fully described and page 325 for an explanation of how to claim such damages while indicating your willingness to forego them if the seller does what you otherwise request.)

Here is sample wording you can adapt and insert after the fourth paragraph of the above letter to describe additional damages you had:

> *"There is now also due from you [$_____] for at least the damages more fully described below which I sustained because the product failed to conform to representations made about it: [Describe the types and amount of damages you could claim]."*

Please note, however, the sample letter is worded so you would, in effect be giving up what you could recover as further damages if the seller does what you otherwise request. If it is important for you to recover such damages, seek legal advice. It is very unlikely a seller would voluntarily pay such damages so you would almost certainly have to sue to collect them. If this is the case, do *not* use the sample letter.

IF A STORE ASKS YOU TO STICK WITH A PURCHASE

It may sometimes not be completely clear that a product actually fails to measure up to representations made about it. If you suspect a problem, promptly tell the business about it anyway, but when you do, the business may refuse to do anything about it and try to convince you the problem is a minor one. In other words, they may try to "re-sell" the purchase by telling you that minor flaws won't really affect the product's usefulness. In the case of the plastic dishes, for example, suppose that only a few dishes are slightly warped; not badly enough to become worthless, but enough to make you wonder whether the seller's claims are accurate. What should you do in a situation like this when a business refuses to take them back?

It won't be timely to use a warning notice because it may not yet be clear whether you really were misled. But now you need a record that you have notified the store of a possible defect in case the problem gets a lot worse. And you need some record to show the store convinced you the product was really all right and to stick with the purchase. Ask the store to put such assurances in writing. Try to get the manager to sign a statement that is dated and addressed to you. Here is an example of such a statement:

"When you returned the set of Plasticware dishes on June 7, I informed you that the slight warping was normal and that you can rely on the representation that the dishes are "dishwasher proof."

If a store's representative refuses to sign such a statement, say that you will write a confirming letter so that there is a record of your attempt to return the goods.

Here is an example of such a letter.

> *1358 Clearview Terrace*
> *Anytown, Rhode Island 00000*
>
> *June 10, 19___*

> *Mr. Wheeler Dealer*
> *Manager*
> *Reliable Discount Shops, Inc.*
> *Meadowlark Plaza*
> *Anytown, Rhode Island 00000*

> *Dear Mr. Dealer:*

> *I am writing to confirm the discussion we had about the set of Plasticware "dishwasher proof" dishes that I returned to your store on June 7, 19___ because they apparently failed to conform to the representations that had been made about them.*

> *I told you that when I purchased the 30-piece set at your store on May 29, 19___, for $89.95, a salesperson told me they were "dishwasher proof." The label on the package said the same thing. I informed you that this feature was important to me because I had intended to wash them in my dishwasher and had asked your salesclerk about this feature to make sure the set would be suitable for this purpose.*

> *But as I showed you, four dinner plates and three salad plates are slightly warped. The warping became noticeable by June 5, after I had washed them in the dishwasher three times. None of the other plastic dishes I own and washed during this period were similarly warped.*

> *Although I asked you to take back the set and requested a refund of its purchase price [(OR) requested that you replace it with a comparable set that was, in fact "dishwasher proof"] before the problem became more serious, you informed me that the slight warping I noticed happened occasionally, but would not get worse. You said I could continue to use the dishes with the assurance that they would otherwise fully conform to the representations that they were, in fact, "dishwasher proof." I therefore*

assented to your suggestion that I continue to use the dishes based on your assurances that the dishes would conform to the claims made for them.

I am, however, doing so while reserving all rights.

Thank you for discussing this matter and I hope that, as you suggested, I won't have similar problems in the future which would require me to pursue this matter further.

Sincerely,

This confirming letter will help strengthen your position if the problem gets worse. It shows when you first told the store how the product has failed to conform, which gave them a chance to solve the problem. It also shows how the store has tried to perpetuate the possible original misrepresentation by convincing you there really isn't anything wrong with the product. Since they have convinced you to keep using the product, it will be easier for you to make the store take back the product later, if necessary, because your additional use of the merchandise has been at their urging. The letter also shows you are serious about making the store live up to its claims.

At this point, one of two things may happen. Either the store may reply to your confirming letter and deny it had given you the assurances you described. Or, you do not hear from the store but the actual problem gets worse so the seller's further assurances turn out to be wrong. See page 97 for the low-keyed warnings you could then use.

STAGE TWO: THE LOW-KEYED WARNING

If the store engaged in a prohibited practice but refuses to correct what's wrong, immediately follow-up with a low-keyed warning letter.

Following is a basic sample low-keyed warning letter you can adapt to your situation. The details in the letter again refer to the hypothetical problem of the "dishwasher proof" dishes; you must obviously supply the facts that fit your situation and your state's law.

If a dispute reaches this point, be sure to put it in writing. The wording of the sample letter assumes you did not put anything in writing when you first told the store about the problem; but if you did, then refer to the initial letter/memo you gave the seller.

You can send a warning letter by certified mail if you don't take it to the store in person. If you take it to the store in person, have someone sign your copy to show the store received it.

If you want the store to take the product back, include a statement that shows your willingness to return it. You could either offer to return the product yourself, or ask the store to pick it up. Such a request is reasonable, especially if the product was delivered to you in the first place.

If, at this stage, you want the seller to take the product back, you must stop using it. If you have already paid something for the product, you would almost always be entitled to keep it until the seller returns at least what you have paid. If you have not yet paid anything, you may be required to return the product or at least offer to do so; but this would be an unusual situation. See Section IV for an explanation of your right to keep a product until a seller returns money you are entitled to get back. You may formally have to invoke the remedies the Uniform Commercial Code makes available to hold a seller accountable for misrepresentations.

If you purchased the goods on credit, requesting a replacement would still be your safest course until you invoke the remedies available under the code. These remedies could specifically entitle you to avoid paying part or all of the outstanding balance.

Certified Letter No. 111222

1358 Clearview Terrace
Anytown, Rhode Island 00000

June 10, 19___

Mr. Wheeler Dealer
Manager
Reliable Discount Shops, Inc.
Meadowlark Plaza
Anytown, Rhode Island 00000

Dear Mr. Dealer:

This is to notify you that the 30-piece set of Plasticware dishes I purchased and received on May 29, 19___, was misrepresented to me when I bought it. The purchase is identified on your sales receipt dated May 29, 19___.

The dishes were represented as being "dishwasher proof" by the salesclerk in the housewares department and by the label on the package. This feature was important to me because I had intended to wash them in my dishwasher and I had asked the salesclerk to make sure the dishes would be suitable for that purpose.

But as I [stated in my letter of June 7, 19___ and] showed you when I came into your store on June 7, 19___, four dinner plates and three salad plates were badly warped after I had washed them in the dishwasher for only the third time. The dishes are no longer usable. None of the other plastic dishes that I own and which I washed at the same time were similarly warped. The representation that the Plasticware dishes were "dishwasher proof" was not, in fact, true.

Since the "dishwasher proof" characteristic of the Plasticware dishes was misrepresented to me, I have been denied an important feature which I was told they had. The misrepresentation also resulted in the dishes being ruined when I used them in a manner that should have been suitable if they had conformed to the representations that were made about them. And the damaged dishes now substantially impair the value of the entire set.

For the purpose of promptly settling this matter, I requested that you take back the set and replace it with one that was, in fact, "dishwasher proof" [(OR) refund its $89.95 purchase price plus sales tax (OR) give me a credit for its $89.95 purchase price plus sales tax toward the price of a comparable set that was, in fact, "dishwasher proof" (OR) describe other solution]. Although you refused to do so when we discussed this matter on June 7, I am still willing to resolve the matter as I proposed if you will promptly replace the set [make the refund/give the credit] as I requested. I am, however, until then retaining and only storing the dishes for you but shall return them upon their replacement [receipt of the refund/credit] I requested. You can call at 333-4444 between 9:30 A.M. and 5:00 P.M. or at 222-5555 after 6:30 P.M.

I hope that we can still satisfactorily resolve this matter so that I will not have to hold you liable at least to the fullest extent provided by the Rhode Island deceptive sales practices law and by the Uniform Commercial Code for misrepresentations.

Sincerely,

NOTE: Louisiana consumers delete the wording referring to the Uniform Commercial Code.

A COMPANY DENIES GIVING ASSURANCES DESCRIBED IN CONFIRMING LETTER

If a company specifically denies it gave you the assurances you described in your confirming letter, the letter may not count for much later. However, the case becomes further weakened if you fail to respond to the company's letter, so it is important to reply. Since the store now claims it didn't give you the assurances, you are left with little choice but to force the issue.

In this case, you would adapt the following letter and insist that the store make a settlement based on the fact that the purchase already fails to measure up to their claims about it.

Certified Letter No. 111222

1358 Clearview Terrace
Anytown, Rhode Island 00000

June 28, 19___

Mr. Wheeler Dealer
Manager
Reliable Discount Shops, Inc.
Meadowlark Plaza
Anytown, Rhode Island 00000

Dear Mr. Dealer:

I am again notifying you that the 30-piece set of Plasticware dishes I bought and received on May 29, 19___ does not conform to the representations that were made to me when I bought it. The purchase is identified on your sales receipt dated May 29, 19___.

I first notified you of the failure to conform when I returned the set to your store on June 7, 19___. I described in my confirming letter of June 10 the representations that had been made and why I felt they failed to conform. I also described the assurances you gave me that convinced me to keep the set even though they apparently failed to conform to those representations.

But in your letter of June 25, you denied that you had given me the assurances I described in my confirming letter.

Since four dinner plates and three salad plates have already warped as I have shown you, and since you now deny even telling me that the dishes would conform to the representations that they were "dishwasher proof," I can no longer rely on your good faith that those representations are, in fact, true.

Since the dishwasher proof characteristic of the Plasticware dishes has been misrepresented, I would be denied important features I was told they had. The dishes could be further damaged by additional use, and your failure to act in good faith prevents me from relying on any further assurances from you.

For the purpose of promptly settling this matter, I had requested that you take back the set and refund its $89.95 purchase price plus sales tax [(OR) and said I was willing to accept a credit for its $89.95 purchase price plus sales tax toward the price of a comparable set that was, in fact, "dishwasher proof" (OR) describe other solution you had proposed]. But I consented to keep the set based only on your assurance that it, in fact, conformed to the representations made which you now deny having given.

So that we can now still promptly resolve this matter, I am prepared to do as I originally proposed if you will promptly make the refund [give me the credit] I requested. I am, however, until then retaining and only storing the dishes for you but shall return them upon receipt of the refund (credit) I requested.

I hope we can still satisfactorily resolve this matter so that I will not have to hold you liable at least to the fullest extent provided by the Rhode Island deceptive sales practices law and by the Uniform Commercial Code for misrepresentations.

Sincerely,

NOTE: Louisiana consumers should not include the reference to the Uniform Commercial Code.

If at this point you feel you cannot trust the store further and want only a refund instead of a credit that you originally requested, simply replace the first sentence in the seventh paragraph with the following wording you could adapt to your situation:

"Since I cannot now rely on you to act in good faith and so that we can promptly resolve this matter, I request that you take back the set and promptly refund its $89.95 purchase price plus sales tax."

SELLER'S ASSURANCES PROVE TO BE UNTRUE

The store's assurances that nothing is wrong could, of course, turn out to be as untrue as the original representations. And despite the store's assurances that nothing was wrong with the plastic dishes in our example, the warping continues until dishes get ruined. You show the store the evidence and now request that it take back the dishes and refund your money, but it refuses. The time has now come to use a low-keyed warning letter.

Following is a sample letter for insisting the store now correct the problem. Note that this sample letter differs from the basic one because it explains the assurances the company gave you.

Certified Mail No. 111222

1358 Clearview Terrace
Anytown, Rhode Island 00000

July 25, 19___

Mr. Wheeler Dealer
Manager
Reliable Discount Shops, Inc.
Meadowlark Plaza
Anytown, Rhode Island 00000

Dear Mr. Dealer:

I am notifying you that the 30-piece set of Plasticware dishes I bought and received on May 29, 19— does not conform to the representations that were made when I bought it. The purchase is identified on your sales receipt dated May 29, 19—.

I first notified you that the dishes did not conform to the representations made about them when I returned the set to your store on June 7, 19—. In my confirming letter of June 10, 19— (a copy of which is enclosed), I described to you the representations that had been made, why I felt the set failed to conform, and my reasons for keeping the set.

But as I showed you when I came into your store again on July 23, 19—, four dinner plates and three salad plates have warped even more despite the assurances you gave me on June 7 that the problem would not get worse and that the dishes would conform to the representations that had been made about them that they were "dishwasher proof". The warping became markedly noticeable by July 20 after I had continued to wash them in the dishwasher. None of the other plastic dishes that I have washed during this period have warped. The representations and the assurances that the Plasticware dishes were "dishwasher proof" were not, in fact, true.

Since the dishwasher proof characteristic of the Plasticware dishes was misrepresented to me, I have been denied an important feature I was told they had. The misrepresentation also resulted in their being ruined when I used them in a manner that should have been suitable if they had conformed to the representations that were made about them and the assurances I received.

For the purpose of promptly settling this matter, I request that you now take back the set and refund its purchase price of $89.95 plus sales tax [OR state other solution you proposed]. Despite your refusal to settle this matter as I had proposed when we again discussed it on July 23, I am still willing to settle it if you will promptly give me the refund [credit] I requested. I am, however, until then retaining and only storing the dishes for you but shall return them upon receipt of the refund [credit] I have requested. You can call me at 333-4444 between 9:30 A.M. and 5:00 P.M. or at 222-5555 after 6:30 P.M.

I hope we can still satisfactorily resolve this matter so that I will not have to hold you liable for misrepresentations at least to the fullest extent provided by the Rhode Island deceptive sales practices law and by the Uniform Commercial Code.

Sincerely,

NOTE: Louisiana consumers should not include the reference to the Uniform Commercial Code.

You can also adapt this letter to make it fit your own particular circumstances, of course, as illustrated on page 92.

If the seller violates the deceptive sales practices law and misrepresents the product, that could entitle you to insist he take back the product and refund its price. If the seller refuses, formally invoking the remedies for rejecting and/or revoking acceptance could then substantially support your position. These are remedies made available by the Uniform Commercial Code as described in Section IV.

You could then take those steps as a follow-up to the seller's continuing refusal to correct the problem. It could be especially important to do this if you made the purchase on credit.

If you are only entitled to recover damages and want to deduct the amount of your damages from the amount still outstanding, see page 324 for the steps to take which could then entitle you do do so.

STAGE THREE: THE ULTIMATUM

If your low-keyed warning fails to solve the problem, then a written ultimatum that describes your rights under the state's deceptive practices law is necessary. You have given the store a chance to settle the matter, and now you are ready to increase the pressure.

Send the ultimatum a few days after the deadline you set for solving the problem, but give the store at least twenty days if you set an indefinite deadline such as "immediately." This way you can show that the store has willfully ignored you.

If you are compelled to go to court—and win your case—the deceptive sales practices law will force the store to pay. That's the pressure point. And referring to the Uniform Commercial Code lets the store know there is another law that could entitle you to a refund of your money because of the store's misrepresentation. See section IV about using the remedies available under that law.

In the following sample letter, the remedies available under the Rhode Island deceptive sales practices law are described for illustrative purposes. But, obviously, your letter should refer to the remedies available under your own state's law. These remedies are listed in Appendix I and you simply adapt the wording of the ultimatum as necessary.

Your ultimatum should be addressed to the president of the company or the owner of the store. But if, for example, you are dealing with a large store and up to now you have only discussed your problem with the company's Customer Relations Department, you might address the letter to the store's manager, rather than the president who may live in another state.

The following sample letter assumes that the store failed to respond to the low-keyed warning letter dated June 10, shown on page 95. You must, of course, adapt the wording to fit your situation.

Certified letter No. 222444

1358 Clearview Terrace
Anytown, Rhode Island 00000

June 30, 19___

Mr. R. U. Smart
President
Reliable Discount Shops, Inc.
Headquarters Lane
Anytown, Rhode Island 00000

Dear Mr. Smart:

I am notifying you of the violation of the Rhode Island deceptive sales practices law which occurred when I purchased a set of Plasticware dishes at your Meadowlark Plaza store on May 29, 19___.

Contrary to the representation that the dishes were "dishwasher proof," they became badly damaged when I washed them in the dishwasher. The misrepresentation, the purchase, and my efforts to resolve this matter are more completely described in my letter of June 10, 19___, to Mr. Wheeler Dealer, a copy of which is enclosed.

I have, to date, received no response.

[Since I can now no longer rely on your good faith to furnish me a set that is, in fact, "dishwasher proof" as the set sold was represented to be] for the purpose of promptly settling this matter, Reliable Discounts, Inc. is to take back the set and promptly give me a credit for its $89.95 purchase price plus sales tax toward the price of a comparable set that is, in fact, "dishwasher proof" [(OR) promptly refund its $89.95 purchase price plus sales tax]. I am, however, until then retaining and only storing the dishes for you but shall return them upon the receipt of the credit [refund] I have requested.

But if my proposal for resolving this matter remains unsatisfied, I shall seek to hold you liable at least to the fullest extent provided by the Rhode Island deceptive sales practices law for deliberate violations and by the Uniform Commercial Code for misrepresentations. Under the Rhode Island deceptive sales practices law, you may be liable for my damages or $200, my attorney's fees and court costs and punitive damages.

Sincerely,

NOTE: Louisiana consumers should delete the reference to the Uniform Commercial Code.

Remember, the last sentence of the letter should always refer to the remedies available under your state's deceptive sales practices law.

The next to last paragraph includes wording in brackets you can adapt if you want to insist on a refund rather than a credit. So use only one or the other set of sample wordings.

If you specifically invoked the remedies available under the code, then adapt and replace the next to last paragraph with the following one:

"Since I can now no longer rely on your good faith to furnish me a set that is, in fact, "dishwasher proof" as the set sold was represented to be, I am now still prepared to resolve this matter as I proposed in my letter/ memo of [date] when I notified you I was rejecting [and/or] revoking acceptance of the product [(OR) I would deduct my damages from the price still due under the contract]".

CALLING IN A GOVERNMENT AGENCY INSTEAD OF THREATENING TO SUE

There are times when threatening to sue may not be an effective ultimatum because, unlike the case of the obviously damaged dishes, for instance, it might be hard to tell whether the company really used a prohibited practice. Determining this might require a good deal of investigation into their methods to show that they had used the prohibited practice on many other occasions. If you're not sure, pressure from a government agency might be more effective, especially if it has received many consumer complaints.

If you decide to call in a government agency, your ultimatum letter to the company should say that you are going to notify the enforcing agency about a possible violation of the law. Obviously, though, a letter like this is not going to be as powerful as one that threatens a lawsuit. It may not bring enough pressure to bear to settle your dispute, and you may not actually get any help from the government agency either. However, if enough consumers complain about a practice, a government agency is likely to investigate the business concerned and take legal action. And previous complaints on file with a government agency can help consumers show a company has deliberately intended to ignore the law. So your complaint could help other consumers, and the complaints of other consumers could help you.

If the dispute involves a local company, contact the state agency that enforces the deceptive sales practices law. If the company operates nationally, contact the FTC.

I caution you, however, to use this approach to back up your request only if the dispute involves a cash transaction.

This is how you should change your ultimatum letter if you are going to contact a state agency or the FTC.

Paragraph (1.) If you are contacting a state agency:

> *"I am notifying you of an apparent violation of the Rhode Island deceptive sales practices law which occurred when I purchased a set of Plasticware dishes at the Meadowlark Plaza store on May 29, 19___."*

If you are contacting the FTC, use the words *"Federal Trade Commission Act"* instead of the reference to the state's deceptive sales practices law.

Paragraph (5.) If you are contacting a state agency, replace it with the following paragraph:

> *"If my proposal for resolving this matter remains unsatisfied, I shall inform the attorney general's office of this apparent violation of the Rhode Island deceptive sales practices law and request the attorney general to investigate this matter. And I shall request that the attorney general take action to protect consumers, including seeking restitution on behalf of consumers who were damaged by a violation of the act, as is authorized by the law."*

(NOTE: The Iowa and West Virginia laws do not allow the state agency to seek restitution for consumers.)

If you are contacting the FTC, the paragraph should say:

> *"If my proposal for resolving this matter remains unsatisfied, I shall inform the Federal Trade Commission of this apparent violation of the FTC Act and request that it take action to protect consumers. The FTC could seek a civil penalty of $10,000 should the practice violate a trade regulation rule or an FTC cease and desist order."*

If you do have to notify a government agency, adapt the sample letter on page 55 for notifying the FTC.

20 · Negotiating Strategy for Disputes Involving Services

If a seller violates your state's deceptive sales practices law in connection with the sale of service, a dispute would then usually be about monetary losses (damages) you sustained as a result of the violation. The damages would amount to the dollar value of your loss. There would, of course, usually be no product for you to return, and generally speaking, the Uniform Commercial Code would not apply. However, it could apply if the transaction primarily involved the sale of products made in connection with services. If the deceptive practice primarily involved the product that was sold, you should usually deal with the matter as the sale of a product rather than a service.

The negotiating strategy included in this chapter primarily focuses on situations in which recovering damages would be an adequate solution for the dispute. Since the deceptive sales practices laws that entitle you to sue always entitle you to recover your damages, these laws would usually be your major legal tool. There are, however, situations in which remedies available under contract law for misrepresentations could entitle you to rescind (i.e. cancel) an agreement so you could get all your money back rather than only the damages you sustained. That could be a more effective remedy than the one the deceptive sales practices law makes available.

Technically speaking, any remedies provided by a deceptive sales practices law are in addition to remedies available under other laws. But without getting into too much detail, contract law usually requires someone to choose among several available remedies. The choice made might then preclude you from using the other alternatives. For example, if you choose to recover damages, this *could* preclude you from later trying to rescind the entire agreement. I caution you, therefore, to seek legal advice if the remedies you initially choose could make a big difference in what and how much you could recover.

If you made the purchase on credit and are seeking to recover damages based on a violation of a deceptive sales law, you could initially ask the seller to pay damages while continuing to pay what was due under the credit agreement. You may, however, be able to deduct your damages from the amount still outstanding under the agreement. You could try to do this by asking the seller/creditor to deduct that amount from the outstanding balance. (See Section VIII for an explanation of how to do this; but when using the sample letters included in that section, delete references to the Uniform Commercial Code.) If the seller/creditor refuses to deduct damages, you may have to pay under the agreement and separately sue under the deceptive sales practices law to recover your damages. Your leverage for convincing a seller to deduct the damages from the outstanding balance is the additional amount you could be entitled to recover under the deceptive sales practices laws.

This book does not, however, specifically cover remedies that could be available for holding a seller accountable under a contract for the sale of services. Seek legal advice about additional remedies that could be available to hold a seller accountable under your contract.

To illustrate how you could try to hold a seller accountable for damages resulting from a violation of a deceptive sales practices law with respect to services, suppose you take your malfunctioning Solux tape deck to the ABC Repair Shop and ask what is wrong with it and how much it will cost to fix. The store identifies the likely problem and estimates that the bill won't come to more than $45. You leave the tape deck but say if the repair costs exceed $45, the store is to call you first for authorization. The salesperson agrees and writes on the repair order that repairs are not to exceed the estimated amount.

When you return to pick up your machine, however, the store presents you with a bill for $110. No one checked with you before the repairs were made, and now the store refuses to return your tape deck unless you pay the bill in cash. Your damages in such a situation could be the entire additional amount the store is now trying to charge.

The following strategy shows how you can assert your rights. Again Rhode Island's deceptive sales practices law is used as an example. Remedies that apply to your own state are listed in Appendix I.

STAGE ONE: OPENING SKIRMISHES

Offer to pay the amount for the agreed upon repairs and insist that the store return the set. The law entitles the store to the money you owe and it can usually keep your property until you pay, but it is not entitled to keep your property as security for money you don't owe. Your offer to pay the $45 and your demand that the store then return your property further weakens the firm's position under another law. That other law is a tort called a "conversion" which, generally speaking, imposes liability on someone who lacks what might otherwise be legal justification for taking or keeping another person's property. Offering to pay what you owe and demanding the return of your property could then trigger the other person's liability under this tort law which could then entitle you to sue and recover the value of the property the person kept.

But sometimes you may not learn about deceptive practices like unauthorized or unnecessary repairs until after you have paid for them. In this case, estimate the cost of the unnecessary repairs and ask for a refund. If you are charged for repairs that weren't made, also demand a refund.

If the matter isn't resolved during these opening skirmishes, immediately move to the next stage of your strategy.

STAGE TWO: THE LOW-KEYED WARNING.

Following is a sample low-keyed warning letter you could adapt for insisting a store pay for damages caused by a violation of the deceptive sales practices law; for example, unauthorized repairs that exceed the estimate.

Certified Letter No. 888111

1125 Elmwood Drive
Anytown, Rhode Island 00000

May 11, 19___

Mr. Freddie Foxy
ABC Repair Shop
Dragoon Place
Anytown, Rhode Island 00000

Dear Mr. Foxy:

I am reasserting my objections to the deceptive repair estimate and the unauthorized repairs that were made on my Solux tape deck, serial num-

ber 34751, identified on your repair order number 15867, which I left for repairs on May 2, 19__. I am also reaffirming my objections to your refusal to return my property on May 10 when I offered to pay the amount due for the repairs I authorized you to make.

You estimated that the needed repairs would not exceed $45. Since I am not knowledgeable about electronic equipment, I relied on your expert judgment and authorized you to make repairs not exceeding that amount. You were to call me before proceeding with any work if the cost exceeded the estimated amount shown on the repair order. The order also stated that the repairs were not to exceed the estimated amount. Instead, you performed unauthorized repairs and billed me for $110 when I returned May 10 to pick up my property. And, despite my objections, you refused to return the tape deck after I offered to pay the $45 due for the repairs I authorized you to make.

For the purpose of promptly settling this matter, I am still willing to pay you the $45 due for the authorized and necessary repairs that you agreed to perform; you are then to immediately return my property with the authorized repairs completed in a satisfactory manner. You may call me at 111-3388 between 9:00 A.M. and 5:00 P.M. or at 317-5588 between 6:30 P.M. and 10:00 P.M. so we can promptly arrange to resolve this matter.

I hope we can satisfactorily settle this matter so that I will not have to hold you liable at least to the fullest extent provided by the Rhode Island deceptive sales practices law for violations and/or for your unlawful retention of my property.

Sincerely,

When a company only charges you for the estimated amount but you later find out that some of the repairs have not been made, ask for a refund. If this is refused, here is a sample low-keyed warning letter you could adapt for requesting an appropriate refund.

Certified Letter No. 555888

1125 Elmwood Drive
Anytown, Rhode Island 00000

July 15, 19__

Mr. Freddie Foxy
Expert Electronic Repair Shop
Dragoon Place
Anytown, Rhode Island 00000

Dear Mr. Foxy:

I am reasserting my objections to the deceptive charges for repairs allegedly made on my Solux tape deck, serial number 34751 that I left for repairs on May 2, 19__. Your repair order number 15867, dated May 2, 19__, identifies the repairs that were allegedly made and for which I was billed $45, which I paid on May 10.

According to the itemized list of charges shown on that repair order, you billed me for the following parts and service: (List what was done or allegedly done).

On July 10, I subsequently discovered, however, that the following parts were not supplied and the following services could not have been performed as claimed on the bill I received: (List what was not done). The parts you claimed were supplied and the services you claimed to have performed but which were not in fact supplied and performed are worth $30 as shown on your bill.

I returned to your shop on July 13 and requested a refund of the $30 I paid which I thought were for parts and services actually furnished but which were not, in fact, furnished.

For the purpose of promptly resolving this matter, you are immediately to send to me at the above address your payment for the $30 I sustained as damages as a result of deceptive charges for repairs not, in fact, made as claimed.

I hope you will resolve this matter as I have requested so that I will not have to hold you liable at least to the fullest extent provided by the Rhode Island deceptive sales practices law for violations.

Sincerely,

Naturally, these sample letters must be adapted to your specific curcumstances. Be sure to mention such things as the written repair order and the itemized bill to help support your claim. If you have not kept such documents, describe the situation as accurately as possible.

STAGE THREE: THE ULTIMATUM.

Give the store a reasonable time to respond—about twenty days. If you receive no reply, it's time for the ultimatum. Here is a sample ultimatum that could be used as a follow-up to the low-keyed warning letter shown on page 103, that describes unauthorized repairs that exceeded the estimate.

Certified Letter No. 444999

1125 Elmwood Drive
Anytown, Rhode Island 00000

June 1, 19__

Mr. Freddie Foxy
Expert Electronic Repair Shop
Dragoon Place
Anytown, Rhode Island 00000

Dear Mr. Foxy:

I am notifying you of a violation of the Rhode Island deceptive sales practices law which occurred when I agreed to have my Solux tape deck, serial number 34751, repaired at your shop as shown on your repair order number 15867 dated May 2, 19__.

Although the repair order said the repairs were not to exceed $45, you billed me for $110 and refused to return the set unless I paid this amount. Your company's misrepresentations and my objections to your demands were described in more detail in my letter of May 11, 19__, a copy of which is enclosed.

For the purpose of promptly settling this matter, I shall, as I have already offered to do, pay you the $45 stipulated in the repair order, and you are then immediately to return my property with the authorized repairs completed in a satisfactory manner.

But if you still fail to do so immediately, I shall seek to hold you liable at least to the fullest extent provided by the Rhode Island deceptive sales practices law for willful violations and/or for your unlawful retention of my property. Under the Rhode Island deceptive practices law, you may be liable for my reasonable attorney's fees and court costs, my damages or $200, and punitive damages.

Sincerely,

- Naturally, if the company no longer has your property, you would delete the phrase *"and for your unlawful retention of my property,"* from the last paragraph of the letter.

- And if you wanted to ask a government agency for help, instead of threatening your own lawsuit, you would change the ultimatum in the way described on page 100 where settlements involving products are discussed. In cases involving services, you would usually ask the state agency that enforces the deceptive sales practices law rather than the FTC.

21 · Legal Weapon No. 3: The Fraud Law

If someone took you to the cleaners in a poker game by dealing from the bottom of the deck or by using marked cards, you would certainly think you were being cheated, ripped off, and swindled because that's not how the game is supposed to be played. Unfortunately, instances of trickery and deception also occur in the marketplace. When they do, common law describes them as frauds.

WHAT THE FRAUD LAW PROHIBITS

What is the difference between deceptive practices, as spelled out in the deceptive sales practices laws, and fraud? Generally speaking, a fraud happens when someone deliberately misleads (or lies to) you about a purchase and you are damaged (suffer some loss) as a result.

Basically, common law fraud is a tort law that says a seller has a duty *not* to deliberately lie or mislead you when he tries to convince you to buy. This law applies to anyone who sells you anything.

Courts use the following formula to describe a fraud: Fraud = falsehood (told by seller) + intent to lie (by seller) + aim to mislead (by seller) + reliance (by consumer, who acted on the lie) + damage (suffered by consumer). If all five parts of the equation take place, then a seller is guilty of committing a fraud.

Let's look a little more closely at each of these aspects of fraud.

1. Falsehood. In this case, the seller must have misled you by lying about the purchase in some way and the lie must have been about something important. Usually the information has to be false at the time the seller tells it to you. An antique dealer tells you a particular wicker chair is a Victorian antique made in England in the 1880s, for example, but he knows at the time that the chair was actually manufactured recently in Hong Kong. Or a car dealer tells you a car is new when, in fact, it is a reconditioned demonstrator the dealership has used during the last six months. The failure to tell you important information can also be considered a lie for the purpose of establishing fraud.

Sometimes a promise a seller makes about what he will do for you in the future will be considered a lie, if it turns out that he never meant to carry out the promise. This could happen, for example, when a seller takes your money and promises to deliver your merchandise some time in the future. The merchandise never arrives because the seller never intended to send it in the first place.

A misrepresentation that would be considered a lie under the fraud law would also be considered a violation of the deceptive sales practices laws. But it is usually much harder to prove your case under the fraud law.

2. Intention to lie. To prove fraud, one must also show a seller knew, or believed, that what he said was untrue. In other words, that the seller told you an intentional lie.

Obviously, this can be hard to prove. In the case of the wicker chair, for instance, suppose the antique dealer had bought it from someone who claimed it was a Victorian chair made in England. The seller might say he didn't know the chair wasn't really an antique. How could you prove otherwise?

Court decisions are beginning to make it easier for a cnsumer to prove that a seller told an intentional lie. For example, it may be enough to show that the seller *should* have known a particular statement was false. A seller would be especially vulnerable if you can claim he was reckless, or should have known better, since he was an expert and you an amateur relying on his judgment.

3. Aim to mislead. The seller must have told the lie with the intention of misleading you. In other words, he must have deliberately used the lie in order to trick you. This can also be difficult to prove. But one way would be to show what happened during a purchase. For example, the antique dealer told you the wicker chair was Victorian. His store claimed it sold only antiques. He charged you the price of a Victorian chair, which was considerably higher than the price of a Hong Kong imitation. So the lie was not just a slip of the tongue; it was meant to convince you that you were getting an antique.

4. Reliance by the consumer. In this case, you must have depended on the false information in some way when you made your buying decision, and usually you must provide a sound reason for having relied on the lie. The law won't allow you to believe an outrageous lie and then claim fraud to get out of a sale. That doesn't mean, though, that you must investigate all the facts before you can say you depended on a lie. Generally speaking, if you were an unsophisticated buyer dealing with an expert, or if there wasn't any reason to suspect a seller was lying, a court would usually allow you to claim you relied on what the seller told you.

5. Damages. To prove fraud, you must show you suffered a significant, tangible loss because you relied on the seller's lie. In practical terms, this usually means you failed to get the value you expected.

FRAUD CAN MEAN FALSE VERBAL PROMISES

Your rights under the fraud law do not depend on the rights you have under contract laws. When you enforce your rights under a written contract, you are usually bound by what's actually stated in that contract. You can, for instance, only force the seller to take a corrective action that enables you to receive what you bargained for under the contract. Fraud law, on the other hand, usually allows you to ignore—or override—some or all of the provisions included in a contract that would prevent you from holding him accountable for frauds he commits.

The key point here is that when you try to enforce a written contract, usually you cannot claim that a seller broke the contract by failing to live up to *oral* representations or promises he made that differ from what is in writing. But when a seller commits a fraud, you can try to prove that he made false, verbal promises. Obviously, it is easier to prove a seller lied if you have something in writing to show what he promised. That's one reason I urge you to use sample forms provided in this book so you can get sellers to put their representations in writing.

But remember, under the fraud law a seller is liable *only* if all five elements of fraud occurred when he induced you to buy. For this reason, it is usually easier for you to win a case under state deceptive practices laws: these laws generally require you to prove only one of the five elements—that the seller used a prohibited practice (the falsehood part of the fraud law). Sometimes, deceptive practices laws also require you to show that the seller intended to violate the law, but they seldom require you to prove more than this.

YOUR RIGHTS AND REMEDIES

When a seller commits fraud, the law entitles you to sue him. It also entitles you to recover any money you may have lost as a result of the fraud. In addition, you may also be able to recover punitive damages, extra money a judge or jury may require the seller to pay as a form of punishment.

When you sue a seller for what he owes you, there are two ways you can go about it. Which one you choose depends on which makes it easier for you to get your money back. One option is to return what you bought, and demand your money back. In other words, you rescind your agreement and sue for the amount of money you paid. If you paid $400 for the "Victorian" wicker chair, for instance, you would sue to rescind the contract and for that amount.

The other option is to stick with your contract, keep the merchandise, and sue for compensatory damages, or the money you lost as a result of the fraud. When you sue for compensatory damages, a court will usually measure your loss as the difference between what the purchase should have been worth, and what it actually was worth. For example, if the imitation chair, made in Hong Kong, was worth only $100 and you paid $400 for it, the compensatory damages would be $300.

You might also be able to collect what are called "consequential" and "incidental" damages: these kinds of damages cover other losses you may have suffered as a result of the fraud. Incidental damages, might include expenses involved in having the wicker chair appraised. You might recover consequential damages, on the other hand, if you suffered a personal injury or damage to property as a result of the fraud.

If a fraud involves the sale of products, the Uniform Commercial Code also entitles buyers to use all the remedies available under this code for holding a seller accountable for breaking a contract. As explained in Section IV, the key remedies that could be available are rejecting or revoking acceptance and cancelling the contract, or recovering damages as provided by the code. This, in effect, means you could then invoke those remedies in place of the ones available under the fraud law.

POSSIBILITY OF PUNITIVE DAMAGES PROVIDES LEVERAGE

Punitive damages are awarded when a seller substantially disregards consumer rights or is especially abusive or reckless. Such extra money, awarded by the judge or jury, may turn out to be much more than your actual losses.

Courts are most likely to award punitive damages when a scheme is directed not at just one consumer, but at the public at large. They are meant to deter the seller from continuing the practice.

Most frauds are, of course, directed at the public at large, since it seldom pays for a seller to engage in fraudulent schemes in order to fleece just one person. But courts have awarded punitive damages in cases involving a single consumer. In 1964, for example, an Alabama consumer paid some $5,000 for what he thought was a new car. The car turned out to be a demonstrator. It also turned out to be defective. When the dealer refused to take back the car, the consumer sued for fraud and asked for punitive damages. The jury awarded him $20,000.

And in a 1961 landmark decision, the New York Court of Appeals issued a ruling in the case of a business that had regularly used false and fraudulent representations. It said it would be proper for a jury to award punitive damages up to $75,000, even though the consumer's actual losses were only $1,380.

The court said it was proper to award these damages because: "Those who deliberately and cooly engage in a far-flung fraudulent scheme, systematically conducted for profit, are very much more likely to pause and consider the consequences if they have to pay more than the actual loss suffered by an individual plaintiff [i.e. the consumer who sued].

"An occasional award of compensatory damages against such parties would have little deterrent effect. A judgment simply for compensatory damages would require the offender to do no more than return the money which he had taken from the plaintiff. In the calculation of expected profits, the wrongdoer is likely to allow for a certain amount of money which will have to be returned to those victims who object too vigorously, and will be perfectly content to bear the additional cost of litigation as the price for continuing his illicit business. It stands to reason that the chances of deterring him are materially increased by subjecting him to the payment of punitive damages."

When you use the fraud law, your leverage is the possibility that a judge or jury might award you hefty punitive damages. That is what makes the seller vulnerable: he could lose a good deal more than it would have taken to settle the dispute.

WHICH LAW TO CHOOSE?

The fraud law can be a potent legal weapon when you have been misled or deceived. But if you can sue a seller under your state's deceptive sales practices law, that law will usually give you more leverage simply because it is often easier to make out a case—and win it. If it also allows you to recover punitive damages, minimum damages, or multiple damages, your state's deceptive sales practices law will always create the most leverage for you.

If your state's deceptive sales practices law does not allow you to sue a seller, which is the case in Arkansas, Iowa, Nevada, New York, North Dakota, and Oklahoma, the fraud law will be the strongest legal weapon you have.

The fraud law may also create more leverage for you if a seller commits a flagrant fraud and your state's deceptive practices law allows you to collect only your damages and attorney's fees.

HOW TO PRESERVE YOUR RIGHTS

When you first discover you have been defrauded, you must immediately take certain steps to preserve your rights under the fraud law.

Rule number one is, if you discover the fraud before a purchase has been completed, don't complete it.

Suppose, for example, that at the time of delivery you see a "Made in Hong Kong" label on the chair you thought was an antique; you should neither accept the chair nor pay for it. You must, however, tell the seller why you are rejecting it. (See page 164 for how to reject goods.)

If you complete the sale when you could have avoided doing so, you won't normally be able to hold the seller liable for fraud. The law assumes that if you complete a sale after you know the seller is lying to you, then the lies are not very important to you.

Rule number two is, if you accept the purchase notify the seller immediately when you notice something is wrong. Tell him how you think you were misled or deceived and ask him to take corrective action. If the case goes to court, notifying the seller quickly will show that his misrepresentations were unacceptable to you early on. If the seller tries to tell you nothing is wrong, have him put his assurances in writing. If nothing is wrong, fine; but if you later find out you were deceived, the written assurances will help strengthen your case.

Rule number three is, stop using the product as soon as you discover the fraud. When you do this, you keep your right to rescind the contract and make the seller take back the product. And definitely do not continue to use the product if the seller has refused to take it back. If you continue to use the purchase, you will almost always lose your chance to rescind your contract based on rights under the fraud law and the Uniform Commercial Code.

22 · Negotiating Strategy: Putting the Fraud Law into Action

Let's take the following example to illustrate how you would use the fraud law.

Suppose you purchased a General Watts freezer on May 10 for $325. You were told you were buying a new freezer and it was delivered on May 16. You used it up until August 20, but because the freezer wasn't cooling properly, you called in an authorized repair service for warranty work.

When you discussed the freezer with the repairman he told you it must be a used model because it showed evidence of greater wear than would have been the case if it were new. The repairman determined that the freezer was at least two years old. Since your new appliance warranty no longer covered your freezer, you had to pay $50 for the service call.

STAGE ONE: OPENING SKIRMISHES

How could you have determined that the freezer was a used model before the repairman discovered the fact? One clue might have been if the freezer was not delivered in a factory shipping carton; a new model probably would be.

If something like this happens to make you suspicious, ask for an explanation. You might be told, for instance, that the store unpacks appliances to make it easier for them to dispose of the packing materials. Have the delivery man write the explanation on your copy of the delivery slip and sign it.

Alternatively, write the explanation on a separate sheet of paper and identify the appliance, the delivery date, and the serial number. You could ask him to write something like this, or write it for him and have him sign it: "When the purchaser, Mr./Mrs./Ms. _____, asked why the General Watts freezer, serial number 3857X88, was not delivered in its original factory packing case, I told him/her it was the company's policy to unpack appliances before delivery. I assured him/her that the appliance was new, and not a used model, and I acknowledge that he/she took delivery only because of these assurances." If the delivery man and the store lie to you, having such a statement will later help you prove your case.

If the delivery man cannot give you a reasonable explanation, or won't note in writing that something is clearly wrong, refusing the goods would then usually be your safest course until the problem is satisfactorily resolved. (The correct way to do this is explained on page 164.) However, if a store is really trying to pull a switch and you get suspicious and press for an explanation, such as in this example, a delivery man is most likely to give an excuse for not delivering the merchandise rather than give you a false explanation which compounds the fraud. He may say he has mixed up his delivery schedule, for instance. (See page 93 for a confirming letter you could use for pinning down assurances given to you after you raised questions about something that could be wrong.)

Say you had no suspicions, though, and didn't learn you had a used appliance until the repairman later told you, as in our example. Your first move should be to make a written memo which describes how the purchase was misrepresented. Immediately return to the store and ask the store representative to sign it. Be sure to have the person state his or her title. Leave room on the memo to write these down before the representative signs.

Here is a sample memo you could adapt. The wording assumes you previously informed the store about the cooling problem involved in the example.

August 21, 19___

> *To: White Appliances, Inc.*
>
> *This is to notify you that the General Watts freezer, serial number 3857x88 which was delivered on May 16, 19___, does not conform to the representations that were made when I purchased a freezer on May 10, 19___. It also fails to conform to the terms stated on your sales receipt, number 152-3928, dated May 10, 19___.*
>
> *At the time of the purchase I was told I was buying a new appliance, and it was identified as a new appliance on the sales receipt. The freezer was also represented as new when it was delivered. A new appliance warranty and an owner's manual were packed inside the appliance.*
>
> *I found out on August 20, however, that the appliance was, in fact, a used model when Amos Appliance Repairs, an authorized General Watts repair service, tried to repair a cooling defect I had previously told you about on August 18. The serviceman informed me that the appliance that had been delivered was an older model manufactured at least two years ago. He said it showed evidence of far more wear and tear than would have been apparent if it had, in fact, been a new appliance when it was delivered three months ago. Amos Appliance Repairs also informed me that the appliance was no longer covered by the manufacturer's new appliance warranty, and I had to pay $50 for a service call that would otherwise have been covered by the warranty.*
>
> *(your signature)*

At the bottom of the memo write:

> *I acknowledge receiving a copy of this memo on (insert date) and discussing this matter with (your name). I then told him/her the following: (Write down any promises or explanations you get from the store's representative.)*

Then ask the store representative to sign your copy and write his or her title.

If the store won't give you any explanation or make any promises, just ask the person to sign the memo to show the store has received a copy. This way you will have written evidence showing when you told the store about the misrepresentation.

Presenting a written memo and asking for a representative's signature puts more pressure on the store to settle your dispute. And even if the representative refuses to sign it, leaving a copy and keeping one for yourself will help you prove when you notified the store.

If the store promises to settle the dispute, or gives you assurances but refuses to put them in writing, write the following confirming letter.

101 Pine Tree Lane
Anytown, USA 00000

August 23, 19___

Mr. John C. Poll
Manager

White Appliances, Inc.
North Woods Plaza
Anytown, USA 00000

Dear Mr. Poll:

This is to confirm the discussion we had on August 22, 19___ when I notified you personally and by written memorandum that the General Watts freezer, serial number 3857X88, which was delivered on May 16, 19___, does not conform to the representations that were made when I purchased a freezer on May 10, 19___, for $325. It also fails to conform to the terms stated on your sales memorandum number 152-3928, dated May 10, 19___.

The written memorandum dated August 21, which I left with you, described the representations and the freezer's failure to conform, and the date I discovered the non-conformity. It also informed you of the $50 expenses I incurred for repairs which should have been covered by a warranty for a freezer that was, in fact, new.

You then informed me that the wrong appliance must have been delivered to me by mistake. You agreed to pick up the appliance at my home between 1 and 5 P.M. on August 30, 19___, and deliver a new appliance as called for by our agreement. And for the purpose of settling this matter, I agreed to accept a $50 credit as reimbursement for the expenses I had.

Thank you for settling this matter promptly as you have promised to do.

Sincerely,

STAGE TWO: THE LOW-KEYED WARNING.

If your informal negotiations fail—if the store refuses to solve the problem, or promises to solve it but fails to do so—you would immediately send a low-keyed warning letter. Here is a sample letter you could adapt.

Certified Letter No. 93847567

101 Pine Tree Lane
Anytown, USA 00000

August 22, 19___

Mr. John C. Poll
Manager
White Appliances, Inc.
North Woods Plaza
Anytown, USA 00000

Dear Mr. Poll:

I am notifying you of the misrepresentation that occurred when I purchased a General Watts freezer at your store on May 10. The purchase is identified on your sales memorandum, number 152-3928, dated May 10, 19___, and the freezer, serial number 3857X88, was delivered to me on May 16.

At the time of the purchase, I was told I was buying a new appliance. Your sales memo identifies the merchandise as a new appliance, and the freezer was represented as new at the time of delivery. But contrary to the representations and the sales terms, the appliance I received was, in fact, a used model. The misrepresentations, how I discovered them, and the expenses I incurred for repairs are described in my memorandum of August 21, a copy of which I left with you when we discussed this matter on August 22.

Since I received a used, not the new appliance I was led to expect, I have been denied the performance and reliability of a new appliance as well as the manufacturer's new appliance warranty which I was told would be part of this bargain.

For the purpose of promptly resolving this matter, when we discussed it on August 22, I requested that you immediately take back the appliance and exchange it for the same model that was, in fact, new [(OR) refund its purchase price of $325 plus sales tax] and pay me the $50 I sustained as damages for the expense of a service call. This service call would have been covered by a new appliance warranty. Although you refused this proposal for resolving this matter, I am still prepared to resolve it as I have proposed if you will promptly replace the freezer with one that is, in fact, new as represented [if you will promptly refund its purchase price and then arrange to pick up the appliance that was delivered but which is not, in fact, new as had been represented].

I hope that we can resolve this matter satisfactorily so that I will not have to hold you liable at least for tortious fraud [and as provided by the Uniform Commercial Code for fraudulent misrepresentations].

Sincerely,

You must, of course, adapt this letter to fit your particular situation. Describe as specifically as possible what representations were made and how they turned out to be false. Include important details that show what happened, and state whether some disadvantage such as age, lack of expert knowledge, or language skills, made it easy for the seller to mislead you.

Suppose, for instance, you had been misled when you had relied upon a repair shop's assessment of needed repairs for a washing machine. Then say something like this in the second paragraph of your letter:

"Since I lack any knowledge about the mechanical characteristics of appliances, I relied on your expert skill and judgment as an appliance repairman to tell me what repairs were needed when I agreed to the repairs noted on your repair order, number 34521, dated January 6, 19__."

Naturally, you would also have to adapt the letter to different negotiating situations. The examples of how to adapt a basic letter on page 92 should help you adapt this letter to deal with violations of the fraud law. If you purchased a product, see section IV about using the remedies available under the Uniform Commercial Code.

STAGE THREE: THE ULTIMATUM.

If the low-keyed warning letter does not produce results, you could adapt and send the following ultimatum.

Certified Letter No. 12938476

101 Pine Tree Lane
Anytown, USA 00000

September 15, 19___

Mr. Tom White
President
White Appliances, Inc.
1811 Great Neck Blvd.
Anytown, USA 00000

Dear Mr. White:

I am notifying you about the tortious fraud involving what was to be a new General Watts freezer I purchased at your Northland Plaza store on May 10, 19___. The purchase is identified on your sales memorandum, number 152-3928 dated May 10, 19___.

I was told at the time of purchase that I was buying a new appliance, which is how it was identified on your sales memorandum and how it was represented at the time of delivery on May 16. The misrepresentations and my efforts to settle this matter are more fully described in my memorandum of August 21 and my letter of August 22 to Mr. Poll, the Northland Plaza store manager (copies are enclosed.)

So far, I have received no reply to my letter of August 22.

I am still willing to resolve this matter as I proposed in my letter of August 22 if White Appliances, Inc. immediately gives me a full credit [refund] for the purchase price of the freezer ($325 plus tax) and pays me $50 to cover the expenses for a service call, and promptly arranges to pick up the freezer at my home immediately upon giving me the credit [refund] for the price. I am until then retaining and only storing the appliance for you.

If my proposal for resolving this matter remains unsatisfied, I shall seek to hold you liable at least to the fullest extent provided by law for tortious fraud and by the Uniform Commercial Code for fraudulent misrepresentation. I shall seek a jury verdict to recover all my losses, and I shall seek punitive damages for the reckless, deliberate, and wantonly fraudulent conduct that occurred. I shall also inform the state attorney general about this matter and seek information about the number and nature of other consumer complaints against your company that may be in the attorney general's files to strengthen my claim for punitive damages.

Sincerely,

Remember that showing there are complaints on file with consumer protection agencies is one important way to prove a company directed its fraud at the public at large. Courts are more likely to award punitive damages in such cases.

If the company doesn't settle the dispute, complaining to the attorney general before seeing an attorney could help; or you could contact the local government agencies that enforce your state's deceptive sales practices law.

SECTION IV
BUYING GOODS: YOUR RIGHTS AND OBLIGATIONS WHEN BUYING CARS, FURNITURE, CLOTHING, FOOD, AND OTHER CONSUMER PRODUCTS

23 · Your Major Legal Tool: The Uniform Commercial Code

During the evening hours of Friday, February 10, 1967, Mrs. Smith took delivery of a brand new 1967 Chevrolet Biscayne sedan her husband had purchased from Zabriskie Chevrolet on February 2. Mr. Smith had given the dealer a $124 deposit, then paid the balance of $2,069.50 by check on February 9.

As Mrs. Smith was driving the new car home—a distance of only two and one half miles—the car began to stall. First, it stalled at a traffic light just seven tenths of a mile from the showroom. It stalled again after traveling another 15 feet. Soon it stalled each time Mrs. Smith had to stop. Then, after she had driven about one and a quarter miles, the car refused to move in "drive" gear: it would only move in "low–low" gear at speeds of five to ten miles per hour. Finally, a disbelieving Mrs. Smith called her husband and he drove the car the last few blocks to their home.

That same evening Mr. Smith called his bank and stopped payment on the check. He also called the dealer and told him the car was a lemon, that he had stopped payment on it, and that the purchase was canceled. The next day, the dealer's wrecker towed the car back to the dealership.

The dealer replaced the faulty transmission with one from another car, then called Mr. Smith and insisted that he pick up and pay for the car. Refusing to do so, Mr. Smith repeated that the sale had been canceled.

Eventually, the dealership sued Mr. Smith, claiming that he owed payment for the car since he had "accepted" it when Mrs. Smith took delivery and drove away. Mr. Smith argued that far from accepting the car, he had rejected it and canceled the purchase when he learned that the car he had received was not what he'd purchased—that is, a new car in perfect operating condition. Smith also sued the dealer for the $124 deposit he had paid.

A New Jersey court ruled in Smith's favor, saying that a buyer doesn't "accept" goods until he has had a "reasonable opportunity to inspect" them. The court said "[Mr. Smith] assumed what every new car buyer has a right to assume and, indeed has been led to assume by the high-powered advertising techniques of the auto industry—that his new car, with the exception of minor adjustments, would be mechanically new and factory furnished, operate perfectly, and be free from substantial defects. The vehicle delivered to [Mr. Smith] did not measure up to these standards."

In Mr. Smith's case, the court said, the "reasonable opportunity to inspect" occurred during the trip home. The court stressed the importance of the right to inspect because, " . . . to the layman, the complicated mechanisms of today's automobiles are a complete mystery. To have the automobile inspected by someone with sufficient expertise to disassemble the vehicle in order to discover latent defects before the contract is signed, is assuredly impossible and highly impractical. Consequently, the first few miles of driving become even more significant to the excited new car buyer. This is the buyer's first reasonable opportunity to enjoy his new vehicle to see if it conforms to what it was represented to be and whether he is getting what he is bargaining for."

The court concluded that the seller couldn't require a consumer to accept a car that was as seriously defective as the one delivered to Mrs. Smith. Nor could the dealer repair the defect with a transmission from another car and expect the consumer to accept the car as factory new.

The court ruled that Mr. Smith did not have to take the car and ordered the dealer to return his $124 deposit.

RULES FOR THE SALE OF GOODS: THE UNIFORM COMMERCIAL CODE

In every state, except Louisiana*, the sale of goods is governed by a law called the Uniform Commercial Code (usually referred to in this book as the UCC or the Code). Mr. Smith won his case because of the rights he had under the Code and because he was willing to take the necessary steps to uphold them.

The UCC is a broad law, but this section of the book covers only those parts that apply to the sale of goods. They include requirements that govern what can be included in an agreement, what both sides may have to do to fulfill an agreement, and what each side can do when an agreement is broken.

Drafted to encourage states to make the laws governing sales uniform throughout the country, the Code itself is a model law. While each state has adopted its own version of the Code, and laws may vary, they are basically the same in every state. For our purposes, then, the rules outlined in this section are taken from the model law. They spell out the basic guidelines that govern the sale of goods under your state law.

Some of the rules are general in nature, such as the requirement that both parties to an agreement deal with each other in "good faith," or in other words behave honestly. Other rules are more specific, such as those that define when a buyer becomes obligated to pay for his purchase, when a seller must deliver the goods, or when a buyer has to accept or can reject the delivered goods.

WHAT KIND OF GOODS ARE COVERED BY THE UCC?

The Code governs only transactions involving "movable" goods, such as cars, furniture, clothing and foods. Lawyers call such goods tangible personal property.

The Code provisions described in this section, therefore, do *not* apply when you buy intangible property such as an insurance policy; investment securities such as stocks or bonds; real property such as land, or a house, or anything permanently attached to them; or personal services such as repair work or medical care. Even when you purchase a personal service that requires the repair person to furnish parts, such as a car repair, for example, the sale of such parts usually is *not* covered by the Code. Instead, such transactions are governed by the common law of contracts or other federal and state statutory laws that may apply.

---

*While Louisiana has adopted some parts of the Code, its laws governing the sale of goods are patterned after French law, which was used during the time the state was a French possession.

ENFORCING YOUR RIGHTS UNDER THE CODE

The Code only requires parties to live up to their agreements, it does not impose penalties—a violator isn't thrown in jail, for instance. No government agency enforces the UCC either, so if a seller does not comply you cannot seek help from an enforcement agency.

How, then, do you enforce the Code? If someone breaks an agreement, or ignores your rights, your main legal weapon under the Code is to sue to recover compensation for your losses.

The fact that you have to take private legal action to enforce the Code, is one of its main drawbacks as far as many consumers are concerned. For if you sue, the seller need only compensate you for what you were entitled to in the first place. You cannot collect anything extra, such as attorney's fees or minimum damages. This doesn't create much leverage to help you settle a dispute, unfortunately, because even if the seller chooses to be completely unreasonable he won't face extra penalties.

However, knowing your rights, and following the requirements of the Code, will allow you to bargain more effectively. And if a dispute winds up in court, the fact that you have taken the right steps will automatically strengthen your position. It may cost you to sue, but it will also cost the business to fight you. The stronger your bargaining position, the more likely your case will be settled before it reaches court.

COMBINING RIGHTS FOR MAXIMUM LEVERAGE

The UCC rules, and how to use them to deal with different situations, are discussed separately here, but when you are trying to settle a dispute remember that several rules can apply. So be sure to identify all those that apply to your dispute and combine your rights so you get maximum leverage when you negotiate.

It's also important to remember that the Code is not the only law that governs consumer transactions involving the purchase of goods. Federal and state consumer protection laws may beef up the rights you have under the Code. The common law of contracts, which governed agreements before the Code was adopted, still applies to certain situations not specifically covered by the Code. And case law which has been established as courts have interpreted the Code, may affect how a Code provision or a specific rule will be applied. The way the court decided Mr. Smith's case, for instance, is an example of how a court applied the Code to a buyer's right to inspect goods and to reject them if they didn't conform to the agreement.

Although you can't know all these legal technicalities, if you understand and follow the basic rules that govern purchases, you can strengthen your bargaining position if a dispute arises. Your knowledge will make you feel more confident about insisting that a seller follow the rules, and—when you are negotiating a settlement—follow them in a way most favorable to you. You can't really lose if you act carefully and base your negotiating strategy on the strongest argument for interpreting a rule in your favor.

24 · Making An Agreement: How Written and Unwritten Terms Count

Generally speaking, a sale involves two basic obligations. The seller must transfer and deliver the goods, and the buyer must accept and pay for them. The sale is completed when both sides have carried out these obligations according to the agreement or contract.

What is an agreement? Every time you purchase something you and the seller reach an agreement that governs the sale. Technically, a contract consists of everything you both agree to, including any specific promises the seller makes to induce you to buy and any promises you make, plus the rights and obligations each side has under the law. (Warranties and financing terms that may be part of an agreement are covered in Sections V and VII of this book.)

SALES TERMS: ORAL AND WRITTEN AGREEMENTS

Formal written agreements are generally the exception rather than the rule, but the savvy consumer *always* makes sure significant terms are put into writing. A written agreement not only makes it easier to prove what you and the seller agreed to, but the Code gives extra weight to what is in writing—especially if terms have been added to a seller's printed form.

It's important to remember that written terms are not necessarily the only thing that may count if you have a dispute, though. As explained in this chapter, there are times when an oral agreement can be just as binding. There are also times when, even though you have a written agreement, you can still hold the seller to oral promises or unwritten sales terms. And sometimes written terms may *not* be binding, especially "unfair" terms in fine print.

WHEN *MUST* YOU HAVE WRITTEN PROOF OF AN AGREEMENT?

The Code spells out the kind of sales agreement that must be in writing, what has to be stated so it is binding, and what can be omitted from—but still be a valid part of—a written agreement.

In general, whenever the purchase price of a product is $500 or more, the Code requires written proof of an agreement for it to be enforceable in court. There are two exceptions to this. One is if a seller accepts payment from you; the second is if you receive and *accept* the goods (see page 160 for what constitutes acceptance). Making payments or accepting goods can bind you and the seller to an agreement, but you would still be in a better position legally if you at least have a written record of the transaction.

When making a cash payment, for instance, make sure the store gives a written receipt that identifies the amount. Have the store note on the receipt what the payment is for: "Payment on the price of a five-piece living room set," for example. If you pay by check, write the same notation on the front of it. In the case of a check, the seller may have to cash, or at least endorse it, before the Code recognizes that he has accepted payment from you.

If a purchase is for less than $500, an oral agreement is as legally binding as if you had written proof. Even so, in today's impersonal marketplace it's best to have some written record or receipt—"proof of purchase"—to show that you have actually bought something from a specific store.

WHAT CONSTITUTES WRITTEN PROOF?

The Code does not require that a written agreement include all the important terms or promises in order to be binding. It requires only enough information to show that you and the seller actually have an agreement. Generally, it is enough that written proof state the quantity of goods involved in the sale, and be "signed" by the person you want to hold to the agreement, in order to be enforceable.

The "signature" of the seller can be any symbol that a business uses to show it is responsible for an agreement: it can be an initial or stamp; it can be typewritten or even printed as long as it shows the business has made the sale. A store's name printed on a cash register receipt, for example, is usually enough to count as a signature.

So if you buy some furniture and the store gives you a signed sales slip that says simply, "Sold one five-piece set of living room furniture," despite the fact that the model, style, brand, color and even the price are omitted, that is enough written proof to show you have an enforceable agreement.

The seller's signature does not necessarily have to be on the sales slip to count, either. If it is used to endorse a check you provide for your down payment, that is usually enough to show you have an agreement. To make sure you can show the signature and the sales slip are part of the same transaction, though, ask the store to note the number of the check on the sales slip: "Down payment made with check number 101," for example. And on the check itself write: "Down payment on five-piece set of living room furniture." This way, you would have the minimum written proof the Code requires to show you have an agreement.

Even if the written sales slip says nothing more about the furniture than "five-piece set," obviously you have still agreed to buy a specific style, model, color, and brand for a specific price. Since those unwritten terms are part of the agreement, that is what the store will have to deliver, and you can use your rights under the Code to make the seller live up to the agreement.

Never hesitate to enforce your rights under the Code to make the seller live up to unwritten terms or oral promises when they are part of your agreement. But, obviously, it is always easier to do so if the receipt or sales slip accurately identifies what you are buying and how much it costs.

HOW WRITTEN TERMS GOVERN AN AGREEMENT

If a dispute arises, anything written into an agreement is always considered especially important because the Code gives it extra legal weight.

Generally speaking, written terms override unwritten terms or oral promises that differ from them. For instance, if you are promised one thing verbally but the written agreement says you are promised another, courts will usually decide a dispute based on the written terms. When there is a conflict like this, you often lose the chance to bring up in court any oral promises the seller has made.

So when you negotiate with a seller about any written terms and he refuses to change them, you will usually be considered to have specifically agreed to them if you go ahead and buy. Before you start negotiating about written terms included in a form contract, then, be aware of the possible consequences of failing to get them changed to your liking.

When unwritten terms or oral promises do not conflict with what is in writing, you can sometimes still hold a seller to them. Suppose, for example, the sales slip says, "No exchanges or refunds." No other conditions are stated. That clause will not get the seller off the hook if the product is defective or doesn't measure up to his promises. If, however, the sales slip also states that the product is sold "as is," it means the seller is not giving any warranties: usually this will get him off the hook.

Written terms can help or hurt you depending, of course, on whether or not they are favorable. For this reason you may sometimes be better off if there is little or nothing in writing about a deal, than if you have a written agreement that includes a lot of *unfavorable* terms in the fine print. You are usually bound by the fine print in a contract even though neither you nor the seller may have specifically discussed or agreed to the terms.

Courts are beginning to discount some fine print clauses, noting that those which seriously hurt consumers either by taking away important rights or by giving a seller special rights he would not ordinarily have, are not considered part of the agreement unless they are so conspicuously stated a buyer would naturally notice them. A fine print merger clause (see below) is one example of this type of clause. A clause that deprives consumers of practical ways of holding a seller accountable for failing to honor an agreement is another.

While courts don't always rule in favor of buyers when they interpret fine print clauses, they are increasingly recognizing that consumers lack the legal knowledge and the bargaining power to change such terms, and that it is often unfair to allow sellers to impose them on a take-it-or-leave-it basis.

Since it is impractical to suggest you negotiate every fine print clause and then ask the seller to change those that are extremely unfair, your best bet if a dispute reaches court is to rely on the judge to rule that you should not be held to them. Be aware, though, that this course can be risky and you cannot rely on it at all when it comes to prominently disclosed written terms. (This book describes how the Code allows you to get out of some fine print terms.)

If a seller tries to hold you to very unfair fine print terms while you are negotiating a settlement, therefore, base your strategy on the assumption that a court won't hold you to them and let the seller know they may not count. Sellers often include in their contracts fine print terms they know won't hold up in court simply to increase their bargaining leverage in case of a dispute. In fact, the authors of a law textbook recommend that lawyers who are acting for sellers include these terms in form contracts for just that purpose. As they point out, a seller has nothing to lose since the worst that could happen is a court could decide the terms are invalid.

So when you are negotiating with a seller who has not honored an agreement, don't throw in the towel just because he claims that certain clauses obligate *you* to do so. Neither you nor the seller can tell in advance whether some fine print clause will really hold up in court, so let the uncertainty work to your advantage.

An important word of caution, however. If issues like this come up in a dispute involving a significant purchase that could cost you a lot of money if you lose your case in court, *don't* hold up payment and give the seller a chance to sue you for breaking the agreement until you first check with an attorney. Make your payment under protest, in order to preserve your rights, as explained on page 127.

MERGER CLAUSES

In the case of a written agreement that is supposed to include *everything* that is part of the deal, unwritten terms or oral promises generally count for little or nothing. Sellers often try to make such an agreement by putting what is called a "merger clause" into the fine print. Basically, this clause says that you and the seller have put into writing everything that you have agreed to, so that in the event of a dispute the written agreement will be the *only* thing that counts. More often than not, the printed terms included in the standard form contract are ones you never discuss or specifically agree to, while those you do discuss are usually the ones omitted from the agreement. Just about every formal agreement you sign includes a merger clause.

Since clauses like this are obviously harmful especially when they are buried in the fine print and a salesperson has assured a buyer that promises don't have to be put in writing, courts are tending to discount them in consumer transactions. That's why you should base your negotiating strategy on forcing the seller to live up to important unwritten terms or promises.

There is a version of the merger clause that can hurt you, though. It goes something like this:

> This agreement signed by both parties and so initialed by both parties in the margin opposite this paragraph constitutes a final expression of all the terms of this agreement and is a complete and exclusive statement of those terms, and any and all representations, promises, warranties or statements by seller's agent that differ in any way from the terms of this written agreement shall be given no force or effect.

This example is taken from a law textbook whose authors recommend it to law students as a really effective way to help a seller bind a buyer to a written agreement and discount unwritten promises.* It doesn't really differ very much from other merger clauses that are used except that the authors suggest it be conspicuously printed and that the consumer be asked to initial it.

Always look out for a clause like this in a contract. If you initial it, you most likely will be held to the agreement.

There is a way to turn this merger clause idea around so it works in your favor, though. Use it to test the seller's honesty. When you are asked to initial such a clause, and the written agreement does not include all the terms and promises the salesperson makes, refuse to initial it or to sign the agreement. Tell the salesperson he is asking you to sign something that is obviously untrue.

If you go through with the deal but don't initial the clause, in the case of a dispute a court will rarely count it as being part of the agreement. You will then be able to hold the seller to unwritten terms or oral promises that were part of the deal.

Alternatively, if you are presented with a merger clause, insist that all the important terms and promises be put into writing just as the clause says. If the salesperson won't do it, how can you trust him?

Of course, if you spot a prominently disclosed merger clause that doesn't say anything about your having to initial it, then insist the salesperson cross it out and initial it himself. And say you want it out of the agreement because it is obviously untrue.

POINTS TO WATCH OUT FOR

Always check to see a sales slip correctly identifies what you've bought. If you buy a new appliance, make sure the written sales slip or agreement describes it as a new appliance. If a salesperson writes "floor model," it obviously is not a new appliance, for instance. If the agreement identifies the appliance model, make, or type, be sure it describes the kind you actually examined and bought.

Take special note of sales terms that are prominently stated in an agreement, and be sure to note any terms a seller asks you to initial or sign separately: these are terms a court is especially likely to say you should have noted and hold you to in case of a dispute.

If the agreement includes prominent terms that conflict with what the salesperson

NOTE: White, James J. and Summers, Robert S, *Uniform Commercial Code,* 2d edition, West Publishing Co., (St. Paul, Minn., 1980), p. 90.

tells you, a statement saying "no terms or exchanges," for example, have the statement crossed out and ask the salesperson to initial it and state the conditions under which you could return or exchange the product.

Also look for prominently displayed store signs that state sales conditions and that can become part of your agreement. If such a sign differs from what a salesperson has told you, then get your conditions in writing.

The time to question terms and to change them is before you buy. If you ignore them, it will be tough to claim the store really agreed to something different.

SIGNING AN AGREEMENT

Signing a blank contract is like signing a blank check. If a salesperson asks you to sign a blank contract, be firm and insist that it be filled in first—then make sure all the terms are stated accurately.

Get a copy *as soon as you sign* to protect yourself against any alterations someone might try to make later. A seller can seldom hold you to terms that differ from those stated on your copy of the agreement.

If for some reason you do sign a blank contract, never take the goods or pay anything until you have checked the completed agreement and made absolutely sure the written terms describe the deal correctly. *Never* assume the store has filled in the agreement accurately. Check everything. And insist that the store show you the *original* pages of the agreement so that you may compare them with the copy. If the terms are not stated correctly, insist the store write a new agreement that is correct. Either rip up the original or write "Void" on it.

CORRECTING MISTAKES IN AN AGREEMENT

Naturally mistakes are sometimes made in agreements. A seller who makes an honest mistake is usually willing to correct it. However, if there is a dispute about what an agreement says, contract law—established before the Code was adopted—is used to settle the matter.

The most important point to remember is that if you make a mistake and the seller has nothing to do with it, you will seldom be able to get out of an agreement because of it. The seller can, in effect, hold you to the deal even though the terms aren't what you thought they were. You might make a mistake of this kind if you fail to read all the terms of a contract, for instance.

When both you and the seller make a mistake about what is an important part of a deal—say you thought you were buying a 19-inch portable TV for $395, while the seller thought he was selling a 17-inch model for $329—the law generally holds there is no deal and therefore no agreement to enforce. Either party can then rescind the "agreement." When an agreement is terminated in this way because of a mistake, both parties must return whatever they may have received. In unusual situations this may not be possible and tricky technicalities could arise about whether the deal could actually be terminated.

If there is a mistake about the terms of an agreement, therefore, have it corrected before you sign or at least before you pay for or receive the goods. This way you have the best chance of calling off a deal.

A seller who makes an honest mistake won't object to writing a new agreement. But if he becomes nasty and balks—especially if you signed a blank contract—call off the deal immediately. In this case, the seller isn't making a mistake. He or she is out to clip you and it would be foolish to do business with him.

Don't let a seller scare you into sticking with an agreement in this situation if he threatens to take you to court, either. As a practical matter, a seller would rarely do so because he would have a hard time showing you had a deal at all. But if the seller persists, use the rights you have under your state's deceptive sales practices law or your state's fraud law.

Say, for instance, a seller claims that the terms of a contract that you signed in blank (and which was later filled in incorrectly) constitute your agreement. If you haven't paid for anything or received the goods, you are in a strong position to argue that both sides were mistaken. Your argument that the seller tried to defraud you by getting you to sign a blank contract will be most convincing in court. But if, in such a situation, you would not be satisfied with simply calling off the deal, seek legal advice.

It is usually much harder to get out of an agreement after you have received and started to use a product. To hold a seller liable for mistakes, you would usually have to show he has violated either your state's deceptive practices law or the fraud law.

HOW FRAUD OR MISREPRESENTATIONS AFFECT WRITTEN TERMS

If a seller commits fraud or makes serious misrepresentations, he usually cannot hold you to your agreement in the case of a dispute. This is one time when the merger clause does not count, even if you haven't got the promises in writing.

The laws that can help you when the seller commits fraud or engages in misrepresentations or deceptions, are described in Section III. You can use the rights available under these laws, as well as the rights you have under the Code to enforce an agreement.

25 · General Rules That Govern Agreements

There are five key rules that affect how a court would interpret and enforce the terms of an agreement. These rules and how they can affect your rights are described in this chapter.

1. KEEPING YOUR RIGHTS

Generally speaking, if a seller breaks a specific term of your agreement, and you ignore the fact, you will usually lose your right to hold him to it later on. So if something goes wrong, it is important to speak up and object right away.

Suppose, for example, you buy a Model X-200 Soyi TV set but the store delivers an X-400 model. Instead of objecting, you keep the TV; but after using it for some time it goes on the blink. Although you will still be able to make the seller honor a warranty on the set, you won't be able to make him take the set back on the grounds that he did not deliver the X-200 model you actually ordered in the first place. To do that, you would have had to make your objection at the time the wrong set was delivered.

2. HOW BREAKING AN AGREEMENT CAN CHANGE ITS TERMS

If a specific term of an agreement is broken and you ignore it, that simply prevents you from compelling the seller to honor that particular term later on. But when an agreement requires one side to perform in some way over a period of time and the other party repeatedly ignores a failure to do so, the continued acceptance could change the terms of the agreement. In effect, this rule says that the way people willingly carry out their agreement over a period of time affects what they can be obligated to do.

In practice, this rule generally affects payment terms. Suppose, for instance, your agreement requires you to make payments on the first of each month but a couple of times you actually make them on the fifteenth. If the seller doesn't raise any objections at the time, he can't later claim you broke the agreement. If a future payment is late, however, the seller can hold you responsible for breaking the agreement if he chooses to. In other words, overlooking a failure simply excuses it without changing the terms of the agreement.

If you *regularly* make late payments and the seller accepts them, his continued willingness to do so could change the due date to the date you actually pay—in this case to the fifteenth of the month. So a continued willingness to overlook someone's failure to carry out an obligation can result in an agreement being changed. And once an agreement has been changed this way the seller usually would not be able to hold you to the terms of the original agreement. For this reason, most form contracts used by sellers include a fine print clause which says the terms of the written agreement can only be changed *in writing,* and that the seller's failure to object if you regularly break some term is not considered a willingness to modify, or change, the agreement.

If that's the case, you might ask, why am I bothering to explain a rule which is unlikely to help you anyway?

There are two reasons. First, such a clause counts in a consumer transaction *only* if the consumer has specifically signed or initialed it. Sellers rarely ask buyers to do this, so in effect the clause is usually invalid. If by chance you are asked to sign such a clause, though, refuse to do so.

Second, even if the seller can enforce such a clause, he must first give you a chance to honor the agreement if he has regularly overlooked your failure to do so. He cannot, for example, suddenly count the next late payment as a breach which entitles him to sue you. Instead, he must first tell you that he wants you to pay on time from now on.

3. RESERVING YOUR RIGHTS IN CASE OF A DISPUTE

Initially you may want to hold off formally holding a seller accountable for an agreement he has broken. You may, instead, be willing to carry out your part of the bargain, and a seller might insist that you do, while you try to work out the problem. In a case like this, it's important to make sure you don't lose rights you could have under the Code because of your willingness to go along with the seller.

Suppose, for example, you sign for goods without inspecting them because the delivery people are "in a hurry" and insist you pay first and look at the goods later. Later you find the goods are defective, but when you inform the seller he claims that you accepted the goods when you signed and paid for them and that you cannot now reject them and insist he take them back.

While it is doubtful the seller's claims would hold up under such circumstances, the Code allows you to specifically reserve your rights at the time of delivery. You can do this simply by stating that you are doing as the seller asks—signing for goods without inspecting them, say—"under protest" or "with a reservation of all rights."

Reserving your rights can be part of any negotiating strategy when you continue to carry out your part of a bargain while a dispute is pending, of course, as this book shows. The rule is especially useful in a payment dispute. Perhaps you don't actually want to withhold payment, but neither do you want to make it appear that you are ignoring the seller's failure to honor your agreement. One way to handle such a situation is to write the following on your check: "This payment due on June 1, 19__, made with a reservation of all rights."

Chapter 6 shows how you can use this rule to notify a creditor you are reserving rights to hold him accountable based on an agreement you actually have with the seller.

4. GETTING OUT OF "UNCONSCIONABLE" TERMS OR AGREEMENTS

The Code makes it possible to get out of what are called "unconscionable" terms or agreements. These are clauses or agreements that are considered so grossly unfair that it would be unconscionable to hold the buyer to them. They are usually fine print clauses that take away rights you might otherwise have under the law; such as a merger clause, or a clause that severely limits what a seller must do to honor warranty obligations.

While the Code does not completely prohibit sellers from using such clauses, it does allow judges to throw out clauses or change an agreement to make it fairer.

While the Code does not set a clear-cut standard that specifically describes what is an unconscionable term or agreement, there is a rough standard. As one judge put it: "Unconscionability has generally been recognized to include an absence of meaningful choice on the part of one of the parties together with contract terms which are unreasonably favorable to the other party."

Generally speaking, a person acts unconscionably when he tries to exploit some-one's weakness, such as his lack of bargaining power, knowledge or skill. This could happen, for instance, if a seller makes a lot of specific promises, uses high-pressure tactics to convince you to buy, and then tries to negate everything he says by putting a merger clause in the fine print, or a clause that says you have given up, or waived, rights you could otherwise use to make the seller honor the agreement.

As noted in Chapter 7, the sanctity of contracts doctrine generally meant that judges enforced whatever was in writing because that is what the two sides had "agreed to." How people arrived at the agreement or what was in it, was not usually considered. The rule about unconscionable terms, however, specifically allows judges to do so. So the rule can help you make a seller live up to actual promises he has made.

In addition, when a seller tries to hold you to what seems to be an unconscionable clause, he may be committing an "unfair" practice prohibited under state deceptive sales practices laws, as explained on page 83. In such a situation, use the rights available under your state law.

5. OBLIGATION TO ACT HONESTLY

The Code specifically requires both sides to act in good faith when dealing with each other. In the case of merchants, it also requires that they live up to reasonable commercial standards of fair dealing. If either side deals dishonestly, it is like breaking the agreement.

For the seller's part, acting in good faith can mean he must make an honest effort to live up to any promises he makes, such as a promise to repair a defective product. And it can mean that if he makes a lot of specific promises and gives you assurances that he will honor them, he should put them in writing and avoid using fine print clauses which deny these promises.

For your part, you must also act in good faith. Broadly speaking, this means being reasonable and honest while seeking to resolve a problem. If you try to act reasonably and the seller fails to act in good faith, your chances of winning in court are usually improved.

To hold a seller accountable, you must show that he did not act honestly when you reached your agreement or when you tried to settle a dispute. Keeping a record of the steps you take to reach a settlement, and copies of any letters involved, can help you prove this.

You can also use this rule in your negotiating strategy. When it becomes clear the seller is not being honest with you, you can add extra pressure by referring to his failure to act in good faith in any written ultimatum you finally send.

If your state's deceptive sales practices law prohibits "unfair" practices, it could give you extra leverage to settle a dispute in such a case. As noted previously, a practice can be considered unfair if it violates some legally established standard of fair conduct. The obligation to act in good faith, required by the Code, *is* such a standard.

26 · Using the Code to Pin Down Favorable Terms When . . .
Ordering by Mail
Buying in Person: Pinning Down a Firm Offer
Buying on Approval
Setting Delivery and Shipment Conditions

This chapter covers ways you can pin down terms and conditions when ordering goods or buying in person, and includes a negotiating strategy for nondelivery of goods.

ORDERING BY MAIL

There are two ways the Code can help you pin down favorable terms.

1. You can write on the order form that the seller may only accept your order *if he ships the goods promptly*. This means that no agreement will really be formed—and no money owing—until he actually ships or promises to ship the goods.

To do this simply write: "This order may be accepted only by the prompt shipment of conforming goods."

If you want to state the condition in a separate letter say the following:

"The order dated (_____) and described on the attached order form

may be accepted only by the prompt shipment of conforming goods." Then state

the following on the order form: *"This order subject to terms stated in letter of*

(_____)."

2. You can *add your own terms and conditions* to the order and then state that the seller can accept your order only by agreeing to all the terms listed, and that any other terms are not acceptable. In effect, you would be making a take-it-or-leave-it offer. The terms you pin down might cover delivery or shipping conditions (see page 139), or a "free trial" offer the seller is making (see page 136), or other conditions.

If you want to add other terms then say the following:

> *"This order may be accepted only by the prompt shipment of conform-*
> *ing goods described on the enclosed order form dated (_____) and*
> *only by your agreeing to all the other terms and conditions stated below.*
> *Any other terms or conditions are unacceptable. Unless the order is*
> *accepted as stated, it shall be deemed canceled and . . ."* (complete the
> *sentence by using either clause (a) or (b) below, depending on how you*
> *would be paying for the purchase):*

(a) "my authorization to charge the $ _____ purchase price to my Master Money account, number 000-0000-00, is revoked."

(b) "please void and return my check for $ _____ which I have enclosed as payment for the purchase price."

Then state the terms and conditions you want included in your agreement.

Of course, the seller doesn't have to accept the conditions you set. If he chooses not to, and you send money with the order form, naturally he cannot keep it. Knowing this can help increase your bargaining leverage to get your money back, or it can help you stop a creditor from collecting for the purchase if you use certain kinds of credit.

If you are going to set purchase terms you insist the seller accept, it is then especially important to state how the seller can accept the offer. Doing this means combining the wording for spelling out how the seller can accept with wording detailing what terms the seller must accept.

You would almost automatically have to write a separate letter to do this. You should then write on the order form that it is subject to the terms and conditions stated in the letter you write, and alter the wording of the order form as appropriate.

Here is a sample letter you can adapt for spelling out the terms and conditions you want to set.

200 Witchtree Lane
Anytown, USA 00000

May 1, 19__

ABC Mail Order Company
100 River Street
Anytown, USA 00000

Dear Sir:

The order dated (_____) and described in the attached order form can be accepted only by the prompt shipment of conforming goods described in the order and as further stipulated below.

THAT ORDER CAN ONLY BE ACCEPTED ON THE TERMS AS INCLUDED BY THE BUYER ON THE ENCLOSED ORDER FORM AND ON THE OTHER TERMS STATED IN THIS LETTER. NO TERMS THAT DIFFER FROM OR ADD TO THOSE TERMS ARE ACCEPTABLE.

(Include here other terms you want to state, but now be careful to include everything that was important. You could adapt the following wording to make clear your order is based on all representations and promises made by the seller: "Buyer is ordering in reliance on all descriptions, representations and promises included in seller's catalogue of (_____date_____) (OR otherwise describe sales representations you are responding to) which are agreed to as part of the basis for any bargain." Then add other terms.

A check for ($_____) is enclosed as a deposit for payment on goods ordered, but payment is due the seller only upon the delivery of conforming goods. (OR) The seller is authorized to charge the ($_____) for this order with my (Master Money credit card, credit card account number 0000-00000-000) but only upon accepting the order *as stated and payment is due the seller only upon the delivery of con-forming goods.*

If the order is not accepted as stated, it is terminated and the entire deposit of ($_____) shall be immediately returned to the buyer (stamped, self-addressed envelope is enclosed) (OR) my authorization to charge the ($_____) with my (Master Money credit card) is revoked.

Sincerely,

ORDERING BY LETTER

If you are ordering by letter rather than using an order form, you would have to describe in the letter exactly what you are ordering and state the price you will pay.

You could do this by describing your order as the opening paragraphs in the sample on page 130 and adapting the remaining wording as would then be appropriate such as by deleting the wording that refers to an order form.

Here is sample wording you can adapt for describing what you are ordering:

"I hereby order the following item(s) as described and for the price and other charges quoted in your catalogue of (date) (OR otherwise describe sales representations you are responding to) as noted below:

1 (describe item   )   price ($_____)
1 (describe item   )   price ($_____)
Shipment and delivery charges ($_____)
TOTAL AMOUNT OF ORDER ($_____)"

Then simply add as appropriate the remaining terms and conditions as illustrated in the sample letter on page 130.

POINTS TO REMEMBER WHEN ORDERING BY MAIL

Following these procedures when ordering by mail can help you strengthen your position should the seller fail to ship or deliver the goods.

- Keep a copy of your order, including any additional terms you spell out about delivery conditions that can later help you hold the seller accountable under your contract.
- Keep a copy of the advertising or brochure to which you responded.
- If possible charge the purchase to an open-end credit account or with a *credit card* rather than paying by check or money order. If you charged the purchase to an open-end credit account or with a *credit card,* you could have available the billing-error or claims-and-defenses protections of the Fair Credit Billing Act to avoid payment. These protections may not apply to some mail order situations, and the seller's failure to comply with the FTC "Mail Order Merchandise" Rule may not count as the seller's failure to make delivery for the purpose of triggering a billing error the creditor would then be required to correct. But the Fair Credit Billing Act protections that could apply at least give you some additional leverage.
- Include in your order terms and conditions that can more fully protect you, especially from non-delivery problems which are the most frequent source of consumer complaints about mail order purchases.
- Be sure the delivery or shipping dates spelled out in the order will give you adequate time to raise a "billing error" dispute under the Fair Credit Billing Act when you charge the purchase. That law requires you to get the complaint to the creditor within 60 days after the transaction first appeared on a periodic statement for the account to which it was charged (see page 472). Do *not* agree to a delayed shipment

date as provided by the FTC "Mail Order Merchandise" Rule if that means you could no longer raise a billing error dispute if the delayed shipment isn't made. (See Chapter 26 where this FTC Rule is covered.)

• You could include a clause in your order requiring the seller to comply with the FTC's "Mail Order Merchandise" Rule as part of the condition of your contract. This could give you extra leverage to hold the seller accountable under your contract for failing to comply with the Rule. Here is sample wording you could adapt to state that your order is subject to the FTC's Rule:

> *"Conforming goods are to be shipped F.O.B. to (address where goods are to be sent). The seller must ship the goods by (insert shipment date) and comply with all applicable requirements of the Federal Trade Commission's "Mail Order Merchandise" Rule. The seller's failure to comply with any requirements entitling the buyer to an option to cancel as provided by that Rule shall also entitle the buyer to cancel as provided by the Rule had the seller complied."*

Such wording is very likely to incorporate the requirements of the FTC Rule into your agreement, and combines it with a destination contract shipment condition. You could delete the destination contract requirement and use only the remaining sample wording, but then a seller would be sending the goods under a shipment contract (see page 139).

REQUESTING REFUND OR CREDIT IF SELLER DOESN'T ACCEPT MAIL ORDER

If a mail order firm accepts the money you send or charges the purchase to your credit card account but then doesn't accept your order as you stipulated, the seller is required to either refund your money or credit your account with the amount charged for the purchase.

Following is a sample letter you can adapt for requesting a refund or credit when the seller fails to accept your order.

> *100 Witchtree Lane*
> *Anytown, USA 00000*
>
> *June 15, 19—*

> *ABC Mail Order Company*
> *100 River Street*
> *Anytown, USA 00000*
>
> *Dear Sir:*
>
> *I am writing in response to your failure to return the ($_____) I sent by check as a deposit with my order of (_____) for (identify products) but which you have not accepted as stipulated in my order. (I am writing in response to your having charged to my (Easy Money credit card account, account number 0000-00000-000) on (date) the ($_____) for my order of (date) for (identify products) but which you did not accept as stipulated in my order.) (A copy of my order is attached.)*
>
> *My order specifically stipulated it could only be accepted by the prompt shipment of conforming goods (and by your agreeing to all the other terms stated in the order) and that the amount I sent was only a deposit unless you accepted the order as stipulated (and that I authorized*

you to charge the amount of the order to my credit account only if you accepted the order as stipulated).

But conforming goods have neither been promptly shipped since I have not received them nor have I been promptly notified that shipment has been or will be made.

Since the order has not been accepted as stipulated, it is cancelled and there is now immediately due me the ($_____) I sent as a deposit (there is now immediately due me a credit of ($_____) to my credit card account identified above).

I therefore request that you immediately return the ($_____) deposit to the above address (that you immediately credit the ($_____) to my account). (I am now also notifying the card issuer about this matter.)

I will appreciate your promptly resolving this matter so I will not have to pursue it further.

Sincerely,

If you charged the purchase to a credit card account, your immediate follow-up step would be to assert rights you had under the Fair Credit Billing Act.

If a firm doesn't return your money within a reasonable time, your most effective follow-up step is to assert the rights you could have under the deceptive sales practices law of your state or the state where the firm is located.

BUYING IN PERSON: PINNING DOWN A FIRM OFFER

Sometimes, when you are shopping, a seller may make you an offer that you want to think about before accepting. In this event, see if he is willing to make you a firm offer that you can consider.

According to the Code, a firm offer is made when the seller agrees to sell under specific terms during a specific period stated in the offer. You may hold him to such an offer even if you don't pay anything down as a deposit. But such an offer is binding on the seller only when it is for a period of three months or less.

Here is a form you can adapt for pinning down an offer:

Firm offer to sell

TO: (Insert *your* name and address)

(Insert name and address of seller _____

_____)

makes a firm (<u>insert period, say 10-</u>) day offer to sell you the following goods for the

prices indicated and other terms stated below:

Quantity	Description	Price
		$

_____

_____

_____

_____

This is a firm offer to sell which you may accept within (10) days of

(insert date of seller's offer).

Shipping terms: (state how goods will be shipped)

Delivery date: (state when goods are to be delivered)

Payment terms: (state how you will pay, as described below)

Other terms: (state any other terms or conditions, such as if the seller gives you a

trade-in allowance for something)

For example: "The seller grants a trade-in allowance of $_____on the buyer's

[describe what you are trading in, including serial number, model and make of

the item]

which will be applied to the purchase price quoted in the offer."

_____   _____   _____
Seller's signature   Title   Date

Page 1 of [   ] pages.
If you can't get all the information on one page, then start the next page as follows:

Firm offer to sell, page _____ of _____ pages dated _____. Other terms,

continued:_____

_____

Make sure the shipping and delivery conditions are exactly what you want. If, for example, you will pick up the goods, then write: "Pick up by buyer." Otherwise, set a specific delivery date, and say where the goods should be delivered to you, such as "buyer's address," (See Chapter 26 for descriptions of how to state various delivery terms.)

Also be sure to state how you will pay; by cash, check, or credit card. If the latter, state the credit account you will use. If the seller will extend credit, state the following: "Seller agrees to arrange for financing on terms acceptable to the buyer."

Finally, see that the offer is dated, and have it signed by someone in authority at the store. Include his or her title. When you use additional pages, ask the seller to initial each one.

If a seller makes a firm offer, you would have to accept it within the time stated or it would automatically lapse. If you accept but the seller reneges on the deal, you could sue him because he would, in effect, be breaking your agreement. But it would seldom be worth the expense to do so.

Why, then, bother to get the offer in the first place?

Asking a seller to pin down a firm offer can give you a better negotiating position when you are discussing a deal. It helps you avoid high-pressure tactics and tests the seller's sincerity. An honest seller should be ready to make a firm offer and hold it open for a few days to give you time to think about it, especially if the purchase involves a lot of money. Asking for a firm offer can be an especially effective way to defend yourself against pressure from a door-to-door salesperson, by the way.

While it may not be worthwhile to hold the seller to an offer, it is tough for him to back out without losing the sale. If his word isn't good on this, you really can't trust anything else he might promise and you would be better off taking your business elsewhere. The seller knows this, which is what gives you practical *bargaining* leverage to get him to honor an offer.

BUYING IN PERSON: PUTTING TERMS IN WRITING

The specific terms, conditions, or promises you want written into an agreement will naturally depend on what you and the seller agree on. Since any agreement can include many different terms and conditions, it is impractical to include sample wording showing you how to state everything that could apply. If you have to make up wording to pin something down, the main point to remember is to make sure the wording clearly and specifically describes what you have agreed to.

As a practical matter, pinning terms and conditions down in writing means adding them to a seller's printed form contract or other sales document. You must make sure all terms and conditions you put in writing become part of the agreement or contract under which you buy.

You can, of course, simply add terms and conditions to a seller's printed form. If you do this, be sure the additions are made to the *original* document. Failing to do this can result in a dispute about whether the additions are really part of the agreement.

A standard printed contract sellers use seldom has much space for adding terms and conditions other than for the items that have to be filled in to make the sale. This is often done purposely to make it as difficult as possible to change anything. You may then have to use a separate sheet of paper.

Here is how you can then make clear that anything stated on a separate document is part of the agreement.

First write the following statement on the original of the printed form: *"This agreement is subject to all the terms, representations and promises stated on a separate memorandum dated [_____] which is hereby included as part of this agreement."* Then make up a memorandum (or prepare forms beforehand and take them with you when you shop), that says something like the following:

Memorandum of sales terms

Date_____

As stated in the seller's printed agreement dated (_____), the sale of (describe purchase as stated in printed form) by (state seller's name and address as in printed form) is subject to the following terms and seller's representations and promises which were specifically agreed to as a basis for that bargain:

(Then add the promises and sales terms that are part of the deal. Make sure to include all the terms and promises you want the seller to fulfill.

If you add things but leave out something important, it will be harder to claim later that the written agreement didn't cover everything.)

Although it is unlikely a seller would go along with it, you can try to include the following wording to make clear that unwritten representations and promises are also part of the deal:

"All other representations and promises made to the buyer by the seller or his agents even though not stated herein."

Asking a seller to include such a clause can help you test his sincerity and give you some practical bargaining leverage for insisting that anything important be put in writing if the seller won't go along with such broad language.

To make sure any additional pages are identified as part of the memorandum, number each page and add this phrase to the top of each one:

"Memorandum of sales terms, page _____ of _____ pages dated _____."
Have the salesperson initial each page. Although it may not be legally necessary to get the seller's signature on the memorandum to make it count as part of the deal, if his signature already appears on another part of the agreement which specifically refers to the memorandum, it is best to ask him to sign anyway. It will help ensure that the terms you add become part of the agreement.

In order to make a duplicate copy on the spot for the salesperson, take along a piece of carbon paper.

Showing that you are prepared in this way is really one-upmanship. It forces the salesperson to take you more seriously. All too often, salespeople deal with consumers who never bother to check the written terms, so when someone does check them they may not be fully prepared to deal with the situation. This gives you an edge in discussing and writing the deal.

As a reminder, if you negotiate about and add terms to a seller's form contract, it is more likely that you would be bound by the printed terms. So be sure to check the printed terms for conspicuously stated clauses that could deprive you of important rights and get them crossed out.

PINNING DOWN A SALE ON APPROVAL (OR TRIAL OFFER)

Some companies try to convince you to buy by offering you a sale on approval—an offer that allows you to return goods for a refund even when there is nothing wrong with them. A seller will sometimes let you keep and examine goods for a specific time; occasionally you can actually try out goods and still return them.

A sale on approval is a special sales condition that can, of course, apply whether you are buying in person or ordering by mail. It is one under which you would be entitled to return the goods delivered by the seller within the time allowed even though the goods fully conform to the contract.

The Code spells out three special conditions that apply to any sale on approval unless the agreement says otherwise:

1. The buyer does not assume the risk of loss for the goods until he or she has actually accepted them. You *accept* goods when you indicate to the seller that you intend to keep them (see page 160 where this rule is explained in more detail).

Sometimes a seller might change this rule by stating on the order form or agreement that the buyer assumes the risk on delivery or at the point of shipment. A seller might then say: "F.O.B. the seller's address," or "warehouse," or any location other than your address. If a seller does this, beware. He is trying to put you at a disadvantage. Either cross out, or write no, next to any statement that says goods are shipped F.O.B. to any address other than your own. Also ask yourself if you really want to do business with the kind of seller who first tries to convince you to buy by making what seems like a risk-free offer, but who then includes clauses that really shift the risk back to you.

2. If the seller's offer says the buyer can try out (use) the goods first, trying out the goods does not amount to accepting them. Ordinarily, using the goods *does* amount to accepting them. You can try out the goods only to the extent allowed by the sale. If you choose to return goods sold on approval, you must notify the seller within a reasonable time (or within the time period of the offer) that you are returning them. (Of course, you would also have to return them.) A failure to notify the seller *would* amount to accepting the goods and you could no longer return them. You must also return or keep all the goods sold on approval.

3. If the buyer notifies the seller that he wants to return the goods, the seller must assume the risk and expense involved in shipping them back.

Sellers often try to modify this condition by including terms that say you must pay for shipping goods back if you don't want them. Don't go along with a clause like this, or any other clause that tries to limit your rights to less than the three conditions you are entitled to under the Code when the seller makes what would be a sale on approval.

INCLUDING SALE ON APPROVAL CONDITIONS IN AN AGREEMENT

Individuals often offer to sell goods under conditions allowing you to return them but hedge the sale with terms that strip you of protections you would have with a sale on approval made under the conditions spelled out by the Code.

You can, of course, go along with the different conditions the seller sets. But if you do, you would have to return the goods as stipulated by the seller.

If your purchase is dependent on the seller accepting all the conditions spelled out by the Code, follow the instructions below so that his offer entitling you to return goods becomes a sale on approval.

Use the following wording when the seller's offer does not specifically allow you to *try out* the goods first (in this case, you would only be able to *examine,* rather than use the goods). (A liberal exchange or refund policy would for all practical purposes amount to a sale on approval even though such a policy may not, technically speaking, count as a sale on approval.)

> *"It is agreed this is a sale on approval of the buyer for _____ days after the buyer received the goods. If the buyer decides not to accept the goods, he/she shall notify the seller and return the goods within _____ days after receipt of the goods by the buyer. Buyer shall be entitled to return the goods C.O.D. for ($____) paid for the price plus return shipping costs (OR for return shipping costs and full credit to buyer's (Easy Money Credit card account, account number 0000-00000-000) for ($____) charged to that account for the price."*

If you are buying goods at a store and can return them yourself, then use only the first sentence of the paragraph. If you are ordering by mail, use the whole paragraph since you want to specify that the seller will have to refund your money when he gets his goods shipped back C.O.D.

If the seller includes a free *trial* period in the offer, then change the first sentence in the sample paragraph as follows:

> *"It is agreed this is a sale on approval of the buyer for a free trial period of _____ days after the buyer receives the goods."*

If you want to order goods you can return but the seller insists you pay for the cost of returning them, delete from the sample paragraph the wording saying the seller would be required to pay for return shipping costs.

The seller may, of course, be unwilling to fill an order if you insist that it is a sale on approval. But if he is really honest and sincere, he should be willing to include the conditions if he is really making that kind of an offer.

RETURNING GOODS BOUGHT ON APPROVAL

If you decide to return a product bought on approval, make sure you notify the seller well within the time period for returning the goods.

Always keep any shipping carton or packing materials until you are sure you want to buy the item. This makes it easier to return the goods. It's especially important to keep the shipping container if the mailing label guarantees return postage, of course.

Here is a sample letter you can use to notify a seller you are returning goods bought on approval. Keep a copy for yourself. If you are returning the goods to a store in person, ask the salesperson to indicate on your copy that the store is taking back the product and what the exchange conditions are, and ask him or her to sign it.

100 Orchard Street
Anytown, USA 00000

June 10, 19___

Mail Order Discount House
300 Lookout Road
Anytown, USA 00000

Dear Sir:

I am notifying you that I have decided not to accept the set of carving knives I bought from you on approval for a fifteen-day trial period from the date I received them, as specified in my order dated May 1, 19___, which you accepted.

Since I received the knives on June 4, as shown on the delivery receipt I signed, I am notifying you of my refusal to keep them within the trial period stated in our agreement.

I am shipping the goods to you C.O.D. for the $29.95 purchase price I paid with my order and the return shipping charges. Since the order you accepted made this a sale on approval under the conditions stipulated in the Uniform Commercial Code, I no longer owe the purchase price and the return is at your risk and expense.

Thank you for your prompt cooperation in this matter.

Sincerely,

Naturally, you would have to adapt the wording to fit your situation and the terms you agreed upon.

If the company doesn't refund your money or give you a credit, you would have to use the negotiating strategy described on page 282 for canceling. But instead of saying that you are canceling as stated in the sample letters, revise the wording to say you are terminating the agreement because you have elected not to accept goods sold on approval. You would then no longer owe any amount still outstanding for the purchase. You would not, however, have a security interest in the goods for any payments already made as stated in those sample letters, so delete such wording.

If you charged the purchase to a credit account covered by the Fair Credit Billing Act, see page 470 for your rights under the billing error procedures (the billing error is your not having accepted the goods), and page 482 for your right to raise claims and defenses against a card issuer (your defense would be you no longer owe for goods you elected not to accept).

SETTING DELIVERY AND SHIPMENT CONDITIONS

The Code allows both parties to agree to any delivery and shipment conditions they choose, then spells out what rights each side has depending on the kind of conditions they set. If an agreement doesn't specify a condition, the Code spells out general terms that apply.

Broadly speaking, a seller's delivery obligations spell out when, where, and what he must do to deliver the goods. Delivery refers to the seller handing over (or at least being prepared to hand over) to the buyer the particular product being sold under the agreement, not the more common meaning of delivery, that is, the sending or shipment of goods by the seller. The shipment conditions cover the additional requirements that apply when the seller is responsible for sending (transporting) the goods to the buyer.

A key point to remember about the difference between delivery and shipment is that, as a general rule, a seller is required to deliver goods (turn them over to the buyer) at the seller's place of business unless the agreement calls for delivery to be made somewhere else. If the seller is responsible for transporting the goods past his doorstep, the shipment conditions that apply then, spell out where delivery to the buyer occurs (that is, where the goods being sent are considered to have been turned over to the buyer) and when the buyer becomes responsible for the loss of or damage to the goods.

So if your agreement calls for the seller to deliver (turn over) the goods to you at his place of business, the key delivery condition is *when* he would be required to make that delivery rather than shipment conditions. If, however, the seller is also responsible for sending (transporting) the goods somewhere else, the type of shipment condition that applies becomes important along with the delivery date.

Let's look first at the different shipment conditions that could apply and how to pin down the condition that protects you when the seller is responsible for transporting the goods you bought.

PINNING DOWN SHIPMENT CONDITIONS

Under the Code, two major kinds of shipment conditions can apply in consumer transactions. They are known as "shipment contracts" and "destination contracts." The latter kind gives the buyer the most protection.

Shipment Contracts

A shipment contract applies when the seller can send the goods by common carrier, such as railroad, air freight, or the postal service and the agreement *doesn't* require him to deliver the goods to a particular destination. Once the seller turns conforming goods over to the carrier, you assume the risk of loss or damage to the goods. So, unless you and the seller specifically agree to handle the problem in some other way, in the case of damage or loss you would have to file a claim against the carrier. You would also probably still have to pay the seller.

However, under a shipment contract, the seller must do at least two things as part of his *delivery* obligations. If he fails to do them, you can "reject" damaged or lost goods and cancel the agreement, even though you would normally assume the risk.

First, he must put the goods in the hands of the carrier and make an appropriate contract for transporting the type of goods being shipped. He must tell the carrier if special handling is necessary to prevent damage or loss, for instance. He must also declare the proper value of the goods. This helps if you have to file a claim against the carrier.

Second, he must promptly notify you that the goods have been shipped, and furnish you written documentation showing that an agreement has been made for transporting the goods.

Watch for clauses in an order form that say the seller does not have to make an appropriate contract, or to notify you when the goods are shipped. If a seller doesn't have to do these things, don't buy. You will have no protection in case of loss or damage in shipment.

Under a shipment contract, a seller is also considered to have delivered the goods to the buyer when and where he placed them in the hands of the carrier. So a delivery date spelled out under a shipment contract governs the date by which the seller must put the goods in the hands of the carrier rather than the date by which they must be delivered to the recipient.

The main point to note is that unless your agreement specifically states otherwise, when the seller can ship goods by carrier, they are automatically shipped under a shipment contract. When the seller transports goods on his own vehicles, however, you *don't* assume the risk of loss or damage until the goods are actually delivered to you. The store remains responsible for any loss or damage up until that point.

Destination Contract

A destination contract, on the other hand, is one requiring the seller to deliver the goods to the point specified as their destination. This could be your home, office, or some other place designated by you.

Under a destination contract, the seller remains responsible for loss or damage until the goods arrive at the specified destination. The goods are considered to have been delivered only when they arrive at their destination and are made available for the recipient to pick up. That's when a delivery date spelled out in an agreement also means the date by which you are supposed to receive the goods.

To be fully protected, therefore, specify in your agreement that the seller must ship the goods under a destination contract. The clause could be written into the seller's form contract, the sales slip, order form, the letter you send with your order form, or the memorandum you use to add terms or conditions to the seller's printed form contract.

This is how you would write such a condition:

*"Goods are to be shipped F.O.B. to (*__address where goods are to be shipped__*.)"*

Just the phrase *"Shipment F.O.B. to (*__address_____*)"*

would do.

The abbreviation F.O.B. stands for "free on board." It usually refers to the price of the goods at the place stated, but when you say shipped F.O.B. to some destination, the phrase means the seller is responsible for getting them to *that* place at *his* risk.

The key point is to specify the destination, either by inserting your address in the brackets, or if it is already identified on the order form, by inserting the words "The buyer's address identified on the order form."

Sometimes a seller will not accept an order if you include a destination shipment condition. In such a case, you are probably better off without the goods. If the seller won't assume responsibility and something goes wrong with the delivery, you might be caught in a buck-passing game between the seller and the carrier.

If your goods are damaged you may be able to "reject" them under the rules of the Code (see page 164). If they are lost, the seller hasn't delivered them which could then entitle you to cancel. And if you charge the purchase to a credit account covered by the Fair Credit Billing Act, see page 470.

PINNING DOWN DELIVERY CONDITIONS

According to the Code, unless an agreement sets a definite date by which either party has to live up to a commitment, each side has a "reasonable" time to carry out its obligations. So if you and the seller do not agree to a specific delivery date, for example, he has a "reasonable" time to make the delivery. This applies whether you buy something at a store, or order by mail.

The term "reasonable" gives a store a lot of leeway, of course. A considerable period of time could pass before you reach a point where you could definitely say it had broken the agreement by its failure to deliver on time.

For this reason, it is important to have a specific delivery date. It increases your bargaining leverage and helps you hold the seller to the agreement.

SETTING A SPECIFIC DELIVERY DATE

You can set a specific date by including this term in your agreement:

"Delivery must be made to the buyer by (insert date)." Or you can set a specific time period within which delivery must be made, such as thirty days, five weeks or two months. In this case you would say: "Delivery must be made within (state delivery period) of the date of this order."

A seller might want to give you an oral promise only. As explained on page 121, you might be able to hold a seller to it if your written agreement is incomplete, but it is obviously better if you include the delivery date in writing on any order. If it is a formal agreement, insist on it. If a seller is unwilling to be pinned down in writing to an early delivery date, it is better to pin down a later delivery date in writing than to accept an oral promise of an earlier date, simply because the latter would be harder to enforce.

There is a way of stating delivery conditions so that the seller must comply or be in danger of breaking the agreement completely. You simply add a "time is of the essence" clause to make clear timely delivery is extremely important. It will generally eliminate any leeway a seller might have even when you set a specific delivery date. This is the clause to write into your agreement in combination with a definite delivery date:

"Timely delivery is of the essence to the buyer, and the seller's failure to deliver on time shall be a breach entitling the buyer to cancel."

Include a clause like this whenever you would suffer some loss if the seller misses the delivery date. Add it to the seller's order form if you order by mail; include it on the seller's printed form contract if you buy at a store; or write it as a separate memorandum (See the example on page 130).

You could add the following wording to the above clause to limit how long the seller has to cure non-conformities in the products he delivers: "The seller has no right to cure after the delivery date." See Chapter 29 about the seller's right to cure. As explained on page 172, including such a limitation can help but could also hurt you.

It is especially important to include a "time-is-of-the-essence" clause for purchases charged to credit accounts covered by the Fair Credit Billing Act. A seller's failure to deliver as required by your agreement is a billing error under the Act which a creditor must correct. The Act doesn't provide much leeway, however, to complain about the possibility of a billing error. A firm date by which the seller must deliver is a key requirement for triggering a billing error since it sets when the seller has definitely failed to deliver as required by your agreement. To give yourself time to complain usually means setting a delivery date not more than seven to eight weeks from the date of purchase or the date you send an order. If a seller doesn't want to accept such a short delivery deadline, don't buy if you want to use the protection available under the act. (See Chapter 56 for more details.)

SELLER'S DELIVERY OBLIGATIONS

The seller must deliver the goods at a reasonable hour and notify you ahead of time, or, if you are to collect them yourself, give reasonable notification that the goods are available to pick up. The rule requiring the seller to notify you about delivery can help if he tries to deliver something when you are not around to receive it because you haven't been notified.

If the seller says you must pick up the goods because he has already tried to deliver them, you can point out that he failed to make a proper delivery as required by the Code because he did not inform you when delivery would be made. Insist on proper delivery by arranging a time when you can receive the goods. And say your payment isn't due until the store makes a proper delivery.

While it doesn't pay to push this kind of an issue to a lawsuit, insisting that the seller comply with the delivery conditions spelled out in the Code can strengthen your bargaining position.

FTC MAIL ORDER MERCHANDISE RULE

Setting delivery and shipment conditions that fully protect you is one way to minimize the risks of buying by mail.

The FTC's "Mail Order Merchandise" Rule can also protect you if a mail order firm fails to ship goods on time, especially if you didn't set delivery or shipment conditions that most fully protect you based on requirements spelled out by the Code.

Most mail order transactions are satisfactorily completed, but when trouble comes, getting it straightened out is usually much harder than when you buy directly from a store. Mail order firms are almost automatically insulated from the direct pressure you could bring to bear in personal dealings. And mail order firms are, for practical purposes, also largely insulated from legal remedies that could be available since suing someone who is far away is much more complicated and costly than suing a local business.

The two most frequent types of mail-order complaints are: "They took my money but never sent the goods" and "I ordered Christmas presents in October but they didn't arrive until Easter." Another frequent complaint is: "The company simply ignored me when I complained about not getting my order."

The FTC came up with a partial answer to such problems when it adopted the "Mail Order Merchandise" Rule which went into effect on February 2, 1976.

This rule spells out 1) what mail order firms are required to do to ship merchandise on time and (2) what procedures a firm must follow when it is unable to make a timely shipment.

This rule applies to any *merchandise ordered by mail* except the following:

- magazine subscriptions after the first magazine for the subscription period has been shipped.
- orders for seeds or growing plants.
- collect-on-delivery [C.O.D.] orders or orders made on credit when the consumer's account is *not* charged for the purchase prior to shipment.

• orders that are governed by the FTC's "Use of Negative Options Plans" Rule (see page 75).

In addition, this rule usually does *not* cover merchandise ordered by various "electronic" methods: ordering by a home computer hooked into a cable TV system or ordering by telephone when the purchase is charged to a credit account. The rule covers only merchandise orders that *you* send by mail rather than orders that would be shipped to you by mail. The rule doesn't cover *services* ordered by mail, the most common of which would be photo developing services.

Ordering by phone or using the fancy "electronic" systems now being developed may be more convenient than ordering by mail, but I caution you against using those methods because there are now many gaps in the protections you could have if things go wrong. For example, you have no written record of what you ordered. The lack of written documentation automatically makes it harder for you to hold the seller accountable if *anything* goes wrong with the order.

SHIPPING REQUIREMENTS MAIL ORDER FIRMS MUST FOLLOW.

The rule requires that mail order firms either tell you when you can expect goods to be shipped, or it sets the deadline for timely shipment. If they cannot ship, they must furnish you a revised shipping date, and they must give you a chance to cancel and make an appropriate refund if you don't want the merchandise.

INITIAL SHIPMENT DEADLINE

The rule sets the initial shipment deadline by which a consumer can expect the shipment of merchandise ordered by mail. A firm's inability to meet this initial shipment deadline triggers the further options the firm must then give you.

This initial shipment deadline is either:

• The time period within which the mail order firm promises to ship the order as specifically stated in the brochure or advertising which prompted you to order.

• Thirty (30) days from the date the firm receives the completed order if *no* shipment date is specified in the advertising or brochures the firm used to get orders. So unless a firm specifically gives you a different shipment deadline, the rule automatically sets that 30 days as the time by which orders must be shipped.

A mail order firm has received your completed order when it receives all the information needed to fill the order and the amount for a credit sale is charged to your account or when payment for the order is received. Those dates set the time after which the mail order firm has to ship the merchandise. (Without going into the details that could otherwise apply, the date by which your check is paid by your bank or the date by which a money order is cashed would usually be considered as the latest date by which payment was received).

NOTIFICATION OF DELAYED SHIPMENT AND BUYER'S OPTION TO CANCEL

If a mail order firm is unable to ship by the initial shipment deadline, the rule then requires the firm to notify you how long the shipment will be delayed and either get your consent to the shipping delay or allow you to cancel the order. If you cancel, it must then give you a refund of money paid or a credit for amounts charged to a credit account.

When a mail order firm sends you the "first delay" notification, the firm must either give you a definite revised shipping date or tell you it cannot provide you with a definite revised shipping date (that is, there will be an indefinite delay).

DEFINITE DELAYED SHIPPING DATE OF 30 DAYS OR LESS

If a firm tells you the shipping delay will be 30 days or less, the seller must give you the option to cancel but the seller can automatically assume you agree to the delay if you do *not* notify the seller you are cancelling.

DEFINITE DELAYED SHIPPING DATE OF MORE THAN 30 DAYS; OR, SELLER CANNOT GIVE A DEFINITE REVISED SHIPPING DATE

If the mail order firm either gives you a definite revised shipping date that is more than 30 days after the initial shipment deadline or the firm says it cannot tell you when it will be able to ship the goods, it must also give you the option to cancel. But in this case, the seller must treat your order as having been cancelled by you *unless* you specifically notify the firm that the longer or indefinite delay was acceptable to you.

Here is how this automatic cancellation works. The seller must treat the order as cancelled unless he either *receives* your consent to the delayed shipment within 30 days after the initial shipment deadline or he ships the merchandise within that time but *before* receiving your notice that you want to cancel. Unless you specifically tell the firm you are cancelling, the firm can still try to fill the order for up to 30 days after the initial shipment date but must then treat the order as being cancelled if you have not by then agreed to the shipping delay.

If you agree to a definite revised shipping date, the seller would then have to ship the merchandise by that date or again notify you there would be a further delay and again give you the option to cancel or go along with further delays. If a seller tells you there will be an indefinite delay and you accept it, the seller must then give you a continuing option to cancel the order.

Since there are a number of triggering mechanisms involved in these situations, here is an outline of what could happen, depending on how you respond to the seller's notification.

• If you specifically cancel, the seller must honor any cancellation received *before* the shipment of the merchandise, unless the seller was otherwise required to treat the order as already having been cancelled.

• If you do *not* notify the seller you are cancelling *and* do *not* specifically consent to the delayed shipping schedule, the seller must treat the order as having been cancelled and make an appropriate refund *unless* he ships the goods within 30 days after the initial shipping deadline.

• If you initially consent to an indefinite shipping delay, the seller must honor any subsequent cancellation he receives (assuming the merchandise was not shipped before then).

• If you go along with a definite revised shipping date that is more than 30 days after the initial shipping dealine, the seller must ship the merchandise by that revised date or make further shipping delay notifications and renew your option to cancel unless you consent to further delays *before* the previous revised shipping date has passed.

REQUIREMENTS FOR REFUNDS UPON CANCELLATION

If you cancel the order or the seller was required to treat the order as cancelled, the rule then requires the seller to make an appropriate refund. How the seller must make the refund depends on whether you paid cash or charged the purchase to a credit account.

If you paid for the purchase by check or money order (or cash, but NEVER send cash), the seller must send a refund within 7 business days after receiving your cancellation or after he is required to treat the order as cancelled.

If you charged the purchase to a credit account you have with someone other than the seller (i.e., usually a bank credit card account), the seller must either send you a copy of the credit memorandum he sent to the other creditor to remove the charge from your account or send you a statement acknowledging the cancellation and notifying you that your account has *not* been charged for the purchase. The seller must do this within 7 business days after cancellation occurs.

If you charged the purchase to a credit account with the seller, the seller must then send you a credit memorandum or account statement reflecting the fact that the charge has been removed from your account. In all credit card sales the seller must make the appropriate adjustments in your account within one "billing cycle" after cancellation has occurred.

The requirement that the seller send you a credit memo or account statement is very important. Once you get the memo, the creditor's failure to credit your account would be a "billing error" under the Fair Credit Billing Act (see page 470).

PENALTIES FOR VIOLATIONS OF THE RULE

A mail order firm that fails to comply with the "Mail Order Merchandise" Rule violates the FTC Act (see page 52.) The firm could then be fined up to $10,000 for each violation, and the FTC could take action on behalf of consumers injured by the firm's failure to comply. (The FTC rarely if ever takes action on behalf of an individual consumer, but may do so if it learns that many consumers have been damaged by a particular firm's failure to comply.)

Consumers *cannot,* however, take action on their own to hold a firm accountable for failing to comply with the Rule. So in situations like this, you would usually have to rely on the actions the FTC might take.

INCLUDING THE FTC RULE PROVISIONS AS PART OF YOUR ORDER

To help you hold a seller accountable under your agreement based on the requirements spelled out by the FTC's Rule, it could be worthwhile to stipulate in your order that the seller agrees to comply with the requirements of that rule (see page 132 for sample wording you could use).

Although doing so would not make it easier for you to take action on your own to hold the seller accountable under the rule, it could help trigger the billing-error or claims-and-defenses protections available under the Fair Credit Billing Act (see Chapter 56). That's because the seller's failure to comply with the rule could then amount to a failure to comply with the terms of your agreement. And if you have those rights as part of your agreement, that would at least substantially strengthen your position to assert the relevant protections available under the Fair Credit Billing Act to avoid having to pay for goods not shipped as required by the rule.

The shipping deadlines spelled out by the FTC Rule designate a delivery date for goods being sent by a seller under a shipment contract condition. Remember, the shipping deadline set by the FTC rule spells out the date by which a mail order firm must put the goods in the hands of the carrier who will deliver the goods to you. It does not set the date by which the goods must be delivered to you.

NEGOTIATING STRATEGY FOR NON-DELIVERY OF GOODS BOUGHT IN PERSON

When negotiating about non-delivery problems, remember that a seller breaches a contract if he fails to deliver within the time called for by the agreement. If that happens, it is also important that you object immediately.

A seller's failure to make a timely delivery almost always puts a buyer in a quandary. On the one hand, a seller may insist he had further time to deliver and refuse to call off the deal and refund what you have paid. On the other hand, you may want the goods and would be reluctant to call off the deal.

Whether the seller could insist on more time depends on how firmly you pinned down the delivery date. If your agreement includes a time is of the essence clause, and if holding the seller to the delivery date is important to you, he will seldom be able to insist on more time. If your agreement includes a definite delivery date but without the time is of the essence clause, a seller can usually insist that you give him a little more time to "cure," or take care of, his failure before you use other remedies. Be prepared to give him more time if he wants it and is willing to assure future delivery, but pin down a definite delivery date. When you specify the new delivery date note that you are agreeing to let him cure his default. Then if he misses the new delivery date, you will be in a stronger position to get out of the agreement altogether.

By immediately objecting to a seller's failure to deliver on time, you show the obligation is important to you. A failure to react quickly could amount to a waiver of your right to hold the seller responsible for failing to make a timely delivery. If the seller is aware of this, he can insist that you stick with the agreement and that you give him even more time to deliver the goods.

If a seller fails to deliver the goods by the time required under your agreement, your basic remedy is to cancel. Upon doing so, you would no longer owe what you haven't paid, you would be entitled to get back what you had already paid and may be able to hold the seller liable for damages. (See chapter 36 for further details.)

If it is acceptable to you and the seller, cancelling for a full refund may be the easiest way to resolve a non-delivery problem. But if that solution is unacceptable taking steps that would demonstrate the seller has clearly breached the contract by failing to deliver can strengthen your position. The key question is whether you still want the goods by an alternative delivery date or whether you would rather call off the deal.

If you want the goods or the seller doesn't want to refund what you have paid, your initial negotiating objectives would be to obtain the seller's commitment for a firm alternative delivery date. His failure to make such a commitment or to keep one that he makes then almost automatically strengthens your position to cancel. The key leverage cancellation gives you in such situations is the chance to hold a seller accountable for damages because of his failure to deliver.

Keep in mind that if your agreement stipulates timely delivery was of the essence to you, your willingness to give the seller much additional time to make delivery is likely to be an acknowledgement that timely delivery wasn't really that important. If timely delivery really was that important, immediate cancellation would then be your main option if you are determined to hold the seller accountable for failing to deliver on time. If the seller won't go along and at least refund what you have paid, the cancellation ultimatum is the step you could then take to hold the seller accountable. But if you could still give the seller some additional time, be sure to pin down a definite alternative date by which the seller must deliver.

There is also one particularly nasty type of non-delivery problem you could face when in effect a seller tries to deliver a substitute for the product you actually ordered. A seller who does this is almost certainly using it as a gimmick to re-write your original agreement so you go along with paying more.

You can, of course, simply accept this, but there are some steps you can take that put you in a better negotiating position for dealing with the seller.

When the seller tells you the product is ready for delivery but it is not exactly what you ordered, your initial step is to make the seller commit himself as to whether he is actually delivering the product as the one called for by your agreement *before* you get involved in a discussion as to how the problem is to be solved. Doing this can help you set the stage for the type of breach you could be entitled to hold the seller accountable for.

You do this by asking whether the seller is *identifying* the product he wants you to take as the one being delivered under your agreement. Simply ask the seller: "Are you identifying this product described as *(give model and serial number)* as the one being delivered under our agreement of *(date)*?"

That gives the seller an option to answer in only one of two ways. If he answers "No, this isn't the product I am identifying as the one being delivered under our agreement." he then has *not* made delivery which could then result in his becoming responsible for failing to deliver. If, on the other hand, he says, "Yes it is the product I am identifying as the one being delivered under our agreement," he is then failing to deliver a product that conforms to your contract so you could be entitled to reject it and insist he cure the non-conforming delivery (see Chapter 28 about your right to reject and Chapter 29 about the seller's right to cure). And to drive home the point you are onto the game being played, insist the seller produce the order he actually sent when you ordered the product. That would make clear who really made the "mistake" for which the seller now wants you to pay extra. Your action would also identify whether you are actually facing a non-delivery problem or a problem involving the delivery of non-conforming goods. In addition, letting the seller know how you could then hold him responsible for breaking the agreement is likely to give you some practical bargaining leverage for negotiating about how much you should really pay for features you didn't order.

STAGE ONE: OPENING SKIRMISHES

It is usually best to return to a store and deal with someone in authority about a delivery problem. Point out that the store has failed to meet the delivery date, tell how this failure is unacceptable to you, and ask for an explanation of why the goods have not been delivered.

Since the seller may be waiting for a shipment from his own supplier or manufacturer, the key question to ask is whether the goods have been shipped and, if not, when the supplier expects to ship them. If you are unwilling to wait, remember that although a store can sometimes insist on a little more time, if it can't, or won't, give you a reasonable delivery date, the failure immediately strengthens your position to get out of the agreement and to get your money back.

PUT YOUR OBJECTION ON THE RECORD

Prepare a written statement before you leave home and take two copies with you. Give one to the manager, or other person in authority you deal with, and ask him or her to sign and date both copies. Here is an example of such a letter:

100 Poplar Court
Anytown, USA 00000

September 11, 19___

Manager
Modern Crafts Furniture Store
250 Main Street
Anytown, USA 00000

Dear Sir:

I hereby object to your store's failure to deliver the six-piece set of dining room furniture I ordered, by the September 10, 19___, delivery date required by our agreement of July 8, 19___.

I was assured at the time of purchase that the furniture would be delivered not later than two months from the date of the order, and our agreement specifically required delivery by September 10.

Although the furniture has not been delivered as required by our agreement, I am willing to proceed with our agreement if you will promptly give me a definite date by which you will make delivery.

I do, however, reserve all my rights. My willingness to give you reasonable time to cure this breach is not to be considered as a modification of our agreement.

I will appreciate your prompt cooperation in this matter so we can still satisfactorily complete this transaction.

Sincerely,

Have the store pin down a definite delivery date by asking the person to complete and sign the following statement addressed to you. You must also prepare this statement beforehand, of course.

Date
_____

TO: (Insert your name and address)

__(Insert name of company)__ gives its assurance it will cure its failure to deliver the

__(Insert description of purchase)__ you ordered by the (__insert agreement delivery date__)

delivery date called for in our agreement of (_____) by making the

delivery not later than (__new delivery date__).

(Signature)
_____

Include title of person

If your agreement did not include a definite delivery date, then adapt the following sample letter which refers to the reasonable amount of time the seller has had to make delivery.

100 Poplar Court
Anytown, USA 00000

September 11, 19___

Manager
Modern Crafts Furniture Store
250 Main Street
Anytown, USA 00000

Dear Sir:

I hereby object to your store's failure to deliver the six-piece set of dining room furniture I ordered within the reasonable time called for by our agreement of June 15, 19___.

I was assured at the time of purchase that the furniture would be delivered not later than ten weeks from the date of the order, which was the reasonable time for making the delivery as prescribed by the Uniform Commercial Code. Your failure to deliver the furniture within a reasonable time is a breach of our agreement.

Although the furniture has not been delivered within a reasonable time called for by our agreement, I am willing to proceed with our agreement if you can promptly give me a definite date by which you will make delivery and cure your breach.

I do, however, reserve all my rights. My willingness to grant you additional time to make delivery is not to be considered as a modification of our agreement.

Thank you for your prompt cooperation

Sincerely,

In this case, ask the store to give you a definite delivery date by signing the following form.

_____ Date _____

TO: (Insert your name and address)

(Insert name of company) _____

gives its assurance it will cure its failure to deliver the (describe purchase) within

the reasonable time called for by our agreement of (insert date of agreement) by

making the delivery not later than (insert new delivery date).

_____
(Signature)

_____
Title of person

STAGE TWO: THE LOW-KEYED WARNING

If the company misses the new delivery deadline, you may be willing to give them another chance. If you are, then state your objections and try to pin down another delivery date by using the following letter.

100 Poplar Court
Anytown, USA 00000

September 30, 19___

Manager
Modern Crafts Furniture Store
Anytown, USA 00000

Dear Sir:

I hereby object to your store's renewed failure to deliver the six-piece set of dining room furniture by September 28, 19___, the date by which the company promised to cure its failure to deliver the furniture by September 10. The September 10 date was the original delivery date required by our agreement of July 8, 19___.

I was willing to give you time to cure the original breach of our agreement because of the signed assurance you gave me that the furniture would be delivered by September 28.

Although the furniture has again not been delivered as required by our agreement, I am still willing to proceed with our agreement but only if you will immediately give me your assurances that this additional breach will be cured by a prompt delivery of conforming goods [OR by a delivery of conforming goods not later than ___(date)___.]

I do, however, reserve all my rights. My willingness to grant you additional time is not to be considered as a modification of our agreement, and I shall be forced to treat any further failure to make a timely conforming delivery as a material breach of our contract.

I hope that you will now promptly perform your delivery obligations so that I will not have to cancel the agreement because of your failure to deliver and hold you responsible for damages as provided by the Uniform Commercial Code.

Sincerely,

Get the new delivery date specified in writing by adapting the sample statement on page 148.

If the store fails to make delivery after you have given them several chances, your most practical course is to call off the agreement and to insist that the store refund any payments you made. If the store refuses, your main remedy then is cancellation (see chapter 36). If you charged the purchase to a credit card account covered by the Fair Credit Billing Act, see page 470.

NEGOTIATING STRATEGY FOR NON-DELIVERY OF GOODS PURCHASED BY MAIL

Your main bargaining leverage for getting a refund or a credit when a mail order firm fails to ship goods ordered would be based on the requirements spelled out by the FTC's "Mail Order Merchandise" Rule unless you insisted on a destination contract shipment condition in combination with a definite delivery date and a "time-is-of-the-essence" clause. If you stated those terms as part of your order, and you don't receive the goods by the stipulated delivery date, you could be entitled to cancel based on the terms of your order. To do so, you could simply use the cancellation ultimatum covered in Chapter 37.

Getting a refund or credit isn't likely to involve a lot of problems if the seller complies with the rule. Your difficulties start with a seller who didn't notify you that you would be entitled to cancel because he is unable to ship.

STAGE ONE: OPENING SKIRMISHES

If the mail order firm complies, notifies you of a shipping delay and gives you the option to cancel, your initial step would be to tell the seller of your decision (most sellers will provide a form you can fill out and return indicating your choice).

Keep a copy of the completed form and get a mailing receipt or, if the order involves a lot of money, send it by certified mail, return receipt requested so you know when the seller receives your cancellation. This tells you when cancellation occurred.

If you charged the purchase to an open-end credit account, especially an account other than with the seller, and you don't have a lot of time to raise a billing error, immediately notify the creditor that a billing error occurred. When you describe the billing error, make clear the merchandise wasn't shipped [delivered] within the time required by the agreement and that you used your option to cancel as provided by the FTC's Mail Order Merchandise Rule. Send along a completed copy of the cancellation form the mail order firm sent. (See page 470 for a description of the billing error correction procedures creditors must follow under the Fair Credit Billing Act.)

If you receive the copy of the seller's credit memo but the amount is not properly credited to your account, then raise as a billing error the creditor's failure to credit the amount to your account.

If you made the purchase and charged it to an account with a credit card issued by the seller, the failure to deliver could also be a defense for not paying as provided by the Fair Credit Billing Act (see page 482).

CANCELING WHEN SELLER FAILS TO NOTIFY YOU ABOUT A SHIPPING DELAY

Here is a sample letter for notifying a seller you are cancelling your order when you failed to receive the goods and were not notified of a shipping delay as required by the Rule.

You could send this letter when the goods have not arrived by the shipping date spelled out by the Rule or a few days later. If a seller has not complied with the mail order rule by notifying you of a shipping delay, my advice is you're wasting your time doing anything but trying to cancel and demanding your money back.

Base your cancellation on both the delivery requirements of your order as well as the cancellation option the Rule requires the seller to give you. Technically speaking, the cancellation option the Rule requires is not part of your contract unless you included it as a condition of your order, but you may as well assert the option.

> *600 Witchtree Lane*
> *Anytown, USA 00000*
>
> *April 1, 19___*

Prompt Mail Orders
300 Horizon Tower
Anytown, USA 00000

Dear Sir:

*This is to inform you I have neither received the [identify product(s)]
I ordered on [_____] nor have I been notified as required by the FTC's
"Mail Order Merchandise" Rule that there would be a shipment delay
beyond the [state delivery or shipping time stated in the order] required
by my order. I sent you my check for [$_____] with the order as payment
in full (as partial payment toward the [$_____]) for the entire order.
([I authorized you to charge the entire [$_____] for the order to my
[identify account] with my credit card, account number 00000-00000-
000.])*

*Unless the merchandise I ordered has, in fact, been shipped by the time
you receive this letter and in which case you are promptly to notify me of
the shipment as required by the Uniform Commercial Code,* my order
is cancelled because of your failure to deliver as required by my order or
our agreement and as provided by the FTC's "Mail Order Merchandise"
Rule [which was also a condition of my order].*

*There is now due me and I request a prompt refund of the [$_____] I
have paid [a prompt credit for the [$_____] which was charged to the
account described above].*

*I am now also notifying [identify creditor with whom you have
account] about the billing error that has resulted from your failure to
make delivery as required by my order or our agreement.*

*I hope this matter will now promptly be resolved as I have requested
so I will not have to pursue it further.*

Sincerely,

*When goods are delivered by shipment contract, the Code requires that the seller
promptly notify the buyer about the shipment. Insisting the seller do so when you
have failed to receive the goods can later help you reject the goods and cancel the
sale if the seller claims the goods were shipped but you failed to get them.

REQUESTING REFUND NOT MADE AFTER CANCELATION

Following is a sample letter you could adapt when the seller fails to make the appropriate refund after you notified the seller you were cancelling as provided by the
Rule.

Give a seller at least two, but perhaps three weeks to get the refund to you.

600 Witchtree Lane
Anytown, USA 00000

May 18, 19__

Prompt Mail Orders
300 Horizon Towers
Anytown, USA 00000

Dear Sir:

*This is to inform you I have not received the refund of [credit for]
[$_____] due me upon having cancelled my order of [__date__] for
[__identify goods__] for the reasons stated in my letter of [__date__] [in
response to your notification of [__date__] that there would be a shipping
delay].*

The refund [credit] is now due for the [$\_\_\_\_] sent with my order as payment in full [as partial payment toward the [$____]] for the entire order [for the [$____] I authorized you to charge to my [<u>identify account</u>] with my credit card, account number 00000-00000-000].

I, therefore, request the immediate return of [an immediate credit for] the [$____] now due me so that I will not have to pursue this matter further.

Sincerely,

STAGE THREE: THE ULTIMATUM

If the mail order firm fails to comply with the FTC's Rule after your initial letter, the only practical follow-up step is an ultimatum demanding a refund. Your main leverage in such situations is possible FTC action.

Following is an ultimatum you could adapt for demanding a refund. It includes alternative wording for situations in which you failed to receive a refund due after telling the seller you were cancelling.

Certified Mail #11112222

600 Witchtree Lane
Anytown, USA 00000

May 1, 19__

Prompt Mail Orders
300 Horizon Towers
Anytown, USA 00000

Dear Sir:

This is to notify you that the [Prompt Mail Orders] is in violation of the Federal Trade Commission's "Mail Order Merchandise" Rule with respect to my order for [<u>identify product(s)</u>] I sent you on [<u>date</u>]. I then also sent you my check for [$\_\_\_\_] as payment in full (as partial payment toward the [$____]) for the entire order. [I then also authorized you to charge the entire [$____] for the order to my [identify account] with my credit card, account number 00000-00000-000.]

You received the order not later than [<u>date</u>] when my check was paid [when the transaction was charged to my credit account]. The order required delivery [to me]* by [state shipping <u>or delivery deadline</u>] [and was conditioned on timely delivery being of the essence to me].

I first informed you by my letter of [<u>date</u>] that I had not received the merchandise nor a notification from you as required by the FTC Rule that there would be a shipment delay. I then also informed you that I was cancelling the order because of your failure to deliver as required by our contract and requested a prompt refund of [credit for] the amount I had paid [the amount charged to my account for the order unless the merchandise had, in fact been shipped by the time you received that letter and you promptly notified me of the shipment. [I received your notice of [<u>date</u>] that there would be a shipping delay to which I responded on [<u>date</u>] to inform you I was exercising my option to cancel and requested a refund of what I had paid [a credit for the amount charged to my account] for the order as provided by the FTC Rule.]

But I have to date still failed to receive the merchandise, nor have I been notified that shipment was made or, as required by the FTC Rule, that there was a shipment delay despite the fact that delivery [shipment] has now been delayed by at least [state period involved] beyond the time required by our contract. [But I have to date still not received the refund due me [a copy of the credit memorandum indicating that the amount charged is to be credited to my account] upon my cancellation.]

Your failure to make delivery as required by our contract and your failure to comply with the requirements of the FTC "Mail Order Merchandise" Rule now prevents me from relying on you to make delivery in good faith.

Any agreement for the sale of the goods I order is now cancelled because of your failure to deliver according to our contract as I informed you in my letter of [__date__] and as provided by the FTC Rule [which was also a condition of my order].

You are now immediately to refund the [$\_\_\_\_] I have paid [to credit to my account the [$____] that was charged to it] for this order as I have already requested and as provided by the FTC Rule.

But if you still fail to comply with the FTC "Mail Order Merchandise" Rule, I shall notify the FTC of this apparently continuing failure to comply with its rule and the Federal Trade Commission Act under which you could be liable for a fine of up to $10,000 for each violation of the Act.

Sincerely,

NOTE: *Refer to the seller being required to make delivery "to you" by the delivery date when you included a "destination contract" delivery condition in your order.]

If you still don't receive the refund due, then notify the FTC about the firm's apparent failure to comply with the Rule. (See page 55) for a sample letter. When you notify the FTC, be sure to include *copies* of relevant documents, including a *copy* of your order, cancelled check or billing statement showing the purchase was charged to your account, any correspondence relating to the problem and the advertising or brochure the seller used for soliciting the order.

REJECTING GOODS THE SELLER CLAIMS TO HAVE SHIPPED BUT WHICH YOU DID NOT RECEIVE

A mail order firm might claim it has shipped the goods but you fail to receive them. The FTC Rule would not help you if the seller actually shipped goods you failed to receive.

Your failure to receive goods can be a problem if they were to be delivered under a shipment contract. With that agreement, the seller, in effect, "delivers" the goods when they are placed in the hands of the carrier. But if you insisted that delivery be made under a destination contract, the seller has not made delivery until you actually receive the goods so that your failure to receive the goods by the required delivery date could entitle you to cancel the agreement for a refund.

If the goods were to be delivered under a shipment contract and the seller tells you when they were shipped and tells you who the carrier was, you will have to discuss the lost or delayed delivery with the carrier.

But if the seller fails to notify you about the shipment and there was a significant delay or the goods were lost, you could be entitled to reject the goods and cancel as explained on page 139.

Following is a sample letter you could adapt for rejecting the goods and cancelling in these circumstances. As a practical matter, however, doing this is unlikely to give you much leverage in getting your money back unless you charged the purchase to an open-end credit account and were still able to raise a "billing error" complaint.

Following is a sample letter for notifying a seller you are rejecting the goods and cancelling when the goods were lost if they were being delivered under a shipment contract and the seller failed to notify you when they were being shipped.

Certified Mail #11112222

> *600 Witchtree Lane*
> *Anytown, USA 00000*
>
> *May 15, 19__*

Prompt Mail Orders
300 Horizon Towers
Anytown, USA 00000

Dear Sir:

I hereby reject the [__identify product(s)__] you claim to have shipped on [__date__] by [identify carrier] pursuant to my order of [__date__] which required delivery by [__date__]. I am now also cancelling the order or any agreement we may have. I have also paid you [$____] for the order by check. [The [$____] for the order has been charged to my [__identify account__] with my credit card, account number 00000-00000-000.]

I am rejecting the goods and cancelling the order or any agreement we may have because you did not promptly notify me of the shipment as required by the Uniform Commercial Code [despite my having insisted that you do so in my letter of [__date__] when I first inquired about the delayed delivery and because the shipment has now either been materially delayed or lost in transit since I still have not received the goods even though more than [indicate time that has passed] have elapsed since the goods were purportedly shipped on [__date__] as you subsequently claimed in your letter of [_____].

Since I have no rejected the goods and cancelled the order or any agreement we may have, there is now due me and you are promptly to return the [$____] I have paid [and you are promptly to take steps to credit my [__identify account__] that was charged with my credit card, number 00000-00000-000 to that account for this purchase].

I hope this matter can be promptly resolved as I have requested so I will not have to hold you liable for this breach at least to the fullest extent provided by the Uniform Commercial Code and by the Fair Credit Billing Act.

> *Sincerely,*

Then take immediate steps to notify the creditor who may be involved and use the recourse the Fair Credit Billing Act could make available to you.

27 · Your Rights When Inspecting and Accepting Goods

Once the seller delivers goods the rest of the purchasing sequence is set in motion. Further steps include your right to inspect the goods to make sure they conform to your contract (and any warranties that are part of the deal); your obligation to accept and pay for them if they do conform, or to reject goods that do not conform; the seller's right to cure, or correct, defects that may cause you to reject the goods; and your right to cancel if the seller fails to cure those defects. As explained when these different steps are described, your agreement can determine how and when you can take each of these steps.

Other steps usually apply if defects appear in the goods *after* you have accepted them. These include any rights you may have under warranties to hold a seller accountable for damages because the goods fail to conform (see Section V), or—if it applies—your right to revoke acceptance and then to cancel the sale.

The first step involves your right to inspect goods after the seller delivers them. Once you have had a chance to do so, you must either reject or accept them. These two steps are closely linked and once you have taken any action that amounts to acceptance, you can no longer reject.

The rest of this section provides a step-by-step guide to these rights plus negotiating strategies for when things go wrong.

Let's first look at inspecting goods.

YOUR RIGHT TO INSPECT GOODS

The Code entitles and obligates you to inspect goods to make sure they conform to your agreement. It also requires you to object to any defects you discover. This rule gives both sides a chance to find and take care of any apparent defects before the sale is fully completed and the goods begin to deteriorate in value.

To conform, the goods must be as they are described in your agreement, and must measure up to any specific claims the seller made, as well as to any model or sample you examined, and any warranties that are part of the deal. (See Section V.)

Unless your agreement specifically states otherwise, the Code entitles you to inspect before you pay for or accept goods.

PAYMENT REQUIRED BEFORE INSPECTION

If your agreement requires you to pay *before* inspection, then you become obligated to pay and the seller can insist on it before giving you a chance to inspect the goods. This might happen if you have to pay for goods at the time you order them; or if goods are sent to you collect on delivery. The post office C.O.D. delivery receipt, for example, says: "Addressee may not examine contents of the C.O.D. package before delivery."

Nevertheless you retain the right to inspect the goods after payment. And you retain the use of all the other rights you have to make a seller live up to an agreement, such as the right to reject non-conforming goods and demand your money back. And naturally, if goods are not delivered when you have paid for them in advance, you also retain your right to demand your money back.

There is one exception to the rule requiring you to pay before inspection as called for by your agreement. If you can immediately see the goods do not conform, without formally inspecting them, you can reject them at once and avoid payment without breaking your agreement. If, for example, you buy a blue carpet to be delivered C.O.D. but the store sends a yellow one, and you can see it is the wrong carpet as it is brought in the door, then you are not obligated to pay first and could instead reject the goods.

If you want to retain the right to inspect goods before having to pay for them in C.O.D. situations, you must note the condition in your agreement by adding words such as "C.O.D., but the buyer may inspect before payment."

RIGHT TO INSPECT BEFORE PAYMENT

Unless your agreement states otherwise, you are entitled to inspect the goods *before* a seller can *require* you to pay.

Whether you have to pay before or after inspection affects who sues whom in the case of a dispute. In cases where payment must be made before inspection, such as a C.O.D. sale, you would have to sue the seller to get your money back if you found and rejected goods that did not conform to your contract. To win, you would have to show he was not entitled to your money.

In cases where you pay after inspection, on the other hand, the seller would have to sue you. To win, he would have to prove that you broke the agreement by not paying and that he had lived up to it by delivering goods that did measure up to the contract. This would be hard to do if the goods did not conform and you rejected them properly, of course.

This is what happened in Mr. Smith's case. When he immediately stopped payment on his check after finding his car was defective, the car dealer sued him. But Mr. Smith was in a strong position to take that step since he was entitled to inspect before having to pay for the car. By stopping payment, Mr. Smith not only put the burden of suing on the dealer, but also the burden of proving that he, Mr. Smith, had broken the agreement while the dealer had lived up to it.

When you are entitled to inspect before payment, always be sure to do so if you would have a reasonable opportunity to make an inspection before payment.

RETAINING YOUR RIGHTS

If you must pay before inspection, you automatically retain the right to inspect and reject faulty goods.

If you are entitled to inspect before paying, however, and *postpone* the inspection until after you pay, even though you have had the opportunity to do so, it may affect your right to reject goods. The Code is not completely clear on this point. If you can show that you did not get a reasonable opportunity to inspect, it is very unlikely the Code would deprive you of your right. If, on the other hand, you saw the goods were faulty and still paid for them, or if you ignored things you could easily have found if you had inspected, you might be deprived of your chance to reject.

The key point to remember is that courts usually count voluntary payment as a sign of satisfaction, especially when it would have been easy to find defects. So, never postpone any inspection you could easily make at a store before paying—especially when it might be hard later to show the store was responsible for a defect such as breakage or damage, for instance. And if a store sign says you must inspect goods before taking them, don't ignore it.

A rule of thumb is, if you use a product before spotting defects you could have found without using it, you probably waited too long to make your inspection.

WHEN AND HOW YOU MAY INSPECT GOODS

The Code entitles a buyer to inspect goods at any reasonable time and place, and in any reasonable manner. Your agreement may specifically spell out how, when, or where you can inspect, but this is not a general practice in consumer transactions.

In effect, the basic rules spelled out in the Code allow a buyer to decide the time, place, and method of inspection as long as the choices are reasonable. If the seller is to deliver or ship the goods, a reasonable time and place to inspect is when and where they are delivered.

Again, the key word is "reasonable." What's reasonable will naturally depend on the type of product you buy, what might be wrong with it, how hard it would be to find a defect, and how easy it might be to show that the seller was responsible for it.

Your right to inspect goods covers more than just the right to *examine* them: it covers any reasonable check for defects in goods whose *surface* appearance is satisfactory. In the case of the Smiths' car, the Biscayne sedan the dealer delivered certainly appeared to be satisfactory. It was only when she actually drove the car that Mrs. Smith discovered the defect. She certainly could not have determined whether the transmission, or any other moving parts, actually worked just by looking at them on the dealer's lot.

When you inspect, you can use any reasonable method that might reveal defects in the kind of product you are buying, including diagnostic testing or expert appraisal. If you buy a car, you can have it inspected by mechanics at a diagnostic center. But if you are going to have an expert inspection, have it done right after you get the product.

Generally speaking, the more complicated the product and the more difficult it is to spot defects, the more time you have to inspect. In the same way it is more likely to be considered reasonable to test a complicated product before formally accepting it.

While the Code entitles you to inspect goods, it does not exactly specify the point when you will be formally considered to have accepted them. This is the tricky part of using your right to inspect when it involves operating or testing the product.

In the Smith case, for example, the court said the question of how long a buyer could drive a new car under the guise of inspecting it, was not an issue because Mrs. Smith found the defect only minutes after leaving the dealership, when she had driven the car only seven-tenths of a mile. The court decided that such a short period of use was well within what could be considered a reasonable opportunity to inspect. The court did not define what general sort of time period could be considered reasonable, however.

What is reasonable will usually depend on the sort of difficulties involved in learning whether goods conform to a contract. It isn't difficult to find out if a dealer has delivered a car with the kind of special radial tires you ordered, for instance; but it is a lot harder to find out if the car has a faulty transmission. What would be considered a reasonable testing period in one situation, therefore, may not be considered reasonable in another.

So the best thing to do is inspect goods as soon and as thoroughly as possible before putting them to full-scale use or altering them any more than is necessary to find a defect. This is especially true when you inspect a product by test-operating it. Remember, the Code only gives you a chance to find out *whether* the goods conform to the contract, and to identify *how* they do not conform if that is the case, at or near the time you receive them and *before* you fully begin to treat them as your property. Other laws—primarily those governing warranties and the chance to revoke acceptance—govern what you can do to make the seller take care of defects that show up after you have accepted a product.

Although specific inspection requirements are not usually spelled out in consumer agreements, sales slips or agreements sometimes state how quickly you must notify the seller about any defects you find after receiving the goods. It could be a statement like this: "All claims must be made within three days after the receipt of the goods." If you wait longer than the three days, when that would be a reasonable time period for notifying the seller about defects, you could easily be stuck with the goods even if they are defective (unless it is a hidden defect you could not reasonably be expected to find within that time). A store may still take back defective goods out of good will, of course. But don't count on it. Waiting too long always weakens your bargaining position.

MAKING AN EFFECTIVE INSPECTION

As soon as you have a reasonable opportunity to inspect, use it effectively. Remember, the purpose of an inspection is to allow you to answer this question: "Is the seller turning over to me the product promised as part of our agreement?" If the answer is no, you have to be able to *show* the seller is responsible.

Conduct your inspection systematically. Look for obvious defects first, then less obvious ones. Go one step at a time, so you don't destroy evidence that might help prove your case. If the product arrives in a damaged packing container, for example, unpack only as far as necessary to find out if there is inside damage. If there is, don't unpack any further. Leave the packing material as you originally found it and leave the product in its container. If the product is wrapped in a sealed plastic bag, for example, and you can see that it is damaged, don't rip open the plastic bag to see how bad the damage is. The battered shipping container, coupled with the damaged item still sealed in its plastic bag, will be convincing evidence the damage occurred in shipment. Your next step should be to check the contents against the order or invoice, to make sure you've received what you ordered. If you haven't, don't unpack further or start trying out the product—unless you are prepared to keep it the way it is. Unwrapping the inside packing materials won't necessarily weaken your bargaining position if you want the seller to take back the product, but using the product certainly will.

Next, check the product itself. Leave the tags on until you are finished and are satisfied everything is okay. Make sure any parts you're supposed to get are there. If, for example, you bought a tent that is supposed to have a zippered window flap, see if the flap is there *before* you open the tent peg and the pole packages and set them up in the back yard. If you get some of the parts dirty, and are later involved in a dispute because some part is missing, you will have a hard time getting the store to take back the product.

If the merchandise comes with several accessories or parts that have to be assembled, make sure everything fits before you test the product by operating it. If some of the parts don't fit and you have not tested the product, you will be in a much stronger position to make the store take it back.

Finally, if the inspection has not revealed any problems, perform any tests necessary on the product. If you test something by operating it, make sure you know how to operate it *properly*. If the seller can show that a defect is due to mishandling, you will probably have a hard time getting him to take it back.

Never put a product to full scale use if you can test it without doing so. If you bought an electric saw or drill, say, you don't have to actually saw or drill with it to make sure the motor works. Nor do you have to cut the grass to test the engine on a new lawn tractor. See if the engine works while the blade is still out of gear; this will eliminate the possibility of accidentally chipping the blade.

Remember, keep the product in its original condition as much as possible while you are inspecting it. And if you find a fault that is important to you, don't proceed and risk damaging the product further.

If you find something wrong, note exactly what the problem is, when you found it, and how the defect became apparent. Note any details that prove the defect is not your fault.

If you receive the goods at a store, make as thorough an inspection as possible in the seller's presence. Take forms so you can make a written list of defects and pin down the seller's promise to take care of them. Being prepared in this way puts you in a strong bargaining position to negotiate a settlement, and demonstrates to the seller that you know what you are doing.

If goods are delivered to your home and you have the right to inspect before paying, insist that they be unpacked. Be prepared to make a written list of defects and ask the delivery people to sign the list. If they are willing to take back a defective product, use the sample forms on page 189 which refer to your rejection of defective goods. A signed statement like this is evidence that the seller or carrier is responsible for the damage. If you are asked to sign a receipt or invoice, describe the defect on the invoice in the same way as you describe it in your statement.

If the delivery people refuse to take back the product, use the form on page 189.

If goods are shipped C.O.D., you cannot inspect before paying, of course, even if the shipping carton is damaged. But when you have paid, ask the delivery people to wait while you open the box to check for inside damage. If they are willing to wait, use the form on page 189, the same statement of defects you would use if you had inspected the goods before paying, and ask them to sign it. If the goods are delivered by a carrier and sent under a shipment contract, you may have to file a damage claim with the carrier. Carriers usually have forms to record damage claims, so ask the delivery person to wait until you have examined the contents and ask him to complete a damage inspection report.

If the delivery people won't wait, have them write on the box exactly where the container was damaged when it was delivered.

SPELLING OUT INSPECTION RIGHTS IN AN AGREEMENT

There may be times when it is inconvenient to inspect goods at a store before payment. And there may be times when you want an expert to inspect the goods. In cases like this, ask the store to write the following on your sales slip or agreement before you buy:

"Buyer is entitled to inspect goods at (_____)
after payment and receipt of goods."

Insert in the brackets the place where you want to inspect the goods; the store, say, or the expert's address, perhaps a diagnostic center or an expert appraiser's office.

If the store refuses to go along with you, insist on your right to inspect the goods, or to use an expert. If the store again refuses, don't buy.

ACCEPTING GOODS

Remember, it is important to use your right to inspect goods before you do anything that might be construed as accepting them. Never, for example, sign for goods at the time of delivery by stating that you "accept" them. If you are asked to sign a delivery receipt, say only that you have "received" the items. And always watch out for written terms that say you are accepting the goods being sold.

Be prepared in advance to take the proper steps to reject goods.

HOW ACCEPTANCE OCCURS

You accept goods by:

- Indicating to the seller, after having had an opportunity to inspect the goods, that they are satisfactory, or that you will keep them even if they do not conform to the contract.
- Failing to reject goods in the proper way after having had a reasonable opportunity to inspect them. These steps are explained on page 164.
- Doing anything that is inconsistent with the seller's ownership of the goods; in other words treating the goods as though they are your own property. Depending on the circumstances, receiving and paying for, using, altering, or repairing the goods are actions that could be considered inconsistent with a seller's ownership and thus count as acceptance. Since almost any action after receipt of the goods might be considered inconsistent with the seller's ownership, courts generally use three main criteria to decide the issue.

1. Actions taken *before* you could have discovered that the goods did not conform are rarely considered inconsistent with the seller's ownership. So receiving or paying for goods, before you had a reasonable opportunity to inspect and discover a defect, would not be considered inconsistent. On the other hand, if you find a defect and continue to use goods or alter, or work on them, without notifying the seller, a court would probably rule your use counts as acceptance.

2. Actions taken *after* you reject goods, such as continuing to use them, or to make regular payments or to keep them after the seller has said he will take them back, will almost always count as acceptance. Once you formally reject goods, play it safe by doing only what the Code allows or requires you to do with rejected goods.

There are occasional circumstances when the continued use of a product will not count as acceptance if the seller refuses to take it back. Continued use would be unavoidable, for instance, if a seller refuses to take back a defective carpet nailed to the floor. Some courts have concluded that a purchaser of a defective mobile home could still reject or revoke his acceptance, even while continuing to live in the home, if the dealer refuses to take it back and refund the buyer's money.

3. Actions taken after notifying a seller about a defect, but before rejecting the goods, may not be considered inconsistent with the seller's ownership but are much less clear-cut. Say the seller tries to repair or adjust complicated machinery, such as a car. In a situation like this courts often say use that occurs while repairs are being made is not inconsistent with the seller's ownership. But sometimes they decide the exact opposite.

You are likely to retain your right to reject in such a case only if it involves a complicated product that may require adjustments and repairs before it is possible to tell whether a defect can be corrected. The defect would also have to be something important and you and the seller must have been working to get it corrected.

For example, in *Sarnecki v. Al Johns Pontiac*, in 1966, a Pennsylvania court decided that Mr. Sarnecki was entitled to reject a defective car five months after his purchase.

In this case, Sarnecki had first told the dealer about the defects within four days of the purchase and the two sides had been engaged in negotiations and repairs until Mr. Sarnecki finally rejected the car when the repairs proved unsatisfactory. Entitling a buyer to reject so long after delivery is unusual, but it illustrates how flexible courts can be when deciding what remedies a consumer is entitled to use. The type of defects involved, and the way the consumer and the seller go about trying to resolve the problem, almost always has an important bearing on the way a court interprets the rules in a particular situation.

The key to reserving your right to reject (or revoke acceptance) in such a situation is to keep good written records of all the defects you tell the seller about and the steps he takes to correct them. Records should include copies of repair orders, statements of what the seller promises to do, descriptions of what the seller does, and notes of conversations. And you must keep after the seller to correct the defects right up to the time it becomes obvious that he can't or won't do anything more and you finally reject the goods.

HOW ACCEPTANCE AFFECTS YOUR RIGHTS AND OBLIGATIONS

If the goods conform to your contract, you must honor the agreement by accepting and paying for them.

Since acceptance is really considered your acknowledgment that the seller has satisfactorily carried out his part of the bargain, taking this step also affects your rights and obligations if you later discover the goods do not, in fact, live up to the contract.

There are three important ways that acceptance affects future steps you can take to enforce your agreement if necessary.

1. Accepting goods cuts off your right to reject them, as previously noted. Unless the seller has committed fraud or made important misrepresentations, normally you will only be able to get out of the agreement completely if you are entitled to revoke your acceptance. This procedure is explained in Chapter 33.

Acceptance does not prevent you from using other remedies available under the Code, of course, such as your rights under any warranty. (See Section V.)

2. If you accept goods knowing that they are defective, you lose your right to revoke acceptance unless the seller has specifically promised to correct the defects, or you have reason to believe he will do so. Normally, you would still have other remedies available under the Code, though, such as having the product repaired under a warranty or recovering damages.

To avoid losing your right to revoke acceptance, get the seller's promises to fix defects pinned down in writing before you do anything that could be considered as accepting the product. For complete details on how to revoke acceptance and the rules that apply, see Chapters 33–35.

3. You could lose your right to use any of the remedies available under the Code—including whatever rights you have under a warranty—if you *fail* to notify the seller about a defect within a reasonable time. Simply by not notifying him promptly, you could let the seller off the hook completely.

YOUR OBLIGATION TO PAY AFTER ACCEPTANCE

Acceptance of the goods also triggers your legal obligation to pay the full amount due under the agreement. If you do not pay, the seller can sue and collect the entire amount. If, on the other hand, you refuse to accept goods even though they conform to your contract, a seller would usually only be able to sue for damages rather than the full purchase price.

Once you have accepted goods, it is up to you to show the seller has broken the agreement in a way that entitles you to avoid payment. Until you have accepted the goods, however, technically speaking it is up to the seller to show that he has fully lived up to the agreement and delivered conforming goods if he is to hold you responsible for failing to accept and pay.

Since acceptance triggers your obligation to pay, in cases where full payment may not be due until later—when you are buying on credit, for instance—a seller is likely to insist that you give written acknowledgment that you are accepting the goods. It's best not to do this unless you at least pin down the seller's assurances to correct any defects you have discovered. And even if there is nothing wrong, ask for the seller's written assurances the product conforms. This can help you revoke acceptance if it turns out that it doesn't.

28 · How to Reject Non-Conforming Goods

YOUR RIGHT TO REJECT NON-CONFORMING GOODS

Rejection is really a self-help remedy. If you and the seller are unable to settle a dispute, you may have to take legal action to enforce your rights. To strengthen your position in any future court action, you must *rightfully* reject goods; that is you must be entitled to reject them and you must reject them in the proper way.

If the seller delivers goods that do not measure up to your agreement, the Code entitles you to reject them. Rejection, in turn, triggers various rights and obligations for both parties. A key follow-up right that may be triggered is the right to cancel and get all your money back.

Sometimes when you rightfully reject goods, you may be able to cancel immediately; in other cases, the seller will first have the right to cure, or correct, the non-conformities before you become entitled to cancel.

Broadly speaking, rejection is a formal way of telling the seller that a product's failure to conform to your agreement is unacceptable and that you refuse to keep it in that condition. You are then also telling the seller he will have to take appropriate steps to cure the non-conformities if he wants to insist on holding you to the agreement and avoid responsibility for breaking it.

Specifically telling a seller you are rejecting goods immediately places everything on a more formal basis, of course, since it triggers various rights and obligations, and can affect your negotiating flexibility. There are less formal ways of asking the seller to correct what's wrong which may well get the problem resolved. So whether you formally reject goods immediately is partly a matter of negotiating tactics. But always be prepared to take formal steps when rejecting goods is obviously more important than negotiating flexibility.

If you don't take the correct steps to reject goods your action will amount to acceptance and you will become obligated to pay the full price. Normally, you could then only make the seller pay for actual damages you suffer because the product does not conform.

When you rightfully reject goods, you acquire two key rights:

1. You are freed of the obligation to pay the price stated in your agreement.
2. You become entitled to get back any money you have already paid. (Technically speaking you only become entitled to demand your money back when you also cancel the agreement.) You may also be entitled to collect damages.

Along with these rights comes the obligation to treat the goods as the seller's property and return them to him.

As explained in the next chapter, a seller does have the right to cure goods you rightfully reject. If he does so, that terminates the rejection, in effect, and cuts off your right to cancel. If, on the other hand, you take the correct steps to reject goods but you are not actually entitled to do so, the seller could hold you responsible for breaking the agreement. In this case, though he can usually only sue for damages he sustained because of your failure to accept the goods rather than for the full purchase price. Such damages would usually include any deposit or down payment you made.

So, in effect, properly rejecting goods cuts off the seller's right to make you pay the full price called for by the agreement even if you are not entitled to reject the goods. This gives you key bargaining leverage.

Your right to reject goods can be limited or modified by clauses included in your agreement. It shouldn't surprise you, therefore, that sellers and manufacturers regularly include clauses in their form contracts or written warranties that say the buyer agrees to limit the remedies he or she can use. One such clause might say a seller only has to repair or replace defective parts, rather than replace the product itself, for example.

But a seller can't take away all your remedies so you have no way to enforce your agreement. So while some clauses may limit your actions, and some may, technically speaking, deprive you of the right to reject goods, rightfully rejecting goods as provided by the Code can still give you substantial bargaining leverage while negotiating with the seller. At the least, it should trigger the remedial steps the seller is obligated to take under the agreement. If the seller doesn't do what the agreement requires, or the limited remedies are inadequate, you would usually be entitled to use all the remedies the Code makes available. (See page 239 for how the seller can limit the remedies you have and what you are entitled to do if they are inadequate.)

WHEN IS A BUYER ENTITLED TO REJECT GOODS?

Technically, the Code allows you to reject goods when they do not fully conform to your contract and when you have done nothing that can be construed as accepting them. But courts usually interpret this requirement to mean that the goods must fail to conform in some fairly important way. A scratch on the highly polished surface of a dining room table, for instance, is likely to be considered an important failure to conform. But a scratch on the rear fender of a car won't be considered serious in the same way because it can be more easily fixed. No court is going to require a seller to deliver an absolutely perfect product.

Goods usually fail to conform in one or more of the following ways:

• They are not what you purchased; the seller delivers a different product from the one described in your agreement.
• They are defective, faulty or damaged. (But remember that under a shipment contract, you may not be able to reject goods damaged *in shipment*.)
• They do not measure up to quality or performance standards, or to other specific claims or promises the seller made, or to a sample he showed you. Such standards or claims are usually governed by any express or implied warranties that apply to the sale. These warranties are described in Section V.

Usually, you would discover defects covered by warranties *after* you have accepted a product and so only remedies that apply to accepted goods would be available— such as revoking acceptance. See Chapter 33. But if you find the product doesn't conform to the warranties *before* you accept it, then you can reject it.

Remember, the specific claims or promises you can hold a seller to depend largely on whether you have an oral or a written agreement. When your agreement is in writing, the unwritten claims or promises that could still count are those which do *not* conflict with the written terms. Even these may not count at all, though, if your agreement includes a merger clause that says the only terms that count are the ones in writing. In that case, the main way out would be if the seller makes material, or important, misrepresentations or commits fraud. Under these circumstances, the Code specifically entitles you to use all the remedies available to enforce a contract, and rightfully rejecting goods is one of them.

• If goods are sent under a shipment contract (described on page 139) and lost in shipment, you would usually have to pay the seller and file your claim against the carrier. If the seller has failed to comply with his shipment obligations, however, and you suffer damage or loss, you can reject the goods. This is because, technically speaking, the seller "delivered" the goods when he gave them to the carrier. The seller's delivery then fails to conform to the requirements of your contract.

While a court may not uphold your rejection if it came to legal action, following the rejection procedure will put you in a strong bargaining position with the seller. If a seller fails to tell you when the goods were delivered to the carrier, or to give you the carrier's address so you can file your claim, you may have a strong case of fraud against him. In a situation like this the initial step of your negotiating strategy should be to make the seller show how he complied with the shipment obligations.

REJECTING ALL OR SOME OF THE GOODS

Under the Code you have three options when it comes to rejecting goods.

1. You can reject all the goods purchased under a contract even when only some of them fail to conform. For example, if you buy an amplifier, two stereo speakers, and a turntable, but only the turntable is defective, you can still reject all the items.

2. You can accept some of the items and reject those that don't conform. You could reject the defective turntable and accept the other items, for instance. But if the goods are part of a set, you cannot reject an individual piece. If you buy a five-piece set of living room furniture, you would have to reject or accept all five pieces.

3. You can accept all the goods even though there is something wrong with an item. It is never wise to do this unless you receive assurances the seller will correct the problem.

HOW TO REJECT GOODS IN THE PROPER WAY

In order to reject goods correctly under the Code you must do three things:

1. *You must notify the seller that you are rejecting the goods.*
A rejection doesn't count unless you specifically notify the seller you are taking this step. To notify him, you must at least make it clear that the goods are unacceptable and that you refuse to keep them. You don't have to use formal legal language, however.

2. *You must reject the goods within a reasonable time after they are delivered.*
For the purpose of rejecting goods, delivery occurs either when the seller gives you the goods or when they arrive at your home or other delivery area. The reasonable time for rejecting goods begins at this point. It comes after you have an opportunity to inspect, and before you have done anything to accept.

What is considered a reasonable time? It usually depends on the following:

• How difficult it is to discover the non-conformity. The easier it is to find a defect, the faster you must act.
• How long your agreement gives you for notifying the seller of a claim.
• The perishability of the goods.

The way you and the seller deal with each other during the period between notification that the goods do not conform and formal rejection can sometimes increase the "reasonable" time allowed—as it did in Mr. Sarnecki's case. In situations like this you must almost always notify the seller about the non-conformity within the reasonable time period, and hold off formally rejecting the goods only while he is actively trying to make repairs or adjustments. (You can't hold off formal rejection when the problem cannot be fixed by repairs or adjustments.) You must also promptly and formally reject the goods once it becomes clear the seller can't or won't fix the defects.

The key point to remember, is that a reasonable time is seldom very long, so always act promptly after delivery. A failure to do so may mean you will lose your right to reject. While this, in itself, will not usually prevent you from recovering damages, it will weaken your bargaining position. It is a lot harder to argue about what the seller owes you in damages when you still owe him something for the goods, than it is to argue you don't owe anything. Failing to notify the seller promptly is one of the most frequent and costly mistakes consumers make.

3. *You must specifically describe the defects that entitle you to reject the goods.*

Naturally, you cannot reject a product simply by saying you don't want it or it isn't any good. You must describe *how* and *why* it does not conform.

If you do not mention specific defects you could have found by reasonable inspection, you cannot use these unstated defects as a reason for rejecting the goods or holding the seller responsible for breaking the agreement, nor can you bring them up later as a reason for getting out of the agreement.

This rule does not prevent you from holding the seller responsible for hidden defects or defects which could be found only by very detailed or expert inspection.

If a dispute goes to court, any defects you have described can be used to justify rejection. So if goods do not conform to important oral representations or claims, notify the seller just as though they were part of the written agreement. If it later turns out the goods did not conform because the seller made misrepresentations or defrauded you, the stated defects could help you justify a rejection based on misrepresentation or fraud.

HOW TO DESCRIBE NON-CONFORMITIES

Always notify the seller in writing about non-conforming goods. Either specifically identify what is wrong ("I received a red sweater instead of the blue one I ordered"), or describe how the product failed to work as it should ("When I first turned on the electric drill, the motor emitted a loud humming sound and blew a fuse").

Always state *when* you discovered the defect, to show how quickly you have acted, and *how* you discovered the defect, to show you used the product correctly.

Keep a record of notification by having the seller sign a copy of the written notice, or by getting proof of mailing. Use certified mail, return receipt requested, whenever you reject an important purchase, to provide additional proof you have notified the seller.

BUYER'S RIGHTS AND OBLIGATIONS WHEN REJECTING GOODS

Once you have rejected goods, the Code specifically states your obligations.

1. *You must treat the goods as though the seller owns them.* In other words, you can't use them. If you do anything that is inconsistent with the seller's ownership, you lose your right to reject.

2. *You must be prepared to give the goods back.* Rejected goods are the seller's property. While the Code does not require you to return goods yourself—it is up to the seller to make arrangements for getting them back—in practice there are times when you may have to follow a seller's reasonable instructions. To make it clear you are prepared to return rejected goods, always insist the seller make appropriate arrangements at the time you reject goods.

How and when you must actually give back rejected goods depends on whether you have already paid anything for them. Let's look at these two points separately.

RETURNING GOODS FOR WHICH YOU HAVE NOT YET PAID

Once you notify the seller you are rejecting goods for which you have not yet paid anything, the Code requires only that you take reasonably good care of them until the seller picks them up.

There are occasions though when you must follow reasonable instructions for returning goods. One instance would be if you bought from a mail-order house. You can insist the seller pay shipping charges, however, unless you had previously agreed to pay them.

If the seller fails to give you instructions within a reasonable time, then you can store the goods or ship them back as you see fit. You could send them C.O.D. and ask the post office to collect the shipping charges, for instance.

As a practical matter you would usually return goods personally when you first notify a store. If the goods are bulky, though, or you would have a hard time returning them yourself, you can insist the seller remove them since the rule requires that you follow only reasonable instructions.

If the goods might be further damaged while you are returning them, ask the seller how he wants them returned, or else insist that he pick them up himself.

Although a seller may claim you are not entitled to reject the goods, or that you failed to do it properly, and sue you for breaking the agreement—as Zabriskie Chevrolet did to Mr. Smith—if you follow the rules for rejecting goods you will be in a strong position if your case goes to court. That's why disputes in these situations are usually settled long before they reach court.

WHAT IF THE SELLER REFUSES TO TAKE BACK THE GOODS?

If you haven't yet paid anything and the seller refuses to take back non-conforming goods, he is in effect, triggering a dispute. By immediately challenging your right to reject, he is actually asserting that you have accepted the goods and are required to pay. In a case like this, you may have to use all the leverage available to reach a settlement.

You have two options in such circumstances. Instead of insisting on formally rejecting the goods, you can simply go along with whatever promises he makes to cure the defects. A seller will almost certainly insist you pay, as called for by the agreement, before he cures. Doing this is likely to count as acceptance, of course.

If the goods substantially fail to conform and you want to establish that you have rightfully rejected them so you can either insist on a replacement or retain leverage for negotiating a more adequate cure than the seller is willing to make, you would have to give prompt notification that you are formally rejecting the goods and insist he take them back. In this case you would not have to pay unless the seller properly cures.

To negotiate effectively in situations like this, you must decide in advance how far you are prepared to go. Then you can promptly take follow-up steps to reinforce your bargaining position.

If you reject the goods and the seller still refuses to take them back, you have two options.

1. You can either leave the goods at the store or ship them back. If you leave them, try to get a receipt; if you ship them, get a mailing receipt. In either case, write the seller a letter to reaffirm that you are rejecting the goods and to state your objections to any inadequate settlement he might have made. Send the letter by certified mail. See the sample receipt and letter on page 211.

2. You can keep and store the goods. This would be an option in the event the seller refuses to give you a receipt for them. You may not use the goods in any way, of course. Write a letter to reaffirm that you are rejecting the goods. Make it clear you are only storing them and restate your demand that the seller pick them up. Also state your objections to any inadequate settlement the seller might have made. See the sample letter on page 211.

RETURNING REJECTED GOODS FOR WHICH YOU HAVE PAID

If you have made payments, or signed a time payment note, you are not obligated to give back rejected goods until the seller is prepared to refund your money. Generally, he would be obligated to do this at the time you become entitled to cancel. This Code rule gives you some leverage; in effect, the goods become your collateral. The Code also gives you a security interest until the seller pays any reasonable expenses you might be entitled to collect for inspecting, storing or transporting the goods. It is seldom worth arguing about collecting these expenses, though, if the seller is willing to correct the defect or return any money you've paid. It smacks of holding out for the last penny, and that is risky since the seller may then refuse to settle and keep your money. Your objective, after all, is to reach a reasonable settlement rather than to fight a lawsuit.

It is not always easy to know if you are entitled to collect for reasonable expenses either. The Code allows the seller to state in the agreement that he is not required to pay such expenses. Form contracts usually say this, for instance.

If the seller refuses to be reasonable, on the other hand, you usually have a stronger case for making him pay these expenses. And if he is totally unreasonable, you may be able to collect them despite the fact that your agreement may specifically state that the seller does not have to pay them. (See page 241.)

While you do not have to actually return rejected goods for which you have paid until the seller is prepared to refund your money, you must take all the other steps to make sure you reject goods in the correct way. You must show you are willing to return the goods, follow the seller's instructions for returning them, take reasonable care of the goods, and give the seller enough time to pick them up. And, of course, you cannot use the goods after you reject them.

If the seller refuses to take back goods for which you have paid, you can hold and store them until he is prepared to take them back and refund your money.

29 · The Seller's Right to Cure Defects

On the one hand, the Code obligates the seller to deliver conforming goods and entitles you to reject them if they don't conform. On the other hand, it also gives the seller the right to cure the defect after you reject goods. If he properly corrects the problem then you must complete the sale. If he does not, you can enforce your rejection by canceling.

It's important not to confuse a seller's normal refund or exchange policy with his opportunity to cure non-conforming goods. A seller who delivers a non-conforming product must cure the defect or you are entitled to reject it and follow through by canceling to get your money back. A seller who delivers goods that do conform to your contract, on the other hand, does not have to take them back unless such a condition is part of the agreement or the store has a liberal exchange or refund policy.

HOW CAN A SELLER CURE A NON-CONFORMING PRODUCT?

Basically, the seller can cure a non-conforming product by delivering one that does conform to the requirements of your contract. But the Code is not entirely clear about what he has to do to accomplish this. Must the seller exchange the defective product, for example, or can he simply repair it and say that because it now conforms you have to accept it? The Code does not address itself to these specifics, unfortunately.

It is when a seller insists on repairing a defective product, rather than exchanging it, that consumers often run into trouble, of course. This is what Zabriskie Chevrolet insisted on doing in Mr. Smith's case. But in Mr. Smith's case, the court said that the defects were so substantial—the transmission had to be replaced completely—that the buyer couldn't really be sure the repairs were adequate. In effect, the court said the dealer could have cured the defect only by delivering a new car.

The court also said that the seller's opportunity to cure a defect did not give him the license to decide arbitrarily what kind of measures would be enough to correct the problem and then force the buyer to accept them. The seller had to do at least enough to cover the *important* requirements of the deal.

But while the seller must do "enough" to cure defects, remember there are no absolute guidelines that spell out exactly what this entails. There are only general principles to go on. If a product has only minor defects that can be corrected easily and the seller repairs them, courts almost always decide the seller has done enough. The most effective thing you can do in such a situation is to notify the seller of the defects in writing and pin down his promises to correct them. This will help strengthen your bargaining position and allow you to revoke acceptance later if necessary. If the defects are so serious the product is inoperable or unfit to use, courts are more likely to decide that repairs are not enough and the buyer is entitled to a new product. Thus, if a product has a major rather than a minor defect you are in a much stronger bargaining position to insist the seller either exchange it or refund your money.

THE SELLER'S RIGHT TO CURE DEFECTS / 171

PRICE REDUCTIONS

Sometimes a seller may offer to "cure" a defect by reducing the price of the product. While the Code does not specifically provide for this solution, it may be one way you could both reach a satisfactory settlement. It is unlikely that a seller could force you to accept a price reduction and you may not be able to force a seller to accept one either. Nevertheless, it is an alternative to consider when there isn't anything seriously wrong with a product and it is easy to figure what a fair price reduction would be.

Suppose, for example, you purchase a 21-inch console TV set but the store sends you a portable model instead which costs $150 less. If the portable model is acceptable, ask the seller to adjust the price you are supposed to pay under your agreement. Don't use the product until the seller agrees to the price reduction, and insist he put the change in writing. This is especially important if you have a written agreement to begin with. (Note: Technically speaking, if you had already received the nonconforming goods you could force the seller to let you keep them for a reduced price by claiming the price reduction as your damages, but if the seller refuses you run the risk of a dispute and a lawsuit.)

Never accept a reduced price as a settlement unless you are willing to live with the defects. There is nothing you can do to make the seller correct them later.

SELLER'S OBLIGATION TO NOTIFY BUYER THAT HE WILL CORRECT DEFECTS

In order to be entitled to the right to cure non-conformities, the seller must notify you within a reasonable time that he will correct the problem.

What constitutes a reasonable time depends on the situation, but usually the more serious the defect and the more you stand to lose by the seller's failure to act, the faster he must move to notify you. If he fails to do so you are fully entitled to reject the goods.

When you notify the seller you are rejecting the goods, ask him to put his plans for correcting the defects in writing to strengthen your position should he fail to respond.

TIME LIMITS ON THE SELLER'S OPPORTUNITY TO CURE DEFECTS

The Code also sets two time limits for the seller to cure non-conformities.

The first is the original delivery date. A seller can always cure up to the time delivery was originally required by your agreement. If your agreement calls only for delivery within a "reasonable time," then he has that reasonable time for curing. Since "reasonable" is a vague term, it's best to have a firm delivery date specified in your agreement so you also have a firm cut-off date for curing non-conformities. (See page 141 for how to specify delivery dates.) You can then follow through with the rejection by canceling unless the second time limit applies.

The second time limit sometimes enables a seller to cure a non-conformity within a reasonable time after the original delivery date. This can happen if he originally sent substitute goods that did not measure up to the agreement but which he had reason to believe would be acceptable to you anyway. In this case the Code allows him reasonable additional time to deliver the products you actually ordered. (The seller may offer to reduce the price of substitute goods but you do not have to accept the goods or a price reduction.) The Code has this provision in order to allow for a seller's *honest* effort to live up to an agreement. He will usually be considered to have made such an effort if the quality of the substitute product is at least as good as the one you originally ordered, the product has only minor imperfections, or if it has been shipped in the manufacturer's sealed packaging. However, to get the extra time after the delivery date has passed, the seller must notify you that he will send the correct product. And he can usually correct such a non-conforming delivery only be replacing it with one that meets the requirements of the contract.

If you make it clear in your agreement that you want the seller to comply strictly with the purchase terms, then he will have no reason to believe that non-conforming goods will be acceptable and will not be able to insist on any extra time to correct the defect. To do this, add the following to your order form or written agreement:

"No replacement or substitute goods will be acceptable to the buyer."

Include a clause like this whenever it will take time for the seller to deliver what you order or whenever it might be difficult to return a product personally, such as in the case of a mail order purchase.

You could also add to the above clause: "The seller shall have no right to cure after the delivery date." If you include this wording, a firm delivery date, and a time is of the essence clause, a seller will almost always have to comply strictly with these terms. If he does not, he will then be considered to have broken the agreement and you could cancel and get your money back. Cutting off a seller's right to cure after the delivery can be a two-edged sword, though. It can help you if the goods obviously do not conform on delivery and you promptly reject them formally. But you cannot expect much leeway for finding less obvious non-conformities. Insisting on strict compliance with the requirements of the contract will apply to both parties. It may, therefore, only be worthwhile to try to restrict the seller's chance to cure in cases where you could immediately spot a non-conformity at the time of delivery.

BUYER'S RIGHT TO DEMAND ADEQUATE ASSURANCES

The Code entitles either party to make a written demand that the other side give adequate assurances that it will perform its obligations. So if you have strong reason to believe a seller may not live up to the contract, you can insist on this provision. It gives you a specific way to test the seller's sincerity. Remember, though, that under the Code the seller is only obliged to give you assurances if you demand them in writing.

What would give you reason to suspect a seller's willingness to perform his obligations? Any of the following would be a tip-off:

• The seller refuses to acknowledge that a product fails to conform when it's obvious that it does not.

• The seller promises but fails to correct the defects, or continues to insist that certain repairs will correct the problem when earlier attempts have shown they will not.

• The seller refuses to commit himself to curing or repairing the defects as he is obligated to do.

When you are justified in demanding assurances from the seller, the Code also allows you to hold off completing your end of the agreement until you receive them. Usually this means delaying acceptance or payment for goods. However, you may delay performing your part of the bargain only for things the seller hasn't done. For example, if you accept some goods, but demand assurances that the seller will correct defects in other products you reject, you must still pay for those you accept.

The Code does not spell out exactly what counts as adequate assurances. It depends on the circumstances—how serious the seller's failure is, how unwilling he is to confirm his readiness to correct it, how seriously you might be hurt by his failure to carry out his obligation should you still go ahead with your part of the deal, what the seller's reputation is for honesty and fair dealing.

The least you should demand, however, is a specific commitment from the seller that he will carry out his obligations under your contract. If your reasons for doubting his sincerity are serious, you could demand that he do more than simply what the agreement requires. Say, for instance, you reject a defective product and the seller's attempt to repair it fails. If he asks for another chance to correct it, you could demand that he give assurances he will take the product back and replace it should this second attempt also fail.

After a seller receives your written demand for adequate assurances, he must furnish assurances within thirty days that he will at least perform the obligations required by your contract. You can insist he give assurances sooner if circumstances warrant it, such as if you need the product urgently.

If the seller fails to give his assurances within thirty days he will be considered to have broken the contract and you can use legal remedies to hold him to it.

Remember, though, you must have *good* reason to doubt the seller's willingness to perform his obligations. If you are not justified, and you withhold payment because you don't receive the assurances, *you* may be breaking the contract, not he.

You should also use your right to demand assurances sparingly; doing so with every little thing that might go wrong can cast doubt on your good faith and make it seem as though you are trying to trap the seller. And *never* try to hold a seller accountable for failing to provide assurances about future obligations without legal advice. Always base claims on the seller's past failure to live up to your agreement.

30 · Summary of Strategy for Rejecting Goods

This chapter provides an overview of the negotiating strategy for rejecting goods. The following two chapters provide step-by-step guides: the first to rejecting goods at the time of delivery, the second to rejecting goods after delivery.

STARTING THE BARGAINING PROCESS

The initial step the Code requires you to take is to promptly notify the seller that the goods fail to conform. You have to do this after you've had a reasonable opportunity to inspect the goods and before you've done anything that could count as acceptance. This step starts the bargaining process that will result in the seller either curing the non-conformity, or in your becoming entitled to cancel and recover any money you've paid plus any damages.

Since a seller is usually entitled to cure a non-conformity, the initial dispute is likely to concern whether or not his proposal for doing so is adequate. This becomes important when either party insists on holding the other side to the deal. So the first thing to find out is what the seller is prepared to do and decide whether it is acceptable. Always make it clear that you are giving the seller a reasonable chance to cure and that you are prepared to live up to your end of the bargain.

Whether you tell the seller you are formally rejecting the goods at the time you first notify him of defects is partly a matter of negotiating tactics. Doing so puts things on a more formal legal footing and both parties tend to assume more belligerent postures. This can usually be avoided simply by asking a seller to correct the problem.

But since you can't tell in advance how accommodating a seller will be, the key to keeping your options open is to be *prepared* to formally reject goods at the initial discussion if necessary. As a matter of tactics, how you open the bargaining process depends on how significant the non-conformity is, how firmly you wish to establish that you want to return goods, what you will insist the seller do to cure the non-conformity, whether you are willing to pay while the seller cures, and the importance of your relationship with the seller.

While it isn't possible to give hard and fast guidelines, here are some points to consider.

● *If the product fails to conform in ways the seller can easily fix and he is likely to do so,* it's normally worthwhile to start out in a low-keyed way. Simply tell him what's wrong and focus on resolving the problem. Either take a written statement with you about the way the product does not conform, or be prepared to write one once you and the seller have agreed on the non-conformity. Pin down any promises he makes about curing the defect and give him a copy of the statement. You should also be prepared to reject the goods formally should it become necessary to do so. Always treat the goods as the seller's property until the matter has been satisfactorily resolved.

There is another reason why it could be worthwhile to avoid formally rejecting goods in this situation. Whatever the seller does to fix the product may cut off your rejection remedy entirely since you could be considered to have accepted the goods. If you later find the product substantially fails to conform in other ways, revoking acceptance may then be your only alternative. If, on the other hand, you do not formally reject the goods initially and the substantial non-conformities show up relatively soon after delivery, you might then still be able to reject and/or revoke acceptance. Retaining the possibility of using both options later could give you some additional legal and bargaining leverage.

• *If the goods substantially fail to conform* and you would not want to go through with the sale unless the seller replaces them, or if you are unsure about the seller's response, promptly triggering the rejection remedy becomes increasingly more important. Bear in mind, though, that this course does involve risks if you are. not actually entitled to reject.

The negotiating strategies for rejecting goods assume that if the seller cures the non-conformities that justified your initial rejection you would be considered to have accepted the goods. This may not be the case, however, in some situations. It is possible that if substantial non-conformities show up after you have rejected the goods but within the time you have for inspecting the cured goods before acceptance, you could still notify the seller about the defects and be entitled to cancel because you had already rejected the goods. Treating the goods as though you had accepted them would almost certainly foreclose such possibilities, though. If you don't want to foreclose this option seek immediate legal advice before doing anything in this situation.

• *You may also be entitled to reject goods because the seller made important misrepresentations that convinced you to buy* or because he committed fraud. But be sure you have a solid case. To trigger your justification to reject, tell the seller why the goods don't conform to the representations he made. If the seller corrects the defects, then using the Code may be all you need to reach a settlement. If not, you may have to combine your rights under your state's deceptive sales practices law or the fraud law with those available under the Code. To do this, immediately follow up with a low-keyed warning step included in the negotiating strategies for these laws, then follow that up by notifying the seller you are rejecting the goods.

Broadly speaking, you usually have more time to find out whether a seller has committed fraud or engaged in misrepresentations than you have for discovering a product's failure to conform. Still, you would have to take the above steps in quick succession as the seller's response makes clear what the real story is.

If a dispute reaches court and you have properly rejected the goods, that strengthens your position to hold the seller accountable under the Code as well as either of the other two laws that apply.

YOUR LEVERAGE WHEN RIGHTFULLY REJECTING GOODS

Rightfully rejecting goods entitles you to avoid having to pay what would otherwise be due until the seller cures the non-conformity. This is the immediate leverage you have in case of a possible dispute.

If the seller refuses or fails to cure, you can then go through with the rejection by canceling. (See page 276.)

RISKS YOU TAKE WHEN FORMALLY REJECTING GOODS

Formally rejecting goods and not paying can trigger an immediate dispute and give the seller a chance to sue you. He might try to claim you owe the money because you had actually accepted the goods, as Zabriskie Chevrolet did in Mr. Smith's case. If the court agrees with you, as it did with Mr. Smith, the seller would not be able to collect anything. That's the best that could happen.

What's the worst that could happen? A court could decide that you did not rightfully reject the goods and the seller could hold you responsible for breaking the agreement. If the court also decided you had accepted the goods, the seller could collect the full contract price, plus additional expenses, plus attorney's fees if your agreement specifically provides for them.

If you pay the full amount, you would be entitled to the goods. But if the goods failed to conform and the seller didn't cure, you could deduct whatever amounts you sustained as damages. If, however, you bought the goods on credit and failed to pay upon rejecting, the seller/creditor to whom you owed the money could be entitled to repossess. If he did so and followed proper procedures for reselling the goods, he could be entitled to collect the difference between what you owed under the agreement and what he got upon properly reselling the goods plus amounts for expenses and perhaps attorney's fees. These are, of course, good reasons for being extra careful about refusing to pay for goods you buy on credit. A judgment against you could also hurt your credit record, although the rights you have under the Fair Credit Reporting Act could help you minimize the damage. (See page 580.)

See page 280 for a summary of the remedies available to a seller, and page 530 for a summary of additional remedies available to a creditor.

The main thing to remember about the negotiating leverage you get by rejecting and withholding payment, unless the seller cures, is that the seller (or creditor) also takes risks if he disputes your right to reject and insists on making you pay instead of trying to reach a reasonable settlement.

He may end up getting nothing, which is what is likely to happen if you have promptly taken the proper steps to reject the goods and try to be reasonable about settling the problem but the seller doesn't properly cure. Following the rules in this way helps to strengthen your bargaining position.

And the seller may not end up winning very much even if the court decides you did not reject the goods properly, or were not entitled to reject them in the first place, especially if the purchase price does not involve a lot of money. And if you have damages to collect because the goods did not conform, you may end up owing the seller less than the full purchase price. And if you properly but wrongfully rejected the goods (that is, you weren't entitled to reject but had done it properly so you would not be considered to have accepted the goods), the seller usually could not collect more than the damages he had rather than the full price.

So while the law puts pressure on you whenever you reject and withhold payments, it also puts pressure on the seller. Other laws might also apply to the situation, such as your state's deceptive sales practices law or the Magnuson-Moss Warranty Act, which could make the seller more vulnerable to legal action. And as more fully explained in Section VII, you can make it especially risky for a creditor to try to repossess goods for which you may not owe the money.

Withholding payment is unquestionably one of the toughest decisions a consumer has to make, especially if payments are due at the time or soon after the seller makes it clear he will fight you. But it is the strongest leverage you have to back up your negotiating strategy when you and the seller cannot reach a settlement.

If you decide to withhold payment, don't do it simply by avoiding payment. Specifically tell the seller that you are rejecting the goods and that therefore payments are no longer due. This demonstrates you are not defaulting on your obligation to pay, but are acting correctly in order to use your rights under the Code. If the seller insists on payment and you do so to avoid giving him a chance to sue you right away, make the payments under protest and reserve all your rights, as explained on page 127.

If you buy goods under certain kinds of credit agreements and are entitled to withhold payment from the seller, you can also withhold payment from the creditor if he is someone other than the seller. In a situation like this, you must deal separately with the seller and the creditor. Section VI tells how you should notify a creditor that you don't owe the money and what other steps you should take.

Although, theoretically, a seller or creditor can sue you as soon as you fail to pay by a due date, as a practical matter this will almost always be his last step. First he will try to convince you to pay or to work out a settlement. This is especially true if you have received the goods.

GETTING THE SELLER TO ACKNOWLEDGE THE PRODUCT DOESN'T CONFORM

Even though you may already have put in writing how the product doesn't conform, always try to get the seller to explicitly confirm the product doesn't conform *before* discussing what he should do to correct the problem. This step is a practical way to test a seller's sincerity before you firmly commit yourself to a bargaining position. The trick is to get the seller to admit the product doesn't conform rather than telling him directly. This may be easy when goods are obviously defective, but if they aren't, you'll have to persuade him the product doesn't conform to your agreement before you can convince him to correct the problem.

To do this, never be accusatory. This will only make the seller defensive. Instead, get him to agree with you by asking questions that prompt him to reach the same conclusion.

Ask questions like these:

"Is this the product I actually ordered?" or, "This isn't the product I actually ordered, is it?"

"It doesn't look as if this is working properly, is there something wrong with it? Can you tell me what it is?" or, "Is this how the product is supposed to work?"

"Is this part attached the way it is supposed to be, or is something wrong with it?"

"Isn't this product supposed to come with (describe what's missing)? What happened to it?"

"Aren't these (describe defects you see) faults that need to be corrected?"

A seller could, of course, answer by denying that anything is wrong. This is unlikely when the defects are obvious because he knows that if he refuses to satisfy you at this point, you can refuse to take or pay for the product and he will then be in a poor position to hold you to the agreement. But if the defect is not so obvious and the seller denies that anything is wrong, immediately refer to your agreement. Have a copy on hand so that you can point to the relevant parts.

Never accuse the seller of cheating you or insist that he is wrong. Instead, ask questions like these:

"But didn't our agreement call for the delivery of (state what your agreement required)?"

"But didn't our agreement and warranties call for the delivery of a product that was (free of defects or state what they called for)?"

Questions which refer the seller to the agreement are another way of testing his sincerity because his replies will reveal whether you can still expect him to honor the agreement. They also make it easier for him to agree with you and to retreat from his initial position without admitting he was wrong.

When you first discuss the matter, either prepare a memo you will use for notifying him in writing so you can insert in it what the seller confirms is wrong or have him acknowledge that what you have written correctly describes what's wrong.

Try to avoid getting picky about minor inconsequential things, otherwise the seller will think that nothing he can do will satisfy you and he'll be less inclined to be accommodating.

Sometimes a seller may try to convince you that what you think is a defect is really "normal" or "what you would expect." Because you may not know for sure whether such reassurances are correct, you may hesitate to reject the goods or to challenge the seller. But hesitation won't help if you are correct: if you don't inform the seller about the apparent defect, you may later weaken your bargaining position.

Instead of hesitating to challenge the seller, test his sincerity by asking him to put his assurances in writing. Notifying a seller about possible defects and getting such assurances is one very important way to hold a seller accountable later.

DECIDING WHAT SETTLEMENT YOU WANT

Once the seller acknowledges the defect or claims nothing is wrong, it is time to negotiate your settlement or to request him to put his assurances in writing.

These are the main settlement options you could negotiate:

• Insist the seller replace or repair the goods while making clear you are then still prepared to complete the sale. These are two main options you can insist on while the seller can still cure. Whether you can insist on a replacement usually depends on how substantially the product doesn't conform. If the defect is covered by a warranty, your first step should be to insist the seller honor it. If the defects are substantial and the seller insists on repairing rather than replacing the product but you are unwilling to accept repairs, then formally reject the product and insist the seller replace it. Doing this shows how serious you consider the problem to be and puts on the seller the burden to insist the repairs he wants to make are adequate if you later decide to go along with it. That can help later if the seller is wrong.

• Tell the seller you would be willing to return the product for a full refund or credit. This amounts to cancelling and may be the most acceptable solution if neither you nor the seller want to hold each other to the deal and you are willing to forget about any damages you might be entitled to recover. You can only *insist* on this kind of settlement *after* the seller has failed to cure the defect within the time allowed. In effect, the seller can hold you to the original deal by insisting that he will cure the defect.

• Ask the seller to reduce the price if you are willing to accept the goods despite the fact they don't conform. Never do this unless you are really willing to live with the defects, and always make it clear that this does not mean you are willing to overlook other defects you may find later.

• Ask the seller to pay for damages you incurred because the goods do not conform. Although this is not a frequent occurrence, don't forget the possibility of collecting damages could increase the seller's willingness to settle. See page 276 for a description of damages you may be entitled to collect, and page 241 for what to do if a seller used clauses to prevent you from collecting these damages.

• Get the seller's assurances to correct the defects and take delivery of the product rather than formally rejecting the goods. In this case, be sure to notify the seller about the defects in writing and pin down his assurances to fix them. Make clear you are taking and paying for the goods only on the condition the defects are corrected. Stating these conditions will strengthen your position to reject the goods later and/ or to revoke acceptance should you get involved in a real dispute. However, it is usually wise to formally reject goods that are *substantially* defective, and request a replacement rather than simply asking or going along with the seller's promises to fix the defects.

• If you purchased more than one product under an agreement, remember you have the option to reject either the faulty product, or all of the items as explained on page 166. If the seller is willing to correct the defective product, it is usually reasonable to take the ones that conform. If the seller refuses to do so, you are usually better off rejecting all the goods in case something later goes wrong with the others.

• Withholding further payments until the seller cures the defects. If you bought the goods on credit, check Section VII for an explanation of when you could withhold payment.

When you start to negotiate, rank the alternatives that would be acceptable to you so you have a fall-back position. Decide what is the least you will accept and be prepared to back up that position if the seller refuses to accept it.

If the seller refuses to acknowledge that the product is defective, or will not agree to what you consider would be adequate measures to correct the problem, it is appropriate to increase the pressure by saying you are rejecting the product and that payment isn't due unless the defects are cured. Refer to the legal remedies you have and the damages you might be entitled to collect if he insists on breaking your agreement.

Make it clear, however, that you are still willing to live up to your part of the bargain as long as he is willing to live up to his and that you are prepared to give him a reasonable opportunity to correct any non-conformities.

MAKING THE SELLER CURE THE DEFECTS

Whether you reach a settlement, or the seller refuses to correct what's wrong, your next step is to hold the seller to his obligation to cure the defects. You do this with the low-keyed warning letters which begin on page 220.

CANCELLING AND DEMANDING YOUR MONEY BACK AND WITHHOLDING PAYMENT

This is your final negotiating step before taking formal legal action. It involves sending an ultimatum letter and using the legal remedies available, such as cancellation, which are described on page 276.

If you have not paid for the goods, be prepared to withhold payment to back up your negotiating strategy if you are determined to go through with rejecting the goods and getting all your money back. But also be prepared for the fact that the seller may sue you. Your willingness to risk a lawsuit can be an effective tool since it demonstrates just how serious you are about the issue. If you are not willing to risk a lawsuit by stopping payment, using an ultimatum letter while continuing to make payments even while reserving your rights will seldom create enough pressure to force a settlement. And if you try to withhold payment later, after continuing to pay even though you say you don't owe the money, your continued willingness to pay could amount to a waiver of the rights that could have entitled you to avoid paying.

As more fully explained in Section VII, cancellation is also a counter-move you can use against a seller and/or creditor who, instead of carrying out his obligation to cure, seeks to hold you responsible for breaking the agreement merely because you had formally rejected the goods and/or because you did not pay. Cancellation could be an especially effective counter-move to a seller/creditor's attempt to repossess when you had purchased the goods on credit.

CONSULTING AN ATTORNEY

To use your right to reject goods, you will almost always have to make the first moves on your own since it is obviously impractical to consult an attorney about every step you take. Also you may not even have time to see an attorney before taking the initial steps.

But when you make an expensive purchase and the seller refuses to take back goods you reject, at least *consult* an attorney while the dispute is still in its early stages. It is often worthwhile, in a situation like this, to consult an attorney before you withhold payment. Remember, the longer a dispute drags on after you have rejected goods, the easier it is for technicalities to complicate the enforcement of your rights. It is in the early stages of a dispute that an attorney can help you preserve your rights most effectively or help undo mistakes you might have made.

If a dispute doesn't involve enough money to make it worth seeing an attorney, acting promptly and taking the correct steps under the Code will almost always put you in a strong bargaining position to reach a satisfactory settlement. And if a seller refuses to refund your money, consider suing him in small claims court.

POINTS TO REMEMBER

1. *Put Things in Writing*
Buyers who did not notify a seller in writing that they were rejecting goods have not generally been successful in court actions. Written notices, and verification that the seller has received them, give you concrete evidence that you have taken the proper steps to reject goods.

It's particularly important that you don't withhold payment if you haven't promptly notified a seller in writing that you are rejecting goods. That is, unless you first see an attorney for advice.

Always make a copy of any letters or memos.

2. *Get Verification the Seller Received It*
Either ask the seller to acknowledge receiving your letter by signing your copy, as shown, or send it by certified mail. At the very least, get a mailing receipt to prove you have sent it.

3. *Key Points to Pin Down in Writing*
Be sure to get written receipts showing you have returned rejected goods. Either get the receipt from the seller, or if you ship back the goods, get a mailing or shipping receipt.

If the seller takes back the goods and you agree to settle by calling off the sale, make sure your receipt clearly shows you no longer owe the money, especially if your agreement is in writing. This will protect you if the seller tries to collect from you at a later time.

If you agree to some other settlement, such as a repair or an immediate exchange, pin it down in writing. If the seller then fails to fix the problem, the written promise will strengthen your position to follow through with a rejection by canceling.

If you purchased the goods on credit and a separate creditor is involved, check Section VI for an explanation of additional steps you might have to take to settle up with a separate creditor and how to pin it down in writing especially when the matter is to be resolved by you and the seller calling off the sale.

See page 578 for sample wording you can adapt to pin down settlements about money you no longer owe and what the seller owes you.

4. *Prepare Memos Ahead of Time*
Prepare copies of memos ahead of time so they are ready when you need them. Write alternative versions that cover negotiating situations that are most likely to occur when you initially discuss the problem. If you are not sure how the seller will correct the defects, or you are willing to settle for more than one alternative, include wording that covers different acceptable alternatives. You can always cross out the ones that don't apply. If the seller objects to some wording delete it only if you are willing to compromise. Don't be hasty about crossing out wording that refers to your rights or the seller's obligations.

Having memos ready strengthens your bargaining position when you negotiate. Remember, most sellers, especially those who are out to gyp you, are aware of one cardinal rule—the more the buyer pins down in writing when trouble first arises, the more trouble he can make if the seller does nothing about the problem.

5. *Leave Room for Inserts*
Prepare the memos so you can easily add extra pages if necessary. For example, end a page by leaving space to list the defects and then add a blank page where you

can add to the list of points after you have discussed the matter with the seller. You should, of course, cross out any blank spaces that are left.

You should also leave blank spaces at other points in a memo so you can easily insert specific agreements you reach.

The memos and letters that follow in the next two chapters show you how to state specific conditions that you might want to pin down in a particular situation. Since it may not be worthwhile to include them all in a form you prepare for general use, you could write such conditions on cards and carry them with you so they will be on hand when you need to put something in writing.

6. *Date and Number the Pages*

When your memorandum is more than one page long, include the following heading at the top of each page: "Memorandum, the date, page ____ of ____ pages." You can also include the following notation at the bottom of each page: "Continued on page ____."

31 · Negotiating Strategy for Rejecting Goods at the Time of Delivery

STAGE ONE: OPENING SKIRMISHES

The sample letters and memos that follow show how to inform the seller the goods don't conform; state that you are rejecting them (or accepting them with non-conformities, as the case may be); and pin down what the seller agrees to do to correct the problem—steps that could be available if delivered goods fail to conform. Alternative paragraphs for stating various conditions that might apply to a situation are included after the basic memo for you to use as necessary. But see page 154 in Chapter 26 for rejecting goods ordered by mail.

In most situations, the delivered goods would, of course, conform so you would have to accept them. But since you can never tell for sure whether the goods actually conform, it could be worthwhile to insist the seller furnish his assurances that the delivered goods conform. A sample memo for getting such assurances is included as part of your opening skirmishes for rejecting goods at the time of delivery since acceptance is the alternative step that happens at this point.

The samples for rejecting goods illustrate what you can do when you purchase more than one product under the same agreement and are either rejecting all of them or only those that don't conform. Naturally, you must adapt the wording to fit your particular purchase, but it would almost always be reasonable to take delivery of conforming goods when the seller gives you his assurances that he will correct defects in the other products. If the seller refuses to do so, however, you would usually be better off rejecting all the goods. There are two reasons for this.

First, if the seller refuses to cooperate, you can expect him to be even less accommodating about taking care of any defects you might discover later. This, in turn, could involve you in a dispute. And second, if you take some of the goods and reject others, you owe the seller part of the amount due. If you pay part of the amount due under a contract, when you could have avoided paying the entire amount, by rejecting all the goods, you give up some of your economic bargaining leverage. Part payment may also make it harder to clarify the remaining rights and obligations each side has, especially if you financed the purchase under the same credit agreement.

If you buy goods on credit, check Chapter 62 for when and how to withhold payments and steps you should at least be prepared to take which can help you counter a seller's and/or creditor's attempt to repossess the goods or otherwise to claim you are breaking the contract by rejecting the goods.

Although you would not necessarily have to state everything included in these samples, remember that the more clearly you nail things down when you negotiate with the seller, the more you strengthen your bargaining position if something goes wrong later.

PINNING DOWN SELLER'S ASSURANCES PRODUCT CONFORMS

Even if nothing seems to be wrong with the product the seller delivers, it can still be worthwhile to pin down the seller's assurances the product conforms. If the product later proves defective, this will help you demonstrate you received and accepted it under conditions that entitle you to revoke acceptance (see Chapter 33 for a buyer's revocation of acceptance remedy).

While it would obviously be absurd to do this with each purchase you make, you should do it when buying a costly or technically complicated product. It is especially important if the seller insists you sign a delivery receipt that states you are *accepting* the product. Remember that when you do this, you are indicating the product conforms to your contract.

Here's how to pin down the seller's assurances that the product conforms even if there appears to be nothing wrong with it. Where applicable, use the alternative wording to confirm the product has been properly installed.

June 1, 19___

(TO: Insert your name and address)

We hereby give our assurances that the (identify product) we sold (and delivered

to you today/delivered today under our agreement of April 15, 19___) fully con-

forms to our contract on delivery and that we have (delivered it so it is ready for

normal use/have properly installed it so it is ready for normal use).

By (Signature and title of store representative) (Date)

My acceptance of the product described above is conditioned on these

assurances.

(your signature)   (Date)

- If you purchase the product for special purposes, and the seller told you it would be fit for those purposes, then add the following after the words "normal use": "and for the following specific uses for which it was sold:" (Describe specific uses)
For example, if you purchase a vehicle which the dealer says can pull a 15-foot, 6,000 pound camper-trailer, then describe that special purpose as: "Towing a 15-foot, 6,000 pound camper-trailer."
- If you rely on the seller's judgment that a product is fit for a special purpose, the merchandise will be covered by an implied "warranty of fitness for a particular purpose" (described on page 303). Be sure to get such a warranty in writing if it is part of your deal.
If you have such a warranty but the seller refuses to give his assurances that the delivered product is, in fact, ready to be used for its particular purpose, see page 199 for how to notify the seller you are refusing delivery and demand assurances the product conforms to your contract.

RESERVING RIGHTS WHEN UNABLE TO INSPECT AT TIME OF DELIVERY

There may be times when you are unable to inspect goods at the time of delivery but the seller (or his delivery people) insist you take the goods and even pay on delivery.

This is most likely to happen when a store delivers goods at your home, but could also happen when you are picking the goods up from the seller.

If you are asked to sign anything showing you have taken delivery, make sure you state only that you have "received" rather than that you have "accepted" the goods. If the seller insists you acknowledge "accepting" the goods, insisting on the right to inspect first would be your safest course. But at the very least, insist the seller give his written assurance the product conforms before you acknowledge accepting them.

Following is a sample memo you can adapt to make clear you are reserving all rights when you are unable to inspect at the time of delivery but the seller insists you take delivery and pay.

June 1, 19__

TO: General Department Store
Retail Plaza
Anytown, USA

At your insistence I received (and paid for) the (describe item delivered) which was delivered on (insert date) according to our agreement dated (insert date of agreement   ) but without having an opportunity to inspect it and with a reservation of all my rights.

(Your signature)

(Signature of person who made delivery)

REJECTING GOODS WHEN SELLER AGREES TO SETTLE

Following is a sample memo you can adapt to confirm you are rejecting the goods when you and the seller have also resolved how he is to cure the non-conformities at the time you reject the goods.

PLEASE NOTE THAT ALL DATES, NAMES, ADDRESSES, PRICES, AND SO ON, USED IN THESE MEMOS ARE FOR ILLUSTRATIVE PURPOSES ONLY.

June 1, 19__

TO: ABC Sales Company
Futurama Mall
Anytown, USA

This is to confirm the results of our discussion of June 1 when I informed you that I was rejecting and refusing to take delivery of (all the products/ the following products) that were included in the shipment delivered on June 1 under our agreement of April 15, 19__ , and that I am doing so because the products did not conform to the requirements of our contract.

Upon examining the shipment at the time of delivery, we agreed that the shipment and the following products did not conform to our contract as described below:
(Identify the defective or missing products, and then list what was wrong with each product)

I then accepted the specific assurances you gave me that the defects would be completely corrected as described below and that these products conforming to our agreement will be delivered no later than (June 20, 19__ /the dates specified below)

(Specifically describe how the seller promises to correct the defects. If more than one product is defective, identify each one and describe how each is to be corrected. State the date by which the seller must deliver each product if he cannot do it all by the same date.)

You shall have no further right to cure these defects if the products still fail to conform on delivery or a conforming delivery is not made by the dates stated above.

I am, however, taking delivery of the products which apparently conformed to our agreement of April 15, 19__ , but my doing so is not to be construed as a waiver of any defects that may be revealed by subsequent examination.

Payment is not, however, now due or owing for the rejected goods until the non-conformities are properly cured.

Thank you for promptly resolving this matter so we can satisfactorily complete this transaction.

(Your signature)

(_____ The ABC Sales Company _____)

hereby acknowledges receipt of and agrees to the terms contained in pages _____

to ____ of your memorandum of June 1, 19__.

By (Signature and title of store representative)   (Date)

• When you list each defect, briefly describe how the product did not conform to your agreement. For example, if the company delivered the wrong product, state: "The General Watts freezer that was delivered is an inferior floor sample 19__ Model X200 and not the 19__ Model X700 I purchased."

• If it was defective or faulty, then state: "The General Watts freezer was defective and faulty because (describe the faults you found)."

• "If the product did not include features you ordered, or included ones you did not order, then say, for example: "The General Watts freezer was not equipped with the fresh juice dispenser I ordered," or "The General Watts freezer was equipped with a fresh juice dispenser I did not order."

• Be sure to list all the things that were wrong with the product to show that it did not measure up to the terms of your agreement, or to any written or implied warranties that covered the purchase. If you give the seller a detailed list of defects but omit something that you should have spotted, the omission could prevent you from bringing up the matter later.

• When you specify what you want corrected, clearly describe what the seller agreed to do. For example, if the seller agreed to replace the defective product, state: "The defective (describe product) will be replaced with a conforming product to be delivered by (June 20, 19__.)"

If the seller will repair, adjust or replace defective parts, then state how the seller agreed to correct each defect. For example, "Replace the damaged freezer door with a factory-new part." Or "Install the following new equipment which was ordered but not delivered with the freezer (describe)." Or "Diagnose and make necessary repairs and adjustments to correct these malfunctions (describe)." Or "Make necessary repairs and adjustments to correct these defects (describe)."

- Leave a blank space above the last paragraph where you could mention other points, such as canceling part of the order if the seller cannot deliver a replacement for some of the defective products within a reasonable time. You could state it like this: "We agreed to cancel the sale of (describe product) which was made as part of our agreement of April 15, 19__ and to deduct its $ _____ purchase price from the $ _____ balance that would have been due under that agreement."

- If you agree to take a product with some defects while rejecting others that don't conform, then state: "I will take delivery of (describe product) with the following defects (describe defects you are willing to ignore) and shall receive an allowance of $ _____ which (shall be deducted from the $ _____ purchase price still due under our agreement/which shall be credited to my Credit Master Account, number 000-0000-00, as of April 15, 19__, when it was charged to the account). My willingness to take the product with these defects is not to be construed as a waiver of defects that may be revealed by subsequent examination."

Since you are really accepting a product with defects that you are willing to ignore, specifically describe those defects so the seller can't claim you had also agreed to ignore other defects you might discover later.

- If the seller assures you that some of the things you noticed were not really defects, include the following paragraph to pin down his assurances:

"This is also to confirm I informed you that the following products seemingly failed to conform to our contract as described below:

(identify products and describe apparent defects)

But at your insistence, I agreed to take delivery of these products with the apparent defects but only because of your specific assurances that the products were not, in fact, defective and fully conformed to our contract despite the apparent defects I described. I am, however, doing so while reserving all my rights."

- If there is a possibility of your having to hold up payment until the seller cures, include the wording making clear you don't owe the money when payment isn't due under your agreement until after delivery. If the seller insists you are to pay but you don't want to trigger an immediate dispute about it, you could instead adapt the following wording to make clear you are paying while reserving your rights: "I am, at your insistence, paying as would otherwise be due but am doing so while reserving all rights."

- If you purchased only one product or a set which you would have to treat as one unit, change the first paragraph as follows:

"This is to confirm the results of our discussion of June 1 when I informed you that I was rejecting and refusing to take delivery of the/set of (describe product or set) which was delivered on June 1, 19__, under our agreement of April 15, 19__, and that I am doing so because it failed to conform to the requirements of our contract."

You should similarly alter the rest of the wording to make it fit the purchase of only one product.

TAKING DELIVERY OF GOODS SELLER PROMISES TO CORRECT LATER

Here is a sample memorandum you could adapt if you take delivery of a defective product which the seller promises to fix later. It should significantly strengthen your position to reject the goods later or to revoke acceptance if necessary.

June 1, 19__

TO: *ABC Sales Company*
Futurama Mall
Anytown, USA

This is to confirm the results of our discussion today when, at your insistence, I consented to take delivery of the products delivered on June 1, 19___, under our agreement of April 15, 19___, even though the (identify the defective or missing products) which were to be delivered under this agreement (seemingly failed and also) did not conform to the requirements of our contract as described below.

Upon examining the shipment at the time of delivery, we agreed that the following products failed to conform to our contract as follows: (Identify the defective or missing products and describe what was wrong with each one)

I consented to take delivery of the products which failed to conform to our contract but only because of the specific assurances you gave that the defects (and the incomplete delivery) will be completely cured as described below no later than (June 20, 19___ /the dates specified below): (Specifically describe how the seller will correct the defects)

My willingness to take delivery of the products which do not conform to our contract and to make payments as due is specifically conditioned on your assurances that the defects described above will be promptly and fully cured, and is not to be construed as an acceptance, or waiver of any rights, or waiver of any defects that may be revealed by subsequent examination.

I also informed you that the following products seemingly failed to conform to our contract as described below: (Identify products and describe seeming defects)

At your insistence, I consented to take delivery of the products with those seeming defects but only because of your specific assurances that the products were not, in fact, defective and fully conformed to our contract despite the seeming defects I described. I am, however, doing so while reserving all my rights.

Thank you for resolving this matter so we can satisfactorily complete this transaction.

_____

(Your signature)

(<u>The ABC Sales Company</u>) hereby acknowledges receipt of and agrees to the

conditions stated on pages ____ to ____ of your memorandum of June 1, 19___.

By <u>(Signature and title of store representative)</u>

<u>(Date)</u>

• If the seller agrees to correct the defects in a way that would be satisfactory but he doesn't want to agree to the conditions stated in the above memorandum, insist that he cure the defects before you actually take delivery. But to avoid a dispute if you are willing to take the goods while waiting for the seller to cure, you might prepare two versions of the memorandum. On one of them, simply change the statement you would ask the seller to sign.

The ABC Sales Company

_____

hereby acknowledges receipt of your memorandum of June 1, 19___.

By <u>(Signature and title of store representative)</u>   (Date)

If the seller refuses even to acknowledge receipt of the memorandum, however, then insist the store correct the defects before you take delivery and use the first version of the form to reject the goods and pin down how the seller will correct the defects.

By clearly spelling out the conditions under which you are still willing to go ahead and take delivery in such a situation, you strengthen your position to hold the seller to them—especially when you can show he was aware of the defects when he delivered the goods.

AGREEING TO KEEP FAULTY GOODS

If the products are defective in minor ways that you are willing to ignore, here is a memorandum you could use to make clear you are ignoring only the defects you specifically describe and which you knew about when you received the product. By doing this, you strengthen your position to hold the seller responsible for other defects that may appear later.

June 1, 19__

TO: *ABC Sales Company*
Futurama Mall
Anytown, USA

This is to inform you that I am taking delivery of the products you delivered on June 1, 19__ , under our agreement of April 15, 19__ , even though the (identify defective products) included in the shipment did not conform to the requirements of our contract as described below:
(Identify products and describe defects you are willing to overlook)
    But my willingness to take these products with these defects is not to be construed as a waiver of any other defects that may be revealed by subsequent examination.
    I am also informing you that the following products seemingly failed to conform to our contract as described below:
(Identify products and describe seeming defects)
    I agreed to take delivery of these products with these seeming defects but only because of your specific assurances that the products were not, in fact, defective and fully conformed to our contract despite the seeming defects I have described. I am, however, doing so while reserving all my rights.

———————————————
(Your signature)

(The ABC Sales Company) hereby acknowledges receipt of your memorandum of June 1, 19__ , (and confirms it gave the assurances described in it). We also confirm we have granted you an allowance of $ _____ which (shall be deducted from the $ _____ amount still due under the agreement of April 15, 19__ /which shall be credited to your Money Master Account, number 000-0000-00, as of June 1, 19__).

By: __(Name and title of store representative)__   *(Date)*

AGREEING TO CANCEL AN AGREEMENT

You and the seller may, of course, also agree to cancel the transaction if the problem can't be corrected in a reasonable time. Either insist on an immediate cash refund, or a written credit memo for any payments you have made, or a note in writing stating how and when your money will be refunded.

If you signed a written agreement be sure to get the cancellation confirmed in writing or have the store return the original and all copies of the written agreement you signed. (See page 186 for how to cancel an agreement and how to get it confirmed in writing.)

REJECTING GOODS WHEN YOU ARE UNABLE TO DISCUSS A SETTLEMENT

You cannot, of course, negotiate a settlement when you find that goods a store delivers to your home do not conform. You have one of two choices. Either reject the goods, refuse delivery and insist the delivery people take the goods back, or take the goods and work out a settlement later.

If you decide to reject and refuse delivery, use the memo on page 194 to notify the seller and have the delivery person sign it. If you haven't prepared a memo in advance, then write the following statement on the invoice, receipt, or delivery slip, and ask the delivery person to sign it:

"This is to notify you I am today rejecting and refusing delivery of these products because they do not conform to our contract as described below: (describe the defects)

      (Your signature)   (Date)

Receipt acknowledged by: (Delivery person's signature)   (Date)

Have a piece of carbon paper handy and make a copy of the statement for yourself.

If you take delivery and pay for the product, even though it doesn't conform, you can adapt the following memo to identify the defects and to reserve your rights. Also ask the delivery people to confirm that the store will take care of the defects.

June 1, 19__

*TO: General Department Store
Retail Plaza
Anytown, USA*

*At your insistence I received (and paid for) the (describe item delivered) identified on your invoice number (_____) and delivered on (insert date) pursuant to our agreement dated (insert date) but am hereby notifying you that, when received, the good(s) failed to conform to our agreement as noted below and that I am reserving all my rights.
(List defects) _____*

_____
_____
_____
_____
_____

_____
(Your signature)

_____
(Signature of person making delivery)

In addition to getting the delivery people to sign your memorandum, state on the receipt they ask you to sign: "Received with a reservation of all rights."

Whether you reject the goods, or take delivery of defective goods, promptly return to the store to arrange a settlement.

1. *If you rejected the goods.*

Take a suitable memo with you in order to pin down the seller's assurances to correct the defects. If you and the seller are unable to agree on how he will cure the defective delivery, use the follow-up letter on page 194 to reaffirm your request for his assurances that he will cure the defective delivery. If you took delivery of some of the goods see number two below.

2. *If you took delivery of the goods.*

Treat the matter as explained in Chapter 32 which describes how to reject goods which you discover to be defective after you receive them but before you do anything to accept them.

REJECTING GOODS WHEN THE SELLER REFUSES TO SETTLE

You would use the following memos to reject goods if the seller refuses to correct the problem in a satisfactory way. At this point, you may be faced with the possibility of having to reject and refuse to pay for the goods. Instead of taking this step on the spur of the moment, tell the seller you would like a few days to decide whether or not you will take the product under the conditions he states.

If the seller is at all reasonable, he should be willing to do this, and it will give you a chance to seek legal advice if you wish. It is at this point that an attorney could be most helpful. The extra time will also give the seller a chance to reconsider, since he now knows that you are dissatisfied with his initial proposal.

Before you leave the store, write down all the defects you found and what the seller said he would do to correct them. Also ask the seller to confirm in writing how much time you have to notify him of your decision.

Here is how to get such confirmation.

June 1, 19___

TO: *ABC Sales Company*
Futurama Mall
Anytown, USA

This confirms our discussion of June 1, 19___ , when I informed you that the products delivered today under our agreement of April 15, 19___ , did not conform to our contract. While we were unable to resolve the matter at this time, we agreed that I would have until June 5, 19___ , to notify you of my decision on whether or not I will take delivery of the goods as you proposed.

(Your signature)

Accepted and approved by:
(Signature and title of store representative)   *(Date)*

- If you decide to take the product, then use the sample memorandum on page 186 to notify the seller of the defects and to pin down how the seller will fix them.
- If, after you have considered the matter, you decide to reject the goods, then here is a sample memo to adapt as necessary. Prepare the outline and take it with you to the store.

Since the seller would usually already have offered to correct the defects in ways that are unacceptable to you, this sample includes wording to inform him what would be acceptable. This letter is really a low-keyed warning follow-up step to insist the seller either replace the defective goods or furnish adequate assurances that the repairs he wants to make will be adequate. (Check page 223 for details of this step and page 224 for a sample memo to pin down the seller's assurances.)

June 4, 19___

TO: ABC Sales Company
Futurama Mall
Anytown, USA

This is to notify you that I have decided to reject and to refuse delivery of (all the products/the following products: identify the defective products you are rejecting when you take delivery of those that conform) that were delivered on June 1, 19___ , under our agreement of April 15, 19___ , and that I am doing so because of their failure to conform to the requirements of our contract as I informed you at the time of delivery. I am, however, electing to take delivery of (describe the items you are taking).

Upon examining the products at the time of delivery, I discovered and showed you that the following products failed to conform to the requirements of our contract as described below:
(Identify each product and how it failed to conform)

And although I informed you on June 1 that I was prepared to proceed with our agreement if I received adequate assurances that you would carry out your obligation under our contract to cure the defective delivery of non-conforming goods (I have received no assurances/your proposal to cure the defective delivery by [describe the inadequate corrections the seller wanted to make] is inadequate because [describe how the seller's proposals are inadequate.])

I am, however, still prepared to proceed with our agreement if you will promptly give me adequate assurances that you will cure the defective delivery by delivering replacement products which fully conform to our contract. But to settle this matter promptly, I am also prepared to have you make the repairs and adjustments you proposed if you will give me your assurances that such adjustments and repairs will, in fact fully cure the defects or you will agree to take back the product and replace it or refund its purchase price should the repairs and adjustments prove inadequate.

Please notify me promptly of your intention to cure the defects by fur-

nishing me the assurances I have requested to avoid a complete breach of our agreement.

But as provided by the Uniform Commercial Code, payment for the rejected product(s) is not due or owing unless the non-conforming delivery is adequately cured.

If I promptly receive the adequate assurances I requested, I would, of course, agree to any reasonable additional time needed to cure the non-conforming delivery.

But if I don't receive these assurances so we can promptly resolve this matter, I shall insist on full and complete performance not later than ten days after the delivery date stipulated in our agreement to accommodate you for the five days you granted me to notify you of my decision.

I hope that you will promptly furnish me the assurances I requested so that we may resolve this matter and satisfactorily complete this transaction.

<u>(Your signature)</u>

<u>(The ABC Sales Company)</u> *hereby acknowledges receipt of your memorandum.*

By <u>(Signature and title of store representative)</u>   <u>(Date)</u>

- When you describe why you think the seller's proposal was inadequate, make it clear that you would be left in doubt about whether the product would really conform. You could say, for example: "You refused to assure me that you would deliver a replacement product that fully conformed to our contract for the purchase price stipulated in our agreement." Or "I would be insecure about whether the adjustments and repairs you proposed to make would, in fact, completely cure the substantial defects I have described so that the repaired product would, in fact, fully conform to the requirements of our contract." Or "The repairs and adjustments would leave the product with unacceptably visible damage that would significantly detract from its appearance and reduce its value considerably below what I had agreed to pay for it." Or "The missing equipment which cannot now be installed (or which you cannot deliver) would leave the product unfit for the purpose for which I purchased it."

Since rejecting the product after you have had a chance to think about your decision is obviously a more deliberate step than if you had decided it on the spur of the moment, it puts more pressure on the seller to be accommodating. It shows you are determined to stick with your position.

But when you return to notify the seller of your decision to reject the goods, be prepared to negotiate again. Take with you an additional memorandum to pin down the assurances you requested and the seller's promises to repair the defects.

Prepare a memo that describes the settlement you are willing to accept. To illustrate how to do this, I have revised the memo on page 184 which you would use when a seller agrees to correct defects before you actually take delivery of a product. The revised version includes the optional paragraph discussed on page 186 which refers to defects you are willing to ignore.

If the seller gives you time to think about your decision, you can obviously tailor the wording of the memo to the kinds of settlements you would be willing to accept. You could also use wording from different samples and combine them in this follow-up memorandum so it is specifically tailored to your negotiating situation.

June 5, 19___

TO: *ABC Sales Company*
Futurama Mall
Anytown, USA

This is to confirm our discussion of June 5, 19___ , when I notified you by my memorandum of June 4, 19___ , that I was rejecting the products delivered on June 1, 19___ , and requested your assurances that you intend to cure the defective delivery of non-conforming products.

We have now agreed that, as described in my memorandum of June 4, the products did not conform to the requirements of our contract of April 15, 19___ , when they were delivered on June 1, but that description is not to be construed as a waiver of any defects that may be revealed by subsequent examination.

I then accepted the specific assurances you gave me that these defects will be completely cured as described below and that conforming products will be delivered no later than (June 30, 19___ /the dates specified below) (Leave space to describe the seller's assurances)

I have, however, agreed to keep (describe products) with the following defects (describe defects you are willing to ignore), but I shall receive an allowance of $ _____ which (shall be deducted from the $ _____ still due under our agreement/which shall be credited to my Credit Master Account, number 000-0000-00, as of June 1, 19___) . My willingness to take the products with these defects is not to be construed as a waiver of any defects which may be revealed by subsequent examination.

There shall be no further right to cure the defects if the products still fail to conform on delivery or if a conforming delivery is not made by the dates shown above.

Thank you for resolving this matter promptly so we can satisfactorily complete this transaction.

(Your signature)

(The ABC Sales Company) hereby acknowledges receipt of your memorandum of June 4, 19___ , and affirms its agreement with the conditions stated on pages ____ to ____ of the above memorandum.

By: *(Signature and title of store representative)*   *(Date)*

- You will, of course, have to make an immediate decision on whether or not you will take the defective goods on the seller's terms if he won't give you time to think about your decision. If you decide to take the goods, be sure to use the appropriate memo to note what the seller agrees to do to correct the defects. If you reject the goods because you don't think the seller's proposal to cure the defects is adequate, or he refuses to promise anything to cure the defects, here is a sample memorandum for informing him of your decision.

I suggest that in this situation you use a memorandum which only describes the defects and notifies the seller you are rejecting and payment isn't due. Then immediately write a follow-up letter spelling out what you want the seller to do.

June 1, 19___

TO: *ABC Sales Company*
Futurama Mall
Anytown, USA

This is to notify you that I am rejecting and refusing to take delivery of (all the products/the following products: describe the faulty products you are rejecting when you decide to keep those which conform) that were included in the shipment delivered on June 1 under our agreement of April 15, 19___, and that I am doing so because they failed to conform to the requirements of our contract. I am, however, electing to take delivery of (describe the satisfactory products you are keeping) which were also included in this shipment and which appeared to conform to our contract. My receipt of these items is not to be construed as a waiver of any defects that subsequent examination may reveal.

Upon examining the products at the time of delivery, I discovered and told you that the following products and the shipment failed to conform to the requirements of our contract as described below, but this description is not to be construed as a waiver of defects that may be revealed by subsequent examination:
(Identify the non-conforming products and list what was wrong with each one)

I therefore request that you promptly furnish me adequate assurances that you will carry out your obligation to cure the defective delivery of non-conforming products by the (date) delivery date of our agreement as required by the Uniform Commercial Code.

But as provided by the Uniform Commercial Code, payment for the rejected product(s) is not now due or owing under our agreement unless the non-conforming delivery is adequately cured.

I will appreciate your promptly resolving this matter so that we may still satisfactorily complete this transaction.

_____
(Your signature)

Receipt of the above memorandum acknowledged by:

_____   _____
(Signature and title of store representative)   *(Date)*

Here is a follow-up letter you could send to the store to renew your request for assurances.

100 Witchtree Lane
Anytown, USA

June 2, 19___

Mr. Rip Seller
Manager
ABC Sales Company
Futurama Mall
Anytown, USA

Dear Mr. Seller:

I hereby reaffirm my request for adequate assurances that you will fully cure the defective delivery of non-conforming goods that was made on

June 1, 19___ , and which I rejected for the reasons stated in my memorandum of June 1, 19___ , when we discussed this matter at the time of delivery.

Although I then informed you that I was prepared to proceed with our agreement if I promptly received (adequate assurances you would carry out your obligation under our contract to cure the defective delivery/your assurances the goods fully conformed despite the seeming defects I described), (I received no assurances the defective delivery can and will be cured/your proposal to cure the defective delivery by:) (describe the inadequate corrections the seller wanted you to accept) is inadequate because (say why the seller's proposals are inadequate.)

I am, however, still prepared to proceed with our agreement if you will promptly furnish me adequate assurances that you will cure the defective delivery by delivering a replacement product which fully conforms to our contract. But to settle this matter promptly, I am also prepared to consent to your making the necessary adjustments and repairs that will fully cure the non-conformities if you will give me your assurances that such adjustments and repairs will fully cure the non-conformities I described or that you will take the products back and either replace them or refund their purchase price should the repairs and adjustments prove to be inadequate.

Please notify me promptly of your intention to cure the non-conformities and furnish me the assurances I requested to avoid a complete breach of our contract.

If you do so, I would, of course, agree to any reasonable additional time beyond the delivery date that you may require to cure the defective delivery.

And to settle this matter if you cannot cure the delivery within a reasonable time after the delivery date specified in our agreement, I am prepared to cancel our agreement (with respect to the non-conforming goods)* if you will promptly refund the $ _____ I have paid toward their purchase price and discharge all remaining obligations relating to those purchases under our agreement.

But if I fail to receive adequate assurances that you will correct the defective delivery so it fully conforms to our contract, or should you refuse my proposal for settling this matter, I shall insist on full and complete performance by the (June 20, 19___ /reasonable) delivery date stipulated in our agreement.

I hope you will now promptly resolve this matter as I have proposed so I will not have to hold you responsible for breach of contract and damages at least to the fullest extent provided by the Uniform Commercial Code.

Sincerely,

*(Note: Include this clause only if you elected to take delivery of goods that did conform when you purchased more than one product under an agreement.)

Since the seller has already refused to cooperate, this follow-up letter includes a low-keyed warning that you intend to hold him liable for breaking your agreement should he refuse to correct the defects and give you the assurances you request. As an alternative, the letter includes a proposal to settle the matter by canceling the agreement for a full refund. Of course, if this is not an acceptable settlement for you, then delete the references to it.

Once you have taken the initial steps to reject the goods, you then have to give the seller a chance to correct the defects as he promised, or wait for him to give you the assurances you requested.

If the seller fails to cure the defects as he is obligated to do, then use the low-keyed warning follow-up steps beginning on page 220.

If it later turns out that the product is defective even though the seller gave his assurances there was nothing wrong with it when you took delivery, your follow-up steps would be the ones you would use to reject goods after you have received them or to revoke acceptance. Whether you can still reject or only revoke acceptance depends on how soon you found out the product really was defective.

If you notify the seller that the product is defective but, instead of rejecting it, take and use it when the seller promises to correct the defects later, you must, of course, give the seller an opportunity to correct the defects before you could then reject and/ or revoke acceptance as the case may be and cancel so you could get all your money back.

REJECTING GOODS AT A STORE WHEN YOU DON'T HAVE A PREPARED MEMORANDUM

What if you discover goods are defective at the time of delivery and you don't have a written memorandum on hand for rejecting them? Although a memorandum strengthens your bargaining position, don't panic. Just try to pin down the most important things in writing.

These are the steps you should take in this situation:

● Make a written list of defects.

● If you decide not to take the goods until the defects are cured, inform the seller you are rejecting and refusing to take delivery and pay for the goods.

● If you refuse to take the goods and you reach a settlement on how the seller will cure the defects, ask him to state in writing what he will do and the date by which he will do it.

● If you and the seller can't reach a settlement, ask for his assurances that he will cure the defects.

● If you don't reject and refuse delivery of the goods but take them because the seller promises to fix the defects later, insist he state in writing that he will fix the defects you have listed in writing and ask him to sign the statement.

● If you are unwilling to withhold payment when the seller insists you pay while he cures the defects (which might happen if you reject and refuse delivery but the seller promises to replace or fix the goods later), make clear to the seller you are reserving your rights when you pay. (See page 127 for an explanation of reserving your rights.)

● If the seller agrees to cancel the agreement and refund your money, and that is acceptable to you, have the seller state it in writing.

The easiest way to resolve the situation, of course, would be if you reject and refuse delivery and the seller agrees to cure the defects.

Although you obviously can't get all the details stated in writing in this kind of situation, the more you put in writing the better off you will be. And take notes of what happens during your conversation.

Here is the sort of wording to use when you don't have a prepared memo and must write something quickly on the spur of the moment:

"I am rejecting the following products delivered on June 1, 19___ , under our agreement of April 15, 19___, because the delivery failed to conform to the requirements of our contract as described below:

(Identify the products and describe how they failed to conform.)"

Write the statement on the seller's copy of the agreement, or on the invoice, delivery slip used as a receipt for delivery, or on a separate sheet of paper addressed to the seller. Get a copy for yourself, if possible.

Promptly write a confirming letter detailing what you told the seller and what agreement you reached at the store. Adapt the sample memo on page 190 that you would normally have used at the time of delivery.

A prompt confirming letter puts everything on the record and makes it clear to the seller you plan to hold him to your agreement. It is especially helpful to do this when the seller is unable to correct the defects until some time after the initial delivery.

If you are unable to reach a settlement at the time of delivery, ask the seller for time to make up your mind. If you later decide to reject the goods, notify him of your decision by using the memo on page 191. If the seller won't give you more time, then either reject the goods in writing by using the sample statement on page 196 or at least do so verbally. In either case, you should promptly follow-up by sending the seller a confirming letter.

Following is a sample confirming memo you can adapt for putting on the record steps you took at the time of delivery when you didn't have a memo available for use.

100 Witchtree Lane
Anytown, USA

June 2, 19___

Mr. Rip Seller
Manager
ABC Sales Company
Futurama Mall
Anytown, USA

Dear Mr. Seller:

This confirms (my verbal notice of/the written note I gave you on) June 1, 19___ that I reject and refuse delivery of (all the products/the following products:) that were included in the shipment delivered on June 1 under our agreement of April 15, 19___ , and that I am doing so because they failed to conform to the requirements of our contract. And while I elected to take delivery of (describe products which appeared satisfactory) which were also included in this shipment and which appeared to conform to our contract, my doing so is not to be construed as a waiver of any rights with respect to defects that may be revealed by subsequent examination.

Upon examining the products at the time of delivery, I discovered and showed you that the following products failed to conform to the requirements of our contract as described below, but this description is not to be construed as a waiver of defects that may be revealed by subsequent examination:
(Identify the non-conforming products and list what is wrong with each one.)

Although I then informed you I was prepared to proceed with our agreement if you furnish me (adequate assurances you will promptly carry out your obligation under our contract to cure the defective delivery/your assurances the goods fully conformed despite the seeming defects I described), (I received no assurances the defective delivery can and will be adequately cured/your proposal to cure the defective delivery by: describe the inadequate corrections the seller wanted you to accept) is inadequate because (say why the seller's proposals are inadequate.)

I am, however, still prepared to proceed with our agreement if you will promptly furnish me adequate assurances that you will promptly cure the defective delivery by delivering replacement products which fully conform to our contract. (But to settle this matter promptly, I am also prepared to consent to your making the necessary repairs and adjustments that will fully cure the non-conformities if you will furnish me your assurances such repairs and adjustments will fully cure the non-conformities I have described or you will take the products back and either replace them or refund their purchase price should the repairs and adjustments prove inadequate.)

Please notify me promptly of your intention to cure the non-conformities and furnish the assurances I requested to avoid a complete breach of our contract.

If you promptly do so, I would, of course consent to any reasonable additional time beyond the delivery date that you may require to cure the defective delivery.

And to settle this matter promptly if you cannot cure the defective delivery within a reasonable time after the delivery date specified in our agreement, I am prepared to cancel our agreement (with respect to the non-conforming goods)* if you will promptly refund the $ _____ I have paid toward their purchase price and discharge all remaining obligations relating to those purchases under our agreement.

But as provided by the Uniform Commercial Code, the $ _____ balance remaining for the price is neither due nor owing for the rejected goods unless the defective delivery is adequately cured.

And if I fail to receive adequate assurances that you will cure the defective delivery so it fully conforms to our contract, or should you refuse my alternative proposal for promptly resolving this matter, I shall insist on full and complete performance by the (June 20, 19__ /reasonable) delivery date stipulated in our agreement.

I hope you will now promptly resolve this matter as I have proposed so I will not have to hold you responsible for breach of contract and damages at least to the fullest extent provided by the Uniform Commercial Code.

Sincerely,

*(Include the wording identified by asterisks only if you elected to take delivery of goods that did conform when you purchased more than one product under an agreement.)

DEMANDING ADEQUATE ASSURANCES

If it appears that the product does not conform but you're not absolutely sure, and the seller refuses to confirm that it does conform, you may be undecided about whether to reject the goods. But taking the goods without assurances could prove risky since you might find the product fails to conform once you start using it. It may also happen that a seller tells you a product is fit for a special purpose when you purchase it, but then refuses to confirm it when the product is delivered. A product sold under these circumstances would usually be covered by what is called a warranty of fitness for a particular purpose which is described on page 303.

In this kind of situation, the best you can do is demand that the seller give you assurances the product conforms and to refuse delivery until he does so.

June 1, 19___

TO: *ABC Sales Company*
Futurama Mall
Anytown, USA

This is to notify you I am today refusing delivery of the (describe product) made under our agreement of April 15, 19___ , and requesting that you furnish me adequate assurances that the product in fact conforms to the requirements of our contract, or that you make a conforming delivery should the product in fact not conform to our contract.

(As I informed you on delivery, the product apparently failed to conform to the requirements of our agreement as described below/As I informed you, I could not rely on the product being fit for the special purpose for which I purchased it, when you refused to confirm that the product was in fact fit for the following special purpose:
describe the seeming defects or the special purpose for which you purchased the product which the seller knew about)

Since you have refused to confirm the product does in fact conform to the requirements of our contract or to confirm that you will cure the defects should the product fail to conform, I can no longer rely on your good faith that you have made a conforming delivery.

Please furnish the assurances I have requested within fifteen days or deliver replacements that, in fact, conform to our contract. I would, of course, be prepared to grant you any reasonable additional time you may need to deliver a conforming replacement should you agree to do so.

I am, however, suspending further performance until you furnish adequate assurances or make a conforming delivery.

And to settle this matter promptly, I would also be prepared to cancel our agreement and to waive my claims for damages I may have if you will refund within fifteen days the $ _____ I have already paid toward the purchase price.

I hope you will promptly furnish the assurances I have requested and make a delivery which fully conforms to the requirements of our contract so that we may still satisfactorily complete this transaction.

(Your signature)
_____

Receipt acknowledged by:
(Signature and title of store representative)   *(Date)*

● If the seller refuses to give his assurances, and you found definite signs the product doesn't conform, then reject it and insist the seller cure the problems. If the seller again refuses to confirm the product is, in fact, fit for the special purpose for which he sold it, your follow-up step would be to use your legal remedies to cancel the agreement and demand your money back.

If on delivery you had refused to accept and pay for the product until the seller gave the assurances you demanded, he could claim that you had broken the agreement. But the seller's refusal to confirm that the product conforms to your contract or to cure seeming defects significantly weakens his bargaining position to hold you to the agreement, particularly if he refuses to confirm that the product was really fit for a special purpose for which he sold it. And if you are determined to hold up payment, then make clear to the seller you are suspending performance.

A seller's refusal to give his assurances that the product being delivered is really fit for the special purpose for which he sold it or that the product conforms even though you have spotted what may be significant defects is an almost sure sign that something is wrong. Insisting the seller furnish his assurances and suspending performance until he does is the way to put the issue to a test without getting and using the product then finding out later it doesn't conform. Remember, a seller's refusal to furnish adequate assurances when you have reasonable grounds to ask for them can then help you hold the seller accountable for breaching the contract.

TAKING DELIVERY OF REJECTED GOODS THE SELLER REPAIRS

When you take delivery of goods the seller repairs after you have rejected them, then get the seller's assurances that repairs have adequately corrected the defects.

Here is a simple notice you can use to pin down the seller's assurances at the time of delivery, or which you can send later as a confirming memo.

June 18, 19__

> TO: *ABC Sales Company*
> *Futurama Mall*
> *Anytown, USA*

> *This is to (inform you that I am, today, taking/confirm that I informed you on June 18 when I took) delivery of the (identify product) which I had rejected on June 1, 19__ , because it failed to conform to our agreement of April 15, 19__ . But I am (doing/did) so only because of your assurances that the defects you were to repair have in fact been cured so the product now conforms to our contract.*

> *My receipt of the product is specifically conditioned on those assurances and is not to be construed as a waiver of any defects that may be revealed by subsequent examination.*

(Your signature)
_____

> *Received and acknowledged by:*

(Signature and title of store representative)   *(Date)*

• The seller should be willing to confirm that the repairs are adequate. But if he refuses, you could increase the pressure by telling him you will refuse to take delivery or to pay for the rejected goods unless he gives you his assurances or replaces the product.

To avoid a confrontation with the seller, if he at least gives you his verbal assurances, send the above memo as a confirming letter.

• If he does not give you assurances, here is a low-keyed warning for demanding them. Since taking this step could immediately bring about a dispute, see page 223 where I discuss the low-keyed warning for demanding adequate assurances from the seller.

June 18, 19___

TO: *ABC Sales Company*
Futurama Mall
Anytown, USA

This is to notify you that I am today refusing your delivery of the (iden-tify product) which I had rejected because of the substantial defects described in my memorandum of June 1, 19___. I am refusing the product because of your refusal to furnish, on delivery, adequate assurances that the repairs you were to make will in fact cure the defects.

While I had agreed to your proposal to repair the product rather than insist that you deliver a conforming replacement, I then also requested, in writing, that you furnish me your assurances that the repairs would, in fact, adequately fix the product so it would conform to our contract.

When you returned the repaired goods, I again asked for assurances that the repairs had adequately corrected the defects, but you refused to give them to me.

Since you refused to furnish the assurances I requested to confirm that the product conforms to our contract, I can no longer rely on your good faith that the repairs have cured the defects.

And as provided by the Uniform Commercial Code, the $ _____ bal-ance of the price is neither due nor owing until you furnish the assurances and carry out your obligation to cure the defective delivery I have rejected.

If you fail to furnish the assurances I have requested and carry out your obligation to cure the defective delivery by replacing it with a prod-uct that fully conforms to our contract, to settle this matter promptly, I am prepared to cancel our agreement for a full refund of the ($ _____) I have already paid.

But if you fail to furnish the assurances I have requested or if you refuse the alternatives I have proposed for resolving this matter, I shall hold you responsible for breaching our contract and for any damages I sustain as a result.

I will appreciate you giving this matter your prompt attention so that we can still satisfactorily complete this transaction.

(Your signature)
_____

Receipt acknowledged by:

_____   _____
(Signature and title of store representative)   *(Date)*

FOLLOW-UP STEPS IF SELLER FAILS TO CURE

If the repairs and adjustments correct the defects or the seller furnishes a conforming replacement as promised, your problems are usually solved. But what if the repairs or adjustments don't do the job, the non-conformities aren't corrected when the seller again tries to deliver the product, or the seller fails to cure within the time he has?

To strengthen your bargaining position, you could then take the appropriate low-keyed warning follow-up steps beginning on page 220 in Chapter 32.

If you purchased the goods on credit from the seller, check Section VII about whether you could be entitled to withhold payment under the credit agreement involved before you take any steps that would call for you to withhold payment. And if you are determined to withhold payment when you could be entitled to do so, be sure to take any further steps that may be necessary to deal with any separate creditor who may be involved as explained in Section VII.

32 · Negotiating Strategy for Rejecting Goods After Delivery

STAGE ONE: OPENING SKIRMISHES

When you reject goods after you have received them you must either convince the seller to take them back or permit the seller to correct what's wrong by making repairs or adjustments.

The following sample letters and memos illustrate how to notify the seller that the goods do not conform, that you are rejecting them, and how to pin down a settlement in various situations that may apply.

REJECTING GOODS WHEN THE SELLER AGREES TO SETTLE

When you inform a seller that you are rejecting goods because of defects and he agrees to correct the problem, write a confirming memo which spells out the settlement you reach.

The sample confirming memo that follows includes alternative wording in brackets so you can easily adapt it to your own circumstances. Be sure to omit wording that doesn't apply. The sample includes wording describing different settlements which you can adapt to suit your needs.

Since you prepare the memo in advance, either leave space so you can later fill in the resolution or include wording describing different settlements that could be acceptable. Cross out the ones that don't apply when you actually reach a settlement at the store. For example, you might include the alternative about keeping the product with some defects if the seller should offer you a price reduction then cross it out if you reach a different settlement. (Also be sure to adapt sample wording for describing what happened. For example, if you already notified the seller about nonconformities but discover others later, adapt the wording to refer to all defects. You could do this by simply combining the alternative wording included in the second paragraph in parenthesis with the first part of the paragraph. In that case, the wording would be " . . . as described below and as I have already described . . .")

June 3, 19—

TO: ABC Sales Company
Futurama Mall
Anytown, USA

This is to confirm the results of our discussion of (today/ or give date) when (as had been suggested by Mr. Helper during our telephone conversation of June 2), I returned the set of (identify defective products or set) which failed to conform to the requirements of our contract. I purchased and received the set on June 1, 19—, as shown on the attached sales receipt. (The set was delivered on June 1, 19—, under our agreement of April 15, 19—.)

We agreed today that the set failed to conform to the requirements of our contract at the time of delivery as described below (OR: as I have already described in my memorandum of June 1, but with such exceptions as are noted below). This description is not to be taken as a waiver of defects that may be revealed by subsequent examination: (Leave space to identify defective product and describe the defects the seller later confirms exist, or, if you have already furnished a list of defects the seller hasn't yet confirmed, leave space to identify the ones you have already described which the seller insists aren't defects.)

I accepted your assurances that the following defects will be completely cured as described below and that these conforming products will be delivered no later than (June 20, 19___ /the dates specified below):
(Leave space to describe how the seller promises to correct the defects you agreed to: see page 185 for how to pin down the seller's promises to correct defects)

We have also agreed that no further payments shall be due for the defective goods until the defects have been satisfactorily corrected. And there shall be no further right to cure these defects should your attempt to cure them prove to be inadequate or if a conforming delivery is not made by the dates stated above.

I have, however agreed to keep the following products with the defects noted below, and shall receive an allowance of $ _____ which (shall be deducted from the purchase price still due under our agreement/shall be credited to my Credit MasterAccount, number 000-0000-00). My willingness to keep these products with these defects is not to be construed as a waiver of defects that may be revealed by subsequent examination.
(Leave space to describe defects you are willing to ignore.)

I am also informing you that (As I had already described in my memorandum of June 1, 19___) the following products apparently failed to conform to the requirements of our contract as described below:
(Describe the apparent defects which the seller assured you were not really defects)

At your insistence, I consented to keep these products only because of your specific assurances that the products were not, in fact, defective and fully conformed to our contract. I am, however, doing so while reserving all my rights.

Thank you for giving this matter your prompt attention so that we can satisfactorily complete this transaction.

_____
(Your signature)

(The ABC Sales Company) acknowledges receipt of and agrees to the terms stated on pages ____ through ____ of the above memorandum of June 3, 19___.

By *(Signature and title of store representative)*   *(Date)*

When you know a seller is willing to settle, but don't know the terms to which he will commit himself, adapt the following kind of memo as an alternative to the one included above. In this case, the wording for pinning down the seller's promises to correct the defects should be included after your signature.

June 3, 19___

TO: *ABC Sales Company*
Futurama Mall
Anytown, USA

As suggested by Mr. Helper during our telephone conversation of June 2, I am returning the (identify defective products or set) which I purchased and (received on June 1, 19___ , as shown on the attached copy of my sales receipt/was delivered on June 1, 19___ , under our agreement of April 15, 19___). I am also rejecting them because they do not conform to the requirements of our contract.

Upon examining the products (on June 2/at the time of delivery on June 1) I discovered that they (apparently) failed to conform to the requirements of our contract as described below (as I have already described in my memorandum of June 1, 19___), but the description is not to be construed as a waiver of defects that may be revealed by subsequent examination:
(Identify the defective products and list what was wrong with each one if you have not already done so at the time of delivery)
Please cure the defective delivery of non-conforming products by replacing them with products that fully conform to the requirements of our contract so that we may still satisfactorily complete this transaction.

But as provided by the Uniform Commercial Code, the $ _____ (balance of the) price for the products I am rejecting is neither due nor owing until you carry out your obligation to cure the defective delivery. (I am, therefore, stopping payment on my check #000 for $ _____ which I gave you on June 1, 19___ , and will now pay when payment is due upon your having performed your obligation to cure the non-conforming delivery.)

I will appreciate you giving this matter your immediate attention so we can resolve it and still satisfactorily complete our transaction.

_____
(Your signature)

June 3, 19___

TO: *Your name*

(_____The ABC Sales Company_____ *) acknowledges receipt of the*
above memorandum.

We accept the return of the following rejected goods and will replace them with goods that conform to the contract. We shall deliver the replacement goods not later than June 20, 19___ , at (our place of business/ FOB your address).
(Leave space to identify products that will be replaced)
We shall make the repairs and adjustments required to cure the defects noted below and give our assurances that these adjustments and repairs will fully cure those defects.
(Leave space to identify the products and defects to be cured)
We give our assurances that the following products fully conform to

*our agreement of June 1, 19___, despite the seeming defects noted below
which you described in your memorandum.*

*(Leave space to identify the products and to list the seeming defects
when the seller claims the product still conforms. And leave space to
include other things you might agree to, such as an allowance to be
deducted from the purchase price.)*

By: *(Signature and title of store representative)*   *(Date)*

Consider the following points when you choose the wording of these memos.

- If you are sure the product is defective, say so and state you are rejecting it to make the issue clear. But you could omit the phrase with a seller you *know* to be reliable if you expect him to exchange the product without any problems. You could also omit the phrase if you told the seller about the defects at the time of delivery but received the goods anyway because you were told the defects would be corrected.

- If you are unsure about whether the product is defective, you could avoid adopting an inflexible position by referring only to the apparent defects and omitting the phrase about rejecting the goods. If the seller claims the product conforms, you still have a written statement if something goes wrong later. If the seller refuses to confirm the product doesn't conform or to assure you that it conforms when something seems to be wrong, be prepared to reject the goods by acting as though the seller refused to cure, or else demand the seller's assurances the goods conform.

- If the seller promises to cure the defects after you have paid, consider stopping payments you have already made and withholding further payments. Since such a step questions the seller's sincerity, and he may still be accommodating, ask him pleasantly to agree that you will withhold payment until the defects are cured. You could also prepare two versions of the memo, one with and one without the paragraph about withholding payments.

If you have used a check that also covers payment for goods you are keeping, don't stop payment on the check unless you make arrangements for immediate payment for the goods you keep. Either give the seller another check, or be prepared to pay cash. (Remember, a seller is not required to take a check in payment, and if you stop payment on one check, he may not accept another one from you.)

- If you purchased the goods under a credit agreement, see Chapter 62.

If a seller promptly agrees to cure non-conformities, it can sometimes be difficult or awkward to put in writing any conditions for keeping the product based on the seller's promises or assurances to cure. In situations like this, you could verbally inform the seller about the conditions under which you will consent to keep the nonconforming product and then confirm it in writing as a follow-up step. Following is a sample letter you can adapt for confirming such conditions. The sample includes alternative paragraphs in parentheses for describing various conditions so use only the ones that apply.

100 Witchtree Lane
Anytown, USA

June 5, 19___

Mr. John Seller
Manager
ABC Sales Company
Futurama Mall
Anytown, USA

Dear Mr. Seller:

Thank you for promptly giving the assurances I requested on June 3, 19___ , when I returned the apparently defective products that had recently been delivered to me.

Since I have consented to keep the (identify the product) when you assured me that it fully conformed to our agreement of June 1, 19___ , despite the apparent defects I described to you, I am reaffirming that I have done so only on the basis of your assurances while reserving all my rights.

(Since I have consented to keep the [identify product] despite the defects noted below when you gave me a $ _____ allowance toward the purchase price, I am reaffirming that my willingness to keep the product with the defects noted below is not to be construed as a waiver of any other defects that may be revealed by subsequent examination.)
(Identify defects you agreed to overlook)

(Since you have assured me that the adjustments and repairs you will make will correct the defects so the [identify the product], as repaired, will fully conform to our contract, I am reaffirming that my willingness to keep the product after it has been repaired is not to be construed as a waiver of any other defects that may be revealed by subsequent examination, nor as a waiver of any rights should the repairs prove inadequate.)

I hope this matter is now fully resolved so that we may satisfactorily complete our transaction of June 1, 19___ .

Sincerely,

There may be situations when you are unable to return the defective product: it might be a heavy piece of furniture, for instance. Since you can't show how it is defective when you first discuss the matter with the seller, and he won't make any commitments to correct the defects until he has examined the product, your first step is to arrange for the seller either to pick up the goods or to examine them in your home. Following is a sample memo you can adapt in these circumstances. The sample memo again includes alternative wording in brackets to cover different situations, so use only the wording that applies and adapt it as required by your specific situation.

June 4, 19___

TO: ABC Sales Company
Futurama Mall
Anytown, USA

I am hereby notifying you that (OR: As I have already informed you at the time of delivery by my memorandum of June 1, 19___/As I informed Mr. Helper by telephone on June 2 when we made arrangements for you to pick up the product at my home on June 3), the (identify products) which I purchased and received on June 1, 19___ , as shown on the attached copy of my sales receipt (was delivered on June 1 under our agreement of April 15, 19___,) (apparently) does not conform to the requirements of our contract. I am also notifying you that I am therefore rejecting it.

Upon examining the product on June 2, 19___ (at the time of delivery), I discovered that it (apparently) failed to conform to the requirements of our contract as described below: (as I described in my memorandum of

June 1 when I also informed you I received (and paid for) the product despite the defects only because I was assured the defects would be cured). (Identify defective products and list what was wrong with each one if you have not already done so at the time of delivery)

(Please make arrangements to pick up or examine the defective product at my home at your earliest convenience and/Since you have already picked up the product on June 3, please) furnish me adequate assurances that you will carry out your obligation to cure this defective delivery of a non-conforming product (by delivering a replacement which fully conforms to our contract) so that we may promptly settle this matter and satisfactorily complete our transaction.

I am, however, only storing the product for you until it is picked up and my doing so is not to be construed as acceptance.

And as provided by the Uniform Commercial Code, the $ _____ (balance of the) price for the goods I am rejecting is neither due nor owing until you carry out your obligation to cure the defective delivery of a non-conforming product. (I am, therefore, stopping payment on check # 000 for the $ _____ which I gave you in payment on June 1, 19__ , and I shall now pay when payment is due upon your having performed your obligation to cure the non-conforming delivery.)

I will appreciate you giving this matter your prompt attention so that we may resolve it and still satisfactorily complete this transaction.

_____
(Your signature)

(_____The ABC Sales Company_____) *acknowledges receipt of the above memorandum.*

(Leave space to write when the seller promises to pick up or examine the product and when he promises to tell you what he will do to fix it.)

By _(Signature and title of store representative)_   _(Date)_

• See the comments on page 206 about selecting the wording included in the memo. But remember that in this situation the seller has not yet promised anything about curing the defects. Thus it is more reasonable to hold up further payment, or even to stop payment on a check, while you wait for him to tell you whether he will cure the defects. This prevents the seller from ignoring his promises to pick up the defective product, or examine it in your home, so you are unable to work out a settlement.

• If the seller examines the product as promised and cures the defects to your satisfaction, the problem is settled. If he promises to cure the defects later, use the wording for the seller's response on page 205 as a guide to pinning down his assurances. And then use the follow-up letter on page 188 to pin down the appropriate conditions under which you agree to keep the product.

REJECTING GOODS WHEN THE SELLER REFUSES TO SETTLE

If you are unable to reach a settlement because the seller refuses to cure the defects, or refuses to pick up the product or examine it in your home, adapt the sample memos which follow page 209 to tell him the product doesn't conform, notify him you are rejecting it, and insist he take back the rejected goods and adequately cure the non-conforming delivery. To be safe, make clear that you are rejecting before you actually give the goods back. This puts the seller on notice that you consider the problem serious. He might refuse to take the goods back since his acceptance could thereby acknowledge you have rightfully rejected them. If this happens, getting the seller to take back the rejected goods is the important first step in resolving the matter.

Keep in mind, however, that if you already know the seller is unwilling to take action, rejecting the goods and insisting that the seller cure could eventually lead to legal action. So before you take that step decide whether rejection is the course you want to take. Remember that it is risky to reject goods after receiving them since you might, in the meantime, be considered to have accepted them. So unless you act on legal advice reject goods you have received *only* if they substantially fail to conform and curing by repairs would clearly be inadequate.

If you have paid something for the goods, you have a security interest in them. If the seller agrees to cure, you would then, of course, also arrange for the return of the goods. But if the seller refuses or fails to cure, you would not be required to hand the goods back until he returns what you have paid.

If you have not paid for the goods, you must give them back to the seller when he is ready to take them once you have announced you are rejecting them. You obviously haven't paid anything if you haven't given the seller any money. But you also haven't paid if you stop payment on a check or if you are still entitled to withhold repayment of the entire amount under a credit arrangement. The most likely situation in which the latter could happen is if you charged a purchase with a credit card and you successfully avoid having to repay by using the rights available under the Fair Credit Billing Act (see page 470 and page 482). If you could avoid having to repay the entire amount, to be safe, handle the goods as though you had not paid anything for them when rejecting them. You should then immediately take steps for asserting rights based on protections available under the relevant credit laws described in Section VII.

The following sample is for situations in which you have already paid the seller something for the product. The paragraphs are numbered only to illustrate how to revise the wording for different situations.

The sample also includes wording to tell the seller of specific damages you might be entitled to recover. Telling the seller about damages you sustained can help you should it come to legal action. You cannot, however, expect a seller to pay such damages unless you force the issue by suing. The sample letter assumes that you are willing to forget about holding the seller accountable for damages if he adequately cures what's wrong. Be sure to note that the wording about damages included in the sample letter is *only* for situations in which you can afford to forget about the damages. (See page 213 for more details about using this wording or omitting it entirely and for alternative wording you could adapt for some situations in which you might insist a seller reimburse you for damages even if he otherwise adequately cures what's wrong.)

REJECTING GOODS FOR WHICH YOU HAVE PAID

June 4, 19___

TO: ABC Sales Company
Futurama Mall
Anytown, USA

(1) This (is to notify you/confirms the verbal notice I gave you on June 3, 19___ that) I am rejecting the (describe the goods) that (I purchased and received on June 1, 19___, as shown on the attached copy of the sales

receipt/was delivered on June 1, 19___ , under our agreement of April 15, 19___). I am doing so because they failed to conform to the requirements of our contract. (I am also hereby notifying you of the damages I sustained because of their failure to conform.)

(2) Upon examining the products on June 2, I discovered that they failed to conform to the requirements of our contract as described below, but the description is not a waiver of defects that may be revealed by subsequent examination:
(Identify the non-conforming products and list how each failed to conform.)

(3) And as described below, there is also due at least $ _____ for damages I have already sustained because the products failed to conform. (Describe and give the amounts for damages you sustained.)

(4) I request that you therefore promptly carry out your obligation to cure the non-conforming delivery by replacing the rejected products with ones that fully conform to our contract (or by an acceptable alternative cure which you assure me will make the products fully conform to our contract) and that you promptly furnish me your assurances you will make a conforming delivery so that we can still satisfactorily complete this transaction. I also request that you promptly arrange for the return of the rejected goods or furnish me your instructions for returning them at your expense and risk. (ALTERNATIVELY, adapt the following wording in place of the previous sentence depending on whether the goods were returned if you want to confirm that you have verbally rejected them: Since you refused to take the product back (refused to make arrangements for examining and picking the product up at my home) when I verbally notified you on June 3 that I was rejecting them, I now again request that you promptly arrange for the return of the rejected goods or furnish me your instructions for returning them at your expense and risk./ Since the rejected products were returned on June 3, I expect that a conforming delivery will be promptly made.)

(5) But as provided by the Uniform Commercial Code, the $ _____ (balance of the) price of the products I have rejected is neither due nor owing until you carry out your obligation to cure the defective delivery of non-conforming products. (I am, therefore, stopping payment on my check #000 for $ _____ which I gave you as partial payment on June 1, 19___ , but) I shall, of course, pay as required upon your having performed your obligation to cure the non-conforming delivery.

(6) And while I am prepared to grant you any reasonable additional time beyond the delivery date in our contract which you may require to cure the non-conforming delivery, I shall insist on strict performance should you fail to give me your assurances. (I do, however, require that the non-conforming delivery be promptly cured since being deprived of the use of the products is causing me great inconvenience [and additional expense for (describe expense involved)].) (I am also prepared to waive claims for damages I have thus far sustained if the non-conforming delivery is promptly and adequately cured.)

(7) In the meantime, however, I am only storing the rejected products for you pending appropriate arrangements for their return. But as provided by the Uniform Commercial Code, I also have a security interest in the products for at least the $ _____ I have already paid on (date) toward their price should you fail to carry out your obligation to cure the non-conforming delivery.

(8) And to resolve this matter promptly should you be unable to cure

the non-conforming delivery, I am prepared to do so for the prompt return of the $ _____ I have already paid and the discharge of any remaining obligations under the agreement with respect to the rejected goods. Upon the refund of moneys I have paid, I would, of course, have the rejected goods available for you to pick up (and would waive my claims for damages).

(9) Please notify me promptly that you intend to cure the non-conforming delivery and furnish me the assurances I have requested so that we can still satisfactorily complete this transaction or promptly resolve this matter as I have otherwise proposed so that I do not have to hold you fully responsible for breaching our contract by compelling me to cancel and hold you liable for all damages.

(10) I will appreciate your giving this matter your immediate attention so that you can still resolve it and satisfactorily complete our transaction.

(Your signature)

Receipt acknowledged by:
(Signature and title of store representative)   *(Date)*

ALTERNATIVE WORDING WHEN YOU TOOK DELIVERY OF GOODS THAT DIDN'T CONFORM

As previously explained, there may be times when goods delivered at your home fail to conform but you receive them anyway because you are told the seller will correct what's wrong.

You should put in writing how the goods you received failed to conform on delivery and make clear that you are receiving them only on the expectation that the seller would adequately cure. If he then refuses to cure, you have additional leverage for holding him accountable. It could now be worthwhile to put his refusal to cure on the record.

You could do so by adapting the above sample memo as illustrated below:

Replace paragraph (2) of the sample memo with the following one:

(2) *"Upon examining the product at the time of delivery on June 1, I discovered it failed to conform to the requirements of our contract as I already described in my memorandum of June 1 when I notified you of the defects at the time of delivery and informed you I received (and paid for) the product despite its defects and only because of assurances the defects would be promptly and adequately cured."*

Add the following paragraph (3A) after paragraph (3) of the sample memo:

(3A) *"But when I first discussed this matter with you on June 4, you refused (to furnish me any assurances you would cure the non-conforming delivery/to make arrangements for examining and picking up the product at my home or to furnish any assurances you would cure the non-conforming delivery). (ALTERNATIVELY, if the seller's proposal for curing was inadequate, adapt the following wording: your proposal for curing the non-conforming delivery by [insert inadequate steps seller wanted to take] are inadequate because [state reason why they were inadequate].)"*

Keep the other paragraphs of the sample memo to the extent they apply to your situation, and adapt the wording as appropriate.

REJECTING GOODS FOR WHICH YOU HAVEN'T PAID

If you have not paid anything for the product, revise the wording of the basic memo on page 209 as follows:

Keep paragraphs (1), (2), and (3) if they apply.

Replace paragraphs (4) through (10) with the following ones:

> *"I request that you, therefore, promptly carry out your obligation to cure the non-conforming delivery by replacing the rejected products with ones that conform to our contract (or by an acceptable alternative cure which you assure me will make the products fully conform to our contract) and that you promptly furnish me your assurances that you will make a conforming delivery so that we can still satisfactorily complete this transaction.*
>
> *"But as provided by the Uniform Commercial Code, the $_____ price of the products I have rejected is neither due nor owing until you carry out your obligation to cure the defective delivery of non-conforming products. (I am, therefore, stopping payment on my check #000 for $ _____ which I gave you as payment in full on June 1, 19__, but) I shall, of course pay as required when you perform your obligation to cure the non-conforming delivery."*

Then use one of the following two paragraphs depending on whether you have actually returned the product:

> *"And since you have refused (to take the products back when I returned them on June 3 /to make arrangements for picking up the products at my home), you are now to make prompt arrangements for the return of the rejected products or furnish your instructions for returning them at your expense and risk. In the meantime, however, I am only storing the products for you at your expense and risk."*
>
> OR: *"And although you refused to take back the rejected goods when I returned them on June 3, I am leaving them in your custody and care at your place of business on (___include address___), and expect that you will now promptly make a conforming delivery."*

If you return the goods, ask the seller to acknowledge receipt of them. If he refuses, you could keep and store the goods—but only do this as a last resort and make clear to the seller you are only storing the goods for him.

Then continue:

> *"While I am prepared to grant you any reasonable additional time beyond the delivery date in our contract which you may need to cure the non-conforming delivery, I shall insist on strict performance should you fail to do so. (I do, however, require that the non-conforming delivery be promptly cured since being deprived of the use of the products is causing me great inconvenience [and additional expense for (describe expenses involved)].) (I am also prepared to waive claims for damages I have thus far sustained if the non-conforming delivery is promptly and adequately cured.)*
>
> *"And to resolve this matter promptly should you be unable to cure the non-conforming delivery, I am prepared to do so by cancelling our contract (and waiving my claims for damages) if you will promptly discharge all obligations remaining under the agreement with respect to the rejected goods.*
>
> *"Please notify me promptly that you intend to cure the non-conforming delivery and furnish me the assurances I have requested so that we can still satisfactorily complete this transaction or promptly resolve this mat-*

ter as I have otherwise proposed so that I do not have to hold you fully responsible for breaching our contract by compelling me to cancel and hold you liable for all damages.

"I will appreciate your giving this matter your immediate attention so that we can still resolve it and satisfactorily complete our transaction."

———————————————
(Your signature)

Receipt of the above memorandum is acknowledged.

(Leave space for the seller to sign receipt for the goods you returned and left at the store)

By *(Signature and title of store representative)*   *(Date)*

If you took delivery of goods even though they failed to conform, then also revise paragraph (2) of the basic memo and include paragraph (3A) as illustrated on page 211.

REQUESTING PAYMENT FOR DAMAGES

If you don't list any specific damages, then naturally omit all the wording that refers to your willingness to waive them. Do, however, keep the wording in paragraph (9) in case you sustain damages later.

If you do want to claim damages, though, it can't hurt you to do so because if the seller refuses to cure the defects, you might be entitled to recover them even if your agreement specifically says the seller wasn't liable. (See page 241.)

An important word of caution. As worded, the sample memos assume you are willing to forget about insisting the seller pay damages if he otherwise resolves the matter satisfactorily.

NEVER use the sample memos as worded if it's important to recover damages even if a seller fully cures what's wrong or refunds the money you have paid. This is not a situation that is likely to arise often, but if you do happen to incur losses, DON'T throw away your chances to recover them by waiving your rights to do so. If you sustained serious injury or significant damage to property, never try to handle these situations by yourself. Always consult an attorney.

There may be some situations in which you might want to insist on your own that a seller compensate you for damages even though the seller was willing to cure the non-conforming delivery or refund your money. Keep in mind, however, that collecting such damages would usually require you to take legal action.

Here is how you could revise the wording of the sample memo to request a seller to compensate you for damages in addition to curing the non-conforming delivery.

Keep paragraphs (1), (2), (5), and (7). Replace paragraphs (3), (4), (6), (9), and (10) with the following and delete paragraph (8):

(3) And as described below, there is now also due at least $ _____ for damages which have already resulted because the product failed to conform and for which I request prompt reimbursement, but I am not hereby waiving claims for additional amounts that may become due. (Describe the damages or injury and state amounts due.)

(4) (The damages caused by these defects now prevent me from relying on these products being adequate and safe for ordinary use.) I request that you, therefore, also either promptly carry out your obligation to cure the non-conforming delivery by furnishing me replacements which fully conform to our contract or that you return the $ _____ I have paid

toward their price and discharge all obligations remaining under our agreement, with respect to the purchase of the products I have rejected. And if you elect to cure by making a conforming delivery, you are also to furnish me your assurances that you will promptly do so (and that any replacements you deliver will, in fact, be adequate and safe for ordinary use). You are also to arrange for the return of the rejected products or furnish me your instructions for returning them at your expense and risk, but I request that, upon the return of the goods, you preserve them as evidence and have them available for any expert examination and testing which may be required.

(6) If, however, you do not furnish me your assurances that you will promptly cure the non-conforming delivery (and your assurances that any replacements you deliver will, in fact, be adequate and safe for ordinary use) should you elect to cure by the delivery of conforming replacements, I shall insist on strict performance and shall treat your failure to furnish those assurances as a material breach of contract. But if you furnish me such assurances, I am prepared to grant you any reasonable additional time beyond the delivery date in our contract which you may require to cure the non-conforming delivery. (I do, however, require that the nonconforming delivery be promptly cured since being deprived of the use of the products is causing me great inconvenience [and additional expenses for (describe expenses involved)].)

(9) Please notify me promptly that you intend to cure the nonconforming delivery, furnish the assurances I have requested, reimburse me for the damages I have sustained, promptly return the moneys I have paid, discharge the remaining obligations under the agreement with respect to the goods I have rejected, and reimburse me for the damages I have sustained so I do not have to hold you fully responsible for breaching our contract and compelling me to cancel and hold you liable for all damages.

(10) I will appreciate your giving this matter your immediate attention so that we can still satisfactorily resolve it as I have proposed.

DEMANDING A REFUND WHEN NON-CONFORMITY CAN'T BE CURED

There are also situations in which a product's failure to conform cannot be adequately cured simply by replacing it with another one. If replacement wouldn't be an adequate cure, then either ask for your money back or insist the seller furnish a product that does conform to the claims and promises made for the original merchandise.

Here is a sample memo you can adapt for rejecting a product in this situation.

June 4, 19___

TO: ABC Sales Company
Futurama Mall
Anytown, USA

This is to notify you I am rejecting the (identify product you are rejecting) which (I purchased and received on June 1, 19___, as shown on the attached copy of the sales receipt/was delivered on June 1, 19___, under our agreement of April 15, 19___). I am doing so because it failed to conform to the requirements of our contract.

At the time of the purchase, it was represented to me (by the salesperson/by the product labels) that the product would (be suitable for/would conform to the following quality/performance standards: describe the special purpose, quality, performance, or specific representations made about the product). This feature was important to me and I asked the salesperson to make sure the product would conform to these requirements.

But contrary to these representations, upon examining the product on June 2, 19__ , I discovered that it failed to conform to those requirements as described below:

(Describe how the product failed to measure up to the representations)

I request that you therefore promptly carry out your obligation to cure the non-conforming delivery by furnishing me a substitute for the rejected product which will conform to the requirements of our contract (or that you promptly credit the $ _____ price of the rejected product toward the price of, and deliver a substitute product which fully conforms to the requirements of our contract), and that you promptly furnish me assurances that you will make a conforming delivery so that we can still satisfactorily complete our transaction. I also request that you promptly arrange for the return of the rejected product or furnish me your instructions for returning it at your expense and risk. (ALTERNATIVELY, adapt the following wording in place of the previous sentence as appropriate: Since you refused to take the product back [refused to make arrangements for examining and picking up the product at my home] when I verbally notified you on June 3 that I was rejecting it, I now again request that you promptly arrange for its return or furnish me your instructions for returning it at your expense and risk./Since the rejected product was returned to you on June 3, I expect that the non-conforming delivery will be promptly cured.)

But as provided by the Uniform Commercial Code, the $_____ (balance of the) price of the product I have rejected is neither due nor owing until you carry out your obligation to cure the defective delivery of a non-conforming product. (I am, therefore, stopping payment on my check # 000 for $ _____ which I gave you in partial payment on June 1, 19__ , but) I shall, of course, pay as required when you perform your obligation to cure the non-conforming delivery.

While I am prepared to grant you any reasonable additional time required to cure the defective delivery beyond the delivery date if you give me your assurances that you will do so, I shall insist on strict performance if you fail to do so.

In the meantime, however, I am only storing the rejected product for you pending appropriate arrangements you make for their return. But as provided by the Uniform Commercial Code, I also have a security interest in the product for the return of at least the $ _____ I have already paid on __(date)_ toward its price should you fail to carry out your obligation to cure the non-conforming delivery.

If you are unable to cure, I am, however, also prepared to resolve this matter by returning the product to you for a prompt refund of the $_____ I have already paid and the discharge of any remaining obligations under our agreement for its purchase.

Please notify me promptly that you intend to cure the non-conforming delivery and furnish me the assurances I have requested so that we can still satisfactorily complete our transaction or promptly resolve this matter as I have otherwise proposed so that I will not have to hold you liable for a complete breach of our contract and for all damages.

I will appreciate your giving this matter your immediate attention so that we can still resolve it and satisfactorily complete our transaction.

(Your signature)

Receipt acknowledged by:

(Signature and title of store representative)   *(Date)*

REJECTING GOODS PURCHASED BY MAIL

If goods purchased by mail fail to conform, you could be entitled to reject them just as if you had made a purchase in person. Nevertheless it is usually much more difficult to resolve such problems unless the seller cooperates with you. You would usually have to resolve everything by correspondence which, of course, takes time. Simply working out arrangements to return the goods for a refund or credit can involve additional complications since a seller may not want to give a refund or credit until the goods are returned (and he can verify they don't conform), but you may not want to return the goods until you get a refund or credit.

If the matter is important enough, it would usually be worthwhile to call the seller immediately so you can at least find out how or if the seller will resolve the problem. If you do, be sure to get the name of the person you talked to and make notes of what you discussed. Then immediately follow through with a confirming letter which puts everything on the record and carry out whatever you have agreed on.

If you were entitled to reject goods ordered by mail, your most practical option would be requesting a refund or credit (assuming, of course, that you had either paid or charged the purchase which would usually be the case). If, however, the seller insists on a replacement rather than a refund or credit, you could at least insist he do so within the time he has for making a conforming delivery.

Keep in mind that you are likely to have the most leverage for resolving a problem involving goods purchased by mail if you charged the purchase with a credit card and were still entitled to avoid having to pay the card issuer based on protections available under the Fair Credit Billing Act. (See page 470 and page 482 for the two ways the Act can protect you in such situations.) You are otherwise unlikely to have much leverage to get your money back since it is almost always extra-hard to sue an out-of-state mail order company.

Following is a sample letter you can adapt for notifying a seller you are rejecting goods purchased by mail. The letter includes alternative wording you can adapt when using it as a confirming letter after having first discussed the matter by phone.

200 Witchtree Lane
Anytown, USA 00000

August 1, 19___

Reliable Mail Order Company
100 Delivery Plaza
Anytown, USA

Dear Sir:

This (is to notify you/confirms the verbal notice I gave [name of person] by telephone on July 31, 19___ that) I am rejecting the (___identify___ ___products) I ordered on (___date___) and which I received on July 30). I am doing so because the product failed to conform to the requirements *of our contract. The $ _____ price of the product plus shipping charges was (paid to you by my check number 000 which I sent with the order/ charged to my Master Money credit card account, account number 0000-00000-00).*

Upon examining the product on July 30, I discovered it did not conform to the requirements of our contract as described below, but the description is not a waiver of defects that may be revealed by subsequent examination:
(Describe how the product did not conform.)

(Since my order, which you accepted, stipulated you would have no right to cure a non-conforming delivery,) I request that you promptly (return the $ _____ I have paid/credit my account for the $ _____ that was charged for the order) and that you furnish me your reasonable instructions for returning the product to you at your expense and risk. (But if you instead intend to cure the non-conforming delivery by furnishing me replacements which fully conform to our contract, please notify me immediately and furnish me your assurances that a conforming delivery will be made by the (___date___) delivery date stipulated in our agreement or an acceptable alternative delivery date by which you will, without fail, make a conforming delivery./As we arranged during the July 30 telephone conversation, you are to return the $ _____ I have paid/credit my account for the $ _____ that was charged for the order) upon receipt of the rejected goods which I am to ship back to you by (parcel post) at your risk and you shall then also reimburse me for return shipping expenses.)

I shall, in the meantime, only store the product for you pending appropriate arrangements you make for their return. And as provided by the Uniform Commercial Code, I have a security interest in the product for the return of all moneys paid for its price.

As also provided by the Uniform Commercial Code, the price of the product I have rejected is neither due nor owing unless you carry out your obligation to cure the non-conforming delivery. (If you do not [make a refund/credit my account] as I have requested or fail to make a timely conforming delivery should you insist on curing your defective delivery,/ If you fail to resolve this matter as we have arranged), the sale is cancelled.

I hope that you will promptly resolve the matter as we have already arranged (I require your immediate response that you will cure the defective delivery or that you immediately refund/credit my account for the amount paid/charged for the price) so that I will not have to hold you liable for this breach. I am, however, immediately notifying the (identify credit card issuer) about this matter should your failure to resolve it require me to assert the rights available under the Fair Credit Billing Act.

I will appreciate your giving this matter your immediate attention so that we can promptly resolve it satisfactorily.

Sincerely,

- You can, of course, alter the wording of this memo to suit the other negotiating situations described in the alternative versions on page 211.

If the seller refuses to correct non-conformities in these situations and appears to have violated the deceptive sales practices law or the fraud law, your follow-up steps would be those needed to enforce your rights under those laws. (See Chapters 19 and 22.)

USING THE MEMOS AS CONFIRMING LETTERS

You could give the seller one of the written memos when you first discuss the matter; or you could adapt it as a confirming letter by altering the wording to show that you had previously discussed the problem and are now confirming your discussion.

• Revise the first paragraph as follows, for instance:

Simply change the opening wording of the first sentence from "This is to notify you that I am rejecting . . ." to "This confirms the verbal notice I gave you on June 3, 19— that I am rejecting . . ."

You should also alter other wording in the sample memos as appropriate to indicate when and to describe what you had discussed or done or any arrangements you wanted to confirm.

The sample memo on page 197 illustrates wording you could adapt when using it as a confirming memo.

RESERVING YOUR RIGHTS AND MAKING PAYMENTS UNDER PROTEST

The sample memos illustrate how to withhold payment until the seller corrects defects. But since withholding payment is drastic and can be risky, you might want to take a safer interim step until you are reasonably certain the seller will not repair or replace the defective product.

This step is making payments under protest and reserving your rights. It makes it clear to the seller that the payments are not a sign of satisfaction, and it helps preserve your right to reject the goods and demand all your money back later should the seller fail to cure the defective product.

Always state in writing that you are paying under protest and reserving all your rights. This is not only a practical negotiating step that keeps the pressure on the seller, it also gives you concrete proof in case the dispute reaches court. It is, in effect, a low-keyed warning which gets over the following message: Although I don't have to pay since I have rejected the goods, I am doing so until I know for sure that you really mean to ignore your obligations under our contract. Once I know that, you can expect me to use all the remedies I have to hold you responsible for breaking our contract.

• If you are paying under protest, rather than withholding payment when you reject goods, substitute the following wording:

"Although as provided by the Uniform Commercial Code, the $_____ balance of the price is neither due nor owing until you carry out your obligation to cure the defective delivery of the non-conforming product, I am (at your insistence/suggestion) making payments as due but all payments are made under protest and I am reserving all my rights."

• If you pay by check, make a formal notation that identifies the goods, such as:

"Payment for rejected set of dining room furniture made under protest with all rights reserved."

If you write such a notation on the check, you do not have to include the statement about paying under protest in the written statement you give the seller. However, *be sure* to include the same notation on any subsequent check you use for payment. It's important to do this because if you include the notation on the first check but omit it from others, it could be construed as a sign of satisfaction with the goods.

You can't keep paying under protest forever, of course. You can do it once or twice, but sooner or later you'll have to use your legal rights to force a settlement. This is more than just a legal technicality, it's a matter of practical bargaining leverage. If this step is to be credible, you must actually be prepared to stop payment once it's clear the seller won't cure the defects; otherwise the warning loses its sting.

If you decide to pay under protest, do not use the rejected goods until you reach a satisfactory settlement with the seller. While reserving your rights allows you to demand your money back, it doesn't give you a chance to *use* the rejected goods.

REJECTING GOODS BOUGHT ON CREDIT

If you purchased the rejected goods on credit, the creditor may be someone other than the seller and you may also have to deal with him when you withhold payment.

Always deal first with the seller: act as you would if you still owed him the money or had bought the goods for cash. Then take the steps that help you enforce your rights against the creditor, as explained in Section VII.

Remember that the rights you could have for holding a creditor accountable depend on the type of credit you used.

When notifying the seller, also identify in your letter the type of credit arrangement involved. The sample letters in Section VII illustrate how to do this. Simply include that information in the first paragraph of the sample letters/memos as shown in Section VII.

If you reject goods bought on credit and have already paid something, be careful about actually returning the goods until you have resolved the matter with the seller. If the seller won't cure but you still have the goods, it is difficult for a seller and/or creditor to claim returning the goods was a voluntary repossession. As explained in Section VII, if you rightfully reject and cancel and are entitled to your money back, you would usually have potent leverage that makes it very risky for a seller and/or creditor to repossess the goods. Finally, if a separate creditor is involved as explained in Section VII, you would usually have to settle with him rather than the seller.

DEMONSTRATING THAT YOU ARE WITHHOLDING PAYMENT IN GOOD FAITH

It is always important to demonstrate that you are acting in good faith when you withhold payment. A way to do this is to set aside the money you owe the seller. While the Code does not require you to set aside money in order to use your rights, doing so will almost always strengthen your bargaining position. The move says, in effect: I had the money for the seller and was prepared to give it to him as soon as he honored our agreement. I had no choice but to withhold payment when the seller showed no intention of living up to our contract.

Such a move makes it much harder for the seller to say you are simply trying to *avoid* payment.

The most clear-cut way to do so is to get a certified or bank teller check, or a money order, made out to the seller for the amount you are withholding but which could be due upon the seller having performed his obligation.

Whenever you withhold payment and set the money aside, make clear to the seller you have done so. This is the additional wording you should include:

"I am, however, prepared to pay the amount due as soon as you carry out your obligations under our contract as I have requested, and have obtained a certified check for that amount (copy enclosed) as payment which I shall hold for you until it is clear that I can no longer rely on you to carry out your obligations."

If you can't make the arrangements to set aside the money at the time you tell the seller you are refusing to pay, adapt this follow-up letter to inform him the money is now available.

100 Witchtree Lane
Anytown, USA 00000

June 3, 19___

Mr. Rip Seller
Manager
ABC Sales Company
Futurama Mall
Anytown, USA 00000

Dear Mr. Seller:

As I informed you in my memorandum of June 1, 19___ , payments are neither due nor owing under our agreement of April 15, 19___ , for the reasons I have already given you.

But as I then told you, I am prepared to pay when you carry out your obligations under our agreement as I have requested you to do in my memorandum of June 1, 19___ . I have, therefore, obtained a certified check for the amount that would be due upon you having carried out your obligations. (A copy is enclosed.) I shall hold this amount for you until it is clear that I can no longer rely on you to carry out your obligations.

I do hope, however, that we can still resolve this matter so that we can satisfactorily complete this transaction.

Sincerely,

STAGE TWO: LOW-KEYED WARNINGS

When you have rightfully rejected goods, your problem is solved if the seller immediately replaces the defective product or agrees to give you a credit or a full refund of the purchase price.

But if he merely promises to cure the defects later, your next step is to give the seller a chance to do so, or request assurances he will do so.

If the seller still fails to correct the defects, there are four situations that call for tougher follow-up action. This would involve a low-keyed warning letter that makes it clear that unless the seller carries out his obligation to cure the defects within the time he has for doing so, you will use your legal remedies to hold him responsible for breaking your agreement.

1. The seller fails to inform you within a reasonable time after you reject the goods that he will cure the defects. In this case, the seller either won't admit the goods are defective or simply ignores his obligations to cure the defects. Follow-up action will let you know whether you can still expect him to honor the agreement.

2. The seller gives what you consider inadequate assurances that he will correct the defects. This might happen when you reject a new product that is substantially defective. Instead of replacing it, the seller may only want to correct the defects by making repairs. However, the repairs in question would leave you quite unsure about whether the defects had really been corrected.

3. The seller promises to correct the defects after you formally reject the goods but fails to do so or does so in an inadequate way.

4. You take delivery of the goods and tell the seller they are defective, but don't formally reject them since the seller promises to correct the defects. The repairs, however, turn out to be inadequate.

LOW-KEYED WARNING TO DEMAND SELLER CURE DEFECTS

If the seller ignores his obligation to cure the defects, it is hard to say exactly how much time you should give him before sending a low-keyed warning letter. But if time isn't critical to you, give him at least fifteen days from the time you notify him you are rejecting the goods. If you believe more time is necessary, then grant it, but thirty days should be the absolute maximum.

The key point here is the time within which a seller must cure based on the delivery date and his obligation to notify you within a reasonable time that he will cure the defects, if he is to retain his right to do so. And he must then make good his promise within a reasonable time.

The first sample letter that follows illustrates the low-keyed warning you would use when you reject and refuse delivery of goods in either of the following two situations. (1) You have paid for the goods but when you return them the seller refuses to correct the defects and you therefore keep/store them. (2) You have not yet paid anything for the goods, and return and leave them at the store or keep/store them when the seller refuses to take them from you.

The sample includes alternative wording and paragraphs that can be adapted to various situations.

It is usually best to return to the store with the letter, try to get the seller's commitment to correct the defects, and then hand the letter to the store representative. (You should, of course, take with you the sample wording included on page 185 to illustrate how to pin down a seller's promise to correct the defects in case you reach a settlement.)

If you mail the low-keyed warning letter, get a post office mailing receipt or send it by certified mail.

100 Witchtree Lane
Anytown, USA 00000

June 16, 19___

Mr. Rip Seller
Manager
ABC Sales Company
Futurama Mall
Anytown, USA 00000

Dear Mr. Seller:

This is to inform you I have not been notified that you will cure the non-conforming delivery of the products I rejected and refused to take on delivery (and returned to you/and am storing for you) as I already notified you by my memorandum of June 1, 19___ (copy attached). Nor have I received the adequate assurances I requested that you will carry out your obligations to cure the defects.

Your failure to cure these defects deprives me of the use of the rejected product (which I need for daily household/family purposes). And as described below, I have already sustained at least $_____ in damages because the product failed to conform to our contract:
(Describe any damages if applicable and give the amount due: see page 276.)
Since I am deprived of the use of the rejected product (which I need

for daily household/family purposes), you are to notify me within (five/ ten) days and furnish me adequate assurances that you will promptly carry out your obligation to cure the defective delivery of non-conforming goods (and arrange for the return of the rejected goods or furnish me your instructions for returning them at your expense).

And while you are obligated to cure the defective delivery by the (June 20, 19___/reasonable) delivery date called for by our agreement, I am prepared to grant you additional time if you will promptly honor your obligation to cure non-conforming delivery. (And to settle the matter promptly, I would also be prepared to waive my claims for damages if you carry out your obligations and I sustain no further damages.)

But as provided by the Uniform Commercial Code, the $___ (balance of) the price of the goods I have rejected is neither due nor owing until you carry out your obligation to cure the defective delivery.*

But should you fail to furnish me your assurances that you will carry out your obligation to cure the defective delivery, I shall insist on strict performance and hold you responsible for breaching our agreement and for any damages I sustain.

I will appreciate your giving this matter your immediate attention so we may still satisfactorily complete this transaction.

Sincerely,

Receipt acknowledged by:

(Signature and title of store representative)   *(Date)*

---

*(Note: If you purchased the goods on credit, see Chapter 62 for the steps you can take.)

• If a seller fails to pick up or examine a product after he has agreed to do so, send a low-keyed warning letter to insist upon it. In this case, be sure to refer to the seller's previous failure to pick up the goods.

Return to the store with the letter and arrange for the goods to be picked up. Give the store the letter even if you succeed in making new arrangements. If the store refuses to make arrangements, give them the letter anyway and make it clear that while you hope the problem can be settled without any further fuss, you will do as you say in your letter.

100 Witchtree Lane
Anytown, USA

June 10, 19___

Mr. Rip Seller:
Manager
ABC Sales Company
Futurama Mall
Anytown, USA 00000

Dear Mr. Seller:

This is to inform you that the (describe product) I have rejected has not been (picked up/examined at my home) on June 9 as we arranged when we discussed this matter on June 4. Although I then notified you I was rejecting the goods (copy of notice attached), I also have not received the

*adequate assurances I requested that you will carry out your obligation
to cure the defective delivery of non-conforming goods.*

*Your failure to cure the non-conforming delivery deprives me of the
use of the rejected product (which I need for daily household/family purposes). You also have only a reasonable time by which you are obligated
to notify me that you will carry out your obligations to cure the defective
delivery.*

*And as described below, I have also sustained $_____ in damages
because the product failed to conform to our contract:*
(Describe any damages if applicable and give the amounts due)

*Please furnish me within (five/ten) days the adequate assurances I have
requested that you will promptly carry out your obligation to cure the
defective delivery of non-conforming goods, and then make arrangements
to pick up the goods at my home.*

*While you are obligated to cure the defective delivery by the (June 20/
reasonable) delivery date called for by our agreement, I am prepared to
grant you reasonable additional time if you will promptly carry out your
obligation to cure the non-conforming delivery. (And to settle this matter
promptly, I would also be prepared to waive my claims for damages if
you carry out your obligations and I sustain no further damages.)*

*But as provided by the Uniform Commercial Code, the $_____ (bal-
ance of) the purchase price of the product I have rejected is neither due
nor owing until you carry out your obligation to cure the defective delivery of a non-conforming product.**

*If you fail to honor your commitment to pick up the product or if you
fail to furnish me the adequate assurances I have requested, you shall
have no further right to cure and I shall hold you responsible for breaching our agreement and for any damages I sustain.*

*I will appreciate your giving this matter your prompt attention so we
can still satisfactorily complete our transaction.*

Sincerely,

Receipt acknowledged by:

(Signature and title of store representative)   *(Date)*

---

*(Note: If you purchased the goods on credit, see Section VII.)

If the store still fails to cure the defects after you send these low-keyed warnings,
your next step is to give an ultimatum based on the legal remedies available to you.

LOW-KEYED WARNING WHEN SELLER'S PROPOSAL TO REPAIR DEFECTS IS INADEQUATE

If a seller only wants to repair rather than replace a substantially defective product
you have rightfully rejected, you may want to force his hand. To do this, you could
refuse the repairs as an inadequate cure and insist he replace the product. You should
be prepared to back up this position by withholding payment, however.

If you do want a replacement, first see page 239 for an explanation of how the
seller can limit your remedies. Check to see if the seller has done so. If he has, you
may have to be satisfied with repairs that would be adequate; if he hasn't, you will
almost always be in a strong position to insist on a replacement.

If you have to settle for repairs (or don't want to withhold payment), you could
still insist the seller give you adequate assurances that the repairs will make the

product conform to your contract, and press him to commit himself to taking the product back and either replacing it or refunding your money, should the repairs prove inadequate. The key in this kind of negotiating situation is to put the seller on the spot, and demand to know what more he will do if his repairs don't take care of the problem.

Here is a sample letter you can adapt either to demand that the seller replace the product, or to ask for assurances about repairs.

100 Witchtree Lane
Anytown, USA 00000

June 15, 19___

Mr. Rip Seller
Manager
ABC Sales Company
Futurama Mall
Anytown, USA 00000

Dear Mr. Seller:

This is to notify you I am rejecting the assurances I received on June 12 when Mr. Helper (verbally informed me/informed me by letter dated June 8, 19___) that you (would cure/have cured) the defective (describe product) by (describe what the seller promised to do or says he has done).

I am also notifying you of the damages I have sustained because the product did not conform. (I am also renewing my request for adequate assurances that you will carry out your obligation to cure the defective delivery by replacing the non-conforming product with one that fully conforms to our contract.)

Your proposal to repair the defects without giving me any assurances that you would still carry out your obligation to cure the defects by replacing the defective product if repairs do not cure the defects is inadequate because (describe how the assurances are inadequate as described on page 192)

And as described below, I have also sustained $ _____ in damages because the product failed to conform:
(Describe any damages if applicable and give the amounts)

But since you have proposed to cure the defects by making repairs rather than by replacing the defective product even though its value is substantially impaired, to settle this matter I am prepared to consent to the proposed repairs if you will give me your assurances that the product then fully conforms to the requirements of our contract, and if you will give me your assurances you will carry out your obligation to cure the defective delivery by replacing the non-conforming product or refunding its purchase price should its value to me be further impaired because the repairs prove inadequate.

As an alternative, however, I am prepared to settle this matter by (canceling our agreement of April 15, 19___ /the terms of our agreement of April 15, 19___, pertaining to the sale of the product I have rejected) and returning the product to you upon the refund of the $ _____ I have already paid toward its price.

If we can promptly resolve this matter as I have proposed, I would be prepared to give you whatever additional time you need to cure the defects beyond the June 20, 19___ , delivery date called for in our agreement (and to waive my claims for damages if there are no further breaches of the agreement by you).

But as provided by the Uniform Commercial Code, the $ _____ (balance of the) price of the product I have rejected is neither due nor owing until you furnish adequate assurances and carry out your obligation to cure the defective delivery.

And since I am deprived of the use of the rejected product (which I need for daily household/family purposes), you are to notify me within (five/ten) days and furnish me adequate assurances that you will carry out your obligations to cure the defective delivery of a non-conforming product (and arrange for the return of the rejected products or furnish me your instructions for returning them at your expense).

Should you fail to carry out your obligation to cure the defective delivery and furnish the adequate assurances I have requested should you insist on attempting to repair the defects, I shall hold you responsible for breaching our agreement and for the damages.

I will appreciate your giving this matter your immediate attention so we can still satisfactorily complete this transaction.

Sincerely,

Receipt acknowledged by:

(Signature and title of store representative)   *(Date)*

- Include the wording about canceling a part of your agreement only if you bought more that one product and kept those that were not defective.
- Include the wording about why a product is important to you and describe what you need it for when it is urgent to get the problem fixed. Remember, the more you need the product, the more reasonable it is to insist on quicker action by the seller.
- A word of caution about using this negotiating step to demand that the seller commit himself to replacing the product if the repairs he insists on making prove to be inadequate. Don't make the demand unless you are prepared to back it up by canceling the agreement and demanding your money back. If you make the demand, then back off and simply go along with the repairs the seller promised to make in the first place, you will more often than not weaken your bargaining position if something else goes wrong later.

But if you reject a product that is substantially defective, insisting the seller spell out what more he is prepared to do to correct the problem if the repairs prove inadequate, is an interim step you can take to keep the pressure on while the seller still has an opportunity to cure defects.

Since negotiations about whether repairs are adequate are seldom settled immediately after you reject goods, visit another expert and ask his opinion about whether the defects could really be corrected by the repairs the seller proposes to make. Another expert may give you specific reasons why the proposed repairs might be inadequate; you can then list these reasons when you explain why the seller's proposal to repair the defects is inadequate.

When you use this negotiating step, prepare your written objections to the seller's proposed repairs and assurances, return to the store and press the seller to tell you what additional steps he is prepared to take to correct the defects. If he refuses to commit himself, ask him, for example, how he can expect you to go along with the suggested repairs when he refuses to confirm that they will really be adequate, or to promise that he will still take the product back if he is unable to fix the problem. If the seller still refuses to commit himself, but insists you go along with repairs you think are inadequate, then give him your written objections indicating what more you want.

If the seller then gives his assurances, or commits himself to taking the product back, this is how to pin down the settlement in writing.

June 17, 19___

TO: (Insert your name)

The (name of the store) acknowledges that the (identify product) we delivered on June 1, 19___ , under our agreement of April 15, 19___ , failed to conform to the requirements of our contract as described below (and that you have rightfully rejected it):
(Describe the defects the seller acknowledges and agrees to correct)
We shall make the repairs and adjustments required to cure these defects and give our assurances these will cure the defects so the product then conforms to the requirements of our contract. The repairs and adjustments will be completed by June 25, 19___ .
But should our attempt to cure the substantial defects described below prove to be inadequate within (___) months after the promised completion date, you shall be entitled to return the product if it has not been subjected to extraordinary use and is otherwise undamaged except as a result of its own defects. We shall then, at your option, either replace it with a product that conforms to our contract or refund the purchase price. We shall make any refund due you within (_____) days of the return of the product to us.
These are the substantial defects referred to in this memo: (Describe the substantial defects the seller agrees to fix)
We agree that a breach of any of the terms relating to the substantial defects referred to above shall be a breach of our agreement of April 15, 19___ , and that you shall then be entitled to cancel.
We hereby agree that our agreement of April 15, 19___ , is modified by the terms of this memorandum but only to the extent provided for by the terms of this memorandum.
Terms agreed to on (June 17, 19___) by:

(Signature and title of store representative)   (Date)

• If the seller promises to replace or refund your money if the repairs turn out to be inadequate, don't give him a second chance to repair those defects unless you specifically reserve your right to hold him to his earlier promise to replace the product.

Here is how you can make clear you are reserving your rights in these situations.

July 15, 19___

TO: ABC Sales Company
Futurama Mall
Anytown, USA

This confirms that the (identify product) was returned to you on July 15, 19___, and that I informed you the (describe the substantial defect the seller was supposed to have repaired) has not been adequately repaired as you had assured me on June 17, 19__ (copy of your memo attached).

I have instead discovered on July 12, 19__, that the defects have not been adequately cured by the repairs which were completed by June 25, 19__, because (describe how the original defect has not been corrected).

You had agreed to take the product back and replace it or refund the purchase price if the repairs proved inadequate within three months of June 25, 19__. I am, however, giving you another chance to correct the defect by July 19, 19__, since you have insisted and assured me that further repairs will in fact fully cure the defects.

But I am giving you this additional opportunity while reserving all my rights to enforce the terms included in your memorandum of June 17, 19__.

(Your signature)
_____

Confirmed and received by:

(Signature and title of store representative)   *(Date)*

If the repairs don't cure the defects, then insist the seller either replace it or refund your money as he specifically promised to do. While you can usually expect a seller to honor this kind of a promise if you get it pinned down in writing, here is a low-keyed warning you can use to demand your money back should he refuse to do so.

June 30, 19__

TO: Mr. Rip Seller
Manager
ABC Sales Company
Futurama Mall
Anytown, USA

This is to notify you that the following substantial defects in the (identify product) which I rejected on June 1 have not been cured by the repairs that were completed by June 25 as had been promised when I consented to your attempt to cure the non-conforming delivery by repairs: (describe the defects that were not properly corrected)

And despite the written assurances you gave on June 17, 19__, that you would take the product back and either replace it or refund its purchase price if the repairs were inadequate, you refused to do so after I told you the product still didn't conform.

Since the defects have not been cured and you have refused to replace the non-conforming product or to refund its purchase price as required by the specific assurances you gave, I can no longer rely on your good faith to perform your obligations under our contract of April 15, 19__.

I therefore request that you promptly (refund the $____ I have paid toward its purchase price/credit my Master Money Credit account, number 000-0000-00, for the $____ I charged to that account for its purchase price/credit its $____ purchase price toward the amount still due under our agreement of April 15, 19__, for the products I elected to keep).

You are also to make prompt arrangements for picking the product up at my home at 100 Witchtree Lane, or to furnish me your instructions for returning it upon the payment or proper crediting of the refund due me.

In the meantime, I am only storing the product for you and holding it as security until the refund due is paid or credited to me.

And as provided by the Uniform Commercial Code, the $_____ (balance of) the price is no longer due or owing because of your failure to cure the defects in the rejected product as required by our contract. (I am, however, prepared to carry out my remaining obligations under our agreement with respect to the products I elected to keep.)

But if you do not promptly give me the refund or the credit I have requested and take back the product so that we can fully resolve this matter as I have suggested, I shall hold you responsible for breaching our contract by canceling and for all damages I sustain.

(Your signature)

Receipt acknowledged by:

(Signature and title of store representative)   *(Date)*

• If the seller still refuses to settle the matter, your follow-up step would be an ultimatum to cancel the purchase which would be based on your legal remedies described on page 276.

• See the sample memo on page 209 which includes wording telling the seller about damages you sustained and that you are willing to waive your claims for damages as part of a prompt settlement.

LOW-KEYED WARNINGS WHEN SELLER FAILS TO CURE AS PROMISED

A seller would cure either by furnishing a replacement product or by returning the goods after repairing defects. Technically speaking, the seller is then re-delivering the goods. You should then inspect to make sure the replacements conform or that the rejected goods have been properly repaired. When you receive the repaired goods see page 200 for a sample memo you could use for pinning down the seller's assurances that they conform.

If the goods still fail to conform when the seller delivers them again, or if the goods are not delivered on time, the seller has then failed to cure. You usually will not have to give a seller another chance. You would now be entitled to use your legal remedies to cancel, demand your money back and hold a seller accountable for damages.

These are the low-keyed warning follow-up steps you could then take depending on how the seller has failed to carry out his promise to cure.

REFUSING DELIVERY OF NON-CONFORMING REPLACEMENTS OR GOODS THAT HAVE NOT BEEN PROPERLY REPAIRED

If your inspection shows the replacement product does not conform or that the seller's repairs have not corrected the defects in the goods you rejected, you should refuse delivery (unless you are willing to take the goods on the seller's promise that he will fix the defects later).

Your strongest option now is to try to get your money back by insisting that you will cancel the agreement unless the seller at least replaces the defective product you have already rejected. If the seller wants another chance to repair the product, you could, as an alternative, demand adequate assurances that these additional repairs will make the product conform or that the seller will either replace the product or refund your money.

Your main bargaining leverage in these situations is that you do not have to give the seller a further chance to cure defects in rejected goods when the time for delivering the goods has expired. If the agreement still allows the seller time to make the delivery later, he may be able to insist on having a further chance to cure the defects, but he cannot do so if the delivery date has passed.

It is unlikely that a reasonable seller will refuse to call off a sale and refund your money if the product still fails to conform by the time he makes the second delivery. But here is a low-keyed warning you could adapt should the seller refuse to do so.

June 20, 19___

TO: Rip Seller
Manager
ABC Sales Company
Futurama Mall
Anytown, USA

This is to notify you that I again reject (and refuse to take delivery of/ insist you take back) the (describe product) you delivered (today/on June 19, 19___) because you have still failed to cure the non-conforming delivery I rejected on June 1, 19___. I am also informing you of the (further) damages I have sustained because your delivery still does not conform to our contract.

Although you had assured me on June 1, 19___, that the non-conforming delivery which I had rejected on June 1 would be cured by (the delivery of a replacement/repairs and adjustments which would make the product conform), the delivery still fails to conform to our contract as described below:
(Describe how the product still fails to conform)

As described below, I have also sustained at least $ _____ in damages due me because a conforming delivery has not been made:
(Describe and list the amount of damages)

Since (you have failed to cure the non-conforming delivery as you had assured me you would do/we agreed you would have no further opportunity to cure the defective delivery if the product still failed to conform on re-delivery), (I can no longer rely on you to make a conforming delivery/you have no further right to cure), and your further breach now prevents me from continuing with our agreement.

In order that we may now promptly resolve this matter, I am prepared to cancel our agreement for an immediate refund of the $_____ I have already paid and the discharge of all remaining obligations under our agreement of __(date)__. (If you do so, I would then also waive my claims for damages.)

And as provided by the Uniform Commercial Code, the $_____ (balance of the) price is neither due nor owing for the product I have rejected.

(Since you have refused to take the product back when I returned it on [__date__]), you are to make prompt arrangements for its return or furnish me instructions for returning it at your expense and risk. But as provided by the Uniform Commercial Code, I have a security interest in the product for the return of moneys I have already paid. In the meantime, however, I am only storing the product for you while you make arrangements for its return.

And since the failure to cure the defective delivery continues to deprive me of the use of the product (which I need for daily household/family purposes), I shall cancel and hold you responsible for all damages I sustain, if you do not promptly return the moneys I have paid and make arrangements for the return of the product as I have requested.

(Your signature)

Receipt acknowledged by:

(Signature and title of store representative)   *(Date)*

You might as well adopt such a position with a seller who refuses to refund your money and take the product back after he has failed to cure defects in the rejected goods. You can't expect to reach a satisfactory settlement in this kind of situation unless you use all the leverage available to you under the Code.

LOW-KEYED WARNING WHEN SELLER FAILS TO DELIVER A REPLACEMENT

• If a seller fails to deliver a replacement on time, you might give him a *little* more time if you think delivery will be made by an acceptable delivery date.
• If you are willing to give the seller a chance to make a later delivery, use the sample letter on page 149 to settle on a firm delivery date.
• If you decide not to give the seller another chance, however, and he refuses to cancel the agreement and to refund your money, here is a low-keyed warning memo to deliver to him to demand your money back.

June 30, 19___

TO: Mr. Rip Seller
Manager
ABC Sales Company
Futurama Mall
Anytown, USA

This is to notify you that our agreement of April 15, 19___, for the purchase of (identify product) has been breached by you since the replacement for the non-conforming product I rejected on June 1, 19___, has not been delivered as required by our contract.

Upon rejecting the non-conforming delivery made on June 1, you gave me your assurances that it would be cured by the delivery of a conforming replacement not later than June 29, 19___. But the replacement has not been delivered by the required delivery date.

Since (your failure to cure the defective delivery according to your assurances prevents me from relying on your good faith to carry out your obligations under our agreement/we had agreed that you would have no further opportunity to cure the defective delivery if the replacement was not delivered as promised), I am no longer prepared to continue with (our agreement/the terms of our agreement pertaining to the product which has not been delivered).

Although you refused the refund I requested when we discussed this matter today, I am still prepared to settle this matter in full if you will promptly (refund the $_____ I have already paid you for the product and discharge the obligations remaining under our contract with respect to *this sale/credit to my Master Money account, number 000-00000-000, the $_____ that was charged to it for this purchase).*

But as provided by the Uniform Commercial Code, the $_____ (balance of the) price of the product I have rejected is neither due nor owing under our agreement because the non-conforming delivery has not been cured. (I am, however, prepared to carry out my remaining obligations under the agreement with respect to the products I took on delivery.)

Since your failure to cure the defective delivery deprives me of the product I bought (which I need for daily household/family purposes), if you do not (promptly refund my payments/or give me a proper credit toward the balance still outstanding under our agreement), I shall cancel (our agreement/the terms of our agreement pertaining to the product I rejected) and hold you responsible for damages I sustain.

(Your signature)

Receipt acknowledged by:
(Signature and title of store representative)   *(Date)*

- It would usually be worthwhile to be accommodating about the delivery of a replacement when you have purchased more than one product under the same agreement and have accepted some of them.
- Of course, if the seller still fails to deliver a replacement when you give him another chance, then it would be reasonable to demand your money back. Use the above low-keyed warning if the seller then refuses to refund your money, but revise it by referring to the subsequent delivery date the seller failed to meet.

SELLER'S REPAIR OF REJECTED GOODS LATER TURNS OUT TO BE INADEQUATE

What happens, if you use a product after the seller has repaired it but then find the repairs are still inadequate or that there are additional defects?

It's difficult to give you a clear-cut answer about what you might be able to do.

On the one hand, it is possible that if the defects were substantial and you discover repairs were inadequate very soon after the seller returns the product, you might be entitled to cancel because of the seller's failure to cure. This option might be available if you had to use the goods as part of your inspection. It is unclear how long you could continue to use them and then try to cancel.

Once you start using the repaired goods it is more likely to be construed as acceptance. In that case, the only alternative available for making the seller take the product back is revoking acceptance, a remedy covered in the following chapter.

The negotiating strategies included in this book assume that you probably have accepted the goods by the time you find the seller's repairs are inadequate. The follow-up strategies you could use would then depend on whether or not you could revoke acceptance or only hold a seller accountable for damages.

But to help strengthen your bargaining position to revoke acceptance, make it clear to the seller when he delivers the repaired product that any acceptance depends on adequate repairs. See page 183 for a sample memo that makes note of such a conditional acceptance.

There are times when you may be entitled to cancel and demand your money back based on the seller's failure to cure the defects by repairs. If a purchase involves a lot of money and the seller's attempt to cure defects for which you formally rejected the goods are inadequate, it could be worthwhile to seek legal advice rather than try to handle the matter yourself.

33 · Your Right to Revoke Acceptance

Sometimes you don't learn that a product is defective until after you've accepted it. And sometimes you accept a defective product because the seller assures you he will correct the problem, then it turns out he can't, or won't, fix the defects. In the meantime, you have either paid for the product or are making payments to the seller or to some other creditor.

Finally, you've had enough and want the seller to either take back the product and replace it with one that really works, or refund your money. But if the product is substantially defective, the seller doesn't want it back any more than you want to keep it, of course.

Situations like these often cause consumers to take self-defeating steps that all too often result in their having to put up with a lemon.

But the Uniform Commercial Code does provide a weapon called "revoking acceptance." Here is an example of how it works.

Mr. Conte's troubles started when he purchased a new Lincoln Continental from Dwan Lincoln-Mercury, Inc. of Connecticut on March 25, 1970. When he picked up the car on March 26, it was dirty and the doors weren't aligned so he insisted the dealer fix the problems before driving it home.

The day after delivery, Mr. Conte discovered the engine and transmission were leaking oil and that the cigarette lighter and windshield wiper didn't work. The dealer fixed the wiper and told Mr. Conte to make a list of defects and he would fix them. But the electric windows then stopped working and the paint started to blister.

Soon after he got the car Mr. Conte also wrote to the Ford Motor Company to complain and continued to correspond with the company. On October 25, the car had to be towed to the dealership for repairs. On October 27, a Ford Motor Company representative examined the car and said the defects would be corrected.

But all the defects weren't fixed. The car became undrivable four more times between October 27, 1970, and May 3, 1971, when it had to be towed back to the dealer because of a broken fan belt. Two weeks before that, the dealer had had to replace the alternator.

In all the dealer had tried to repair the car at least eight times between March 1970 and May 1971, and the car had been out of commission for some six to eight weeks since Mr. Conte had bought it.

When the fan belt snapped on May 3 and the car had to be towed back to the dealer's once more, Mr. Conte's patience finally ran out. He refused to pick up the car again, and he refused to accept any further assurances from the dealer or from the Ford Motor Company that the car was in a good and safe condition. He revoked acceptance and demanded his money back.

The dealer refused to pay him and eventually Mr. Conte was forced to sue. The jury agreed with his claim and ordered the dealer to refund the purchase price. So did the Connecticut Supreme Court which upheld the jury's decision on appeal.

The dealer and manufacturer claimed Mr. Conte wasn't entitled to revoke acceptance for two reasons. First, because he had already had the car for fourteen months. And, second, because his warranty said the dealer's only obligation was to repair or replace defective parts.

Not so, said the Connecticut Supreme Court.

Taken together, all the defects Mr. Conte found had substantially impaired the value of the car, which is one important requirement for being entitled to revoke acceptance as provided by the Code.

While Mr. Conte had waited almost fourteen months to revoke acceptance, waiting that long was not unreasonable in his case since he and the dealer were in almost constant touch about the condition of the car and the dealer had kept trying to repair it. Moreover, Mr. Conte had promptly informed the dealer he was revoking acceptance after the car was towed back for the eighth set of repairs and it finally became apparent that repeated attempts to correct the defects were inadequate. While the court agreed the seller had a chance to cure the defects by repairs, as spelled out by the warranty, the opportunity to do so does not last indefinitely it said.

As to the argument that Mr. Conte had to be satisfied with repairs or replacement of defective parts as spelled out in the warranty, the court pointed out that the Code recognizes that an essential element of any sales contract is that it provide minimum remedies to the buyer when a purchase doesn't conform to the contract. Since the car did not operate as a new car should—that is, free of defects—even after numerous repairs, the limited remedies included in the warranty failed to provide the essential element of the sales contract. Mr. Conte could therefore use the remedies the Code makes available to a buyer.

This case illustrates the basic principles involved in revoking acceptance, but a word of caution is in order. Mr. Conte's case is an extreme example of how long a buyer can wait to revoke acceptance. He discovered the first defect immediately after he received the car, and kept on finding new ones each time the dealer corrected previous ones.

While the Code does not set a fixed time limit for revoking acceptance, in most situations you would have to act much sooner than Mr. Conte did. Generally speaking, the time allowed depends on the seriousness of the defects, what happened after you told the seller about them, and how much you used the product. The longer you keep the product, the harder it is to revoke acceptance, so if you don't learn that a product is substantially defective until after you have used it for a long time, see an attorney before you formally revoke acceptance and stop payments, especially if the purchase involves a lot of money.

Revoking acceptance is really a legal way of saying you are "calling off" your previous acceptance. It is a way of telling the seller: Had I known at the time I accepted the product that it had all the defects I finally found, or had I known that you could not repair the defects as I expected you to do, or as I promised to do, I would never have accepted the product in the first place. I am now taking back my acceptance and am, in effect, rejecting the goods as I would have done had I known all this at the time of delivery.

The Code sets tougher standards for revoking acceptance than it does for rejecting a product before acceptance. The rest of this chapter tells you:

- When you are entitled to revoke acceptance.
- Your obligation to notify the seller of defects found after acceptance.
- How soon you must act.
- The seller's chance to repair defects before you can revoke acceptance.
- How to revoke acceptance.
- Your rights and obligations after revoking acceptance.
- How a sales agreement or product warranty can limit your remedies and how you can get around these limitations.
- How your rights to revoke acceptance and enforce a warranty fit together.
- How your rights under the Magnuson-Moss Warranty Act and your agreement fit together.
- Revoking acceptance for fraud or material misrepresentation.

WHEN IS A BUYER ENTITLED TO REVOKE ACCEPTANCE?

Generally speaking, the Code entitles you to revoke acceptance of a product when *all four of the following conditions apply at the same time.*

1. *The product fails to conform to the requirements of your contract.*
Although technically the right to revoke acceptance could apply whenever the seller breaks some part of your contract, in practice this usually means that the product fails to measure up to warranties. In other words, you can usually revoke acceptance only for defects that are covered by a warranty that is part of the agreement. A warranty is the seller's or manufacturer's specific promise that a product will have the quality, characteristics, capacity or performance set by the warranty. (See Chapter 38 for an explanation of warranties and how they become part of an agreement.)

Since almost all new products sold are covered by warranties, the right to revoke acceptance could apply whenever you buy a new product.

The right seldom applies, though, if the seller specifically sells a product "as is" or "with all faults," or uses other wording that amounts to the same thing, such as: "This product is sold without any express warranties or implied warranties of merchantability or fitness for purpose." When the seller uses such wording, he is saying that he is making *no* promises about how the product will work or how good it is. (Note: When a seller uses these phrases, he is disclaiming warranties you would otherwise be given under the Code. But the seller isn't off the hook unless he *properly* disclaims the warranties. So before you give up in a situation like this, check page 306 which describes how disclaimers work.)

Remember that used products, seconds, damaged goods, and products significantly reduced in price, are usually sold "as is." The right to revoke acceptance seldom applies in these cases, unless the seller commits fraud or makes important misrepresentations to convince you to buy.

2. *The defects substantially impair the product's value.*
The product must not only fail to conform, the defects must significantly reduce the product's value to you as well. In other words, the benefits or uses for the product must be significantly less than it would have been if the product had conformed.

While it is difficult to pin down precisely what the Code means by "substantial impairment of value," one court said: "The reason why a 'substantial impairment of value' must exist before a buyer can justifiably revoke his acceptance is to preclude revocation for trivial defects or defects that may be easily corrected."

Normally, a product's value to you would be substantially impaired if it has one very important defect, such as an engine that can't be fixed, or many different defects that together result in a product of impaired value.

You must, of course, be able to demonstrate how the product's value is impaired. A defect usually impairs a product's value when it prevents the product from performing important functions it is meant to perform; the cost of repairs is high in relation to the product's price; the product's quality is significantly below what you could expect; or your confidence in the dependability of the goods is strongly shaken by things that go wrong. A car that keeps breaking down, a washing machine that continually tears up clothes, a refrigerator that doesn't keep food cold, are examples of how a product's value could be substantially impaired by defects.

3. *You must have accepted the product under either of the following two circumstances:*

• *You knew about the defects but accepted the product anyway on the reasonable assumption the seller would cure them, but the seller did not do so within a reasonable time.* (As previously noted, it is risky to accept a product that you know is defective, especially if you don't first pin down in writing the seller's assurance that he will correct the defects.)

This rule does not entitle you to revoke acceptance because of defects you cannot expect the seller to cure. Say, for example, a seller delivers a red sweater instead of the blue one you ordered, but you accept it anyway by wearing it. You cannot later revoke acceptance because you don't like the color. You could, however, still revoke acceptance if the sweater turned out to be defective in other ways.

To be safe, if you know the product does not conform before you accept it, *do not do anything* that amounts to accepting it until you get the seller's assurances that he will cure the defects. The easiest way to get stuck with a defective product is to assume the seller will fix the defects and go ahead and use the product. As previously noted, using a product is one of the fastest ways to accept it. It is especially risky to accept a complicated product, such as a car, without first telling the seller about what may seem to be only minor defects. An apparently minor defect could later cause major damage if left uncorrected.

This rule would, however, still enable you to revoke acceptance if you accepted a product knowing it was defective but did so on the assumption the seller would later correct the defects under your warranty. This simply means that this rule does not automatically prevent you from revoking acceptance if you accepted a product knowing it was defective but failed to get the seller's specific assurances the defects would be corrected. But if—before you tell the seller about them—the defects resulted in a major problem, the negotiating steps described in this section are unlikely to help you settle a dispute because you will have significantly weakened your bargaining position.

• *You accepted the product without discovering the defects either because it was difficult to discover them, or because of the seller's assurances that the product conformed.*

It is sometimes difficult to find a defect during even a reasonable inspection, so if you accept a product with latent or hidden defects, the Code says you can still revoke acceptance later. At the same time, be sure to inspect the product as thoroughly as possible because if you accept it, you could later lose your right to revoke acceptance if the seller fails to cure defects that you could have found by careful inspection.

Don't ignore potential *signs* of a defect, such as a flickering oil warning lamp in a car. Few of us are experts on the workings of complicated machines, of course, but try to look for anything that could be a defect when you inspect the product. The seller is supposed to be the expert, so ask him whether there really is anything wrong when you spot potential trouble.

A key point to remember about your obligation to spot defects is this: the more complicated a product is or the more expert knowledge is required to spot a defect, the more likely it is to be considered a hidden defect that you could not find until it actually shows up after you have accepted it. In turn, the more knowledgeable you are about the product involved, the more thoroughly you will be expected to inspect it for defects before you accept.

The Code also says you can revoke acceptance if you didn't discover defects before accepting the product because of assurances the seller gave the product conformed. Generally speaking, this rule covers situations in which you failed to discover defects before accepting a product because of things a seller did to convince you it conformed—that is, it wasn't defective—rather than because it was difficult to discover the defects before accepting the product. A seller could give such assurances by words or actions which led you to believe the product conformed. Although the Code is unclear how far you can simply rely on a seller's assurance a product conforms rather than inspecting it yourself for defects before you accept, this rule is most likely to help you in situations in which you spot what seem to be defects or signs of defects which you tell the seller about before you accept, but the seller assures you the product conforms. If you then accept only to find out afterwards the product really didn't conform, your failure to find out for sure that the product didn't conform before you accepted it wouldn't prevent you from revoking acceptance. This rule in effect prevents a seller from, on the one hand, giving you assurances that a product conforms to convince you to accept it, and then, on the other hand, claiming the assurances don't count because it was up to you to find the defects on your own.

So if you spot possible defects before you accept a product, tell the seller and either get his assurances the product conforms or his assurances that he will cure the defects. Always get such assurances in writing. If you are buying a complicated product, as an added precaution obtain the seller's assurances that the product conforms and is ready for use at the time of delivery, even if you see nothing wrong with it, especially if a seller insists you state in writing you are accepting the product.

4. *You must revoke acceptance before there is a substantial change in the condition of the product which is not caused by the defects.*

In other words, you usually cannot revoke acceptance of a product and make the seller take it back, after its condition has been significantly changed because you've used it. Although it's hard to determine exactly what a "substantial change" is in a product, you can seldom revoke acceptance if defects don't show up until after you have had significant use out of it. Your only alternative at this point would be to hold the seller accountable for damages you sustained because the product fails to measure up to your warranty.

On the other hand, changes in the condition of a product usually won't prevent you from revoking acceptance if they occur while the seller is trying to repair defects that begin to show up soon after you get the product, especially if the seller insists he will only repair rather than replace the goods.

To retain your right to revoke acceptance while you keep using a product, you must constantly keep after the seller to repair defects that show up until it is clear repairs are inadequate.

Of course, any changes in the product's condition which *are* due to the defects would not prevent you from revoking acceptance, no matter how badly the product is damaged as a result of those defects.

These, then, are the four conditions under which you are entitled to revoke acceptance. Ask yourself these questions to determine if you would be able to revoke acceptance.

1. Does the product fail to measure up to a warranty that applies to the purchase, or to another major requirement of your contract?

2. Does the product's failure to measure up substantially impair its value to you?

3. Did you accept the product under either one of the following circumstances:

• Did you have reasonable grounds for believing the seller would cure the defects you knew about when you accepted the product, but now find he has failed to do so?

• Did you accept the product without knowing about the defects because it was difficult to discover them, or because the seller gave you assurances the product conformed?

4. Has the condition of the product changed substantially because of use? (Exceptions are changes caused by the defects or changes that occurred when the seller insisted on fixing them.)

In order to revoke acceptance, you should be able to answer yes to the first three questions and no to the fourth. If you do revoke acceptance and must sue the seller to get your money back, you will have to convince the court you have good answers to these questions. The burden will then be on the seller to convince the court otherwise.

YOUR OBLIGATION TO NOTIFY THE SELLER ABOUT DEFECTS IN ACCEPTED GOODS

If the seller breaks the contract after you have accepted goods, you must notify him about it within a reasonable time. If you don't do this, you could lose your right to use the remedies available.

The Code does not specify a particular method for notifying the seller. But while verbal notification is enough, a written record is obviously preferable: it shows when you notified the seller and what you told him.

HOW SOON MUST YOU ACT TO REVOKE ACCEPTANCE?

You are required to act only *after* you are, or should have, been reasonably sure you are entitled to revoke acceptance. Since it is often difficult to tell whether a product is so defective its value is substantially impaired, or whether the seller can fix it as he is supposed to do, the Code does not require you to revoke acceptance at once.

As soon as it becomes clear you are entitled to revoke acceptance, though, you must act promptly by clearly telling the seller you are doing so. If you don't act reasonably fast, you will usually lose your right to revoke acceptance. And never hold off telling the seller about *any* defects you discover after acceptance.

Courts tend to be generous about how long you can wait to notify a seller about a defect, especially when a consumer has suffered a personal injury, damage to other property or the delay has not hurt the seller. And you have a reasonable time to notify a seller you are revoking acceptance once you are or should have been reasonably certain you could be entitled to do so. But if you delay telling the seller about a defect and the problem gets worse or becomes more costly to fix as a result, courts are likely to prevent you from holding a seller responsible for anything that could have been prevented had you acted promptly. Thus, the longer you delay, the weaker your bargaining position.

SELLER'S OPPORTUNITY TO REPAIR DEFECTS

Although the Code does not specifically require it, courts have almost always said a buyer must first give the seller a chance to cure a defective product before he can revoke acceptance. Exceptions to this would be cases where the defects are so substantial, or cause such other damages, that repairs would clearly be inadequate.

One reason for giving the seller a chance to repair defects, is that the written warranties that come with many products usually limit your remedies to repairs or replacement. (See Chapter 39.) If the seller repairs the defects as he is supposed to do under a warranty or agreement, you usually cannot revoke acceptance. Such limitations may not hold up, however, so you could be entitled to revoke acceptance despite terms in an agreement or warranty which, in effect, say otherwise. But you can usually get around such limitations only after it is clear the seller's attempts to repair defects is inadequate. (See page 239).

Another reason is that the Magnuson-Moss Warranty Act gives you important leverage to enforce your rights under a written warranty or an implied warranty, but only after you have given the seller or manufacturer a chance to cure the defects and he has failed.

There isn't any clear-cut rule that spells out exactly how many chances you should give a seller to repair a defect. Generally speaking, though, the more complicated the product, and the more things that can go wrong with it, the more chances you have to give a seller to correct problems. So in a situation like this you would usually have to give the seller several chances to fix defects.

HOW TO REVOKE ACCEPTANCE

The Code requires that you notify the seller you are revoking acceptance. The notice must make clear to the seller you are taking this step.

While the Code does not specifically require that you notify the seller in writing, always do so and keep a copy. To show the seller received the notice, ask him to acknowledge receiving it if you hand-deliver it or send it by certified mail.

The Code also doesn't require you to use any particular wording when notifying the seller you are revoking acceptance. In your letter, you should, however, make clear you are revoking acceptance, indicate your reasons by briefly describing the defects, how the product's value is impaired to you and previous attempts to correct defects, and state what you want the seller to do (which would usually be a refund of what you have paid). You should also make clear what the seller is to do about the goods based on the rights and obligations you have after revoking acceptance of the goods.

YOUR RIGHTS AND OBLIGATIONS AFTER REVOKING ACCEPTANCE

Once you revoke acceptance, you acquire the same rights and obligations as you do when you rightfully reject goods.

You acquire two basic rights—you no longer owe the seller the money, and you are entitled to get back what you have paid. You also acquire the obligation to return the goods.

Since you will already have paid the seller at least something for the goods, you need only follow the rules for returning rejected goods for which you have paid when you revoke acceptance. Remember to treat the goods as the seller's property; that is, don't use them, except if you find yourself in a very unusual situation where continued use is impossible to avoid and the seller refuses to take the product back.

When you revoke acceptance, the Code also gives you a security interest in the goods for the return of at least what you have paid for them. But generally speaking, you have this security interest only as long as you still retain possession of the goods. So whether you or the seller have the goods when you revoke acceptance can be very important from a bargaining and legal standpoint, especially if there is still an outstanding balance for the goods.

If you tell the seller you are revoking acceptance only after you have returned the goods (perhaps you return the product because it is defective but then decide to revoke acceptance), you cannot then take the goods from the seller if he insists he has repaired them. Taking the goods back from the seller after he has supposedly repaired them in these circumstances is usually a sign of satisfaction and would amount to you giving up your right to revoke acceptance. So if you are determined to revoke acceptance, you cannot take back from the seller goods you have already returned to him. You can then demand your money back (but may have to sue the seller to get it), and would no longer owe the outstanding balance for the price (assuming you justifiably revoked acceptance). Keep in mind, however, that a seller—or creditor—could sue you for payment if you don't pay, and having returned the goods makes it easier for them to claim they repossessed it. (See Section VII).

If, however, you tell the seller you are revoking acceptance *before* you have returned the goods to him, you can't use them, but you have a security interest in the goods until the seller returns at least what you have paid. This can entitle you to prevent the seller from taking the goods back until he refunds money you have paid for the price so that a seller or creditor who tried to take them by repossession could incur substantial liabilities for legal wrong-doing (assuming, of course, you were entitled to revoke). (See Section VII).

If amounts are still outstanding for goods you bought on credit, always insist the seller—or creditor—settle the outstanding credit obligation in a way that makes clear you do not "owe" the money. In other words, never simply leave the goods with the seller and stop making further payments. The seller may not sue you for the money but he may treat the matter as a repossession and tell a credit reporting agency that your account is delinquent or that he wrote the account off as a bad debt, which would damage your credit rating.

If the seller refuses to refund what you have already paid or won't agree that you no longer owe the money, in order to protect your credit rating you may have to force the issue by suing the seller for money due you or to get a judgment saying you don't owe the money. You can often at least sue for money back in small claims court without having to get an attorney.

If you are not prepared to insist on a settlement to protect your credit rating or for possible legal action if you don't pay, you may be better off keeping the product and demanding the seller fix the defects rather than revoking acceptance and withholding further payments.

One way to encourage the seller to settle an outstanding credit obligation is to let him keep part or all of the money you have already paid, especially if you've had at least some use out of the product. Although the Code technically entitles you to a full refund, to protect your credit rating it may be worth letting the seller keep part of the money due in return for settling the credit obligation.

To help protect your credit rating, insist the seller state in writing that he will not furnish anyone with adverse information about the transaction. See page 579 for how to do this. Also see Chapter 70 for an explanation of laws that can help you protect your credit record, and rights you have for holding a creditor accountable based on the seller's failure to honor your contract.

HOW CLAUSES IN AN AGREEMENT OR WARRANTY CAN LIMIT REMEDIES . . . AND HOW TO GET AROUND THEM

The Code allows the parties to include clauses in an agreement that limit the remedies available if the agreement is broken. Clauses like this can prevent you from revoking acceptance and demanding your money back. It's perhaps not surprising, then, that most written agreements and warranties include clauses that limit the remedies to those that are actually stated.

A typical clause that sellers and manufacturers use to limit your remedies reads something like this, "All warranties shall be fulfilled by the selling dealer . . . at his place of business . . . replacing any defective part with a genuine part . . . or repairing any defective part free of charge." Another might read: "The manufacturer warrants the completed work against defective material and workmanship . . . for the period of one year from the completion thereof. Its liability under this warranty shall be limited to the replacement . . . of any defective work or material . . . and it shall be liable for no other damages or losses . . ."

In effect, what the seller or manufacturer is saying is, if the product doesn't live up to the warranty or the requirements of the contract, you can only expect him to repair or replace the defective parts or product—or perhaps get a refund of the purchase price—but you can't use the remedies the Code would otherwise make available to you.

A warranty or agreement also usually says that you are not entitled to recover incidental or consequential damages. A clause like this can prevent you from suing the seller of your new refrigerator, say, if the machine suddenly stops working and all your food spoils.

Such a clause is intended to prevent you from using the much tougher remedies the Code makes available when you incur damages as a result of the seller's failure to live up to the contract or warranty.

As long as the seller or manufacturer at least repairs defects and you don't have substantial additional losses, there is nothing basically wrong with such limitations. But if you do incur losses, such as personal injury, what happens? And what if the seller doesn't repair the defects? Do you get stuck with the lemon, having to return it again and again for further repairs?

No, you do not, because the Code provides three important ways to get round these clauses.

1. LOSSES FOR PERSONAL INJURY

If you suffer a personal injury as a result of a defect in a product covered by a warranty, the Code says that any clause that tries to prevent you from recovering losses is considered "unconscionable." For all practical purposes, then, you can ignore any such clause if a loss involves *personal injuries*. Keep in mind, however, that the negotiating strategies included in this book are not meant to help you resolve such disputes.

2. "EXCLUSIVE" CLAUSES

Another way clauses may be discounted is if they do not clearly spell out that the limited remedies are exclusively the ones you have to use. The Code says that limited remedies are considered optional or additional, *unless* the agreement or warranty clearly expresses that they are exclusively the ones the buyer has under that agreement or warranty.

Suppose, for example, a warranty on a watch says something like: "During the warranty period, the watch movement, dial and hands will be repaired promptly without charge." If it says nothing more about what remedies you can use if the watch does not measure up to the warranty, the wording is likely to be considered an optional rather than exclusive remedy under the Code.

But suppose your agreement or warranty includes something like the following wording: "The parties agree that the buyer's *sole and exclusive* remedy against the seller shall be for the repair or replacement of defective parts as provided herein. The buyer agrees that *no other remedy* (including, but not limited to, incidental or consequential damages for lost profits, lost sales, injury to person or property, or any other incidental or consequential loss) shall be available to him." (Emphasis added.)

This wording, suggested in a textbook for law students, tries to take everything away from the buyer except the repair or replacement of defective parts covered by the warranty. And although the attempt to limit remedies for consequential damages involving personal injury would rarely hold up in court in a consumer transaction, the authors suggest their students include such a clause anyway since it would at least give the seller more bargaining leverage in case of a dispute.

A tough clause like this will almost certainly prevent you from using the remedies you would otherwise have under the Code, at least as long as the seller sticks to the remedial measures promised in the warranty.

A weaker but still effective clause might say the seller or manufacturer would not be liable for the buyer's incidental or consequential damages, but would only be responsible for, say, repairing or replacing defective parts or refunding the purchase price. This version is also likely to prevent you from using the Code's remedies—at least when you first discover a defect.

When you first buy a product, you could try to insist the seller take tough limitation of remedies clauses out of your agreement, but he will most likely refuse. If a problem arises, check the wording of any written warranty or agreement carefully so you know what you're entitled to. Your first step should almost always be to insist the seller fulfill his obligations under the agreement or warranty.

3. WHEN LIMITED REMEDIES FAIL TO SOLVE A PROBLEM

The third important way around tough limitation of remedies clauses is when the limited remedies included in the agreement or warranty fail to solve the problem or the obligations that are spelled out are not honored.

The basic purpose of limited remedies is to give the seller a chance to make a defective product conform. Those remedies fail when the seller is unable, or refuses, to correct a problem within a reasonable time by doing the limited things he specifically promised to do. If that happens, the Code specifically entitles the buyer to use the remedies available under the Code, rather than being stuck with limited clauses that turn out to be inadequate for taking care of the defects, or which the seller refuses to honor.

This almost always means you would then be entitled to use any remedies available under the Code for holding a seller accountable for what went wrong with the purchase itself, such as revoking acceptance. And since the Code says you can, in effect, use any remedies available, you would also be in a strong bargaining position to claim you could recover incidental and consequential damages.

HOW YOUR RIGHTS TO REVOKE ACCEPTANCE AND ENFORCE A WARRANTY FIT TOGETHER

The Code makes two basic remedies available when accepted products don't measure up to the requirements of your contract, or warranty and the seller is unable, or refuses, to correct the problem. One is to revoke acceptance (but as more fully explained in Section V on warranties, this remedy usually would only be available if a product failed to measure up to warranties that are part of your agreement with the seller—that is, this remedy may not be available at all if the seller has no responsibility for honoring a warranty covering the product like a separate manufacturer's warranty which had to be honored *only* by the manufacturer); the other is recovering any monetary loss (damages) you had because the product itself failed to conform (plus additional amounts you could recover for incidental and consequential damages).

If revocation of acceptance isn't available, your main option then would be recovering damages (see Chapter 42 where this remedy is more fully described). But if you are entitled to revoke acceptance, you could, instead, seek to recover damages. If you could use either remedy you would, of course, normally use one or the other, but you may sometimes decide to combine rights you could have by using both remedies as part of your negotiating strategy.

There's one major difference between these choices. When you revoke acceptance, you cannot keep using the product and must return it to the seller as provided by the Code. If you don't, you cut off the revocation option. When you only try to recover your losses, on the other hand, you can continue to use the product since using this remedy means you are keeping the product rather than seeking to make the seller take it back as would be the case when you seek to revoke.

While you would usually be in a much stronger bargaining position if you chose one of these options when mapping out your negotiating strategy, if you are in doubt, the Code does not say that it would be inconsistent for you to combine the rights. In this case you would demand the seller take back the product and refund all your money (as you would do when you revoke acceptance) and demand the seller only pay for your damages (which allows you to keep the product). Doing this obviously weakens your bargaining leverage, though, since you are letting the seller know you are not sure exactly what you require him to do.

It would really only make sense to combine the two steps as part of the same negotiating strategy, if the damages you can recover are about the same as the purchase price you want refunded. You could then strengthen your bargaining position by making it clear to the seller that you have two ways to get your money back.

If you combine both steps, remember to stop using the product once you revoke acceptance, otherwise you will most likely cut off the option.

(See Chapter 42 for the steps to take when you are enforcing your rights under a warranty only.)

HOW YOUR RIGHTS UNDER THE MAGNUSON-MOSS WARRANTY ACT AND YOUR AGREEMENT FIT TOGETHER

The Magnuson-Moss Act regulates almost all written warranties. It also affects rights under warranties created by the Code, which may or may not be written. It does this by providing important rights and remedies you can use to enforce the seller's or manufacturer's obligations.

But, as explained in detail in Chapter 39, if a written warranty regulated by the act was given by a manufacturer, it may have to be honored only by the manufacturer of the product rather than the seller. If this is the case, and the manufacturer fails to honor the warranty, you may not be entitled to revoke acceptance and demand your money back from the seller. (Chapter 41 shows you how to avoid this situation at the time you buy.)

In most situations, though, you would be able to hold the seller accountable when the manufacturer fails to honor the warranty by taking some simple but important steps as soon as you learn the product doesn't measure up.

First, and most important, notify the seller even though the written warranty says that the manufacturer (or someone other than the seller) is responsible for correcting the defects. Remember, an important requirement for revoking acceptance is promptly notifying the seller about defects.

When you return to the store, you might be told the seller has nothing to do with the problem and you should go straight to the manufacturer. Tell the seller about the defect anyway, just as you would if he were obligated to correct the defects, and then do what the warranty says. The seller may not know it, but notifying him can make him responsible if the manufacturer fails to honor the warranty in ways that still entitle you to revoke acceptance.

Some sellers, primarily car dealers, have tried to include clauses in their agreements that get them off the warranty hook entirely—even though you have a separate written warranty from a manufacturer. It is unclear whether the seller really could avoid all warranty obligations under the agreement for product defects when you get a written warranty from someone else. But one thing is clear. Unless the seller properly includes special clauses in his agreement to get out of his warranty obligations as spelled out by the Code, you have all the implied warranties the Code creates whenever you have a written warranty regulated by the Magnuson-Moss Act and that enables you to hold the seller responsible for ignoring such obligations.

Unless the seller specifically promises you he will take care of the problem in some way, such as by replacing the product or refunding your money, your next move should always be to notify the manufacturer and take the steps required by the manufacturer's written warranty. If the warranty says to return the product to the manufacturer but the seller corrects the problem, notify the manufacturer about the defect and how it has been corrected. If the seller's first attempt at repairs fails to work, and you didn't notify the manufacturer initially, do so now.

Dealing with both the seller and the manufacturer may be inconvenient, and may also seem pointless when one corrects the problem. But unless you're sure the problem will be fixed, do not just deal with the one who initially does the job. If the defect is not corrected, the one you ignored may later tell you that he won't help because you failed to notify him.

REVOKING ACCEPTANCE FOR FRAUD OR MATERIAL MISREPRESENTATION

You could also be entitled to revoke acceptance if the seller engages in fraud or material (important) misrepresentation. All the conditions for revoking acceptance still apply. The value of the product, for example, still has to be substantially impaired as a result of the seller's actions.

Since a seller who engages in fraud or material misrepresentations will, more likely than not, also be violating your state's deceptive sales practices law, you should use the remedies available under those laws in addition to the remedies available under the Code.

To get the most leverage in such situations, take the initial steps for revoking acceptance by notifying the seller about the product's failure to measure up to the false promises he made, then use the follow-up steps for enforcing your rights described in Section III, and then formally revoke acceptance (assuming the remedy applied).

34 · Summary of Strategy for Revoking Acceptance

YOUR SETTLEMENT OPTIONS

The main settlement options for your negotiating strategy are these:

- Insisting the seller, or where appropriate the manufacturer, correct the defects covered by the warranty as your agreement or warranty requires them to do—providing, of course, the defects can be repaired. At the same time, ask for and try to pin down the seller's assurances that the repairs will be adequate.
- Asking for a replacement or your money back when you first discover substantial defects, or when it appears the defects cannot be adequately repaired. In the case of substantial defects, specifically ask the seller to replace the product or refund your money even though your agreement or warranty may say the seller only has to repair defects. Make the seller insist that he only has to repair the product. This helps you demonstrate the seller forced the repair option on you, and strengthens your position to revoke acceptance later if the seller doesn't get the job done by the method he insisted on.
- Demanding the seller take back the product and refund your money. You can insist on this settlement when you are entitled to revoke acceptance.
- Withholding further payment after revoking acceptance. If you select this option, be prepared for the possibility that you may be sued. If the purchase involves a lot of money, check with an attorney before you actually withhold payment. Also check page 219 for the steps to take to demonstrate you are withholding payment in good faith.
- Insisting the seller pay for damages you sustained. (See page 276 for damages you may be entitled to recover when the seller breaks your agreement.) While it usually isn't worthwhile to hold out for damages, you should always notify the seller if you have any. Your willingness to forget about damages if the seller reaches an acceptable settlement, will usually put some extra pressure on him to settle. But *never* say you are willing to forget about damages, if they are substantial or if they are important to you.
- Insisting the seller furnish adequate assurances that repairs will be adequate, and asking him to pin down what more he will do if the repairs turn out to be inadequate.

Which option you select depends on what the seller is obligated to do at the time. Remember that when you first discover defects in accepted goods, the seller's initial obligation is usually to repair the defects or to replace the product, rather than to refund your money and pay for your damages. A seller's initial obligations are usually spelled out in the agreement or written warranty; they may be covered by limitation of remedies clauses, as explained on page 239.

Rank the alternatives that would be acceptable to you, so you have a fall-back position when you start to negotiate. And be prepared to back up your position with tougher follow-up steps if the seller refuses to perform his obligations.

DOCUMENT EACH STEP

The most difficult part of planning a negotiating strategy for revoking acceptance is the fact that you can seldom tell ahead of time whether you will actually be *entitled* to do so. So you must take the initial steps before you know for sure you will be able to follow through.

This means building a file as you go along. Each step you take must be documented. At the time of delivery pin down the seller's assurances that the product conforms to your agreement, or his promises to repair the defects. Then document each step you take to have the defects repaired.

If the problem is corrected right away, you will have a very thin file and can happily throw it away. But if the problem isn't corrected and you have only a very thin file—or no file at all—to demonstrate what happened, you will have a very hard time filling in the gaps later and proving you are entitled to revoke acceptance.

For example, there was the case of a man who complained to the Michigan Consumer's Council about a dealer refusing to do anything more to repair defects in the engine of a new car after the warranty had expired. He had, however, complained to the dealer about the defects while the car was still under warranty and had returned it for repairs on several occasions. The dealer had apparently fiddled around with the engine until the warranty period expired, then refused to do any more about the problem.

Unfortunately, the consumer kept a copy of only one repair order—and that didn't clearly identify the defects he had complained about. He had also changed the oil himself, but failed to keep written records of when he had done it or receipts to show he had purchased the amount of oil required. Since he couldn't demonstrate that he had actually notified the seller about the defects during the warranty period, or that he had properly serviced the car, both the dealer and the manufacturer refused to do any more about the defective engine.

The consumer didn't think it was important to keep records and his story did not have a happy ending. Failing to have written documentation for everything does not, of course, automatically prevent you from having a case—verbal testimony can also be used to prove a case. But not having written documentation makes it much harder to win.

So, when a seller returns a product after repairing defects, ask for confirmation that the problems have been solved, especially when you cannot fully verify the matter yourself. There are three ways to do this. If the seller gives you a copy of the repair order for the work, for instance, ask him to note on it that the defects described have been repaired or that he has checked the problem but found nothing wrong. If the seller does not give you a copy of the repair order, and you notified him in writing about the defects, ask him to note on your copy of the memo what he did to correct the defects. If neither of these alternatives is convenient, send the seller a confirming letter that spells out what happened, and what he did, or told you he would do about the defects.

Keep one point in mind when planning your negotiating strategy and while you negotiate with the seller after having at least notified him about any defects (or other breach of your contract occurring after you have accepted the goods). You must promptly notify a seller you are revoking acceptance once it is reasonably clear you would be entitled to do so. But if you have notified the seller the product doesn't conform, it is almost always reasonable for you to try to resolve the matter with the seller before you formally revoke acceptance.

The timing of your notification you are revoking acceptance can, therefore depend on how the seller responds to your attempt to resolve the matter after you have notified him the product fails to conform. If you start to negotiate with a seller about how he is to correct defects that could entitle you to revoke acceptance, you could usually hold off formally notifying him you are revoking acceptance but only until it is clear that further attempts to resolve the matter would be fruitless.

The key to negotiating with a seller about how he is to cure defects in accepted goods is to get him to commit himself as to what he is prepared to do and then negotiate about whether that would be adequate given what wrong and what more you could reasonably insist the seller do. If the defects are substantial enough to entitle you to revoke, and you are determined to make the seller take the product back, revoke promptly after it is clear the seller will not adequately correct the defects.

1. INITIAL STEPS AT THE TIME OF DELIVERY

At this stage document either that you accept the product with defects because the seller promises to correct them, or that you accept the product without knowing about any defects because of a seller's assurance it conformed.

2. OPENING SKIRMISHES WHEN YOU DISCOVER DEFECTS

Immediately notify the seller or manufacturer, or both, when you first discover the defects, and push them to correct the problems as they are supposed to do under your contract and warranties.

Be prepared for three possibilities at this point:

- The seller agrees to remedy the problem in a way that is acceptable to you.
- The seller agrees to correct the problem in a way that is unacceptable to you. This is likely to happen when the defects are substantial and the seller only wants to repair them, while you want him to replace the product or perhaps refund your money.
- The seller denies the defects are covered by your warranties.

In the case of the last two possibilities, you must be prepared for follow-up action.

3. LOW-KEYED WARNINGS WHEN REPAIRS ARE INADEQUATE

You reach the low-keyed warning stage when the defects are so substantial that repairs would be inadequate to make the product measure up to your contract. You also reach this point when the seller is still unable to correct defects, after you have given him or the manufacturer enough chances to do so, and he insists on making further attempts.

Two kinds of low-keyed warnings can be used in both these situations. One kind demands a seller give you assurances that repairs will be adequate if he insists on repairing rather than replacing a substantially defective product; or, in the case of repeated attempts to repair defects, demands that he take back the product should further repairs prove inadequate. If the seller's previous failures to correct the defects have already impaired the product's value considerably but perhaps not enough to entitle you to revoke acceptance, making clear to the seller you now expect the problem will be finally and adequately corrected if he still insists on making further repairs should help strengthen your bargaining position to revoke acceptance if he is still unable to correct the defects.

The other kind of low-keyed warning is to give the seller notice that you are formally revoking acceptance. At this point, you would demand the seller take back the product, refund your money and make clear you no longer owe whatever might still be due. Once you formally revoke acceptance, remember to stop using the product. If you purchased the goods on credit, see Section VII about resolving the matter with any separate creditor depending on the type of credit arrangement you used.

If you cannot promptly settle the matter with a seller and/or separate creditor you could also hold accountable, you should then be prepared to withhold further payment and to back up revocation with cancelling. You could, however, still try to resolve the matter in a way that could enable you to complete the sale, such as by insisting the seller furnish a replacement for the goods. If the seller and/or creditor insisted you had to pay, you might do so while reserving your rights until it is clear you will be unable to resolve the matter. Withholding payment is then your practical as well as legal bargaining leverage for settling up with the seller and/or creditor.

I caution you against revoking acceptance unless you are determined enough to follow through by also withholding payment when you could be entitled to do so based on your rights under laws governing the type of credit transaction you used.

4. ULTIMATUM TO CANCEL THE AGREEMENT AND DEMAND A REFUND

If the seller and/or separate creditor involved refuses to settle after you revoke acceptance, then use an ultimatum to cancel the agreement and demand your money back. (See Chapter 36 about your right to cancel.)

Take this step only if you are actually determined to withhold any further payments. Since cancelling when you are entitled to do so ends any remaining obligations with respect to a purchase you cancel, continuing to pay undermines your position from both a legal and practical bargaining standpoint for negotiating a final settlement. You would, however, have to keep paying a creditor when the credit arrangement under which you financed the purchase required you to pay the creditor back regardless of whether you were entitled to avoid paying the seller.

As explained in Section VII, be prepared in advance to cancel as an immediate follow-up step to revoking acceptance. Assuming you are entitled to revoke acceptance, cancelling gives you significant additional leverage against a seller or creditor who might try to repossess the goods rather than resolving the matter because they could then become liable for various kinds of legal wrong-doing if a court decided you were right and they repossessed anyway.

35 · Negotiating Strategy for Revoking Acceptance

STAGE ONE: OPENING SKIRMISHES

If you discover defects in accepted goods your first step is to notify the seller and make arrangements for the problem to be corrected. You will have to pick the settlement that is most satisfactory to you, given the options available.

If you accepted a product with defects a seller promised to correct later, you would, of course, have to give the seller a chance to do so. In situations like this, make sure you get written records showing the seller has had a chance to fix those defects.

NOTIFYING THE SELLER ABOUT DEFECTS AND GETTING ASSURANCES HE WILL CORRECT THEM

Here is a sample memo you can adapt for notifying the seller about defects. The numbered paragraphs, and alternative wording in brackets, may be used or dropped according to circumstances.

Be sure to note these and other sample memos refer to damages you sustained and wording that you are willing to ignore them as long as the seller otherwise takes care of the problem. See page 213 in Chapter 32 for a further explanation about using such wording. NEVER use such wording if it is important for you to collect damages even if a seller otherwise corrects what's wrong with the product. If the matter of collecting damages is an important issue, seek legal advice before you take steps on your own to resolve the matter.

June 15, 19__

TO: ABC Sales Company
Futurama Mall
Anytown, USA

(1) This is to inform you that the (describe product) which I (purchased and received on June 1, 19__/which was delivered on June 1, 19__, under our agreement of April 15, 19__) fails to conform to the requirements of our contract. (This notice is also to inform you of damages I have sustained because the product did not conform.)

(2) (Contrary to your assurances that the product conformed despite the apparent defects I told you about at the time of delivery,) I have as of now discovered the following (apparent) defects which have become evident since delivery (but this description is not a waiver of defects that may be revealed by subsequent examination):

(Describe the defects, or how the product is not operating properly, and when you first discovered them or noticed the problem)

(3) And as described below, I have also sustained $ _____ in damages

and will incur the following expenses because the product failed to conform:

(Describe the type of damages you sustained and the amount of the loss)

(4) Please make such adjustments and repairs as would be required to correct the defects so the product conforms to the requirements of our contract (or furnish me a replacement which conforms to our contract/ and/or reimburse me for the damages I have sustained).

(5) But since I regularly use and need the product for (describe use) and I have already sustained damages because the product was defective, should you elect to repair the defects, then please furnish me your assurances that the repairs will be adequate so that I can rely on the product for future use.

(6) I would appreciate your (picking up the product at my home and) either repairing it by June 20, 19___ , or replacing it within a reasonable time.

(7) Thank you for giving this matter your immediate attention.

_____
(Your signature)

Receipt acknowledged.
(Leave space for noting what the seller promises to do)

By _____   _____
    (Signature and title of store representative)   *(Date)*

IF YOU ARE NOT CERTAIN THE PRODUCT IS DEFECTIVE

If you are not sure the product is actually defective, but want to put on record that you told the seller it was not operating properly, so he has a chance to take care of the problem before something more serious happens, then ask him to examine the product and make whatever adjustments and repairs are necessary.

If the seller claims there is nothing wrong, have him say so in writing on your copy of the memo. If you don't want to press him hard to put his claims in writing, send him a confirming letter to get what he tells you on the record.

Here's how to do it:

200 Witchtree Lane
Anytown, USA

June 16, 19___

Mr. R. P. Seller
Manager
ABC Sales Company
Futurama Mall
Anytown, USA 00000

Dear Mr. Seller:

This is to confirm our discussion of June 15, 19___ , when I gave you a copy of the attached memo describing how the (describe product) I purchased from you seemingly failed to conform to our contract of April 15, 19___ .

You then specifically assured me that the apparent defects I described did not mean the product was defective and that I could rely on the product operating normally if I continued using it in the condition you found it when you examined it on June 15, 19___.

Please notify me promptly and take whatever corrective actions may be required should you have any reason for reconsidering the matter.

Thank you for giving this matter your prompt attention and reassuring me that the product is operating normally. I am, however, reserving my rights should I subsequently discover that the product is, in fact, defective.

Sincerely,

• Use the same basic memo to notify the seller about any further defects you discover or about the inadequacy of any repairs that are made, by revising paragraphs (1) and (2):

(1) "This is to inform you that the (describe product) which I (purchased and received on June 1, 19___/which was delivered on June 1 under our agreement of April 15, 19___) still fails to to conform to the requirements of our contract because the repairs completed by June 20, 19___ have not adequately corrected the defects I told you about on June 15, 19___ (and because of additional defects I was only able to discover since the last repairs on June 20)."

(2) "(Contrary to the verbal assurances you gave on June 20 that the repairs had adequately corrected the defects I had described,) the following defects have not been corrected (and I have up to now discovered these additional defects since the last repairs on June 20, 19___) (but this description is not a waiver of defects that may be revealed by subsequent examination):

(Describe the defects that have not been corrected and/or new ones you've found)

If you had not previously asked the seller to replace the product, you could ask him to do so now especially if you have incurred damages or expenses.

• If you use paragraph (5) to request the seller's assurances that further repairs will be adequate, you could refer to the inadequacy of the past repairs by inserting the following clause at the beginning of the sentence: "But since previous repairs have already proved inadequate and since . . ."

• Use these memos to keep notifying the seller about inadequate repairs, or additional defects, until you reach the point where it would be reasonable to give him a low-keyed warning that draws the line on further repairs.

REQUESTING THE SELLER TO REPLACE SUBSTANTIALLY DEFECTIVE PRODUCTS

Sometimes defects are so substantial that repairs are unlikely to be adequate. If you discover such defects while you can still revoke acceptance, a seller might be willing to replace the product or to refund your money. But if it would cost him more to replace the product than to repair it, you can be sure he will insist on trying to repair it.

If you don't think repairs will be adequate, then insist—at least initially—that the seller replace the product. Put the onus on him to declare that repairs will turn out to be satisfactory.

If you are asking for a replacement, use the basic memo on page 248 but revise it as follows:

Replace paragraphs (4) through (7) with the following ones:

(4) "Since the product is substantially defective (so that I can now no longer rely on it being adequate/and I have already sustained damages because the product failed to conform) please cure this breach by replacing the defective product with one that fully conforms to the requirements of our contract (and reimburse me for the damages I have sustained)."

(5) "I am, however, also prepared to resolve this matter (in full)* by returning the product to you for a (prompt refund of the $ _____ I have already paid toward the price [plus related charges]/and the discharge of all further obligations for this purchase under our contract, as well as reimbursement for the damages I have sustained.)"*

(6) "But since I regularly use and need the product for (_____(describe use)_____) and my being deprived of its use is causing me great inconvenience and additional expense for (describe expense), it is important that you promptly furnish a replacement or that you promptly make the refund as I have requested which I need to enable me to obtain a replacement. (I will return the defective product/Please pick the defective product up at my home) as we arrange."

(7) "Please contact me promptly so that we can resolve this matter in a manner that will still enable us to complete the transaction satisfactorily or according to the alternative I have proposed for minimizing any further damages."

(8) "Thank you for giving this matter your immediate attention."

*As previously noted, if the seller is willing to take care of the problem, it is usually not worthwhile to insist he pay damages; unless, of course, you sustained significant damage. Never say you are willing to settle "in full" if collecting damages is important; always add the phrase asking for the payment of damages. Seek legal advice rather than trying to handle the matter yourself if damages are very important.

Your problem would usually be solved if the seller agrees to take the defective product back and replaces it or refunds your money. Be prepared to pin such a settlement down in writing. (See page 185)

If, however, the seller insists on repairing the defects, you then have to decide whether to accept his offer or continue insisting he replace the product.

If you decide to go take the first course, pin down the seller's promises and ask him to state the repairs will be adequate to correct the problem. Since you are backing off from what you initially stated as a satisfactory way of resolving the problem, it could be especially important to make clear you are doing so based on the seller's insistence as to what was adequate. (See page 249 for a sample memo you can adapt for pinning down the seller's assurances repairs would be adequate. If the seller doesn't want to put anything in writing, get his verbal commitment and then adapt the sample memo on page 249 for putting it on the record.)

If you use a confirming memo but the seller denies giving the assurances you describe (an unlikely event since doing so amounts to denying you can count on the adequacy of the repairs he insisted on making), see page 257 for a low-keyed warning you could adapt to demand that he furnish such assurances. If you take these follow-up steps, don't use the product until you get the seller's assurances. Not using the product avoids further changing its condition, which can then help you preserve your right to revoke acceptance should you be entitled to do so.

If, however, you decide to insist that the seller replace the product, you should immediately make clear why the repairs are inadequate and repeat your request that the seller replace the product. Remember that once you know the seller wants to repair rather than replace the product your continuing insistence that the seller replace the product (or refund your money as an alternative) could lead to a further dispute in which you would eventually have to accept the repairs the seller insists on making or revoke acceptance. Therefore, it is only worthwhile to continue insisting on replacement if the product is so defective you are entitled to revoke acceptance. This initial follow-up step can, however, help you negotiate about the adequacy of the repairs the seller wants to make and to negotiate for assurances on what more the seller will do if the repairs turn out to be inadequate. The seller's refusal to give any assurances that you can count on the adequacy of the repairs he insists on making can strengthen your position to revoke acceptance.

If the seller insists on repairing the defects and is prepared to make commitments about taking the product back if repairs are inadequate, be sure to pin them down in writing. (See page 226)

If the seller refuses to do anything about the defects, or the defects can't be repaired but he refuses to replace the product or refund your money, see page 254 for the follow-up steps you could then take before you formally revoke acceptance.

Keep in mind, however, that you should promptly notify the seller you are revoking acceptance when you could be entitled to do so and it becomes clear that any further attempts to negotiate about repair would be fruitless.

REQUESTING A REPLACEMENT IN PLACE OF INADEQUATE REPAIRS

Although the seller initially could refuse to replace a substantially defective product, he may often change his mind after you begin to negotiate.

If the seller initially insists on making repairs that clearly are inadequate and/or he initially won't even give any assurances that his repairs will be adequate, you should refuse the repairs and at least initially insist the seller replace the product. It is unlikely that you will reach an immediate settlement in this situation, but you will put pressure on the seller.

Following is a sample memo you can adapt for making clear the seller's proposed repairs are unacceptable and to renew your request the seller replace the product to avoid further problems as a way of keeping open further negotiations about how the seller is to correct the defects.

If you did not initially notify the seller about the defects in writing, you could now confirm having told him and describe the defects in writing.

June 25, 19___

TO: *ABC Sales Company*
Futurama Mall
Anytown, USA 00000

This is to (inform you/confirm I verbally informed you on June 24) that your proposal to repair the (____(identify product)____) by (describe repairs seller proposed) is inadequate and unacceptable. (This also confirms my having informed you of the damages I sustained because of this breach.)

As you know, this product was delivered on June 1, 19___ under our agreement of (__date__) (copy of receipt/sales memorandum is attached). But as I notified you in my memo of June 23 which I gave you, I have discovered the product substantially fails to conform to our contract. (As I verbally informed you on June 24, I have up to now discovered [that, contrary to the assurances you gave me at the time of delivery that the product conformed/despite the seeming defects I then described to you]) the product did not, in fact, conform to the requirements of our contract because of the following substantial defects, but this description is not a waiver of defects that may be revealed by subsequent examination: (Describe the defects, or how the product is not operating properly, how and when you first discovered them, and what happened as a result of the defects.)

And as described below, I have now sustained at least $ _____ in damages because of this breach: (Describe the damages and state the dollar amount of the loss)

Since the product (is substantially defective/(and) was extensively damaged during normal use because of its defects), it is now unfit for further use and I cannot now rely on repairs being adequate to ensure the product would then, in fact, fully conform to our contract. (Since I also need and regularly use this product for (_____ (describe uses) _____) and have already sustained damages because of its failure to conform, I would suffer considerable further inconvenience and could sustain additional damages should repairs prove unreliable.)

I therefore again request that you replace the product rather than seek to repair the defects so that we can still satisfactorily complete this transaction and avoid any further impairment of the product's value to me and any additional damages. (I also request prompt reimbursement of the amounts now due me as damages.)

If, however, you are unable to replace the product promptly, I am now also prepared to resolve this matter by returning the defective product for the prompt refund of the $ _____ I have already paid toward its price, the discharge of any obligations remaining for this purchase under our contract (and the prompt reimbursement of amounts due me for damages.)

In the meantime, I shall make payments as due under our contract while we seek to resolve this matter, but am doing so while reserving all my rights.

Since the defects deprive me of the use of the product which I regularly need for (household/family) purposes (and is causing me additional expenses for (_____ describe _____), please replace the product promptly or refund payments I have made toward its price which I need so I can promptly purchase a suitable replacement.

Please contact me promptly so we can now still satisfactorily resolve this matter and complete this transaction to avoid my having to hold you fully responsible for this breach and all damages I sustain.

Thank you for giving this matter your immediate attention.

_____
(Your signature)

Receipt acknowledged.
(Leave space for writing down a settlement the seller may be prepared to reach after you make your position clear.)

_____   _____
(Signature and title of store representative)   (Date)

• If you bought the goods on credit and are unable to reach a prompt settlement, make any payments that come due while you are still negotiating, but make it clear you are reserving all your rights. If you owe the money to someone other than the seller, be sure to notify the creditor about the dispute to let him know you may be entitled to withhold payments. (See Section VII.) Since you may have to act quickly to preserve your right to withhold payment if you used a credit card, make it a point to notify the card issuer promptly.

• If the seller insists he will only repair the product, you will then have to decide between going along with his offer or revoking acceptance.

• If you are determined to refuse the repairs because the product was so substantially defective that repairs would clearly be inadequate, your follow-up steps will then be the low-keyed warning to revoke acceptance and the ultimatum to cancel (assuming, of course, the revocation remedy applies). Keep in mind, however, that revoking acceptance without giving a seller any chance to make repairs is likely to be available only if attempts at repair would clearly be inadequate. If you are determined to revoke, do this promptly after the seller makes clear he won't replace the product. If you revoke acceptance, you could still seek to resolve the matter by requesting the seller replace the defective product rather than return your money. If the seller refuses, you would have to cancel. So revoking acceptance rather than accepting a seller's attempt to repair very substantial defects can help you put more pressure on the seller to replace the product or refund your money. But it also could trigger a more serious dispute that could lead to legal action. If the purchase involves a lot of money, seek legal advice before you decide what to do.

• If you decide to go along with the seller's repairs, it is important to put on the record you are doing so at his insistence. Doing this will make the seller more accountable if the repairs are inadequate. If it is clear the seller will insist on repairing, you could follow up with a low-keyed warning requesting assurances that the repairs will be adequate. See page 257 for the warning to use in this situation.

STAGE TWO: LOW-KEYED WARNING FOR REVOKING ACCEPTANCE

There are several low-keyed warning steps you could use as part of a negotiating strategy for revoking acceptance. Below are the negotiating steps you could take before you revoke acceptance and the final step you can take to notify the seller you are revoking acceptance.

If you purchased a product on credit, and are entitled to withhold payment from the creditor because of the seller's failure to honor your contract, you can often put extra pressure on the seller simply by telling him this fact. To do it effectively, prepare a letter to the creditor to assert rights you have to hold that creditor accountable for the seller's failure to honor the contract and show it to the seller. (Since rights for holding a separate creditor accountable depend on the type of credit you used, see the appropriate chapter in Section VII for sample letters.)

A seller will usually make some effort to repair defects covered by a warranty. But if he refuses, or won't even acknowledge that the product is defective, adapt the following memo to demand he cure the defects as required by your contract.

If the seller still refuses to correct the defects, your demand that he do so will strengthen your bargaining position when it comes to holding him accountable for breaking your agreement. If the seller denies the defects are covered by warranties, see Chapter 38 on warranties in general, and page 341 for a memo you could use to remind him about warranty obligations that he has tried to avoid.

June 15, 19—

TO: ABC Sales Company
Futurama Mall
Anytown, USA

(This is to inform you that/As I have already verbally notified you on June 14, 19___) the (identify product) which (I purchased and received on June 1, 19___/was delivered on June 1, 19___, under our agreement of April 15, 19___) fails to conform to the requirements of our contract (and to inform you of the damages I sustained because it did not conform). I am also requesting that you furnish me adequate assurances that you will promptly perform your obligation under our contract to cure these defects.

(Contrary to your assurances that the product conformed on delivery despite the apparent defects I described to you/I have as of now discovered the following defects since delivery) (but this description is not a waiver of defects that may be revealed by subsequent examination):

(Describe the defects, or how the product is not operating properly, and when you first discovered them or noticed the problem)

And as described below, I have also sustained $ _____ in damages because the product failed to conform:

(Describe the damages and state the amount of the loss)

Since you have refused to cure the defects either by replacing the product or by repairing the defects as I had proposed (when we discussed this matter today/on June 14, 19___,) I can no longer rely on your good faith unless you give me adequate assurances that you will promptly carry out your obligation under our contract to cure the defects.

Since these defects deprive me of the use of this product (which I need for daily household/family purposes) and since I have already sustained damages because of this breach of our contract, you are either promptly to replace the product with one that conforms or make the adjustments and repairs required to make the product conform and furnish me your assurances within (five) days that you will do so.

I am, however, also prepared to resolve this matter (in full)* by returning the product to you for (a prompt refund of the $ _____ I have already paid toward the price (plus related charges)/and the discharge of all further obligations for this purchase under our contract, as well as reimbursement for the damages I have sustained.)*

And although I am still prepared to make payments that are due while we try to resolve this matter, any further payments are made with a reservation of all rights.

If you fail to furnish me the assurances I have requested and do not promptly carry out your obligations to cure the defects, I shall hold you responsible for breaching our contract and for all damages I sustain.

Please contact me promptly and either resolve this matter so we can still satisfactorily complete this transaction or as I have otherwise proposed to avoid my having to hold you liable for your breach.

_____
(Your signature)

Receipt acknowledged by:

_____   _____
(Signature and title of store representative)   *(Date)*

---

*Note: *Never* say you are willing to settle the matter "in full" if collecting damage is important to you; always add the phrase asking for the payment of damages. I personal injury or significant damage to other property resulted, seek legal advic rather than trying to handle it yourself.

• If you don't have this alternative memo with you when the seller first refuses to correct the defects, then use it as a follow-up step to demand the defects are corrected.

• If you have not notified the seller in writing about the defects when you first return to the store, then use the follow-up memo to put everything on the record. In this case, simply change the first sentence to say "This is to confirm my verbal notice of June 15, 19__ that the . . ." Then use the rest of the wording as appropriate.

• If you have already given the seller a written notice of the defects, then replace the first paragraph as follows:

"I am requesting that you promptly furnish me adequate assurances that you will perform your obligations under our contract of April 15, 19__, to cure the defects I described to you in my memorandum of June 15, 19__, which I gave you when we first discussed this matter."

Omit the wording for describing the defects and the damages you sustained if you have already told the seller, but use the rest of the paragraphs.

THREE OPTIONS FOR FOLLOW-UP ACTION

If the seller still refuses to correct the defects after you have demanded his assurances, you have three main options:

1. *Revoke acceptance if you are entitled to do so.* If the seller refuses to repair *substantial* defects, for instance, take this step immediately by adapting the sample low-keyed warning letter on page 269. Even if the seller is entitled to repair defects, his refusal to do so as required under a warranty almost automatically triggers your right to use the remedies available under the Code. This is an important pressure point: it is why sellers will generally at least go through the motions of trying to repair defective products.

2. *Recover damages you've sustained because the seller hasn't repaired the defects.* These are losses you've sustained because the product isn't worth what it would have been had it conformed to your contract. This is your main remedy when revocation is not available. (See chapter 36.)

3. *Use your negotiating strategy to enforce your rights under your state's deceptive sales practices law or fraud law if applicable.* If you have told the seller about the product's failure to measure up to important representations and he refuses to remedy the situation, use the low-keyed warning step on page 94 in Chapter 19. If this doesn't work and you could be entitled to revoke acceptance because of material misrepresentations or fraud, notify the seller you are revoking acceptance before you send him the ultimatum included in Section III.

A key point to remember when a seller (or manufacturer) refuses to repair defects, as he is obligated to do, is that if your agreement or written warranty includes clauses limiting your remedies, his refusal almost automatically entitles you to ignore such clauses. This is an important pressure point—it makes the seller vulnerable to all the actions you could take under the Code to enforce your contract. Always keep this in mind.

SELLER INSISTS ON REPAIRING SUBSTANTIALLY DEFECTIVE PRODUCT

If you initially discovered very substantial defects, or the product is badly damaged because of its defect, and the seller insists on repairing the product rather than replacing it as you have requested, you are faced with a dispute about whether repairs will be adequate to correct the problem.

The key to reaching an agreement is flexibility. Be accommodating and always make it clear that you are open to reasonable alternatives that will give you a product which fully conforms to your contract. It is important to leave some bargaining room to make it easier for both sides to back away from their initial bargaining positions.

Once you have notified the seller in writing about the defects, there is no need to state every bargaining position in writing while you are discussing a settlement. Instead, keep good notes of your conversations.

While you should be prepared to keep trying to negotiate a settlement, once it is clear the seller will only repair substantial defects without promising to do anything else, don't drag the matter out.

Choose between the following low-keyed warning follow-up steps if you decide to go along with the repairs rather than revoke acceptance.

- Insist the seller furnish his assurances that the repairs will be adequate and seek further commitments on what more he will do if they are not. Then put those commitments in writing as a condition for consenting to the repairs. If you consent to the repairs, also make clear you are doing so at his insistence and are reserving your rights.

- If the seller insists on repairing the defects but refuses to give you any assurances, give him a low-keyed warning that you are consenting to the repairs only because of his insistence, that you are reserving your rights, and will hold him responsible for breaching the agreement once it is clear the repairs are inadequate.

If a seller insists on repairing substantial defects and such repairs can correct the problem, you often have little choice but to go along with him. Since the seller is, in effect, forcing you to accept the settlement he wants, make clear that's the only reason you are going along with him. Doing this will usually strengthen your bargaining position to revoke acceptance later.

A key point to remember, however, is that the seller is in a weaker bargaining position to insist that repairs are adequate if your agreement or applicable warranties do not include limitation of remedies clauses, or such clauses call for the replacement of defective products.

DEMANDING ASSURANCES REPAIRS WILL CURE SUBSTANTIAL DEFECTS

Adapt this low-keyed warning to insist the seller give a specific commitment that repairs will correct substantial defects.

July 1, 19___

TO: R. Seller
Manager
ABC Sales Company
Futurama Mall
Anytown, USA

I am hereby (requesting/reaffirming the verbal request I made on June 29) that you furnish me your assurances that your attempt to repair the substantial defects in the ((identify product)) I purchased under our contract of (___date___) will, in fact, be adequate to make the product fully conform to our contract. I am also requesting your assurances that you will carry out your obligation to replace the product with one that conforms if its value to me is further impaired because your repairs fail to cure the defects.

The product was delivered on June 1, 19___, under our agreement of

April 15, 19___, but I subsequently discovered defects that considerably impair its value to me (and sustained damages) as I have described in my memorandum of June 25, 19___, which I gave you when we first discussed this matter. I then requested that you replace the product with one that conforms to our contract.

But during our discussions of this matter, you have continued to insist you would only repair the defects (and resulting damages to the product) rather than to replace it even though the product is substantially defective. I have pointed out that I consider the repairs inadequate to cure this breach because (describe why you think the repairs are inadequate—see page 192 for examples)

I have, however, also informed you that to avoid a dispute and complete this transaction, I am prepared to consent to repairs that are, in fact, adequate to make the product fully conform to our contract since you have insisted you will only repair the product rather than replace it. But since I must also depend on your skill and expertise in this matter, I cannot rely on repairs being adequate without your assurances.

If, however, you have any doubts about the adequacy of repairs, I urge you to replace the product rather than seek to repair it so we can avoid any further breach and additional damages.

If you, therefore, still insist in repairing the defects rather than replacing the non-conforming product, please furnish me the assurances I have requested and promptly complete the repairs required to make the product fully conform.

As an alternative, however, I am also prepared to settle this matter by returning the product to you for a prompt refund of the $ _____ I have already paid toward its purchase price (and a settlement in full of all outstanding obligations for this purchase.)

In the meantime, I shall, as you insist, make payments as due while we seek to settle this matter, but I am doing so while reserving all my rights.

I hope that we can now promptly settle this matter so that I will not have to hold you responsible for a complete breach of our contract and for all damages I sustain.

_____
(Your signature)

Receipt acknowledged.
(Leave space for pinning down a settlement you might reach.)

By _____   _____
(Signature and title of store representative)   *(Date)*

When you describe why the repairs are inadequate, be sure to describe how the repairs the seller wants to make would be incomplete or insufficient to make the product conform. He may, for example, want to replace damaged or defective parts with used or rebuilt ones in a new product.

CONSENTING TO REPAIRS SELLER INSISTS ON MAKING WITHOUT SPECIFIC ASSURANCES

If you finally consent to repairs the seller insists on making, even though he refuses to give you any written assurances, here is a memo you can adapt to put on the record the fact that you are consenting only at the seller's insistence.

July 15, 19__

TO: *R. Seller*
Manager
ABC Sales Company
Futurama Mall
Anytown, USA 00000

This is to notify you I am consenting to your proposal to repair the substantial defects in the (identify product) which I described in my memorandum of June 25, 19__ (copy attached) but only because you have insisted that our contract of April 15, 19__ under which I purchased it now only obligates you to repair those defects despite the reservations I have expressed about repairs being adequate to make the product fully conform.

Since you have refused to replace the substantially defective product or to furnish me your assurances that repairs would be adequate to cure the defects and have insisted that I must consent to the repairs as an adequate cure since our agreement now limits my remedies to the repairs you will make, I shall do as you insist.

But since I am compelled to rely on your expertise and skill for the adequacy of the repairs, please ensure that you make all the repairs required so the product then fully conforms to our contract to avoid any further material breaches.

I also request that you now complete the repairs promptly upon arrangements we make for returning it to you.

If, however, you have any doubts about the adequacy of your proposal for curing this breach, please notify me so that we can promptly make alternative arrangements for resolving this matter to avoid any further breach of this contract.

I am, of course, prepared to perform my remaining obligations under our agreement, but I am doing so while reserving all my rights.

And while I hope that your repairs will fully cure the defects so we can still satisfactorily complete this transaction, if it becomes clear the product's value is substantially impaired because the defects were not, in fact, adequately cured by repairs you have insisted on or because of further breaches I discover, I shall hold you responsible at least to the fullest extent provided by the Uniform Commercial Code.

_____
(Your signature)

Receipt acknowledged by

_____   _____
(Signature and title of store representative)   *(Date)*

When you agree to repairs, *do not* sign anything that says the repairs have been completed to your satisfaction, simply acknowledge *receiving* the product.

Follow-up actions would depend on how much the product's value has been impaired by any further defects you find.

Give the seller a chance to repair any minor defects that appear (use the sample memos for notifying the seller about subsequent defects). But if the repairs fail to correct major defects, request a replacement. If the seller insists on further repairs, leave open the possibility of giving the seller a final chance to repair the defects. If, however, you become reasonably sure you cannot rely on further repairs and could now be enitled to do so, revoke acceptance.

Here is a sample memo you can adapt to notify the seller he has failed to cure substantial defects and to request a replacement, while at the same time putting the onus on the seller to insist that repairs would still work.

September 5, 19__

TO: Mr. R. Seller
Manager
ABC Sales Company
Futurama Mall
Anytown, USA 00000

This is to inform you that our contract of April 15, 19__ , under which I purchased a (identify product) has again been breached as described below. (I am also notifying you of the damages I sustained as a result of this breach.)

I initially notified you on June 25, 19__ , about the substantial defects I had discovered after receiving the product. Although I requested that you replace it because it was substantially defective and repairs seemed unlikely to be adequate to cure the defects, at your insistence, I consented to your proposal for repairing those defects as I described in my memorandum of July 15, 19__ .

The product was returned to me on July 20, 19__ , but despite your attempts to repair the defects, it still fails to conform to the requirements of our contract as described below:
(Describe the defects that were not repaired adequately and any further defects you found)
(And as described below, I have sustained at least $ _____ in damages as a result of this further breach.)

Since you had previously insisted on repairing the defects, and since the inadequate repairs (and additional defects) have now further impaired the product's value to me, I request that you now promptly replace the defective product with one that fully conforms to our contract to avoid further breaches and so that we can still satisfactorily complete this transaction.

But as an alternative to replacement, I am also prepared to settle this matter by returning the defective product for a prompt refund of the $_____ I have already paid (and a settlement in full of all outstanding balances for this purchase).

(And there is now also due from you the $ _____ I have sustained in damages.)

I am, of course, also prepared to return the defective product to you (Would you make arrangements to pick up the defective product at my home) when you are prepared to replace it.

(Although I am still prepared to make payments as due while we seek to settle this matter, my payments are made with a reservation of all my rights.)

Since your previous attempt to repair the substantial defects has already proved inadequate, I urge you to replace the product rather than seek to make further repairs so we can complete the transaction without further breach and additional expense and inconvenience to me.

Please contact me promptly so we can now resolve this matter and avoid my having to hold you liable for a complete breach of our contract and all damages I sustain at least to the fullest extent provided by the Uniform Commercial Code.

_____
(Your signature)

Receipt acknowledged.
(Leave space for pinning down what the seller promised to do.)

By _____   _____
(Signature and title of store representative)   *(Date)*

• If the seller still insists he is only obligated to repair the defects, and you are prepared to go along with him, then use the memo on page 263 to make it clear you have again consented to his repairs at his insistence. Add wording as appropriate to make it clear the seller is still insisting he is only obligated to make repairs, despite the inadequacy of his previous attempt, and that your further willingness to consent doesn't mean you are waiving rights you previously asserted.

• If you are unwilling to consent to further repairs, though, and it is now reasonably clear you are entitled to revoke acceptance, then use the low-keyed warning on page 269 to revoke acceptance and demand your money back.

GIVING A SELLER A FINAL CHANCE TO REPAIR DEFECTS

If the seller's efforts fail to repair the defects, but he still insists on further chances, you can adapt the following low-keyed warning to make it clear this is his final chance.

September 20, 19___

TO: J. Seller
Manager
ABC Sales Company
Futurama Mall
Anytown, USA 00000

(1) This is to notify you that our contract of April 15, 19___, under which I purchased a (describe the product) has again been breached because the product still fails to conform to the requirements of our contract despite your previous attempts to repair defects. (And I am informing you of [further] damages I have sustained because the product still fails to conform.)

(2) I received the product on June 1 and initially notified you on June 15, 19___, that the product failed to conform to our contract as (I described to you in the memorandum I gave you/as was noted on your repair order number A111222). Although you then (verbally) assured me that the repairs would make the product conform to our contract, I have had to return the product on June 20 (list other dates on which you returned the product) because of defects (I described in the memos I gave you/as was noted on your repair orders numbered A1111333, _____).

(3) But contrary to your continuing assurances that the repairs would make the product conform to our contract, the repairs have still failed to correct the following defects (and I have discovered these additional

defects which only became apparent since the product was last repaired on September 1, 19___): (Describe defects that still have not been corrected and/or additional defects you discovered)

(4) And as described below, I have sustained $ _____ in (further) damages because the product has not conformed.

(5) Since our contract has now been repeatedly breached and the defects have deprived me of the use of the product and have continued to impair its value to me (and have resulted in the damages I have described), while you have insisted you would only repair the defects I am prepared to grant you only one more opportunity to comply with your obligations to furnish a product that fully conforms to our contract. You are, therefore, either to replace the defective product with one that fully conforms to our contract or, if you still insist on attempting to repair the defects, to make the repairs and adjustments necessary to correct all defects. (But since past repairs have already proved inadequate, if you still insist on making further repairs, please furnish me adequate assurances that you will now fully carry out your obligations to furnish me a product that conforms to our contract.)

(6) But as an alternative to further repairs or a replacement, I am also prepared to resolve this matter by returning the product to you for a prompt refund of the $ _____ I have paid (and a settlement in full of all outstanding charges for this purchase).

(7) And there is now also due from you $ _____ I have sustained in damages.

(8) (Since I have already returned the product to you/Please pick the product up at my home by September 23 and) replace it promptly or, if you insist on repairing it, please complete the repairs by (give date) and furnish me the assurances I have requested.

(9) Although I am prepared to make payments as due while we try to settle this matter, I am making payments while reserving all my rights.

(10) And since previous efforts to repair the defects have already proved inadequate to cure the repeated defects I have described which continue to impair the product's value to me, any further failure to cure the product's defects will prevent me from relying on assurances that further repairs would still be adequate to make the product conform.

(11) I hope that you will now either complete the repairs required to make the product conform so we can still complete the transaction without further breach and additional expenses and inconvenience to me or that you resolve it as I have proposed to avoid my having to hold you responsible for a complete breach of contract at least to the fullest extent provided by the Uniform Commercial Code.

_____
(Your signature)

Receipt of this memorandum is hereby acknowledged.

[Leave space to pin down seller's promises to correct the defects and to state the assurances you requested.]

By _____   _____
(Signature and title of store representative)   *(Date)*

• If the seller insists on repairing the goods after past attempts have already proved inadequate, try to get a commitment from him to take back the product if further repairs don't work. It's usually easiest to get such a commitment in the early stages, soon after you receive the product. This way the goods haven't yet changed very much because of use. That's when a seller is more likely to make such a commitment to try to convince you to keep the product since it is then that you are usually in a strong position to use remedies for making the seller take the product back, such as revoking acceptance if the seller won't do enough to correct the defects.

See page 226 for a memo to pin down such a commitment. But in this case, omit the wording about rejecting the goods.

If the seller refuses to make such a commitment, press for written assurances that the repairs will be adequate. Here is wording you can adapt to pin down the seller's assurances:

> *"We shall make the repairs and adjustments necessary to correct all the defects described in (your memorandum of September 20, 1990/ the above memorandum) and assure you these repairs and adjustments will correct all defects so the (describe product) will fully conform to the requirements of our contract of April 15, 19___ ."*

You could also use the memo included on page 249 to confirm any verbal assurances the seller gives you.

• If further repairs are still inadequate, your follow-up step would be the low-keyed warning to revoke acceptance (on page 269) and demand your money back if you are now entitled to take this step. The seller's insistence that he is only obligated to repair the defects, and his assurances that further repairs will correct them, will almost always substantially strengthen your bargaining position to revoke acceptance after his efforts clearly fail to work.

• If the seller has refused to make further repairs, as he is obligated to do, your follow-up steps would be the low-keyed warning to revoke acceptance if you are entitled to do so or, if you are not entitled, a low-keyed warning that you will hold him responsible for damages. If you can only recover damages because the seller refuses to repair defects, see page 322.

• If the seller insists on repairing defects, but won't make any promises about what he will do if further repairs prove inadequate, adapt this follow-up letter to make it clear you are only going along with the repairs at the seller's insistence. If it's already clear that you are entitled to revoke acceptance, and the seller still insists on repairing defects rather than replacing the goods or refunding your money, then obviously you do not have to go along with further repairs.

> *100 Witchtree Lane*
> *Anytown, USA 00000*
>
> *September 28, 19___*

Mr. Rip Seller
Manager
ABC Sales Company
Futurama Mall
Anytown, USA 00000

Dear Mr. Seller:

This confirms that I consented to another attempt to repair defects I described in my memorandum of September 20, 19___ , only because you insisted that you would do no more than to repair the (identify product) I purchased under our contract of April 15, 19___ , despite the fact that previous attempts to make this product conform to our contract have proved inadequate as I described to you.

Although I requested you either replace the product or furnish me adequate assurances that further repairs would, in fact, cure all defects after you refused my request for a replacement, you refused to do so. (Although you gave me your verbal assurances that the further repairs would cure all defects so I could now expect the product to conform to our contract, you stated in your letter of September 24, 19___, that you had not given those assurances I had described in my confirming letter of September 21.)

While I consented to the repairs because you insisted you were still only obligated to repair the product (and I was convinced you had given me the assurances described in my confirming letter), since (you refused to assure me/now deny giving me any assurances) further repairs will cure the defects so I can expect the product to conform to the requirements of our contract despite its repeated failure to do so, the repairs you completed by (date) must now make the product fully conform to the requirements of our contract.

I am, however, only consenting to the repairs at your insistence (and shall continue further payments under our contract) with a reservation of all rights.

(Since I have been compelled to rely on your expertise and skill for the repairs you insist on making) if you therefore have doubts about the adequacy of the repairs you completed, please notify me immediately so that we can promptly make alternative arrangements for resolving this matter to avoid any further breach of contract.

But if you do not respond to this proposal for making alternative arrangements that would avoid any further breach of our contract, your failure to cure the defects (and the denial you gave me assurances the repairs you completed would, in fact, be adequate to make the product conform), prevents me from relying on any assurances (or your good faith) that the product can (and will be) made to conform by further repairs if I discover any further breach.

I, therefore, urge you to reconsider whether the repairs you have completed are, in fact, adequate and that you promptly take such steps as you deem appropriate to ensure the product conforms to avoid my having to hold you responsible for a complete breach of contract and all damages I sustain at least to the fullest extent provided by the Uniform Commercial Code.

Sincerely,

REVOKING ACCEPTANCE

When you are entitled to revoke acceptance, return to the store and see if the seller will take back the product and exchange it, or refund your money. If he is cooperative, your problem will usually be solved—though be prepared to put the settlement in writing if doing so could be important. If the seller refuses to take back the product, on the other hand, you should be prepared to give him your written low-keyed warning for revoking acceptance.

SELLER AGREES TO TAKE BACK THE PRODUCT

If you made a cash purchase, it is seldom necessary to pin down anything in writing when the seller takes back the product and refunds your money.

It can be important to pin down a settlement in the following situations, though:

1. *The seller gives you a credit instead of a cash refund or only credits the account to which you charged the purchase.* It is important to pin down in writing that the seller now either owes you a refund of what you have already paid, or that any amounts you had charged to an account are, in effect, wiped out. Having written proof that you are entitled to a credit for the entire amount you had charged to a credit account is the easiest way to clear up an outstanding credit obligation. The written credit record should identify the defective product, the date, the amount of the credit, the account to which the credit will be applied, and when the amount is to be credited to the account if it is different from the date when you returned the product.

2. *There are outstanding payments under an agreement which you no longer owe after the seller takes back the product.* You must pin down in writing that you no longer owe the outstanding payments to the seller, or any other creditor to whom you may be making payments, and get a refund or proper credit for any amounts you have already paid for the product.

This situation would usually occur when you bought the product under an installment credit agreement calling for regular monthly payments. How you clear up these outstanding obligations can depend on the type of credit you used, whether you are still making your payments to the seller or some other creditor, whether you are entitled to withhold payments from the creditor (other than the seller) because of the seller's failure to honor the agreement, and whether you still owe money for other products purchased under the same agreement. See Chapter 64 for an outline of what to do if any of these conditions apply.

It is important to remember that when you purchase a product on credit from the seller, you have, in effect, two separate sets of rights and obligations under that agreement. One covers the purchase of the product; the other the terms under which the credit was extended. The remedies described in this chapter tell how you can hold the seller accountable for breaking the sales terms of your agreement. The laws described in Section VII spell out how and when you can hold a creditor responsible for the seller's failure to honor your sales agreement, so that you do not have to repay the creditor what you no longer owe the seller.

3. *The seller replaces the defective product.* If you are willing to have the seller replace the product, it means, in effect, you are continuing with your original agreement. You should note that the seller has taken back the faulty product and describe what he delivers as a replacement. If the replacement will not be delivered until later, pin down an absolutely firm delivery date and note that you will be entitled to your money back if the product isn't delivered by that date. Also note any specific conditions that would entitle you to your money back if the replacement does not conform.

In short, if the seller replaces the defective product—when you are entitled to revoke acceptance and could demand your money back—give him as little room as possible to argue about whether you will be entitled to your money back if the replacement isn't delivered on time, or if there is anything wrong with it. If the seller refuses to agree with these terms, then press for a refund instead; you don't want a replacement that would simply be another headache.

4. *Arrangements for returning the product.* When you are entitled to revoke acceptance of a product for which you have paid, be especially careful about the circumstances in which you actually return the product, especially if payments are still outstanding. If you cannot take the product with you when discussing the matter with the seller, you may then be unable to resolve the matter fully until after the seller has picked it up or at least examined it at your home (or elsewhere) to confirm it is really defective as you say.

If the seller is willing to take the product back, refund your money and settle the outstanding obligation on your complaint that the product is defective, get such commitments in writing before you return the product. (If a separate creditor is involved, see page 537 for more details about additional arrangements you should make with him before you return the product.) If the seller is unwilling to make any commitments until he has examined the product, ask him to look at it and then work out the settlement before he picks up the product. Be careful about the circumstances in which you return a product. The Code gives you a security interest in it for the return of what you have paid, but you have that security interest only as long as the product is still in your possession.

If you simply assumed the seller was going to resolve the problem after he picked the product up, you might then be faced with the following unpleasant alternatives.

If you then revoke acceptance, you no longer have the product or a security interest in it and the leverage that can give you to settle up with the seller and/or creditor.

If, however, the seller again tries to repair the defects and insists on returning the product and you take it even though it should be reasonably clear you were entitled to revoke acceptance, you would then almost certainly give up that right.

Whether you notify the seller you are revoking acceptance before or after he picks a product up from you probably won't matter very much if you've already paid for the product, since in either case you would have to sue the seller to get your money back if he refuses to refund it. But if the seller gets the product back while you still owe money on it and you then try to revoke acceptance, instead of going along with further repairs, it is then much easier for the seller to claim that he is keeping the product as a voluntary repossession, and report your account as a bad debt if you try to withhold payment. So, in this situation, revoking acceptance while you still have the product at least gives you some leverage while you try to reach a settlement.

Pinning down how the seller will settle the matter after he picks up the product, significantly strengthens your bargaining position if you then have to formally revoke acceptance because the seller reneges on his promise.

The key point to remember is to pin down the commitments the seller agrees to and get his signature. You can do this on a settlement form he provides, or on the original copy of the agreement you signed.

Sample wording is not included for pinning down settlements where it is usually easy to get needed documentation, such as when a seller gives you a credit on your account. (If a seller doesn't give you adequate written documentation, your alternative is to get a cash refund.)

The sample memo that follows is for use in the following circumstances when you have already paid for the product:

• The seller gives you a credit instead of a cash refund, but you want to retain the option of getting a cash refund in case you cannot use the credit.
• The seller agrees to replace the defective product but the new one won't be delivered until later.
• You must first ask the seller to pick up the product and want to pin down a preliminary settlement.

The memo identifies the problem; sample wording for pinning down different settlements is then included and the appropriate wording should be placed at the bottom of the memo, *after* you have reached a settlement.

A word of caution about using any wording for pinning down a settlement. If you agree to settle a problem in a particular way, you are usually stuck with that settlement. So never agree to a settlement in writing unless you are satisfied with the solution that is spelled out. And to avoid any possible trouble, *never* use the sample wording when you have significant additional damages for which you may want to hold someone accountable. Seek legal advice before you settle anything in these circumstances.

Remember, you may also have to make a separate settlement with a creditor when you still owe money. See page 578 in Chapter 69 for sample letters or memos to tie down settlements involving outstanding payment obligations under a credit agreement.

September 15, 19__

TO: *ABC Sales Company*
Futurama Mall
Anytown, USA 00000

I am revoking my acceptance of (and returning/ requesting that you pick up) the (describe defective product) which I bought from you on (under our agreement of) April 15, 19__ , because it is still defective as described below despite previous attempts to correct all defects.

(Identify the defects especially if you are asking the seller to pick up the product.)

I have (paid its $ _____ purchase price to you as shown on the attached copy of my receipt/charged its $ _____ purchase price to my Easy Money Credit Account, number 000-0000-0000).

_____
(Your signature)

Then pin down the appropriate settlement at the bottom of the memo, and use continuation pages if necessary.

PINNING DOWN A CASH REFUND OPTION WHEN YOU GET A CREDIT

The (_____(ABC Company)_____) accepts the return of the product identified above and has given the buyer a credit of $ _____ but the buyer shall, at (his/her) option, be entitled to a cash refund.

Agreed to by:

_____   _____
(Signature and title of store representative)   *(Date)*

PINNING DOWN CONDITIONS FOR THE LATER DELIVERY OF A REPLACEMENT

The (ABC Company) accepts the return of the defective product identified above and shall deliver a replacement by (insert delivery date). The replacement shall conform to the requirements of our contract of April 15, 19__ . (Delivery shall be made F.O.B. the buyer's address.)

The (ABC Company) agrees that timely delivery is of the essence to the buyer and that the company shall have no right to cure if the replacement fails to conform to the requirements of our contract. If timely delivery is not made or the replacement does not conform to our contract (before acceptance by the buyer),* the buyer shall be entitled to cancel the

*purchase. The transaction shall otherwise be subject to the terms of the
original contract.*

 Agreed to by:

_____ _____

(Signature and title of store representative) *(Date)*

Accepted by buyer with reservation of all other rights.

_____ _____

  (Your signature)   Date)

*Note: You can try to leave out the phrase "before acceptance by the buyer" if the seller agrees to take back the replacement should it turn out to be defective after acceptance. You can be pretty sure, though, that the seller would rather refund your money than go along with this kind of a settlement.

If the seller insists that you formally agree to the settlement, then try to reserve any other rights you might have.

PINNING DOWN A PRELIMINARY SETTLEMENT WHEN YOU ASK THE SELLER TO PICK UP THE PRODUCT

The (ABC Company) will pick up the product identified above on (September 17, 19__) at the buyer's home and will accept its return if it does not conform to our contract.

 If the product does not conform, the buyer shall be entitled to cancel the purchase and to a refund of $_____ unless an alternative settlement is arranged by (September 17, 19__).

 Agreed to by:

_____ _____

(Signature and title of store representative) *(Date)*

If the seller reneges on this promise to settle, your follow-up step should be the ultimatum to cancel. So the memo you write when asking the seller to pick up the product should specifically state you are revoking acceptance. (You don't have to say that in your memo when you return a product yourself, however.)

• Don't type a settlement option at the bottom of your memo. When you return to ask the seller to take back the product, take the wording with you and then add it after you have reached the settlement. Also take with you a low-keyed warning memo for revoking acceptance in case the seller refuses to settle.

SELLER REFUSES TO TAKE THE PRODUCT BACK

Following are sample memos you can adapt for notifying a seller you are revoking acceptance in different circumstances when the seller refuses the take the product back from you and settle. Keep in mind that revoking acceptance can now trigger a dispute that could lead to legal action.

(If you are making payments to a creditor at this point, and are entitled to withhold payments as described in Chapter 62, be sure to notify the creditor you have revoked acceptance and may no longer owe the money. If the seller and/or creditor insist you do owe the money, see Chapter 62 for follow-up steps you can take to settle credit terms.)

REVOKING ACCEPTANCE WHEN YOU STILL HAVE THE PRODUCT

Adapt this memo to revoke acceptance if the seller refuses to settle and you still have the product.

September 15, 19___

TO: Mr. Rip Seller
Manager
ABC Sales Company
Futurama Mall
Anytown, USA 00000

(1) "I am hereby revoking my acceptance of the (identify defective product) which (I purchased and received from you on June 1, 19___, as shown on the attached copy of my receipt/which you delivered on June 1, 19___, under our agreement of April 15, 19___). I am also notifying you of the damages I have now sustained."

(2) "I am revoking acceptance because the product still does not conform to our contract, despite your previous attempts to cure the defects, and which has now substantially impaired its value to me."

(3) "The product still does not conform to our contract because of the following defects (which have not been adequately repaired/(and) which I have only discovered since your last attempt to repair it on (date)): (Describe the defects the seller has still failed to correct and/or additional ones you found since the seller's last attempt to repair the product)

(4) ● Choose whichever of the following applies to your situation:

"I originally accepted the product on your assurances it conformed to our contract but which it failed to do as I informed you on (list the dates on which you notified the seller about defects you discovered later)."

"I originally accepted the product without knowing of the defects which I was unable to discover until after acceptance and which I told you about on (list the dates on which you notified the seller about defects you discovered later)."

●"I initially rejected the product on June 1, 19___, because it failed to conform to our contract as I described to you in my memorandum of that date. When I received the product again on June 18, 19___, I accepted it only on the condition those defects had, in fact, been cured by (describe how the seller was supposed to correct the defects) but which were not, in fact, cured as I informed you on (dates). I also accepted it without knowing of the additional defects I was unable to discover until after acceptance and which I told you about on (list the dates)."

●"I originally accepted the product on (your assurances/the assumption) the defects I told you about on June 3, 19___, would be cured by (describe what the seller had promised to do or what you expected him to do to correct the defects) and without knowing of additional defects I was unable to discover until after acceptance and which I told you about on (list the dates when you notified the seller about defects you discovered later)."

(5) "But (contrary to your continuing assurances that the product would be made to conform by your attempts to make repairs and adjustments, your last attempt to make the product conform again proved inadequate/

although you have continued to insist that you are obligated only to repair the defects even though the product has repeatedly proved to be defective, your last attempt to repair the defects is again inadequate)."

(6) "Since these defects again deprive me of the use of this product which I regularly need for (household/family purposes), I can no longer rely on further assurances from you that the product can be made to conform to our contract by any further adjustments and repairs. (Your previous refusal to give me your assurances that the product would be made to conform by the repairs and adjustments you performed and to which I consented at your insistence now prevents me from believing that any further repairs will make the product conform to our contract.)"

(7) "I have now also sustained at least the damages described below for which there is now due from you $_____ . (describe and give the amounts due for damages caused by the defects)."

(8) "Although you have already refused to do so, in order that we may promptly resolve this matter, I am now still prepared to do so for the prompt return of the $_____ I have already paid toward the price (and related charges), (and) the discharge of all obligations still remaining for this purchase under our contract (and the reimbursement of the $_____ I have now sustained as damages). You are also to make arrangements for picking the product up at my home or furnish me your instructions for returning them at your expense and risk upon the return of at least the $ I have paid toward the price. (I am, however, also still prepared to continue with our agreement if you will now cure this breach by promptly replacing the defective product with one that conforms to our contract. If you will not do so,) I require a prompt refund of what I have paid so I can purchase a suitable substitute to minimize my further expenses and your damages."

(9) "But as provided by the Uniform Commercial Code, I now have a security interest in the product for the return of at least the $_____ I have paid toward the price. I am now only holding the product for you at your risk (and am reserving my right to resell it as provided by the Uniform Commercial Code if you do not return the $_____ I have paid toward the price (and any outstanding instrument/and properly account for the amount no longer due or owing under our contract for this purchase) within ten days from (date))."

(10) "And as also provided by the Uniform Commercial Code, the remaining balance for this purchase is now no longer due or owing under our agreement. (I shall, however, continue to make payments as due for the other products I have also purchased under this agreement.)"

(11) "Please contact me promptly so that we can still satisfactorily resolve this matter."

(12) "But if you refuse my proposals for resolving this matter, I shall hold you responsible for breach of contract and for all damages I sustain to the fullest extent provided by law."

———————————————
(Your signature)

———————

Receipt acknowledged by:

————————————————————————   ———————
(Signature and title of store representative)   *(Date)*

- If the seller refuses to acknowledge receipt of your memo, leave a copy anyway, and then promptly send him another copy by certified mail with a covering letter.
- If there is still an outstanding balance when you purchased the product on credit, prepare a cancellation letter available for immediate use in case the seller/creditor tries to repossess as explained in Chapter 67. And if repossession is a possibility, see page 559 for additional wording you could add to the last paragraph to warn the seller about cancellation and risks he could then take if he still tried to repossess.
- If you purchased the goods on credit, also see page 543 for sample wording you could adapt and include in the first paragraph to identify the type of credit arrangement involved.
- The amounts you could include in "the price" the seller could be required to return may also depend on the type of credit arrangement you used. See page 539 for more details about what amounts could be included in "the price" and how you might estimate it when it doesn't include amounts paid for other items like finance or credit insurance charges.
- The sample wording included in paragraph 9 to tell the seller you are reserving your right to resell the defective product if he fails to refund what you have paid could make a seller/creditor very nervous and prompt attempts to repossess since if you did resell as you could be entitled to do, they would be out the collateral. But saying that you are at least retaining your right to do so warns them about that possibility and puts more pressure on them to settle. But NEVER actually try to resell goods in such circumstances without legal advice. You could, of course, simply omit the wording about reselling.

REVOKING ACCEPTANCE WHEN YOU DON'T HAVE A WRITTEN MEMO WITH YOU

If the seller refuses to take the product back but you don't take a written memo with you when you return to the store, then at least verbally notify the seller you are revoking acceptance and spell out the things you would have included in a memo. Then immediately send a low-keyed warning to revoke acceptance in writing. Use the sample memo on page 269 but revise the first paragraph as follows, and alter other wording as appropriate.

"This is to confirm the verbal notice I gave you on September 15, 19__, that I was revoking my acceptance of the (identify defective product) . . ." Then continue with the rest of the first paragraph.

REVOKING ACCEPTANCE AFTER YOU HAVE RETURNED THE PRODUCT

Although I strongly urge you not to do this, there are times when it might happen that you return a defective product to the seller before you revoke acceptance and make a settlement. Obviously, in this case you lose the leverage of having the product in your possession while you are trying to settle. A situation like this usually occurs when you have to ask the seller to pick up the product. One answer is to try to arrange a preliminary settlement, as described on page 268.

But if you simply returned the product first, be prepared to revoke acceptance in writing when the seller again tries to return the goods to you. Here is how you can adapt the memo on page 269 to fit this situation.

Replace numbered paragraphs (1), (2), (8) and (9) with the following ones, and use and modify the other paragraphs as appropriate.

(1) "I am hereby revoking my acceptance of the (identify defective product) which I (purchased and received from you on June 1, 19___, as shown on the attached copy of my receipt/which you delivered on June 1, 19___, under our agreement of April 15, 19___). (I returned the product to you on September 15, 19___/The product was picked up by your company on September 17, as we had arranged on September 15) when I informed you the product was still defective. I am also notifying you of the damages I have now sustained."

(2) "I am now revoking acceptance because the product still does not conform to our contract despite your previous attempts to cure the defects and its value to me has now been substantially impaired as a result."

(8) "Although you have already refused to do so, in order that we may promptly resolve this matter, I am now still prepared to do so for the prompt return of the $_____ I have already paid toward the price (and related charges), (and) the discharge of all obligations still remaining for this purchase under our contract, (and the reimbursement of the $_____ I have now sustained as damages). (I am, however, also still prepared to continue with our agreement if you will now cure this breach by promptly replacing the defective product with one that conforms to our contract. If you will not do so,) I require a prompt refund of what I have paid so I can purchase a suitable substitute to minimize my further expenses and your damages."

(9) "But as provided by the Uniform Commercial Code, the remaining balance for this purchase is no longer due or owing under our agreement. (I shall, however, continue to make payments as due for the other products I have also purchased under this agreement.) And although the product has already been returned to you, you are not to treat it as a repossession."

REVOKING ACCEPTANCE WHEN THE SELLER INSISTS ON REPAIRS THAT ARE UNACCEPTABLE

There are, of course, times when defects are so substantial, or cause such substantial damage to the product, that repairs would be inadequate. If the seller insists on making repairs that are unacceptable, your next step is to revoke acceptance (assuming, of course, you would be entitled to do so).

Here is a sample memo you can adapt for revoking acceptance in such situations.

July 10, 19___

TO: Mr. R. Seller
Manager
ABC Sales Company
Futurama Mall
Anytown, USA 00000

I am hereby revoking acceptance of the (identify defective product) which (I purchased and received from you on June 1, 19___, as shown on the attached copy of my sales receipt/which you delivered to me on June 1, 19___, under our agreement of April 15, 19___.) (I returned the product to you/You picked the product up on) (date) (when/after) I informed you it failed to conform to our contract.

I am revoking acceptance because the product does not conform to our contract as I have already described in my memorandum of June 25,

19__, when I also informed you of the damages I sustained (copy attached).

I originally accepted the product (on your assurances that it conformed to our contract/without knowing about the defects which I could not discover until after acceptance).

Since the substantial defects I later discovered (and the extensive damage to the product which was caused by those defects) prevented me from relying on repairs as being adequate to cure this breach, I initially proposed that you replace the product with one that conformed to our contract. But when you refused to do so when we discussed this matter on (list dates when you discussed it) and insisted instead that you would only repair the defects, I then informed you on July 1, 19__, that I would be prepared to consent to those repairs if you furnished me your assurances that the repairs would, in fact, be adequate to make the product conform to our contract, and that you would carry out your obligation under our contract to replace the product or refund its purchase price if the repairs turned out to be inadequate.

But on July 9 you told me you would furnish no written assurances and have continued to insist you would only seek to repair the defects.

Although you have continued to claim the substantial defects (and resulting damage) could be adequately repaired, your refusal to furnish the assurances I requested prevents me from relying on those repairs being adequate to cure this breach and on your continued willingness to carry out your obligations under our contract in good faith.

(Then complete the memo by adapting paragraphs (8) through (12) of the basic memo included on page 269 when you still have the product or by adapting the alternative paragraphs included on page 272 when the product has already been returned to the seller.)

_____

(Your signature)

Receipt acknowledged by:

_____   _____

(Signature and title of store representative)   (Date)

REJECTING AND REVOKING ACCEPTANCE AFTER SELLER FAILS TO CURE DEFECTS

There are situations in which it could be unclear whether you might still be entitled to reject goods or only revoke acceptance. This may happen if a seller delivered goods that failed to conform and you received them with the seller's promises to correct the defects which he then failed to do. It may also be true if you discovered defects within the time you had to inspect before accepting. Since the Code is unclear just how long you can take to find defects after you start using the product and still be entitled to reject rather than only revoke acceptance, it could be important to avoid foreclosing the rejection option in such situations when you may be entitled to revoke.

If you then assert you are only revoking acceptance and indicate you had accepted the product, that would almost certainly foreclose the rejection option that might still be available. So if a product's failure to conform and/or the seller's failure to correct defects could entitle you to revoke acceptance but the rejection option might still be available, you could then notify the seller you are "rejecting and/or revoking acceptance" to strengthen your bargaining position. But remember you cannot combine these options unless you have found and notified the seller about the defects within the time allowed for rejecting the product in the first place.

You can adapt the following sample memo for notifying a seller you are rejecting and/or revoking acceptance when that possibility could still be available. The wording of this memo assumes you did not leave the product with the seller when you told him you are taking this step.

Use the alternative wording on page 272 as a guide for adapting this memo if you reject and revoke acceptance only after the product has been returned.

July 7, 19___

TO: Mr. R. Seller
Manager
ABC Sales Company
Futurama Mall
Anytown, USA 00000

I am hereby rejecting and/or revoking my acceptance of the (identify the product) which (I purchased and received on June 1, 19___, as shown on the attached copy of my sales receipt/which you delivered on June 1, 19___, under our agreement of April 15, 19___). I am also notifying you of the damages I have now sustained.

I am now doing so because the product still does not conform to our contract, despite your previous attempts to cure its defects, and which has now substantially impaired its value to me.

The product still does not conform to our contract because of the following defects (which have not been adequately repaired/(and which I have only discovered since your last attempt to repair it on (date)):

(Describe the defects the seller has still failed to correct and/or additional ones you found since the seller's last attempt to repair the product)

As you know, (I informed you at the time of delivery the product did not conform but received it on your assurances/I first informed you on (date) that the product failed to conform but you then assured me) the defects would be cured by the repairs and adjustments you were to complete by (date) (or state how else the seller had promised to cure the defects).

(But of these defects, the ones already identified still have not been repaired despite further repairs and adjustments made after I had to return the product on (give dates). /Although these defects have now apparently been cured, I was required to return the product for further repairs on (give dates) before they were apparently cured.)

(Atlhough these defects were apparently cured,) I subsequently discovered and notified you on (give dates) about further defects I discovered and for which I had to return the product for additional repairs on (give dates).

(Then complete the memo with paragraphs (5) through (12) of the basic memo included on page 269.)

_____
(Your signature)

Receipt acknowledged by:

_____   _____
(Signature and title of store representative)   *(Date)*

• If the seller agrees to a satisfactory settlement after you formally revoke acceptance, then pin down the settlement in writing as outlined on page 578.

• If the seller refuses to settle, your next step is to issue an ultimatum based on your legal remedies for enforcing an agreement. (See the next chapter.)

If you purchased the product on credit, be sure to check Section VII.

36 · Buyer's and Seller's Legal Remedies for Enforcing An Agreement

The Code makes several legal remedies available to the buyer when the seller breaks an agreement. Generally speaking, these remedies spell out what corrective actions you can take on your own, and what damages you may be entitled to collect.

Some of the remedies may be used only when you are entitled to cancel all or parts of an agreement. Others may be used only when you cannot undo acceptance of a product. Still others can be used in every situation.

Remember, though, that remedies available under the Code may be limited by "exclusive" terms included in your agreement or warranty. (See page 239.)

BUYER'S RIGHT TO CANCEL

The Code entitles you to cancel an agreement when:

- The seller fails to deliver the products as required by the agreement.
- You rightfully reject or justifiably revoke acceptance of the products the seller delivers.
- The seller repudiates the agreement; that is, he makes clear in advance he will not perform future obligations. Although a seller is considered to have repudiated an agreement when he fails to furnish assurances that you are entitled to demand (see page 172), trying to cancel an agreement merely because of such a failure can involve you in tricky legal technicalities. Always get legal advice before canceling an agreement in this kind of situation.

In cases where you purchase more than one product under the same agreement, and the seller fails to deliver or you reject or justifiably revoke acceptance of only *some* of the products, you may cancel only the parts of the agreement that cover the products involved rather than the entire agreement.

REMEDIES AVAILABLE WHEN YOU ARE ENTITLED TO CANCEL

When you are entitled to cancel an agreement, these are the remedies available:

1. *Right to refund of amount paid for price and discharge of remaining obligations.*
Cancellation entitles you to a refund of what you have paid for the price. Cancellation also discharges (i.e. it legally ends) any obligations remaining under the agreement except that the person entitled to cancel keeps remedies he has for holding the other party accountable for breaching the contract. The discharge of obligations remaining under the agreement means, for example, you legally no longer owe any unpaid amounts for the cancelled purchase. If a seller won't refund your money, you can sue. (If you purchased goods on credit, you could also be entitled to get your money back from a creditor other than the seller and would also no longer owe the outstanding amount to that creditor depending on the type of credit used for financing the purchase. See page 523.)

But while a buyer entitled to cancel normally has the right to a refund of all amounts paid for the price, this has tended to make the courts more reluctant to rule in favor of buyers seeking to use remedies that would entitle them to cancel (such as revoking acceptance) after having gotten some use out of the product. That's because ruling for the buyer in effect means forcing a seller to assume the entire loss for a transaction even though the buyer gained some benefit from the use he got. But if courts strictly followed the rules spelled out by the Code, they can avoid making the seller assume the entire loss only by ruling a buyer wasn't entitled to use remedies that would enable them to cancel, which results in the buyer being stuck with a faulty product and having to pay the full amount except for what a buyer might be entitled to get back for damages because the product failed to measure up to the contract.

To avoid such all or nothing results, courts have, in some cases, said a buyer was entitlted to reject and/or revoke acceptance and cancel but have required the buyer to pay the seller a reasonable sum for the use he got out of the product. Decisions like this have usually been made in situations where the seller had refused to take back the product after the buyer had revoked acceptance, and it was difficult for the buyer to avoid using it.

This was the solution a Tennessee court adopted in 1972 in the case of *Moore* v. *Howard Pontiac-American, Inc.* It allowed Mr. Moore to revoke acceptance of a defective car, even though he had used the car after doing so, because he found other kinds of transportation prohibitively expensive. But it required Mr. Moore to pay the dealer a reasonable amount for the use of the vehicle.

Although courts have not established clear-cut rules in such cases, your willingness to pay the seller for reasonable use of a product *could* strengthen your position to revoke acceptance. In this way you would be able to get most of your money back at least. Whether such a partial refund would be a reasonable settlement would depend, of course, on the situation. I don't suggest you automatically offer to pay the seller just for the use of the product when you are entitled to revoke acceptance; but it is something to consider as a way of settling the matter. Remember, as a general rule, you must stop using the product after revoking acceptance.

2. *Damages for buying a substitute product*

If you are entitled to cancel because the seller fails to deliver the product, you rightfully reject or justifiably revoke acceptance, you then also do not have the product the seller was required to furnish under your contract.

Since the seller has then failed to furnish the product you were entitled to get, you may now have to go out and buy a substitute from someone else. The substitute may cost more than you were supposed to pay for the product you were to get under your agreement, and under certain circumstances, the seller may have to pay the difference. This would be considered a form of damages because the seller failed to furnish the product you were supposed to get for the price called for under your agreement.

Buying a substitute in a situation like this is called making a "cover" purchase, and your damages are the "cost of cover." To hold a seller accountable for such damages, you must make a substitute purchase without unreasonable delay, in other words, soon after rejecting or revoking acceptance, or soon after the seller fails to deliver the product.

Suppose, for example, you buy a $350 General Watts freezer. Unfortunately, the deal turns sour because the store fails to deliver the product and you cancel upon being entitled to do so. But now you have to buy the freezer from someone else—and the cost turns out to be $500. The $150 extra you have to pay could be considered damages for the original seller's failure to furnish the freezer under your original agreement.

While a substitute product does not have to be identical to the original, it must be at least very similar. If you first purchased a stripped-down economy model, you couldn't buy a super-deluxe substitute, for instance.

Nor may you collect the cost of cover expenses you "saved." If the original seller was going to charge you $25 extra for delivering the freezer, for example, but the delivery charge was included in the $500 price of the second freezer, then the cover purchase obviously cost you $125 extra rather than $150.

3. *Buyer's damages when he doesn't make a substitute purchase*

The Code doesn't require you to make a substitute purchase, of course, but if you don't make one, you can recover only the difference between the market price for the kind of product involved and the purchase price under your agreement.

If you purchase the goods at a store, the market price is the one prevailing in the locality where you buy the product. If you buy some other way, such as via mail order, there are other ways to figure the market price. It is, of course, up to the buyer to show what the market price is.

4. *Other remedies that could be available*

There are other remedies you can use when canceling a purchase, but they are seldom practical moves unless you have legal advice. They are:

• Obtaining possession of the specific product a seller fails to deliver. In special circumstances, such as when a seller fails to deliver a product you could not buy elsewhere, you could be entitled to go to court to force the seller to deliver the actual product rather than simply trying to collect damages.

• Reselling the goods yourself if you have rightfully rejected or justifiably revoked acceptance of them, but the seller refuses to take them back and refund your money. If you resell the goods for more than the refund you would receive, you would have to return the rest to the seller. If you don't get enough to cover the refund you are entitled to get, you could sue the seller for the rest. This is seldom a practical option when goods are defective.

• Resales must be made according to specific rules, so you do need legal advice.

A WORD ABOUT FINANCE CHARGES

When you are entitled to cancel a purchase, the Code allows you to get back the purchase price. But the purchase price may not include finance charges or payments for other services, such as for credit life insurance. (See section VII.) You may, however, be entitled to recover such payments as either incidental or as consequential damages. (See page 276 about these types of damages.)

USING THE REMEDIES AVAILABLE WHEN YOU ARE ENTITLED TO CANCEL

Getting your money back and settling any outstanding payment obligations should be your main objective. But damages could be the seller's weak spot and threatening to hold him accountable for them could convince him to settle.

Mention the damages that you could recover. And to demonstrate that you're serious, find out and tell him what you would have to pay elsewhere for a substitute product. Get specific price quotations from other stores soon after you learn the seller has broken the agreement.

But while the Code entitles you to recover these damages, you obviously can't expect the seller to pay them willingly. So, as a practical matter, these remedies aren't very useful when the seller refunds your money since it would seldom be worthwhile to sue him. But if you have to sue the seller anyway to get your money back, you might as well try to recover other damages as well. (Check to see if your agreement or warranty includes "exclusive" limitation of remedies clauses which could prevent you from collecting such damages.)

YOUR RIGHTS WHEN ACCEPTANCE CANNOT BE UNDONE

When your acceptance of the goods is considered final, and you are no longer entitled to revoke acceptance and get a refund, the Code makes two remedies available. They are:

- Recovering damages you sustain because the product fails to measure up to the requirements of the contract or the warranties.
- Deducting damages from any amounts still due under the contract.

These are also the main remedies available to enforce your rights under a warranty when you can no longer revoke acceptance. They are discussed in more detail in Chapter 36.

DAMAGES A BUYER COULD RECOVER IN ALL SITUATIONS

The Code makes two other remedies available which can apply in all situations. These are the rights to recover what are called "incidental" and "consequential" damages.

AMOUNTS RECOVERABLE AS INCIDENTAL DAMAGES

Although they are not specifically defined by the Code, incidental damages generally refer to reasonable out-of-pocket expenses you incur as a result of the seller's breach of the contract. The Code lists the following expenses which you may claim as incidental damages:

- Reasonable expenses for inspecting, transporting, or storing goods when you rightfully reject or justifiably revoke acceptance.
- Reasonable charges, expenses, or commissions you incur when making a cover purchase.
- Any other reasonable expenses that are due to the seller's breach of contract.

Examples of incidental damages might include towing charges for a defective car; rental fees for a substitute product; or fees paid for insurance coverage on a product while you are storing it. They might include finance charges paid under an agreement.

Courts have given buyers considerable leeway when it comes to incidental damages, so don't overlook any reasonable expense that *results from* the seller's breach. You cannot, on the other hand, hold the seller responsible for avoidable or unnecessary expenses.

AMOUNTS RECOVERABLE AS CONSEQUENTIAL DAMAGES

Generally speaking, consequential damages are losses caused by the defect itself, or the seller's breach of contract. In consumer transactions, injury to a person or damage to property are the types of consequential damages that are most likely to occur. Here are some examples:

- A purchaser bought antifreeze to protect an engine to be stored over the winter. The antifreeze was defective and the engine and equipment were damaged as a result. The buyer recovered the reasonable cost for the labor and parts required to repair the damage.

• A defect in a car caused a fire in the owner's house. He recovered $90,000 as consequential damages from the manufacturer.

• The cost of unsuccessful repairs of defects covered by a warranty, and amounts paid as finance charges, could count as consequential rather than incidental damages.

To recover consequential damages, you must be able to establish the actual dollar value of the loss. And you *cannot* recover any losses you could have avoided. Say, for example, consequential damages occur after you continue to use a product, when you know about or should have known about, the defects. You can seldom hold the seller, or other warrantor, accountable for the losses because, in this case, the law considers that, in effect, you brought them on yourself.

One consumer was prevented from recovering $62,000 in consequential damages when a fire, caused by defective wiring in an "instant-on" TV switch, swept through his house. Even though the switch had given off sparks and smoke on two previous occasions, the owner had continued to use the set and kept it plugged in all night. It was decided that the consumer had had fair warning something was amiss with the set.

If you have a loss you could recover as consequential damages, promptly make an itemized list of the damage incurred and, if at all possible, keep some evidence, such as the defective product, or what's left of it. Try to take pictures that show the extent of the damage to help substantiate your claim.

COLLECTING DAMAGES RECOVERABLE IN ALL SITUATIONS

Since incidental or consequential damages can amount to a lot of money, a seller—or a manufacturer who gives a written warranty—obviously wants to avoid paying them. The Code allows them to do so by including limitation of remedies clauses in your agreement or warranty. See page 239 for a description of these clauses and how you may be able to get around them.

If your agreement or warranty does not include such clauses, theoretically you may collect all the damages the Code entitles you to recover. Even so, you can seldom actually do so unless you sue. For all practical purposes, then, the chance to recover damages is usually useful mainly as bargaining leverage to get your money back.

If you sustain significant incidental or consequential damages, promptly seek legal advice rather than trying to handle the problem yourself. This is especially important when you sustain a personal injury or damage to property caused by a defect covered by a warranty.

OUTLINE OF SELLER'S REMEDIES WHEN YOU BREAK YOUR AGREEMENT

Of course, the Code also entitles a seller to use various remedies if a buyer breaks the agreement.

Generally speaking, the seller can hold you accountable when you:

• Wrongfully reject or revoke acceptance of a product.
• Do not make payments due on or before delivery.
• Repudiate the contract; that is, specifically tell the seller in advance that you won't perform your obligations under the contract.

Broadly speaking, these are the steps the seller can take against you:

- Refuse to deliver goods he still has available, or stop the delivery of goods already turned over to a carrier.
- Resell goods he has rightfully withheld from you after you have broken the agreement. If the goods are resold in good faith and in a commercially reasonable manner, the seller can then hold you accountable for the difference between the agreed price and the resale price, plus damages for any incidental expenses he incurs.
- Sue you for damages resulting from your non-acceptance of the product or repudiation of the agreement. The seller's damages would *usually* be the difference between the market price and the agreed price for the goods, plus his incidental expenses. If the difference does not fully compensate him for his loss, the seller could, instead, recover lost profits.
- Sue you for the full purchase price, plus incidental expenses. A seller can only do this, however, when you do not pay for goods you have *accepted* (in other words you wrongfully revoke acceptance); or when conforming goods are lost or damaged within a reasonable time after you have assumed the risk of loss but before you have accepted them. (See page 139 for details on shipment and destination contracts.) A seller can also sue you for the purchase price of goods you wrongfully refuse to accept and which cannot be resold for a reasonable price. A case in point would be custommade or special order goods that no one wants. (Other remedies are also available to the seller of custom-made goods.)

A seller's incidental expenses usually cover amounts for reasonable charges, expenses or commissions he must pay after a buyer breaks an agreement. These could include items like commission paid to make a resale, and transportation or storage charges.

- Cancel the agreement and use other remedies available.

37 · The Ultimatum to Cancel a Purchase

A written ultimatum canceling the purchase would be your last step before suing the seller. When you send the ultimatum, you would again demand your money back, insist the seller take back the product, and note what damages you have sustained.

The Code does not require that, before bringing a lawsuit, you formally notify the seller that you are canceling the agreement. But this step almost always strengthens your bargaining position should the dispute get to court, because it shows you gave the seller one more chance to settle the problem.

Remember that if a dispute reaches this stage and you say you are canceling the agreement, you would have to withhold any further payments. You should, therefore, already have taken the steps described in Section VII regarding your rights to withhold payment from a creditor.

There are two sample memos you can adapt for notifying a seller you are canceling an agreement (or canceling just one of several purchases you made as part of an agreement). The first covers situations in which you are canceling because of the seller's failure to deliver the product; the second covers situations in which you are canceling after rightfully rejecting or revoking acceptance of the product.

The samples include alternative wording and paragraphs to cover different situations, and they refer to various laws that may apply. Naturally, you should check whether the points apply in your particular situation before using the wording.

ULTIMATUM TO CANCEL FOR FAILURE TO DELIVER THE PRODUCT

_____date_____

TO: Mr. R. Seller
Manager
ABC Sales Company
Futurama Mall
Anytown, USA

I am hereby canceling our contract of April 15, 19___, under which I purchased (identify product) but which has not been delivered as required by our contract. (I am hereby canceling the purchase of [identify product] which I made as one of several purchases under our contract of April 15, 19___, but which has not been delivered as required by our contract.) I am also notifying you of amounts now due me as damages because of this breach of our contract.

Although our agreement required delivery by June 1, 19___, and stipulated that timely delivery was of the essence to me, the product was not delivered by that date. (Although the product was be delivered within a reasonable time which I was told would be about June 1, 19___, delivery was not made by that date nor by the June 28 revised delivery date we agreed to on June 3, nor the July 15 delivery date by which I notified you that delivery had to be made to avoid a material breach of our contract.)

I am, therefore canceling our contract because of your failure to make delivery as required. (I am, therefore canceling my order for the product which has not been delivered as required by our contract.)

There is now due me and I request a prompt refund of the $_____ I paid on (give date) for the product. (I now (also) request that you promptly deduct from the balance outstanding under our agreement all amounts no longer due or owing for the canceled order and furnish me a complete accounting which verifies that the proper deductions have been made, indicates the remaining balance, and which revises the remaining payment schedule to reflect the amounts no longer due or owing under our contract.)

Since I have now canceled our contract (I have now cancelled this purchase), no further payments are due or owing (for the purchase I have cancelled). (I am, however, prepared to pay as due my amounts still payable for the products that were delivered.)

And as described below, there is now also due from you at least the $_____ I have sustained up to now as my damages for your failure to make delivery as required by our contract:
(Describe and state the amount due for damages you could be entitled to collect)

While I hope we can satisfactorily resolve this matter, if my payments are not promptly refunded (and if the amounts no longer due or owing are not promptly deducted and a complete accounting of the remaining balance is not made), I shall then also hold you liable for all my damages at least to the fullest extent provided by the Uniform Commercial Code.*

_____
(Your signature)

Receipt acknowledged by:

_____   _____
(Signature and title of store representative)   *(Date)*

*Note: This wording says, in effect, that you are willing to forget about your other damages if the seller does the other things you request. Do *not* use it if it is important for you to collect those damages; seek prompt legal advice instead. If you want to try collecting such damages on your own even if the seller refunds what you have paid (I caution you against trying to do this if collecting is really important), you could substitute the following for the last paragraph in the sample letter:

"If my requests are not promptly satisfied, I shall hold you liable for this breach at least to the fullest extent provided by the Uniform Commercial Code."

• The seller's failure to deliver the product as required by your contract and refusal to refund payments you made, *could* amount to a violation of your state's deceptive sales practices law. So if a refund isn't forthcoming, you could try the ultimatum step of the negotiating strategy for using that law. (See page 99.) In this case, refer to the seller's refusal to refund payments made for an undelivered product as the deceptive practice. Use the above sample letter as a guide for rephrasing the ultimatum letter on page 99.

ULTIMATUM TO CANCEL AFTER REJECTING OR REVOKING ACCEPTANCE

In this situation you would state why you are now entitled to cancel, so the sample refers to previous steps, describes requests you could have made, and identifies various ways the seller could have failed to carry out his obligations. You must obviously adapt this wording as necessary to describe your particular situation, and add any important things that happened which the sample doesn't refer to.

Although your rights under warranties and credit agreements are described in the next section of the book, you must often combine the rights under different laws as part of the same step of a negotiating strategy. That is what the wording of this letter does.

The type of credit arrangement used and whether a separate creditor was involved affects who and how you could hold a seller and/or creditor accountable. Be sure to check Section VII.

The following sample memo covers situations in which you are initially notifying the seller about the cancellation when the purchase was a cash transaction, the seller has been paid from the proceeds of a loan or the purchase was financed by the seller and when you are cancelling before any attempt was made to repossess if you purchased the goods on credit. See page (562) for sample memos included for situations in which you prepare a cancellation letter in advance for possible use at the time of repossession.

> *200 Witchtree Lane*
> *Anytown, USA 0000*
>
> ___date___

Mr. R. Seller
Manager
ABC Sales Company
Futurama Mall
Anytown, USA 00000

Dear Mr. Seller:

I am hereby canceling our contract of April 15, 19___, under which I purchased (identify product). (I am hereby cancelling the sale of (identify product) which was one of several purchases I made under our contract of April 15, 19___. I am not, however, hereby waiving any rights with respect to defects I may yet discover in other products I have purchased.) (The price, plus tax and related charges totalling $_____ was paid in full on (__(date)__) (with a down-payment of $_____ made on (__(date)__), plus $_____ for the (identify product) I traded in and with the proceeds of a (purchase money) loan from the (Discount Finance Company.)

I charged the purchase on (__(date)__) with my (Master Money) credit card, account number 0000-00000-00./The sale was (one of several purchases I) made and financed under our (consumer credit contract) of (April 15, 19___) (which has been assigned to the (Discount Finance Company).

(I am canceling the contract/canceling this purchase which I made under that contract) because I rejected the product on June 3, 19___, for the reasons I then described to you and because of your failure to cure the non-conforming delivery (and because our agreement specifically does not give you an opportunity to cure a non-conforming delivery). Although the non-conforming delivery was to have been cured by the delivery of a conforming replacement, the conforming replacement has not been delivered (the replacement that was delivered also failed to conform as I informed you on June 20, 1990). (Although the non-conforming delivery was to have been cured by the repairs and adjustments you were to make [you had insisted on making instead of replacing the product as I had requested], the defects were not cured as I informed you on June 15,

19___ .) (Although I informed you upon rejecting the product that repairs and adjustments were inadequate to cure the substantial defects I described, you have continued to refuse to furnish me a replacement that fully conformed to our contract and have refused to furnish your assurances that repairs would, in fact be adequate to cure the defects and that you would carry out your obligation to furnish me a fully conforming replacement if the repairs turned out to be inadequate. I had requested these assurances on June 15 when I informed you that, in order to settle this matter so we could still satisfactorily complete our transaction, I would consent to your proposed cure under those circumstances, but you have refused to furnish them so I cannot rely on repairs being adequate to cure.)

(I am canceling the contract/canceling this purchase which I made under that contract) because of my having (rejected and/or) revoked acceptance of the product on September 15, 19___ , for the reasons I then described to you.

Because I have now cancelled the (sale of [identify product] made under this) contract, there is now, as provided by the Uniform Commercial Code, no further outstanding obligation under that contract (with respect to the cancelled purchase and any balance remaining is reduced at least by the amount no longer due or owing for it and which I calculate to be $ _____).

(And/Because I have now cancelled the (sale of [identify product] made under this) contract,) I am now entitled to, and request the prompt return of, all moneys I have paid for this purchase. I calculate this amount to be the $_____ I have paid (which includes the $_____ down-payment, $_____ for the (identify product) I traded in and (the $_____ paid with the proceeds of the (purchase money) loan except as, and only to the extent that the balance remaining for that loan is otherwise satisfactorily resolved by the (Discount Finance Company)/the (portion of the) $_____ in monthly payments I have made (which have been applied to the amount included for the cancelled purchase in the entire balance).) (I calculate this amount to be at least the $_____ down-payment and $_____ for the (identify product) I traded in plus the portion of the $_____ in monthly payments I have made which have been applied to the amount included for the cancelled purchase in the entire balance but which I am unable to calculate accurately. I therefore request that you do so and furnish me a prompt and accurate accounting.)

There is now also due me (and I request prompt reimbursement for) at least the $_____ I have up to now sustained as damages as more fully described below:
(Describe and state the amount due for damages you could be entitled to collect)

(And so we can promptly settle accounts with respect to any remaining balance, I request that you promptly furnish me a complete accounting of the balance still outstanding under our agreement upon the proper deduction of the amounts no longer due or owing for, and the prompt crediting to my account of amounts now due me for payments made toward, the sale now cancelled. I calculate the amount still outstanding is no more than $_____ which I am, of course, prepared to pay as due. (I calculate that there would then be no further amounts still due or owing under the contract [and that there is, instead, due me a credit balance of at least $_____ which is to be promptly returned to me].)

(Since there is no further outstanding obligation, neither you nor any

creditor still has a security interest in any goods sold under this contract./ Since there is no further outstanding obligation under our contract with respect to the sale now cancelled, neither you nor any creditor has a security interest in the product involved. And since all payments due for any balances remaining under the contract are, in fact, paid in full as due, and shall pay as due all amounts still, in fact, owing, I am not in default.)

(And as provided by the Uniform Commercial Code, I instead have a security interest in the (identify product) for the return of all moneys I have paid for it and which, (including down-payment and trade-in plus other payments) totals at least $_____ . I am, therefore, only holding the product for you until that amount is paid to me (or properly credited to the balance remaining under our contract) (and, since there is then no further obligation under our contract, any outstanding instrument is returned to me)./Since you have refused to take back the product upon my having notified you I want(rejecting/(and/or) revoking acceptance of) it, I am only storing it for you and again request that you make prompt arrangements to pick it up from me or furnish me your instructions for returning it to you at your expense and risk.)

(Since there is now no outstanding secured obligation you are, as provided by the Uniform Commercial Code, to file a termination statement within 10 days to terminate your security interest if a financing statement covering the goods has been filed. If you fail to do this, you will be liable under the Uniform Commercial Code for $100 plus any losses I suffer as a result./ And since there is no now further outstanding obligation under our contract with respect to the sale now cancelled, you are to indicate that you no longer have a security interest in the product involved and to specify the goods in which you still retain a security interest.)

If you still refuse my proposals for resolving this matter, I shall seek to hold you liable for this breach at least to the fullest extent provided by the Uniform Commercial Code, and as provided by the Magnuson-Moss Warranty Act for failing to comply with obligations under a written (and) implied warranty. That Act also makes you liable for my damages and can entitle me to recover my legal expenses, including attorney's fees, should your continuing failure to carry out your obligations compel me to take legal action.

(And since there is no further secured obligation/And since I am not in default on any payments still actually due or owing under our contract), any attempt by you or your agents to repossess will be wrongful and subject you to liability for conversion and for any other tortious conduct for which I shall seek to hold you liable to the fullest extent provided by law. Under the Uniform Commercial Code, your liability for wrongful repossession would be at least ten percent of the amount financed plus the finance charge. Your liability for conversion or other tortious conduct could include punitive damages.)

I therefore urge you to contact me promptly so we can still quickly resolve this matter. (And to avoid any further dispute so we can promptly resolve it, I am now still prepared to waive my claims for damages I have thus far sustained.)

Sincerely,

Receipt acknowledged by:

_____   _____

(Signature and title of store representative)   *(Date)*

Try to get a signature acknowledging receipt if you return the letter to the store yourself. If you mail it, send it by certified mail, return receipt requested.

Here are some important words of caution about using certain wording included in the sample letter above.

- *Never* say you are willing to waive your claim for damages if it is important to you to recover them. But seek legal advice rather than trying to handle the matter yourself at this point.
- The sample includes alternative wording for describing amounts you have paid which the seller is to refund and proposals for settling up when you still owe something for other products purchased under the same agreement. The wording you use for describing the amounts to be returned would, of course, depend on what you have paid and the type of financing arrangement used, so be sure to adapt the wording to your situation. The wording does not specifically refer to finance and other charges that might be included in the total amount you have repaid. You may not be entitled to get all those amounts refunded. (See Section VII.)
- The sample also includes alternative wording and paragraphs which describe amounts you may no longer owe upon canceling, the security interest you may have in the goods and the security interest a seller/creditor may no longer have when you don't owe anything. Use only the wording that applies to the particular situation and omit the alternatives.
- Be sure to note that if you have not paid anything for the goods when you become entitled to cancel, you would not have a security interest in the goods. If you have the goods because the seller previously refused to take them back, then omit the wording that refers to the security interest you have and insist instead that the seller take the product back.
- The sample refers to the Magnuson-Moss Warranty Act and how it may entitle you to hold the seller accountable. That law could apply in this situation since it covers the seller's failure to honor obligations under written or implied warranties. See Chapter 39 for a full explanation of this law.
- The next to last paragraph also refers to a seller's or creditor's potential liability for wrongfully repossessing a product, conversion and other tortious conduct. It may be unnecessary to state things this harshly, of course, but it could be worthwhile to caution the seller (or creditor) about these potential liabilities especially if he has threatened to take such steps. See Chapter 63 where the seller's liability for wrongful repossession is explained. While this book does not cover tort laws governing someone's liability for injuring your reputation, generally referred to as libel and slander laws, a person who makes false statements about you *could* be liable under those laws.
- If you are making payments under the agreement to someone other than the seller, you must also settle up with that other creditor. (See Chapter VII.) Under some financing arrangements, you may have to pay back a separate creditor even though you might no longer owe the money to the seller. In such situations, the seller would, of course, have already been paid in full so you would have to try to get all your money back from the seller while still paying the creditor. (See Chapter 64 about settling up in these situations.)
- See Chapter 67 for a sample memo you can adapt and have ready for immediate use in case a seller/creditor tried to repossess after you cancel.

SECTION V
WARRANTIES: YOUR RIGHTS AND HOW TO ENFORCE THEM

38 · Different Kinds of Warranties

WHAT IS A WARRANTY?

How can you be sure a product you buy will really work, or that its quality will measure up to your expectations? How can you be sure, for instance, that a self-cleaning oven will really clean itself? Or that an "all-wool" rug is really made only of wool?

Sometimes you can tell about a product's quality and potential performance just by examining it. But more often than not you have to depend on a seller's or manufacturer's promises about the product. Generally speaking, such promises are called "warranties." If the product doesn't measure up to the different kinds of warranties that become part of a deal, then you have a legal basis to enforce the warranties.

In some ways warranties are like insurance policies. If you have a warranty that covers a particular problem that arises, then the warrantor assumes the risk and becomes responsible for what goes wrong. If you don't have a warranty that covers the problem, you may have to take the risk and pay for whatever loss results. (But from a legal standpoint, warranties are *not* insurance policies.)

Every warranty spells out:

• The coverage that you have and what, if anything, you must do to obtain it. This coverage is given either by specific warranties from the seller or manufacturer, or by special warranties created by law, usually by the Uniform Commercial Code.

• What the warrantor is required to do to remedy the situation if a product doesn't measure up.

Remember, however, that what warranties you have must be pinned down as part of your deal before you have agreed to buy except for some unusual situations in which you could hold a seller accountable for warranties he makes after you have already agreed to buy.

DIFFERENT KINDS OF WARRANTIES

The Uniform Commercial Code and the Magnuson-Moss Warranty Act are the principal laws that govern different types of warranties applied to a purchase. (Some states have additional laws covering specific types of products, but since they usually vary considerably, they won't be covered in this book.)

Written warranties are governed by the Magnuson-Moss Warranty Act. Express and implied warranties are governed by the Uniform Commercial Code. The provisions of these laws each limit their protection to the type of warranty covered. Yet, often the protection you have under one law can extend your protection under another. It is therefore important to see how these laws operate.

WRITTEN WARRANTIES GOVERNED BY THE MAGNUSON-MOSS WARRANTY ACT

Almost all new products are covered by written warranties; a few used ones are too. It may be given by either a seller and/or manufacturer and spells out standard promises he is willing to make. Although it is not tailored to fit the individual customer, such standard warranty coverage does give you important protection. Just knowing about your coverage and what you can do to enforce it can often help you get a problem solved with little effort.

The Magnuson-Moss Act spells out requirements that govern written warranties as defined by the Act. It includes most but not all written warranties that could count as express warranties under the Code.

EXPRESS WARRANTIES GOVERNED BY THE CODE

An express warranty is a specific promise or factual assertion a warrantor makes (expresses) about a product. Normally, it consists of a promise about a product's quality, capacity or performance, made in order to convince you to buy. Such a warranty may be created by the warrantor's words or conduct, and so may not be written.

An express warranty is one type of warranty governed by the Uniform Commercial Code. But when an express warranty is put in writing and qualifies as a written warranty as defined by the Magnuson-Moss Act, such a warranty would then also have to comply with the requirements spelled out by that act.

IMPLIED WARRANTIES GOVERNED BY THE CODE

There are two types of implied, or silent, warranties. One is called the *implied warranty of merchantability,* the other is called the *implied warranty of fitness for a particular purpose.* They cover such basic promises about a product that the law assumes they are part of every deal, *unless* they are specifically excluded in an agreement.

Implied warranties are created and governed by the Code which also spells out what must be done if they are to be properly excluded from an agreement. The Magnuson-Moss Act can help you keep such warranties as part of an agreement when the product you buy is covered by a written warranty governed by the Act. This can help strengthen the warranty coverages you could have as part of your agreement.

DON'T BE FOOLED BY SCARE TACTICS

Warranties aren't just something to throw away or put into a desk drawer and forget about; they can be extremely important in helping you achieve satisfaction with a purchase. But if you don't know what a warranty can do for you, it may be easy for a seller to fool or scare you into thinking that there's nothing to be done when you have a problem with a purchase.

A conversation I had with a salesperson at a New York City paint store shows how this can happen.

The paint store listed a number of warranty conditions on the *back* of a sales slip that customers received only *after* paying for the merchandise. These conditions referred to terms that had never been discussed. Since a buyer usually would not learn about these conditions until after a sale had been completed and the terms already "set," they probably would not count at all. The paint store was, nevertheless, trying to intimidate its customers with important-sounding language.

These were some of the warranty conditions listed on the back of the sales slip:

"Any and all warranties are strictly those of the manufacturer.

"[The seller] assumes *no* liability for damages resulting from the use of the purchased materials *beyond* the purchase price.

"At its discretion, [the seller] reserves the right to replace same or refund the price of goods or material supplied by [seller] proven upon inspection to be defective in material or workmanship."

At first glance, these terms certainly made it seem as though I and the other customers had very few rights if we happened to buy defective paints or supplies from the store.

But this is what a salesman actually admitted about those terms when I asked him about them a few days after I had purchased paint and venetian blinds from the store. I was then simply curious about what he would tell me.

"I have no idea what the terms mean," he said. "They are just printed on the back and nobody can figure them out. It's too technical for me and I've never tried to make out what they mean."

"But what does this point mean about all warranties belonging to the manufacturer?" I asked.

"Well, that's to shift all the warranty obligations to the manufacturer," he replied. (So, I thought, he really has tried to figure out what they mean.)

"But, what about the implied warranties the Uniform Commercial Code automatically makes part of an agreement?" I asked. "This doesn't say anything about those warranties not being part of the agreement."

"I know it doesn't," he responded, "but what we say sounds good." (So, he did recognize that the buyer had warranty protections that weren't mentioned at all.)

Then I asked about the second paragraph which, in effect, stated that *the store* could be responsible for damages up to the purchase price. "Doesn't this mean that you have some responsibility for defects under the warranty?"

"Well," he said, "that paragraph does seem to contradict the first one."

"And then what about the third paragraph which says the store would refund the purchase price of or replace defective goods," I went on. "Doesn't that also contradict the first paragraph since you are assuming responsibility for products that are defective in materials or workmanship?"

"Well, not really. We say we will only do it at our option so it isn't really like giving a warranty," he replied. (So, the salesperson really had studied all the paragraphs.)

"Maybe," I argued, "but according to the Magnuson-Moss Warranty Act, what you are saying about refunds and replacements makes that into a written warranty and your wording may not comply with the law."

"I don't know anything about the Magnuson-Moss Warranty Act," he blurted out. "Look, we just put these things in to score points as part of the game. It sounds tough when you go through them with the customer."

He should have completed the sentence by adding, "a customer who doesn't know anything about the rules governing warranties." But as you can see, a few simple questions based on the warranty laws make it obvious that those warranty "conditions" on the sales slip were not nearly as intimidating as they seemed to be and that the salesperson really knew it.

Do such scare tactics pay off for the seller? You bet they do. I once saw a customer picketing a cabinet store in Manhattan as a warning to other customers that the store had ripped him off. He didn't think there was anything else he could do when the store refused to correct defective merchandise he'd bought.

The store manager had pointed to a clause on the back of the man's sales slip which said something like: "We are not responsible for any *damage* to goods unless a claim is made within five days after delivery." Well, that clause could have got the store off the hook if the product had been damaged during delivery and the consumer failed to report the damage within five days. But it wasn't enough to get the store off the hook for defects in the product itself. The consumer had a very important type of silent warranty that covered those defects: the implied warranty of merchantability created by the Code. He could also have used the Magnuson-Moss Warranty Act to hold the store accountable for defects. If the consumer had known about these remedies and how to enforce his rights, he might not have had to picket the store on a cold winter day.

YOUR RIGHTS WHEN WARRANTY COVERAGE DOES NOT APPLY

There may be times when you either have no warranty coverage or what you do have does not enable you to hold someone accountable for losses. Nevertheless, there may be alternative ways to hold a seller or manufacturer accountable anyway.

Generally speaking, there are two other important sources of legal redress. These are laws covering product liability, and laws dealing with fraud and misrepresentation.

1. *Product liability law* is a specific tort law which makes a *seller or manufacturer responsible* for personal injuries, or for damage to property, caused by an unreasonably dangerous or harmful product. In effect, it spells out minimum safety standards for products a seller or manufacturer must satisfy, regardless of any warranty promises made about a product.

There is a major difference between your rights under product liability law and your rights under warranties. Under product liability law your legal recourse depends on obligations imposed on sellers or manufacturers rather than on the warranty coverage included as part of your agreement. And a seller or manufacturer can rarely, if ever, use contract terms to alter or modify the obligations imposed on him by product liability law or to limit the amounts you can recover as damages.

Thus under product liability law you can sometimes hold a seller or manufacturer accountable for defects which make a product dangerous or unhealthy, even though the defects were not covered by warranties. If you sustain significant losses, never let a seller or manufacturer dissuade you from pursuing your claim by saying the defect isn't covered by your warranty. Promptly see an attorney for advice.

2. *Laws dealing with fraud and misrepresentation* can also be used to hold a seller accountable for false or misleading promises he makes about a product. Specific promises count as express warranties. If the promises turn out to be fraudulent or violate your state's deceptive sales practices law, you can use those laws to give you extra leverage. In that case, your legal recourse depends on what is defined as seller misconduct, rather than the terms specifically mentioned as part of your deal.

39 · Your Main Legal Tool for Written Warranties: The Magnuson-Moss Warranty Act

THE MAGNUSON-MOSS WARRANTY ACT

The Magnuson-Moss Warranty Act (MMW Act), enacted by Congress in 1975, regulates the rights you have under most written warranties. (Exceptions would be some kinds of written statements or promises that could count as express warranties, but would not necessarily also count as written warranties as defined by the act.)

The act also strengthens the rights you have under express warranties and implied warranties governed by the Code.

Before the act became law, a written warranty could be used in all but a few states to take away the broader protections you would have had under implied warranties created by the Code and to limit your warranty protection to whatever promises the seller or manufacturer spelled out in the written warranty. Often these warranties consisted of long-winded legal gobbledegook that few consumers could understand. It was easy for the warrantor to use clever wording to make promises that actually offered very little protection once the implied warranties were taken away.

The MMW Act eliminated most of the problems previously caused by written warranties but, in the process, created some new ones. For instance, the remedies the act makes available for enforcing your rights under a written warranty can generally be used only against the person who actually gives the written warranty rather than anyone who may be involved in the sale. So, for example, if you receive a written warranty from a manufacturer, the remedies the act makes available for enforcing the warranty usually can be used only against the manufacturer and not against the seller unless the seller was also considered to have given that warranty.

The written warranties governed by the Act will usually help you keep as part of your agreement with the seller the implied warranties created by the Code. The seller would then have to honor the implied warranties. This can give you leverage for holding a seller accountable under your agreement based on implied warranties. But it is still possible for a seller to avoid all implied warranty obligations under an agreement through *his* agreement with you.

It is therefore important to look at what the seller's written agreement says about warranty obligations and, if necessary to eliminate wording that says the seller is not giving any warranties.

WRITTEN WARRANTIES AND SERVICE CONTRACTS COVERED BY THE ACT

The act regulates only written warranties and service contracts on consumer products; that is, any tangible personal property used for personal, family, or household purposes. This is how the act defines the terms "written warranties" and "service contracts."

1. A written warranty includes:

• A written statement of fact or promise which refers to the nature of the product's material or workmanship *and* which says either that the material or workmanship is free of defects, or that the product will meet a specified level of performance over a stated period of time.

This definition covers such promises as: "This watch is free of defects in materials or workmanship," and "The ingredients in the paint will prevent peeling or flaking within five years of application."

Promises such as "Made of one hundred percent wool," or "This watch is waterproof," are not covered, on the other hand, even if they are in writing, since they do not say the product is free of defects or designate a time period during which you can expect the materials or workmanship to measure up to a specified level of performance. (Such statements would usually count as express warranties under the Code, though.)

By itself this first definition would give very little protection, but there is a second definition extending coverage.

• Any written promise to refund, repair, or replace the product, or to take other remedial action if it fails to meet the specifications spelled out by the promise. This definition covers promises such as: "If this watch is defective in materials or workmanship, the seller will repair or replace defective parts," or "The buyer's remedies in case of defects in materials or workmanship shall be limited to the repair or replacement of defective parts or a refund of the purchase price."

This definition covers warranties promising only that specific remedial action will be taken. It is also likely to cover any clauses a seller or manufacturer might use to limit his liability to specific remedial action rather than the remedies the buyer would have under the Code.

So, under this definition, you have a written warranty when someone makes a written promise to take remedial action should the product fail to meet certain specifications. The apt irony is that clauses meant to limit a buyer's remedies are likely to count as written warranties under the Magnuson-Moss Warranty Act.

Here is how a New Jersey court explained these facts of life to a car dealer.

Hoping to evade all obligations under the manufacturer's written warranty the dealer included the following clause in his agreement: "It is expressly agreed that there are no warranties . . . except, in the case of a new motor vehicle, the warranty expressly given to the purchaser upon the delivery of such motor vehicle or chassis. The dealer also agrees to promptly perform and fulfill all the terms and conditions of the owner service policy."

A New Jersey court ruled that since the dealer specifically undertook to perform obligations under the owner service policy, his promise to take remedial action amounted to a written warranty governed by the act. This definitely was not what the dealer had in mind when he included the wording in his agreement.

A written warranty must be one of the reasons you bought the product. It would be considered as part of the basis for the bargain as long as you are given it at the time of sale and you don't have to pay anything extra for it. If you do have to pay extra for what would be a written warranty as defined by the Act, the warranty would then be considered a service contract.

2. A *service contract* includes any written contract to perform maintenance or repairs on a consumer product during a fixed period of time, such as one year, or for a specified duration, such as during the first 36,000 miles of use.

HOW THE ACT PROTECTS CONSUMERS

The Magnuson-Moss Warranty Act sets up a regulatory system which covers different warranties in different ways.

First, the act regulates *written warranties* and *service contracts* by:

- Spelling out the information that must be clearly disclosed about your warranty coverage.
- Requiring that any written warranty regulated by the act be labeled either a "full" or a "limited" warranty.
- Establishing minimum standards of protection for *"full"* written warranties.
- Prohibiting the disclaimer of implied warranties by the person who gives a written warranty or who sells a service contract on the product within a certain time after the sale. (As you now know, this prohibition applies only to the person who gives the written warranty or sells the service contract rather than anyone else.)

Although these protections are triggered whenever someone gives you a written warranty as defined by the act, or sells you a service contract on a product, the act does *not* require that anyone give you a written warranty or sell you a service contract in the first place. It only spells out requirements if someone does so. And the act leaves it up to the warrantor to decide what coverage to give under the written warranty.

ENFORCEMENT FOR WRITTEN AND IMPLIED WARRANTIES

The act also sets up a two-part enforcement mechanism by:

- Making the Federal Trade Commission responsible for enforcing compliance with the act. Any violation of the act and of the rules issued by the FTC, which further define your protection, is specifically designated an unfair or deceptive practice under the FTC Act, and the FTC can use all its powers to enforce that act (see Chapter 11). Since someone who violates the requirements of the Magnuson-Moss Warranty Act and the FTC rules is, in effect, engaging in an unfair or deceptive practice, he may also be considered to be in violation of your state's deceptive sales practices law. You may then be entitled to use remedies under that law (see Chapter 18).
- Giving consumers their own legal recourse to hold someone accountable for violating the act, or for failing to honor obligations under a written warranty, service contract, or an *implied warranty* created by the Code, even though the consumer may have *no* written warranty or service contract on the product.

Let's look more closely at the different protections you have under the act.

WHAT INFORMATION MUST BE DISCLOSED IN A WRITTEN WARRANTY?

The act allows warrantors to decide what coverage to include in a written warranty, but it requires them to use simple and readily understandable language to disclose the terms and conditions.

Any written warranty on a consumer product costing more than $15 must spell out at least the following information:

- If warranty coverage will not be available to more than one owner during the warranty period, the person entitled to the coverage must be identified. For example, if the coverage is available only to the original purchaser, that fact must be disclosed.

But if no limitations are stated, then the coverage is transferable to other owners during the warranty period.

• The products, parts, characteristics, components or properties of the product covered by the warranty must be clearly described and identified. You must also be told what the warranty does *not* cover if that is not made clear by the coverage. This requirement can be important if the warrantor later tries to claim that something is not covered when the wording of the warranty makes it seem as though it is.

• The actions a warrantor will take if the product has defects, or if it malfunctions, or fails in some other way to conform to the written warranty, must be disclosed. Will he, for example, repair or replace the product, or will he refund your money? If the warrantor will pay for certain items or services, the information must be disclosed. You must also be told what won't be provided or paid for, if that information is needed to clarify what the warrantor will do.

• The beginning of the warranty period must be stated, if it is different from the date of purchase, and the duration of the coverage. The latter can be a specific time period or some other measurement of duration, such as mileage.

• An explanation of what the consumer must do to get the warranty coverage has to be included. The warrantor must identify those authorized to perform warranty service, and provide the names and addresses of the warrantor, names and addresses of those responsible for performing warranty obligations, and/or telephone numbers consumers can call free of charge to learn about warranty service.

• Any limitations the warrantor puts on the *duration* of implied warranties created by the Code, must be stated on the front page of the warranty. If the warrantor does this, he must also include a statement saying that such limitations may not apply to you because they are prohibited by some state laws. (See the next chapter.)

• Any limitations the warrantor sets on the recovery of incidental or consequential damages must be disclosed. The warrantor must also include a statement saying that some state laws do not allow such limitations and that therefore they may not apply to you. These are "limitation of remedies" clauses that try to keep you from recovering losses or using remedies the Code would otherwise make available to you. They are discussed in detail in Chapter 33.

• The following statement about your legal rights must be given: "This warranty gives you specific legal rights, and you may also have other rights which vary from state to state." These other rights would usually be those governed by the Uniform Commercial Code and other state laws specifically governing consumer product warranties.

• The conditions under which you must return a warranty or ownership registration card in order to receive coverage must be included. If the warrantor uses such a card but you are not obliged to return it in order to obtain coverage, that fact must be disclosed. A warrantor can require that you provide proof of the date of purchase, or other evidence to show when the coverage started, though. Here are two questions consumers often ask about registration cards.

Should I return the card to be sure of getting the coverage? If the warrantor requires it as a condition for getting the coverage, to be safe it is best to return the card. Failing to return the card can result in your losing the coverage because it gives the warrantor a way out. But most warrantors honor claims anyway, so if you have failed to send in a card make a warranty claim if necessary. If the use of the card is optional and you don't return it, be sure to keep adequate proof of when the coverage began.

Do I have to answer all the questions the warrantor asks when he requires me to return the card? Questions about your income or purchasing habits may be asked by companies for marketing purposes, for instance. The answer is no. Simply fill out the information needed to verify proof of purchase and when the coverage started.

• As a condition for keeping warranty coverage, a warrantor can require that you follow use and maintenance instructions. For example, when it comes to having defects fixed, failing to follow instructions such as "This warranty void if the watch case has been opened or the watch has been tampered with" can be costly. On the other hand, a warrantor can only require that you use his company for services or parts supplied without charge under the warranty. In other words, he cannot use a clause such as, "This warranty is void if service is performed by anyone other than an authorized ABC dealer and all replacement parts must be genuine ABC parts," to prevent you going elsewhere for services or parts not covered by your written warranty.

• The FTC rules also require that warranties for products costing more than $15 be available for the buyer's inspection before purchase. At a store, a seller can comply with this requirement by having the written warranty available, or by displaying it with the product. In the case of mail order or catalogue sales, the warranty must either be printed in the catalogue or you must be told that you can get a copy by writing to the seller. In a door-to-door sale, the salesperson must tell you that a written warranty is available for your inspection and he or she must allow you to examine it before you buy.

WHAT INFORMATION MUST BE DISCLOSED IN A SERVICE CONTRACT?

Although the act requires that the terms and conditions of service contracts be fully, clearly, and conspicuously disclosed, it doesn't give specific guidelines.

Generally speaking, though, the person who sells a service contract on a product must disclose in readily understandable language what maintenance and repair services the contract covers so you know what you are getting.

HOW WARRANTIES MUST BE LABELED

Any written warranty on a product costing more than $10 must be clearly and conspicuously labeled as either a "full" or "limited" warranty. A product can be covered by more than one "full" or "limited" warranty, but each one must be clearly labeled. A label may also include a statement about the duration of the coverage, such as "full one year warranty."

The difference between these two types of warranties is that the Magnuson-Moss Warranty Act establishes minimum coverage standards for "full" warranties. Any warranty that does not meet the minimum standards has to be labeled "limited" warranty.

MINIMUM COVERAGE STANDARDS FOR "FULL" WARRANTIES

These are the minimum coverage standards the act requires for "full" warranties:

• If the product is defective, malfunctions, or fails to conform to the written warranty, the warrantor must, within a reasonable time, either repair or replace the defective product without charge or refund your money. A warrantor *cannot,* however, choose to refund your money rather than repair or replace the product unless a refund is acceptable to you, or the product cannot be replaced or repairs aren't practical or can't be made within a reasonable time.

• When you have a "full" warranty, the warrantor may not shorten the duration of any implied warranties.

• The warrantor cannot exclude or limit consequential damages for breach of any written or implied warranty on the product *unless* such limitations are clearly and conspicuously spelled out in a clause stating that the warrantor would not be liable for consequential damages caused by a product's failure to conform to the written warranty or implied warranties. The MMW Act requires that the clause be on the first page. If it appears elsewhere, you can safely ignore it. The clause may also be invalid because of Code requirements governing its use. A few states completely prohibit such clauses in consumer transactions.

• The warrantor must give you the option of taking a refund or a replacement product or component, when a product or component is still defective or malfunctions *after* a reasonable number of attempts to correct the problem. This is the so-called "lemon remedy" which applies only if you have a "full" warranty, and which is, in effect, like the buyer's right to revoke acceptance under the Code. To use this provision, you must show that the warrantor has had the opportunity to make a reasonable number of attempts to correct the defects and that the product still fails to conform. Although the act does not specify what constitutes a reasonable number of attempts, generally the less important the defects, the more chances you would probably have to give; the more important the defects, the fewer the chances.

• A warrantor can require you to notify the company of a defect, but he cannot impose other conditions on you for obtaining the remedies available under the "full" warranty *unless* he can demonstrate that such conditions are reasonable. This provision prohibits warrantors from requiring you to return a product at your expense, for example, if that involves costly transportation charges. (He may be able to require you to do so if the costs are minimal.) This provision is also likely to prevent a warrantor from including unreasonable use or maintenance requirements. The restriction on setting other conditions is meant to prohibit the warrantor from giving you a "full" warranty, then adding burdensome conditions that make it easy for him to evade his obligations.

• The coverage under a "full" warranty extends during the warranty period to anyone who is a consumer. This usually includes anyone who buys the product or to whom it is transferred during the warranty period. (It sometimes also includes a person who is injured by the warranted product.) This means that if the "full" warranty is for a set time period (like a year) or duration (like 36,000 miles), the coverage cannot then be restricted to the original purchaser but would extend to any consumer during the warranty period. But if the warranty period is based solely on the first purchaser's ownership, such as a car battery warranty that said "full warranty for as long as you owned your car," the warranty coverage would then not extend beyond the first purchaser.

• The warrantor's obligation to remedy defects without charge does not mean he must compensate you for any incidental expenses you might have, such as minimal transportation costs. However, if the warrantor fails to provide the required remedy within a reasonable period, or imposes unreasonable conditions, then the act does entitle you to recover incidental expenses.

YOUR RIGHT TO IMPLIED WARRANTIES

The person who actually gives you a written warranty, or who sells a service contract on a product at the time you buy (or sells the service contract within ninety days after you buy), *cannot* disclaim or modify any implied warranties created by law (the Code). The only exception is in the case of a "limited" warranty; the warrantor can limit the *duration* of the implied warranty to the same period as the "limited" warranty.

Any wording for disclaiming implied warranties in violation of the Act is also void so you can ignore it.

Before the Magnuson-Moss Warranty Act was adopted, you would generally have found something like the following clause in a warranty: "This warranty is expressly in lieu of any other express warranty or implied warranty, including any implied warranty of merchantability or fitness for a particular purpose, and any other obligation on the part of the seller." Now, the Magnuson-Moss Act prohibits the use of such "take away" clauses by the warrantor who gives you the written warranty or a person who sells a service contract.

Remember, though, that the prohibition may not apply to everyone involved in the transaction, such as the seller, for example, if the written warranty is given by the manufacturer. If a seller really wants to disclaim the implied warranties when he might be allowed to do so (and the state law permits him to do so), he must make the fact clear. If he doesn't take the proper steps, then you would have the implied warranties automatically as part of your agreement with him.

Generally speaking, the seller will not be able to disclaim implied warranties if:

- He fails to use the methods that could enable him to do so (see page 307).
- He includes wording in the agreement which could count as a written warranty under the Magnuson-Moss Warranty Act even though the agreement is not labeled as a warranty (see page 294).
- He sells you a service contract on the product within ninety days after you buy it and/or the seller is also considered to be the person giving someone else's written warranty.
- Your state's law prohibits the disclaimer of implied warranties when the MMW Act still allows it.

YOUR RECOURSE UNDER THE MAGNUSON-MOSS WARRANTY ACT

Your basic recourse under the act is to sue for damages. If you win your case you may also be able to recover your legal expenses.

Consumers can sue when a business fails to comply with its obligations under the act. If someone gives you a written warranty or service contract but doesn't spell out the terms in the way the act requires, fails to label the warranty as "limited" or "full," or includes prohibited clauses, among other things, you could sue if you sustained any damages as a result.

You are also entitled to sue a business if it fails to comply with its obligations under a written warranty, a service contract, *or* an implied warranty. So the remedies available under the Act can be used to hold someone accountable based on implied warranty obligations he had even though he did not give you a written warranty or sell you a service contract. (The Act does not entitle you to sue someone who fails to honor an unwritten express warranty or a written *express* warranty that does not fit the definition of a written warranty under the Act.)

There are two basic restrictions on your right to sue:

1. You must first give a business a reasonable opportunity to comply with the requirements spelled out by a written or implied warranty, or service contract: in other words you can sue only after a business has failed or refused to correct defects covered by warranties or to perform maintenance or repairs called for by a service contract.

2. To enforce your rights, the act only entitles you to sue the person or company that actually gives the written warranty.

In the case of *implied warranties,* however, the Act entitles you to sue someone who failed to honor implied warranty obligations the person had even though the person did not give a written warranty or sell a service contract.

The act authorizes warrantors to establish independent mechanisms for settling warranty disputes; such as independent offices or agencies set up by one or more warrantors and operated according to rules established by the FTC.

If a warrantor has such a mechanism, he can require you to use it before going to court if he includes that requirement in your warranty. But very few such mechanisms have been set up.

WHAT CAN YOU RECOVER IF YOU SUE?

If you are entitled to sue, and win your case, broadly speaking the act allows you to recover money in two ways.

You can recover damages sustained because of, or seek any other legal or equitable relief available to hold someone accountable for, a violation of the Act or breach of warranty or service contract obligations. The Act does not spell out the types of damages for which you could sue, but this almost certainly includes any amounts you could be entitled to recover based on remedies the Code entitles you to use. You are also entitled to sue under the Magnuson-Moss Warranty Act to enforce remedies made available by other laws for enforcing rights under warranties, such as the right you could have under the Code to revoke acceptance which in effect helps you tie everything together into one nice legal package.

The second way is by enabling you to recover your legal expenses, including reasonable attorney's fees as allowed by a court. So when you tie everything together into a legal package, by using the Magnuson-Moss Warranty Act to enforce remedies made available by other laws for enforcing warranty rights, the act then also enables you to try to recover your legal expenses. Your chance to recover legal expenses can make it costly for someone to ignore his obligations under written or implied warranties or service contracts.

Although courts are not required to award legal expenses to consumers who win their cases, they have usually done so. Take the following cases, for instance:

• In *Adams* v. *General Motors* (an Alabama case decided in 1979), the consumer was awarded $7,000 in damages, collected $5,800 in attorney's fees, and $4,800 for legal expenses.

• In *Curtis v. Ford Motor Company* (a Minnesota case decided in 1978), the consumer recovered $10,000 in damages, $2,600 in attorney's fees, and $74 in court costs.

• In *Ventura v. Ford Motor Company* (a New Jersey case decided in 1980), the consumer recovered $6,745 in damages from the *dealer,* and $5,165 in attorney's fees from the Ford Motor Company.

40 · Your Rights Under Express and Implied Warranties

The Uniform Commercial Code governs two types of warranties you could have on a product: express and implied warranties.

Express warranties cover promises specifically or expressly made about the quality, capacity, or other characteristics of a product. You get express warranties only when a seller (or manufacturer) makes specific promises to you.

To have this type of warranty, you must specifically get it from the seller (or manufacturer). So to have this kind of warranty, it must be included as part of the deal, which can make it important to pin it down in writing as part of your agreement.

Also keep in mind, however, that when put in writing, what would count as express warranties under the Code could then be written warranties governed by the Magnuson-Moss Warranty Act. And as explained in more detail in Chapter 41, if such a written warranty is given by someone other than the seller, it may not be part of your agreement with the seller unless you pin down that it is.

Implied warranties, on the other hand, cover such basic promises about a product that the law assumes they are automatically part of a deal *unless* they are specifically—and legally—excluded from the agreement. Implied warranties are, in effect, "silent warranties" because nothing has to be said about them for them to count, but if it is properly done and it is legal to do so, these warranties can be specifically excluded from the deal (i.e., disclaimed), in which case you would not have them. So to have these warranties, you would have to prevent them from being excluded from the deal.

Each of these two kinds of warranty can give you important protections not available under the other, so let's look more closely at what they cover and how you get them.

HOW IMPLIED WARRANTIES PROTECT YOU

Two kinds of implied warranties—the *implied warranty of merchantability* and the *implied warranty of fitness for a particular purpose*—spell out basic promises covering a product.

IMPLIED WARRANTY OF MERCHANTABILITY

A warranty of merchantability is given only by someone who sells goods in the ordinary course of business or one who holds himself out as having special skills or knowledge with respect to goods bought (such as a repair person who sells goods). Products bought at a private sale are never covered. If John Jones sells you his car, for example, it will not be covered. If you buy a car from John Jones Car Dealership, on the other hand, it will be covered by the warranty unless specifically excluded.

Generally speaking, the warranty of merchantability says that any merchant who sells goods automatically promises that they are merchantable; that is, that they measure up to certain minimum standards, *unless* he properly disclaims or alters the promise when the law allows him to do so. (See page 307.)

The warranty of merchantability requires that:

• The product you buy must at least conform to ordinary standards and be of the same average grade, quality, or value as other products sold under similar circumstances. If you buy a TV set, for example, it must work at least as well as other TV sets in the same price range.

• The product must be fit for the ordinary purpose for which you would use it. A car must be fit to use for transportation, for instance. An air conditioner must cool the air, and so on.

• The product must measure up to whatever promises or factual statements are made about it on its container or label (such promises or statements could also count as express warranties).

• The product must be adequately labeled, packaged, or packed in a container appropriate for the product.

Here are a few examples of products that courts decided were not merchantable:

• A linoleum tile that turned yellow shortly after installation. A court said the discoloration meant the tile was not of fair average quality since a tile must not only be durable but must also hold its patterns and color for a reasonable length of time.

• A two-week-old car that lost a wheel while going twenty-five miles per hour.

• A training device called a "Golfing Gizmo" meant to help unskilled golfers improve their game. The company's sales catalogue described the product as a "completely equipped backyard driving range." The label on the shipping carton and the cover on the instruction booklet said: "Completely safe, ball will not hit player." But when the consumer involved used the "Gizmo" as instructed, the ball hit him and knocked him unconscious. A court decided that the product wasn't merchantable because it did not conform to the affirmations of fact made on the label and wasn't fit for the ordinary purpose for which it was supposed to be used.

• A *used* product may also be considered unmerchantable. But to be considered unmerchantable, a used product would generally have to be defective in ways that could not reasonably be expected. For example, a consumer bought a used car which developed engine trouble only twelve days later. The car was repaired several times and the buyer paid half the repair costs. But problems continued and within forty days of the purchase the engine was completely ruined because of oil pressure defects. A court decided that the car was not merchantable because forty days after the purchase the buyer did not have a car fit for its ordinary purpose, namely transportation.

In general, however, the warranty of merchantability on a used product would seldom cover minor defects, or parts that need replacement or repair because they have been worn out by normal use.

These examples show the sort of things likely to make a product unmerchantable, based on the requirements spelled out by the Code. But since merchantability often depends on the type of product involved and the circumstances under which it is bought, here are some additional guidelines.

• Trade usage, or standards generally followed by merchants selling a particular type of product, is normally a good guide to what would count as a defect. If your product does not measure up to trade usage, that's usually strong evidence that it isn't merchantable.

• The price paid for a product is usually taken as a strong indicator of a seller's obligations under a warranty of merchantability. The quality you can expect is often set by the quality you would get if you bought a similar product within the same price range.

- In the same way, the characteristics and capacity of similar products made by other manufacturers would usually be a strong indication of the characteristics you could expect to find in the one you bought. If your product does not measure up, that would be a strong indication that the product isn't merchantable.
- Many state and federal laws set standards for particular types of goods, or they require that certain labeling information be stated. If a product does not measure up to these requirements, that is often strong evidence it is not merchantable. To find out about product standards or labeling requirements that might apply in your case, contact the appropriate agencies listed in the back of this book.

In summary, the primary requirements of the warranty of merchantability are that the product be fit for the *ordinary* purposes for which it is used, and that it *work* at least as well as someone would normally expect that type of product to work.

Always keep in mind, however, that an implied warranty of merchantability fails to cover things you normally could not expect from the type of product you are buying. So this type of warranty does not mean the product you are buying will automatically measure up to everything you expect.

IMPLIED WARRANTY OF FITNESS FOR A PARTICULAR PURPOSE

This second kind of implied warranty is given by a seller when you buy a product in the following circumstances:

- You buy a product for a particular use or purpose and the seller *knows* you need it for that particular purpose.
- You depend on the seller to tell you which product is suitable for your specific purpose and you buy the one that he recommends.

In these instances, the seller automatically gives an implied warranty that the product is fit for the particular purpose you've stated, *unless,* as explained on page 307, he makes it clear that he is *not* giving this warranty as part of the deal.

To get this kind of warranty, make sure the seller knows about the special purpose or use you have in mind, and make it clear you are relying on him to recommend a product that is suitable for that purpose. Suppose you want a vacuum cleaner that will clean a 3-inch shag rug, for example. You tell the seller about the thickness of your rug and ask him to recommend a model that will be suitable for cleaning it. He picks out a model that he says will do the job and you buy it. But when you try to use it, the machine won't move on the rug and the shag tangles in the cleaning mechanism.

Since you can't vacuum the rug with the machine, the warranty of fitness for a particular purpose has been breached—even though the vacuum cleaner is working perfectly in every other way. If you can't sort the matter out with the seller, you then use your remedies for enforcing your rights under your contract.

Although an implied warranty of fitness for a particular purpose is automatically part of the deal when you purchase a product under circumstances in which you get this warranty (unless it was specifically and properly excluded), to enforce it, you would have to demonstrate the seller knew about the particular purpose for which you were buying the product and that you bought it on his recommendation that it was fit for that purpose.

Assuming this implied warranty was not legally disclaimed, it is possible to demonstrate that you bought the product under circumstances in which you have an implied warranty of fitness for a particular purpose without anything having been put in writing about it.

If, however, you buy a product under circumstances in which you would have this warranty and a mistake about its suitability could be costly, then ask the seller to put in writing that you have this warranty. See page 319.

See page 306 for how implied warranties can be disclaimed so you would not have them, and how a seller can try to avoid all warranty obligations under your agreement even though the product you buy is covered by someone else's written warranty.

EXPRESS WARRANTIES

As previously noted, express warranties are specific promises a seller (or manufacturer) makes about the quality, capacity, performance, or other characteristics of a product. They are, in effect, assurances that the product will conform to the specific promises made about it. But the promises that would qualify as express warranties count as such only if they are also part of the basis for the bargain (that is, the promises made at least partly convinced you to buy the product).

Express warranties are created by the warrantor's words or conduct. The words may be written, printed, or spoken, or they may be symbols, labels, or advertising which indicates what you can expect from a product. Conduct may include a demonstration that shows you how a product will work. To create an express warranty, a seller does not have to use specific words or formal phrases, such as, "I warrant that . . ." or "I guarantee that . . ." as long as he does or says things which indicate what you can specifically expect the product to be like or how it will perform.

A warrantor creates express warranties by:

• Making any factual affirmations or promises about what you can specifically expect a product to be like. Although the dividing line between the two is not always clear-cut, a factual affirmation is generally considered to be a statement about what is true when it is made, such as: "Made of one hundred percent wool," or "All-transistor TV."

Promises, on the other hand, refer to expectations that are to be realized later; the truthfulness of a promise necessarily depends on what actually happens in the future, when the product is put to the test. Thus, statements such as: "This tire won't have a blow-out within 36,000 miles;" and "This housepaint won't flake or peel within five years," are promises.

• Describing a product in specific ways that identify it. Descriptions may include pictures and illustrations; or words that appear in your agreement, or in catalogues, brochures, and advertising, or on the product's container or label. When, for example, an airplane was described in advertising as an "Aero Commander, N-266B, Number 135, FAA, Flyable," a court decided that description meant the plane was supposed to conform to the instrument and visual flight requirements spelled out in the Federal Aviation Regulation Part 135.

• Showing you samples or models from which you select your product. Say, for example, you select a fabric and color from a sample the seller shows you. This gives you an express warranty that the fabric and color of your product will at least closely match it.

SOME POINTS YOU NEED TO KNOW ABOUT EXPRESS WARRANTIES

• An express warranty covers only the *specific* promises that a seller makes or the specific impression he creates when he convinces you to buy a product, and nothing else.

Suppose, for example, a dealer says he is selling you a "warranted used car." If you think the warranty covers a defective engine, for instance, you'll certainly be disappointed. The only promise your "express" warranty is actually making is that you are getting a used car. The warranty says nothing about defective parts or how well you can expect the car to work.

Similarly, if an express warranty says that a product is "free from defects in factory material or workmanship," it will only cover problems actually due to those defects, and no others. If you buy a set of dishes covered by such an express warranty, for instance, and they crack when you wash them in a dishwasher, your warranty will not cover the problem unless you can show the dishes were ruined because of defects in materials or workmanship. So never let an express warranty fool you into thinking that it gives you broad protection. The coverage is limited to what has been specifically promised.

• Express warranties that have been created do not necessarily have to be put in writing to count as part of the deal. But it is up to you to demonstrate you got them as part of the deal. Pinning them down in writing is, of course, the surest way to demonstrate that you got them. The next best thing is to keep anything that can help you document what you were told about the product and which could count as express warranties. And it is especially important to check what a written agreement says about warranties. Although anyone who creates an express warranty is then, technically speaking, stuck with it (always assuming you could prove it was created), a written agreement can include clauses which, in effect, strip away express warranties that were not put in writing.

• Express warranties are *not* created by statements which consist merely of the seller's opinion about a product or its value. Such statements are simply considered to be "puffing" or "sales talk"; they usually include general or vague claims or promises about what you can expect from a product. Statements like: "This is a top-notch car," or "This is the best refrigerator on the market," or "This product will give you good value for the money," or "I've had no complaints about the product and I've used one like it for three years," are examples.

The Code specifically does not allow a buyer to hold the seller accountable for such statements because, as the law sees it, a reasonable person would automatically disregard such statements. This is the old *caveat emptor* rule at work, so the best advice is to ignore such sales talk.

There is one major exception to this, however. If the seller makes himself out to be an *expert,* and you aren't knowledgeable about the product and ask for his opinion, you may be able to count on his expert opinion as an express warranty. Suppose, or example, you go to a locksmith and ask him to furnish you the best pick-proof lock on the market. He gives you one and tells you it is the best you can get. Such a statement is likely to count as an express warranty, and if it turns out the lock can easily be picked, you could probably hold the locksmith accountable (providing, of course, you can prove he gave you the express warranty).

• If specific factual affirmations or promises made are obviously untrue, they may not count as express warranties even though they were specific enough so they would otherwise qualify as such. This is also the old *caveat emptor* rule at work and which in this situation in effect says that an obviously false statement could not have convinced you to buy. So if a seller tells you specific things that you can tell are false but you buy anyway, you may be unable to hold a seller accountable for it later. It is, unfortunately, not clear-cut just how obvious it must be to you that something is false before you can, in effect, depend on and hold a seller accountable for what you were specifically told about a product. Failing to check things you could easily have found out on your own were actually false can still hurt you. But also keep in mind that it is very difficult for someone to get off the hook this way if he created what would qualify as an express warranty even though it consisted of a false factual affirmation or promise (and remember your state's deceptive sales practices act or fraud law could then apply as well).

• You can usually hold a seller accountable only under express warranties created *before* you buy a product. There are some exceptions, however. One would be if he tells you a new and important fact about the product around the time you complete the deal. Such a post-sale promise usually must refer to a characteristic which leads you to believe the product can be used in a certain way.

Another instance would be if you order a product and at the time of delivery you ask whether it has certain important characteristics, and the seller specifically promises that it does. In a situation like this, you would, in effect, be asking the seller to modify your original agreement by making additional promises about what you can expect from the product. The seller does not have to give such promises, but if he does, you could hold him to them.

You must always be considered to be acting in good faith when you ask the seller for what would now be post-sale warranties. Simply ask whether the product has the characteristics you now know will be important to you: "I didn't ask about this before, but I'd like to be sure that the product I ordered will . . ." If the seller unhesitatingly tells you the product has those characteristics, that's very likely to count as an express warranty. But if he says it doesn't, and your original deal didn't cover it, the seller could hold you to it. If those characteristics were really important, you could try to negotiate a new deal but you have no legal leverage to make the seller do so.

A seller could also be considered to have given you a post-sale warranty if you ask whether a product has some characteristic after you receive it, and he specifically tells you it does but it turns out the product doesn't have it and something goes wrong when you use the particular feature involved.

• The seller's post-sale conduct can help you demonstrate what warranties are part of the deal. If, for example, he corrects or promises to correct defects that turn up, his willingness to do so will usually help you prove he had given warranties covering those problems. On the other hand, if you show willingness to ignore the seller's refusal to take care of problems covered by promises, it can be taken as a sign that those problems weren't covered in the first place. Keep in mind, however, that this kind of post-sale conduct doesn't create express warranties you didn't have in the first place or take away from you express warranties you had; such post-sale conduct with respect to how you and the seller handle defects that show up is instead usually taken as a sign of what warranties the parties considered as being part of the deal in the first place.

HOW BUYERS CAN LOSE WARRANTY COVERAGE

In order to minimize their potential liability, it is obviously to the seller's or manufacturer's advantage to make the fewest promises possible to convince you to buy. This is one important reason why most advertisements make only bland, vague, meaningless or fanciful claims about products: they seldom provide express warranties for which you could hold a company accountable.

The Code also enables the seller (or manufacturer) to limit—or eliminate—express or implied warranty obligations under an agreement. This would be their way of trying to avoid promises that could become very expensive to keep. Normally, the seller would try to use clauses to knock out both these kinds of warranties at the same time, but since different rules apply, let's first look at how a seller could eliminate express warranties.

ELIMINATING EXPRESS WARRANTIES

Once a warrantor has made promises about a product that would count as express warranties, and you have *written them into your agreement,* the Code rarely allows him to eliminate those warranties. Writing express warranties into your agreement is practically a fool-proof way to hold a seller accountable.

It's not impossible for a seller to eliminate *unwritten* express warranties, though, especially when you buy a product under a formal written agreement.

He can do this by combining a properly worded *merger clause* (which says, in effect, that the *only* terms that count as part of the agreement are those which have been spelled out in writing) with a clause that says either you have no express warranties, or that you have no express warranties other than those that are specifically spelled out. See page 312. A seller could also use such a clause for saying he wasn't obligated to honor a written warranty on a product which was given by someone else (the manufacturer).

Although clauses like this can be used to knock out express warranties that were created but which were not pinned down in writing, they also may not hold up. That's because according to the Code, any express warranty that was created is considered part of the basis for the bargain unless good reason can be given it wasn't supposed to be part of the deal. So once you can demonstrate an express warranty was created, it is then usually up to the seller to show it wasn't part of the deal. A clause that says so is one way to demonstrate that express warranties not put in writing weren't part of the deal, but it may not be enough to get a seller off the hook under express warranties that were created, especially if such a clause is buried in fine print.

Do not, therefore, give up merely because a seller can point to such a clause as a way of trying to avoid having to honor express warranties he did create. You should, at the very least, notify the seller in writing how the product failed to conform and what had been promised.

If a dispute like this involves a lot of money, seek prompt legal advice.

ELIMINATING IMPLIED WARRANTIES

On the one hand, the Code creates implied warranties that are automatically considered part of your agreement. On the other hand, the Code allows such warranties to be completely excluded (disclaimed) except in states where the law has been changed. And the Magnuson-Moss Warranty Act now also prohibits the disclaimer of implied warranties but only under certain circumstances. In order for a disclaimer clause to count, however, when it can still be used, the person doing so must follow important rules spelled out by the Code and use wording that *properly* eliminates the warranties.

So the key points to remember about such disclaimer clauses are:

• They do not count at all when their use is prohibited by your state's law and/or the Magnuson-Moss Warranty Act.
• They would rarely count in cases where they could still be used if they were not properly worded.

WHEN IMPLIED WARRANTIES CANNOT BE DISCLAIMED

Since the legality of the implied warranty disclaimer clause depends first on whether your state's law still allows it, I will first list the states where the clause is prohibited. If it is prohibited in your state, you can skip the rest of the chapter except for parts that cover how you could still lose some implied warranty coverage without the implied warranties having been disclaimed. See page 311.

STATES WHERE IMPLIED WARRANTY DISCLAIMERS ARE PROHIBITED OR RESTRICTED

Kansas, Maryland, Massachusetts, Mississippi, and West Virginia flatly prohibit the disclaimer of implied warranties involving the sale of goods in consumer transactions. There may, however, be exceptional circumstances in which some implied warranty coverage could be eliminated.

The District of Columbia, Maine, and Vermont prohibit the disclaimer of implied warranties, with exceptions that usually apply to the sale of used goods sold "as is."

While the state of Washington prohibits the disclaimer of all implied warranties, it allows a seller to eliminate them with respect to product characteristics or qualities that are specifically identified. This is an unusual law which, in effect, only partially prohibits disclaimers.

California and Minnesota have laws which regulate the use of written warranties and prohibit the disclaimer of implied warranties *when the product is sold with a written warranty*. (While the implied warranty disclaimer prohibition is triggered by a written warranty, a provision similar to the one in the Magnuson-Moss Warranty Act, these laws may *not* define the written warranty in exactly the same way as the act.) The duration of the implied warranty also can be limited to the duration of the written warranty.

If you live in one of these states and a warrantor uses a disclaimer clause, contact a local or state consumer protection agency or the state attorney general's office. Ask for a pamphlet or brochure which explains how your state's law prohibits the disclaimer of implied warranties. This should identify the specific circumstances in which a disclaimer clause would be valid.

WHEN THE MAGNUSON-MOSS WARRANTY ACT PROHIBITS THE DISCLAIMER OF IMPLIED WARRANTIES

The Magnuson-Moss Warranty Act also prohibits the disclaimer of implied warranties but only by the person who gives you a written warranty regulated by the act, or who sells you a service contract within the time period stipulated by the act. (Remember, though, that the act does *not require* anyone to give you a written warranty or service contract.)

When two different people are involved in supplying you with a product—a seller and a manufacturer—the one who gives you a written warranty or sells you a service contract is specifically prohibited from disclaiming the implied warranties. The act does not directly prohibit the other one from doing so, however, providing he *properly* disclaims the warranties.

It is possible that your state law governs implied warranty obligations in such a way that you may be unable to hold a *manufacturer* accountable even when the Magnuson-Moss Warranty Act prohibits him from disclaiming implied warranties. But this sort of situation involves complicated technicalities, and you would need an attorney's advice on the matter.

WHEN IMPLIED WARRANTIES COULD STILL BE DISCLAIMED

Generally speaking, implied warranties can still be disclaimed when your state's law or the Magnuson-Moss Warranty Act does not prohibit it.

Given the way the Magnuson-Moss Warranty Act prohibits the disclaimer of implied warranties, this could now happen in one of two ways

• The product sold is *not* covered by a written warranty or service contract regulated by the Act.

• The person disclaiming the implied warranties is someone other than the one who gave the written warranty or service contract governed by the act. This would usually happen when a seller tries to disclaim such warranties even though the product you are buying is covered by a manufacturer's written warranty.

PRACTICAL REASONS THAT MAKE IT HARD TO DISCLAIM IMPLIED WARRANTIES PROPERLY AND HOW THAT HELPS YOU

While sellers and manufacturers are still allowed to disclaim implied warranties under the Code (and the Magnuson-Moss Warranty Act), they often trip up and don't do it properly. That, of course, helps buyers.

Although the requirements for disclaimer clauses are somewhat technical, they are not that hard to understand. Nor is it very difficult for someone to follow them if his *only* concern is complying with those requirements. But the seller and his attorney are usually concerned with something much more fundamental—namely, staying in business. The seller must keep convincing people to buy his products. If he, or a manufacturer, is determined to disclaim something as fundamental as the implied warranty of merchantability he is, in effect, telling you that he sells junk. How then can he convince you to buy the product in the first place?

Forcing the seller (or manufacturer) to be upfront when he tries to strip you of the implied warranties, is the basic purpose behind all the Code's requirements for disclaimers. The main reason why sellers often fail to disclaim implied warranties properly is because they are trying to avoid implied warranty responsibility and trying to convince buyers that the merchandise is satisfactory at one and the same time.

HOW IMPLIED WARRANTIES CAN BE ELIMINATED

Generally speaking, implied warranties can be eliminated in the following ways:

• The most usual way is by making such terms part of your agreement.

• By your examination of the product *before* you buy it. Technically speaking, even if the seller or manufacturer has not specifically disclaimed the implied warranties, your examination of the product can do so if you go ahead and buy the product despite defects you did or could have found by an examination you made before buying.

• By the seller's and your post-sale conduct, which may clearly indicate that neither of you consider the implied warranties to be part of the agreement. This issue would only arise, of course, if the implied warranties had not been properly disclaimed and there was a dispute about the matter.

Let's look at these points in more detail.

INCLUDING DISCLAIMERS OF IMPLIED WARRANTIES IN CONTRACT TERMS OR SALES CONDITIONS

There are three key rules a seller (or manufacturer) must follow in order to properly disclaim the implied warranties.

1. He must use particular wording or expressions

The implied warranties can be disclaimed only if the following wording or expressions are used.

Disclaiming the warranty of merchantability.

With one important exception, the basic rule is that the language used must specifically refer to the word "merchantability" and must make it clear you are not being given this warranty. An example of such wording would be: "The seller excludes all implied warranties of merchantability from this sale," or "There is no implied warranty of merchantability in connection with the sale of this product." Normally a seller would combine this disclaimer with wording that also eliminates the implied warranty of fitness for a particular purpose.

Technically speaking, the warranty of merchantability can be disclaimed without putting it in writing, but it would then be up to the seller to prove it.

Disclaiming the warranty of fitness for a particular purpose.

In this case, the seller can use any wording that makes it clear the warranty is not part of the deal. He might simply say, for instance: "There is no implied warranty of fitness for a particular purpose." The Code, however, does specifically allow someone to eliminate this warranty by using the wording: "There are no warranties which extend beyond the description on the face hereof."

This warranty can only be disclaimed in writing (except when a seller used a single expression that could enable him to eliminate all implied warranties).

Alternative expressions for eliminating all implied warranties

All implied warranties can be excluded from the agreement by the use of the expressions "as is" or "with all faults." This exception permits the disclaimer of the implied warranty of merchantability even though the word "merchantability" isn't used. Such disclaimers don't have to be put in writing to count, but a seller would almost certainly do so.

Occasionally, some courts have gone further and allowed sellers to use other wording which clearly calls the buyer's attention to the fact that the product is being sold without any implied warranties, such as: "No other warranty, whether express or implied, shall exist."

Such alternative expressions were mainly meant to cover purchases made in circumstances which would already alert buyers to the fact that the purchase might be risky: when buying a used product, a new product that had been damaged, or one containing imperfections, for instance.

But courts have sometimes allowed such alternative expressions to hold up when the purchase was made in other circumstances.

Whether such expressions are likely to count usually depends on how they are included in an agreement and the circumstances of the sale. If for instance, such an expression is handwritten or typed—indicating that you and the seller are likely to have talked about it—and the sale was made in circumstances that involved obvious risks, it would almost always hold up.

If the expression was *pre-printed* on the agreement, without the seller having done anything else to call your attention to the fact that the warranties were being disclaimed, it would not be nearly so likely to hold up.

The way to treat an alternative expression which a seller may use in a printed form depends on when you spot it. If you spot the clause *before* you finalize the deal, treat it as a proper disclaimer clause when deciding whether to negotiate about having it deleted. If you don't spot the clause until *after* you conclude the deal, then treat it as though it is not a proper disclaimer of the warranty of merchantability, because the word merchantability had not been used, so you can hold the seller accountable. Let the seller worry about whether such a clause will get him off the hook.

Courts have almost uniformly held that implied warranties cannot be disclaimed unless the proper wording is used. Phrases like "We make no exchanges or refunds," and "We are not responsible for defects," and "All warranties are strictly those of the manufacturer" do *not* eliminate the implied warranties created by the Code, so don't take such wording seriously when a seller points to them as a way of avoiding his implied warranty obligations.

2. Written disclaimer terms must be conspicuous

Implied warranties can be disclaimed by written terms *only* if conspicuous clauses are used.

To be conspicuous, a printed clause must stand out and be so placed that any reasonable person would notice it.

Courts have shown very little mercy to sellers who have disregarded this rule. *Fine print* clauses that try to eliminate the implied warranties are worthless, even if all the proper wording is used.

A disclaimer clause would usually be considered conspicuous if the clause is in a different size, color, or typeface than the rest of the form. It could also be made conspicuous by headings that clearly and accurately identify it, such as "EXCLU- SION OF WARRANTIES" or "WARRANTY DISCLAIMERS."

The wording cannot be misleading. Phrases such as "APPLIANCE WAR- RANTY" or "NOTICE TO THE BUYER," for example, cannot be used to identify a clause which actually eliminates warranties.

Regardless of how conspicuous such a clause is, though, a seller can effectively hold you to it by getting you to initial or sign it to indicate you have specifically agreed to the clause. He can also hold you to it if you specifically discuss the clause, the seller insists on keeping it in the agreement, and you buy anyway. *Never* do this unless you are willing to agree to the terms of such a clause.

Remember, too, that terms that are *handwritten* or *typewritten* on a printed form are very likely to be considered conspicuous, and to be taken as a sign that you and the seller specifically discussed and included them as part of your deal.

3. Timing of the disclaimers

Generally speaking, a disclaimer counts only if it is made part of the agreement while you are negotiating and *before* you and the seller have concluded the deal.

Watch for statements by salespeople or store signs that say a product is being sold without implied warranties. In this way, a seller could be properly making a disclaimer clear before the sale is completed. He could do this by attaching a prominent sign to the product saying it is being sold "as is" or "with all faults," for example.

On the other hand, disclaimer terms cannot be added *after* you have settled on a binding deal. Disclaimer terms included on a statement or invoice sent after you have bought and paid for a product would rarely, if ever, count unless you later agreed to them. Similarly, if your receipt includes a disclaimer but it is not handed to you until after you have bought and paid for the product, it is unlikely to count.

ELIMINATING IMPLIED WARRANTIES BY EXAMINING THE PRODUCT

If you examine a product as fully as you wish before buying, or the seller *insists* on your examining it, you thereby eliminate implied warranties with respect to any defects or product faults which you find—or should have found—during the inspection.

This condition does *not* apply to hidden defects, or faults that an unskilled buyer couldn't be expected to find, however. Nor does it eliminate implied warranties when the seller says or does specific things to indicate the product is okay.

The Code does not, however, *require* you to examine a product to keep implied warranty coverages on defects you could have found. But if you do examine it, it then behooves you to check it for defects you could find because such defects might then not be covered by implied warranties. If, however, the seller *insists* you examine the product before buying and you fail to do so, the implied warranties would then not cover defects you could have spotted. In effect, the seller is letting you know that you cannot automatically assume the goods are free of defects.

(The pre-purchase examination which can affect your coverage is not the same thing as the *post-delivery inspection* the Code entitles and requires you to make, of course.)

HOW IMPLIED WARRANTIES CAN BE ELIMINATED BY POST-SALE CONDUCT

Finally, implied warranty coverage may be eliminated by the way in which you and the seller actually carry out the agreement. The way two parties willingly carry out an agreement is usually taken as a sign of what they thought the agreement consisted of in the first place.

Say the seller insists your implied warranties don't cover defects you find, or that the warranties weren't part of your deal, and you willingly go along with him by, for example, paying for repairs. In this case, your behavior could help demonstrate that you didn't consider the coverage was part of your deal in the first place.

On the other hand, if the seller corrects the defects, his willingness to honor the terms of the implied warranties helps demonstrate that he considered they were part of the deal originally.

PRESERVING RIGHTS IN DISPUTES INVOLVING WARRANTY COVERAGE

If a seller insists you pay for some repairs that an implied warranty might cover, but you don't want to make a big issue of it, then agree to the seller's demands while preserving your rights. (See page 127 for an explanation of how the Code allows you to reserve your rights in such situations.)

Situations like this arise when it is unclear whether a defect is covered by implied warranties; or when you have a written warranty, which requires you to pay for repairs, and implied warranties which may not require you to do so. There might then be a dispute about what the seller's obligations are under each warranty.

If a warrantor fully honors a written warranty in a way that results in most things being taken care of, it is seldom worthwhile to insist he honor the implied warranties which might require him to do a little more. But reserving your rights in these situations can help you keep the implied warranty coverage in case you need it later.

EXAMPLES OF WARRANTY DISCLAIMER/MERGER CLAUSES AND HOW THEY HURT YOU

As noted previously, a seller usually cannot eliminate express warranties he created to convince you to buy a product. But he can try to eliminate unwritten express warranties by using merger clauses that say only the written terms count. Generally, a seller would then usually try to knock out the implied warranties as well. He could do this with a combination merger/warranty disclaimer clause. Here is an example:

"MERGER CLAUSE: Buyer may have seen advertisements or other seller literature and seller's salesmen may have made oral statements about the goods described in this contract. The parties agree that such statements or representations, even if made, do not constitute warranties, shall not be relied upon by the buyer, and are not part of this contract for sale unless specifically included in this contract. The seller neither assumes nor authorizes another person to assume for it any other liability in connection with this contract. This writing constitutes the final expression of the parties' agreement, and is a complete and exclusive statement of the terms of that agreement.

"WARRANTY DISCLAIMER: THE PARTIES AGREE THAT THE IMPLIED WARRANTY OF MERCHANTABILITY AND FITNESS FOR A PARTICULAR PURPOSE AND ALL OTHER WARRANTIES, EXPRESS OR IMPLIED, ARE EXCLUDED FROM THIS CONTRACT AND SHALL NOT APPLY TO THE GOODS SOLD."

A seller may insist you initial such clauses. In addition, the clauses may include wording that says by initialing them you specifically agree to them.

Always look for clauses like these when you buy a product under a written agreement, even if it is covered by a written warranty given by someone other than the seller, who would not be entitled to disclaim the implied warranties because of the Magnuson-Moss Warranty Act.

Remember that any express warranties pinned down in writing cannot be eliminated by such clauses. If you spot a clause that tries to do so, you either have to get the clause out or pin down in the agreement any express warranties the seller created.

The sample clauses include wording most likely to hold up in court, so you can be sure that any seller who uses such wording really means business. He may, however, try to use a shorter version of a disclaimer clause that could also be effective, such as this one:

"WARRANTY DISCLAIMERS: The seller hereby expressly disclaims having made any express or implied warranties as part of the basis for this bargain and hereby specifically EXCLUDES ALL IMPLIED WARRANTIES OF MERCHANTABILITY AND FITNESS FOR A PARTICULAR PURPOSE from this contract and the seller neither assumes nor authorizes another person to assume for it any warranty liabilities in connection with the sale of this product."

While a clause like this would not eliminate express warranties included in writing, and *may* not be enough to eliminate unwritten express warranties the seller created to convince you to buy, if the agreement does not also include a merger clause, it could make it harder for you to convince a court he made them. And a clause like this is likely to exclude the implied warranties from your contract. If the product is covered by someone else's written warranty, a seller may add wording which says that *only* the manufacturer is obligated to honor it.

Warranty disclaimer/merger clauses are among the nastiest conditions a seller can include in your agreement. They are his way of saying that, legally speaking, he is selling you junk. This is why courts usually show little mercy to sellers who don't strictly follow all the rules that allow them to use such clauses.

If, before buying, you spot clauses that are likely to hold up, you have to decide between taking a chance on living with them or getting them out.

HOW THE MAGNUSON-MOSS ACT HELPS YOU KEEP IMPLIED WARRANTIES

The Magnuson-Moss Warranty Act only prohibits the disclaimer of implied warranties by the person who gives you a written warranty or sells you a service contract. But by doing so, it often automatically helps you keep those warranties as part of the agreement and helps you negotiate with the seller, so it becomes more difficult for him to disclaim such coverage.

This is how the act helps you:

• If you get a written warranty from a manufacturer, and the seller wants to disclaim the implied warranties, the act now forces him to take positive action on his own in order to do so. If he does not take such action, the implied warranties automatically become part of your agreement with the seller.

Before the Act, sellers had little incentive to negotiate warranty terms because they could simply give the standard one furnished by the manufacturer. It was easy for a seller to shift all the responsibility onto the manufacturer and he didn't have to worry about what his competitors were up to: they were up to the same thing. All this meant that consumers had very little bargaining leverage, of course.

But now the seller has to take positive action to disclaim implied warranties if the product is covered by a manufacturer's written warranty, so he cannot be certain his competitors are doing the same thing. This can give you some bargaining leverage. When you negotiate about getting disclaimer language out of an agreement, a seller who insists on keeping it in can risk losing the sale to a seller who doesn't.

• A product covered by a written warranty is often sold without an additional written agreement, which makes it inconvenient for a seller to specifically disclaim the implied warranties as he is required to do by the act.

• It may not be worthwhile for a seller to disclaim the implied warranties: it is easy to scare away customers if you make it clear to them that you won't stand behind a product in any way.

• Strange as it may seem, many sellers *and* lawyers haven't the foggiest idea how the Magnuson-Moss Warranty Act works. Because of this some sellers still use disclaimer terminology which was fashionable and effective *before* the act, but which no longer holds up.

41 · Negotiating and Pinning Down Warranties When You Buy

IS IT WORTH NEGOTIATING ABOUT A DISCLAIMER/MERGER CLAUSE AND PITFALLS YOU FACE IF YOU DO

If a seller insists on using a clause to strip you of warranty protections, refusing to buy is your main bargaining leverage.

If you're unwilling to say no, then you're unlikely to convince the seller to change the terms to suit you. Convincing a seller to delete or change such clauses is one very important way to protect yourself.

But a word of caution before you start to negotiate. If you negotiate unsuccessfully about such clauses and buy anyway, you are then much more likely to get stuck with the wording included in the agreement than if you had never said anything. Thus your only safe course is to get such a clause out of the agreement, or refuse to buy because you could be stuck with it whether or not you negotiate about it.

Is it, then, ever worthwhile to negotiate with the seller about deleting an offensive clause?

It may be if there is a lot of competition among those selling the product you want to buy. You may be surprised how accommodating a seller will be when you make it clear that he either gets rid of the clause or loses the sale. If you can't get a clause deleted after a couple of tries, though, and you still want to buy the product, you're probably better off ignoring it and hoping that in the case of a dispute, a court will say the clause shouldn't count.

HOW TO NEGOTIATE WITH THE SELLER

The following questions can help you to get a seller to acknowledge his real intentions. This, in turn, will help demonstrate just how unfair a disclaimer clause really is to you.

When you spot a clause, ask what its purpose is. Then ask questions like:

"Doesn't that wording say that I won't have the implied warranty of merchantability?"

"What warranty coverage am I giving up if that clause stays in the agreement?"

"Doesn't that warranty mean that I can at least expect the product to be fully suitable for the ordinary purposes for which it would be used?"

"If you keep that clause does it mean the product isn't good enough to measure up?"

"If I can really expect the product to measure up to those standards, why is the warranty being eliminated as that clause says?"

Having to answer such questions practically forces the salesperson to "unsell" the product. He or she can see the sale slipping away even though you haven't directly demanded that the clause must go.

Such questions will also help you find out very quickly if the seller really wants to make the sale, and if he is likely to keep the clause in the agreement.

If the seller still wants to save the deal, he is likely to start "re-selling" you on the product and to try to deflect your attention from the disclaimer clause.

He might try to re-emphasize the value of the product, for instance. If he does, you could then say:

"In other words, I can expect the product to be as good as the warranties say?" Any answer in the affirmative gives you the opening to say: "In that case, why don't we delete this clause which really says the opposite and which you obviously don't mean?"

The seller might also try to avoid eliminating the clause by either minimizing its importance, or by saying that he can't change printed terms (meaning he refuses to). You can try to counter these attempts by saying something like:

"If the wording isn't really that important, and you are willing to stand behind the product as you say, then why keep the clause in the agreement? We can quickly complete the deal and settle everything simply by deleting it."

If the seller still won't budge, you must make clear you don't want to buy.

Here's how to negotiate about merger/express warranty exclusion clauses when the seller is seeking to avoid being bound by someone else's written warranty as well as implied warranties.

"But doesn't this wording say that no express warranties are part of this agreement?" "Does that mean the written warranty covering the product isn't really part of this agreement?" Or ask, "Where does it say in the agreement that those warranties are part of my agreement with you?"

The seller could then try to deflect you by saying that the manufacturer provides the warranties. You could then try to counter this by saying something like:

"But I am buying the product from you, not the manufacturer. Does this wording mean you won't stand behind the product at all?" Or you could say, "But since I am buying the product from you, how can I rely on that warranty if you don't back it up by making it part of our agreement?"

Once you have made it clear you don't like the wording that tries to eliminate someone else's written warranty from your agreement, then refer back to the implied warranty disclaimer clause with questions like:

"But doesn't this clause really mean that I don't have any warranty coverage as part of the agreement with you? What would happen if this product turns out to be defective?"

If the seller has not foreclosed further discussion by giving you a take-it-or-leave-it answer, he will most likely ask what it is you want. Now you spell out what wording you would like to have deleted from the agreement, and what wording you want to include to make a manufacturer's written warranty part of the agreement with the seller.

If you cannot convince the seller to make the changes you want after asking the sort of questions illustrated, I strongly urge you not to buy because you are very likely to be stuck with the clause—unless its use is specifically prohibited by law.

If you haven't yet formally agreed to the seller's written terms or paid any money, you can for all practical purposes ignore any pressure he might bring to convince you to complete the deal.

WRITTEN WARRANTIES

Formal written warranties that come with products, and which may be given by either the seller or manufacturer, are regulated by the Magnuson-Moss Warranty Act. Since they consist of standardized promises, there is seldom anything you can do to negotiate coverage.

Nevertheless, it's a good idea to find out what type of warranty you have (is it "full" or only "limited"?) and what it will and will not cover. Ask yourself if the warranty covers everything that could be important to you, and check whether particular parts or problems are specifically excluded. While the warrantor cannot take away coverage under the implied warranty of merchantability, if particular parts, product capacities, or other characteristics are specifically excluded under a written warranty, it could mean that under ordinary circumstances you could *not* expect the product to have those attributes. In this case the implied warranty of merchantability may give you little or no protection.

If your written warranty is provided by the manufacturer, check whether it includes conspicuous wording that says the seller won't be responsible for honoring the written warranty or any implied warranty (see page 312 for how a seller can do this). To make the seller accountable, get him to agree in writing that the written warranty is part of the agreement. If he refuses, then at least make sure he has not included wording that would eliminate the warranty of merchantability.

Keep a record of any promises the seller or manufacturer makes that convince you to buy a product. Identify the most important ones in the agreement so the seller understands they are important conditions of the deal and that he must be accountable for them under your contract.

PINNING DOWN EXPRESS WARRANTIES

Sometimes you might negotiate express warranties with a seller; promises he makes only to you. Because most products today are mass-produced and mass-marketed, and thus come with standard promises, you obviously can't negotiate warranty coverage that says the product is tailor-made for you. But what you can do is find out whether a particular product will measure up to specific expectations.

You do this by asking the seller whether the product possesses the specific qualities, capacities, or characteristics that are important to you. Don't be satisfied with vague, hedging answers like: "I think it does," or "It probably will." If the seller specifically confirms that the product possesses the qualities, that usually counts as an express warranty. Say, for example, you're thinking about buying a used car and ask: "Has this car ever been damaged or involved in an accident?" If the answer is, "No, it has not," that's likely to be an express warranty. If, on the other hand, the answer is something like: "I can't be sure, but I don't think so," you've got the person's opinion but not much else.

GETTING PROMISES IN WRITING

If the seller makes express warranties, be sure to identify them on the sales slip you get, the written agreement you sign, or on a separate document that specifically refers to your agreement (see page 135 for a form you can use to incorporate the promises into an agreement).

How careful you should be in nailing down such promises depends, of course, on how costly the product is, what's important to you, what's already covered by a written warranty, what could go wrong, and how expensive repairs would be.

Here are ways to identify different kinds of express warranties in your agreement:

- Insist the product be *accurately* identified and described. Such a description constitutes an express warranty that the product will conform to the description.
- If the product is covered by a written warranty given by the manufacturer, try to include the following wording: "Agreement subject to manufacturer's written warranty given to the buyer." (If the seller refuses to do this, then at least make sure the agreement *does not* include clauses which say the *seller* is not giving you any warranties.)
- If the product is described or specific promises are made in separate sales liter-

ature, advertising, or labels then say: "As (described/represented/advertised) in (seller's/manufacturer's catalogue/advertising/label) dated April 10, 19___."

• If the product is demonstrated either to you personally or in the seller's or manufacturer's advertising, then say: "As demonstrated (to the buyer/in TV commerical on April 15, 19___)."

• If the seller shows you a sample or model of the product, then make sure the goods correspond by adding: "As shown to buyer on April 15, 19___, by (display sample/model) identified as (describe specific sample or model number if not already specifically described in the agreement)."

• If you are buying a very expensive product, or one that could be hazardous, find out if the product conforms to applicable government health, safety, or construction standards, and then note: "Product shall conform to all applicable government or other consumer health, safety, or construction standards, regulations, and codes."

• If the seller makes verbal statements about qualities or characteristics you can expect from the product, put them in writing by saying, for example: "Car sold has not been damaged in an accident," or "Mileage on car does not exceed the 37,958 miles shown on the odometer." Make sure to state such promises as clearly and exactly as possible.

MAKING PROMISES COUNT

Is it necessary to include each promise a seller makes in your agreement?

The Code says that all specific statements or promises about a product that count as express warranties become part of the basis of a sale *unless* good reason can be given that the promise wasn't supposed to be part of the deal. So if the seller tries to show that a promise wasn't really part of your deal, you have to be able to *demonstate* that he actually made the promise. Obviously the more significant the statement or promise about a product, the harder it usually is for a seller to show it wasn't part of the deal.

Thus, while it may not be necessary to formally pin down every promise, remember that unwritten promises are hard to prove, and that unwritten terms may not count at all if they differ from what is said in writing, or if the agreement says that the only terms that count are those that are in writing.

Obviously, then, the key to making promises count is the ability to demonstrate the warrantor made them to convince you to buy. One way to do this is to keep a record of any promises that you don't pin down in your agreement. So long as you have at least some tangible proof of what the seller said or did to convince you to buy, you are likely to be able to hold him accountable—especially if very little is formally put in writing about the agreement. (See page 121 about how unwritten terms count.)

For example, a consumer purchased a set of tubeless polyglass tires that cost twice as much as regular ones. He paid the extra money because he was concerned about his family's safety and had seen a TV ad that demonstrated the tires traveling over glass and rocks at high speed without any problems. When he went to buy the tires, he still had doubts about spending the extra money but the salesperson assured him the tires were "well worth" the higher price. Once on the road, however, one of these "better" tires had a blow-out. When the consumer sued the manufacturer and the tire store, he was reimbursed not only for his medical expenses and damage to his car, but also got new tires. Although everything was not put in writing, this buyer could point to an ad which demonstrated an important product characteristic. He could show he paid much more for the polyglass tires than for regular tires. And he took the trouble to get the store to confirm that the tires were as good as they appeared when demonstrated on TV and well worth the extra money.

IMPLIED WARRANTIES

Although you do not have to pin anything down in writing to make implied warranties count as part of the deal (assuming such warranties were not properly and legally disclaimed), it could be important to pin down in writing the fact that you made a purchase under circumstances in which you would have the implied warranty of fitness for a particular purpose.

You could do this by including the following sentence in your agreement:

"Seller knows the (identify product) purchased under this agreement must be fit for the following (purpose/use) (describe the particular purpose, such as "vacuuming a 3"-high shag rug") and has sold it as being fit for that particular (purpose/use)."

If you are ordering a product, here's how to make this condition part of the order:

"The (identify product) is being purchased for the following particular (purpose/use) (describe the purpose or use) and the product supplied by the seller under this order must be fit for that particular (purpose/use)."

In effect, putting this warranty in writing creates an express warranty which the seller cannot disclaim.

If you don't put this warranty in writing, be sure to check any written agreement for wording that the warranty of fitness for a particular purpose *isn't* part of the deal. It is pointless to rely on a seller's recommendation, then allow him to put a disclaimer in your agreement that says, he won't be responsible if the product he selects is unsuitable.

Of course, it is possible a seller won't recommend or sell a product as being fit for a particular purpose if you make it clear you expect to hold him accountable under the implied warranty. But if he's unwilling to stand behind his recommendation, how can you trust him in the first place?

HOW TO AVOID COMPLICATIONS

In some cases, your only effective bargaining leverage will be to refuse to buy. To avoid complications that could later make it harder for you to do this, both practically and legally, *always* wait until you have settled on written terms before you:

1. Pay the seller any money, and
2. Turn over any goods or sign over any title to the seller in cases where the deal involves any kind of trade-in.

In the case of trade-ins *never,* turn your property over to the seller until *after* you have settled on the written terms. If you do, and you get involved in a big dispute about the written terms and the seller refuses or cannot return your property, you will most likely need legal advice to untangle the mess. You would not be without legal recourse, or bargaining leverage in this situation, of course, but it could be very hard to settle the matter unless both you and the seller were willing to call off the deal completely.

A problem like this is only likely to occur with a purchase that involves a lot of money. Always seek legal advice because the initial steps you take and the settlement options you select can be critical. By selecting one option, for instance, you can easily foreclose another and make it more difficult to assert your rights.

WHAT TO DO IF YOU'VE PUT DOWN A DEPOSIT

But suppose you and the seller reach a verbal agreement and you put down a cash deposit to hold the deal while he "finishes the paperwork." Then you find that the seller has included printed terms you did not agree to and he refuses to change them.

While putting down a deposit is certainly one important way to indicate that you and the seller had reached a deal, if a dispute arises the seller stands little—if any—chance of holding you to terms you had not already specifically agreed to. At this point, the simplest solution from both a practical and a legal standpoint is to call off the deal, and insist the seller refund your deposit. Any bargaining leverage created by the earlier verbal "agreement," would be all on your side because a seller cannot hold you to any terms you haven't previously agreed to.

Naturally, any reputable store will automatically refund your deposit, and even a store that is trying to use preprinted or written terms to rework your verbal deal will probably do so.

If a seller refuses to refund your deposit, it's almost a sure sign you're dealing with a crook. Here is a sample letter you can adapt to demand your deposit back, based on the contention that there is no agreement that entitles the seller to keep it if the seller insists on holding you to written terms you have not agreed to.

Certified Mail #111222333

200 Witchtree Lane
Anytown, USA 00000

April 13, 19___

Mr. A. Slyfox
Manager
Slippery Discounts, Inc.
100 Main Street
Anytown, USA 00000

Dear Mr. Slyfox:

This is to notify you that you are, without legal justification, retaining the $ _____ deposit I made on the (describe product). I gave you this deposit only on the expectation that I would be making the purchase according to the terms we had negotiated on April 11, which were to be put in writing by April 13 when we were to complete the transaction.

But the written terms which were first presented to me today include additional terms which we had neither discussed nor agreed to (and differed from those we had actually discussed). The terms which were put in writing neither reflect nor conform to any bargain we may have reached. The unacceptable additional terms include (a clause disclaiming the implied warranty of merchantability/a clause denying that any express warranties were part of our bargain/and list any other objectionable terms). Your written terms also differed from those we had specifically agreed to in the following respects: (identify any specific ways).

Since your written terms neither reflected nor conformed to the terms we had discussed as a basis for a bargain, I requested that they be altered to the extent necessary so we could still complete the transaction according to the terms we had previously discussed. I was, instead, told that we could complete the transaction only according to the terms that had been put in writing and which were the only basis for a bargain.

We therefore do not, and cannot, have an agreement on the basis of the terms you now unilaterally insist on imposing as the basis for a bargain, and I cannot any longer rely on your willingness to act in good faith with respect to any bargain.

But when I requested a refund of my deposit so we could promptly settle this matter, it was refused.

I am still prepared to settle this matter if you will immediately refund the $ _____ deposit you are no longer entitled to have.

But if my money is not immediately returned to me, I shall seek to hold you liable to the fullest extent provided by law for your having retained my money without legal justification.

Sincerely,

The seller's refusal to refund your deposit in such circumstances is likely to be a violation of your state's deceptive sales practices law or may even amount to fraud. Your follow-up steps would be to send the ultimatum for using your rights under those laws, and then, if the matter is still not resolved, to sue the seller in small claims court.

42 · Your Remedies under the Uniform Commercial Code

Section IV covers your rights to reject and/or revoke acceptance when goods fail to conform to warranties. This chapter focuses on the rights you have under the different kinds of warranties.

In general, the steps covered here supplement those described in Section IV. So when you first discover a defect, always look first in Section IV for the initial steps you should take, then use the steps covered here to beef up the negotiating strategies if necessary.

YOUR REMEDIES UNDER THE CODE

Leaving aside some fine-point technicalities, a warranty can be breached in two ways. The first occurs if the product fails to conform to your warranties. The second occurs if the warrantor fails to carry out his obligations to correct the non-conformity.

In order to enforce your rights under warranties, you are obligated by the Code to notify the warrantor about the product's failure to conform. You must also take certain steps to hold the seller accountable.

What are your remedies under the Code? They generally consist of two options:

1. Rejecting or revoking acceptance of the goods, canceling the agreement and demanding all your money back as explained in Section IV. These remedies may only be available for holding a seller accountable for warranty obligations that are part of the contract under which you bought the product. That is, you may be unable to use these remedies to hold a manufacturer accountable under written warranties that only he, rather than the seller, was obligated to honor.

2. Recovering damages which make up for the amount by which the product's value is reduced by its failure to conform to your warranties. This is one of your main options after you *accept* a product. It is also your only choice when you are not entitled to revoke acceptance of the product. Recovering compensation may also be your only recourse for holding a separate warrantor accountable under a written warranty the seller is not obligated to honor.

The specific remedial actions a warrantor spelled out in a written warranty and/or your agreement would, of course, usually spell out the minimum the warrantor was obligated to do about a product's failure to conform to warranties. Depending on the wording, you could be limited to the remedial actions the warrantor specifically promised to take in place of the remedies the Code makes available.

ADDITIONAL DAMAGES YOU MAY BE ENTITLED TO RECOVER

If you are entitled to use either of these two main options, the Code may also allow you to recover other losses which either result from, or are directly caused by, the product's failure to conform. Normally, these would be any incidental and/or consequential damages. (See page 279 for a description of these damages.) If your agreement includes any limitation of remedies clauses you may be prevented from recovering these additional damages, of course. But, check page 241 to see if you are entitled to disregard any such clauses.

REMEDIES FOR PERSONAL INJURY

While detailed remedies for a personal injury, or damage to other property, caused by a defective product are outside the scope of this book, always seek legal advice at once. There are two important things to do in such situations: *keep the product* (or what's left of it), and make a prompt record of what happened. When it's important to collect for harm caused by a defective product, do not even try to hold the seller accountable for the defect in the product itself.

Remedies under warranties and/or product liability law are the two forms of legal recourse that can entitle you to hold someone accountable for a product that injures you. If you are injured and entitled to sue under a warranty, you will usually be in a very strong position legally to hold the warrantor accountable for resulting damages for personal injury. In the case of injury, the Code in your state spells out who beside the buyer can also sue under the warranty covering the product. This would always include members of the buyer's immediate family but could also include guests in the buyer's home and, in some states, other third persons. This book does not go into the details that could apply since you should seek legal advice in such situations.

AMOUNTS YOU CAN RECOVER AS COMPENSATION FOR DEFECTS

When you are entitled only to recover damages for a product's failure to conform, the Code spells out two ways of measuring such compensation.

The Code includes a general as well as a more specific rule for how to measure the amount of compensation due because the product did not conform.

The general rule says a buyer can recover losses resulting from the ordinary course of events from the breach. Under this rule, the loss can be measured in any reasonable way that demonstrates the monetary amount. Generally speaking, this would cover losses involving the product itself rather than incidental or consequential damages.

This general rule is most likely to be important when the defect covered by warranty further damaged the product itself. And you can use this rule for measuring the loss only with respect to defects you have notified the warrantor about. So this rule can usually help you hold a warrantor accountable for further losses that occur after you have notified him about a defect which he does not properly correct.

The more specific rule allows a buyer to recover for a breach of warranty the *difference* between the value of the product as accepted and the value it would have had if it had been as warranted unless special circumstances show that someone should be entitled to recover a different amount.

This specific rule can be expressed as an equation: Value of the goods as warranted (minus) value of the goods as accepted (the actual value of the defective product) = the amount of loss buyer can recover.

Broadly speaking, there are two ways to compute the amounts.

One way is by directly measuring the amount of the actual loss. This would usually be the cost of repairing and/or replacing defective parts. If, for example, you buy a new refrigerator that turns out to have a defective motor, the simplest way to measure the loss is to equate it to the cost of repairing or replacing the defective motor. The dollar amount could be either the actual or estimated cost. If repairs—or a replacement—fail to bring the product up to its warranted value, then you can still recover any difference. This method would usually be used when repair or replacement of defective parts would correct the defects.

The other way to measure the amount of the loss is to compute the difference between the value of the product as warranted and its value as accepted (that is, given the defects). This method would usually be used when repair or replacement of defective parts isn't feasible or doing so would be more costly than what the difference in value would be.

If you use this method, the product's value as warranted would usually be its fair market value at the time, and place where you accept it. As a practical matter, that's usually the purchase price, but it could be higher or lower. If, for example, you buy a product on sale, its value could be its regular price rather than its sale price.

While it's usually easy to determine a product's value as warranted, it can be much harder to determine its value as accepted (that is, as a defective product). You can usually come up with a reasonable estimate, though. Pick the lowest amount that would be reasonable given the situation. In cases where products have been substantially defective, courts have allowed buyers to set the value of the goods as accepted at zero, which entitled them to recover the entire purchase price.

Courts usually give consumers considerable latitude in fixing losses, so the formula you use for measuring compensation is rarely as important as having adequate proof of the loss. From both a practical and legal standpoint, your best bet in such situations is to claim any measurable monetary loss that directly involves the product itself, since the worst that can happen is that your claim will be turned down.

BUYER'S RIGHT TO DEDUCT DAMAGES FROM AMOUNT STILL DUE

If you sustain damages because your contract has been breached, the Code specifically entitles you to deduct those damages from the balance of the purchase price still due. Normally, a seller's failure to honor warranty obligations would count as such a breach. (A word of caution: this would only apply if the seller, rather than the manufacturer, was obligated to honor the written warranty in the first place. The Magnuson-Moss Warranty Act then entitles you to recover your loss directly from the manufacturer who gave the written warranty rather than from the seller who wasn't obligated under that warranty.)

The Code sets two restrictions on this remedy. They are:

1. You may deduct damages only from the amount still due under the contract the seller has *breached*. In other words, you cannot deduct damages for one breach of contract from amounts that may be due under another contract.

2. You may deduct damages in this way only if you have first *notified* the seller that you intend to do so. If you simply withhold payment without notification, you could be in default under your agreement.

If, in this situation, the seller goes along with the price reduction, your problem is settled. If he refuses to go along, after you have notified him, deduct only the amounts you could clearly be entitled to recover, rather than all the amounts you might be able to claim (unless, of course, you take this step based on legal advice). Reserve your right to hold the seller accountable for any amounts you did not deduct.

If you and the seller dispute the amount you can deduct but you pay the amounts you believe are still due under the contract, then see page 395 for an explanation of how you can use a check to make a partial payment that can count as payment in full when your check is cashed.

If you bought the product on credit and owe money to a creditor other than the seller, your right to withhold payment from that creditor generally depends on the laws regulating the kind of credit you used. See page 523.

43 · Negotiating Strategy for Holding a Warrantor Accountable

The strategies covered in this chapter are:

• Retaining rights to hold a seller and/or a manufacturer accountable under different warranties you may have, based on the Code and the Magnuson-Moss Warranty Act.

• Holding a warrantor accountable under a "full" warranty regulated by the Magnuson-Moss Warranty Act.

• Reserving your rights when you are not yet willing to hold a warrantor fully accountable under a warranty because the issue is not really clear-cut.

• Responding to a warrantor's denial of warranty coverage based on your rights under the Code, the Magnuson-Moss Warranty Act, and your state's deceptive sales practices law.

DESCRIBING AND REQUESTING PAYMENT FOR DAMAGES

The sample letters included in this and the following chapter illustrate how you could describe and request reimbursement for amounts you may be able to recover as incidental or consequential damages.

A word of caution about using the sample wording. NEVER use the sample letters included in this and the following chapter when it is important for you to hold a seller and/or manufacturer accountable for such damages and they involve large sums. Seek legal advice instead. If you *must* try to collect on your own, specifically request reimbursement and never say you are willing to waive claims for such damages. (Keep in mind it is unlikely a warrantor will reimburse you for such damages unless you sue.) So if the warrantor at least takes care of what's wrong with the product itself, it normally isn't worthwhile trying to insist on being reimbursed for additional damages you sustained as a result. Also keep in mind that limitation of remedies clauses are likely to prevent you from recovering such damages at least as long as a warrantor properly corrects what's wrong with the product itself based on what he was required to do. So as a practical matter, you are seldom giving up very much if you don't insist on being reimbursed for further damages as long as the warrantor corrects what's wrong with the product itself.

If you are willing to forget about collecting further damages as long as the defects are corrected, then omit the wording requesting reimbursement. But if you refer to damages while proposing a settlement that doesn't demand the seller pay them, you are almost certainly giving up your chance to collect those damages later. Doing this, however, demonstrates your willingness to be reasonable and can give you some practical bargaining leverage to convince a warrantor to correct what's wrong with the product. So that's how the sample letters are worded.

It is up to you to decide whether to press for additional damages you could be entitled to recover. Notifying the warrantor about, and requesting reimbursement for damages strengthens your position to hold the warrantor accountable for them especially if he refuses to perform warranty obligations. But you could be waiving rights by proposing settlements based on the wording included in the sample letters

326 / THE CONSUMER PROTECTION MANUAL

if you do *not* insist on being reimbursed for the damages you describe. It may, however, be easier for you to reach a settlement if you make clear your willingness to give up something to get something, while the seller who refuses to give you anything may then end up owing you for everything, if you had to sue because he failed to honor his warranty obligations.

But again, I caution you to seek legal advice rather than try to handle the matter yourself when it is important to recover additional damages.

RETAINING YOUR RIGHT TO HOLD A SELLER AND/OR A MANUFACTURER ACCOUNTABLE UNDER DIFFERENT WARRANTIES

One of the toughest warranty problems you are likely to face is if a seller and a manufacturer could each be accountable under different warranties.

STAGE ONE: OPENING SKIRMISHES

The way to go about this problem is to always deal with the seller first by notifying him about the defect in writing—*regardless* of what a separate manufacturer's written warranty might tell you to do. Even if a defect is specifically covered by a manufacturer's written warranty, a seller could also be accountable for the defect based on warranty obligations he has under your agreement, such as the implied warranty of merchantability.

Your next step depends on what the seller does. If he insists the manufacturer is responsible for correcting the defect, it may be pointless to argue—at least initially. So return the product to the manufacturer for servicing under the manufacturer's warranty, but reserve your rights under your contract with the seller in case you later need to hold him accountable under his warranties.

If the seller does assume responsibility for the defect, it may still be worthwhile to notify the manufacturer and explain the action you have taken in case you might later have to hold *him* accountable. This would be the case, for instance, if the seller's attempt to cure turns out to be inadequate. Do not, however, allow a seller to repair defects covered by a manufacturer's warranty if the seller is not qualified to do so and the warranty specifically requires repairs by someone who is qualified. Such action could result in the manufacturer disclaiming responsibility. Instead, notify the seller about the defect, then—unless he is willing to exchange the product or refund your money—seek warranty servicing as specified by your written warranty.

Caution: retaining your rights to hold separate warrantors accountable under different warranties can get very complicated, and trying to hold the wrong person accountable can be very costly. If the product involved is an expensive one, seek legal advice.

If the seller assumes responsibility for correcting defects covered by any warranty, it could be advantageous to you; he is then very likely to be considered responsible for having to honor the warranty as part of your agreement. However, the seller who refuses to honor someone else's separate warranty, doesn't get off the hook as far as his own obligations under the agreement are concerned.

RESERVING YOUR RIGHTS WHEN THE SELLER INSISTS THE MANUFACTURER IS RESPONSIBLE

If you have notified the seller of the defects in writing and he insists you return the product to the manufacturer, reserve your rights under your contract with the seller with a confirming letter, such as the following:

100 Witchtree Lane
Anytown, USA 00000

June 15, 19___

Mr. R. Seller
Manager
ABC Sales Company
Futurama Mall
Anytown, USA 00000

Dear Mr. Seller:

As I have already notified you in writing on June 14, when we discussed this matter, the (identify product) (I purchased from you on June 1, 19___/which was delivered on June 1, 19___, under our agreement of April 15, 19___) fails to conform to the requirements of our contract.

But since your company insists that I return the product to (identify separate warrantor) for obtaining the remedial action promised under the written warranty with which I purchased the product, I shall do as you insist.

I am, however, confirming that I am doing so only while reserving all my rights.

Sincerely,

NOTIFYING MANUFACTURER WHEN SELLER CORRECTS DEFECTS

You could adapt the following sample letter for notifying a manufacturer about a defect covered by his written warranty when the seller assumes responsibility. Send it to the person or office identified on the written warranty, or to the company's main office.

100 Witchtree Lane
Anytown, USA 00000

June 15, 19___

Warranty Service Center
XYZ Manufacturing Company
100 Industrial Park
Anytown, USA 00000

Dear Sir:

(1) This is to notify you that the (identify product) I purchased on June 1, 19___, from (identify seller) failed to conform to your written warranty (as described below/as described in the attached copy of the notice I gave the seller when I returned the product on June 10, 19___).
(Describe the defects and/or seller's inadequate attempt to correct them if you are not attaching a copy of your notice to the seller)
(2) According to the ABC Company, the defects have been corrected by the repairs or adjustments which were completed by June 13, 19___, and which were described to me (as follows/as noted on the attached copy of their service order)

(Describe repairs seller said were made if you don't have a copy of his service order)

(3) I hope the repairs and adjustments made are adequate to make the product conform, but please notify me immediately if the repairs are inadequate or other repairs or adjustments would be required to correct the defects I have described, and furnish me your instructions for obtaining the appropriate corrective actions.

Sincerely,

• If you have not already notified the manufacturer, and the seller's attempts to correct the defects fail to work and the product continues to be defective, you should now definitely inform the manufacturer of the situation.

• If you have notified him previously, send a follow-up letter about the seller's failure to correct defects by using the following replacement paragraphs:

(2) "Since the seller's attempts to correct defects I previously discovered have proved inadequate (and since I have now discovered additional defects) as described in the attached copy of the notice I gave the seller, I now request that the XYZ manufacturing company promptly take whatever actions are necessary to make the product conform to its warranties. And as described to the seller, I have sustained $_____ in damages."

(3) "(I returned the product on July 1 to the [ABC Company, Futurama Mall, Anytown, USA] and request that your company's representative examine it promptly to determine what repairs or adjustments are now still necessary to make the product conform, and that your company then either take steps to ensure that the product is made to conform to your warranties or replace it with one that does. Please contact me promptly so we can make arrangements to make the product available for your examination to enable your company to determine what repairs or adjustments are now still necessary to make the product conform so that your company can then either take steps to ensure that the product is made to conform to your warranties or replace it with one that does.)

"You can contact me at (111) 333-2222 between 9:00 A.M. and 5:00 P.M. or at (111) 444-5555 after 6:00 P.M."

"Thank you for your prompt cooperation."

Sincerely,

Naturally, you must adapt these letters to fit your particular situation. You may have to expand on the seller's failure to correct defects, for example. (See Chapter 35 for sample letters for notifying a seller about defects).

NOTIFYING THE MANUFACTURER WHEN SELLER DOES NOT ASSUME RESPONSIBILITY FOR DEFECTS

If you have to obtain warranty servicing from the manufacturer because the seller refuses to assume responsibility, spell out when and where you bought the product, say how you are returning it to the warrantor, and describe the defect, as in this sample letter.

200 Witchtree Lane
Anytown, USA 00000

June 16, 19___

Warranty Service Center
XYZ Manufacturing Company
100 Industrial Lane
Anytown, USA 00000

Dear Sir:

(1) I am hereby returning by insured parcel post and notifying you that the (identify product) I purchased from the (identify name and address of seller) on June 1, 19__, does not conform to your warranties as described below:
(describe the defects or how the product is not operating properly)
(2) And as described below, I have also sustained $____ in damages and will incur at least the following expenses because of the product's failure to conform:
(describe the types and the amount of the loss)
(3) Please replace the product with one that fully conforms to your warranty or make whatever adjustments and repairs will make the product conform (and reimburse me for my damages).
(4) But since I regularly need the product for (describe use) and have already sustained damages and will incur expenses because it failed to conform, should you elect to repair rather than replace the product, please furnish me your assurances that the repairs will in fact be adequate so that I can rely on the product for future use.
(5) I would appreciate the product being promptly replaced or properly repaired and returned to me at the above address, properly insured and shipped at your expense.
(6) Thank you for giving this matter your immediate attention.

Sincerely,

- If you have to ship back a product covered by a "full" warranty, the warrantor may be required to reimburse you for your shipping expenses (see page 297 for an explanation of your rights under a "full" warranty). If so, request reimbursement for your shipping expenses by inserting the following paragraph after paragraph (3) or (4) as appropriate.

"Since the requirement that I return the product at my expense is an unreasonable condition for securing my remedies under your "full" warranty as provided by the Magnuson-Moss Warranty Act, I request that you promptly reimburse me for the $____ in shipping and insurance charges I incurred for returning the product for warranty servicing."

- If you must return the product for further warranty servicing, use the same basic letter but adapt the wording by using the follow-up memos included on page 250 for notifying the seller about subsequent defects as part of your negotiating strategy for revoking acceptance. Use the follow-up steps for holding a seller accountable for further defects even though you are dealing with the manufacturer. These are the steps for revoking acceptance.

- If you buy a product you might have to return to a manufacturer for servicing, try to keep the packing materials to make it easier to ship back safely. Ask for a return receipt to verify delivery.

Remember, the warrantor usually won't be responsible for damage in shipment. If you could have trouble shipping the product back safely, contact the manufacturer to find out how he wants to handle the problem.

STAGE TWO: THE LOW-KEYED WARNING

The warrantor may not return the product to you within a reasonable time. Your initial follow-up step should be to request the prompt return of the repaired product, or a replacement.

Generally speaking, a warrantor has two main obligations when you send him your property for servicing. One is to correct the defects as covered by your warranty; the other is to return your property. You can adapt this sample follow-up letter to demand that he do both.

200 Witchtree Lane
Anytown, USA 00000

July 15, 19__

Warranty Service Center
XYZ Manufacturing Company
100 Industrial Lane
Anytown, USA 00000

Dear Sir:

This is to notify you that the (identify product) has not been replaced, or repaired, and returned to me as I requested in my letter of June 16, 19__, which I enclosed when I shipped the product to you on June 16 by parcel post (copy of letter is attached).

I therefore request that you promptly carry out your obligations under your warranty and return to me a conforming replacement for the defective one I returned, or that you properly repair and return the product I shipped.

Please return the conforming replacement, or the repaired product, by August 5, 19__.

I hope that you will now promptly carry out your obligations so that I will not have to hold you accountable for breaching your warranty and for failing to return my property.

Sincerely,

STAGE THREE: THE ULTIMATUM

If the product still isn't repaired, or replaced, and returned to you, use an ultimatum for setting a final deadline.

The following sample ultimatum is based on two ways the warrantor could be accountable to you at this point. One is for breach of warranty because of his failure to correct the defects; the other is for refusing to return your property. Generally speaking, the unauthorized taking or keeping of property belonging to someone else is called conversion. While the manufacturer obviously has your authorization to keep the product while he is trying to correct the defects, that authorization doesn't entitle him to keep it forever.

Certified Mail #11112222

100 Witchtree Lane
Anytown, USA 00000

August 20, 19__

Warranty Service Center
XYZ Manufacturing Company
100 Industrial Lane
Anytown, USA 00000

Dear Sir:

This is to notify you of the breach of your warranty which has occurred because of the failure to ship a conforming replacement for, or to repair and return to me, the defective (identify product) which I shipped to you on June 16, 19___ .

The company has now had more than a reasonable time to carry out its obligations under its warranty on the product as I requested when I returned the product as called for by the warranty. And even though I wrote to the company on July 15, 19___ and (list other dates) to renew my requests that the company carry out its obligations, I have to date received no response. (Copies of previous letters are attached.)

And as described below, I have now incurred $_____ in further damages because of the company's failure to carry out its obligations: (list further damages and amounts, if any)

Moreover, since I need the product for (describe purpose) as I explained when I returned the product, I shall be compelled to purchase a replacement because of the company's failure to carry out its obligations under its warranty.

To cure this continuing breach of warranty, a conforming replacement or the repaired product must be shipped to me at the above address, properly insured and at your expense, within five days upon receipt of this certified letter.

But if the company still fails to cure this breach of warranty and does not return to me a conforming replacement or the fully repaired product, I shall hold you liable for damages as provided by the Uniform Commercial Code and for failing to comply with your obligations under a written warranty as provided by the Magnuson-Moss Warranty Act which makes you liable for the damages I sustain and which could make you liable for my legal expenses should I be compelled to enforce my rights by legal action.

Sincerely,

If this step does not produce satisfactory results, your legal recourse is to sue.

REVOKING ACCEPTANCE AFTER MANUFACTURER FAILS TO CURE DEFECTS

If the seller insists you return the product to the manufacturer for servicing under the manufacturer's warranty, but the seller is *also* obligated to honor warranties that cover the defects, the manufacturer's failure to correct the defects *could* entitle you to revoke acceptance under the circumstances described on page 234.

Technically speaking your right to revoke acceptance would, in effect, be triggered by the product's failure to conform to the warranties the *seller* is obligated to honor as part of your contract (but remember there are other conditions that govern your right to revoke acceptance). That's why it is so important for you to deal with the seller as well as the manufacturer.

If you are entitled to revoke acceptance with the seller, proceed as you would if dealing with the seller alone, by using the basic low-keyed warning on page 269 and substituting the following paragraphs as appropriate.

Substitute paragraphs for memo on page 269.

> *(2) "I am revoking acceptance because the product does not conform to our contract despite my having returned it to the (XYZ Manufacturing Company) to have the defects corrected as you had insisted upon my first having notified you about the defects on _____ . The product's value to me is now substantially impaired because of its continuing failure to conform.*
>
> *(5) "(But despite your insistence that the product would be made to conform by the repairs and adjustments the [XYZ Manufacturing Company] was to make to which I consented while reserving my rights, the company's last attempt to make the product conform again proved inadequate./Although you insisted that I return the product to the [XYZ Manufacturing Company] for servicing under their warranty as an alternative to your assuming your warranty obligations under our contract and to which I consented while reserving my rights, the product has repeatedly failed to conform and the company's last attempt to repair the defects is again inadequate.)*
>
> *(6) "(Since these defects again deprive me of the use of this product which I regularly need for [household/family] purposes, I can no longer rely on further assurances from you or the [XYZ Manufacturing Company] that the product can, in fact, be made to conform to our contract by any further adjustments and repairs./Your previous refusal to furnish me your assurances that the product would be made to conform by the adjustments and repairs and your refusal to assume responsibility for the product's failure to conform to our contract now prevents me from believing that the product could still be made to conform to our contract if I returned it for further servicing.)*
>
> *"Nor can I continue to incur the added expenses of returning the product for the repairs and adjustments which have been required because of its failure to conform to our contract."*

• If you shipped the product back to the manufacturer, you should at least *claim* those expenses as damages.

• Use the above wording as a guide for adapting the other memos for revoking acceptance.

HOLDING A WARRANTOR ACCOUNTABLE UNDER A "FULL" WARRANTY REGULATED BY THE MAGNUSON-MOSS WARRANTY ACT

The Magnuson-Moss Warranty Act automatically creates the so-called "lemon remedy" for any "full" warranty. It entitles the buyer to choose a refund or a replacement when a product, or product part, is defective or malfunctions after a reasonable number of attempts by the warrantor to correct the problem.

The lemon remedy is like your right to revoke acceptance under the Code, except that the Magnuson-Moss Warranty Act entitles you to demand a refund or replacement without satisfying the same requirements. And since the act automatically makes the lemon remedy part of any "full" warranty, it cannot be changed by limitation of remedies clauses.

STAGE ONE: OPENING SKIRMISHES

In order to be entitled to this remedy, you must first notify the warrantor about the defects and give him a reasonable number of chances to correct them. These initial steps of your negotiating strategy are the same as those used for notifying a seller about defects when rejecting and/or revoking acceptance, as described on page 248. Remember, however, that this written warranty gives you recourse only against the person who actually gave it. So if it was given only by the manufacturer, you would have to get a replacement or refund from the manufacturer. But if the seller had given it or he had also become bound to honor it as part of your agreement, you would then also have recourse against the seller.

When the refund or replacement remedy is triggered, you could at least initially request the store to honor it even if the written warranty was only given by the manufacturer. The store may be willing to do so. If not, you could then go to the manufacturer.

REQUESTING A REFUND OR REPLACEMENT

Here is a sample note you can take to a store when you want to request a refund or replacement and pin down a settlement.

September 15, 19—

> *TO: ABC Sales Company*
> *Futurama Mall*
> *Anytown, USA*

> *I am hereby (returning/requesting that you pick up) the (identify product) which I bought from you (on/under our agreement of) April 15, 19—, but which is still defective as described below despite previous attempts to correct all defects.*
> *(Identify the defects, especially if you are asking the seller to pick up the product)*
> *Since the product was sold with a "full" (one year) warranty but the product continues to be defective despite the reasonable number of attempts to correct all defects, I now request that you (promptly refund its $___ purchase price/promptly furnish me a conforming replacement) as provided by the Magnuson-Moss Warranty Act.*

> _____
> *(Your signature)*

Then pin down the appropriate settlement at the bottom of the memo.

RESERVING YOUR RIGHTS IF THE SELLER INSISTS MANUFACTURER IS RESPONSIBLE

If the seller claims the manufacturer is responsible for refunding the purchase price or replacing the product, then reserve your rights. This could help you hold the seller accountable later should the manufacturer fail to honor his obligations and the seller is also bound by the warranty as part of your contract.

200 Witchtree Lane
Anytown, USA 00000

September 16, 19__

Mr. R. Seller
Manager
ABC Sales Company
Futurama Mall
Anytown, USA 00000

As I have already notified you on September 15 when we discussed this matter, the (identify product) I purchased from you on June 1 (under our agreement of April 15, 19__) with a "full" (one year) warranty continues to be defective despite the reasonable number of attempts to correct all defects.

But since you insisted that the (XYZ Manufacturing Company) was responsible for (refunding the purchase price/replacing the product) as required by the Magnuson-Moss Warranty Act, I shall as you insist request that company to (refund the $____ purchase price/to replace the product) as I have already requested you to do.

Since I did, however, purchase this product from you with this "full" (one year) warranty, I am doing so while reserving all my rights under our contract.

Sincerely,

REQUESTING A REFUND OR REPLACEMENT FROM MANUFACTURER

If the seller insists you request a refund or a replacement from a manufacturer, notify the company and ask how it wants the product returned before sending it back. This sample letter assumes that, at the seller's insistence, you have previously returned the product to the manufacturer for warranty servicing.

200 Witchtree Lane
Anytown, USA 00000

September 16, 19__

Warranty Service Center
XYZ Manufacturing Company
100 Industrial Lane
Anytown, USA 00000

Dear Sir:

I am notifying you that the (identify product) I purchased and received from the ABC Sales Company, Futurama Mall, Anytown, USA, on June 1, 19__, for $____ with your company's "full" (one year) warranty is still defective as described below despite your company's previous attempts to correct the defects. (copy of proof of purchase showing amount paid is attached).

(Describe the defects and malfunctions)
I have returned the product to the ABC Company on (_____)

and Mr. Checker has verified that the product is still defective as noted on the attached copy of the memo he gave me.

And as noted below, I have now sustained $_____ in damages because of the product's failure to conform:
(describe and state the amount of your damages)

The product continues to be defective despite the three previous attempts to correct defects that I notified you about on (give dates) when I had to return the product at great inconvenience to me. These attempts provided you a reasonable number of opportunities to remedy all defects and malfunctions, and the failure to do so deprives me of the reliable use I expected to get from this product.

I therefore request that you (promptly ship me a conforming replacement/promptly reimburse me for the $_____ purchase price) as required by the Magnuson-Moss Warranty Act (and that you reimburse me for the damages I have sustained). I am prepared to return the defective product at your expense and according to any reasonable instructions you furnish. I shall return it (upon receiving the replacement/refund I have requested/ upon receipt of your confirmation that you will send the replacement/ refund I have requested).

(Please remit the refund or arrange a complete settlement without delay to minimize expenses I am incurring for finance charges and [list any other expenses you are continuing to incur]).

Thank you for giving this matter your prompt attention.

Sincerely,

- If the seller insists you request a refund or a replacement from the manufacturer, ask him to verify in writing that the "repaired" product is still defective and include a copy of that verification with your letter to the manufacturer. This simple step can help settle a lot of questions.

- And if you are seeking a refund, refer to any specific expenses you are incurring. As explained on page 298, the Magnuson-Moss Warranty Act could entitle you to hold the warrantor accountable for incidental expenses incurred because of his failure to remedy a defect or malfunction within a reasonable time. So let the warrantor know that an expense meter could be ticking away while he delays.

STAGE TWO: THE LOW-KEYED WARNING

If the seller does not insist that the manufacturer is responsible, but nevertheless refuses to give you a replacement or a refund, give him a low-keyed warning letter. If matters reach this stage, you are probably better off demanding a refund rather than a replacement.

If you don't take the memo with you when you return to the store, promptly send it as a confirming letter. Naturally, only use the paragraphs that are appropriate to your situation.

September 15, 19__

TO: ABC Sales Company
Futurama Mall
Anytown, USA

(1) (I am hereby informing you that/This is to confirm that, as I verbally informed you today when I discussed this matter with [identify

representative]) the (identify product) which/(I purchased and received from you on June 1, 19___/which was delivered on June 1, 19___, under our agreement of April 15, 19___) is still defective despite previous attempts to correct all defects. These defects are (Identify the defects or malfunctions)

(2) And as described below, I have also sustained $_____ as damages because of the product's failure to conform:
(Describe the types of damages and amount of loss)

(3) I purchased this product for $_____ with a "full" (one year) warranty but it continues to be defective despite the (three) previous attempts to correct defects that I notified you about on (give dates). These attempts provided you a reasonable number of opportunities to remedy all defects and malfunctions and the failure to do so deprives me of the reliable use I expected to get from this product.

(4) Although I requested (that you promptly furnish me a conforming replacement/that you promptly refund the $_____ purchase price I have paid/that you promptly refund the $_____ I have paid toward its purchase price and give me a full credit for any balance still outstanding for the price under our agreement, including all finance and other charges) as provided by the Magnuson-Moss Warranty Act and offered to return the product, my request was refused.

(5) I am, however, still prepared to resolve this matter if you will now promptly perform your obligations by doing what I originally requested when we discussed this matter (and by reimbursing me for my damages). I am then prepared to return the defective product to you at your expense and according to any reasonable instructions you give.

(6) And since a full refund of the price is now due me, any outstanding balance under our agreement for the price, (including all finance and other charges), are no longer due or owing. I am, however, prepared to make payments as due for other products I purchased under that agreement.

(7) I hope that we can now resolve this matter promptly as I have proposed so that I will not incur any further expenses or damages because of your failure to carry out your obligations. But I reserve my rights to hold you liable to the fullest extent provided by law should you still fail to carry out your obligations.

_____
(Your signature)

Receipt acknowledged by:

_____
(Signature and title of store representative)   _____
(Date)

MEMO FOR DEMANDING REFUND OR REPLACEMENT FROM SELLER AFTER MANUFACTURER FAILS TO DO SO

This memo covers situations in which you seek a refund or a replacement from the seller after a manufacturer has failed to carry out his obligations. It would follow your memo to reserve your rights on page 327.

Remember, a seller may not be bound by someone else's written warranty, but you can at least try to hold him accountable since he could also have become responsible for having to honor the written warranty as part of your contract if you had made the warranty part of your agreement or the seller had specifically used it to convince you to buy the product.

October 15, 19___

TO: *ABC Sales Company*
Futurama Mall
Anytown, USA

As I already informed you on September 15, 19___ , the (identify product) I purchased (from you on June 15, 19___ ,/under our agreement of April 15, 19___) for $_____ with a "full" (one year) warranty continued to be defective despite the reasonable number of opportunities which have been provided for remedying all defects and malfunctions.

And as described below, I have now sustained $_____ as damages: (Describe and give the amounts due for damages)

Since I had purchased the product from you with a "full" (one year) warranty, I initially requested that you carry out the obligations under that warranty as part of our contract by (replacing the product/refunding the $_____ purchase price I have paid/by refunding the $_____ I have paid toward its purchase price and giving me full credit for any balance still outstanding for the price under our agreement, including all finance and other charges) as provided by the Magnuson-Moss Warranty Act. But since the ABC Company insisted that the (replacement/refund) I requested was to be furnished by the (XYZ Manufacturing Company), I consented to seek a (replacement/refund) from that company but made clear to you I was reserving my rights under our contract.

I notified the XYZ Manufacturing Company on September 16 about the product's failure to conform and requested a (replacement/refund), but the company has failed to respond. That failure now prevents me from any further relying on that company to provide the (replacement/refund) due me under our contract.

I therefore request that the ABC Sales Company now carry out its obligations under the "full" (one year) warranty with which I purchased it as part of our contract by promptly furnishing me (the conforming replacement/refund of the $_____ purchase price) as I have stated above, and that it reimburse me for my damages.

I am then prepared to return the defective product to you at your expense and according to any reasonable instructions you give, but until then, I am merely storing it for you.

And since a full refund is now due me, any outstanding balance under our agreement for the price, including all finance and other charges, are no longer due or owing. (I am, however, prepared to make payments as due for other products I purchased under that agreement.)

I hope that we can now promptly resolve this matter as I have proposed so that I will not incur any further expenses or damages because of your failure to carry out your obligations. But I reserve my rights to hold you liable to the fullest extent provided by law should you still fail to carry out your obligations.

_____
(Your signature)

Receipt acknowledged by:

_____   _____
(Signature and title of store representative)   *(Date)*

STAGE THREE: THE ULTIMATUM

If a refund or a replacement isn't forthcoming within a reasonable time, adapt and send the following ultimatum. You can send it to either the seller or the manufacturer, depending on who you are trying to hold accountable. The sample includes alternative wording to cover both these situations. Use the wording enclosed in brackets and identified with one asterisk only when writing to the manufacturer, and the wording enclosed in brackets and identified with two asterisks only when writing to the seller.

> *200 Witchtree Lane*
> *Anytown, USA 00000*
>
> *October 15, 19__*

Address letter to
seller or manufacturer

Dear Sir:

This is to notify you that your company has not yet complied with its obligation to (refund the purchase price of/furnish a conforming replacement for) the (identify the product) as I requested on September 15, 19__, when I informed you that the product was still defective despite the reasonable number of opportunities you have had to remedy the defects or malfunctions (copy of letter attached).

I purchased the product for $____ (from the ABC Sales Company, Futurama Mall, Anytown, USA 00000)* with a "full" (one year) warranty and informed you on September 15 that I was electing (a refund of the purchase price/a conforming replacement for that product) as provided by the Magnuson-Moss Warranty Act.

And as described below, I have now sustained $____ in (additional) damages.

(Describe and state the amounts you sustained as damages)

(Although I initially requested a conforming replacement for the defective product,) I now request the immediate refund (of the product's [$____] purchase price/the immediate refund of the [$____] I have paid toward the purchase price and an immediate, full credit for any balance still outstanding for the price under our agreement, including all finance and other charges)** as provided by the Magnuson-Moss Warranty Act. (You are also to reimburse me for my damages.)

I am, as I have already informed you, prepared to return the product to you upon receipt of the refund due me for payments made toward the purchase price.

(And since I am entitled to a full refund of the purchase price, no payments for this purchase are still due or owing under our agreement.)
**[NOTE: Use only when writing to seller]

You also owe me amounts I have already sustained as damages, and I shall hold you accountable for all further damages I sustain.

While I hope that we can still settle this matter, if the amount paid for the purchase price is not promptly refunded as required by the Magnuson-Moss Warranty Act, I shall hold you liable for failing to comply with your obligations under a "full" warranty to the fullest extent provided by the Uniform Commercial Code for breach (of contract and)** warranty and as provided by the Magnuson-Moss Warranty Act for failing to com-

*ply with obligations under a written or implied warranty which can make
you liable for my damages and my legal expenses should your continuing
failure to carry out your obligations compel use of legal action. (And if
you continue to ignore your obligations, I shall also notify the Federal
Trade Commission about this matter and request it to investigate whether
your failure to comply with your obligations is now a violation of the
Magnuson-Moss Warranty Act as an unfair or deceptive act or practice
under the Federal Trade Commission Act so that the agency can use its
authority to seek redress for injuries sustained by other consumers.)*

Sincerely,

● One follow-up step would be to contact the Federal Trade Commission. The
wording in brackets in the last paragraph helps generate extra pressure since a failure to comply with the requirements of the Magnuson-Moss Warranty Act counts
as an unfair or deceptive practice under the FTC Act described in Chapter 11.

If you still do not receive satisfaction, your next step would be to contact an attorney and perhaps initiate a suit.

RESERVING YOUR RIGHTS WHEN YOU AREN'T YET WILLING TO HOLD A WARRANTOR FULLY ACCOUNTABLE

There may be times when you don't want to hold a warrantor fully accountable for
the cost of repairs, or for damages, because the issue is not entirely clear-cut. It could
happen, for instance, that in the case of a defect your written warranty requires you
to pay part of the cost of repairs, but your implied warranty makes the warrantor
fully responsible for the entire cost.

Usually, it isn't worth making a big issue out of such a problem. You may, for
example, be willing to pay for repairs rather than hold the warrantor accountable.
On the other hand, your willingness to pay could indicate that you don't consider the
warranty coverage part of your agreement. This could obviously hurt your position
if something more serious goes wrong later.

To protect yourself, you could pay while reserving your rights, or, in the case of
damages, you could make it clear to the seller that you are not waiving any rights
by ignoring his refusal to reimburse you.

There are two ways you can reserve your rights if the seller insists you pay for
repairs. The first is if you pay by check, or charge the amount to a credit account.
Simply state on the back of the check or charge slip saying something like: "This
payment/charge for repairs described on invoice/repair order no. 000 is made with
a reservation of all rights."

The second way is if you pay cash. Make it clear you are reserving your rights,
and put the above notation on the seller's copy of the repair bill. If you can't do this,
then adapt the following confirming letter:

*200 Witchtree Lane
Anytown, USA 00000*

June 15, 19___

*Mr. R. Seller
Manager
ABC Sales Company
Futurama Mall
Anytown, USA 00000*

Dear Mr. Seller

This is to confirm that, as I verbally informed you today when, at your insistence, I paid the $_____ for the repairs on (identify product) as described on your repair order #111, I only paid for the repairs while reserving all my rights under our contract of April 15, 19___, for the sale of this product.

Sincerely,

If you requested reimbursement for damages, which the seller and/or warrantor refuses to pay, here is a follow-up letter that puts on the record the fact that your failure to pursue the matter does not mean you are waiving your rights.

200 Witchtree Lane
Anytown, USA 00000

June 30, 19___

Mr. R. Seller
Manager
ABC Sales Company
Futurama Mall
Anytown, USA 00000

Dear Mr. Seller:

I am responding (to your letter of June 28 in which you/your telephone call of June 28 when you) informed me that the company would not reimburse me for the damages I described in my letter of June 15.

Although I consider that such damages are due me for the reasons I have described in my letter of June 15, I will forgo the matter at this point to avoid a dispute so that we can, instead, otherwise satisfactorily complete this transaction.

My willingness to do so is not, however, to be construed as a waiver of any defects that may be revealed by subsequent examination, and I am specifically reserving all my rights under the contract pertaining to this matter and all applicable warranties.

Sincerely,

A follow-up step like this enables you to back away from an earlier position while getting in a last word. This shows that you are not simply caving in, but have *decided* not to pursue the matter further because a satisfactory and good faith completion of the transaction is more important. You are saying, in effect: We've had a problem which I am willing to forget about if you will do the same. The message also carries with it a very low-keyed warning that this does not mean you will overlook future problems.

A seller cannot respond nastily to a follow-up letter like this without calling into question his willingness to act in good faith, and this could hurt him in a future dispute.

Be careful about using this step if you have already established a good relationship with a seller. Standing on legal formalities can destroy a relationship which previously has been firmly based on trust.

RESPONDING TO WARRANTOR'S DENIAL OF COVERAGE OR FAILURE TO CARRY OUT OBLIGATIONS.

STAGE ONE: INITIAL SKIRMISHES

When you first notify a warrantor about a defect, it's seldom necessary to spell things out in great detail as long as you state what is wrong with the product.

But what if the seller responds by saying your warranty does not cover the defect?

STAGE TWO: THE LOW-KEYED WARNING

To counter a seller's denial, you have to make it clear the specific warranty coverage in question is part of your deal and that the product fails to conform to it.

The following sample letter illustrates how you could do this. It refers to the requirements in the Magnuson-Moss Warranty Act and the Code which show you are entitled to certain warranties. Before you use any of the wording, it's very important to check the sections where these requirements are described to see whether they are likely to apply. And, if the dispute involves a lot of money, seek legal advice rather than trying to handle the dispute yourself past this point.

Trying to counter denial of warranty coverage is probably the most difficult step of a negotiating strategy. In effect, it means you have to state positively that you have certain warranties when the question of whether you do or not can be very complicated.

The most you can do on your own is to describe the specific warranties and coverage that should have been part of your contract, based on the circumstances at the time and the wording of your agreement and/or separate warranty. You obviously cannot prevent the seller from denying that he is legally bound; nor can you be sure that he really is. But by making it clear to the seller what his obligations could be, you can help convince him to rethink his refusal to honor those obligations and perhaps avoid legal action.

200 Witchtree Lane
Anytown, USA 00000

    date

Mr. R. Seller
Manager
ABC Sales Company
Futurama Mall
Anytown, USA 00000

Dear Mr. Seller:

I am (responding to your letter of _____ in which you informed me that/responding to the claims made by (Mr. Adjuster) on _____ that) the contract of April 15, 19__, under which I purchased a (describe product) did not make you responsible for the non-conformities I described in my letter of _____ .
(Adapt and use one or more of the following numbered paragraphs depending on which ones describe the type of warranty in dispute):

1. (But contrary to the position you now take, I purchased this [refer to product] expecting it to be merchantable and fully fit for the ordinary purpose for which it is used as required by the Uniform Commercial

Code. We had neither discussed nor had it been brought to my attention that the warranty of merchantability would not, in fact, be part of our bargain. I [also] expected the product would be fit for the particular purpose of [describe purpose] as was stated in writing [which I described when I informed the ABC Sales Company that I was relying on its judgment to furnish me a product suitable for that purpose and which is the one I purchased. And although the company claims that no implied warranties created by law are part of our contract and has pointed out wording in the agreement which seemingly deprives me of such warranties, those terms were never discussed by us, brought to my attention or conspicuously disclosed so that I had not, in fact agreed to them as part of the basis of our bargain.)

2. (I purchased this [refer to product] based on representations that it was covered by a written warranty which was part of the basis for my purchasing it from you and which I therefore considered to be part of the basis for our bargain especially since it was not brought to my attention that the obligations under that warranty were not, in fact, part of our contract.)

3. (The written warranty states that [describe coverages as stated in warranty] and does not, as required by the Magnuson-Moss Warranty Act, clearly disclose that the warranty does not apply to [state defects which company claims warranty doesn't cover when warranty wording otherwise seems to say defects are covered], or that the warranty does not obligate you to [state what the warrantor claims it doesn't have to do to remedy a defect but which isn't clear based on what the warranty says the warrantor will do about defects].

4. (And since a written warranty as regulated by the Magnuson-Moss Warranty Act is, in fact, part of the basis for our bargain, that Act makes it unlawful to disclaim any implied warranty created by law. [Since our agreement specifically provides that the [ABC Sales Company] will [describe remedial actions stated in the agreement which could count as written warranties under the Magnuson-Moss Warranty Act], it is obligated under a written warranty governed by the Magnuson-Moss Warranty Act which then makes it unlawful for the ABC Sales Company to disclaim the implied warranties created by law.]

5. [Our agreement specifically provided that the product would [describe specific promises pinned down in writing]. The product was sold as conforming to the following statements and claims made [by (identify the salesperson)/on the label/in your advertising/catalogue]: (describe specific claims made about the product). The product was sold as conforming to the demonstration made to me on [give date] which showed me that [describe what the demonstration showed about the product's capabilities]. The product was sold as conforming to the sample/model identified as: (describe sample or model).]

(Then complete the letter with the following paragraphs):

And contrary to these warranties which are, in fact, part of the basis for our bargain, the product does not conform to those requirements as I have already described to you in my letter of (_____). Its failure to do so deprives me of substantial benefits and uses I expected to get based on the warranties made about the product's qualities and characteristics and has caused me great inconvenience and forced me to incur losses and expenses which continue while the product fails to conform to our contract.

I therefore urge that your company retract its repudiation of its obli-

gations under our contract and that it instead promptly honor its obligations as I requested in my letter of (date) so that we may still satisfactorily complete this transaction.

But if the ABC Sales Company does not promptly carry out its obligations under our contract, I shall hold the company liable for its failure to do so at least to the fullest extent provided by the Uniform Commercial Code and the Magnuson-Moss Warranty Act.

Sincerely,

IF THE SELLER FAILS TO REPLY TO YOUR REQUEST FOR REMEDIAL ACTION

Here is an alternative and more low-keyed follow-up step you can take to reaffirm your request for remedial action when the seller fails to respond.

200 Witchtree Lane
Anytown, USA 00000

___date___

Mr. R. Seller
Manager
ABC Sales Company
Futurama Mall
Anytown, USA 00000

Dear Mr. Seller:

This is to inform you that the ABC Sales Company has not yet responded to my request that it carry out its obligations to (describe what you asked the company to do to honor its warranty obligations) for the reasons I already described in my letter of (_____), a copy of which is attached.

Although the (identify product) I purchased under our contract of April 15, 19__ , does not conform as I have already described to you, the ABC Sales Company has, to date, failed to respond to my proposal for resolving this matter.

I therefore urge that your company promptly carry out its obligations under our contract as I have proposed so that we may satisfactorily resolve the matters relating to the breach of contract (and warranty) I have described.

But if the ABC Sales Company still fails to carry out its obligations as I have proposed, I shall hold the company liable for its breach of (contract and) warranty at least to the fullest extent provided by the Uniform Commercial Code and the Magnuson-Moss Warranty Act.

Sincerely,

FOLLOW-UP ULTIMATUM BASED ON DECEPTIVE SALES PRACTICES ACT VIOLATION

A warrantor *could* be liable for violating your state's deceptive sales practices act if he fails, or refuses, to perform warranty obligations or makes warranty promises that turn out to be false. (These laws are described in section III)

While such an issue is not always clear-cut, there is at least a chance that a court would decide it was the case if a seller refuses to perform obligations he has under a warranty. So if a seller or manufacturer still refuses to return money you are entitled to recover, or refuses to perform other warranty obligations after you have taken all the other steps to hold him accountable, decide whether you want to send this follow-up ultimatum. Please note that the sample letter refers to the Rhode Island law. You will have to adjust the wording to refer to the rights you could have under your state's law. For details, see Appendix I.

When you take this follow-up step, refer to the previous reasons for requesting the remedial actions the warrantor refused to take. The sample includes alternative wording to identify different reasons that could apply.

> 200 Witchtree Lane
> Anytown, USA 00000
> ___date___

Mr. R. Seller
Manager
ABC Sales Company
Futurama Mall
Anytown, USA 00000

Dear Mr. Seller:

I am notifying you that the ABC Sales Company may now be in violation of the state deceptive sales practices law because of its continuing refusal (to carry out its obligation to refund/reimburse me for the $_____ due me/to credit the $_____ no longer due or payable under our contract) for the reasons I have already described in my letter of _____, a copy of which is attached.

(Although I have previously [rejected/revoked acceptance of] the [identify product] I [purchased and received on June 1, 19__/which was delivered to me on June 1, 19__, under our agreement of April 15, 19__. Although I previously requested reimbursement for the damages I sustained because the [identify product] I [purchased and received from you on June 1, 19__/which was delivered to me on June 1, 19__ under our agreement of April 15, 19__) failed to conform to our contract], the ABC Sales Company has to date failed to refund to me [reimburse me for] the amounts due me [failed to credit the amounts no longer due or payable under our contract] and to take such other steps as I have proposed for carrying out your obligations in good faith so that we may finally resolve matters relating to the breach [of contract and] warranty I have already described.

I am still prepared to resolve this matter as I last proposed in my letter of _____ if the ABC Sales Company agrees to do so by (set a reasonable deadline).

But if the ABC Sales Company deliberately continues to ignore its obligations to (refund/reimburse me for the amounts now due me/refuses to credit the amounts no longer due or payable under our contract) because of its breach of (contract and) warranty, I shall now also seek to hold the company liable to the fullest extent provided by the Rhode Island deceptive sales practices law should I be compelled to bring suit. This could *result in your company being liable for my attorney's fees and court costs, my damages or $200, and punitive damages.**

Sincerely,

*(The phrase about the amounts you could recover refers to the Rhode Island law. Alter this wording so it refers to the amounts your state's law could entitle you to recover. See Appendix I.)

44 · Negotiating Strategy for Recovering Damages for Defects in Accepted Goods

Recovering damages for defects is your main option under the Code when you either choose to keep the defective product or you cannot make the seller take it back.

STAGE ONE: OPENING SKIRMISHES

The initial steps of such a strategy are described in Chapter 35.
  Here, the following situations are covered.

  • When you have defects repaired by someone other than the warrantor without first notifying the warrantor about them. This might happen in an emergency or some other unusual situation. You would then request reimbursement for the repairs as an initial step of your negotiating strategy, rather than as a follow-up step.
  • When the seller and/or manufacturer does not correct the defects and your only option is to recover damages.

SEEKING REIMBURSEMENT FOR THE COST OF REPAIRS

There are times—usually emergencies—when you must correct defects before you have a chance to notify the warrantor.
  The fan belt on a new car I'd bought broke while I was on an out-of-town trip, for instance. Although it happened around midnight, luckily I was able to have the belt replaced at a service station. The manufacturer fully reimbursed me for the cost of the replacement, even though I had to buy a more expensive belt than the one normally used for that car.
  I substantiated my claim with a written receipt on which I had the mechanic state the time the repairs were made, and the fact that the belt used was the only one available which fit the car. I also returned the torn fan belt to the dealer.
  If at all possible in such situations, try to contact the warrantor for instructions before authorizing any repairs. Make written notes of the conversation, and note the time of the call and the name of the person you talk to. Get written documentation from the person who makes the repairs, and try to keep the defective parts if possible.
  Here is a sample memo for notifying a seller about defects and requesting reimbursement for repairs. Take the repaired product along with the memo if possible.

June 15, 19__

TO: ABC Sales Company
Futurama Mall
Anytown, USA 00000

  This is to inform you that the (identify product) which (I purchased and received on June 1, 19__/was delivered on June 1, 19__, under our agreement of April 15, 19__) failed to conform to our contract as described below and that I had to have the following repairs made by the

(Able Repair Company) for the reasonable cost of $ _____ . A copy of their itemized bill is attached. (I am also informing you of other damages I sustained because of the product's failure to conform.)

(Contrary to your assurances that the product conformed despite the apparent defects I described at the time of delivery,) I discovered the following defects on June 14, 19__ , and had to have the described repairs made immediately to minimize my damages:

(Describe the defects, how and when you discovered them, what repairs were made and the circumstances that required immediate repair. If you are returning defective parts that were replaced, identify them and state that you are returning them)

(And as described below, there is also due from you $ _____ for the other damages I sustained because of the product's failure to conform: [Describe and state the amount due for other damages you could be entitled to recover])

Please (reimburse me promptly for the reasonable cost of the repairs I was compelled to incur [and the other damages I sustained] because of the product's failure to conform/or deduct those amounts from the balance still due for the product under our agreement).

(I am also returning the product and request that you examine it to ensure/I request that you advise me whether) the defects have been properly repaired, and that you make such other adjustments or repairs as may be needed to make the product conform.

Thank you for giving this matter your prompt attention so we can satisfactorily resolve it.

_____

(Your signature)

Receipt acknowledged by:
(Leave space to describe what the seller promises to do about reimbursing your expenses, to confirm the adequacy of repairs made, or to describe additional repairs the seller will make.)

_____   _____

(Signature and title of store representative)   *(Date)*

If the seller refuses to reimburse you, your follow-up step would be a low-keyed warning saying you will deduct the damages from the amount still due under your agreement, or that you intend to hold the seller responsible for your damages.

SEEKING DAMAGES AFTER SELLER FAILS OR REFUSES TO CORRECT DEFECTS

You can usually seek reimbursement for damages in accepted goods if:

1. The seller refuses to correct the defects covered by your warranties.
2. The product can't be repaired or you aren't willing to accept further repairs, but you are not entitled to revoke acceptance.

The initial step in these situations is to notify the seller of the defects, as described on page 248. You could then use the following low-keyed warning steps when the seller fails or refuses to correct the defects. If you are trying to recover damages for defects in accepted goods, describe the reason for the loss and the amount, and state your intention to deduct your losses from the amount still due under the contract. This will stake out your bargaining position.

See page 325 about describing and requesting reimbursement for amounts you could recover as incidental or consequential damages, but remember to be reasonable and flexible.

STAGE TWO: THE LOW-KEYED WARNING

Use this low-keyed warning to let the seller know you will have the defects repaired at his expense and hold him accountable for any other damages. (Use the sample letter on page 329 as a guide to how to revise the wording when you are contacting a manufacturer instead.)

The sample may be used as a letter, or memo to take to the store.

June 30, 19___

TO: *ABC Sales Company*
Futurama Mall
Anytown, USA

This is to inform you that the defects in the (identify the product) which I notified you about on June 15, 19___, will result in my sustaining at least $_____ as damages for the reasonable cost of having the defects repaired as estimated by the (Able Repair Company).

And as described below, there is now also due from you $_____ for other damages I have sustained up to now because of the product's failure to conform: (Describe and state the amounts due for other damages)

(I purchased and received this product from you on June 1, 19___/This product was delivered to me on June 1, 19___, under our agreement of April 15) and I already requested that the ABC Sales Company carry out its obligations to cure the defects as I stated in my memorandum of June 15, 19___, when I notified the company the product failed to conform to the requirements of our contract. But the company has so far failed to do so.

The ABC Company therefore is promptly to honor its obligations to (replace the product with one that conforms/make the product conform to our contract) as I have already requested and to contact me so we can make arrangements for me to return the product.

But if the ABC Sales Company still fails to carry out its obligations as I have requested, I shall have the necessary repairs made and hold the company liable for my damages to the fullest extent provided by law (and deduct those damages from the price still due for this product under our agreement). I am not, however, hereby waiving any claims I may have because of defects that may be revealed by subsequent examination.

_____
(Your signature)

Receipt acknowledged by:

_____   _____
(Signature and title of store representative)   *(Date)*

Notifying the seller in this way will almost certainly strengthen your bargaining position for recovering damages.

LOW-KEYED WARNING: REQUESTING REIMBURSEMENT FOR DEFECTS IN ACCEPTED GOODS

This is a follow-up step to take in the following situations: you have had the product repaired and want reimbursement; or you are trying to recover the difference between the product's value as warranted and as accepted if repairs are not feasible. In the latter situation, you could request that the seller replace the product rather than pay for your damages. This may be an attractive alternative if the damages you could recover almost equal the purchase price.

When you are trying to recover damages for defects in accepted goods, you must describe the type of loss and state the dollar amount of the damages. (See page 323 for the formulas used.) Sample wordings are included after the letter that follows. You can also tell the seller that you will deduct all or part of your damages from the balance still due under your contract at this point, or can reserve such action and use it as a tougher follow-up step later.

The letter includes alternative wording and paragraphs to cover different situations. It also includes several paragraphs illustrating various ways to describe the product's failure to conform, and describing previous steps you might have taken to get the seller to correct the defects. These alternative paragraphs are identified with asterisks, and you obviously must adapt them to fit your particular situation. Be sure to describe other important things that may apply. The sample also identifies things you could do to verify your claim, but don't use this language unless it applies to your case.

> 200 Witchtree Lane
> Anytown, USA 00000
>
> _____date_____

Mr. R. Seller
Manager
ABC Sales Company
Futurama Mall
Anytown, USA 00000

Dear Mr. Seller:

_I am notifying you that, as described below, there is now due me from the ABC Sales Company at least $_____ as damages I have sustained because the (identify product) which (I purchased and received from you on June 1, 19__ /was delivered on June 1, 19__ under our contract of April 15, 19__) failed to conform to the requirements of our contract as I have already notified you on June 15 and (list other dates on which you notified the seller about defects you found). This notification is not, however, a waiver of any other defects that may still be revealed by subsequent examination._

*(Although I first notified the ABC Company on June 15 that the product failed to conform to our contract and requested that [the breach be cured by repairs or adjustments that would make the product conform/ the prompt delivery of a conforming replacement], the breach was not cured [even after I notified the company on June 30 that I would have the defects repaired and hold the company responsible for any damages].)

*(Although I first notified the ABC Sales Company on June 15 that the product failed to conform to our contract and requested the prompt *delivery of a conforming replacement since the defects could not be repaired and rendered the product unfit for ordinary use [and for the particular purpose I intended to use it, as I informed you at the time of the sale and relied on your judgment to select a product suitable for that purpose], the company failed to do so.)*

*(Although I first notified the ABC Sales Company on June 15 that the product failed to conform and subsequently notified the company on [list other dates] about the product's continuing failure to conform to our contract, the product still fails to conform to our contract as I informed you on [give date] when I requested that this continuing breach be cured by the prompt delivery of a conforming replacement since I cannot rely on further repairs or adjustments being adequate to make the product conform to our contract. This breach has not been cured even though the product, as furnished me, was and continues to be unfit for ordinary use [and for the particular purpose I intended to use it, as I informed you at the time of the sale and relied on your judgment to select a product suitable for that purpose].)

*(Although I first notified the ABC Sales Company on June 15 that the product failed to conform and subsequently notified the company [list other dates] when I requested that this continuing breach be cured by the prompt delivery of a conforming replacement since I could no longer rely on further repairs or adjustments being adequate to make the product conform to our contract. But this breach has not been cured even though the product, as furnished to me, was and continues to be unfit for ordinary use [and for the particular purpose I intended to use it as I informed you at the time of the sale and relied on your judgment to select a product suitable for that purpose].)

*(Although the ABC Sales Company insisted on repairing the defects that I informed the company about on June 15, the product as repaired still fails to conform to the requirements of our contract because [describe how the repairs did not completely correct the defects which in effect reduces its value].)

The company's failure to deliver a conforming product has deprived me of the use I expected and has caused me great inconvenience and expense which has resulted in my sustaining at least the following amounts as my damages:

(Describe and state the amounts due as damages: first list the amounts you could recover as damages for the defects in the accepted product, and then items you could recover as incidental or consequential damages. Sample wording for describing amounts you could be entitled to recover is included after the letter.) This list does not, however, limit any claims I could have for further damages.

I therefore request that the ABC Sales Company now promptly (reimburse me for the $_____ now due me as my damages/deduct the $_____ now due me as my damages from the balance of the price still due under our contract and reimburse me for the amount by which my damages exceed the price still due under our contract. If the damages are deducted from the price, please furnish me a prompt and complete accounting to verify the proper deductions from the price and to indicate what balance remains and revise the remaining payment schedule to reflect an immediate credit for the deductions for the damages).

([If I am not reimbursed for my damages/if the amounts are not properly deducted from the balance still due for the price under our contract]

I then intend to deduct from the balance still due under our contract the amounts due me as my damages and hold the company liable for any further amounts still due me. I am, of course, prepared to pay as due any balance that is still due and owing under our contract.)

Alternatively, we could settle this matter by the company promptly furnishing me a conforming replacement for the defective product (and reimbursing me my damages).

I have retained the defective parts which were replaced and which I will make available for your examination under reasonable circumstances.

I hope we can now promptly resolve this matter satisfactorily as I have proposed so that I will not have to hold you liable for your breach to the fullest extent provided by law.

Sincerely,

Receipt acknowledged by:

_____   _____

(Signature and title of store representative)   *(Date)*

Here are some sample wordings to describe damages for defects in the product:

- "$_____ for the reasonable cost of repairs I was required to make because of the defects as shown on the attached copy of my repair bill." (Note: If you don't have a bill, describe what repairs were made.)
- "$_____ for the reasonable cost of purchasing a replacement for the product (which was defective beyond repair/which was damaged beyond repair by its own defects) as verified by the (Able Repair Company) which examined it on (give date)." (Note: This would be an unusual situation, but the replacement cost could be a reasonable way to measure your damages, based on the Code's general rule for measuring damages.)
- "$_____ for the difference between the value of the product as warranted which is at least its $ _____ purchase price and its value as accepted which does not exceed $_____ because (state why and by how much the defects would have reduced the product's actual value at the time you accepted it)."

(Note: Indicate the extent to which the defects made the product unfit. It is usually difficult to establish this kind of value difference because it has to be based on the product's value at the time of acceptance, so it usually isn't worthwhile trying to fix a dollar amount unless the defects made the product completely unfit or very substantially reduced its actual value.)

If you mail the letter, send it by certified mail. If you hand deliver it and the store refuses to acknowledge receiving it, leave it with the store representative and then send a copy by certified mail.

If you purchased the product on credit and must make payments to someone other than the seller, see Section VII.

LOW-KEYED WARNING: NOTIFYING SELLER OF INTENTION TO DEDUCT DAMAGES FROM PRICE

If you haven't yet told the seller you intend to deduct your damages from the balance still due, it is an appropriate follow-up step in situations where you have requested reimbursement for your damages, or requested the seller to deduct the damages from the price, and he has refused.

Here is a sample letter you could use to give this kind of low-keyed warning.

Certified Mail #1111122222

> *200 Witchtree Lane*
> *Anytown, USA 00000*
> ___*date*___

Mr. R. Seller
Manager
ABC Sales Company
Futurama Mall
Anytown, USA 00000

Dear Mr. Seller:

Since the ABC Sales Company has to date failed to respond to my request to be reimbursed for the $_____ due me for my damages (or that those amounts be deducted from the balance still due for the price under our contract of April 15, 19__) for the reasons I have already described in my letter of (_____), a copy of which is attached, I am now notifying you that I intend to deduct from the price still due under our contract the amounts due me as my damages as provided by the Uniform Commercial Code. I am, of course, prepared to pay as due any remaining balance under that contract.

While I am prepared to settle this matter as I have already proposed in my letter of (_____), your continuing failure to carry out your obligations under our contract will compel me to hold you liable for this breach to the fullest extent provided by law unless you now resolve the matter as I have proposed.

> *Sincerely,*

STAGE THREE: THE ULTIMATUM

If your damages are less than the amount still due under your contract, then obviously you can recover all of them simply by refusing to pay that amount. The Code specifically entitles you to do this. But remember this action also gives the other side a chace to sue you. I caution you, therefore, not to take this step without legal advice, especially if the dispute involves a lot of money, and if the question of your being entitled to recover incidental and/or consequential damages is not clear-cut.

The sample letter includes wording to tell the seller you will actually deduct only part of your damages, while reserving your right to hold him accountable for the rest. In effect, it offers a compromise: you will forget your chance to hold him accountable for the full amount if he at least agrees to the partial deduction. If it is important that you recover all your damages, you should not, of course, use this sample. You should instead seek legal advice.

By spelling out the minimum amount you will settle for, and backing off from the positions stated in the low-keyed warnings, you show your willingness to be flexible in order to reach a settlement. This attitude will usually strengthen your bargaining position if the seller continues to be unreasonable and the dispute is forced into court.

If you have already paid for the goods and must sue to get any of your money back, then you may as well insist that the seller pay for all the damages you could recover. The sample does include wording you could use to indicate your willingness to settle for less than the full amount, however.

If you are seeking reimbursement for damages from a manufacturer rather than a seller, ask the company to reimburse you for all your damages rather than stating that you will deduct them from the balance remaining under your contract. Also delete wording referring to your contract. This would involve situations in which only the manufacturer was obligated to honor his written warranty rather than the seller and in which case you may be unable to get the money from the seller.

Also see page 395 in Section VI for how you could use a "payment-in-full" check for settling a dispute with the person to whom you owe money under the agreement.

Certified letter #1111122222

200 Witchtree Lane
Anytown, USA 00000
<u>   date   </u>

Mr. R. Seller
Manager
ABC Sales Company
Futurama Mall
Anytown, USA 00000

Dear Mr. Seller:

This is to notify you that there is still due me from the ABC Sales Company at least $_____ for damages for the reasons I have already described in my letter of (insert date) a copy of which is attached.

Although in that letter I requested prompt reimbursement for the amounts due me as damages (or that the amount be promptly deducted from the balance still due for the price under our contract of April 15, 19__) and subsequently notified the company on (insert date) that I would do so, the company has (describe the company's inadequate response, if any)

I therefore now urge that the ABC Sales Company reimburse me for my damages by give date. (But to avoid a dispute about the amount of my damages, I am prepared to resolve this matter if the ABC Sales Company reimburse me by [give date] for the $_____ due as damages for [describe the damages as you initially did]./While I previously stated that I would deduct the full amount due as my damages from the balance still due for the price under our contract, to avoid a dispute about this amount, I am prepared to resolve this matter if the ABC Sales Company promptly agrees to deduct the $_____ due as my damages for [describe the damages as you initially did].)

But if the company still ignores its obligation to reimburse me for my damages, I shall then immediately deduct from the $_____ balance still due for the price under our contract the $_____ described above and that all amounts due or owing for the price under this contract will have been paid upon the payment of $_____ that still remains due based on my calculations. If you consider that my calculations are in error, then please furnish me a prompt and accurate accounting of what the amount should be.

And since I am only deducting a part of the damages due me, I am reserving my right to hold you liable for all other amounts I could recover.

While I hope we can still satisfactorily resolve this matter, if the ABC company continues to ignore its obligations to reimburse me for my damages, I shall hold the company liable for damages at least to the fullest extent provided by the Uniform Commercial Code for breach of (contract and/or warranty) and as provided by the Magnuson-Moss Warranty Act for failure to comply with obligations under the (written/implied) warranty that applied.* This can make you liable for my damages and my legal expenses should your continuing failure to carry out your obligations compel me to take legal action.

Sincerely,

*(Refer to the Magnuson-Moss Warranty Act only when the defects involved were covered by a written warranty or an implied warranty.)

SECTION VI
DIFFERENT PAYMENT METHODS: HOW TO PROTECT YOURSELF

It's a harsh fact of life that sooner or later you must pay for what you buy. How much sooner or later depends on the payment method and terms you arrange.

When you pay cash, the transaction is pretty straightforward. But in today's world of checking accounts, electronic fund transfers, credit cards, debit cards, retail charge accounts, installment credit agreements, check overdrafts, instant cash advances and financial packages that tie together several kinds of deposit accounts and several lines of credit, paying is no longer as straightforward as cash payment. Paying can, instead, get very complicated.

This section therefore covers the various other ways of making payment; any problems that may be associated with them; and major laws you can use to protect yourself.

Often, the protection available depends on the *kind* of payment method you use. Knowing about such legal protection ahead of time, therefore, can make a big difference in achieving the maximum leverage should a dispute arise.

Increasingly today, payment systems and different kinds of credit are being linked together in various financial service packages. Instead of simply using a checking account just for writing checks say, or a credit account just for buying on credit, you may connect the two in ways that make them, in effect, multi-purpose accounts. You can, for example, use a check to buy on credit: your checking account is linked to an overdraft line of credit which is automatically triggered when your checking account has insufficient funds to cover a check.

Because of this kind of complexity, the rights and remedies you have as protection are not always neatly and conveniently packaged in one place or in one law. Instead, it may be up to you (or your attorney) to tie the remedies together when a particular problem arises. This section can help you do that.

HOW TO CHOOSE THE RIGHT METHOD

Since obtaining the right protection can be very important, when you make a purchase ask yourself the following questions before choosing your method of payment or type of credit:

- If I complete payment now would it affect matters later?

If the answer is no, because you don't expect anything to go wrong after payment, simply select the most convenient and cheapest method.

If the answer is yes, and you feel something might go wrong, then it could be important to find ways to protect yourself . . .

- How long do I need the protection that refusing to pay could provide in case of a dispute?
- What method and/or type of credit gives me protection for the length of time I need?
- What steps should I take to ensure that I have the protection I need?

- If I use a particular payment method, am I actually using other kinds of credit as well and what protection would I have?
- Are there other payment systems tied to the type of credit I am using and how could these affect my protection?

Here is an illustration that shows how various payment systems may be linked together in a service package, and the different kinds of protection available when you make payment with a check.

Payments and kinds of protection in series of transactions initiated by a check

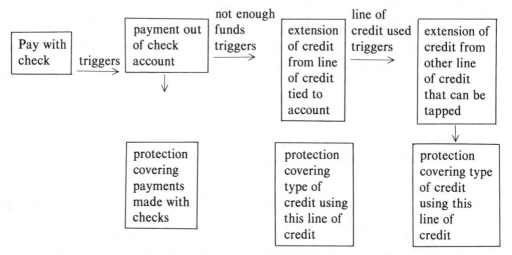

Prepare a similar chart to help you figure out how financial transactions are linked together in any financial package you have. You will then know at a glance when it would be worthwhile to use one rather than another payment method or type of credit.

45 · All About Negotiable Instruments

When money first became the grease of commerce many centuries ago, people almost immediately began looking around for cash substitutes to prevent their loot being lost or stolen. Thus were born various specialized instruments that eventually acquired special legal status. Collectively, they became known as "negotiable instruments." The laws governing them have become part of the Uniform Commercial Code.

A negotiable instrument is simply a written obligation calling for payment of money. The ordinary check is the most familiar and commonly used negotiable instrument in consumer transactions, but there are others, such as certificates of deposit, and promissory notes.

It is important to know whether you're using a negotiable instrument because, if you are, you acquire special payment obligations which need to be handled with care.

DIFFERENT KINDS OF NEGOTIABLE INSTRUMENTS

There are three basic types of negotiable instrument:

1. *A check* is a special kind of draft, or written order, made out by one person which calls on another person to pay a specific amount of money to a third party. In the case of a check the person ordered to pay must be a bank, and the check must be payable "on demand." (Since drafts other than checks are rarely used in consumer transactions, the requirements that apply to them will not be covered here.)

2. *A certificate of deposit* is written acknowledgment by a bank for receipt of a specific amount of money which it is committed to repay on a certain date, usually with interest. When money is deposited in this way, the bank is not required to repay it until the designated date, though it may allow you to "cash in" a certificate early. In this case, it will always charge a hefty interest penalty.

Despite their name, savings instruments which are normally used by consumers and generally referred to as "certificates of deposit"—six-month money market CDs, for example—usually aren't issued in the form of negotiable instruments. They therefore cannot be transferred to someone else. But if you get a certificate that is issued as a negotiable instrument, then treat it with care.

3. *A promissory note,* also called "a note," is a written promise that a person will pay a certain sum to someone else. Since the person promising to pay thereby commits himself, this type of negotiable instrument is used for extending credit. In the past, promissory notes were freely used to extend consumer credit and they were often deadly. But their use has now been severely restricted, primarily by what is known as the Federal Trade Commission's "Preservation of Consumers' Claims and Defenses" Rule (see Chapter 62) and by state laws. Promissory notes can still be used in some situations, though, particularly if you are only borrowing money rather than buying under a credit agreement. And such instruments might be used in violation of the FTC Rule or state law which can still hurt you. So it is still important for you to see whether you are being asked to sign a promissory note when credit is being extended.

Since checks are the type of negotiable instrument you are most likely to use, this chapter will focus primarily on checks rather than the other types of negotiable instruments. This chapter will, therefore, usually refer to negotiable instruments as checks, but keep in mind that the requirements described usually apply in the same way to other types of negotiable instruments.

REQUIREMENTS FOR NEGOTIABLE INSTRUMENTS

A negotiable instrument must conform to certain requirements. Knowing what these requirements are will help you protect yourself when using one, or help you decide not to use one altogether when it could be especially risky to do so.

1. *Must be in writing and signed*

To be negotiable, the instrument must be in writing and all the required information about payment must be stated in the instrument itself. The signature of the person ordering payment or promising to pay the money must appear on the instrument in a way that clearly indicates the fact; normally this means the signature must be on the front.

Technically speaking, a signature can be any symbol or mark, such as initials, that a person has adopted to authenticate instruments. But when you are signing an instrument as an individual consumer, *never* use anything but your full written signature. (A key difference between a negotiable instrument and an ordinary agreement is that it is possible to have a binding agreement without someone's signature actually appearing on it.)

When you are signing a negotiable instrument on behalf of someone else, such as an organization or another person for whom you are acting as an agent, never just sign your name. If you do, you could become obligated to pay if the other party turns out not to have the money. Always add the name of the organization or person involved and your title or position, such as "Cycling Club, by J. Consumer, Treasurer." Never just say "J. Consumer" when you are signing as treasurer, for instance.

2. *Unconditional order or promise to pay*

The instrument must unconditionally order or promise the payment of money without hedging or qualifying it in any way, such as, "Pay $1,000." A conditional promise would be one like "pay $1,000 when the furnance is properly installed."

3. *Payment in money and for a certain amount*

The payment called for must be in money—not in such assets as stocks, goods or property. And it must either be for an exact amount, or for an amount that can be computed exactly at any time based only on the information given: such as, for example, "$2,000 plus interest payable at maturity at the rate of 18% per year."

If there is a difference between the amount stated in figures and the amount stated in words, it is the amount in words that counts; except in very unusual situations when it's clear that the amount stated in figures is actually correct.

4. *Must be payable on demand or at a definite time*

The instrument must call for the payment of the money on demand or at a definite time.

Generally speaking, an instrument is payable on demand when: (1) it specifically says payment will be made "on demand"; (2) the amount is payable when the instrument is presented for payment; or (3) no time for payment is specified. Checks are almost always payable on demand.

An instrument is payable at a definite time when it states some fixed time or date. Promissory notes and certificates of deposit are usually payable at some definite future date, and these instruments are called time deposits or time paper. (There are situations in which the due date for payment can be "accelerated." This usually occurs when the person who promises to pay fails to make payment on time: failing to make some payments as due can trigger the acceleration of all later payments and so make the entire amount outstanding payable immediately.)

5. *Must be made payable "to the order of" or "to bearer"*

The key requirement for a negotiable instrument is that it be made payable "to the order of" or "to bearer." These phrases are used to make clear that payment is not restricted to the person originally identified as the payee, or person to be paid. These phrases also designate who can properly transfer the instrument to someone else. An instrument is made payable "to order" when it is made payable "to the order of" someone specifically identified as the one to be paid. When made payable "to order", only that payee can endorse and transfer the instrument on to someone else. All printed checks include the words "Pay to the order of."

An instrument made payable "to bearer," says the amount called for is payable to *anyone* holding the instrument. An instrument can be made payable "to bearer" by (1) specifically making it payable "to bearer"; (2) making it payable to a specific person or to bearer such as, "pay to the order of J. Seller or to bearer"; or (3) making it payable "to cash," "to the order of cash," or to some other designation that isn't meant to identify a specific payee.

6. *Identifying the drawee*

To be negotiable, a check must clearly identify the drawee, the person who will pay on behalf of the person who is ordering payment. In the case of a check, this is a bank.

RULES GOVERNING THE USE OF NEGOTIABLE INSTRUMENTS

Different rights and obligations govern negotiable instruments at various stages of their use.

ISSUING THE INSTRUMENT

Completing, signing, and issuing a negotiable instrument is the first stage. Technically speaking, an instrument made payable "to the order of" a named person is not considered to be properly issued until it is transferred to that person. An instrument made payable "to bearer," on the other hand, counts as having been issued as soon as it passes into someone's hands.

What are the kinds of things that can go wrong at this stage?

• One possibility is that someone forges your signature as drawer on a check. The law almost completely protects you from this kind of trouble because, as an individual, you are not liable for paying out on an instrument you didn't actually sign. Since it is your bank that actually pays out your money, it is liable if it pays a forged check and you would almost always be entitled to your money back. (You could lose this right if you are negligent, though, see page 381). In the case of a promissory note, if someone forges your signature your only sure protection is not to pay.

The best way to avoid forgeries is to sign your name clearly, and to keep blank checks separate from any items containing your signature.

• You don't fill in all the payment terms before signing. Although, technically speaking, an instrument isn't negotiable until all the payment terms are filled in, once signed, of course, the missing terms can quickly be filled in by someone else. Normally, you would then have to pay just as if you had completed the terms.

The only way to protect yourself is *never* to sign a negotiable instrument until all the required information about payment terms is correctly filled in and all blank spaces completely crossed out. Don't make exceptions to this rule for anyone.

• You make a mistake filling in the required information. If you spot a mistake before you actually give the instrument to the other person, never try to correct it. Void the instrument immediately and write a new one—or, if the instrument is being filled in by someone else, insist that a new one be completed.

If you don't spot a mistake, you might just have to live with the consequences. Failing to make the instrument payable to the right person can result in the money being paid to someone else, of course, and payment will still be owing to the first party. Not paying the right amount can result in your bill not being considered paid in full. Once, when paying a charge account bill that I intended to pay in full to avoid a finance charge, I accidentally transposed the numbers for the cents, writing 89 instead of 98 cents. That small error triggered a hefty finance charge.

The following illustrations show how easy and how difficult you can make it for someone to alter payment terms.

Never use a pencil (erasures are easy to make) and always fill out the instrument with the same colored ink (different colored ink is a clue that alterations have been made).

• Your check, or other negotiable instrument, gets lost or is stolen in the mail.

If the person to be paid never received the check, you still owe the money.

There are two main points to watch when making payment with a check.

1. *Never* send a check unless you make it payable *only* to "the order of" a named person. It will not be considered "issued" until it is transferred to that person. An instrument made payable "to bearer" is like putting cash in the hands of anyone who finds it.

2. Get a record that the person accepted the check as payment. You can do this simply by asking the payee to note on your copy of the agreement, "Paid with check number_____," or get a receipt which identifies the bill you are paying and your check number. Making a note on the check is another way of getting a record of a bill you have paid. (It counts as payment only *after* the instrument has been properly negotiated and paid, of course.) It also gives you written evidence that you had an agreement with the person.

• Someone asks you to sign a promissory note in connection with a purchase you are making on credit. Refuse to do this because of the protections you have under the Federal Trade Commission's "Preservation of Consumers' Claims and Defenses" Rule, see page 524.

NEGOTIATING THE INSTRUMENT

"Negotiating" an instrument, or properly transferring it from one person to another, is the next stage.

How an Instrument Must Be Negotiated
If made payable "to the order of" a named person, an instrument can be properly negotiated further only if it is signed (endorsed) by the payee. An instrument made payable "to bearer" can be negotiated simply by transferring it to someone. The person who gets the instrument can insist that it be signed by the person transferring it, however, and should always do so.

Endorsing an Instrument
Broadly speaking, endorsing an instrument means "signing it over." If an endorsement is required for negotiating an instrument further, one of two types must be used. The first is called a *blank,* the second a *special* endorsement.

• A *blank* endorsement simply consists of a signature written on the back of the instrument by the person transferring it. Endorsing an instrument this way makes it payable "to bearer," in effect, and places no restrictions at all on how or to whom the money is to be paid. It is very unsafe to carry, keep, or send anyone an instrument endorsed with only your name.
• A *special,* or "full," endorsement consists of the signature of the person transferring the instrument, plus wording that designates the person to whom the money is to be made payable. "Pay to the order of J. Seller" (or simply "Pay to J. Seller") above the signature, for instance. When endorsed this way, the instrument can be properly negotiated further only by J. Seller. This is the safest way to sign over an instrument made payable to you.

There are two other types of endorsements that can be used in conjunction with blank and special endorsements.

• A *restrictive endorsement* consists of words added to your signature to designate a specific purpose for which the money has been signed over or to specify other conditions. Such an endorsement places limitations on how the funds may be properly paid. "For deposit only" is the most frequently used example of a restrictive endorsement. When a check endorsed this way reaches the first bank, that bank can only deposit the funds into the account of the person who endorsed it that way; if that bank does anything else with the money, it would then be liable to you for the amount of the check.

If you want to deposit a check either in person or through the mail, the safest way is to use the following restrictive endorsement: "Pay to (Hometown Bank) for deposit only into the acount of" then sign your name and add your account number. The words "For deposit only" over your signature accomplish the same thing for most practical purposes, but they make it easier for a clever person to play games with your endorsement, especially if you place the wording and your signature in a sloppy way.

Restrictive endorsements can also be used to place conditions on when the money is to become payable or how the instrument is to be used. Such a condition might say "Pay to J. Dealer upon the delivery of 1990 model J, 4-door, Astro car." Remember, though, this refers only to an endorsement you make on a check originally written by someone else and made payable to you. Trying to protect yourself in this way can become very complicated, though, and such endorsement conditions are rarely used in consumer transactions.

• A *qualified endorsement* is the second kind of endorsement you can couple with either a blank or special endorsement. It consists of specific wording stating that you, as the person signing over the instrument, refuse to be liable if the person who originally ordered payment fails to do so.

You make this endorsement by adding the words "without recourse": "Pay to J. Seller, without recourse," for example, followed by your signature. This kind of endorsement is rarely used in consumer transactions, however, since few people would accept a check under such conditions. *Never* use such an endorsement when depositing a check; your bank will simply return it as unacceptable for deposit under those conditions.

Warranties Made when Transferring an Instrument

When you transfer an instrument you make certain warranties, or promises, to the person. If you endorse the check, you also make those promises to everyone else who later gets the instrument.

Without going into great detail, these warranties say:

• The person who transfers the instrument also owns it and that the transfer itself is legal.
• All signatures on the instrument are genuine or authorized.
• No material alterations have been made.
• No one has legal justification for refusing to pay the money to the person who is transferring it.
• The person transferring the instrument doesn't know of any bankruptcy proceedings involving the person who originally ordered payment.

If these promises turn out to be untrue—previous signatures were forged, for instance, or someone has a legally justifiable reason for refusing to pay you the money—the payee or payees can demand their money back from you.

There are some important differences between warranties given by endorsers who only transfer the check to someone else and warranties given to the person who pays out the money as called for by the instrument. The main one involves warranties about the genuineness of drawer signatures. If you run into this kind of problem, it's best to seek legal advice.

If a dispute arises over a payment because you broke a warranty (this would usually involve a check you signed over to someone else), seek prompt legal advice before saying whether you will repay the money. Simply tell the person to put his claim in writing and inform him that you will respond after seeking legal advice.

The way to avoid risks when passing on someone else's check, is *never* to accept a transferred check from someone you don't know in the first place, and *never* accept one from someone whom you know is involved in bankruptcy proceedings.

Endorsing Instruments when Name Is Misspelled

If your name is misspelled on any instrument that is actually made out to you, you can endorse it either by signing your name as it was misspelled or by signing it with the proper spelling, or by doing both. The person accepting the check can insist that you sign both ways.

If there is a question about who a check is actually meant for, ask the person who issued it to write another that spells your name correctly.

Endorsing or Making Instruments Payable to More than One Person

An instrument can be made payable to more than one person: the question then arises as to who should endorse it.

If an instrument is made payable to one named person *or* another named person, such as to "J. Consumer *or* T. Consumer," it can be properly negotiated if either person signs it. If it is made payable to both named persons, such as "T. Consumer *and* J. Consumer," then both payees have to sign before the instrument can be further negotiated.

The *and/or* ways of making an instrument payable can be important if you owe money to more than one person. You then make the check payable to both people so each one has to sign in order to receive the money. The same point is true of course if someone owes you and another person money. Make sure the check is made payable to you both.

This could be important if you were borrowing money to pay someone else, and the lender insisted the loan proceeds were to be paid out by a check that was also payable to the seller. This is likely to happen if the lender wants to use the goods being purchased as collateral for the loan. In that case, insist the lender make the check payable to you and the person you are paying. Do *not* sign the check until that person is to be paid based on your purchase agreement. If, on the other hand, a check in this situation is made payable to you *or* the person you are paying, and the check is handed to the seller, or you immediately endorse the check before the other person is entitled to payment, the other has your money. (See page 524 for how the FTC's "Preservation of Consumers' Claims and Defenses" Rule can protect you more fully in such situations.)

HOW NEGOTIATION AFFECTS THE RIGHT TO PAYMENT

Once an instrument is negotiated, two kinds of "holders" can acquire an instrument and demand payment. This becomes significant if you need to stop or withhold payment.

One kind, simply called a holder, is anyone having possession of an instrument made payable to him, properly endorsed to him, or made payable "to bearer."

Someone can qualify as a holder of a negotiable instrument only if he is the one who was originally to be paid or the instrument has been properly negotiated to him. For example, you would be a holder of a check made payable to you, but not one made payable to someone else. But anyone can be a holder of one made payable "to bearer." As a practical matter, whether someone qualifies as a holder in the first place is primarily important in the case of forged endorsements of instruments made payable "to order." Once an instrument like this is negotiated over a forged endorsement, no one who later receives it can qualify as a holder entitled to payment. That person's recourse is to get the money back from those who previously negotiated the instrument.

The person to whom an instrument is originally made payable almost always qualifies only as a holder with respect to the person who issued it to him. That is, the person you originally deal with in a transaction and to whom you issued a negotiable instrument in connection with that transaction would only qualify as a holder. For example, if you gave someone a check as payment for a purchase, the seller would only qualify as a holder. The same would apply if you gave someone a promissory note in connection with a loan or a purchase made on credit (but this should now rarely happen when you make purchases on credit from a seller because of the FTC Rule described on page 523).

The other kind of holder is called a "holder in due course." This is someone who qualifies as a holder of a negotiable instrument but who also has special rights to demand payment of the money with few strings attached, unlike someone who only qualifies as a holder. But if an instrument does not qualify as a "negotiable" one the person demanding payment cannot qualify as a holder in due course.

Without going into all the details, a person can become a holder in due course only by taking the instrument in good faith (by acting honestly); for value (by giving something for it, usually money); before maturity (before payment was overdue); and without knowing there is anything wrong with the instrument (that is, there is something wrong with how the instrument is written or that someone had a legal justification for not having to pay at the time the person obtained the instrument).

In the case of instruments calling for payment by a specific date, they are considered overdue if payment has not been made by the due date. In the case of instruments calling for payment on demand, like checks, they are considered overdue if issued for longer than a reasonable period, which in the case of checks is thirty days from the date of issue.

Anyone would usually be considered to be acting in bad faith if he took the instrument knowing there was something wrong with it or took it under suspicious circumstances that should have alerted him that something was definitely wrong.

Here is an example to illustrate who could become the holder in due course of a check or promissory note you issued.

Suppose you made the check or promissory note initially payable to Mr. Seller. He, in turn, signs it over to and gets the money from, Mr. Banker. The second person who gets it—Mr. Banker—or anyone else who later obtains it, could qualify as a holder in due course.

The key difference between the two types of holders is that a person who qualifies as a holder in due course would be entitled to demand payment of the amount called for by the instrument even though you had legal justification for not paying someone who only qualifies as a holder.

Since the person who qualifies as a holder in due course acquires substantial leverage to collect the full amount called for by the instrument (even though your legal justification for not paying the person to whom you originally gave the check or note), a person must satisfy all the requirements that enable him to qualify as a holder in due course. If those requirements are not met, the person would not qualify as a holder in due course.

These are situations in which you could run into problems involving a holder in due course.

• You stop payment on a check you gave someone who has already cashed it (which is likely to be that person's bank). If that bank has actually paid out the money, it would almost always qualify as a holder in due course entitled to collect the full amount.

• You signed a promissory note in connection with a loan the proceeds of which were used for making a purchase. (See page 524 for how the FTC's "Preservation of Consumers' Claims and Defenses" Rule can protect you in such situations.) If the loan agreement or any separate promissory note you signed does not include the clause required by the rule or the rule does not apply to the transaction, anyone to whom the note is then negotiated could qualify as a holder in due course.

• You signed a separate promissory note when making a purchase on credit from the seller. A situation like this would now almost always involve a violation of the FTC's Rule and/or state law and which makes it questionable whether anyone to whom the note was negotiated could qualify as a holder in due course, but it could happen.

If a negotiable instrument is involved in your transaction and you have justification for not paying someone who only qualifies as a holder, seek legal advice before you refuse to pay someone who could qualify as a holder in due course. It is especially unsafe for you to refuse payment to such person when the instrument involves a promissory note. (See Chapter 62 for an explanation of how the FTC's Rule prevents the use of negotiable instruments in consumer credit transactions and what to watch for so you keep those protections when the Rule applies.)

Justifications for Refusing to Pay a Holder

For the purpose of justifying non-payment, anyone who qualifies simply as a holder is, in effect, in the same shoes as the person you originally dealt with in the transaction. If you had justification for refusing to pay the person you originally dealt with those justifications would also apply to anyone who qualified as a holder.

There are two main legal reasons that would enable you to avoid paying a holder.

- Any legal justifications based on rights or remedies available under a contract such as fraud involving the sale, non-delivery of the goods, or the product's failure to conform to the contract.
- Evidence that you paid the money, or that the instrument called for a larger payment than you actually owed a holder trying to collect.

For example, evidence of payment you made to a holder prevents him from collecting again. But if the instrument is negotiated further to someone who qualifies as a holder in due course, that person could collect again. Generally speaking, however, this could happen only if you pay before payment was due on the instrument. It is, therefore, very important that you insist payment be noted on the instrument itself or that you get the original back when it is paid in full if you pay before payment is due.

And if, for example, you gave someone a check for more than you owed and stopped payment on the check, that person could only collect what you owed rather than the full amount of the check. But if the check has already been cashed by that person's bank, for example, the bank could collect the full amount.

Justification for Refusing to Pay a Holder in Due Course

You could refuse to pay a holder in due course only for the following reasons. (They would, of course, also apply to anyone who qualifies merely as a holder):

- Fraud involving the instrument itself rather than the purchase. Such a case would have to involve someone who convinces a person to sign by falsely telling him the instrument is a contract rather than a negotiable instrument such as a promissory note. Normally, this would apply to someone who is illiterate or who is otherwise unable to find out what he or she is actually signing.
- A person's signature as drawer or maker is forged.
- The terms stated on the instrument at the time it is signed have been materially altered. But the holder in due course could collect according to the terms originally stated. If you sign an incomplete instrument which is later completed by someone else, however, a holder in due course can demand payment as per the instrument completed.
- The person signing the instrument is a minor.
- The person signing is considered legally incompetent for reasons of insanity, or signs under duress, or the transaction is illegal so that the person's payment obligation is legally void to begin with.
- The payment obligation is discharged, or terminated, by a bankruptcy proceeding.
- The holder who takes the instrument is aware that the payment obligation has already been terminated. This could happen, for example, if a holder takes a check already marked "paid."

LOST OR STOLEN INSTRUMENTS

If you give someone an instrument and it is then lost or stolen the person would still be entitled to the money and could demand it from you. Two things can happen in this situation.

1. The instrument is permanently lost or destroyed so no one can try to cash it.
2. The instrument is negotiated further and the money is paid to someone over a forged endorsement. (If the instrument is payable "to bearer" it would be like losing cash for all practical purposes.)

If the instrument is permanently lost or stolen, the payee can request that you issue a replacement. If you refuse, the person can sue if he or she is still entitled to the money and can show why the instrument itself cannot be produced. But since a lost or stolen instrument could turn up again, and perhaps be negotiated further—if the person losing the instrument had signed it in blank so it was payable "to bearer," for instance—the payee would almost always have to put up security to protect you.

If a lost or stolen instrument is negotiated over a forged endorsement, then the wrong person has been paid. No one who has obtained an instrument over someone's forged endorsement can become either a holder or a holder in due course who can properly demand payment. This is what you could do in a case like this:

• If you are the payee, you would usually be entitled to do any of the following: (1) demand the money from the *first* bank that paid; (2) demand the money from a drawee who paid the money out which, in the case of a check, would be the bank of the person who wrote it; or (3) demand the money from the person who issued the instrument to you. If they refuse to pay, you would be able to sue and should seek the advice of an attorney.

• If an instrument you issued was lost by or stolen from the person to whom you gave it, you could do either of the following depending on the circumstances: (1) the person to whom you gave the instrument could demand the money from you, but you could make him sue and prove he was entitled to payment on the instrument and insist he put up adequate security; (2) if the check involved has been paid out by your bank, you could demand that it recredit the money to your account. You, in turn would have to pay that money to the person whose endorsement was forged. Alternatively, your bank could charge your account and pay the money to the person entitled to it, leaving it up to your bank to get the money back from those to whom it should not have been paid.

ALTERED INSTRUMENTS

An alteration can occur if someone changes the terms of an instrument, by "raising" the amount, for instance, or if someone fills in an incomplete but signed instrument other than as authorized.

If an instrument is altered, you would only be obligated under the original terms—unless you were negligent in ways that contributed to the alterations. There are also circumstances under which you may not be obligated to pay at all. You should therefore seek an attorney's advice.

If someone fills in an incomplete instrument you signed, there is very little you can do after it gets into the hands of a holder in due course.

Therefore, always write checks so they cannot easily be altered and never sign a blank or incomplete instrument.

PAYING OR COLLECTING ON NEGOTIABLE INSTRUMENTS

The last stage of the negotiation of an instrument—the actual payment of the money—triggers various rights and obligations depending on the circumstances.

In the case of a check, it is, of course, your bank that is called on to pay the money. If the bank doesn't pay—whether it does so properly or not—then you as the drawer are obligated to pay and if you don't, you could be sued. In the case of a promissory note, you as the maker of the note are obligated to pay and a failure to do so triggers the other party's right to sue.

When Is Liability for Non-Payment Triggered?

The maker of a promissory note calling for payment by a certain date can be sued if payment is not made by the day after payment was due. In the case of a note payable on demand, the maker can be sued if payment isn't made on the date it can be demanded.

In the case of a certificate of deposit, a depositor can demand payment only on or after the certificate's maturity date. If the money is not paid at that time, he is entitled to sue.

Technically, the drawer of a check or any endorser can be sued only after a check has been presented for payment, payment has been refused, and he has been notified of that fact. As a practical matter, though, people do not usually sue at the drop of a hat. However, if you are called upon to pay an instrument and it appears something is wrong and that you are entitled to withhold payment, you should sort the matter out quickly.

PAYING THE MONEY

When the holder of an instrument makes presentment for payment (that is, requests payment of the money), the person being called on to pay can require that:

- The instrument be shown to him.
- The person requesting payment show proper identification and evidence of his authority to request payment on behalf of the holder.
- The instrument be shown for payment at the place where payment is to be made as stated in the instrument. If no place for payment is stated on the instrument, it must be produced at any reasonable place, such as the maker's home or office.
- A signed receipt for partial payment be noted on the instrument, or that the instrument itself be surrendered if paid in full.

In the case of a check it is, of course, your bank that takes care of all these things. But if someone asks you to pay an instrument you signed or that someone claims you signed; or you are making partial or full payment on a promissory note *before* the due date, then you must make sure that you are paying the money to the right person and that partial payment is noted on the instrument itself or that the *original* instrument you signed is returned to you when it is paid in full. If you don't pay the right person, you would still owe the money. If you don't note partial payment on the instrument or if you don't get the original back when it is paid in full, it might be further negotiated and end up costing you more money.

46 · Checking Accounts, 1: Procedures and Negotiating Strategy for Collecting Funds

Paying by check is still the most widely used cashless payment method. It's a relatively safe way to send money through the mails, and in most circumstances a canceled check is an automatic payment receipt.

While checks and checking accounts normally work quite smoothly, things can sometimes go wrong. Over a two-year period, for instance, my bank managed to do the following:

- Deduct $50 more than the amount of a check I wrote.
- Pay out 80 cents less than the amount of another check.
- Bounce a check I wrote when its computer incorrectly showed I had "insufficient funds."

This chapter and the next cover steps you can take to correct various things that can go wrong with checks and checking accounts.

OPENING A CHECKING ACCOUNT

Opening a personal checking account normally involves little more than signing a signature card and depositing funds into the account. Once the account is set up, you write checks, deposit cash or checks into your account, and leave the collection of checks payable to you in the hands of the bank.

The following points can help you to avoid trouble:

- Minimize the risks of something going wrong by always being very careful about the way you write and endorse checks so money is paid out only as you want it to be.
- Always keep accurate and complete records of checks you write, of automatic payments, and deposits.
- Promply review canceled checks and balance your account. Make sure the bank has paid out the proper amounts, and that your account has been properly debited.
- Immediately notify the bank if something is amiss and insist that it properly correct a problem. The faster you act, the better.

In effect, your checking account is the connecting link between separate sets of procedures that are governed by different rules. There is one set of procedures a bank must follow when collecting and crediting funds to your account. They are covered in this chapter. There is another set of procedures for paying out and debiting your account. They are covered in the following chapter.

Both sets of procedures are governed by the Uniform Commercial Code. The Code prevents banks from using clauses that could relieve them of liability for failing to carry out their responsibilities. No bank can legally use a clause like this, for example: "The bank will not be liable for the unintentional payment by accident or oversight of a check on which payment has been stopped." Always ignore any such clause in a deposit agreement. While there are legal grounds that can prevent you from holding a bank accountable in certain circumstances, a "waiver of liability" clause is rarely—if ever—one of them.

WAYS OF COLLECTING MONEY

When a check is made payable to you, there are two ways you can collect the money: you can either go to the drawee bank involved and collect payment yourself, or you can deposit the check in your checking account and have your bank collect it for you.

If you go to the drawee bank, it must either pay or refuse payment by midnight of that day. If it does not do either of these things, the check is dishonored. (See further on in this chapter for more details on this subject.)

If you deposit the check in your account, it can pass through any number of banks before it is finally "cashed" and the funds are transferred to your account. The different steps taken by the various banks are usually referred to as the "check collection process," and the Code provides various rules that banks must follow during it. In general, these requirements spell out when your bank could be accountable to you if something goes wrong.

A BANK'S CHECK COLLECTION RESPONSIBILITIES

When you deposit a check, your bank has the following collection responsibilities:

* Presenting or sending the check through the collection process for presentment at the drawee bank.
* Sending you a notice that the check has been dishonored for non-payment, if necessary, and returning the unpaid check to you.
* Giving you credit for money the bank receives. (Banks rarely transfer actual money when checks are sent out for collection; instead they "settle up" among themselves by using various accounting methods that simply credit or debit the funds to the bank's own accounts.)
* Notifying you when necessary that the check has been lost or delayed in the check collection process. The bank must do this within a reasonable time after discovering the delay.

In general, a bank must complete each step for which it becomes responsible no later than midnight of the following banking day. If the bank does not act within this time it would usually be considered to have failed to carry out its responsibilities properly. So timing and fixing the dates on which your bank took specific actions is the key to establishing its potential liability.

GETTING CREDIT FOR FUNDS DEPOSITED IN AN ACCOUNT

The Code spells out in great detail when a bank must credit your account and have available for withdrawal funds you have deposited.

These are the key requirements:

DEPOSITS MADE IN CASH

A cash deposit is considered final when made and the depositor has the right to withdraw the money when the bank opens for business the next day.

DEPOSITS MADE BY CHECKS

The time allowed your bank for crediting and having available for withdrawal funds deposited by check depends mainly on which bank the check is drawn upon.

If your bank is also the drawee bank, it must credit your account and have the funds available for withdrawal at the opening of the second banking day following receipt of the deposit check—assuming, of course, the check is "good." If you make a deposit on Monday, for instance, the bank has until Wednesday morning to credit the money to your account, or to refuse payment.

Things get more complicated if your bank has to collect the money. In that case, once your bank has a final settlement with the other bank, it then owes you the money and must give you final credit for the amount no later than midnight of the following banking day. The actions taken by the paying bank will usually determine when a settlement is final. Broadly speaking, that bank must pay or refuse to pay a check by midnight of the banking day on which it receives it, but it could have up to midnight of the following banking day to take back the payment and refuse to pay the check instead. This second deadline for refusing payment could sometimes be extended, however. Once the paying bank fails to refuse payment within the proper time after receiving the check, any settlement becomes final and it must pay the money. Once the other bank's payment is considered final, your bank owes you the money and it can no longer charge the amount back to your account.

If you run into a problem, pinning down the exact date on which your bank first took action, or failed to take action, will usually make it clear whether it properly carried out its responsibilities.

Technically speaking, if you deposit a check the bank does not have to allow you use of the money until it has been collected. And it's becoming more common for banks to put "holds" on deposits for a specific number of days—usually up to seven banking days, for local checks but it may be up to fourteen *banking* days, depending on the location of the bank paying out the money. If you write a check against your deposit before the hold has been cleared, you may find that it's bounced.

Many banks arrange for customers to draw on funds deposited by check before they have actually collected the money. You should ask about your bank's policy. See page 372, where this subject is gone into in detail.

BANK'S LIABILITY FOR FAILING TO EXERCISE ORDINARY CARE

The Code makes a bank liable for damages if it fails to exercise ordinary care in handling a check. Normally such damages are limited to the amount of the check involved. There are two situations in which a bank may *not* be considered liable, though.

One is if the amount could not have been collected anyway, even if the bank *had* properly carried out its responsibilities. If, for example, your bank delayed forwarding a deposited check for collection and it was returned upaid because of insufficient funds, the bank probably wouldn't be liable as long as the check would not have been paid even if your bank had forwarded it promptly for collection. This exception would also apply if the check wouldn't have been payable for other reasons, such as a forged drawer signature.

The second situation occurs when the bank doesn't notify you in time that a deposited check has been returned unpaid. Although the bank does not become liable for the amount of the check in this case, in a few instances it *may* become liable for damages you sustain because of its failure to notify you in time, such as if you write checks that bounce, for instance. You should seek the advice of an attorney in a matter like this. In most cases the bank would not be liable if it bounces a check you wrote because a check you deposit is returned unpaid.

WHAT CAN GO WRONG?

In general, there are four things that can go wrong when you deposit a check:

• The check is returned unpaid. Usually this happens because there are insufficient funds in the account of the person writing the check, but it may also be because of lack of a proper endorsement or a discrepancy between the amount written in numbers and words. In a case like this, of course, you have to deal with the person who wrote the check or the one who endorsed it to you.

• The check isn't handled properly during the collection process and the money is not correctly credited to your account. In this case, your recourse would usually be against the bank acting as your collection agent to the extent your bank was responsible. The situation is automatically extremely complicated if anyone else is responsible.

• The check is lost or stolen in the mail. In this case, your bank would not be accountable since the check hasn't actually been deposited. Yor usual recourse would be to ask the person who wrote the check to issue another one.

• The check is restrictively endorsed "For deposit only" to your account but is mistakenly paid to someone else. In this case, you could demand the money back from the first bank that paid out the money.

PREVENTING TROUBLE

There are steps you can take to minimize trouble when you deposit checks. There are also steps you can take to hold a bank accountable if things go wrong.

USING ENDORSEMENTS THAT WILL PROTECT YOU IN CASE OF LOST OR STOLEN CHECKS

When a check is payable to you, always use the kind of endorsement that will prevent it from being properly negotiated by anyone other than yourself or a person to whom you endorse it. See page 360.

When you discover that a check payable to you is lost or stolen, immediately inform the person who wrote it and ask for a replacement. (Don't be surprised if he or she asks you to pay for the cost of stopping payment on the first check.) If the person refuses, seek legal advice about collecting the money.

GETTING RECEIPTS FOR DEPOSITED CHECKS

If your bank loses a check you deposited, it would be very important for you to have a written receipt verifying that your bank actually got it.

But if the deposit slip verifying a deposit only identifies a check by the amount, that may not be enough proof your bank received a particular check. To avoid this kind of trouble, specifically identify the check on your deposit slip, such as by including the name of the person who issued it and the check number.

DEPOSITING CHECKS BY MAIL OR INTO A DEPOSITORY BOX

Depositing checks by mail, rather than in person, is a more convenient but riskier way to do your banking since you do not have an immediate written record that the bank has received your check. You take the same risks when you deposit a check in a depository box or even in an automated teller machine.

Before you use these methods, find out if the bank *promptly* mails receipts. If it does not do so and, in effect, acknowledges receipt of checks only when it sends out monthly statements, don't use the service unless you have sufficient funds in your account to cover all checks until you know *positively* the amounts have been credited to you. If you do not have any other receipt showing your bank got the check, it will be very hard to prove your bank actually received it.

If you're supposed to get a receipt at an automated teller machine, but don't because it is not functioning properly, always contact your bank promptly. Such deposits are usually covered by the Electronic Fund Transfer Act, but receipts you get at a terminal do not necessarily prove that you actually deposited a check. Such receipts usually only help you prove whether the bank credited the funds to the proper account once the amount was collected.

If a check you deposit by mail isn't received by your bank within a reasonable time, treat it as a lost or stolen check and ask the person who wrote it to issue you another one.

That may also be the most practical solution if a check you put into a depository box is "lost" by your bank. You may be able to hold your bank accountable in such a case but you would need an attorney's advice on the matter. The first thing to do, though, is promptly notify the bank so you help establish its potential liability for the loss.

NOTIFYING YOUR BANK WHEN A CHECK IS "LOST"

The following sample letter shows how you could notify your bank and the sort of information you should obtain and include in the letter to verify your claim. You could take the letter to the bank in person or send it as a follow-up confirming letter after an initial phone call.

> *200 Witchtree Lane*
> *Anytown, USA 00000*
>
> *April 1, 19___*

Mr. J. Teller
Manager
Riverview Branch
Hometown Bank
River Street
Anytown, USA 00000

Dear Mr. Teller:

This is to confirm the verbal notification I gave Mr. Counter by telephone on March 31 that the receipt of a check for $1,115.80, made payable to me by the XYZ Company and drawn on the Republic National Bank, has not been acknowledged by your bank. I placed the check in the depository box at the Riverview branch on March 24, 19___, endorsed "For deposit only" into my checking account, number 000-00000-0.

When I contacted Mr. Counter about this matter, I was informed that your bank had no record of this check.

I am enclosing a copy of a memo from the XYZ Company confirming that a check for that amount was issued to me on March 22, 19___, and that the company's bank has verified that this check has not been presented for payment. I have also regularly deposited similar checks in the depository box on or about the same date each month.

I therefore request that the bank conduct a prompt and comprehensive search to find the check and that it promptly take all appropriate and necessary steps to collect and credit my account for the amount of the check. If the bank is unable to find the check, I am asking that it certify to me that it is unable to locate it.

I hope this matter can be promptly resolved by your locating and taking the steps required to have the amount of the check credited to my account, but I reserve my rights to hold the bank liable for its failure to exercise ordinary care in the handling of this item.

Sincerely,

Seek prompt legal advice if the person who wrote the check refuses to issue a replacement, or if your bank can't locate the check and refuses to give you credit for the money.

ARRANGEMENTS TO AVOID CHECKS BOUNCING

As previously noted, a bank doesn't have to credit your account for amounts deposited by check until after it has received the funds through the check collection process. How long this takes depends on how many banks handle the check, but normally it takes between two to five banking days. Nevertheless, some banks are putting "holds" of seven to fourteen days on deposits.

To avoid having checks you write bounce in this situation, it is very important to learn your bank's policy on this matter. Usually, banks follow one of the following policies, but sometimes they combine policies.

• Allowing depositors to draw on funds as soon as a check is deposited. The funds are only temporarily credited to your account, and if the check is returned unpaid, the bank is almost always entitled to debit the amount from your account. This policy is likely to be used only by small banks who know their customers. It is becoming rarer and rarer.

• Allowing depositors to draw on funds only after they have been collected, *unless* special arrangements have been made which would allow you to draw on the funds immediately. A bank may do this with respect to checks it is sure will clear, such as payroll checks issued by a well-known company. Such funds are also only temporarily credited to your account until actually collected, though.

• Allowing depositors to draw on funds immediately if a check is "deposited as cash" *against* an amount already on deposit in another account or, in some cases, against a line of credit tied to the checking account. In this case, the hold is placed on the funds in the other account. If, in such a case, a check is returned unpaid, the bank would usually be able to "charge back" the amount to the account on which the hold was placed.

Normally, you don't have to worry if you're sure the person whose check you are depositing is "good" for the money. If you aren't sure, your only real protection is to insist on payment in cash or by certified check. If you do take a check without being absolutely sure it will be honored, *do not* write checks on the amount until the check actually clears.

If it is ever important for you to obtain immediate use of funds made payable to you by check, ask first how and when your bank will credit the amount to your account and what, if any, arrangements you can make to obtain immediate use of the money.

• Allowing depositors to draw on funds only after a specific waiting period to allow the check to clear. This holding period can be any number of *banking* days following the date of deposit. (In some situations such a waiting period may be questionable under the Code's deadlines for crediting funds to a customer's account, but challenging a bank on this issue involves technicalities that are beyond the scope of this book.)

If the money hasn't actually been collected—a rare occurrence—a bank might or might not count the money as being in the account at the end of the waiting period, depending on its policy.

HOLDING A BANK ACCOUNTABLE FOR FAILING TO PROPERLY CREDIT AMOUNTS DEPOSITED

The easy way to learn that proper amounts have not been credited to your checking account is if you discover it when you review your monthly statement. The hard way is to have your checks returned unpaid because of "insufficient funds."

In either case, contact your bank immediately. If the bank has failed to credit your account for a deposit and, as a consequence, bounced a check, be prepared to deal with these two problems separately (see page 382 for the bank's potential liability for wrongfully dishonoring a check). Your initial step should be to ask the bank to furnish you with an exact account of what happened and to insist that it correct the problem. The nice part is that, as a practical matter, the bank usually has to do this; a failure or refusal to do so is likely to be taken as a sign it is acting in bad faith. Getting an exact account of what happened will usually demonstrate whether or not your bank is responsible. If it is, it gives you key bargaining leverage for settling the problems.

When you contact the bank, be sure to take along the following:

1. The receipt you have for the deposit. This should pinpoint the date, the amount, and the account to which it was made.

2. Your checking account statement. This will either indicate the date the deposit was credited to your account, or the fact the deposit was not credited at all.

3. Any notice you have received that indicates the date on which your bank returned an unpaid check, or on which a check overdraft was triggered.

Also be prepared to ask some questions that will help pin down whether or not your bank carried out all its responsibilities.

Here are some questions that are likely to apply.

• If you do not know when or whether the bank credited a deposit to your account, ask on what date did it do so.

The answer will either pinpoint when the bank made the deposit available to you, or show it has not yet done so. The following questions try to ascertain whether it was responsible for crediting the deposit sooner.

• If you made a cash deposit, did the bank credit the amount to the proper account and make it available for withdrawal at opening time of the following banking day? (NOTE: A bank can set any time after 2:00 P.M. as the close of its banking day, and anything that happens after that time can be counted as occurring on its next banking day. This can apply to any actions for which the bank is responsible.)

If the answer is no, your bank is almost certainly responsible for anything else that went wrong with your account as a result.

• If you deposited a check which the bank arranged to treat as a cash deposit, was it credited to the correct account, and was the amount available for withdrawal according to the arrangements made?

Again, a negative answer almost certainly makes the bank accountable.

• If the bank placed a hold on a deposit for a certain period, and it follows the policy of making the amount available for withdrawal at the end of that time, did the bank then credit the amount to the correct account?

If the answer is no, your bank is almost certainly accountable.

If your bank says a deposit is only available when the amount is actually collected the following questions might apply.

• If your bank is supposed to pay the check from someone else's account at the same branch, has the amount been debited to that account? Were there sufficient funds to pay the check on the same day or the next banking day after your deposit? If the answer to either question is yes, did the bank then credit the amount to your account and have it available for withdrawal as of the opening of the *second* banking day?

If the answer to the last question is no, your bank is almost certainly accountable.

• If your bank has to collect the money from another bank, you may have to ask these additional questions.

On what date did the bank present or forward the check? If it failed to do so by midnight of the banking day following the day of deposit, your bank could be accountable for the amount.

Suppose, for example, you deposit a check on Monday morning, June 1. It should be forwarded for collection that day, and at the latest by midnight June 2, but the bank fails to forward the check until June 8. The check is paid and credited to your account on Thursday, June 11. In the meantime, on Tuesday, June 9, your bank bounces a check you've written—something which would not have occurred at all if it had acted promptly when collecting the check. In this case, your bank would usually be accountable only for any money that could not be collected because of its failure, and *may* become responsible for improperly bouncing a check for insufficient funds only if it acted in bad faith.

A second question would be, on what date was final settlement made by the drawee bank, and by what date was it *required* to do so? These are the key dates.

• If the drawee bank made final payment on the check, did your bank then credit the amount to your account and have it available for withdrawal by midnight of the banking day following final payment?

A negative answer almost certainly makes your bank accountable. (But remember banks may be able to withhold amounts deposited until the end of the waiting periods they set—or so they say.)

• If your bank puts a hold on amounts deposited by check but still doesn't allow you to draw on a deposit until the money is actually collected, did it notify you of a delay in the collection process?

If the answer is no, your bank is likely to be accountable for the amount of the check and you may be able to hold it accountable for failing to pay checks you wrote.

If the answers you get to the appropriate questions indicate your bank has failed to handle a deposit properly, insist it take immediate steps to credit the money to your account and to correct any problems resulting from this failure. If it turns out there is an abnormal delay in the collection process, ask the bank to credit your account while the problem is corrected.

If it turns out the bank has properly carried out its collection responsibilities, and a check you wrote bounces because it gets to your bank before the money you deposited is actually available to you, that is, of course, your responsibility and not the bank's.

NOTIFYING YOUR BANK ABOUT PROBLEMS WITH DEPOSITS

The first sample letter covers situations in which it is already fairly clear that a deposit has not been properly credited to your account, and a check has bounced as a result. The second sample letter covers situations in which a check has bounced but you are not sure what the problem is. The letters include alternative wording for charges triggered to an overdraft line of credit. Obviously, all dates used are for illustrative purposes only.

Whichever letter fits your circumstances, it can be taken to the bank in person or adapted and used as a confirming letter.

Of course, if the only problem involves a bank's failure to credit a deposit properly, omit all the wording referring to a check you wrote having bounced.

200 Witchtree Lane
Anytown, USA 00000

June 1, 19__

Mr. J. Teller
Manager
Riverview Branch
Hometown National Bank
Anytown, USA 00000

Dear Mr. Teller:

This is to (inform you/confirm the notification I gave Mr. Counter today) that the ($800) I deposited by check on May 10, 19__, in my checking account, account number 000-00000-0, apparently was not properly credited to and available for withdrawal from my account. As a result, the check identified below was returned unpaid by the bank (a charge as described below was made to my overdraft line of credit).

The check I deposited was from (identify person), dated May 7, 19__ and drawn on (identify bank), account number 00000. This check (was deposited as cash against my savings account and) should have been credited to and been available for withdrawal from my account by (include date). I have not been notified that the deposited check was either returned as unpaid or that there has been a delay in transit affecting the collection of the check.

But the checking account statement I received on May 30 for the period ending May 26 does not reflect this deposit had been credited to my account. (And on May 28, I received the bank's notification that check number 0000 I issued on May 20 for $683.50 and made payable to the ABC Company, had been returned as unpaid on May 27 for insufficient funds in my account.) (And $443.50 was charged on May 27 to my Master Credit account, account number 00000-000000-0000, as a cash advance for a check overdraft which resulted because sufficient funds were not available to pay my check number 0000 for $625 as shown on periodic statement for the billing period ending May 28.)

Sufficient funds should, however, have been available in my account to pay this as well as other checks if the deposit of May 10 and all other deposits I have made since had been properly credited to and been available for withdrawal from my checking account.

I therefore request (Since Mr. Counter was unable to resolve this matter fully when we discussed it, I reaffirm my request) that the bank imme-

diately take all necessary and proper steps to account for and have avail-
ble for withdrawal all amounts that should have been properly credited
to my account as of the dates on which I was entitled to withdraw them
and that all checks properly payable out of the account be paid by the
bank without fail. And should it become necessary, I request that the
bank issue me a certified check for making payments to payees whose
checks were improperly returned. However, I am not waiving any further
claims for damages. (And the bank is to reverse the amounts improperly
charged to my Master Credit account and credit my account for any
finance charges that may have been imposed on that amount.)

Please notify me promptly of the steps the bank has taken to make a
proper accounting with respect to all items involved in this matter.

Thank you for your prompt cooperation.

Sincerely,

This alternative version is for situations in which a check bounces but you are not
sure what's wrong with your account.

200 Witchtree Lane
Anytown, USA 00000

June 1, 19___

Mr. J. Teller
Manager
Riverview Branch
Hometown National Bank
Anytown, USA 00000

Dear Mr. Teller:

This is to (inform you/confirm the notification I gave Mr. Counter
today) that the bank apparently failed to account properly for amounts
that should have been credited to and available for withdrawal from my
checking account, number 0000-00000-0, since I was notified on May 31,
19___, that the check described below was returned unpaid by the bank
because of insufficient funds (since as described below a charge to my
overdraft line of credit was made on May 31 because of insufficient funds
in my checking account).

Sufficient funds should, however, have been credited to and available
for withdrawal from my account if the bank had properly accounted for
each of the deposits I have made since the accounting period ending April
30, 19___. These deposits are identified below (copies of deposit receipts
are attached):

1. Cash deposit of $450 made on May 3.

2. Deposit by two checks totaling $1250.50 made on May 10. This
deposit consisted of one check for $850.50 issued by the XYZ Company
and drawn on the Hometown State Bank, Anytown, and one check for
$400 issued by Money Funds Investments and drawn on Outstate
National Bank, Somecity USA.

3. (List any additional deposits.)

Since each deposit made by check was deposited as cash against my
savings account and the bank has not informed me that any check was
returned unpaid, all these deposits should have been credited to and avail-

able for withdrawal from my account by no later than (<u>include date based on deposit arrangement</u>). (Since the bank has not informed me that any of the checks were returned unpaid or that there was a delay in transit involving any of the checks I deposited, all the amounts should have been credited and available for withdrawal no later than (<u>indicate date based on deposit arrangements</u>.)

But I was notified on May 31 that my check number 000 for $625 issued on May 25 and made payable to the ABC Company was returned unpaid on May 28 because of insufficient funds. (But $450 was charged on May 25 to my Master Credit account, account number 000000-00000-0000, as a check overdraft loan resulting from insufficient funds to pay my check number 000 for $625 as shown on the periodic statement for the billing period ending May29.)

I therefore request (Since Mr. Counter was unable to resolve this matter fully when we discussed it, I reaffirm my request) that the bank immediately take all necessary and proper steps to account for and have available for withdrawal as required by the Uniform Commercial Code all amounts that should have been properly credited to my account and to prevent without fail the return of any other item that was properly payable out of my account. And should it become necessary, I request that the bank issue me a certified check for making payments to payees whose checks were improperly returned unpaid. I am not, however, waiving any further claims I may have for damages. (And the bank is to reverse the amount improperly charged to my Master Credit account and credit any finance charges that may have been imposed on that amount.)

If the bank contends, however, that any of the deposits described above were not available for withdrawal by (_____) the bank is then to furnish me the information which confirms that it has, in fact, exercised ordinary care in carrying out its responsibilities as a collecting bank with respect to each deposit by check which it claims were not available for withdrawal by that date.

Please notify me of the steps the bank has taken to make a proper accounting of all items involved in this matter.

Thank you for your prompt cooperation.

Sincerely,

If the bank does not promptly correct the problem, you might consider taking one follow-up step as a final attempt to get the problem settled before seeking legal advice. It puts the bank on notice that it has not promptly corrected the problems for which it could be held accountable, and is likely to strengthen your position.

Always take such a follow-up step within a few days after your initial notification to the bank.

200 Witchtree Lane
Anytown, USA 0000

June 5, 19___

Mr. J. Teller
Manager
Riverview Branch
Hometown National Bank
Anytown, USA 00000

Dear Mr. Teller:

This is to notify you that the bank has still failed to furnish me the full and proper accounting I requested on June 1, 19___, with respect to deposits I made into my checking account, number 000-000000-0. I requested this accounting when I learned the bank failed to pay checks drawn on that account as I described in my letter of June 1 which I gave to Mr. Counter at the time we discussed this matter that day (as I verbally informed Mr. Counter on June 1 and confirmed by my letter of June 1). A copy of that letter is enclosed.

I therefore now insist the bank take immediate steps to comply with the requests I made, so that this matter can be resolved by a full and complete accounting and the making available for withdrawal of all deposits in question as of the date required by the Uniform Commercial Code. I also insist the bank do whatever will be necessary and proper to rectify its failure to pay checks drawn on my account, which would have been payable had the bank properly credited deposits to my account, and that the bank now prevent without fail the return of any checks properly payable out of my account.

Please notify me promptly of all necessary and proper corrective steps the bank has taken or will take to rectify this matter.

I hope this matter will now be promptly and fully resolved as I have requested to avoid any further liability for the bank's failure to exercise ordinary care in this matter. I do, however, reserve my rights to hold the bank liable to the fullest extent provided by law.

Sincerely,

DRAWEE BANK REFUSES TO CASH CHECK PRESENTED IN PERSON

If you personally try to cash a check at the drawee bank but it refuses to pay within the proper time, technically speaking, the bank would be dishonoring the check. This could entitle you to demand payment from the person who wrote it and/or from anyone who had endorsed the check to you. But drawee banks may refuse to pay out cash over the counter because they can't be sure they are paying the right person. The easiest solution usually is to deposit the check in your account and collect the money through the bank collection process.

But if you're not sure the person giving you the check is "good" for the money, then ask his bank to:

- Verify that the person has an account at that bank, and has sufficient funds to pay the check.

If the person who wrote the check doesn't have an account (say he simply wrote the check to you) or doesn't have enough funds, it is to your advantage to have the bank formally state it is refusing to pay. This way you can take prompt action against the person who wrote the check.

COLLECTING UNPAID CHECKS

If a check is returned unpaid, promptly notify the person who wrote the check or who endorsed it to you, and specifically demand immediate payment. Although such notification can be given verbally or in writing, it's obviously better to establish a written record.

Here's how you could do it.

200 Witchtree Lane
Anytown, USA 0000

June 1, 19__

Mr. A. Bouncer
100 Elm Street
Anytown, USA 00000

Dear Mr. Bouncer:

This is to notify you that payment on your check number 280, dated May 20, 19__, for $681.50 which was drawn on the Hometown State Bank has been refused by your bank because (state the reason given by bank for refusing to pay the check).

You are to pay me immediately the $681.50 in cash at my address. I would also accept immediate payment by a currently dated check made payable to me and certified by your bank or by a postal money order. There is now also due from you ($0.00) for charges I had to pay because your check was returned.

If payment for the full amount due me is not made immediately, I shall hold you liable for the full amount and shall take steps to have this matter prosecuted to the fullest extent provided by law.

Sincerely,

Get a mailing receipt for the letter.

If the issuer still refuses to pay, your only option is to sue. Never, therefore, return an original unpaid check until after the issuer has made it good, because you will need it as evidence.

Many states have enacted so-called "bad check" laws which make an issuer criminally liable under specified circumstances. Contact your local prosecutor to find out if your circumstances are covered.

47 · Checking Accounts, 2: Procedures and Negotiating Strategy for Paying Out Funds

When it comes to paying money out of a checking account a bank has a two-fold obligation to a depositor. It must pay checks that are properly payable when presented for payment, and it must *avoid* paying those that are *not*.

These obligations are also important when you initiate payments out of a checking account by alternative payment methods, such as debit cards or electronic fund transfers (covered in later chapters). Things can go wrong with these methods as well, of course: holding a bank accountable will then depend partly on rights you have under laws governing those payment methods, and partly on those governing checking accounts.

WHAT AMOUNTS ARE PROPERLY PAYABLE OUT OF YOUR ACCOUNT?

A bank is entitled to charge your checking account for any amounts that are properly payable. This would, of course, include any payments you ordered to the extent they were properly payable when presented for payment. In addition, it may sometimes charge fees for such things as the use of the account, stopping payment on checks, and returning any unpaid checks deposited in your account which it could also deduct. And if you owe the bank money, it can sometimes debit that amount from funds on deposit.

A bank can also be required to freeze or pay out funds from your account based on proper legal orders served on the bank, such as a garnishment.

Also remember that if your bank temporarily credits your account with an amount deposited by check, and the check is returned unpaid, it can "charge back" the amount to you. Normally, though, it cannot do this after it has made final settlement with you for the item.

AMOUNTS A BANK IS NOT ENTITLED TO CHARGE TO YOUR ACCOUNT

In the following situations a bank would not be entitled to charge your account for amounts it might have paid out.

- A check lacks your signature as drawer, or your signature is forged. A check is paid over a forged endorsement of the person to whose order it was payable. A bank would usually have to recredit your account, but you would, of course, still owe the money to the proper payee. Alternatively, the bank could pay the proper payee and then charge your account.
- A check is altered after you sign it, usually by someone who "raises" the amount. If the face amount of a check you write is increased and your bank pays out the higher amount, it would then be liable for the additional amount unless you could be considered negligent. If the bank pays in good faith and has no reason to suspect the amount was altered, it could charge your account for the original amount.
- A post-dated check you write is paid too soon. In this case, your bank is unlikely to be held liable for improperly deducting the amount from your account, unless the

action results in the bank then bouncing other checks that would have been properly payable, or in making it impossible for you to stop payment on the check.

• A check is paid out after you've put a valid stop payment order on it. Your bank could then be liable for any loss you suffer, and would normally be required to re-credit your account for the amount. But, as explained in more detail on page 383, there are situations in which a bank may not be required to do this.

The Code does not clearly cover situations in which a bank could debit your account for amounts made payable by other methods, such as electronic fund transfers or debit cards. Generally, though, laws governing those payment methods would apply. Amounts would then be properly payable if made in accordance with those laws and your account agreement governing the payment method used.

DEPOSITOR NEGLIGENCE

In the case of forgeries, the Code makes a depositor responsible for any negligence with respect to alterations or forgeries involving checks.

You would be considered negligent if you substantially contribute to the alteration of a check or to the forgery of an endorsement or your signature as a drawer. This could happen, for instance, if you write a check in a way that makes it easy for someone to raise the amount, or to forge your signature. Mechanical signature writing machines are usually involved in the latter situation, so this would rarely apply to forged signatures involving consumer transactions. Generally speaking, however, you would usually be considered negligent only if you pre-signed blank checks.

The Code requires depositors to promptly review bank statements and paid checks. Failing to notify the bank promptly of forgeries or alterations can relieve it of any liability, especially in the following situations:

• The bank can show it suffered a loss because you failed to notify it.
• The same person forges or alters a second check, but you fail to notify the bank about the first forgery within fourteen days of receiving your bank statement and forged check. If your bank pays a second forged check after that period, you may as well forget about trying to get the money back from your bank.

The Code also completely prevents you from holding your bank accountable if:

• You do not discover and report to your bank an alteration, or forged drawer signature, within one year after receiving the relevant bank statement and canceled check.
• You do not discover a forged endorsement and report it to your bank within three years after receiving the relevant statement.

The following tips can help you to avoid trouble:

• Be careful with blank checks and promptly report their loss or theft to your bank.
• Make sure all checks are properly and fully completed *before* you sign them, and that all blank spaces are crossed out to make alterations difficult and more easily detectable.
• Promptly balance your checking account and report any discrepancies.

EFFECT OF MAKING PAYMENT BY CHECK

Generally, once a person accepts a check you give in payment, the underlying payment obligation is suspended so that you would not be in default on it until the check is dishonored. But this would usually be important only when the check you gave was lost by or stolen from the person to whom you gave it.

And once a check you gave is properly paid, the underlying payment obligation is also paid.

BANK'S LIABILITY FOR WRONGFULLY DISHONORING A CHECK

The Code imposes a special liability on drawee banks that fail to pay properly payable checks. A bank wrongfully dishonors a check when it refuses to pay within the time it is required to do so even though you have sufficient funds in your account. It then becomes liable for damages directly caused by its failure, including any monetary losses you sustain as a direct result.

If the bank simply makes a mistake, you would usually only be able to recover the actual damages you can prove you suffered. These may include compensation for being arrested and prosecuted for writing a bad check, and other consequential damages, such as harm that ensues to your credit standing. Damages would also include:

- Late payment fees you may owe as a result of the bank failing to pay the check.
- Returned check charges you have to pay someone else.
- Losses you sustain because an agreement falls through when the check is wrongfully dishonored, or damages you sustain because failure to pay results in your breaching a contract.

Depending on your state's common law, a bank that acts deliberately or recklessly when it wrongfully dishonors a check, might also be liable for punitive damages. For example, a bank would be acting deliberately if it dishonors a check after refusing to credit your account with amounts that should have been available for withdrawal, or if it deducts and then refuses to re-credit your account with amounts that aren't properly payable.

Normally, a bank that wrongfully dishonors a check is only liable to its depositor, not to the payee involved. If, however, it issues a certified check, then refuses to pay, it becomes liable to the payee.

A bank does not, however, wrongfully dishonor a check if it has justification for not paying it such as when it wasn't properly payable because of a forgery or insufficient funds, no drawer signature or improper endorsements.

A bank is not required to pay a check that is more than six months old. If a check is not cashed within this time, tell the bank whether you still want it paid. Telling your bank not to pay amounts to issuing a stop payment order. If the bank then pays the check anyway, it would usually be liable for the amount. See page 391 for what to do when a bank wrongfully dishonors a check you write.

YOUR RIGHT TO STOP PAYMENT ON A CHECK

As a checking account customer you can order your bank to stop payment on a check. If the bank does not heed the order it could be liable for the amount. It must be given enough time to act, of course: this could be several hours, depending on the bank's policy.

Such an order can be given orally or in writing. An oral stop payment order is binding for only fourteen days, unless it is confirmed in writing within that time. A written order, on the other hand, is binding for six months and can be further renewed in writing.

Stopping payment is a way of gaining some bargaining leverage in a dispute. You can be sued if you don't pay, of course, but that may be just what you want—it may be the only way to settle the matter.

Stopping payment would not enable you to avoid paying someone who qualifies as a holder in due course, though. The holder in due course would be entitled to collect the money regardless of whether you actually still owe the amount to the person to whom you gave the check. Since checks written by consumers are almost always simply deposited in the bank of the payee, the depository bank would usually be the first to qualify as a holder in due course. This is most likely to happen in cases where that bank has already paid out the money without being entitled to charge it back to the depositor's account by the time your bank returns the check unpaid. But given the way the bank collection process works, if your bank properly stops payment and returns the check, the depository bank would then usually still be entitled to charge the check back to the account of its own customer. So keep in mind that stopping payment on a check may have little practical value if the bank in which the check is deposited becomes a holder in due course because it paid out the check without being entitled to charge the amount back.

If your bank improperly fails to stop payment, there are situations in which it could charge the amount to your account anyway. But these involve fine-point technicalities that are far beyond the scope of this book.

If your bank improperly fails to stop payment on a check, insist that it re-credit your account. If it refuses and you are determined to get your money back from the bank rather than from the payee, promptly seek legal advice.

Only the drawer of a check can stop payment. If you endorse a check over to someone else you cannot do so.

WHEN AND HOW TO STOP PAYMENT

Stopping payment on a check can give you extra leverage for settling a dispute if you find out something has gone wrong with a purchase. It can also be worthwhile to stop payment on a check that is lost or stolen if you have issued a replacement, since in that case both checks could end up in the hands of the person who is entitled to negotiate them and both could be cashed.

Remember, though, that stopping payment costs money, and taking this step may be unnecessary if a lost or stolen check is made payable to the order of a named person who lost it or from whom it was stolen. In this case, no one else can properly negotiate the check and it would not be properly payable by your bank over a forged endorsement.

You must provide your bank with sufficient information for it to identify the check on which you want payment stopped, including: (1) the printed check number; (2) your account number; (3) the name of the person to whom the check is made payable; and (4) the amount of the check. If you are unsure about a point don't guess just to fill in the blanks, because giving the wrong information can result in the bank losing its liability.

When trying to stop payment, the first thing to do is find out if the bank has already paid the check. If not, then ask how long it takes to implement a stop payment order. If the normal procedure takes too long, and stopping payment is very important, ask about any special procedure the bank may have for speeding up matters.

Because timing is critical, most stop payment orders are initiated by phone. Be sure to make a note of the person's name and title, the date and time of the call, and the information you provide. As noted previously, to make the order effective for more than fourteen days you must send written confirmation within that time.

Banks usually have forms for stop payment orders, but you could also use this sample letter to confirm your verbal request.

200 Witchtree Lane
Anytown, USA 00000

June 1, 19___

Mr. J. Teller
Branch Manager
Riverview Branch
Hometown National Bank
Anytown, USA 00000

Dear Mr. Teller:

This is to confirm the verbal stop payment order I gave to Mr. C. Stopper on May 31, 19___ , at 4:00 P.M. requesting that the bank stop payment on check number 410 drawn on my checking account number 000000-00 and made payable to the ABC Company for $1,1250.73. (Mr. Stopper confirmed the bank would take special steps to implement the order immediately.)

I am requesting the bank stop payment on this check because the amount is no longer due or owing to the payee (or identify other reason for stopping payment, such as: the check was issued by mistake; the check was apparently lost or stolen and I issued my check number 459 as a replacement on May 31, 19___) and I would therefore sustain a loss should my check number 410 be paid. (And since my check number 410 has apparently been lost or stolen, it would be advisable for the bank to take appropriate precautions to avoid payment over unauthorized endorsements.)

Thank you for promptly implementing my stop payment order and ensuring that the bank does not make payment on my check number 410.

Sincerely,

If you stop payment, don't add the amount back to your account until you are sure the check has actually been stopped.

If your bank improperly pays a check over a stop payment order, you can adapt the following sample letter to insist the bank re-credit your account.

100 Witchtree Lane
Anytown, USA 00000

June 15, 19___

Mr. J. Teller
Manager
Riverview Branch
Hometown National Bank
Anytown, USA 00000

Dear Mr. Teller:

This is to notify you that the bank has improperly paid, and charged to my account, check number 410 for $1,250.73 drawn on account number 000000-00 and made payable to the order of the ABC Company, despite my having given the bank a stop payment order on the check.

I gave the bank my verbal stop payment order at 4:00 P.M. on May 31,

19___, which I then confirmed in writing on June 1, 19___. I requested the bank to stop payment on the check because (give the reason).

But when the bank returned the canceled checks with my account statement for the period ending June 10, 19___, which I received on June 14, I discovered that the bank had, instead, paid check number 410 on June 5, 19___ and charged the amount to my account even though the bank had by then had more than enough time to implement my stop payment order.

I have now sustained a loss equal to the amount of the check paid by the bank since that amount was not, in fact, due or owing to the payee for the reasons I described when I requested the bank to stop payment. The payee would not have obtained payment but for the bank's negligence in failing to stop payment.

The bank is, therefore, immediately to re-credit my account for the amount of the check which it had an obligation not to pay and which it cannot properly charge to my account as provided by the Uniform Commercial Code.

I hope you will give this matter your prompt attention and immediately recredit my account so we may resolve it without my having to hold the bank liable for its failure to stop payment and for improperly charging my account for the amount of that check.

Sincerely,

If, after initially notifying the bank, you are not able to settle the problem promptly, seek legal advice.

TAKING CORRECTIVE ACTION WHEN THINGS GO WRONG

There are specific steps you should take when you encounter the following problems:

- Loss or theft of blank checks.
- Loss or theft of checks you have written.
- When your bank wrongfully dishonors a check.
- Amounts improperly charged to your account and/or items that were not properly payable by your bank.

LOSS OR THEFT OF BLANK CHECKS

The loss or theft of blank checks can result in someone trying to loot your account. Although it's up to your bank to avoid paying checks if your signature has been forged, promptly notifying the bank about the situation eliminates the possibility of negligence on your part.

The following sample letter illustrates how to go about it. It is best to hand the letter to a bank official in person. Tak a duplicate with you and ask him or her to sign your copy.

200 Witchtree Lane
Anytown, USA 0000

June 1, 19___

Mr. J. Teller
Manager
Riverview Branch
Hometown National Bank
Anytown, USA 00000

Dear Mr. Teller:

   *I am notifying you that my checkbook register and checkbook contain-
ing (an unknown number of blank checks numbered from 201 to 225/eight
blank checks numbered from 218 to 225) were lost or stolen on or about
May 30, 19___ . My checking account number is 000000-00.*

   *(Since my checkbook register is missing along with the blank checks, I
cannot accurately determine the number of missing blank checks, but they
are included within the series of check numbers described above.)*

   *Having notified the bank of the loss or theft of these checks, I expect
the bank to refuse to pay any checks not properly payable.*

Sincerely,

   Once you know about the loss or theft of blank checks, promptly review all canceled checks the bank returns and immediately report any forgeries.

   If you lose a large number of checks and are worried someone will loot your
account, either withdraw all but the approximate amount of money needed to cover
any outstanding checks and close the account when they have cleared, or close the
account and be prepared to settle up with those to whom your outstanding checks
will be returned unpaid.

   Since your bank must refuse payment of checks not actually signed by you (or
someone else specifically authorized to do so), it isn't necessary to stop payment.
Notifying the bank about the loss or theft prevents all questions about whether your
negligence contributed to any forgeries that result.

LOSS OR THEFT OF CHECKS YOU HAVE WRITTEN

If a check you send to someone is lost or stolen, the potential problems depend on
whether the loss occurs before or after the check is received. If it occurs beforehand
then you haven't paid; if it occurs afterwards your obligation to pay under your
agreement is suspended so you will not be in default for non-payment.

   If the loss occurs before the payment is received, you may first learn of it from a
late payment notice or, worse, from the fact that the check is not cashed and returned
by your bank within a reasonable time.

   If a missing check involves a situation in which timely payment is especially important, then immediately contact the person to see if they've received the check. If they
have not, find out what you can do to make up for the late payment. Remember that
"the check is in the mail" ploy is one of the oldest dodges people use for putting off
creditors so be prepared for a skeptical response. If you have a record of timely payment and it is obvious that you are trying to sort out the matter, your problem will
be taken a lot more seriously, of course.

   When a check goes missing you face a dual problem. On the one hand you have
not paid; on the other, you have a valid check out there that can be cashed by someone and later may even end up being cashed by the original payee.

   If the consequences of being considered in default could be very costly, you may
have little choice but to send a replacement check. If the consequences aren't likely
to be costly, then you could wait a while to see if the check turns up.

   If the check you sent was made payable to the order of a named person, your key
protection is the fact that the check cannot be negotiated further by anyone else. If
the bank pays over a forged endorsement it could be liable.

   When sending a replacement check, it's always wise to send a cover letter, too.
The following sample tells the company what you expect it to do if your first check
shows up, and establishes a rightful claim for a refund if it cashes both checks.

200 Witchtree Lane
Anytown, USA 00000

June 1, 19___

Mr. H. Biller
Accounting Department
ABC Company
100 Main Street
Anytown, USA 00000

Dear Mr. Biller:

Enclosed is my check number 516, dated today, for $728.50 which I am sending as a replacement for check number 462, dated April 27, which I had sent you on April 28 as payment for the amount due by May 15, 19___, under our agreement of January 18, 19___ (or otherwise specifi-cally identify the account or agreement).

(As I explained to Mr. Billing on May 30 when I called about this matter, my check number 462 for $728.50 was apparently lost since you had not received it as of that date./Since I was notified on May 29 that payment was overdue when my check number 462 for $728.50 should already have been received and paid, it was apparently lost.)

I am, therefore, immediately sending a replacement to ensure prompt payment and hope that this will satisfactorily resolve this matter.

I am, however, only authorizing you to obtain payment on one of the two checks I have now issued for the same payment and if you receive my original check number 462 before or after receiving the enclosed replace-ment, then please void and return to me whichever of the two checks is received last.

And if the replacement check is cashed, please verify for me that the company neither received nor obtained payment on my check number 462 and that it will not do so should it be received at some later date.

Thank you for your cooperation.

Sincerely,

If you plan to stop payment on the original check, replace the last two paragraphs with the following:

"Since I am sending you a replacement, I am stopping payment on my check number 462. If you receive that check or if it is returned to you unpaid, please void it and return it to me upon obtaining payment on the replacement check I am enclosing."

It's up to you how far you want to trust someone with two checks for the same amount. A reputable company should honor your request and cash only one of the two checks, but slip-ups are made. If the amount for both checks is more than you can cover in your account, your best bet is to stop payment on the original check. Stopping payment is also your safest course if the payment of both checks would result in your paying more than the total amount still owed. This way, any overpay-ment can't simply be credited toward other amounts you may owe and so necessitate a battle to try to get the money back. If both checks end up being cashed by the payee, immediately request a refund or at least insist the overpayment be promptly credited to any amount outstanding if that is what you wish. (See page 465 for how the Truth in Lending Act can help you recover overpayments involving credit arrangements.)

The following sample letter illustrates how you could request a refund.

200 Witchtree Lane
Anytown, USA 00000

June 20, 19___

Mr. H. Biller
Accounting Department
ABC Company
100 Main Street
Anytown, USA 00000

Dear Mr. Biller:

I am hereby requesting that the ABC Company immediately (refund to me/credit to the outstanding balance now due under our agreement of January 18, 19___/credit to my Easy Money account, account number 000-00000-000), the $728.50 overpayment which resulted when the ABC Company obtained payment on my check number 462 dated April 27, 19___, and my check number 516 dated June 1, 19___.

As I explained in my letter of June 1, 19___, check number 516 was sent as a replacement for check number 462 which had been set for the amount due May 15, 19___. I issued the replacement because your company had apparently failed to receive the one I originally sent (copy of my letter enclosed).

But contrary to my request that the company avoid cashing both checks, it has, in fact, obtained payment on both (copies of the canceled checks are enclosed).

There is now immediately due me the $728.50 overpayment which occurred as a result of the company's gross failure to exercise due care in this matter.

This amount is to be immediately refunded (credited to my account) as I have already indicated.

Since time is of the essence to me, I expect that the ABC Company will promptly and properly account for this overpayment as I have requested. I do, however, reserve my rights to hold the company liable for damages I sustain because it has obtained payment on both checks despite my specific authorization to obtain payment on only one of the two checks.

Sincerely,

If you don't issue a stop payment order, you could put the bank on notice about the possibility the check could be cashed over a forged endorsement.

200 Witchtree Lane
Anytown, USA 00000

June 1, 19___

Mr. J. Teller
Manager
Riverview Branch
Hometown National Bank
Anytown, USA 00000

Dear Mr. Teller:

I am notifying you that my check number 462 dated April 27, 19___, for $728.50 made payable to the order of ABC Company and drawn on my checking account, number 000000-00, is apparently missing. I have been informed by the payee that the check has not been received as of this date.

Since this check has therefore apparently been lost or stolen, it would be advisable for the bank to take appropriate precautions to ensure that payment for this check is not made over unauthorized endorsements.

Thank you for your cooperation.

Sincerely,

If the check you issued was lost by or stolen from the payee, he or she could then ask you for a replacement. As noted previously, if you refuse the person can sue you for the amount. If he does, however, the courts may require him to put up adequate security to protect you from paying twice and to cover other expenses you may incur. So it could be advantageous to refuse to issue a replacement and make the other person sue you for the money. Your payment obligation under your agreement is suspended so you wouldn't be considered in default; and it can be risky to issue a replacement check in such situations because you cannot be sure how the other person endorsed the check before it went missing so that it could be properly negotiated further.

There are alternative initial steps you can take in such situations; one is refusing to issue a replacement check, the other is replacing the check under certain conditions.

If a lot of money is involved, always seek legal advice.

The following sample shows how you can state your refusal to issue a replacement check.

100 Witchtree Lane
Anytown, USA 00000

June 1, 19___

Mr. T. Billing
Accounting Department
ABC Company
100 Main Street
Anytown, USA 00000

Dear Mr. Billing:

This is to inform you that I am declining to issue a replacement for check number 462 for $728.50 dated April 17, 19___, sent as payment for the amount due May 15, 19___, under our agreement of January 15, 19___ (or otherwise identify agreement involved).

You notified me on May 25 that, according to your records, the check is missing, and requested that I issue a replacement. I decline to do so since I lack adequate security that I will not also become obligated to pay the amount of the check I originally issued and which you received as payment.

Since you received the check I issued for $728.50 as payment due under our agreement of January 15, 19___, my obligation to pay that amount is suspended and you may not consider me as being in default under our agreement with respect to that payment.

To reduce the possibility of that check being cashed over any unauthorized endorsements, I am notifying my bank that the check is missing so that the bank can take appropriate precautions to prevent improper payment.

I am, however, prepared to reconsider my position and issue a replacement for check number 462 if the (ABC Company) reimburses me for the $_____ it will cost to stop payment and furnishes me adequate security which will fully indemnify me for all losses and expenses I may incur with respect to the missing check.

I am, of course, fully prepared to cooperate with you to resolve this matter to our mutual satisfaction.

Sincerely,

Always remember to be reasonably accommodating. If the company furnishes the adequate security mentioned in the last paragraph, that's likely to obligate you to issue a replacement. Such security could be a very definite written commitment to pay the amount of the lost check and all expenses you may incur because that check was properly or improperly paid. If you don't want to issue a replacement under any circumstances, then leave off that paragraph. Remember, however, that forcing the other person to sue you for the amount of the missing check does not build good relationships.

The following sample letter shows how you can notify the other person that you would be willing to issue a replacement under proper safeguards.

100 Witchtree Lane
Anytown, USA 00000

June 1, 19___

Mr. T. Billing
Accounting Department
ABC Company
100 Main Street
Anytown, USA 00000

Dear Mr. Billing:

This is in response to your letter of May 25, 19___, in which you requested a replacement for my check number 462 for $728.50, dated April 17, ___, sent as payment for the amount due on May 15, 19___, under our agreement of January 15, 19___ (or otherwise identify agreement involved). You indicated the check was apparently lost or stolen after you had received it as payment on May 5.

I am prepared to issue a replacement check as you requested if the ABC Company:

Furnishes me proof of the loss or theft, and certifies that the check was endorsed in a manner that prevents further negotiation of the check by anyone not authorized to obtain payment.

Reimburses me the $_____ it will cost to stop payment on the missing check.

Furnishes me adequate security which will fully indemnify me for the amount of the missing check, and all losses or expenses I may incur because of the proper or improper payment of the missing check.

I will not, however, issue a replacement check until the ABC Company satisfies these conditions since I otherwise lack adequate security that I would be fully compensated for losses and expenses I may incur in case the missing check is paid.

In the meantime, I am notifying my bank about the loss or theft of the check so it can take appropriate precautions to prevent the improper payment of the check.

And since you received as payment the check I issued for the $728.50 due on May 15 under our agreement, my obligation to pay that amount is suspended and you may not consider me in default under our agreement with respect to that payment.

I am, of course, prepared to cooperate with you in promptly having this matter resolved to our mutual satisfaction.

Sincerely,

Use the sample letter on page 388 to notify the bank, but alter the wording to make clear the check was lost by the payee or stolen.

WHEN YOUR BANK WRONGFULLY DISHONORS A CHECK

Two things will usually happen in quick succession when a bank bounces a check you write. Your bank will notify you that it has refused to pay your check and that it is charging you a check overdraft fee, and the person to whom you owe the money will demand payment.

If you had sufficient funds in your account, the bank would be responsible for wrongfully dishonoring your check. You would then still have to pay the person who failed to get the money, but you could at least hold your bank responsible for damages you sustained as a result of its actions.

If you didn't have sufficient funds but you do have a check overdraft credit line, you bank's failure to pay could also count as wrongfully dishonoring a check. A bank may argue otherwise and the issue is not clear-cut, but you may as well argue the point, at least initially. Then let your bank decide how pleasant it could be to fish in those waters.

Although you may not know exactly what has gone wrong when you first learn your bank has wrongfully dishonored a check, the following sample letter shows how you can notify the bank and insist that it correct its mistake. Leave open the possibility of holding the bank accountable for damages.

You should, of course, revise the wording to identify more than one check that was wrongfully dishonored.

200 Witchtree Lane
Anytown, USA 00000

June 1, 19___

Mr. J. Teller
Manager
Riverview Branch
Hometown National Branch
Anytown, USA 00000

Dear Mr. Teller:

This is to notify you that the bank has wrongfully dishonored my check number 510 dated May 20, 19___, for $250 which was drawn on my *checking account, number 000000-00, and which was made payable to the order of the ABC Company for payments due June 1, 19___, on my Easy Money credit account.*

I was informed that the bank had dishonored this check when its written notification of May 25 was delivered to me on May 31, 19___.

Contrary to the bank's claim that my account lacked sufficient funds to pay the check on May 24, 19___, my records show that at all times the account had sufficient funds to pay all properly payable checks as long as the bank had properly credited and debited my account. On May 5, 19___, I had reviewed the checking account statement for the period ending May, 19___, and found that the amounts in my checkbook records and in the bank's statement balanced, and I have not since then issued checks for more than the amounts that should have been credited to and available for withdrawal from my account. I cannot, therefore, see how my account lacked sufficient funds to pay all items in question.

I therefore request the bank immediately review and take all appropriate steps to account for and make available for withdrawal all amounts that were and should be available for withdrawal. The bank is also to take immediate care to prevent the dishonoring of any further checks that are properly payable out of my account. The bank is also immediately to reverse all charges it has imposed on my account as fees for the return of the check.

Prompt action by the bank is essential if I am to minimize my damages and have made available to me the funds deposited in the account so that I can promptly pay those whose checks were wrongfully dishonored.

Although I hope to resolve the matter of the wrongfully dishonored checks with the payee so as to minimize my damages, I do reserve the right to hold the bank liable for all damages I may suffer. And to help minimize the damages, I request the bank notify the payee involved that the failure to pay the check was not, in fact, due to insufficient funds in my account as reported by the bank, but due to the bank's error.

I will appreciate your giving this matter your immediate attention.

Sincerely,

If the bank dishonors other checks before the problem is corrected, make appropriate changes in the basic sample letter above to inform the bank. To avoid this problem, though, you are better off transferring enough funds into the account to make up whatever shortage the bank claims exists.

NOTIFYING THE BANK OF DAMAGES

The following sample letter shows how to notify the bank of damages you sustained because it wrongfully dishonored your check. If the damages involve a lot of money, seek legal advice.

100 Witchtree Lane
Anytown, USA 00000

June 15, 19___

Mr. J. Teller
Manager
Riverview Branch
Hometown National Bank
Anytown, USA 00000

Dear Mr. Teller:

This is to notify you that there is now due from the bank $_____ I have sustained as damages because the bank wrongfully dishonored my check number 510 as described in my letter of June 1, 19__ .

As described below, this amount is due as damages for the following losses I incurred as a result of the bank having wrongfully dishonored that check:

(Describe and state the amounts due as damages for losses)

I request that the bank promptly reimburse me for these damages.

I do, however, reserve my right to hold the bank liable for other damages I may sustain at least to the fullest extent provided by the Uniform Commercial Code.

I will appreciate your giving this matter your immediate attention so that we may promptly resolve it.

Sincerely,

If the bank doesn't pay the damages, your only real leverage is to sue. It is, however, usually worthwhile to request reimbursement for damages, especially for actual out-of-pocket expenses.

PAYING A DISHONORED CHECK

Whether or not a check is wrongfully dishonored, you still have to pay the amount, of course.

When you do so, insist the person requesting payment present the returned check before you pay it. Ask the payee to mark the original check "paid" to avoid further complications. Also get a receipt.

If you cannot deal with the payee in person, explain that the check was wrongfully dishonored and ask the person to deposit the check again. (You can also ask your bank to suggest the person put the check through.)

If the payee insists on a different means of payment this time, such as a certified check, there is no easy way to get the unpaid check back. Your most practical alternative may be to simply pay the amount with a certified check, ask the payee to mark the original check paid and to return it to you, and stop payment on that original check.

The following sample is a cover letter you could adapt when sending payment for the returned check, but obviously you must alter the wording to fit your situation.

100 Witchtree Lane
Anytown, USA 00000

June 10, __

Dear Mr. Billing:

As requested by you on June 3, 19__, I am enclosing a certified check for $735 as payment for the $728.50 due on my check number 462 which was (wrongfully dishonored/returned as unpaid) by my bank. The enclosed payment includes the $7.50 for charges due because the check was returned unpaid.

The amount of check number 462 was for the payment due on May 15, 19__, under our agreement of January 15, 19__ (or otherwise identify the bill your are paying), and I am now making this payment with the enclosed certified check.

Upon receipt of the certified check, please mark as paid and return to me check number 462 and credit my account for the payment I had made with that check.

And since I am sending you a certified check, I am stopping payment on check 462.

I regret that my check number 462 was returned unpaid (but it was due to circumstances beyond my control. My bank wrongfully dishonored the check, and I have asked the bank to verify this for you).

Sincerely,

Put the following kind of notation on the front of the certified check:

"As payment for amount due on May 15, 19___, made by check number 462 which was returned unpaid."

Put the following kind of notation on the back of the check:

"This check can be accepted by payee only as payment in full of check number 462 drawn on account 000000-00 at Hometown National Bank and which was returned unpaid to payee."

Getting a written record that you have paid the amount called for by a dishonored check would almost always be enough to prevent anyone else from collecting the amount if the check was negotiated further. Remember, no one can become the holder in due course of a negotiable instrument after it has been dishonored; a fact which the bank would note on any check it refused to pay. So proof of having paid the amount would count as proof of payment against anyone else trying to collect on the check.

If you use a certified check, and note on it that it is being issued as payment for the dishonored check, ask the bank to provide you with a copy of the paid certified check.

CONTESTING AMOUNTS IMPROPERLY CHARGED TO YOUR ACCOUNT

The following sample letter can be adapted to notify your bank that it has charged your account with an amount that is not properly payable and to insist it take appropriate corrective steps. Identify the amount as specifically as you can and state the reasons why the bank should not have paid or deducted it from your account. If someone forged your signature as drawer, for instance, say something like: "The signature on check number 224 made payable to James Conman is unauthorized." (See page 380 for the most common reasons why amounts may not be properly payable.)

If the problem involves an obvious error the bank is likely to correct without fuss, you can, of course, tone down the letter.

Ask a bank official to acknowledge receiving the letter if you hand it over in person, or else send it by certified mail.

100 Witchtree Lane
Anytown, USA 00000

June 3, 18___

Mr. J. Teller
Manager
Riverview Branch
Hometown National Bank
Anytown, USA 00000

Dear Mr. Teller:

This is to notify you that the bank has improperly charged $_____ to my checking account, account number 000000-00 (which has also resulted in the bank wrongfully dishonoring check number 510 for $250 about which I notified the bank on June 1, 19__).

I discovered on June 2 that the $_____ had been improperly charged to my account when I reviewed the account statement for the period ending June 1 and the canceled checks which the bank furnished me on June 1. I then found the bank had (describe what has happened based on the information furnished by the bank). I discovered on June 1 that the bank had improperly charged $_____ to my account when, upon my having notified the bank that it had wrongfully dishonored the check described above, the bank informed me that it had (describe what has happened based on the information the bank supplies).

But that amount was not properly payable, nor should it have been charged to my account because (state why). (I had, in fact, informed the bank about this possibility when I notified the bank on May 1 that [describe].)

I therefore request the bank immediately re-credit to my account the $_____ which was improperly charged to it (and which should have been available for the payment of check number 510 when it was presented for payment on May 25, 19__, when the bank, instead, wrongfully dishonored it./The bank is also to reverse immediately the $_____ it charged to my account for returning the check.) And the bank is to take immediate care to prevent without fail the dishonoring of any other checks that are properly payable out of my account. I am not, however, hereby limiting my claims for any further damages for which the bank would be liable.

I hope the bank will promptly carry out its obligations with respect to this matter so I sustain no further damages.

Sincerely,

USING A PARTIAL PAYMENT CHECK FOR SETTLING A DISPUTE

If you give someone a check for the full amount owed and the check is properly paid, it counts as payment of the underlying obligation.

But if you are involved in a dispute about how much you owe, giving someone a "payment-in-full" check for less than the total amount can result in a full settlement of the dispute if the other person cashes the check. Doing this is regarded as making an offer of an "accord and satisfaction" which the other party accepts by cashing the check. The person who cashes the check in such circumstances in effect gives up his claim for the rest of the money (i.e., the amount in dispute which you didn't pay when you gave a payment-in-full check).

A payment-in-full check that a seller cashes counts as a settlement of the dispute *only* if you and the seller are involved in a good faith dispute about what you owe. In other words, you must have a valid claim that could entitle you to pay less than the amount the seller claimed was due.

If you make a partial payment, you must *notify* the seller. As explained on page 324, the Code entitles the buyer to deduct from the price still due, any damages suffered because the seller breached the contract. But to use this right, you must notify the seller first.

You must also identify on the check the reason why you don't owe the rest of the amount, and make clear that the check is as payment in full of all amounts due under the agreement. See page 397 for sample notation.

To be sure that the cashing of a payment-in-full check will count as a full settlement, pay something more than the amount you claim is actually still due. The reason for this is that some courts have ruled that payment of just the amount the buyer claims is due does not result in a settlement in full even though the seller may cash the check. The "something more" you pay should be a reasonable amount in relation to what you think you owe; a compromise offer for settling the dispute. In effect, you will be saying something like: "I only owe you $100, but to settle it right now, I am willing to pay you $_____ , and if you take it, that's the end of it because I am giving you more than I would have to pay if I took my claim into court."

A seller who cashes a payment-in-full check under such conditions almost certainly gives up any further claims. Paying only what you owe can also work the same way, but paying something more is the surer way to do it. There is one possible exception to this: if the seller cashed the check and states he is doing so "under protest, all rights reserved." Very few courts have gone along with such a ploy; however, including the sample notation on page 397 should further reduce the seller's chances of success.

Using a payment-in-full check can be a quick way of settling a dispute. But keep the following points in mind:

• The seller doesn't have to accept the partial payment. You could then be in default under your agreement for failing to pay what you owe and the seller retains the right to demand payment of the disputed amount.

• You must put a dollar value on what you claim as damages, or—in other words—what the seller's breach of contract cost you.

• You must, of course, also be able to pay off the full amount that you admit you actually owe under the agreement.

• *Never* use a payment-in-full check as a way of trying to settle a dispute with someone if it's still important to continue a business relationship with that person. This method is one step away from a lawsuit, and using it doesn't foster good business relationships.

Here are some guidelines which give a general idea of when this technique is and is not likely to work.

It's not likely to work if you have a weak claim and/or if the payment you offer means the seller has to forgo a large portion of the amount due. If, for example, the agreement calls for you to pay $1,000 but you offer only $200, the seller is obviously more likely to refuse.

Of course, the stronger your claim that you don't owe the money, the stronger your bargaining position.

As a practical matter, a seller is likely to consider the following when deciding whether to accept your offer:

• What do I stand to gain and lose if I accept the offer? How likely is it that I could really collect more? How much more might I be able to collect despite the buyer's claims? Is any further amount I could collect enough to make it worth refusing this offer? How much could it cost me to collect a higher amount?

It's the very "iffiness" of a situation like this that may create the leverage for you to reach a settlement. Giving someone a payment-in-full check is, in effect, an ultimatum you could use after low-keyed steps of a negotiating strategy have failed to work and you want to force the issue to a showdown.

If it doesn't work and the seller refuses your check, there usually isn't much bargaining room left. Your options are then very simple: either pay what the seller demands, or prepare for a lawsuit.

Always send a payment-in-full check with a covering letter that explains your reason for doing so. The following sample letter assumes you have previously notified the seller about the breach and includes wording referring to previous steps you might have taken while trying to settle the dispute. Naturally, you must adapt the wording to fit your situation.

If you bought the goods on credit, see page 523 for how you could be entitled to withhold payments from a creditor.

100 Witchtree Lane
Anytown, USA 00000

August 10, 19___

Mr. P. Seller
Manager
ABC Sales Company
Century Mall
Anytown, USA 00000

Dear Mr. Seller:

Enclosed is my check for $____ which can only be accepted by you as payment in full for all amounts due under our agreement of April 15, 19___, for the purchase of (identify purchase).

But as I have already notified you on _____ , the product failed to conform to the requirements of our contract because (describe what was wrong).

And as more fully described below, I have sustained $____ in damages because of the product's failure to conform and your company's failure to carry out its obligations under our contract.

(Describe the damages and amount of the loss)

I (also notified you on _____ that unless we could promptly resolve this matter, I would deduct my damages from the $____ price still due under our agreement, but I have not, as of this date, received a response/am hereby notifying you that I am deducting those damages from the $____ price still due under our agreement).

Since I have already paid $____ of the price due under the agreement, I calculate that, upon deducting the $ ____ now due me as my damages, no more than $_____ would still be due or owing under our agreement.

But in order that we may promptly and fully settle your breach of our contract, I am enclosing my check for $175 which can, however, be accepted by you only as payment in full of all amounts due or owing under the agreement I have described.

Sincerely,

You should include the following notations on your check. On the front write: "Payment in full of disputed amount as noted on reverse side." On the back write (or type): "Buyer disputes the amount due and this check is offered and can only be accepted by payee as payment in full of all amounts due and owing under the agreement of _____ for the purchase of (briefly identify). This check must be endorsed by payee."

Wording like this, when combined with an explanatory letter, almost certainly settles a dispute and the seller can't claim any further payment once he cashes the check. Insisting that the payee endorse the check is a way of getting proof he accepts your terms.

Less elaborate wording can work just as effectively and at the same time increase the possibility the seller will take the check. For example, you could simply say: "Payment in full of disputed amount due under agreement of April 15, 19__, for purchase of (identify purchase)."

The seller can, of course, challenge the effectiveness of any wording by trying to collect the rest of the money anyway. But the more clearly you spell out the conditions, the less successfully he will be able to challenge them.

If your check is refused, and the seller demands payment there is one more step you could try. That is getting a certified check for the amount you had previously offered to pay and letting the seller know you are willing to send it as payment in full.

If you do this, make it clear that you are prepared to contest the seller's claim in court and that you will then hold him liable for all amounts you could be entitled to recover.

This is an extreme step, of course, and you should *never* take it unless you are fully prepared to push the dispute into court. If you cannot afford to lose, never take this step without seeking legal advice first. In effect, what you are saying with this offer is: "Take the money I am prepared to send or you can wait until hell freezes over before you get more—unless you can get a court to force me."

If you show you are determined not to pay more, the seller *may* reconsider and accept the settlement. The following sample letter only shows *how* you can demonstrate your determination. *You* have to decide whether you are willing to risk sending it.

200 Witchtree Lane
Anytown, USA 00000

August 18, 19__

Mr. P. Seller
Manager
ABC Sales Company
Century Mall
Anytown, USA 00000

Dear Mr. Seller:

I am acknowledging your return of my check for $_____ which I had sent you on August 10, 19__, as payment in full as I had stated in the accompanying letter (copy of that letter enclosed).

Although you claim the full amount is due, your claim is completely unwarranted for the reasons I have already described in that and other correspondence and discussions relating to this matter.

But in case we may still be able to settle this matter as I have already proposed, I have in the meantime secured a certified check for the $_____ I have already offered to pay as settlement in full as described in my letter of August 10. A copy of this certified check is enclosed.

I shall hold this check for you and am prepared to send it as soon as you tell me that you are prepared to accept it as payment in full for all amounts due under our agreement of April 15, 19__, for the purchase of (identify purchase).

If, however, you persist in demanding payment in full despite your breach of our contract rather than seeking to settle this matter as I have proposed, you leave me no choice but to contest your claim in court as a way of determining what amounts, if any, may actually still be due or owing after the deduction, to the fullest extent provided by law of all amounts due me as damages.

Sincerely,

If your payment-in-full check is cashed, *be sure* to keep the canceled check, or get a copy of the certified check from the bank after it has been paid.

If you decide not to take the extreme step just outlined, but to pay in full, here is a sample letter you could use for trying to preserve your rights. It helps you bow out of the dispute gracefully without completely caving in to the seller. To get damages, though, you would have to sue to collect them. Paying could weaken such a claim, so seek legal advice first.

100 Witchtree Lane
Anytown, USA 00000

August 18, 19

Mr. P. Seller
Manager
ABC Sales Company
Century Mall
Anytown, USA 00000

Dear Mr. Seller:

I am acknowledging your return of my check for $_____ which I sent you on August 10, 19__, as payment in full for all amounts due under our agreement of April 15, 19__, for the reasons stated in my letter of August 10, 19__ (copy of letter enclosed).

Although the claim you make in your letter of _____ that payment of the full amount is still due is unwarranted for the reasons I have already stated in my letter of August 10, and in other correspondence and discussions relating to this matter, since you insist that payment in full is due as originally called for by our agreement despite the damages I have sustained because of your breach, I shall, as you demand, pay the amount you claim is due. Enclosed is my check for $_____.

I am, however, paying under protest and to avoid being in default under our agreement, and I am reserving all rights to hold you liable to the fullest extent provided by law for all damages I have sustained.

But I am still prepared to settle this matter if you will now promptly reimburse me for the $_____ due and owing for damages I have sustained as a result of the breaches I have described.

Sincerely,

Alternatively, you could pay the seller only the amount you admit you owe and make it clear that your payment is payment in full but without using the payment-in-full notation on the check. Paying under these conditions wouldn't count as a settlement of the dispute, even if the seller takes the check. It leaves open the question of whether or not you still actually owe the disputed amount, and the seller could sue you for it—and/or try to take back any collateral he has. So making this kind of a partial payment can also be risky because you will simply be paying out more money without having any assurances the seller won't try to squeeze you for the rest. If the dispute involves a lot of money, you should not take this step without legal advice.

The following is a sample covering letter for this situation: it makes clear that a partial payment is payment in full and that you have deducted amounts you no longer owe. It includes wording for goods purchased on credit, describing risks the seller could be running if he considers you in default.

Certified Mail No. 1111122222

100 Witchtree Lane
Anytown, USA 00000

August 18, 19___

Mr. P. Seller
Manager
ABC Sales Company
Century Mall
Anytown, USA 00000

Dear Mr. Seller:

I am acknowledging your return of my check for $_____ which I sent you on August 10, 19___, as payment in full for all amounts due under our contract of April 15, 19___, for the reasons stated in my letter of August 10 (copy enclosed).

Although you insisted in your letter of _____ that payment in full is due, your claim is unwarranted for the reasons I have already stated in my letter and in other correspondence and discussions relating to this matter.

I am, therefore, as provided by the Uniform Commercial Code, deducting the $_____ no longer due or owing under our contract for the reasons I have already described to you, and am enclosing my check for $_____ which is as payment in full of all amounts due or owing for the price of (identify purchase) purchased under our agreement of April 15, 19___.

Please acknowledge immediately receipt of payment, credit my account as paid in full, and confirm your acceptance of my proposal for resolving this matter.

And since the payment I am making is payment in full of all amounts still due or owing under our contract, I am not in default under our contract and shall hold you liable for wrongful repossession and/or for deliberately and maliciously injuring my reputation if you make any untrue statements to anyone about the status of my account. Under the Uniform Commercial Code, your additional liability for wrongful repossession is equal to at least ten percent of the product's purchase price plus the finance charge. It could also subject you to further liability for conversion and punitive damages.

Moreover, upon this payment in full, there is no further outstanding obligation. And if a financing statement covering the product has been filed, you are to file a termination statement to terminate your security interest within ten days as required by the Uniform Commercial Code. If you fail to do so and do not cooperate in removing the lien, you will also be liable under the Uniform Commercial Code for $100 plus any losses I suffer because of your failure to do so.

Sincerely,

The last two paragraphs refer to the seller's potential liability and to obligations that are triggered when you have actually paid in full in situations where the goods were purchased on credit, and the seller (creditor) has a "security interest" in the goods, that is, they are collateral for the credit extended.

Although payment of less than the full amount would not count as settlement in full which prevents the seller from suing for more, if you actually owed only the amount you paid, the seller would also be unable to collect the rest. And if you didn't actually owe the amount you deducted after telling the seller you were doing so, you almost certainly would not be in default if you had paid everything you actually owed. That can make it very risky for a seller/creditor to treat you as being in default. The seller/creditor's liabilities are briefly described on page 532.

If your payment-in-full check is cashed, the seller might still try to collect the rest even though he would almost certainly no longer be entitled to it. The following sample letter illustrates how you could make it clear that you no longer owe the money.

100 Witchtree Lane
Anytown, USA 00000

September 15, 19___

Mr. P. Seller
Manager
ABC Sales Company
Century Mall
Anytown, USA 00000

Dear Mr. Seller:

This is in response to your letter of September 8 in which you request payment of the $_____ I had deducted from the amount due under our contract of April 15, 19___, for the reasons I have already explained to you.

But the amount you now claim is no longer due or owing under that contract since I sent you my check for $_____ dated _____ which was as payment in full of all amounts due or owing under that contract as I made clear both in my letter of (August 18, 19___), with which the check was enclosed, and on the check I used for making payment. This check was cashed by you and then paid by my bank on _____ so that you thereby accepted the settlement as payment in full of all amounts due or owing under that contract.

You are, therefore, to cease all further efforts to collect since there are now no outstanding obligations under that contract.

And if I discover that you have made any adverse reports about this account to any person or if you take any action based on my being in default which is contrary to fact, I shall then hold you liable for actual and punitive damages to the fullest extent provided by law.

Sincerely,

48 · Electronic Fund Transfers

Computers, electronic impulses, and plastic cards have given us a new method of payment: electronic fund transfers (EFT's).

Congress enacted the Electronic Fund Transfer Act in 1978 to protect consumers. It also authorized the board of governors of the Federal Reserve System to adopt regulations to flesh out the act's basic requirements. These are known as Regulation E.

States can also adopt their own laws to regulate EFT's, and a few have done so. If your state law differs from the federal law, your state's law applies when it provides more protection than the federal law.

WHAT ARE ELECTRONIC FUND TRANSFERS?

An EFT is a transfer of funds *initiated* through an electronic terminal, telephone, computer, or magnetic tape which authorizes a bank or other financial institution to pay out of or deposit funds into a consumer's account. This would, for example include payments you initiate at a point of sale terminal or automated teller machine, direct deposit or withdrawal of funds you initiate from your accounts, or a deposit you initiate at an automated teller machine to designate the account into which funds are to be deposited, such as when you deposit a check. It would cover payments you initiate by phone payment services or home computer terminals that can be directly hooked into your bank. It would also cover payments directly made into or out of your account by magnetic tapes.

Transferring funds by magnetic tape is a relatively new technology which has been developed as a way to eliminate checks. Here is how it usually works. The person who is paying you or the person you are paying would deliver the payment information to an originating bank which processes it and sends it by magnetic tape or other electronic means to a clearing house. The clearing house then sends the information to different banks holding the accounts to be credited or debited for the payments being made and the banks do so based on the payment information they receive. This method usually makes it possible for someone else to make direct deposits into your account or obtain direct payments from it without the use of checks. Such transactions require the pre-authorization of everyone involved, not only because of the EFT Act but also because the transfers would have to be validated so the funds could be properly credited or debited to your account by the financial institution involved.

Electronic fund transfers do not, however, include transfers *initiated* by checks, drafts or other *paper based* transactions. If you are making a deposit by check but initiate the deposit by using an automated teller machine, on the other hand, the depositing of the collected funds into the designated account would count as an electronic fund transfer.

WHEN THE EFT ACT DOES NOT APPLY

The act does *not* apply to the following:

• Check guarantee or check authorization services if they do not result in funds being directly debited or credited to your account. If the service does result in a direct credit or debit to your account, the transaction would be covered by the act.

The difference is that some check services merely "okay" or guarantee payment of a check without the funds being debited to your checking account until the check actually clears. But such services can also be electronically hooked into your bank so the amount of the check is debited to your account when the guarantee or authorization is given, rather than when the check actually clears, and, in effect, the check verifies the transaction.

- Wire transfers of funds you ask your bank to make for you.
- Transfers primarily involving the sale or purchase of securities or commodities that are regulated by the Securities and Exchange Commission or the Commodity Futures Trading Corporation.
- Certain automatic transfers a bank may make under an agreement with you, such as moving money from your savings to your checking account, at the same institution, crediting interest, or making a loan payment to itself.

Always ask at your bank or other financial institution if you're not sure whether a service is covered by the act.

THE ACCESS DEVICE

An *access device* is a card or code that can be used to access your account to initiate an EFT. It becomes an accepted access device when you:

- Request and receive or use the device, or allow others to do so.
- Request the validation of an unsolicited device that you may receive.
- Receive an access device as a renewal or as a substitute for one you formerly accepted.

The question of whether or not you have accepted a device affects your liability for unauthorized use.

OTHER DEFINITIONS THAT GOVERN HOW EFT'S ARE COVERED

Here is how the act defines other terms that spell out how EFT's are covered.

A *pre-authorized electronic fund transfer* is one the consumer authorizes in advance and which is to occur at regular intervals.

An *unauthorized electronic fund transfer* is one initiated from a consumer's account by someone other than the consumer when the other person doesn't have actual authority to do so and the consumer receives no benefit from the transfer. The act limits your liability for unauthorized transfers. But once you give someone your access device and allow transfers out of your account, you could become liable for further transfers made by that person unless you previously notify your bank that transfers by that person were no longer authorized. If a dispute arises, it is up to your bank to prove that a transaction was authorized (which could be hard to do) or that you are liable for unauthorized use according to the requirements spelled out by the act. But beware. If you claim someone used your access device for unauthorized transfers but you continue to use it for making transfers that are clearly authorized, it is likely to be easier for the bank to show the other transfers were also authorized. There are, of course, clear exceptions such as if someone duplicates or forges your access device.

An *electronic terminal* is any electronic device a consumer can use to initiate EFT's and includes point-of-sale terminals, automated seller machines or cash dispensing machines but it does not include a telephone operated by the consumer for initiating EFT's (and home computer terminals also may not be covered as electronic terminals). Transfers initiated by phone or home computers could be covered, but the phone (or home computer terminal) would not be an electronic terminal as defined by the act. As explained later, your bank must furnish documentation at the time you make a transfer at an electronic terminal as defined by the act.

An *account* includes any demand deposit (i.e. checking account), savings or other asset account held by a financial institution. A *financial institution* includes any bank, savings and loan association, mutual savings bank, credit union or anyone else who holds a consumer's asset account. For simplicity, this book refers to such institutions as "banks."

Let's look at the protections you have if you use electronic fund transfers.

RESTRICTIONS ON ISSUING ACCESS DEVICES

A bank or other financial institution can issue an access device only in response to a written or oral request, or as a renewal or substitute for one already accepted.

It can, however, distribute unsolicited access devices to account holders if *all* the following conditions are satisfied:

• The access device is not validated for use when distributed, the institution explains this fact, and tells you how to dispose of the card if you don't want it.
• An account of the rights and liabilities you would have upon validation are sent along with the card.
• The device can be validated *only* on your oral or written request and only *after* the bank verifies your identity by reasonable means, such as via a photograph, a fingerprint, a personal visit, or a signature comparison.

If someone sends you an unsolicited access device, think about whether you really want it before taking steps to validate it. Consider the mix of services that may be offered and the risks involved. If the device can only be used for initiating fund transfers from one account to another, for instance, or for paying particular bills by phone, or making deposits into your account, the potential for misuse is very limited. If the device can be used to make cash withdrawals, or to pay for purchases directly out of your account, there is obviously a much greater chance of unauthorized transfers occurring.

TERMS AND CONDITIONS THAT MUST BE DISCLOSED

A financial institution must disclose the key terms and conditions that affect the use of EFT services in a readily understandable written statement. The statement must be given to you at the time you contract for the services or before the first transfer is made.

These are the main terms and conditions a bank must disclose:

• A summary of your liability for unauthorized use of an access device.
• The telephone number or the address where the bank can be notified about unauthorized transfers.
• The bank's business days.
• The kind of transfers that may be made and any limitations on their number or monetary amount. (Details about the number or amount of transfers that can be made do not have to be disclosed if it is important for maintaining the security of the bank's system.)
• The charges imposed for making transfers.
• A summary of your right to obtain documentation for transfers.
• A summary of your right to stop payment of preauthorized transfers and the procedures involved.

• A summary of the bank's liability if it fails to stop payment of preauthorized transfers.

• The circumstances under which the bank would disclose information about your account to others.

• A notice worded in substantially the following way which spells out the procedures for resolving errors and your rights under those procedures:

"IN CASE OF ERRORS OR QUESTIONS ABOUT YOUR ELEC-TRONIC FUND TRANSFERS

"Telephone us at [_____]

or

"Write us at [_____] as soon as you can if you think your statement or receipt is wrong, or if you need more information about a transfer listed on the statement or receipt. We must hear from you no later than sixty days after we sent the first *statement on which the problem or error appeared.*

"(1) Tell us your name and account number (if any).

"(2) Describe the error or transfer you are unsure about, and explain as clearly as you can why you believe it is an error or why you need more information.

"(3) Tell us the dollar amount of the suspected error.

"If you tell us orally, we may require that you send us your complaint or question in writing within 10 business days.

"We will tell you the results of our investigation within 10 business days after we hear from you and will correct any error promptly. If we need more time, however, we may take up to 45 days to investigate your complaint or question. If we decide to do this, we will re-credit your account within 10 business days for the amount you think is in error so that you will have the use of the money during the time it takes us to complete our investigation. If we ask you to put your complaint or question in writing and we don't receive it within 10 business days, we may not re-credit your account.

"If we decide there was no error, we will send you a written explanation within three business days after we finish our investigation. You may ask for copies of the documents that we used in our investigation."

In general, the terms that *must* be disclosed cover the protection you have in case things go wrong, but your agreement may also spell out additional terms and conditions.

DOCUMENTATION THAT AN INSTITUTION MUST PROVIDE ABOUT ELECTRONIC FUND TRANSFERS

An institution must provide a written receipt at the time an EFT is initiated at an electronic terminal. The receipt must include the following information if applicable:

• The amount of the transfer, which can include any charges made for the transfer if the terminal used was owned or operated by someone other than the institution holding the consumer's account).

• The date the transfer was initiated.

• The type of transfer made and account(s) involved ("withdrawal from savings," for instance).

• The number or code which specifically identifies you as the initiator of the transfer, your account, or identifies the access device used.

• The name of the person from whom or to whom the funds are transferred. The bank does not have to provide this information if you furnish the other person's name in a way that prevents it from being duplicated on the receipt.

The information that must be documented helps verify the transfer you actually made in case something goes wrong. Be aware, though, that if you deposit funds, say by check, your receipt would not serve as proof of your actually having deposited the check or that the bank received it. See page 370 for possible problems you could run into when making deposits in automated teller machines, for instance. The written documentation of the transfer would, however, verify the account to which the deposited funds were to be credited.

PERIODIC ACCOUNT STATEMENTS

A bank must provide you with a periodic monthly or more frequent statement for the period in which electronic fund transfers are made. If no transfers occur, it must provide at least a quarterly statement.

The statement must show the following information:

• The account number(s) involved.
• The total fees and charges imposed for transfers. (Finance charges must be disclosed separately as required by the Truth in Lending Act.)
• The opening and closing balances for the account(s) during the period covered.
• Information about each transfer made, which must include, as applicable:

... The amount of the transfer, which can include certain fees charged for the transfer as shown on your receipt.
... The date on which the transfer was debited or credited to your account.
... The kind of transfer made and the type of account involved.
... The location of the electronic terminal where the transfer was initiated (this information is not required for deposits of cash or checks made at an electronic terminal).
... The name of the party to whom or from whom the funds were transferred. (Such names do not have to be included when deposits are made by check at an electronic fund terminal).

Note: The periodic account statement doesn't have to be furnished when a passbook (savings) or other type of asset account can *only* be accessed by preauthorized transfers. The institution can use other means to inform you of these transfers.

HOW DOCUMENTATION SERVES AS PROOF OF PAYMENT

What happens if an EFT payment doesn't get completed?

In this situation documentation can help you. If either the receipt you obtain when you initiate the transfer at an electronic fund terminal or your periodic statement shows the transfer was made to the person, it counts as evidence of the transfer if the payee sues you for non-payment. While such documentation is not considered complete proof in the same sense as a canceled check is, it would usually help show you are not in default. And it would help you hold the bank accountable for failing to complete the transfer.

It is very important to keep receipts and statements since they are the only written records you will have of making payments by electronic impulses.

PREAUTHORIZED TRANSFERS INTO YOUR ACCOUNT

There are different requirements for preauthorized EFT's depending on whether they involve transfers of funds into or out of your account.

Transfers into your account usually include various types of direct deposits by others. The EFT Act spells out how a bank must let you know whether transfers have been properly made.

If preauthorized transfers from the same person or company are to be made into your account at least once every sixty days, the bank must use one of the following methods to inform you whether the transfer has been made *unless* the depositor specifically tells you payment has been made:

- It must give you oral or written notice within two business days after the transfer occurred.
- If a transfer does *not* occur as scheduled, it must provide you with a written or oral "negative" notice within two business days after the date when the transfer was supposed to have occurred.
- It must make a telephone line readily available for inquiries about transfers. The number must be listed on the initial disclosure notice, and on each periodic statement.

The act also requires an institution to credit your account for the amount as of the date preauthorized transfers are received. Usually this would be the date on which the institution is notified of the transfer to be made, but the act does not specify when such transferred funds are actually "received." That would instead be governed by other state or federal laws that apply to the payment being made. The easiest solution is to find out from your bank when preauthorized transfers count as being received. If time is important and you can get the money sooner by having it paid to you by check, then forget about electronic transfers.

The act's requirements only help you find out if a transfer has been completed as scheduled, of course. If it hasn't, you have to query the person who is supposed to pay the money.

PREAUTHORIZED TRANSFERS OUT OF YOUR ACCOUNT

Preauthorized transfers for payments out of your account require your written authorization, and you must be provided with a copy of the authorization.

- There are different ways of preauthorizing transfers. You can authorize your bank to do so as a way of paying recurring bills. Or you can authorize the payee to initiate the transfers.

If the payments are for a fixed sum, only one authorization is needed for the series of payments. If the payments vary in amounts, then your bank or the payee must notify you in writing of the amount and scheduled date of transfer at least ten days beforehand. In the latter case, you have the option of choosing to have advance notification only in certain circumstances. Say, for instance, you preauthorize the telephone company to collect your monthly phone bill. Instead of insisting the company notify you in advance about each bill, you could request notification only if the bill is more than $50, say, or only if the bill is $20 more or less than the last one.

YOUR RIGHT TO STOP PAYMENT OF PREAUTHORIZED TRANSFERS.

The EFT Act entitles you to stop payment of any preauthorized transfer. To do so, you must give the bank written or oral notice at least three *business* days before the scheduled date of the transfer. As long as you comply with this requirement, the bank has no leeway for failing to stop payment. The act, however, only entitles you to stop payment of preauthorized EFT's. Other EFT's are considered completed when initiated so you cannot stop payment on them unless your state's law or your account agreement could entitle you to do so. So unless you can still stop payment, any payment by EFT is like paying cash.

If you give your bank an oral stop payment order, it can request that you confirm the order in writing within fourteen days. If you don't do so, the order is no longer binding and the bank could proceed to make the transfer.

Once you stop payment of a preauthorized transfer, you may have to reauthorize further payments later.

But as with checks, stopping payment on a preauthorized transfer doesn't mean that you no longer owe that money.

YOUR RIGHTS IF TRANSFERS ARE NOT COMPLETED BECAUSE OF SYSTEM MALFUNCTIONS

What happens to your payment obligation if the transfer is not properly completed and the payee doesn't get credit for the amount debited to your account?

Providing the person agreed to be paid by an EFT, your payment obligation is suspended until the malfunction is corrected and you would not be considered in default. Having documentation that you initiated the transfer, such as the receipt from an automated teller machine or your periodic statement, helps verify that non-payment is a banking error.

If the payee later makes a written request for payment by a method other than an EFT, the request would end the suspension of your obligation and you would then have to pay by other means or you could then be considered in default.

If this happens and your account is debited for a payment that has not been completed, immediately insist your bank re-credit your account.

YOUR LIABILITY FOR UNAUTHORIZED TRANSFERS

Under the EFT Act and Regulation E a consumer is liable for an *unauthorized* transfer only under the following conditions:

- The access device used has been accepted by you. (A forged or duplicated device would not count.)
- The bank has provided some way of identifying the consumer to whom the device was issued, such as a signature, photograph, fingerprint. While the law does not actually require a bank to do this, if it fails to do so, it cannot hold you liable for any unauthorized transfers.
- The bank must have provided you with a written summary of your liability for unauthorized use, as provided by the EFT Act, other state law that applies, and the agreement involved, and has furnished you with the telephone number or address of the person or office to be notified about possible unauthorized transfers.

AMOUNTS FOR WHICH YOU COULD BE LIABLE

You have no liability for unauthorized transfers that occur *after* you notify the bank about the loss or theft of an access device or about the possibility of unauthorized transfers. Your maximum initial liability *before* you notify your bank is either $50 or the amount of the unauthorized transfer—whichever is less.

Under certain circumstances, though, your liability can substantially exceed $50. These circumstances occur if either or both of the following happen:

1. You fail to notify the bank within two business days after learning about the loss or theft of an access device. In this case, your maximum liability for unauthorized use could be as high as $500 unless the *sum* total of the following amounts would result in your owing less:

• The amount of unauthorized transfers occurring before the two business days you have for notifying the institution about the loss or theft up to a maximum of $50.
• The amount of unauthorized transfers occurring after the two days and up until you finally give notification, which could leave you liable for an additional $450 above the initial maximum. To hold you accountable for this amount, the bank in effect has to prove it suffered the loss only because of your failure to notify the institution.

2. You fail to notify your bank about an unauthorized transfer within sixty days after the periodic statement on which it appeared was sent to you. Your liability could then be the *sum* total of the following amounts:

• The amount of unauthorized transfers occurring within the sixty-day period up to a maximum of $50.
• The amount of unauthorized transfers occurring after the sixty-day period and up until the time you finally notify your bank. (Again, your bank would have to show it suffered the loss because of your failure to notify it.)
• The amount of unauthorized transfers occurring after you fail to notify your bank about the loss or theft of a device within two business days after learning about it, up to the $500 maximum. (It is again up to the bank to prove it suffered the loss because of your failure to notify.)

So if you fail to notify an institution, your liability could match what's in your account. If this should happen, seek prompt legal advice.

The law governing your liability for unauthorized use of a *credit card* is quite different. But financial institutions are now making it possible for some credit cards to be used as access devices. When you have a multi-purpose card, therefore, which law governs your liability?

The EFT Act applies if the card is used for making an unauthorized electronic fund transfer from any asset account, or that results in an extension of credit by triggering any kind of overdraft loan arrangement tied to the asset account.

The law which governs the use of credit cards, the Truth in Lending Act, applies if the unauthorized use of a multi-purpose card results in a direct charge to your line of credit or credit card account (such as if the card was used for getting a cash advance that was directly charged to your credit card account as an extension of credit).

HOW TO NOTIFY YOUR BANK ABOUT UNAUTHORIZED TRANSFERS

Since you must notify your bank or other financial institution about the possibility of unauthorized transfers to avoid liability, what counts as correct notification?

You are considered to have notified the institution once you have taken such steps as are reasonably necessary to provide the institution relevant information about the possibility of unauthorized transfers.

You may give notification in person, by phone, or in writing. If you send a written notice, it is considered given when you deposit the letter in the mail; or, in the case of a telegram, when you deliver the notice for transmission.

If you mail your notification, get a mailing receipt. If you notify the bank in person, make a copy of the notice and get it signed to acknowledge receipt. If you notify the bank verbally, make a note of the date and time you called, and the person you spoke to, then send written confirmation. While the act doesn't require you to take these specific steps, it does require you to take "reasonable" steps to notify your bank. The above procedures will verify that you have done so. If you notify a bank by phone, it is likely to give you a verification code number which confirms your notification and which you should be sure to write down.

If you've made the mistake of keeping your personal code or identifying number alongside the access device and both have been lost or stolen, don't waste a second before notifying your bank.

ERRORS A BANK MUST INVESTIGATE

The act and Regulation E require a financial institution to investigate and correct the following types of errors:

- An unauthorized electronic fund transfer.
- An incorrect electronic transfer from or to your account. (Which usually means a transfer that wasn't properly completed.)
- Omissions from a periodic statement of transfers, such as a deposit or payment you made. Such an omission doesn't mean the item will appear on next month's statement; it is a sure sign the transfer wasn't made correctly.
- A computational or bookkeeping error. Your bank may have made the transfer correctly but failed to account for the amount properly on your statement.
- The payment of an incorrect amount of money from an electronic fund terminal. A cash dispensing machine might give you an envelope containing $20 rather than the $50 you requested, for instance. Mistakes like this happen occasionally.
- A transfer that is not correctly identified on your receipt or periodic statement. (See page 405 for the identifying information that must be included.)
- A consumer's request for clarification about a transfer, or other additional information.

NOTIFYING AN INSTITUTION ABOUT AN ERROR

The summary of your billing error rights that an institution must give you spells out what you must do to notify an institution about an error to trigger the billing error resolution procedure.

You must notify the institution about an error within sixty days after either of the following:

- The date the statement contining the error was sent to you.
- The date additional documentation or clarification was sent at your request.

PROCEDURES FOR INVESTIGATING ERRORS

A financial institution can follow one of two procedures while investigating errors.

1. It may conduct an investigation and tell you the results within ten business days after receiving your notification. It must, of course, make appropriate corrections if necessary.

2. Alternatively, the bank may take up to forty-five *calendar* (not business) days to investigate the error and give you the results. If your bank uses this option, though, it must re-credit your account with the amount you have specified to be in error and any applicable finance charges within ten business days after receiving your notification. It must also inform you that it is doing so, and that you have the full use of those funds while it investigates the matter, not more than two business days after it re-credits your account.

There is one exception to the requirement for re-crediting the entire amount in dispute. If the error involves a possible unauthorized transfer, your bank does not have to re-credit up to the $50 maximum amount for which you could be liable.

If the investigation shows that no error has occurred, the bank can debit your account for the amount. It must first notify you that it is doing so, however, and it must continue to pay certain items as described below.

If your bank requires that you confirm a verbal notification in writing, but you fail to do so, it must still comply with the requirements for investigating and correcting errors; but it does *not* have to re-credit the amount for the period of the investigation, and it would *not* be liable for the triple damages you could otherwise recover for certain violations (see page 412).

REQUIREMENTS FOR CORRECTING ERRORS

If the investigation shows an error has been made, your bank must correct it and make appropriate adjustments to your account; including crediting finance charges, and refunding any other fees and charges imposed as a result. But your bank does not have to return, or re-credit your account for up to the $50 maximum amount for which you could be liable in case of unauthorized transfers.

If there is a dispute about your liability, you may have to sue to get your money back. However, the bank must be extremely careful of liability because if it turns out to be wrong you may be entitled to recover triple damages under the civil liability provisions of the act (see page 412).

REQUIREMENTS IF NO ERROR OCCURRED

If your bank determines that no error has been made, or that the amount in dispute differs from your estimate, it must then:

- Send you a written explanation within three business days after completing its investigation. The notice must also inform you that you can request the documentation on which the findings are based.
- If your bank debits your account for the amount it temporarily re-credited during the investigation, it must inform you when the debit is completed. It must also let you know that it will continue to honor checks, drafts, and any pre-authorized transfers for five business days after transmitting the notice.

Different requirements govern billing errors involving open-end credit accounts (see page 470). But if an electronic fund transfer triggers a credit extension under a separate agreement for extending credit when an account is overdrawn, your bank must comply with procedures governing electronic fund transfers rather than open-end credit accounts. (There are some exceptions to this rule which involve fine-point technicalities that are beyond the scope of this book.)

There are situations in which the requirements governing open-end credit accounts give you more protection than those involving EFT's. (See Chapter 56.)

WHEN REQUIRING YOU TO USE EFT'S IS PROHIBITED

The act makes it illegal for anyone to force you to use electronic fund transfers in the following circumstances:

• To require you to repay a credit obligation by using preauthorized transfers.

• To require you to establish an account at a particular financial institution for the direct deposit of pay by EFT's as a condition for employment, but an employer can require you to have such an account as long as you are given a reasonable choice of what institution you can use.

WAYS A FINANCIAL INSTITUTION BECOMES LIABLE

There are three basic ways the EFT Act enables you to hold financial institutions accountable.

1. Liability for mishandling transfers

The act makes a bank liable for *all* damages directly caused by the following circumstances:

• A failure to make a transfer according to the terms and conditions of the account agreement, in the correct amount or in a timely manner, when it has been properly instructed to do so, unless:

(a) The account lacks sufficient funds.

(b) The funds are subject to legal restrictions, such as a garnishment.

(c) The transfer exceeds established credit limits.

(d) The electronic terminal runs out of money and you are unable to make a withdrawal.

• A failure to make a transfer because of "insufficient funds" if the bank has not correctly credited a deposit.

• A failure to stop payment of a preauthorized transfer when properly instructed to do so.

The act entitles you to hold your bank accountable for all damages that you suffer as a direct result of such failures. Suppose, for example, you are making fire insurance policy payments on your house by preauthorized transfers, but your bank fails to make them and your policy is canceled. If your house burns down while you are without coverage, your damages would be the amount of the loss the policy would have covered.

There are two ways the institution can get off the hook, though.

1. If it can demonstrate that its failure resulted from an act of God, or other circumstances beyond its control, or from a malfunction in the equipment which you, the consumer, knew about at the time.

2. If it can demonstrate that the failure resulted from a *bona fide* error, despite procedures it had instituted to avoid such errors.

In either of these two cases your bank's liability would be limited to actual damages you can prove resulted; a restriction that is intended to prevent consumers from recovering damages for such conditions as mental distress.

2. Liability for failing to correct billing errors

An additional liability is imposed on a bank that fails to correct an error as required by the act. This liability is triggered when:

• Your bank did not provisionally re-credit your account for the amount of the error within the required ten business-day period; *and* either did not make a good faith effort to investigate the error, or did not have a reasonable basis for believing the account was not in error.

• Or if your bank knowingly and willfully decided the account was not in error when that conclusion wasn't reasonable based on the evidence.

If you are suing your bank for failing to comply with the act, and a court finds that either of these points apply, you could recover three times the amount of your damages.

3. Civil liability for failing to comply with the EFT Act

A person or institution that fails to comply with the requirements of the act or with Regulation E may be liable for:

• Actual damages you sustain because of that failure.

• A minimum amount that is recoverable in addition to damages; not less than $100 but not more than $1,000.

• The cost of bringing suit plus attorney's fees as determined by a court.

There are some exceptions which could enable an institution to avoid civil liability, but as a practical matter they rarely apply. There is one exception, though, that can be very important. It involves errors that are resolved in accordance with the error resolution procedure, but which resulted in you sustaining additional damages even though the institution corrects the actual error that occurred. The requirements covering error corrections and the recovery of damages are very complicated and affect what damages you could recover if you initiate the error correction procedures and the institution *corrects* the error. If an institution's failure to comply with the act or mishandling of an EFT results in substantial losses, seek prompt legal advice rather than trying to do anything on your own to settle the problem. (You must, of course, still notify the bank about the loss or theft of an access device, or the possibility of an unauthorized transfer.)

ADMINISTRATIVE ENFORCEMENT AGENCIES

The EFT Act is enforced by different federal agencies depending on the type of financial institution involved, as the following list shows.

Type of institution	*Enforcement agency*
National Banks ("N.A." or "National" will be in bank's name)	Comptroller of the Currency Deputy Comptroller for Customer and Community Affairs 6th Floor—L'Enfant Plaza Washington, DC 20219
State banks that are members of the Federal Reserve System	Board of Governors of the Federal Reserve System Division of Consumer and Community Affairs 20th and C Streets, N.W. Washington, DC 20551
Banks that are NOT members of the Federal Reserve System but insured by FDIC (such as state banks and savings banks)	Federal Deposit Insurance Corporation Office of Consumer Compliance Programs 550 17th Street, N.W. Washington, DC 20429

Savings institutions insured by FSLIC and members of FHLB System (savings and loan associations)	Federal Home Loan Bank Board Department of Consumer and Civil Rights Washington, DC 20552
Federally Chartered Credit Unions	National Credit Union Administration Office of Consumer Affairs 1776 G Street Washington, DC 20456
Air Carriers	Civil Aeronautics Board Director, Bureau of Enforcement 1825 Connecticut Avenue Washington, DC 20428
Securities brokers and dealers	Securities and Exchange Commission Office of Consumer Affairs and Information Washington, DC 20549
Retail, department stores, consumer finance companies, all non-bank debit cards and certain other institutions	Federal Trade Commission Electronic Fund Transfers Washington, DC 20580

SOME PRECAUTIONARY MEASURES

You can help protect yourself by taking various precautions when using transfers.

• *Never* use an EFT to pay for a purchase, or to trigger an extension of credit, if it could be important to retain protection under the Fair Credit Billing Act for refusing payment. That act can help you when a seller doesn't deliver goods you have ordered, for example, or when you are involved in a dispute over a purchase made with a credit card.

• Electronic fund transfers that directly access an asset account are, generally speaking, considered payments rather than extensions of credit, even though a line of credit is tied into the account and can be triggered by a transfer. So if you initiate a transfer to pay for a purchase it means you can't take the payment back in case of a dispute. If a transfer triggers a line of credit, such as an overdraft loan, you would not have the protections the Fair Credit Billing Act makes available for disputes involving purchases made with credit cards.

• While it can be advantageous and convenient to link several kinds of accounts together so you can automatically access all the funds in several different ways, doing so is rather like building a battleship without watertight compartments. It's probably best to establish separate accounts for different purposes so you can limit trouble if it occurs.

You could set up a checking account, for instance, simply for initiating EFT payments and keep in it only the amount needed for making such payments. This would minimize the amount someone could tap by unauthorized transfers, and confine problems involving transfers to one account. You could then have another checking account which you could access only with checks; an account like this protects you against unauthorized withdrawals since you are not liable for a single penny paid out on a forged check unless you are negligent. As explained on page 381.

• Keep a composite account balance for all transfers made—particularly if you use various methods to access an account. Be sure to enter pre-authorized transfers on the scheduled payment date; not doing so can easily result in your account being overdrawn.

• If you are paying bills by pre-authorized transfers, be sure to have sufficient funds in the account on the scheduled dates. If you don't, your bank isn't liable for not making the transfers.

• Always keep transfer receipts and your periodic statements. A statement helps you demonstrate when an error first appeared. A receipt serves as evidence of a transfer made and is the only written record you have that could help you substantiate an error on a statement. Although it may not seem that way, EFT's are payments of money; throwing away these documents is like paying a bill in cash without getting a receipt.

• If you are making payments or transfers under circumstances in which you do not get a receipt, such as by a pay-by-phone service or a home computer terminal, write down all the details of the transfer and *be sure* to note any authentication code your bank supplies for verifying the transaction. If something goes wrong, the code may be the only record that you actually made the transfer.

• Promptly review periodic statements for accuracy and notify the institution about any unauthorized or incorrect transfers or other errors. Remember, you have sixty days to do so. If your bank's failure to make a transfer results in substantial damages, seek legal advice *before* you initiate the error resolution procedure.

• Keep the mailing envelope that shows when your bank sent you a periodic statement, or any other documentation you requested, until you are sure there is no error. If there is an error, it can help you show that you gave notification within the proper time period.

• Immediately report the loss or theft of any access device.

• *Never* keep your personal identification number (PIN) with your access device, and *never* give the number to anyone or use it in a way that someone else could copy. The PIN code and access device are two separate combinations that must be joined together to open the vault. If you let others in on those combinations, don't be surprised to find your account looted.

49 · Negotiating Strategy for Disputes Involving Electronic Fund Transfers

This chapter covers steps for settling the following problems involving electronic fund transfers:

- Reporting the loss or theft of an access device, or stopping its further use.
- Stopping preauthorized transfers.
- Notifying your bank about errors and losses resulting from incorrect transfers.

Since EFT's are usually hooked into accounts which can be accessed by other payment methods, one problem can trigger another, such as having a check bounce, for instance. If you have multiple problems, deal with each one separately and use different letters for covering each problem. In each letter, refer to the problem mentioned in the other letters.

STAGE ONE: OPENING SKIRMISHES

The initial step is to notify your bank as soon as possible about the problem. You could do so in person, or on the telephone. But always follow up by putting everything in writing. If you hand over the letter personally have your copy signed by the person you talk to. If you are dealing with a large institution, you may be told to call a specific number or to send a letter to a certain address where problems are handled.

REPORTING THE LOSS OR THEFT OF AN ACCESS DEVICE, OR STOPPING ITS FURTHER USE

The following sample letter shows how to notify your bank about the loss or theft of a device and/or to confirm verbal notification. It also includes alternative wording for informing your bank that a person is no longer authorized to make transfers. Naturally, all details are for illustrative purposes only and you must adapt the wording to fit your own circumstances.

200 Witchtree Lane
Anytown, USA 00000

July 1, ___

EFT Service Department
Hometown Bank
100 River Street
Anytown, USA 00000

Dear Sir:

This (is to notify the bank/confirms the verbal notice I gave Mr. Electron at 9:00 A.M. on June 30) that the electronic fund transfer access device that was issued to me (also list name of other person to whom it was issued, if any) was lost or stolen on or before June 29, 19___ . The number on the missing access device is _____ , the personal identification number for the authorized user is _____ , and the card can be used for making transfers from (identify type of accounts which can be accessed and account numbers if available).

(The loss or theft was first discovered at 10:30 P.M. on June 29 when I tried to make a withdrawal at an automated teller machine but found the card missing from my wallet. The last time the device could have been used for making an authorized transfer was on June 27 when a $50 withdrawal was made from an automated teller machine at the Riverside branch office.)

[This is (to notify the bank/confirm the verbal notice I gave Mr. Electron at 9:00 A.M. on June 30] that whatever authorization [identify person] had to make electronic fund transfers from [identify type of accounts and account numbers] with access device issued to [list name of person and/or other information that identifies the device or user] is hereby [was thereby] terminated. And since any future transfers made by [identify person] with that device are completely unauthorized, the bank is to take such steps as are necessary to prevent such transfers.])

Since unauthorized transfers may have occurred or could occur, the bank is not to charge such transfers to the accounts which can be accessed by that device and is to recredit my account in full for all unauthorized transfers which may have been charged to those accounts.* [Note: See explanation below before using this wording.]

And having notified the bank, my account is not to be charged for any unauthorized transfers that may occur.

Thank you for handling this matter promptly.

Sincerely,

*Note: Including this paragraph may trigger the error resolution procedure by calling on the institution to watch for and correct unauthorized transfers that may have occurred. It may also trigger the bank's obligation to investigate, find and correct unauthorized transfers that occurred. If you simply report the loss or theft of a device and don't say anything about unauthorized transfers, your notification may not trigger the error resolution procedure to search for and correct any unauthorized transfers that have occurred. Since triggering the error resolution procedure could affect how you could hold your bank accountable for damages (even though it may correct the error), you may want to seek legal advice first, and simply report the loss or theft, especially if you think unauthorized transfers have been made.

Make sure you give an accurate description of the circumstances in which you discovered the loss or theft, especially with respect to when you discovered it.

STOPPING PREAUTHORIZED TRANSFERS

Your bank will normally inform you of procedures to follow when stopping preauthorized transfers. The following sample notification may be adapted to include specific information your bank may require.

200 Witchtree Lane
Anytown, USA 00000

July 1, 19___

EFT Services Department
Hometown National Bank
100 River Street
Anytown, USA 00000

Dear Sir:

(I request/this is to confirm the verbal stop payment order I gave to Mr. Electron on June 30, 19___, at 9:00 A.M. requesting) that the bank stop payment of the preauthorized electronic fund transfer for $ _____ to the (ABC Company) scheduled to be made on July 5 from my (identify account).

I will appreciate your implementing this stop payment order as I have requested.

Sincerely,

Bear in mind that stopping payment of a preauthorized transfer can result in your bank also stopping other related transfers. So if you want to stop just one payment, take whatever action is appropriate to continue later ones.

REPORTING ERRORS AND LOSSES

By notifying your bank about an error within the proper time limit you trigger its obligation to investigate the matter and, if necessary, correct it.

If you suffer damages as a result of the bank's error, you could either request reimbursement in your initial letter or in a separate one. Examples of both follow. Seek legal advice before triggering the error resolution procedure if it is important for you to collect damages.

The following sample letter is general in nature; adapt it to identify the type of error involved and decribe the details. See page 410 for the type of errors institutions are required to correct.

200 Witchtree Lane
Anytown, USA 00000

July 6, 19___

EFT Services Department
Hometown National Bank
100 River Street
Anytown, USA 00000

Dear Sir:

This is to (notify you/confirm the oral notification I gave to Mr. Electron on July 5) of an electronic fund transfer error involving my (identify accounts and account numbers) which first appeared (on the periodic account statement dated [July 2] for the June 1 to June 30 accounting period/on the written documentation I received for a transfer I initiated July 4 at the Riverview Branch electronic terminal).

The error consists of (identify the error, such as: "an unauthorized electronic fund transfer," or "an incorrect transfer," or "the omission of a transfer that should have appeared on the periodic statement").

*(Nor did the bank comply with the requirement that [*identify how your bank failed to comply with some requirement of the act*].)*

The (periodic statement I received on July 5/written documentation for the transfer I initiated on July 4) (indicates/fails to indicate) that (describe the transfer(s) involved, or the missing item).

*But contrary to the documentation furnished me about (the transfers occurring during the accounting period/transfer I initiated on July 4), the transfer described above (should have been made as follows according to my records [*describe*]/the transfer described above should not have been made because [*describe*].)*

According to my best calculations, the error is for the $ _____ which was (not properly paid from/improperly deducted from/not properly credited to) the account identified above.

*(There is now also due me $ _____ as damages I sustained because of the bank's failure to [*identify the failure, such as: "transfer the correct amount from my savings account to my checking account"*] resulted in [*describe the harm that resulted such as: "the bank wrongfully dishonoring my check number 510 for insufficient funds about which I separately notified the bank on [*date*].)*

I therefore request the bank furnish me such documentation or additional information as will fully identify the transfer I have described so I can determine whether it was properly completed.

(I therefore request that the bank immediately investigate and correct the error, that it promptly reimburse me for the damages I sustained, and that the bank take the necessary steps to prevent me from sustaining additional damages because of this error.)

I will appreciate the bank promptly taking the appropriate steps to resolve this matter.

Sincerely,

If you are sure that an unauthorized transfer was somehow made, even though no accepted devices could have been used and none were lost or stolen, you could use the following wording to make that clear.

"This unauthorized transfer could not have been made by an accepted access device (since I have not accepted an access device for making electronic fund transfers from any of my accounts with you/since all accepted devices have at all times been in the possession and control of authorized users) so that I am not liable for any amount involved in the transfer."

If an unauthorized transfer was made from your account without an accepted device, you would not be responsible for the amount transferred. But a word of caution. Do *not* say all devices have been in your control unless you are very sure that no one could have used them. If it turns out that they have been used, it will then be extremely difficult for you to claim an unauthorized transfer was made.

Separate Letter for Requesting Reimbursement for Damages

Here is a follow-up notice for requesting reimbursement for damages if you didn't refer to them in your initial letter.

200 Witchtree Lane
Anytown, USA 00000

July 12, 19—

EFT Services Department
Hometown National Bank
100 River Street
Anytown, USA 00000

Dear Sir:

This is to notify the bank that there is now due me $ _____ for damages I sustained because of the bank's failure to (identify) which resulted in (describe the harm that resulted).

I have already notified the bank about this matter on (July 5) when I more fully described the electronic fund transfer involved. A copy of this letter is attached.

I will appreciate the bank promptly reimbursing me for these losses and taking such other actions as would be appropriate to minimize any further losses that may result.

Thank you for your cooperation.

Sincerely,

STAGE TWO: THE LOW-KEYED WARNING

If your bank fails to correct the error according to the required procedures, or if it denies there was an error and you are convinced one has been made, it is time for follow-up action.

Here, low-keyed warnings are given for the following situations:

- Requesting the documentary evidence used by the bank to deny there was an error.
- Demanding the bank correct an error after it has refused or failed to do so.

REQUESTING DOCUMENTARY EVIDENCE

If, after completing its investigation, a bank claims that no error has occurred, it is not obligated to reinvestigate the problem. However, if the documentation used in the investigation actually shows otherwise, your bank could become liable for three times your actual damages. So if you are convinced a mistake has been made, your first follow-up step is to request all the documentation used—in a way that suggests the bank promptly give the matter a further review to avoid possible trouble.

Here is a sample letter for requesting documentation.

200 Witchtree Lane
Anytown, USA 00000

August 1, 19__

EFT Services Department
Hometown National Bank
100 River Street
Anytown, USA 00000

Dear Sir:

I am requesting the bank furnish me copies of all documents it relied on to conclude there was no electronic fund transfer error as I had described in my written notification of July 6 when I told the bank about an error involving my (identify accounts and account numbers). A copy of my notification is enclosed.

I was notified on (July 30) that upon completing its investigation, the bank had determined no error occurred (and that my account would be debited for the amount that had been recredited while the bank conducted its investigation). (And even though the bank has now claimed that no error occurred, it failed to recredit my account for the amount of the error while it took more than ten business days to investigate.)

Since I do not understand how the bank could have reached its conclusion based on any reasonable interpretation of the evidence it should have about the transfer, please furnish promptly the documentation on which the bank relied for reaching its conclusion, as required by the Electronic Fund Transfer Act, so I may determine what further course of action is appropriate.

Should you in the meantime decide to reconsider your position, I would, of course, be prepared to resolve this matter if the bank takes all appropriate steps to correct the error and to reimburse me for the damages I have sustained and which I have already described to you. [Note: See explanation below before using this paragraph.]

I will appreciate your cooperation so we can still resolve this matter satisfactorily.

Sincerely,

You can be pretty certain that requesting the relevant documents in this way will set off alarm bells, and that someone will re-examine them before sending them to you. Telling the bank you are still prepared to settle the matter gives it a chance to make quick amends.

However, technically speaking, if the bank deliberately ignored evidence of an error, you could be entitled to recover triple damages rather than settling for the error being corrected as stated in the paragraph of the letter. Including the paragraph stating you will settle for a correction could amount to waiving your claim for triple damages if the bank corrects the problem as you request. Do *not* include this paragraph if you want to keep that option open even if the bank corrects the error.

DEMANDING BANK CORRECT AN ERROR

If your bank fails to correct an error according to the proper procedures, and/or fails to reimburse you for damages you could recover because it mishandled transfers, you could use the following low-keyed warning letter as a guide. It includes alternative wording for different situations and naturally must be adapted to fit your own circumstances.

The wording assumes you could hold your bank liable for failing to comply with the act if it doesn't reimburse you for damages you may be entitled to recover because it mishandled an electronic fund transfer. While the act is unclear on this point, especially if the institution corrects an error according to required procedure, you have nothing to lose by claiming you could hold the bank accountable. Your bargaining leverage is that the bank cannot be sure what a court is going to decide either.

200 Witchtree Lane
Anytown, USA 00000

August 15, 19___

Mr. G. Banker
President
Hometown National Bank
100 River Street
Anytown, USA 00000

Dear Mr. Banker:

This is to inform you of the bank's failure to correct an electronic fund transfer error involving my (identify accounts and numbers) about which I notified the bank on (July 6), (and the bank's failure to reimburse me for the damages I sustained as a result and which I then also described/ about which I separately notified the bank on _____). Copies of letters are enclosed.

Although I fully described the error (and the damages I sustained as a result) and requested the bank to correct the error (and reimburse me for my damages), the bank has not as of this date (describe what the bank has failed to do, such as: "completed its investigation," or "corrected and credited my account for the amount of the error," or "reimbursed me for my damages." Alternatively, if the bank's response was inadequate, say: "The bank has, instead of fully correcting and crediting my account for the actual amount of the error and reimbursing me for my damages, only [describe the bank's inadequate response based on its responsibilities]). (Nor does it appear reasonable for the bank to have concluded that no error occurred based on the documentation it supplied since [describe how the documentation fails to substantiate its claim].)

The bank's failure to correct and credit my account for the $ _____ amount of the error continues to deprive me of those funds (and its failure to reimburse me for the $ _____ in damages imposes on me additional financial burdens and hardship).

I therefore request that the bank promptly correct and credit my account for the amount of the error (and reimburse me for my damages) and take steps to ensure I incur no further damages as a result of the error.

I hope this matter can now be fully resolved so that I will not be compelled to hold the bank liable as provided by the Electronic Fund Transfer Act.

Thank you for giving this matter your prompt consideration.

Sincerely,

If the Bank Debits the Amount Too Soon and a Check Bounces

There is another low-keyed warning follow-up step you may have to take if the institution denies there was an error after temporarily re-crediting your account, then fails to wait the required five business days to debit the amount—which results in a bounced check.

When you take this follow-up step, find out the name and title of the person in charge of the department that handles consumer accounts and/or EFT transactions and direct the letter to him or her.

200 Witchtree Lane
Anytown, USA 00000

August 10, 19__

Mr. P. Transferman
Vice President
Consumer Accounts Department
Hometown National Bank
100 River Street
Anytown, USA 00000

Dear Mr. Transferman:

This is to notify you that the bank has (improperly refused to honor my check number 810 drawn on checking account number 00000000-00/ failed to make a preauthorized electronic fund transfer from my checking/savings account number 00000000-00) for $ _____ that was payable to the (ABC Company), and that I have now sustained $ _____ in damages and may sustain further damages as a result.

Upon transmitting to me on (August 1, 19__) its notification that it would debit my account for the amount of the electronic fund transfer error about which I notified the bank on (July 1), the bank debited my account for the $ _____ amount of the error on (August 4, 19__) and then refused (to pay the check/make the transfer) described above. The bank asserted my account did not have sufficient funds.

But as required by Regulation E, the amount of the error should not have been debited to my account until at least five business days after I was sent the notification that the bank would do so. My account would have had sufficient funds to pay the amounts described above had the amount of the error not been debited until the time specified by Regulation E.

I therefore request that the bank pay the amount as it should have done and promptly reimburse me for the damages I have sustained. I also insist the bank promptly take such steps as will enable me to minimize any further damages, including notifying the payee that payment was improperly refused.

I am not, however waiving any further claims for damages I may have (nor am I acknowledging the validity of the bank's conclusions with respect to the electronic fund transfer error involved in this matter).*

I hope this matter can now be fully resolved as I have requested so that I will not be compelled to hold the bank liable at least to the fullest extent provided by the Electronic Fund Transfer Act.

Thank you for giving this matter your prompt consideration.

Sincerely,

*Note: Only include the wording in brackets if you think the bank wrongfully concluded there was no error.

STAGE THREE: THE ULTIMATUM

If you are convinced you have a valid claim but your bank still refuses to settle the matter you could seek legal advice and initiate suit even if the amount in dispute does not involve a great deal of money.

Short of seeking legal advice, you could try the following ultimatum, which should be addressed to the president. If your dispute reaches this point, of course, your relationship with the bank is likely to be damaged to the point where it is probably worth switching banks. This is something to keep in mind when you decide how far to push a dispute.

200 Witchtree Lane
Anytown, USA 00000

August 31, 19___

Mr G. Banker
President
Hometown National Bank
100 River Street
Anytown, USA 00000

Dear Mr. Banker:

This is to inform you that the bank has still failed to comply with the requirements of the Electronic Fund Transfer Act and Regulation E with respect to an electronic fund transfer error involving my (identify accounts and numbers). It has also failed to reimburse me for the damages I sustained as I had last requested in my letter of (August 15, 19___) which more fully describes this matter (copy enclosed).

I therefore request the bank promptly correct and credit my account for the $ _____ amount of the error (and reimburse me for the $ _____ in damages I sustained).

But if the bank still fails to settle this matter as I have requested, I shall hold the bank liable at least to the fullest extent provided by the Electronic Fund Transfer Act. And the bank could now be liable for my actual damages, a minimum of $100 or a maximum of $1,000, (treble damages)* plus costs and reasonable attorney's fees I incur to hold the bank liable. (And I shall then also notify the [identify the enforcing agency] about the bank's apparent failure to comply with the requirements of the EFT Act and Regulation E.)

Sincerely,

*Refer to treble damages if that provision could apply (see page 412).
If this step still doesn't result in a settlement, you would have to sue.
You could also inform the appropriate regulatory agency about the bank's failure to comply with the act, but the bank's civil liability for failing to comply is likely to give you more leverage for resolving the matter.

50 · Debit Cards

It can work something like a check, it can work like a credit card, and it can be used for initiating EFT's. In effect, a debit card is a multi-purpose payment device.

HOW DEBIT CARDS MAY BE USED

Debit cards may have a combination of any of three features that identify the kinds of financial transactions for which they may be used.

1. A feature that allows you to make a purchase, or obtain money, that can be directly "charged" to a credit account. When used this way, a debit card would be considered a credit card and the transaction would be governed by laws that apply to credit cards.

2. A feature that allows you to initiate EFT's from an asset account. In this case the card would be considered an electronic fund transfer access device and would be covered by the EFT Act.

If such a transfer triggers an extension of credit tied into the asset account, it would almost certainly not count as a credit card transaction and you would not have the protection that could apply to a credit card purchase in the case of a dispute.

3. A feature that allows you to make a purchase with a paper-based payment authorization. The instrument you sign authorizes and verifies payment: it works something like a check, and the amount is simply debited to your account.

Again, if a payment initiated this way triggers an extension of credit tied into the asset account, the transaction would almost certainly not count as a credit card purchase.

When debit cards are used for making paper-based payment authorizations, they may be processed in one of two ways; this affects the protection you could have.

One way of making and processing the transaction would be for the seller to use the card to obtain electronic verification and authorization for the amount of the purchase. If this also results in the funds being immediately transferred from your account to the seller's, the transaction would count as an EFT and would be governed by the EFT Act. For all practical purposes such a transaction would be like paying cash and you would not be able to stop payment. The authorization would merely be documentation for the EFT.

The second way of making and processing the transaction would be if the seller forwards the written authorization for collection, usually through his bank.

In this case, the transaction probably would not count as an EFT. Neither would it count as a check or a credit card purchase if the extension of credit was triggered from a line of credit tied into the asset account that was initially accessed. In short, the purely paper-based payment authorization feature of the debit card falls between the cracks when it comes to the protection you could have.

The following clause, which appears on many charge slips, describes what's involved: "The issuer of the card identified on this item is authorized to pay the amount shown as TOTAL, upon proper presentation. I promise to pay such TOTAL (together with any other charges due thereon) subject to and in accordance with the agreement governing the use of such card."

While a purely paper-based payment authorization is signed and presented to the card issuer for payment, it is not a negotiable instrument, like a check, and so it does not automatically give you protection in case of forgeries. And the limitations on your liability for unauthorized use as spelled out by the EFT Act and the Fair Credit Billing Act are very unlikely to apply.

Once the written authorization is processed and debited to your account, the purchase has, in effect, been paid. So if a credit extension is triggered when you don't have enough funds in the asset account, you would have to pay the money back to the card issuer even if something goes wrong with the purchase.

Your rights, obligations and potential liability when using purely paper-based debit card transactions is simply *not* as clear cut as when using other payment methods or types of credit.

TERMS YOU SHOULD CHECK ON

You should think long and hard before obtaining a debit card which has a paper-based authorization feature because, as of early 1984, there was no law that specifically provided protection for purely paper-based authorizations. What "protections" you had would, instead usually depend on the terms and conditions of your agreement.

Before getting such a debit card, check how the agreement covers the following:

• What amounts are actually properly payable when the card is used, and/or what counts as unauthorized use? One key point to note is what it takes for a transaction to count as being authorized by you when only a paper based transaction is made— is it, for example, simply the use of the card or must it be coupled with your signature or some special validation code that must be separately furnished? Another key point to note is what counts as unauthorized use and what your liability could be if it occurred? A debit card issuer may include in the account agreement the same provisions with respect to unauthorized use and altered amounts as those required for credit cards or EFT's; but no law says they have to with respect to purely paper-based debit card transactions. An agreement that doesn't at least follow the liability limitations the law sets for credit cards is a *bad* agreement.

• How does reporting, or failing to report, the loss or theft of a card affect your liability? If the terms do not specifically say that you are *not* liable for any unauthorized use that occurs after you report the loss or theft of a card by easily usable means, it is a *bad* agreement.

Also check any limitations on your right to cancel the agreement: you should have no obligations for payment authorizations made after canceling your agreement.

• What about disputes involving differences between an amount debited and an amount shown on the copy of your payment authorization? Usually the amounts on written copies must agree if you are to be held to it. You should certainly be able to argue that any amount that differs from your copy of the payment authorization is not properly payable.

• What does the agreement say about the possibility of stopping a payment?

• Do you have the right to avoid paying the card issuer in case of disputes about a purchase? If the agreement allows you to do so within a certain time period, providing you follow certain procedures, you should be informed of the procedures and follow them carefully. If your agreement doesn't specifically entitle you to do this, you may have no chance to avoid paying the debit.

• From which accounts are payments to be made? The key question is whether the agreement authorizes the card issuer to debit the amounts only to a specific account, or to any account you have at the institution? If more than one account can be accessed, then how are accounts debited? A debit card agreement that allows the card issuer to debit any asset account is generally a *very bad* agreement.

PROTECTION YOU COULD HAVE WITH PAPER-BASED PAYMENT AUTHORIZATIONS

If amounts are payable out of your checking account, the key protection you are likely to have is that covering checking accounts.

Such protection is described below, but remember that your debit card agreement terms will spell out the specific conditions involved in your case.

Stopping Payment

The Uniform Commercial Code specifically entitles an account holder to stop payment on any *item* calling for payment out of an account—and this almost certainly includes a purely paper-based debit card payment authorization.

Since debit card transactions are a new payment method, though, you could end up in a dispute with the bank about whether the right applies. The bank may be able to collect the money based on your having authorized the payment under the terms of your debit card agreement. It is certain, however, that the right to stop payment is *not* limited to checks so you could have a strong case that the right applies.

To stop payment, you should follow the steps for stopping payment on a check.

Amounts Not Properly Payable

Whether or not a purely paper-based transaction is properly payable would largely depend on the terms and conditions of your agreement.

If you wouldn't owe the money based on these terms, you would almost certainly have the same rights as those involved if a bank improperly charged such an amount to a checking account when a check was used, and taking the same steps to correct the matter should help you deal with the problem.

Amounts that would not be properly payable would usually involve unauthorized use.

Notifying Issuer about Loss or Theft

Be sure to follow procedures spelled out in your agreement for notifying the issuer about the loss or theft of debit cards and for limiting your liability for unauthorized use. Following such instructions unquestionably terminates your liability.

SECTION VII:
CONSUMER CREDIT PROTECTIONS

51 · Consumer Credit: Some Key Characteristics

Until the late 1950s and early 1960s few consumers used credit, except to make a large purchase such as a house or car. Today, it is the norm rather than the exception and many of us depend on credit to make daily purchases. It's a financial service that would be hard to do without.

This section primarily covers protections you have under federal laws governing consumer credit and key rights you could have under the Uniform Commercial Code when disputing what you owe a creditor.

Most of the federal laws covered in this section are part of what is called the Consumer Credit Protection Act, an umbrella title given to several separate laws Congress enacted and which have their own names. This is important because there are times when the protections available under one law that is part of that act are keyed to protections available under another law that is also part of that act.

Broadly speaking, using credit is having the right to pay later what you owe now. How you get and can use the credit you have, and how you have to pay it back depends, of course, on the type of credit arrangement you have and the terms of the agreement under which credit is extended. It's important to know the different types of credit arrangements and their distinguishing characteristics because it is these characteristics that often identify other rights and obligations that could apply. Lines are not always neatly drawn between different arrangements, though, simply because new financial services packages offered by financial institutions are blurring distinctions that used to be fairly clear-cut.

OPEN-END/CLOSED-END CREDIT

This feature identifies how you can *use* the credit.

As its name implies, **open-end** credit consists of an on-going arrangement under which repeated transactions may be made under the terms spelled out by the agreement that governs the account. Revolving retail charge accounts and bank, oil company, department store and other credit card accounts are the most familiar examples of open-end credit. They are usually accessed with credit cards. But there are also open-end credit accounts that can be used without credit cards.

Credit cards have some special protections built into them which are available, under certain conditions, in cases where there is a dispute about a purchase. However, these protections do not apply to all transactions involving open-end accounts, even though all purchases made with a credit card would usually be charged to an open-end account. Using a check to trigger an extension of credit under a check overdraft loan arrangement is one example of what would be an open-end credit transaction that would not give you the protections you could have with respect to purchases made with credit cards.

Closed-end credit almost always involves a single extension of a specific amount of credit which must be repaid at the end of a specific time period. The total amount, the finance charges involved, and the monthly payments are usually fixed at the beginning of the loan period; but, depending on your agreement, the rate charged may vary over the period of the loan. A monthly installment loan, or installment credit purchase, is the most familiar example of a closed-end credit transaction.

It is possible to add new purchases to an existing closed-end agreement: this results in the old and new amounts being consolidated under one new closed-end credit agreement. It is rarely worthwhile to make such an arrangement, though, because all the purchases, old and new, usually end up as collateral until most, if not all, the outstanding balance is repaid. And such an arrangement makes it much more difficult to untangle what you still owe in case of a dispute about one purchase.

BUYING ON CREDIT/BORROWING MONEY

Another important distinguishing characteristic of the credit you use is whether the extension of credit involves a *credit purchase* or a *loan of money* which was then used to make a purchase. Generally speaking, you would be "using credit" to buy in either case; but the distinction between the two can make a big difference in the protections available in case of a dispute about a purchase.

A **credit purchase** involves an extension of credit by a seller; an arrangement under which you repay him "over time." Retail charge accounts (open-end), and retail installment agreements (closed-end) credit are examples.

A **loan of money**, on the other hand, means using credit by borrowing money under a loan agreement. When using this kind of credit, the loan and the purchase are usually completely separate transactions and your rights and obligations under one agreement usually have nothing to do with the other, unless a law specifically protects you by making the separate lender accountable for the seller's failure to honor your sales agreement. So unless you are protected this way as more fully explained in the chapters that cover when you could be entitled to withhold payment based on rights you have under the Fair Credit Billing Act or the FTC's "Preservation of Consumers' Claims and Defenses" Rule, if you use the proceeds from a loan to buy something and you have a dispute with the seller, you would still have to repay the loan.

The distinction between these two forms of credit buying used to be fairly clear-cut but it is not always so now. When bank credit cards came along, these two separate transactions were, seemingly at least, merged since the purchase and extension of credit were both achieved simply by signing one charge slip. In some cases, the distinction has been further blurred: various financial services packages tie different transactions together into a sequence of transactions that are triggered almost automatically.

SECURED/UNSECURED CREDIT

A final important distinction is whether the credit you obtain is secured or unsecured.

Secured credit involves putting up some collateral that the creditor can take to satisfy the debt in case of default. The type of collateral used usually determines the procedures the creditor has to follow in order to collect:

• Personal property, such as a car or household furniture. In this case, a creditor has what is known as a "security interest" in the goods, and it must be stated in writing.

• Real property, such as your home. In this case, a creditor has a lien or mortgage on the property. Such a mortgage has to be stated in writing, but there are circumstances in which someone could obtain a lien on your property based simply on the law entitling the person to have the lien, such as if someone does work on your home.

- Liquid assets, such as money you have on deposit in a savings account, for example, that could be used as security for the loan. The amount put up is usually frozen until the loan is repaid. Such arrangements usually have to be put in writing.

It is possible that your bank or other financial institution may be able to tap the funds you have on deposit in order to collect money you owe them under a loan agreement. This is usually referred to as a bank's right to "set off" money you owe.

Unsecured credit means that a creditor does not acquire collateral to secure repayment. Instead, in cases of default, he has to sue to recover the money.

PREVENTING A CREDITOR FROM HAVING A SECURITY INTEREST IN GOODS PURCHASED LATER

When the credit you get (whether a loan or credit sale) is secured by personal property, a creditor usually acquires a security interest only in the property you purchased with the credit being extended or property specifically identified in the agreement. But it is also possible for a creditor to include a clause saying that he could use as collateral any other personal property you purchase later. This is usually referred to as a security interest in "after acquired" personal property. This would apply to goods bought with funds other than credit exended by the creditor.

Without getting into the details, the Uniform Commercial Code which governs security interests involving personal property provides that, in the case of consumer goods, a creditor can use such a clause to obtain a security interest in any other after acquired property only if you purchase it within ten days after the creditor gives value (usually meaning when you get the money or credit).

You avoid this kind of a problem simply by not buying any goods with other funds within that ten day period.

52 · Getting and Keeping Credit: Your Main Legal Tool—the Equal Credit Opportunity Act

This chapter provides some suggestions that might help you qualify for credit if you don't already do so. It then describes the federal law that can be your main tool if you are unjustly denied credit.

The following chapters cover protections you could have under various laws as you use credit.

QUALIFYING FOR CREDIT

There are no hard and fast rules to help you qualify for credit the first time, but here are some tips that can help.

● Establish a checking and savings account. Be sure to use the checking account prudently; bounced checks definitely won't help.
● Promptly pay any recurring bills, such as utility or rental payments. Although your payment record for such bills usually isn't reported to credit-reporting agencies, a record of consistently fast payment can help. Utility companies may put a note on your bill thanking you for prompt payment, for instance. These could help you prove your reliability to a prospective creditor.
● Apply for credit at your bank, or at good retail or department stores, and ask for an amount that is reasonable for your financial circumstances.
● Obtain credit from creditors who report to credit-reporting bureaus. Obtaining credit from other sources obviously isn't going to help you establish a credit record.
● When you move, find out how you can have your credit history transferred to a credit-reporting agency in your area.
● Pay what you owe as due. Getting behind with payments will quickly be reflected in your credit record, especially when you obtain credit from someone who regularly reports information about the promptness of each payment to a credit bureau.

There are certain actions that probably *won't* help and could make it harder for you to establish a good credit history.

● Obtaining credit from a small loan or a finance company, for instance. Such credit is usually weighed negatively by other creditors.
● Obtaining credit from creditors who don't report your credit history, or from creditors who extend credit too freely.
● Applying for credit at too many places within a short period. Credit-reporting agencies usually note the number of credit inquiries they receive from creditors, and a number of inquiries within a short time period would count heavily against you.

One word of caution when applying for credit. If a creditor's application asks you to list *all* your creditors or *all* your debts, do *not* leave any off merely because you run out of space on the form. Add them on a separate sheet. By listing everything, you may give the impression you are over-extended and not get the credit, it's true, but omitting debts could hurt you later if you get into financial trouble and declare bankruptcy. It is possible that a creditor from whom you withheld information could claim fraud and be entitled to repayment in full regardless of the bankruptcy.

EQUAL CREDIT OPPORTUNITY ACT

Enacted in 1974, the Equal Credit Opportunity (ECO) Act became effective the following year. It was designed to stop lenders from using certain discriminatory practices in order to deny credit.

Before the act was adopted, for instance, it was not unusual for a newly married woman to discover that credit was no longer available to her except in her husband's name—even if she continued to work and the couple actually relied on her income for support.

In the same way, a widowed or divorced woman often had no credit history in her own name on which to base an application for credit. Thus, women, and members of some other groups, were put in a catch-22 situation since lenders first refused to extend credit in their own names while they were married, then refused to extend credit when they were no longer married because they had no credit history.

Broadly speaking, the ECO Act prohibits creditors from using certain criteria to deny credit, and spells out broad practices a creditor must adhere to during the credit application process. Regulation B, a regulation adopted by the board of governors of the Federal Reserve System, backs up the act and provides detailed provisions creditors must follow.

Let's look at the key requirements.

WHO MUST COMPLY WITH THE ECO ACT?

The act applies to creditors who regularly extend credit, and so covers lenders such as banks, small loan or finance companies, retail and department stores, credit card companies, credit unions, and other kinds of businesses that regularly extend credit.

But certain credit transactions are given specialized treatment and creditors in such situations would not have to comply with all the requirements that would otherwise apply. Broadly speaking, the following types of transactions are given specialized treatment:

- Public utilities credit (that is, credit extended by public utilities).
- Securities credit (that is, credit extended by securities brokers or dealers regulated by the Securities and Exchange Commission).
- Incidental credit (which normally involves credit extended by someone not involved in the business of extending credit or when the credit was not extended under a credit card account, no finance charge is imposed and, amount is not payable under the agreement in more than four installments).
- Business credit (that is, credit extended for business or commercial purposes).

The requirements that do not apply to such transactions will be identified where they are described and where these types of transactions will be referred to as public utilities, securities, incidental and business credit.

DISCRIMINATION PROHIBITED BY THE ACT

The act prohibits discrimination in a credit transaction on the basis of race, color, religion, national origin, sex, marital status, or age. (The person must be of legal age to enter into a binding contract, and there are a few other exceptions with regard to age.) The act also prohibits discrimination because a person receives income from public assistance; or because a person has, in good faith, already used rights available under the Consumer Credit Protection Act.

The law prohibits creditors from treating one applicant less favorably than another applicant on the basis of those prohibited criteria.

Creditors are also prohibited from using written or oral statements which would, on a prohibited basis, discourage a reasonable person from making or pursuing a credit application. This applies to advertising, brochures and letters; and to oral statements made during inquiries. To count as a violation, such a statement would have to be strong enough to discourage a reasonable person. So while not every discouraging reference that implied a creditor was discriminating on a prohibited basis would count, you should be aware of the prohibition and be prepared to ward off such references.

CREDIT DENIALS THAT ARE NOT PROHIBITED

While the act makes certain discriminatory practices illegal, it does not require creditors to extend credit to everyone, nor does it assume that everyone is entitled to credit.

Creditors can still decide to whom they will extend credit, *and under what conditions.* Thus, a creditor wouldn't be violating the act merely by denying you credit.

REQUIREMENTS COVERING CREDIT APPLICATIONS

A creditor may *not* ask you for the following types of information when you apply for credit, except as otherwise indicated:

- *Information about your sex. The application must use terms that are neutral as to sex. A creditor cannot require you to use a courtesy title such as Mr., Mrs., Miss, or Ms., but can make provision for one on the application form if you are clearly told the use of such a title is optional.
- Information about your race, color, religion or national origin. A creditor may, however, ask about your residence or immigration status.
- **Information about your marital status if you are applying for individual, unsecured credit. That is you are applying only in your own name, without putting up any property or other collateral to secure the loan. A creditor can ask about your marital status even if you apply for individual, unsecured credit when you live in a community property state, however, or the property you are relying on for repaying the loan is in a community property state. The states involved are: Arizona, California, Idaho, Louisiana, Nevada, New Mexico, Texas and Washington.

If you apply for anything other than individual, unsecured credit, a creditor may ask about your marital status: if you apply for credit jointly with your spouse, for instance, or if you put up collateral for a loan. However, the creditor can only ask whether you are "married," "unmarried," or "separated"; you cannot be asked if you are divorced or widowed.

On the other hand, a creditor can ask for relevant financial information that may indirectly indicate your marital status, such as:

. . . Your obligation to make alimony, maintenance, or child support payments.

. . . The income source used as a basis for repaying the credit requested (this could disclose that it's your spouse's income).

*Does not apply to securities or incidental credit.
**Does not apply to utilities, securities, incidental or business credit.

... Whether any of the credit obligations you disclose involve someone else (this person could, of course, be your spouse or former spouse).

... The ownership of assets you are relying on for getting credit (this could disclose a spouse's ownership interest).

... Other names and addresses under which accounts you list are carried, and any other names under which you have previously obtained credit (this information could inform the creditor of your current or previous marital status).

- *Information about your spouse or former spouse may not be requested *unless;*

... Your spouse is permitted to use the account, as in the case of open-end credit accounts such as revolving charge accounts or credit card accounts.

... Your spouse is applying with you and therefore both you and your spouse would be obligated to repay the money.

... You are relying on your spouse's income for repaying the credit requested.

... You are relying on alimony, maintenance or child support payments from a spouse or former spouse as a basis for repaying the credit requested.

- *Information about whether any of the income stated on the application is from alimony, child support, or separate maintenance payments unless the creditor first tells you that such information is voluntary (unless, of course, you are relying on those sources to get credit).
- Information about birth control practices, or any childbearing plans. A creditor can ask about the number and ages of your children, though.

AN EXCEPTION: REAL ESTATE LOANS

There is one important exception to the prohibition on a creditor requesting information about an applicant's sex, race, national origin, marital status or age. If you are applying for a real-estate loan to buy a home, a creditor is required to ask for this information in order to help federal agencies enforce the law. He or she must make it clear that it is up to you to supply the information, though, and you do not have to supply it.

The Federal Reserve Board has prepared a model application form which illustrates how the creditor can comply with these requirements. (Use of this form is not mandatory.) See Appendix IV for a model form that was prepared for closed-end secured or unsecured credit. This gives you an example of the kind of information creditors are likely to request.

EVALUATING AN APPLICANT'S CREDITWORTHINESS

When deciding to extend credit, a creditor's key concern is whether the money will be repaid and how to minimize the risk that it won't be.

In making the decision, creditors usually consider what are called the three "C's" of credit: capacity—enough income to repay; character—a willingness to repay; and collateral—property put up as security if the money isn't repaid. Some creditors extend credit only to those whom they are almost certain will repay; others set lower standards and take a bigger risk.

Creditors use one of two methods, or a combination of the two, for evaluating creditworthiness. These are known as the "judgmental" and "credit-scoring" methods.

---

*Does not apply to securities or incidental credit.
*Does not apply to incidental credit.

When a credit officer uses the judgmental method he or she simply evaluates the information according to the criteria for extending credit and decides whether an applicant qualifies. The decision is usually based on instinct and experience in judging other applications given the creditor's criteria for extending credit.

A statistically based credit-scoring system, on the other hand, consists of a creditor assigning various "points" to characteristics he considers to be reliable indicators that the applicant will repay. He might assign ten points to someone who owns a house, for example, and five points to someone who rents; ten points to someone who has worked at one job for between two to five years, but only five points to someone who has been on the job between six to ten years. The creditor then makes his decision based on the total points scored. Creditors, of course, use many other specific characteristics in assigning points that are to be used for scoring the application. The points assigned to various characteristics are based on complicated statistical studies.

Although credit-scoring systems have been touted as a more objective way of evaluating creditworthiness because they eliminate personal biases that may creep into the judgmental system, they do have their own flaws. How valid are the characteristics selected by the creditor, for instance, and how valid are the points assigned to them? The entire scoring system may, in fact, be unduly biased against applicants with certain characteristics. One major California bank substantially revamped its system in 1982 when it discovered it was turning down a large number of applicants without really reducing its losses for bad debts.

REQUIREMENTS GOVERNING THE EVALUATION OF CREDIT INFORMATION

Since creditors may consider many different characteristics when evaluating creditworthiness—and some might simply be disguised forms of prohibited characteristics—it can be hard for a consumer to show a creditor is actually engaging in discrimination.

For this reason Regulation B spells out specific items a creditor may not consider when evaluating creditworthiness.

APPLICANT'S INCOME

While a creditor can consider the amount of your income and the likelihood that it will continue, he *cannot:*

• Discount or exclude from consideration your income, or your spouse's income, because of sex, or marital status, or because of any other prohibited basis. When considering whether a couple's income is high enough to qualify for the credit they requested, he cannot, for example, count one hundred percent of the husband's income but only seventy-five percent of the wife's income.

• Discount or exclude income from part-time employment or from an annuity, pension, or other retirement program. Income from such sources must be treated in the same way as income from other sources.

• Refuse to consider alimony, child support or separate maintenance payments. But a creditor has to consider such payments as income only if they are *consistently* made, and can ask for proof to that effect. The creditor can consider at least the following factors when evaluating whether such payments are made consistently: are payments being made under a written agreement or court decree; how long and how regularly payments have been received in the past; what procedures are available for enforcing payments due; and the creditworthiness of the person making the payments.

• Refuse to consider public assistance income, but the creditor can consider how reliable those payments may be.

LIKELIHOOD OF HAVING CHILDREN

A creditor *cannot* make assumptions about the likelihood that any group of persons (i.e. women) will have, or will raise, children or that they will, for this reason, receive less or no income in the future. Creditors are also prohibited from using statistical data that may indicate that a particular group of women are likely to have children and are therefore less creditworthy.

APPLICANT'S AGE

A creditor *cannot* consider your age, providing you are of legal age to sign a contract, *unless:*

• You are sixty-two years or older and the creditor treats you more favorably than others because of your age.
• A creditor uses age as a factor in a statistically-based scoring system, but a person sixty-two years or older cannot be assigned a lower score in such a model.
• A creditor uses a judgmental system in which age is taken into account only for the purpose of evaluating other relevant factors affecting creditworthiness. A creditor could, for instance, consider your occupation and the length of time before you retire to determine whether your income (including retirement income) would be adequate for repaying the loan. A creditor could also consider your age to assess the importance of length of employment or residence.

A creditor cannot refuse to extend credit or terminate an account if you are sixty-two years or older because credit life, health, accident or disability insurance is unavailable because of your age.

TELEPHONE LISTINGS

A creditor cannot consider whether a telephone is listed in your name, but he can consider whether your residence has a phone.

APPLICANT'S CREDIT HISTORY

If a creditor considers credit history from credit bureau reports when evaluating the creditworthiness of applicants for similar types and amounts of credit, if you then apply for that type and amount of credit, he *cannot:*

• Refuse to consider, at your request, any available credit history about accounts specifically identified as those which you shared, or for which you were contractually liable with your spouse or former spouse. He cannot refuse to consider the credit history of accounts held only in your spouse, or former spouse's, name if you can show that it is an accurate reflection of *your* creditworthiness. This usually means being able to demonstrate you were contractually obligated for the account, had used or shared payments on it.
• Use unfavorable information about an account you shared with a spouse, or former spouse, if you can show that the information does *not* accurately reflect on your creditworthiness. The law says you don't have to be stuck with a spouse's bad credit history, but you must be able to demonstrate that it does not involve you. You could indicate this by showing you didn't have anything to do with the account, or,

if your name was on the account, that it was used by your spouse and he or she was completely responsible for handling it.

Whether favorable information is considered or unfavorable information is discounted, depends on the creditor's normal *use of* credit histories when evaluating creditworthiness for the type of credit involved. If the creditor doesn't take such information into account when considering other applicants, he doesn't have to take it into account in your case.

REQUIREMENTS GOVERNING THE EXTENSION OF CREDIT

Regulation B also spells out your rights and specific protections when a creditor extends credit.

OBTAINING INDIVIDUAL CREDIT

If you apply for individual credit, you cannot be denied it on a prohibited basis. But when it comes to evaluating creditworthiness, a creditor can take marital status or income source into account for the purpose of determining what rights the creditor would have to collect. The creditor could also require the signature of the person whose income is being relied on for the credit.

HAVING CREDIT IN YOUR OWN NAME

A creditor must allow you to obtain and keep credit in your own first and last name (e.g. Mary Single), your first name and spouse's last name (Mary Married), or your first name and combined last names (Mary Single-Married).*

*KEEPING EXISTING OPEN-END CREDIT ACCOUNTS

If you already have your own open-end (revolving) charge account, a creditor *cannot* ask you to reapply for credit, change the terms of the account, or terminate the account, on the grounds that you have reached a certain age, are about to retire, or changed your name or marital status—unless he has evidence of your unwillingness or inability to repay.

A creditor can ask you to reapply if your marital status has changed and the credit currently extended to you was originally based on your spouse's income because your own income at the time of the original application was not enough to support the amount of credit currently extended to you.

**REQUIRING THE SIGNATURE OF SPOUSES OR CO-SIGNERS

Unless you are applying for credit with your spouse, a creditor cannot require your spouse's signature, or the signature of any other co-signer, if you otherwise already meet the creditor's standards for the amount and type of credit extended.

A creditor can require the signature of a spouse or co-signer, however, if you are relying in part on property to repay the debt; are applying for secured credit; or live in a community property state and the signature of your spouse is needed to enable the creditor to obtain the property in case of default. But when you are applying for individual secured credit, the creditor can generally require the signature of your

*Does not apply to securities credit.
*Does not apply to securities credit.
**Does not apply to securities and incidental credit.

spouse only on the security agreement (that is, the terms governing the collateral used) rather than the credit agreement itself. This means the spouse gives up rights in the property if you default, but the spouse would not be obligated to repay if you don't.

If a creditor simply wants a co-signer, though, he cannot insist that it be a spouse.

*REQUIREMENTS FOR NOTIFYING APPLICANTS

Regulation B sets specific deadlines by which a creditor must inform you of his or her decision about an application, or of other actions taken with regard to your account.

TIME LIMITS FOR CREDITORS

A creditor must take the following actions within the time limits spelled out below:

• You must be notified of the approval or denial of credit within thirty days of the creditor receiving a *completed application.* (A completed application is one that contains all the information a creditor regularly obtains or uses for evaluation purposes, so the thirty-day period doesn't start until he has that information. If you could supply any missing information, the creditor must ask you for it. If the creditor has to get the information elsewhere, he must make a reasonable effort to do so. In other words, he can't simply duck the thirty-day time limit by claiming the application isn't complete while doing nothing to get the missing information.)

There are many ways a creditor can tell you an application has been approved. He must, however, take specific steps to inform you if an application is turned down.

• A creditor must also notify you within thirty days after denying an uncompleted application.
• If the creditor does not receive the missing information, he can deny the incomplete application but he must notify you within thirty days of making that decision.
• A creditor must also notify you within thirty days of taking adverse action regarding an existing account.
• If the creditor first offers to extend credit on terms or for an amount that is substantially different from your request (you ask for $1,000 credit, for instance, and he is only willing to extend $500) and you refuse the offer, he must notify you of the action he decides to take on the original application within ninety days after the creditor offered to extend credit on different terms.

REQUIRED NOTIFICATION OF ADVERSE ACTIONS

If the creditor takes the following adverse actions on an application, or with respect to an existing account, additional notification requirements are triggered.

• The creditor refuses to extend credit on substantially the terms or for the amount you requested (unless the creditor first offers to extend credit on different terms or for a different amount).
• The creditor terminates an existing account or makes an unfavorable change in its terms (such as an increase in the finance charges, or a reduction in the credit limit) if a termination or change in terms does not also affect all, or at least a substantial portion of, the creditor's other accounts.

---

*Notification requirements do not apply to incidental and business credit.

• The creditor refuses to increase the amount of existing credit after you have made your request according to procedures previously spelled out by the creditor.

Before the ECO Act, it was often difficult for a consumer to learn why a credit application had been turned down. At best, you might simply be told the application had been denied. Now the creditor must notify you about adverse actions as follows:

1. Notification must be in writing, except in the case of very small creditors who may notify you orally.

2. The notification must state the action taken by the creditor, provide a summary of the discriminatory actions prohibited by the ECO Act, and furnish you the name and address of the federal agency that enforces the act with respect to the creditor who turned you down. The act is enforced by different federal agencies depending on who the creditor is.

All creditors must also give the *specific* reason (or reasons) for denying you credit or for other adverse action taken, and it must be the real one used. A statement that only states a vague or general reason is not adequate. It isn't enough to say you failed to achieve a passing score under the creditor's scoring system, for instance.

A creditor may automatically supply the reason when he notifies you about the adverse action taken. Or he may withhold the reason until you specifically ask him to supply it. In the latter case, the creditor's notification must inform you that you are entitled to the information if you request it within sixty days after the initial notification was furnished to you. The creditor must then supply the reason within thirty days of receiving your request. He may do so orally, as long as he informs you that you are entitled to written confirmation if you, in turn, put your request in writing.

Requiring the creditor to furnish the specific principal reason (or reasons) for the adverse action is one of the most important enforcement tools you have. Creditors who have not complied with this regulation have been found to be in violation of the act.

A creditor is also required to tell you about information he may have obtained from others, such as credit bureaus or other creditors. Exactly what a creditor must tell you about information obtained from others is spelled out in the Fair Credit Reporting Act rather than the ECO Act (see page 580). Most creditors supply that information when they furnish you with the notification required by the ECO Act, but they could furnish it separately.

SAMPLE NOTIFICATION FORM

The Federal Reserve Board has prepared a sample form—shown below—that can be used to notify consumers of adverse actions. It includes the information a creditor may be required to supply under the Fair Credit Reporting Act. Although creditors don't have to use the form and may alter it or use a letter instead, many do so in order to be considered in compliance with the act and avoid trouble.

STATEMENT OF CREDIT DENIAL, TERMINATION OR CHANGE

DATE _____

Applicant's Name: _____

Applicant's address: _____

_____

Description of account, transaction, or requested credit: _____

_____

Description of adverse action taken: _____

_____

PRINCIPAL REASON(S) FOR ADVERSE ACTION CONCERNING CREDIT

_____ Credit application incomplete

_____ Insufficient credit references

_____ Unable to verify credit references

_____ Temporary or irregular employment

_____ Unable to verify employment

_____ Length of employment

_____ Insufficient income

_____ Excessive obligations

_____ Unable to verify income

_____ Inadequate collateral

_____ Too short a period of residence

_____ Temporary residence

_____ Unable to verify residence

_____ No credit file

_____ Insufficient credit file

_____ Delinquent credit obligation

_____ Garnishment, attachment, foreclosure, repossession or suit

_____ Bankruptcy

_____ We do not grant credit to any applicant on the terms and conditions you request

_____ Other, specify: _____

_____

DISCLOSURE OF USE OF INFORMATION OBTAINED FROM AN OUT-SIDE SOURCE

_____ Disclosure inapplicable

_____ Information obtained in a report from a consumer reporting agency.

Name: _____

Street Address: _____

_____

Telephone number: _____

_____ Information obtained from an outside source other than a consumer reporting agency. Under the Fair Credit Reporting Act, you have the right to make a written request, within 60 days of the receipt of this notice, for disclosure of the nature of the adverse information.

Creditor's name: _____

Creditor's address: _____

_____

Creditor's telephone number: _____

The Federal Equal Credit Opportunity Act prohibits creditors from discriminating against credit applicants on the basis of race, color, religion, national origin, sex, marital status, age (provided the applicant has the capacity to enter into a binding contract); because all or part of the applicant's income derives from any public assistance program; or because the applicant has in good faith exercised any right under the Consumer Credit Protection Act. The Federal agency that administers compliance with this law concerning this creditor is (<u>name and address to be supplied by creditor</u>).

*Note: At the end of this statement, the creditor can refer to any state law that is similar to the ECO Act and the name and address of the state agency that enforces it. See page 445 for a list of federal agencies.

*HOW THE LAW APPLIES TO MARRIED WOMEN

Before the ECO Act, credit histories of married women were usually reported not in their own names but in their husbands' names, which usually made it extremely hard for women to obtain credit.

Now women are specifically entitled to obtain individual credit in their own names and the history of such accounts would, of course be reported under her name.

Regulation B also spells out procedures creditors must use when reporting information about shared credit accounts. These are accounts on which both spouses are liable; and on open-ended accounts that both spouses can use even though only one is contractually obligated on the account.

How the creditor must report information about these types of credit accounts depends on whether the account was established on or after June 1, 1977, or before that date.

ACCOUNTS ESTABLISHED ON OR AFTER JUNE 1, 1977

For accounts established on or after June 1, 1977, a creditor must determine whether an applicant's spouse can also use the account or whether both spouses are obligated under the credit agreement.

If a creditor reports information about such accounts to anyone it must report it in the names of both spouses so the information can, in turn, be reported to others in the name of either or both spouses.

When such credit was established after June 1, 1977, a creditor must automatically follow these procedures and report the account in the name of both spouses if he reports such information.

ACCOUNTS ESTABLISHED BEFORE JUNE 1, 1977

In 1977 creditors were given a choice of action when handling the above kinds of accounts which had been established before June 1 of that year.

First, they could report information in the names of both spouses; the same way they were required to treat new accounts. But very few creditors did this because it involved a lot of work and expense.

Second, they could mail a specific notice to customers telling them they could request the creditor to report information about their account in the names of both spouses.

Literally millions of such notices were mailed out to account holders in 1977, but very few consumers returned the forms. As a result, many accounts continued to be reported in the husband's name only.

Fortunately, you can still request a creditor to report information about such accounts in both names simply by sending him or her a notice to that effect. It may be signed by either spouse. A creditor then has ninety days to fulfill the request. Neither the request nor the reporting of credit information in both names changes the legal obligations of either party.

As a practical matter, such action is most likely to apply to mortgage loans and revolving charge accounts initiated *before* June 1, 1977.

Remember, however, that the rule requiring creditors to report information about shared accounts in the name of both parties applies only to creditors who report such information. Creditors like oil companies usually do not report such information, and the act would not then require them to report such information about you.

---

*Does not apply to utilities, securities, incidental and business credit.

The following is a sample notice you could use.

REQUEST FOR REPORTING
CREDIT HISTORY FOR MARRIED PERSONS

As provided by the Equal Credit Opportunity Act and Regulation B, I request that you report all credit information on the following account in both names. As provided by Regulation B, this request does not alter the legal obligations involving the account.

(Identify account and account number)

First   Middle   Last
Name (print or type)

First   Middle   Last
Name (print or type)

Street address, include apartment number

City, state, ZIP Code

(Signature of either spouse)

CONSUMER REMEDIES FOR VIOLATIONS

A creditor who does not comply with the act or Regulation B can be held liable for the sum of the following amounts:

- Any actual damages you sustain as a result of the violation. While these may be hard to show, damages could include compensation for embarrassment, humiliation, mental distress, and harm to your reputation or creditworthiness.
- Punitive damages of up to $10,000 in an individual suit, even if you have no actual damages.
- Reasonable attorney's fees and costs of bringing the suit if you win.

Consumers can also initiate a *class action* suit on behalf of a number of others harmed by the same violation. In addition to covering the actual damages sustained by all such consumers, a creditor could then also be liable for minimum punitive damages of either $500,000, or one percent of his net worth, plus attorney's fees and costs of bringing suit—whichever is less.

ADMINISTRATIVE ENFORCEMENT

The act is also enforced by various federal agencies, depending on the type of creditor involved, who can also take action against creditors. Although these agencies cannot represent you personally or take action on your behalf, it can be worthwhile to notify them about possible violations. Some types of discriminatory actions can be hard to prove in individual cases; reporting possible violations helps an agency to build a pattern of behavior that indicates a creditor is not complying with the law.

These federal agencies enforce the act against the different types of creditors you are most likely to deal with.

Type of creditor	*Enforcement Agency*
National Banks ("N.A." or "National" will be in bank's name)	Comptroller of the Currency Deputy Comptroller for Customer and Community Affairs 6th Floor—L'Enfant Plaza Washington, DC 20219
State banks that are members of the Federal Reserve System	Board of Governors of the Federal Reserve System Division of Consumer and Community Affairs 20th and C Streets Washington, DC 20551
Banks that are NOT members of Federal Reserve but insured by FDIC (includes such state banks and savings banks)	Federal Deposit Insurance Corporation Office of Consumer Compliance Programs 550 17th Street, N.W. Washington, DC 20429
Savings institutions insured by FSLIC and members of FHLB System (savings and loan associations)	Federal Home Loan Bank Board Department of Consumer and Civil Rights Washington, DC 20552
Federally chartered credit unions	National Credit Union Administration Office of Consumer Affairs 1776 G Street, N.W. Washington, DC 20456
Securities brokers and dealers	Securities and Exchange Commission Office of Consumer Affairs and Information Services Washington, DC 20549
Air carriers	Civil Aeronautics Board Director, Bureau of Enforcement 1825 Connecticut Avenue Washington, DC 20428
Common carriers regulated by ICC	Interstate Commerce Commission Office of Consumer Protection Washington, DC 20423
Federal land banks, federal land bank associations	Farm Credit Administration 490 L'Enfant Plaza Washington, DC 20578
Retail, department stores, consumer finance companies, all non-bank credit card issuers and any other consumer creditors	Federal Trade Commission Credit Practices Washington, DC 20580

53 · Negotiating Strategy for Asserting Your Rights under the ECO Act

The protections of the ECO Act apply only if the creditor uses a prohibited factor for taking adverse action, or violates a specific requirement spelled out in Regulation B. The act does not *require* creditors to give you the credit you've requested.

Some violations of the act may be obvious—when a creditor refuses to extend credit in your own name, for instance. Other violations may be less clear-cut such as when a creditor turns you down for what seems an odd reason. He may say you have "insufficient credit references," for instance, when, in fact, your references are good. The creditor may simply have made a mistake; he may have incredibly high credit standards; or he may actually have turned you down for a very different reason which he doesn't want to reveal because it involves a violation. How do you tell? You are most likely to spot discrimination when the creditor gives you reasons that don't quite make sense given your financial circumstances, the kind of credit involved, and the conditions under which the creditor usually extends that type of credit to others (if you have that information).

What can you do in a situation like this? Creditors don't make money by turning down creditworthy applicants so if he or she made a mistake, or you can provide further information to indicate you really are creditworthy, a creditor will usually be willing to reexamine your application.

In the case of a violation, you would be entitled to sue without giving the creditor a chance to "make up" for it by reconsidering and extending the credit. Proving anything but a very clear-cut violation can be hard, though, especially when the creditor has most of the important evidence, such as the specific standards used for making a decision and the factors he considered when deciding your application. Often, the easiest and cheapest way out for both you and the creditor is to make it clear that you won't be satisfied with a reason that doesn't make sense, and that you would like the matter to be reexamined.

Generally speaking, then, the negotiating steps included in this chapter are designed to do two things: help you get the credit you want while at the same time obtaining information that could help you demonstrate a creditor did, in fact, violate the law. If it becomes necessary to sue, seek legal advice. See if the attorney will accept the case on a contingency, based on the fees awarded if you win.

STAGE ONE: OPENING SKIRMISHES

If applying for credit involves nothing more than sending in a written application form, you aren't likely to find evidence of discrimination until after you have been turned down—unless the form itself asks you to furnish prohibited information. If applying for credit involves personal contacts or interviews, you could find discriminatory conduct initially. If this happens, try to verify it and then firmly but tactfully make it clear that you not only find it unacceptable but know that it is illegal. (See page 448 for a follow-up letter.)

There are some things for which you should prepare in advance. If, for example, you are relying on alimony, child support, or separate maintenance payments based on a court decree, have the decree handy; and take along bank deposit records to show that the payments have been regularly deposited. The requirements described in the previous chapter identify the kind of information you might have to furnish in other kinds of special situations.

If it is really important to get the credit you're seeking, find out first what kind of credit information is being reported on you. You can do this by asking a credit bureau to provide you with the information they have in their files. See page 580 for details of the Fair Credit Reporting Act: it spells out how you can get access to your credit file and have erroneous and incomplete records corrected.

REQUESTING SPECIAL FACTORS BE CONSIDERED

The following sample letter, which asks a creditor to consider special factors, can be adapted to fit your particular circumstances.

100 Witchtree Lane
Anytown, USA 00000

January 15, 19___

Mr. G. Lender
Consumer Credit Department
ABC Department Store
100 Main Street
Anytown, USA 00000

Dear Mr. Lender:

I request that you give full consideration to the following factors to complete my application for (describe credit) which I (submitted on January 10/am submitting today): (I am, as requested, furnishing the following information so you can fully consider it as part of my application for [describe credit] which I submitted on January 10:)

(1) (The credit histories on the following accounts which were reported in my spouse's name [identify spouse and current address if different from yours], and which accurately reflect my creditworthiness since I was [am] either equally liable on those accounts or had [have] full use of those accounts during the periods indicated:

[list each account or credit obligation].)

(2) (Do not consider the credit histories on the following accounts which were reported in my name as well as my spouse's [identify spouse or former spouse] but which do not accurately reflect my creditworthiness for the reasons indicated below:

[Identify the account(s) and explain why it doesn't accurately reflect on your creditworthiness].)

(3) The income I received from (identify source) which has been and should continue to be a reliable income source because (describe, based on how you received it in the past and what makes it reliable in the future). I can, upon your request, furnish copies of documents needed to verify the amount and reliability of the income I have described.

I will appreciate your giving these factors full consideration when evaluating my application for credit.

Sincerely,

If you have been turned down for credit because the credit application was incomplete, find out what information was lacking and then adapt the above letter to furnish the missing information and ask the creditor to reconsider your application.

REQUESTING A DECISION

If you do not hear from the creditor within a reasonable period (well over thirty days), after submitting an application, adapt the following sample letter to indicate you expect an answer.

100 Witchtree Lane
Anytown, USA 00000

February 28, 19___

Mr. G. Lender
Consumer Credit Department
ABC Department Store
100 Main Street
Anytown, USA 00000

Dear Mr. Lender:

I am inquiring about the status of my application for (describe type of credit) which I submitted on January 15, 19___ .
If the application is not yet completed, please indicate the additional information needed so I may complete it. If the application is complete, or if you still need information that you obtain, I would then appreciate it if you would use reasonable diligence to obtain the information needed to complete the application and promptly notify me of your decision.
Thank you for your cooperation and I hope that my application will now soon be approved.

Sincerely,

IF A PROHIBITED PRACTICE IS USED DURING PERSONAL INTERVIEWS

If you encounter a prohibited practice during personal dealings with company officials, adapt the following sample letter as a follow-up step to contact someone higher in the company. Although you might treat the situation as a violation, this low-keyed approach is more likely to help you obtain the credit you are requesting—assuming you qualify.

100 Witchtree Lane
Anytown, USA 00000

January 18, 19___

Mr. C. Creditor
Manager
Consumer Credit Department
ABC Department Store
200 Retail Mall
Anytown, USA 00000

Dear Mr. Creditor:

This is to notify you that when I discussed my application for (describe) with Mr. G. Lender on January 15, I was informed that to complete my application and to qualify for this account, I would be required to: (describe the prohibited information requested or prohibited requirements that were spelled out to you).

But since I was applying for (describe the type of credit as covered by Regulation B) while relying on (describe income source) and was prepared to furnish any relevant information you may need to evaluate my application, I cannot undertand how the additional matters requested by Mr. Lender could either be required for completing my application or considered when my application was evaluated.

I do hope this very unfortunate experience was the result of a complete misunderstanding rather than an example of a policy to discourage or deny credit applications on a prohibited basis. I would, therefore, still prefer to apply for the credit as I had originally planned.

Please let me know promptly with whom I can now discuss this matter so that I can apply for the account and have the application given due and proper consideration.

Thank you for giving this matter your prompt attention.

Sincerely,

REQUESTING THE REASON FOR AN ADVERSE ACTION

The following sample letter shows how you can request that the creditor furnish the reason, or reasons, for any adverse actions taken, if this information is not provided in your notification of the decision.

100 Witchtree Lane
Anytown, USA 00000

February 16, 19___

Credit Department
ABC Department Store
100 Main Street
Anytown, USA 00000

Dear Sir:

I request that you furnish me the specific principal reasons why my application of January 10 for (indicate type of credit) was rejected (or describe other adverse action) on February 12 as I was notified by your letter dated (   ).

Thank you for promptly furnishing me the specific reasons involved.

Sincerely,

Remember the creditor can tell you the reasons orally, in which case you would have to confirm in writing that you want written notification.

If you do not receive the reasons within thirty days, send a further request and get a mailing receipt (or send the letter by certified mail) to obtain proof you requested the information within the time limit set by the act. Be sure to indicate that this is your second request for the information.

Once the creditor tells you the specific reasons, your next step is to figure out whether they really make sense given your situation. If it appears that the decision was based on a prohibited factor, you could use a low-keyed warning follow-up step. If the reasons are appropriate, it is unlikely this step will help unless the creditor follows a policy of re-examining all decisions that are queried by applicants.

If the creditor tells you that information from outside sources was used to evaluate your application, see page 582 for how the Fair Credit Reporting Act enables you to correct any erroneous information. Take such steps promptly and *before* contacting the creditor again.

STAGE TWO: THE LOW-KEYED WARNING

The low-keyed warning follow-up step gives the creditor a chance to reconsider if he has used a prohibited factor or violated Regulation B. If he insists on sticking with his original action then your letter also strengthens your position to hold him liable because it may indicate that whatever he did was deliberate.

Adapt the following low-keyed warning sample letter to your particular situation, and check the previous chapter for a description of the ECO Act and Regulation B requirements in order to spell out how the creditor failed to comply.

> 100 Witchtree Lane
> Anytown, USA 00000
>
> February 20, 19___

Mr. T. Creditor
Manager
ABC Department Store
100 Main Street
Anytown, USA 00000

Dear Mr. Creditor:

(1) I am requesting that the ABC Company (reexamine its decision not to extend the [describe credit] for which I applied on January 10/reexamine its decision to terminate my [describe account and account number] about which I was notified on February 17).

(2A) Although I supplied all the information requested on your application form (and requested on [_____] that you specifically take certain factors into account when evaluating my application), I was notified on (February 17) that (I did not qualify for the credit/that my account was terminated) because (include in quotation marks the specific reasons you were given).

(2B) Since I was applying for (describe type of account, such as: an individual, unsecured account) while relying on (describe income source) and had submitted information that would have enabled the company to give full and due consideration to relevant factors reflecting on my creditworthiness, I do not see how I could, in fact, have failed to qualify for the reasons stated.

(2C) (I have in the meantime obtained information about my credit record from the outside sources referred to in your notification and, contrary to your notification, that record, in fact, indicates the following: [describe; or, if the information is wrong, note that fact and indicate you are correcting it—see Fair Credit Reporting Act.])

(2D) (ALTERNATIVELY, include here your own paragraph describing other reasons indicating that prohibited factors were used.)

(3) Despite this apparently unwarranted decision, I still prefer to obtain the credit I applied for on January 10 (to retain the account that was terminated) and thus minimize any damage done to my credit standing.

I hope, therefore, that the (ABC Department Store) will promptly reexamine its decision by giving full and due consideration to all, and only those, relevant factors which it may consider when evaluating an applicant's creditworthiness, as provided by the Equal Credit Opportunity Act, so that we can either satisfactorily complete the credit transaction or so that I be furnished with the actual, specific and principal reasons for any adverse action the company still considers warranted.

Please inform me at your earliest convenience of any further decision so I won't have to pursue this matter further by requiring me to discover that your decision was in fact unlawfully discriminatory.

Thank you for giving this matter your prompt attention.

Sincerely,

It is by filing a law suit that you could become entitled to discover exactly how the creditor made his decision since that is when your attorney can use legal procedures available for compelling a creditor to disclose the information as part of a suit. And that's precisely what a creditor doesn't want you to discover if he really used a prohibited basis.

STAGE THREE: THE ULTIMATUM

Your next step, short of a lawsuit, would be to send an ultimatum. If the creditor is clearly failing to comply with the law, you now approach the matter from the standpoint that a violation has probably occurred.

The following sample letter tells the creditor that you are now prepared to hold him accountable. Adapt the wording to fit your situation and to identify the probable violation based on the requirements of the ECO Act and Regulation B. Send this letter to the president of the company.

100 Witchtree Lane
Anytown, USA 00000

March 15, 19__

Mr. A. Grant
President
ABC Department Store
100 Main Street
Anytown, USA 00000

Dear Mr. Grant:

This is to inform you of your company's apparent failure to comply with the requirements of the Equal Credit Opportunity Act and Regulation B which occurred in connection with my application for (describe credit) which I submitted on January 10.

I was informed on (_____) that my application was rejected because (state reasons given). Although I requested on February 20 that your company reexamine its decision for the reasons more fully described in my letter (copy enclosed), I have to date received no response.

Contrary to the requirements of the ECO Act and Regulation B, the company (refused to consider/insisted on considering) (describe, based on the requirements of Regulation B).

And the reasons given for the company's decision not to extend credit appears incomprehensible if full and due consideration had in fact been given to all, and only to, factors relevant for determining my creditworthiness. (Indicate how the reasons given don't make sense based on the information you had furnished.)

(Moreover, it now appears the company seeks to make it as difficult as possible for persons like myself to apply or to qualify for credit since [describe any discriminatory practices you encountered during the application process].)

I still prefer to conclude this matter by obtaining the credit for which I originally applied and now request the company to evaluate my application by giving due and full consideration to all, and only those, factors which it may consider when evaluating the creditworthiness of applicants. The company has either failed to do so, or has not given me the actual principal reasons on which it based its decision despite my having given it other opportunities to do so.

I therefore request that the company now reexamine its decision and inform me of its determination within (_____) days. [Note: allow two to three weeks.]

Unless the company now treats my application for credit so that it complies with all applicable requirements of the Equal Credit Opportunity Act and Regulation B and refrains from engaging in any unlawful discrimination, I shall seek to hold the company liable at least to the fullest extent provided by that act for all damages I sustained, for the maximum $10,000 of punitive damages recoverable, and for reasonable attorney's fees and costs that can be assessed against you.

Sincerely,

54 · The Truth in Lending Act: Disclosures that Must Be Made about Credit Terms and Conditions

This chapter, and the following chapters, focuses primarily on key protections you have under federal laws when you use various types of credit. Every state also has its own laws governing consumer credit, which generally strengthen the protections you have under federal laws. State laws are likely to be important in cases which require legal action.

TRUTH IN LENDING ACT

The first consumer credit protection law enacted by Congress, the Truth in Lending Act passed in 1968. Today, it's just one part of what is known as the Consumer Credit Protection Act, an umbrella title that incorporates the various consumer credit protection laws enacted by Congress.

The Truth in Lending Act was significantly revised in 1980, and creditors were required to comply with the revisions by October 1, 1982. The description that follows is based on the revised version. The act is backed up by Regulation Z, adopted by the Federal Reserve Board, which spells out the regulations creditors must follow in more detail.

It's important to recognize at the outset what the act does and does not do. Generally speaking, it does *not* regulate the terms and conditions under which credit can be extended; such matters as interest rates on loans, for instance. Congress left it up to the individual states to regulate the terms a creditor may include in an agreement, and your state is likely to have a number of separate laws governing the extension of specific kinds of credit.

What the act does do, however, is require creditors to make specific disclosures about the most important terms and conditions under which they extend credit and to make certain disclosures about transactions made under open-end credit plans. These may be included in the credit agreement itself, or they can be given in a separate document. So while your agreement may include terms other than those that must be specially disclosed, the act has simplified and standardized the way the most important conditions must be described.

WHAT DOES THE TRUTH IN LENDING ACT COVER?

The act applies to anyone who regularly extends credit to consumers for personal, household, or family purposes. (Commercial credit is not covered.) Normally credit is extended whenever you are called on to pay a finance charge, or to repay the entire amount in more than four installments, not counting the down payment. But in the case of credit cards, the card issuer must comply with any relevant requirements governing open-end credit and credit cards even though no finance charges were imposed in connection with the account or the amounts were not repayable in more than four installments. This requirement applies to what are usually called travel and entertainment cards, like those issued by companies such as American Express and Diner's Club so that they are covered just like credit cards even though no finance charges are imposed in connection with the account.

There are a few kinds of transactions that are not covered by the act. These exceptions are as follows:

• Extensions of credit for more than $25,000, unless it is secured by real estate or personal property that is used as your principal residence (a mobile home, for instance).

• Extensions of credit involving public utility services if rates and charges are regulated by a government agency.

• Transactions made through a securities or commodities account and the credit is extended by a broker-dealer registered with the Securities and Exchange Commission or the Commodity Futures Trading Commission. This exception could include central assets accounts offered by brokers, such as Merrill Lynch's "cash management" account. At the moment though it isn't completely clear whether credit extended by brokers under such arrangements is exempted.

• Home fuel budget plans under agreements that call for installment payments for purchase of home fuels without finance charges and which a consumer can terminate at any time.

DISCLOSURE REQUIREMENTS FOR COST OF CREDIT

While the act and Regulation Z set up different requirements that creditors must follow when disclosing terms for *open-end* and *closed-end* credit, the same disclosures covering the cost of the credit must be made for both.

The two key terms that tell you how much credit costs are the *finance charge,* and the *annual percentage rate* (APR) which is based on the finance charge. Detailed requirements spell out the amounts that must be included in the finance charge, and how the APR must be computed so it accurately states the rate you are paying.

The finance charge identifies the dollars and cents cost, and must include amounts described as interest, time-price differential, any add-ons or discount charges, or any other fees for which creditors might dream up any number of names but which are imposed as a condition for extending credit.

There are certain amounts that can be *excluded* from the amounts disclosed as the finance charge under certain conditions even though such amounts are imposed in connection with extending credit and might otherwise count as finance charges.

• A creditor does not have to include application fees that everyone applying for credit must pay whether or not the credit is extended; late payment or delinquency fees; check or transaction overdraft fees unless a written agreement states that overdrawn items would be paid and such charges would then be imposed; a credit plan participation fee such as an annual charge for using a credit card account.

• If the credit transaction is secured by real property or involves a residential mortgage transaction (an extension of credit used for financing purchase of a consumer's principal dwelling, such as a house, a condominium or cooperative unit, or a mobile home or trailer), the following fees and charges could be excluded: title examination, title insurance, abstract of title and property survey fees; deed, mortgage, and similar document preparation fees; notary, appraisal and credit report fees; amounts payable into an escrow or trustee account when such amounts would not otherwise be included in the finance charge.

• Premiums charged for credit life, accident, health, or loss of income insurance can also be excluded from the finance charge but *only* under the following conditions: such insurance is not required by the creditor and that fact is disclosed to you; the premium for the initial term of the insurance is disclosed; and you sign or initial a statement specifically indicating you want the coverage.

• Premiums for property or liability coverage insurance may be excluded if you have the option of obtaining such insurance from an insurer of your choice and this fact is disclosed to you.

• Taxes or fees which are payable to public officials for recording liens on property being used as security can be excluded if they are separately itemized and disclosed.

In effect, fees and charges that may be excluded from the finance charge are included as part of the amount of the credit being extended to you; the amount on which you pay a finance charge, in other words. The more the creditor can exclude from the finance charge, the larger the amount financed, and the larger the amount financed, the more the creditor can collect in finance charges while—at the same time—lowering the rate he discloses as the cost of the credit.

The annual percentage rate identifies the dollar cost of credit on an annual basis. It is a yardstick for measuring what the finance charge is as a percentage of the amount financed, and shows you the relative cost regardless of how long it takes you to repay a loan.

Many state laws set ceilings on the maximum amount a creditor can charge for credit but they do not define the finance charge (or interest the creditor can collect) in the same way as the Truth in Lending Act. Thus, what counts as the finance charge for the purpose of setting rate ceilings, and what counts for the purpose of making an accurate rate disclosure under the Truth in Lending law, can result in a creditor charging apparently different rates for the same transactions.

If you think a creditor is charging more than he might be entitled to collect, one way to find out is to contact the state agency that enforces laws governing the type of credit you are using, or the type of creditor involved. In the case of creditors who lend money, that would usually be the state agency responsible for regulating banks; in the case of retail credit sales agreements, it would usually be your state's attorney general. Send a copy of the agreement involved and ask whether the amount charged complies with the applicable rate ceilings set by state law.

DISCLOSURE REQUIREMENTS FOR OPEN-END CREDIT

There are two sets of disclosure requirements governing open-end credit. The first covers the *initial disclosure statement* that must be given about a credit plan; it tells you important information about the terms under which you can use the plan and what it will cost. The second covers the *periodic statement* that must be regularly provided about your account giving details of transactions you have made and the charges involved.

The disclosure requirements for open-end credit also apply to credit card accounts for which no finance charges are imposed like travel and entertainment card accounts, only to the extent they would be relevant to such accounts.

THE INITIAL DISCLOSURE STATEMENT

A creditor must furnish the initial disclosure statement before the first transaction is made. It must state the legal obligations between the parties, and include the following information, though some of these requirements don't apply to credit card issuers who do not impose finance charges:

• A description of when you must begin paying finance charges on amounts you charge, and whether there is a period during which you can repay without incurring them; a so-called "free ride" period. A creditor does not have to provide such a period, but if he does he must explain it.

• The periodic rate (the percentage rate for a particular calculation period, such as a week or month), or rates, that will be used to compute the finance charge, the range of balances to which each rate is applied, and the corresponding APR for each one.

If the creditor will use more than one rate for calculating the charge and/or use different rates for different types of transactions, that must be disclosed.

• An explanation of how the creditor computes the outstanding balance on which the periodic rate is imposed. There are four basic methods used. The Federal Reserve Board has prepared model clauses creditors can use to disclose their methods and most creditors use them.

1. Adjusted Balance Method

Under this method, the creditor takes the outstanding balance at the end of the previous billing cycle (say $500 on June 30) and subtracts from it payments received or credits due you during the current cycle (say $200 during the billing period ending July 31). In this case the finance charge would be imposed on the $300 balance. (Creditors may also deduct unpaid finance charges included in the previous balance since state law may not allow them to impose finance charges on outstanding finance charges.)

2. Previous Balance Method

Under this method, the creditor imposes the finance charge on the balance owing at the end of the previous billing cycle without taking into account payments you make or credits you received during the current cycle. Say, for example, you owe $500 at the end of the previous cycle and pay $200 during the current cycle: you would pay finance charges on the $500 rather than the $300.

Some states don't allow creditors to use this method since they can collect finance charges on amounts you have already repaid.

3. Average Daily Balance Method Without Current Transactions

Under this method, the creditor imposes the finance charge on the average daily balance. To arrive at this figure, he adds the balance outstanding for each day of the billing cycle, then divides that sum by the number of days in the cycle. To get the figure for the balance outstanding each day, the creditor subtracts payments received or credits received each day but does not add transactions made during the current cycle.

Suppose, for instance, you owe $500 during the first fifteen days of the billing cycle (that total would be fifteen times $500, or $7,500), then paid $200. The balance during the remaining fifteen days of the cycle would be only $300 (a total of $4,500) for a grand total of $12,000. The creditor would then divide the $12,000 by the thirty days in the cycle, making your average daily balance $400. The periodic rate would be imposed on that amount.

When current charges are not included in the daily balance, and you do not repay the entire balance due to avoid further finance charges, purchases made during the current cycle may then be counted into the *next* month's daily balance as of the date they were added to the account. So if, for example, there is a $100 purchase on the account for fifteen days during the current billing cycle it would be counted into the sum used for computing the average daily balance for the following billing cycle, and fifteen times $100 would be $1,500.

4. Average Daily Balance Method Including Current Transactions

Under this method, the creditor uses the same formula for figuring out the average daily balance but he also adds any new charges posted to the account each day during the current billing cycle. Payments received are still subtracted, but it means you pay finance charges on all amounts outstanding each day if you have not repaid the entire balance.

Say you make a $200 charge on the first day of the billing cycle. Using the previous examples, your average daily balance would then be $200 plus $500 for the first day times fifteen days, or $10,500; plus $700 minus the $200 payment times fifteen days, or $7,500; for a grand total of $18,000 divided by the thirty days in the billing cyle for an average daily balance of $600. If you then repaid the entire balance due, the creditor would not impose a finance charge for the following billing period.

As you can see, the method used by a creditor can make a big difference in the finance charges you pay. For instance, if the periodic rate was 1.5 percent per month (18 percent APR) for each of the computation methods described, your finance charge would be $4.50 for the adjusted balance method; $7.50 for the previous balance method; $6.00 for the average daily balance method without current transactions; and $9.00 for the average daily balance method including current transactions.

- An explanation of how the finance charge is computed, along with a description of how finance charges based on a method other than the periodic rates will be determined, must be disclosed.
- The amounts of other charges that are part of an open-end plan, an annual fee, for example, or an explanation of how they are computed must be given.
- Any security interest the creditor has, or will acquire, must be disclosed.
- A summary of your billing error rights, and right to avoid payment in case of disputes about certain purchases made with credit cards, must also be given.
- If applicable, a creditor must make additional disclosures of your right to rescind certain credit transactions secured by your dwelling (see page 462), and tell you about the limitations on your liability for the unauthorized use of credit cards (see page 466).

THE PERIODIC STATEMENT

A creditor must also furnish a periodic—or billing—statement for all open-end credit plans.

A statement must be provided for each billing cycle at the end of which you have a credit or a debit balance of more than $1, or during which a finance charge is imposed. A billing cycle is defined as the time between periodic statements, and it must consist of almost equal periods. These periods may not be longer than quarterly. Most creditors send monthly statements.

A statement must disclose at least the following items (see important note on page 458 about items marked with asterisks):

* ● The previous balance.
* ● An identification of each transaction. The method of identification depends on whether the transaction involves sale or nonsale credit.

Sale credit includes purchases made with a credit card, or purchases charged to an account with a seller. Depending on the billing method used, the following information could be included as applicable:

. . . If an actual copy of the receipt or other written documentation is included with the billing statement, the transaction can be identified simply by listing the amount involved, and either the date of the transaction or the date on which it was debited to your account.

. . . If a receipt or other documentation is not provided with the billing statement and the creditor and seller are the same, the transaction must be identified by a brief description of the property or service purchased along with the amount and date. (This can be a code or reference number that is also included on the copy of the receipt you obtained at the time of purchase.)

... If documentation is not provided with the billing statement and the creditor and seller are *not* the same, the transaction must be identified on the billing statement by including the amount, the date of the transaction, the seller's name, and the city and state or country where the transaction occurred. (There are some exceptions as to how the address must be identified if the transaction was not made in a fixed location, such as an inflight charge for a ticket, or was made in your home, or involved a telephone or mail order.)

Nonsale credit refers to loan credit, such as cash advances or check overdraft loans. It can be identified with a brief description, the amount involved, and either the date of the transaction, the date on which it was debited to your account, or the date appearing on any written document you signed. The description can be omitted if you are given a copy of the receipt which states the amount and the date.

* • Credits made to your account during the billing cycle. The amounts and dates of the credits must be identified, but the date can be omitted if delay in crediting does not result in a finance charge.

• The periodic rate, or rates, used for computing the finance charge, the balance to which each rate applies, and the corresponding APR.

• The balance, or balances, on which the finance charge was computed and an explanation of how it was determined.

• The dollar amount of the finance charge debited to or added to the account. The term "finance charge" must be used to identify the amount or amounts and the components must be individually itemized if more than one periodic rate is used.

• The APR for finance charges imposed during the billing cycle.

• Any other charges made during the billing cycle must be separately itemized and identified.

• The closing date of the billing cycle and the new balance as of that date.

• The free ride period, if any. A creditor could use wording like: "To avoid additional finance charges, pay the new balance before _____ ."

* • The address where you should send notification of a billing error; it can be part of the billing error notice included on the statement.

(Note: A creditor who does not comply with requirements for disclosing items marked with an asterisk, would *not* be liable for the minimum damages amounts consumers could otherwise be entitled to collect for violation of the act, as explained on page 488.)

WRITTEN NOTICE OF A CHANGE IN TERMS

If a creditor changes the terms governing an open-end plan, he must mail notices to those affected at least fifteen days before the date the changes go into effect. This does not apply if you have already agreed to the change, or if the periodic rate is increased because of a delinquency or default, though a notice must still be sent before the date of the change. Nor does it apply if the change involves the termination or suspension of future extension of credit, late payment charges, and some other matters. (But remember the Equal Credit Opportunity Act requires creditors to send you a notice of any adverse action taken, though it can be sent after it occurs.)

DISCLOSURE REQUIREMENTS FOR CLOSED-END CREDIT

Broadly speaking, closed-end credit includes any credit that isn't open-end credit.
The terms of a closed-end credit agreement are those that spell out:

- Your financial obligations, such as the amount financed, finance charges, fees not part of the finance charges, the rate charged, and the loan period. These are terms you can usually negotiate to some extent.
- The collateral the creditor would acquire, and any additional amounts you could owe, if you fail to repay according to your agreement.
- What you may be required to do to protect the collateral, such as keeping it in good repair, obtaining insurance on it, and so on. This usually applies to cars, mobile homes, or other dwellings used as security.
- Your rights and obligations if you pre-pay the entire amount. An agreement usually specifies the amount you would have to pay as a penalty, or whether you would owe less than the full finance charges.

If the financing involves a credit sales agreement, under which you are also buying the goods or services being financed, you should make sure all the important purchase conditions are included or else that specific reference is made to another document in which important terms are spelled out.

Usually, a credit sales agreement must include a special clause called for by the FTC's "Preservation of Consumers' Claims and Defenses" Rule (see page 523). Always make sure that clause is included in any credit agreement when it is supposed to be there according to that rule.

Other terms may be included in your credit agreement, but normally only the payment terms are likely to matter. Although the chief characteristic of closed-end credit agreements used to be fixed payments and a fixed interest rate for the entire credit period, this is no longer a general rule you can count on, especially when it comes to mortgages and other types of long term installment credit. Variable rate mortgages and consumer credit agreements are becoming more common and they are obviously much riskier.

The Truth in Lending Act requires creditors to disclose key credit terms in a clear and uniform way so they stand out. (See Appendix IV for model disclosure forms prepared by the Federal Reserve Board.) Generally, a creditor must make the required disclosures about these terms before you become legally bound by them. But a creditor can delay making the required disclosures until the due date of the first payment when you order by mail, or by telephone or other electronic means (such as home computer terminal); and also for a particular transaction which is financed under a closed-end credit agreement that specifically provides for adding new purchases to the balance due under the agreement.

SPECIFIC DISCLOSURES

A creditor must disclose at least the following information if it is applicable to the transaction. There are some differences depending on whether you are making a purchase on credit or just borrowing money.

* • The identity of the creditor.
  • The amount financed. This item identifies the *amount of credit* extended to you. It can be stated as a total rather than the creditor having to itemize different charges included in the total. The total disclosed must be calculated by:

Taking the principal loan amount (which is the actual amount of credit being extended) or the cash price of items purchased on credit being extended (and subtracting any down payment or trade-in);

Adding to that amount other amounts financed by the creditor which do not have to be included in the finance charge (fees for credit insurance, for example, provided the creditor complies with the requirements); and

Subtracting from the above amount any prepaid finance charge.

* ● A separate written itemization of the amount financed which identifies at least the following amounts:

. . . The amount you receive.

. . . The amount credited to an account with the creditor (such as a previous loan being paid off by the new one) *or* the cash price of items being financed.

. . . Amounts the creditor pays to other persons on your behalf and who must be identified (such as an insurance company being paid for credit life insurance premiums or other creditors being paid from the proceeds of the loan you are getting).

. . . The prepaid finance charge.

A creditor can either automatically itemize the amount or give you a total and inform you that you can request an itemization. If you request the itemization, it must be furnished at the same time as the rest of the disclosures and be separated from them. (See Appendix IV for a model form that illustrates how an amount could be itemized.)

Always ask for an itemization. Compare the figures for accuracy with whatever amounts the creditor/seller must itemize in the actual agreement *before* you sign the agreement. Having an itemized list which identifies who the creditor is supposed to pay money to on your behalf could help you hold him accountable if he fails to make payments.

● The amount of the finance charge, which is the dollar cost of the credit.

● The APR, which must be identified using that term.

● Variable APR. If the creditor can increase the APR, the following information must be disclosed:

. . . The circumstances under which the rate could increase.

. . . Any limitations on the increase (such as a ceiling of two percentage points during the repayment period).

. . . The effect of any increase with an example of the payment terms that would result.

● The payment schedule, which gives the number, amounts, and timing of payments.

● The total of payments you would be called on to repay (as called for by the payment terms in effect at the beginning of the agreement).

* ● Any demand or "call" feature, a condition entitling the creditor to demand payment of the entire outstanding amount without you being in default. (Most credit agreements include a clause enabling a creditor to demand payment of the entire amount after you fail to pay as due, a clause which differs from a demand feature allowing this without default.)

* ● For a credit sale, the total sale price, using that term to identify the total amount you would pay for a purchase made on credit. The total sale price is the sum of the cash price, the amounts that can be added to that price when computing the amount financed, plus the amount of the finance charge.

* ● Prepayment terms or your financial obligations when you repay the amount financed ahead of schedule. If the finance charges are computed periodically and are due only on the unpaid balance, the creditor must include a statement telling you

whether there is a penalty for paying early. If this statement is filled in on the disclosure form, the finance charges due are *not* pre-computed and included in the total amount due under the agreement; the finance charges are instead only owing as of each payment becoming due.

If, on the other hand, the finance charge is computed in advance and included in the total amount owing, the creditor must say whether any portion of the finance charges would be due for a rebate if the obligation is fully repaid ahead of schedule.

* ● Late payment fees. The dollar amount or percentage charge that could be imposed for late payment.

● The creditor's security interest; which is the collateral you have to put up. For disclosure purposes, it includes any collateral in real or personal property the seller could acquire as part of the agreement. The creditor must disclose that the creditor will or has acquired a security interest in the property being purchased with the credit extended or in other property, in which case the property or type of security interest must be identified.

● Insurance premiums not included in the finance charge but sold as part of the credit agreement must be separately disclosed if the premiums are to be excludable from the finance charge.

● Official fees and security interest charges, such as those paid to check, record or release security interests, which are not included in the finance charge.

* ● A reference which refers you to the appropriate contract if you want further information about terms governing default, pre-payment penalties or rebates, or the creditor's right to accelerate due dates of payments.

* ● The creditor's assumption policy regarding residential mortgage transactions. Can someone else assume the mortgage under the original terms of the agreement used for extending credit to purchase a residential dwelling (a house, cooperative unit, condominium or mobile home)?

(*Note: A creditor who does not comply with the disclosure requirements for items marked with asterisks would *not* be liable for paying the minimum amounts consumers could collect for a violation of the act as explained on page 488.)

The model forms, prepared by the Federal Reserve Board, illustrate how creditors can make the required disclosures for closed-end credit.

COMPUTING FINANCE CHARGES FOR CLOSED-END CREDIT

Generally, three methods—or combinations of them—are used to compute and fix your payment obligation for the finance charges due under a closed-end credit agreement. They are the so-called "add-on," "discount," and "unpaid balance" methods.

1. *Add-on finance charges.*

With this method, the creditor pre-computes the total amount of finance charges due on the amount financed for the entire term of the agreement and adds it to what you owe. You are then obligated to repay the total amount.

If you make late payments, you are, in effect, underpaying the finance charges since you have the money longer than scheduled. Creditors protect themselves against this possibility by adding delinquency fees for late payments. If you pay sooner than scheduled, you are, in effect, overpaying the finance charges. Naturally enough, creditors are not too concerned about protecting you against this possibility, but most state laws require them to refund a portion of the unearned finance charges if the total amount of credit extended is repaid ahead of schedule.

2. *Discount finance charges.*

This method is the opposite of the add-on method. Here, the creditor pre-computes the total finance charges due on the entire amount extended, then *deducts* them from that amount. The actual amount of credit you receive, therefore, is the amount left after the deduction.

This method of pre-paying the finance charge is normally only used when you are actually borrowing money. It enables the creditor to collect more in finance charges than the add-on method, even though he uses the same computation rate (the rate would not be the APR that must be disclosed, however). Your state law may require a creditor to refund a portion of the finance charge upon early payment of the entire balance.

3. *Unpaid balance method.*

With this method, a creditor computes and collects finance charges only on the actual balance outstanding during the period between payments, much as in the case of open-end credit. This is much the fairest way of computing finance charges since they aren't owing until the creditor has, in effect, earned them.

With this method, creditors may pre-compute the total finance charges for the entire loan period, assuming you repaid the loan as scheduled, but only actually collect them as they are earned. This method involves more calculations then the other two, of course.

RIGHT TO CANCEL CREDIT CONTRACTS SECURED BY PRINCIPAL DWELLING

The Truth in Lending Act gives you three business days to think about and to cancel certain credit transactions for which your *principal* dwelling is used as security.

This right applies when the credit extended (1) is secured by a mortgage or other type of security interest on your principal dwelling which the creditor acquired as part of the agreement under which the credit was extended; or (2) when the person doing work for you would have a legal right to acquire a security interest (lien) on your principal dwelling based simply on the work done. In the first situation, the credit extended would usually be secured by what is called a second mortgage but it could also be a first mortgage if your home was paid for. In the second situation, someone doing major repairs or remodeling work on your dwelling could be entitled by law to have a security interest (lien) on it, even though you did not specifically agree to give one.

This right to cancel is only triggered when your principal dwelling was being used as security (the principal dwelling could be a house, a cooperative or condominium unit or a mobile home). (The right to cancel does not apply when you are buying the principal dwelling with the credit, and the dwelling serves as collateral.) And it would not apply, for example, if the security was on a second home.

Your right to cancel is usally triggered when you *first* enter into a credit transaction. The situation gets more complicated, however, if you enter into a credit arrangement secured by your dwelling but the credit is actually extended later under a separate credit transaction, like an open-end account secured by your dwelling. Your right to cancel would apply when you first make the arrangement, but you cannot count on it applying to each subsequent transaction; it would depend on how the arrangement was set up and some fine-point technicalities. In a situation like this, seek legal advice.

CONSUMER'S CANCELLATION PERIOD

When you are entitled to cancel a credit transaction secured by your principal dwelling, you can do so up to midnight of the third *business* day following the latest of these events:

- The date of the transaction.
- The date you received the required Truth in Lending Act disclosure statement pertaining to the transaction. But in this case, you might be entitled to cancel after the cancellation period is over only if the creditor fails to make certain key disclosures.
- The date you received the written notice of your right to cancel the transaction. (See below.)

If the creditor fails to furnish key disclosures or the written notice of your right to cancel, you could still cancel after the three day period but only if you do so within three years after the date on which the transaction became a legally binding obligation, and before you sell or move from the dwelling.

REQUIRED NOTICE OF YOUR RIGHT TO CANCEL

Whenever the Truth in Lending Act entitles you to cancel a credit transaction, the creditor must furnish you with two copies of a notice that tells you about your cancellation rights. This notice must clearly and conspicuously disclose that:

- Your principal dwelling will secure the credit.
- You are entitled to cancel the transaction.
- What you must do to use your cancellation right.
- How cancellation affects you.
- The date on which the cancellation period ends.

Here is a sample form prepared by the Federal Reserve Board. Forms may vary for various transactions, but they should all include the same basic information.

NOTICE OF RIGHT TO CANCEL

Your right to cancel

You are entering into a transaction that will result in a [mortgage/lien/ security interest] [on/in] your home. You have a legal right under federal law to cancel this transaction, without cost, within three business days from whichever of the following events occurs last:

(1) the date of the transaction, which is _____ ; or

(2) the date you received your Truth in Lending disclosures; or

(3) the date you received this notice of your right to cancel.

If you cancel the transaction, the [mortgage/lien/security interest] is also canceled. Within twenty calendar days after we receive your notice, we must take the steps necessary to reflect the fact that the [mortgage/ lien/security interest] [in/on] your home has been canceled, and we must return to you any money or property you have given us or to anyone else in connection with the transaction.

You may keep any money or property we have given you until we have done the things mentioned above, but you must then offer to return the money or property. If it is impractical or unfair for you to return the property, you must offer its reasonable value. You may offer to return the property at your home or at the location of the property. Money must be returned to the address below. If we do not take possession of the money or property within twenty calendar days of your offer, you may keep it without further obligation.

How to cancel

If you cancel this transaction, you may do so by notifying us in writing, at

(_____ *creditor's name and business address* _____)

You may use any written statement that is signed and dated by you and states your intention to cancel, or you may use this notice by dating and signing below. Keep one copy of this notice because it contains important information about your rights.

If you cancel by mail or telegram, you must send the notice no later than midnight of (__date__) or midnight of the third business day following the latest of the three events listed above. If you send or deliver your written notice to cancel in some other way, it must be delivered to the above address no later than that time.

I WISH TO CANCEL

_____   _____

Consumer's signature   *Date*

CANCELING THE TRANSACTION

To cancel, you *must* do so in writing within the three business day cancellation period.

If you send written notice of cancellation by telegram, notice is considered given at the time it is filed for transmission at the telegraph office. If you send notice through the mail, it is considered given when the letter is put in the mail. If you use either of these methods, be sure to get a receipt showing you sent the notice in time. If you use other methods, your notice must *reach* the creditor within the three-day cancellation period.

See page 493 for a sample cancellation letter, which also offers to return money or property furnished by the creditor.

CREDITOR'S OBLIGATION TO DELAY PERFORMANCE

A creditor is not supposed to disburse any mony for you (he may only put it into an escrow account), furnish any service, or deliver any materials during the cancellation period. This is to prevent him from making it more difficult for you to cancel since you could be required to return or pay for materials you receive. Make sure a creditor, and anyone who is going to start any work for you, sticks to this, otherwise it may become practically impossible to use your rights.

If you need work done immediately in a genuine emergency, you can modify or waive your right to cancel. To do this, you must give the creditor a written, dated and signed statement which describes the emergency and which specifically waives or modifies your right to rescind. It must be signed by everyone who could be entitled to cancel the transaction. Printed forms cannot be used for this purpose, so the statement would usually have to be handwritten.

Since it is in an emergency situation that you are most vulnerable, it is precisely at this moment that you need the extra time to think over a deal. If you sign away your right to cancel, you may be stuck with a deal that doesn't look so good next morning.

To protect yourself in a real emergency, waive your right to cancel only with respect to work or services that must be performed immediately and have the charges firmly pinned down in writing first. Say a water pipe bursts, for instance. Have a plumber stop the water flow if you can't do it yourself, but don't immediately sign a contract to redo the plumbing and waive your cancellation rights for the entire job simply because you need emergency assistance.

EFFECTS OF CANCELLATION

If you properly cancel a credit transaction the security interest in your home is void, and you are not liable for any amount, including finance charges.

If the creditor delivered any materials or furnished money during the cancellation period, you must *offer* to return it. If the creditor does not take back the money or materials within twenty calendar days of your offer, you can keep whatever is involved.

If you have given the creditor any money or property in connection with the transaction, he must return it within twenty calendar days after receiving your notice to cancel. He must also take whatever steps are necessary to terminate the security interest involved.

REQUIREMENTS FOR THE PROMPT CREDITING OR REFUNDING OF AMOUNTS DUE TO CONSUMERS

The Truth in Lending Act also spells out what a creditor must do if you end up with a credit balance of more than $1 in connection with a credit transaction because:

- You paid more than the total balance due on an account.
- You were entitled to a rebate of unearned finance charges or insurance premiums upon prepayment of the entire balance due.
- A creditor otherwise owed or held amounts for your benefit which, in effect, resulted in your having paid more than you owed. The act does not spell out when a creditor ends up holding a credit balance for this reason. But it could apply once the creditor owes a refund of what you paid. This requirement is, however, unlikely to help you resolve a dispute about whether a creditor is required to refund what you had paid, but it can help you get money back once a creditor agrees a refund is due you.

In these situations the creditor must do the following:

1. Credit your account with the amount due you and apply it to any other amounts you owe.

2. If there is still an amount due after the credit balance is applied to what you owe, it must be refunded upon your written request. A creditor can make the refund before you request it, but *must* do so afterward. In the case of an open-end credit account, the refund must be made within seven business days of a written request. In the case of a closed-end account, the refund must be made *upon* receipt of the request.

3. If you don't request a refund, a creditor must make a good faith effort to return any credit balance remaining on his books for more than six months.

These requirements apply to closed-end or open-end credit transactions, including the "no finance charge" credit cards.

These requirements can help you get refunds, especially if a creditor is legally required to rebate finance or insurances charges upon prepayment of a credit transaction or after a creditor admits you are entitled to a refund of what you have paid.

55 · The Truth in Lending Act: Your Liability for Unauthorized Use of Credit Cards

The Truth in Lending Act sets limitations on your liability for unauthorized use of your credit cards. These limitations apply to any device that can be used repeatedly for making purchases or obtaining money on credit, including "charge cards" issued by companies that do not impose finance charges.

Broadly speaking, the term "unauthorized use" covers use of a card by someone who has no legitimate basis for doing so and which brings no benefit to the cardholder.

The act sets your maximum liability at $50 for unauthorized use; though the card issuer or your state law may set it at less than this amount.

REQUIREMENTS CREDITOR MUST MEET

However, you are liable for unauthorized use only if the following requirements have been met by the card issuer:

- The card is an *accepted* credit card; that is, you have signed, used, or authorized someone else to use it. A card issued as a renewal or a substitute is deemed an accepted card only after you *receive* it. That is why companies usually send a follow-up letter asking whether you have received your card.
- The card issuer has adequately notified you in writing about your maximum liability and the methods you should use to notify him of the loss or theft of your card. You can notify the card issuer orally or in writing.
- The card issuer has provided some way of identifying you as the cardholder or as a person authorized to use the card; such as a signature on the card or a photograph or other method for verfiying the identity of the card user. This requirement protects you if a card or other adequate identification wasn't used for making an unauthorized transaction, such as mail or telephone orders when only your account number is used for charging the purchase to your account.

While the card issuer is not compelled to comply with these requirements, if he does not, he can't hold you liable for unauthorized use.

TWO LAWS MAY APPLY

If your credit card can also be used as an access device for making electronic fund transfers, one of two laws may apply depending on which feature is used.

- The Truth in Lending Act would cover unauthorized use which results only in a credit transaction.
- The EFT Act would apply when a credit card is used as an access device for initiating an EFT from an asset account, which then triggers a sequence resulting in the extension of credit. See page 402 for an explanation of the EFT Act.

HOW TO NOTIFY THE CARD ISSUER

You may notify a credit card issuer about the loss, theft, or possible unauthorized use, in person, by phone, or in writing.

You are considered to have given notification when you have taken reasonable steps to do so, such as, reporting the loss to the telephone number provided. When you give written notification, you are considered to have done so when it is *received* by the issuer, so this is a slow method to use. If your notification is lost in the mail, then you are considered to have given notice as of the time it would normally take for the letter to be delivered. If you mail a notification, at least get a mailing receipt or send it certified mail, return receipt requested. (The time requirement for electronic fund transfer access devices and credit cards is different: see page 409.) Be sure you also follow those requirements if card is also an EFT access device.

Calling is always the quickest method to use. Be sure to note the date and time of the call, the number reached, and the name of the person you spoke to or any identification or verification code the person gave you. You may want to follow up with a confirming letter that indicates when you gave initial notification.

To minimize the risk of loss or theft, carry only the cards you normally expect to use. Although the law limits your liability to $50 for each card, that figure quickly zooms up if you lose several cards.

To make it easier to notify card issuers promptly, keep a list of the relevant phone numbers and addresses handy. Delays can be costly, and a list like this can save you time and trouble.

56 · Fair Credit Billing Act: Billing Requirements Covering Open-End Credit

The Fair Credit Billing (FCB) Act, enacted in 1974, protects you in two main ways when you use open-end credit.

First, it covers certain billing practices and error-correction procedures creditors must follow. They are outlined in this chapter. Second, it provides a set of protections that apply when you make some kinds of purchases with credit cards and have a problem with the quality of the goods or services involved. Under certain circumstances, the FCB Act entitles you to withhold payments, which gives you important leverage that can help settle a dispute. This second set of protections is covered in Chapter 58.

Although Congress enacted the FCB Act as a separate law, its requirements are part of the Truth in Lending Act; a creditor's failure to comply, therefore, makes him liable for violating the Truth in Lending Act. (See Chapter 59 for a creditor's liability.)

The FCB Act sets up the following ground rules for billing practices.

PROMPT MAILING OF PERIODIC STATEMENTS

If a creditor gives a time period within which you can repay your balance due and avoid additional finance charges, he must mail or deliver a periodic statement to you at least fourteen days *before* that date. This requirement also applies if there is a delinquency charge for late payments.

If a creditor fails to send a statement before the fourteen-day period, the act prohibits him from collecting any finance or delinquency charges imposed as a result of the creditor's failure to send the statement on time.

If you move, the periodic statement must be sent to your new address—providing you give the creditor written notification of the change at least twenty days before the end of the billing cycle involved. If you still do not receive your statement at your new address, it would be considered a billing error.

If you use a change of address form included on your billing statement, you would normally have to notify the creditor two billing periods in advance. Make copies of the front and back of the statement to help verify you included the address change. Of course, notifying a creditor so far ahead can be risky—things often get fouled up, as we all know. In some ways it's safer to wait until you've actually moved, but in this case remember the creditor won't be responsible for mailing delays.

The following steps can help you keep a creditor accountable for failing to follow the fourteen day mailing requirement:

- Keep the mailing envelope in which the statement was mailed, especially when the envelope has a dated post-mark.
- If delays result because a periodic statement is sent to your old address despite your having notified the creditor about the address change in time, keep the statement so you can show how it was addressed.
- Keep the next periodic statement, too, the one on which finance or other charges are imposed because of the creditor's failure to mail the first statement on time. It

will show when a "late" payment was received by the creditor and posted to your account. You could then demonstrate that the charges are the result of the creditor's delay in mailing the first statement, and insist they be deducted from your account. If you then pay the rest of your balance, make clear that it is payment in full for amounts actually due and owing for that billing cycle.

There is a drawback to not paying avoidable charges that you should consider, though: it can lead to a continuing dispute about further finance charges that are added to your account because supposedly you have not paid your balance in full. While you would almost certainly win in the end, you would also create extra problems that could take further time and trouble to straighten out.

An alternative, though not without *its* problems, is to pay the charges and at the same time notify the creditor in writing that you are merely making an overpayment for accounting purposes, in order to avoid further payment problems, and insist he promptly and properly adjust your account. This could be said to be a situation in which a creditor owes you money, which triggers the requirement that the credit balance be credited to your account or refunded upon your written request (see page 465). If a creditor fails or refuses to do this, he could then be liable for violating two requirements of the Truth in Lending Act.

Paying in this way, then insisting the creditor return amounts he wasn't entitled to collect, can create problems if you end up having to sue to get the money back. You have to decide which of the two alternatives you think is best.

PROMPT CREDITING OF PAYMENTS

A creditor must credit payments to open-end accounts on the date they are received, *unless:*

1. No finance or other charges are imposed as a result of any delay.

2. The creditor specifies on your periodic statement the requirements you are to follow when making payment, and you fail to follow them, such as that you send only checks or money orders, or that your payment be accompanied by your account number or by a payment stub furnished by the creditor. If, however, the creditor accepts the payment anyway, he can delay crediting your account for up to five days. So it behooves one to follow payment instructions. (A creditor may not set requirements that are difficult to satisfy, though, such as demanding that payment be made only in person between 10:00 A.M. and noon, for instance.)

If the creditor does not credit payment in time, he is required to adjust your account so that any charges imposed as a result are credited during the following billing cycle. If he fails to do so he becomes liable for violating the Truth in Lending Act.

The date of receipt, by the way, generally means just that and *not* the date the money is actually collected through the check collection process. Since delays in crediting can result in hefty finance charges, the requirement prevents creditors from using delays to their advantage and your disadvantage. You can make a fairly accurate estimate of whether a payment was promptly credited by comparing the date specified on your periodic statement with the earliest date stamped on the back of your canceled check. (The latter definitely fixes the date of receipt.) If you used another method, then check the payment date and the date payment was received. If the creditor debited the payment to one of your asset accounts held by that creditor it received payment as of the date of the debit. If the date on which payment was credited to your account was *later* than the earliest date stamped on the back of the check (or the payment date when using another payment method), or if these two dates are off by more than the five-day delay period, if it is allowable, then the creditor has almost certainly failed to credit your payment in time.

BILLING ERROR CORRECTION PROCEDURES

Is your creditor billing you for someone else's purchase? Are you being charged twice for the same purchase? Did you fail to get credit for a refund due you? If you answered yes to any of these question, you are not alone. A Federal Reserve Board survey found that almost fifteen percent of the consumers interviewed had found these kinds of billing mistakes.

The FCB Act sets specific procedures creditors must follow when you complain about billing errors, and it penalizes those who fail to do so. In general these procedures apply to extensions of open-end credit (including "no finance charge" credit cards such as American Express), with the exception of those initiated by electronic fund transfers from an asset account. This would usually involve some kind of overdraft loan arrangement and the error resolution procedures of the EFT Act would normally apply.

There is one key point to remember when considering which of these two resolution procedures applies. The differences between the acts mainly affect the amount of your liability for unauthorized use and what is considered a billing error. The Truth in Lending (Fair Credit Billing) Act covers some delivery problems and some disputes that may result in your refusal to accept goods or services: the EFT Act does not apply to such problems. (See page 482 for more details about the protections available under the Truth in Lending Act in this situation.) Naturally, then, it's best to use the payment method that offers the most protection.

WHAT IS A BILLING ERROR?

The FCB Act includes the following problems in its definition of the term "billing error," and the resolution procedure applies to them alone.

- You are billed for an item that wasn't sold to you or to someone authorized to use the credit card or open-end account involved.
- You are billed for an item not identified on the periodic statement as required by Regulation Z. (See page 457 for how specific transactions must be identified.) If the identifying information about a transaction is incorrect, the creditor must either treat and correct it as a billing error or the failure to furnish the required information would be a violation of the Act. Always treat incorrect information as a billing error.
- You are billed for an item but you want more information about it from the creditor.
- The creditor fails to mail or deliver the periodic statement to your last known address provided you have given him notification at least twenty days before the end of the billing cycle.
- The creditor makes a computational error, or other kind of accounting mistake. (See the next chapter for computation methods used.)
- You are billed for property or services purchased which you haven't yet *accepted,* or which have not been delivered *as agreed.*

This is a special kind of "billing error" that covers certain kinds of disputes with a seller. What constitutes "acceptance" is spelled out by the Uniform Commercial Code with respect to goods, see page 160, and by general contract law with respect to services which is not specifically covered eleswhere in this book. But generally speaking, you could refuse to accept services only if those performed substantially failed to conform to your contract. Whether the goods or services have been delivered "as agreed" depends, of course, on what you ordered and the delivery conditions spelled out in your agreement or purchase order. But generally speaking, the types of disputes covered include refusal to take delivery because the goods fail to conform to your contract in some way or because they are "sale on approval" items; and late delivery or one that is not made in accordance with your agreement.

Whether such problems actually count as billing errors usually depends on what you agreed to and how you charged the purchase. This, in turn, means planning ahead and making sure you do the following so you would be enitled to cancel if necessary:

1. Clearly identify in your agreement the goods you are ordering, and spell out other conditions that could entitle you to refuse the merchandise.

2. Set a definite delivery deadline by which goods or services must be delivered to *you* (not the date the seller must ship). Allow enough time to notify the creditor about a billing error should a seller fail to meet the deadline involved. (See the next section in this chapter.)

3. Follow the correct procedure for refusing to accept goods that don't conform (see page 164).

4. Charge the purchase itself to an open-end credit account, such as a retail charge account or credit card account, so it will count as *sale credit* rather than nonsale credit on your periodic statement.

ESTABLISHING BILLING ERRORS

You must, of course, identify a billing error and establish that it has occurred. (No creditor has to correct errors you do not identify.)

An error may be so obvious it's easy to spot—you are billed for a purchase you never made at a place you never visited—but few mistakes are this simple. The following points can help you identify and prove a billing error.

1. Get and keep accurate written sales records.

The written documentation you get about credit purchases should accurately identify all the sales terms—what you bought, when you bought it, how much it cost. They should note any special conditions that apply, such as if the store will make an exception to its normal policy and allow you to return the item.

Be sure to keep copies of any separate sales agreements or order forms that govern the terms of a purchase you charged. These also spell out what you agreed to and could help you to verify a billing error. Make sure the terms are filled in before you sign, then immediately take your signed copy with you. This way you have proof if somebody changes the terms.

It's especially important to keep copies of your charge slips. If a creditor only provides "descriptive billing" statements that simply describe what or where you bought something, you will have little chance of finding billing errors. And even if charge slips are provided along with your billing statement, you'll find it hard to prove an amount was altered without your own copies on hand. And alterations can happen. I received an American Express charge slip on which the amount owed had been changed by a restaurant. I had no trouble spotting the "mistake" and American Express promptly corrected it when the error was pointed out to them.

There are times when you may have to sign a charge slip without knowing what the charges will be. Most car rental companies won't rent a car, for instance, unless you sign a charge slip when you take the car out. The amount you owe is filled in when you return the car.

Because you are being asked to sign a blank check, in effect, you should be very careful about keeping copies of the documents you are given. You will be asked to sign a separate rental agreement, for example, which will be completed when you return the car. Make sure it is filled in first to show the charges you will have to pay per day or per mile. When you return the car, make sure the rental agreement is completely filled in and shows all charges that are due. If possible, have the company complete the charge slip you originally signed. To protect yourself further, you could also write something like the following on the charge slip when you take the car: "Charge only for amounts due per lease agreement # _____ dated _____ ."

2. Put delivery terms into your contract or order.

As previously noted, certain problems with a purchase would be treated as a billing mistake if you had not yet *accepted* the goods or services or they were not delivered *as agreed.* So when you buy, use the kind of credit that would make this provision applicable and include terms and conditions in your agreement. This can be especially important in mail order situations, but delivery problems can come up at any time, of course. (There is a separate provision of the act which can help you deal with a dispute over a purchase you *have* accepted, see page 482.)

See Chapter 26 for how you can state purchase and delivery conditions. And remember to insist that delivery be made under the terms of a destination contract; this will significantly strengthen your position to turn a problem about non-delivery into a billing error. Timing is crucial. You must choose a delivery date that allows you enough time to complain to the creditor about a billing mistake. He must receive your complaint within sixty days of the mailing date of the first billing statement that contained the mistake.

How much time should you allow for delivery? You can never be sure exactly since the time allowed for complaints depends on how soon the purchase is posted to your account, when the creditor mails the statement, and how soon your complaint reaches him. So, to be on the safe side, the delivery date should be no later than seven to eight weeks from the date of the purchase. Seven weeks will usually give you a considerable margin for error and also allow you at least eleven days to make your complaint to the creditor.

3. Check periodic statements for mistakes.

Check for errors as soon as you receive a statement or other information you need to verify an error. Some mistakes may be obvious at once, others may not occur until there is an additional sequence, such as a seller's failure to deliver goods or services.

The periodic statement must include identifying information about each transaction so you can match it with your own documentation (see page 457); a failure to do so is itself a billing error. If lack of information prevents you from knowing whether there was an error, ask for clarification or documentary proof.

YOUR OBLIGATION TO NOTIFY A CREDITOR

The FCB Act specifies when and how you must notify a creditor about a billing error. If you don't follow the requirements, you can lose the protections the law provides.

TIME REQUIREMENT

You must send written notification of the error so the creditor *receives* it within sixty days of the date on which the *first* periodic statement containing the error was sent. It must be sent to the specific address noted by the creditor on your statement for handling such matters. Normally, it is identified as the place to send "billing inquiries." You may not include notification on the return payment stub if the creditor specifies this fact.

If you don't notify the creditor within the time limit he may still correct the error to maintain good will, but you have no special leverage to make him do so.

DEMONSTRATING CORRECT NOTIFICATION

The following precautionary steps can help you show you have correctly notified a creditor.

• Keep the mailing envelope in which the relevant statement is sent. The postmark fixes the beginning of the time period.
• Often you will have time to use regular mail. A creditor must acknowledge receipt of your notice within thirty days. If he does not do this, follow-up with a certified letter, return receipt requested. If time is important, always send your notice by certified mail, return receipt requested.

INCLUDING THE RIGHT INFORMATION

Your notice must include the following information:

• Your name and account number.
• The fact that you believe the periodic statement contains an error, the amount involved, and the reason why you believe the error occurred.

If you want further information about the transaction, you must specifically ask the creditor to provide it.

ERROR RESOLUTION PROCEDURE CREDITORS MUST FOLLOW

Properly notifying a creditor about a billing error activates the resolution procedure which spells out the following under the act:

• How soon a creditor must respond to your claim.
• What both you and the creditor can and cannot do with regard to your account while the complaint is under investigation.
• Actions a creditor must take if he admits the error occurred.
• Actions a creditor can take after telling you there was no error.
• What you can do if the creditor denies there was an error and you still see a mistake has been made.

It is important to remember that the procedures a creditor must follow do not require him to admit to and correct what you claim is an error. They only require the creditor investigate the claimed error and that he either correct what he admits is an error or tell you why he doesn't believe there is an error. A creditor can resolve a billing error by doing either of those things within the time he has under the act.

A creditor cannot, however, "resolve" billing errors simply by denying there has been an error. He must conduct at least a reasonable investigation, and he would be failing to comply wih the error resolution procedure and the act if he does not conduct a reasonable investigation.

But if, after such an investigation, the creditor decides there was no error, the billing error resolution procedure no longer covers a dispute about the error. You would then have to raise the error as a dispute based on the terms and conditions governing the agreement under which the credit was extended.

Let's look at these resolution procedures in more detail.

HOW SOON A CREDITOR MUST RESPOND

Once a creditor receives your notice, he must either:

1. Resolve the billing error by taking appropriate action within thirty days; or
2. If he is unable to resolve the matter within thirty days, he must acknowledge receipt of your notice within that period, but may then take up to ninety days from the date of receipt to resolve your complaint.

YOUR RIGHT TO WITHHOLD PAYMENT

Until the error is resolved, you are entitled to withhold payment of the disputed amount, plus any finance or other charges imposed on it.

The disputed amount itself can be:

• The dollar amount of the error you specify.
• The amount of the transaction, if the error involves the description or identification of a particular transaction.
• The entire balance owing if the error involves the failure to mail or deliver a periodic statement to your last known address (which includes your new address if you notified the creditor in time about an address change).

You must, of course, pay undisputed amounts as called for by your agreement, but a creditor cannot impose any additional finance or other charges on the undisputed amount that you pay as called for by the agreement. Say, for instance, your agreement enables you to avoid finance charges by paying the entire balance by the due date and you pay all but the disputed amount. A creditor cannot then impose finance charges on the undisputed amount because you had not paid the "full," or disputed, amount. Nor can he impose a finance charge on the undisputed amount retroactively if it turns out that no error occurred and you had, as a result, not actually paid the entire balance that might have been due.

But I caution you *not* to take advantage of this by making up billing errors or padding the amount of a "claimed" error to gain extra time to pay the entire balance due. If you want to play those games, you are on your own.

A CREDITOR'S OBLIGATIONS

A creditor may not take any of the following actions while a billing error dispute is pending:

1. Speed up payments you are required to make for undisputed amounts you owe. You are entitled to continue paying such amounts under the original payment terms.
2. Restrict or close your account because you have, in *good faith*, used your billing error rights. This would be not only a violation of the Fair Credit Billing Act but also of the Equal Credit Opportunity Act (see page 432).
3. Deduct any portion of the disputed amount, or related finance or other charges, from a deposit account that he holds in your name (in this case the creditor would usually be a bank). This would apply in situations involving automatic payment arrangements, of course. However, the bank (or other creditor) is prohibited from doing this *only* if it receives your billing error notice at least three business days before the scheduled payment would be debited.

4. Make, or threaten to make, an adverse report about your credit standing to anyone; or to report that your account is delinquent because you failed to pay the disputed amount or related finance or other charges. This requirement protects your credit record only while the dispute is pending.

5. Try to collect the disputed amount or related finance or other charges while the dispute is pending. A creditor cannot, for example, initiate suit at this time.

WHAT A CREDITOR CAN DO

A creditor can, on the other hand, do the following while a billing error dispute is pending:

1. The disputed amount and related charges can be applied against a credit limit on your account.

2. The disputed amount and related charges can be reflected on your periodic statement—providing the creditor specifically informs you that you do not have to pay them while the dispute is pending. And the creditor can impose finance or other charges on the disputed amount while the dispute is pending. If the dispute is resolved by the creditor claiming there was no error, he may then collect those amounts.

ACTIONS A CREDITOR MUST TAKE TO RESOLVE AN ERROR

A creditor must resolve an error by taking one of the following actions within the time limits.

If the Error Occurred as Claimed

If the creditor admits the error occurred in the way you claim, he must then:

- Correct the error and credit the disputed amount and any related charges to your account.
- Mail or deliver to you a written confirmation that an error occurred and what has been done to correct it.

Creditor Claims No Error Occurred or that Error Differed from the One You Claimed

A creditor could also resolve the error by either claiming there was no error at all or that the error that occurred differed from the one you claimed. In these situations, a creditor must:

- Mail or deliver a written explanation stating the reasons why the creditor believes that you are partly or completely incorrect about the error you claimed occurred.
- Furnish copies of documentary evidence of what you owe, but only if you request it.

If the creditor admits an error occurred but it differed from the one you claimed (which would usually involve a difference about the amount), the creditor must then correct the error the creditor admits occurred and credit that amount and related finance or other charges to your account.

As already noted, a creditor must conduct a reasonable investigation before claiming that no error occurred or that it differed from the one you claimed. And in the case of errors involving the non-delivery of goods or services or your failure to receive a credit that was given to you by someone who honored a credit card, a creditor cannot claim there was no error until he conducts a reasonable investigation and determines that the product or services actually were delivered, mailed, or sent as agreed; or that the information about the credit you failed to receive is actually correct. (See page 486 for requirements covering a credit you are supposed to get from someone who honored a credit card.)

While there are no definite guidelines as to what qualifies as a "reasonable" investigation, the requirement gives you some leverage: it means the creditor must supply specific reasons. In general, the less the creditor does in the way of an investigation, the greater the likelihood he has not complied with the resolution procedure—a violation of the act which could prove costly.

If the creditor claims any portion of the disputed amount is owed, he must:

• Promptly notify you in writing and state what portion of the disputed amount is owing and when it must be paid.

• Give you as much time to pay the disputed amount he claims is due (plus related charges that have accrued on it) as you would have had to pay originally without imposing additional finance charges. A creditor must, however, give you at least ten days to pay. If, for example, your agreement gives you a "free ride" period, the creditor must allow you that much time to pay the disputed amount (plus accrued charges) without imposing additional finance charges. But if you could not have avoided finance charges, you must be given ten days to pay.

• Can report you as being delinquent only at the end of any "free ride" period that applies or after the ten-day minimum period.

PROCEDURE THAT APPLIES IF YOU STILL THINK AN ERROR HAS BEEN MADE

If a creditor claims there is no billing error, and you still think he is wrong, you can reassert that the error occurred. This step simply obligates a creditor to furnish additional information to credit reporting agencies.

To reassert an error you must do so in writing within either the "free ride" period or the ten-day minimum period—whichever is relevant. If you do this and still refuse to pay the disputed amount, a creditor cannot report that your account is delinquent *unless* he *also:*

• Promptly reports that the amount or account is in dispute.

• Mails or delivers to you a written notice of the name and address of each person to whom he reports such a delinquency at the time he does so.

• Promptly reports any subsequent resolution of the reported delinquency to those same people.

Once he has fully complied with the billing error resolution procedure, though, a creditor has no further obligation. If you still refuse to pay the disputed amount, he can initiate collection action, such as a lawsuit. So if you take this step seek legal advice and be prepared for possible legal action. If you were right and did not owe the amount claimed by the creditor under your agreement, he could not then collect.

As an alternative, you could pay the disputed amount under protest while reserving your rights, and then try to get your money back. Do not do this, though, if you insist on holding a credit-card issuer accountable for a seller's failure to honor an agreement (see page 482).

CREDITOR'S SPECIAL LIABILITY FOR A FAILURE TO COMPLY

A creditor who fails to comply with any of the requirements for correcting billing error disputes, forfeits the right to collect the disputed amount plus finance or other charges imposed on that amount up to a maximum of $50.

If, for example, he does not respond to your notice within the time limit, he can be out up to the $50 maximum even if no error actually occurred.

A creditor who fails to comply could also become liable under the civil liability provision of the Truth in Lending Act (see page 488).

57 · Methods Used to Calculate Finance Charges, and Average Daily Balance for Open-End Accounts

Accounting errors that are usually the hardest to spot are those involving the computation of the finance charge, a rebate due for a finance charge, and the average daily balance.

While it may be difficult, and sometims impossible, to calculate these amounts to the last penny, you can make a rough estimate to see whether it would be worth activating the billing error resolution procedure.

CALCULATING PERIODIC FINANCE CHARGES

There are two ways you can roughly calculate the amount due for finance charges on an open-end account when the calculation is based on a periodic rate.

The first is simply to multiply the balance on which the finance charge is computed by the periodic rate used. (See your periodic statement for these figures.)

If, for example, your balance is $600 and the periodic rate is 1.7 percent per month, the finance charge would be about $10.20 (or $600 × .017 = $10.20). While your calculation may not match the creditor's calculation exactly, if the difference is more than a very small amount, he is likely to be way off the mark.

The second way to estimate is to divide the annual percentage rate for the applicable periodic rate by 360 (which is usually the number of days in a creditor's year). For example, if the periodic rate is 1.75 percent per month, the annual percentage rate would be 21 percent (or .21 when using it for computations). The daily percentage rate would then be about .000583, or .0583 percent (that is .21 divided by 360 = .000583, which equals .0583 percent).

Using the daily rate is generally the easiest way to estimate the amount of finance charges due on a particular amount outstanding for a specific number of days. For example, if $600 is outstanding for twenty days and the creditor imposes a periodic rate of 1.75 percent per month, the finance charge would be about $6.99 (or $600 × 20 × .000583 = 6.99). Since the creditor might be using a slightly different computation method there could be a small difference in the sums.

You cannot use the daily finance charge rate computed as per the above method to make an accurate estimate of the finance charge due for a billing period when the creditor applies the periodic rate to the balance for that period. Unless the billing period is for 30 days, differences in the number of days in each billing period will throw your calculation off.

CALCULATING THE AVERAGE DAILY BALANCE

Figuring whether a creditor has correctly calculated the average daily balance can sometimes be impossible. For example, if the dates on which amounts are posted to your account are not identified, you won't know when they are counted as part of the daily balance, and you won't be able to check the creditor's accuracy.

In some other cases, though, if a creditor makes an error in his calculations, the mistake is likely to be a substantial one which could be costly to you but which should also be easy to spot. For instance, if the periodic rate is 1.5 percent per month (or .015 for calculations), a $100 error in the creditor's calculation would cost you about $1.50 per month (or $100 x .015 = $1.50).

The following method allows you to make a rough estimate of a creditor's accuracy.

If you have not paid the entire balance due and charges are imposed on transactions added to the account during the current billing period, the average daily balance should *not* exceed the sum of the previous balance and the new amounts added. If the previous balance for the period ending September 30, say, was $400 and $600 is added for new transactions, the average daily balance cannot then exceed $1,000. If it does, the creditor has made an accounting error.

Just how much less the average daily balance should be than this maximum depends on how much and when you pay and when new transactions are posted to your account. Consider a 30-day billing period for which the previous balance was $500. If your $300 payment isn't posted to the account until the last day of the billing period and a $400 transaction is added on the second day, the average daily balance would be about $876; or very close to the sum of the previous balance and the amount added for new transactions. But if the $300 payment is posted to your account on the second day of the billing period and the $400 transaction is added on the last day, the average daily balance would be about $223; or very close to the total you would get by subtracting your $300 payment from the $500 previous balance. As you can see, the average daily balance can vary considerably (over $600 in our example) depending on when payments and transactions occur.

However, if amounts added to the account are spread out over the billing cycle, and you make a payment exceeding the total for new purchases at least by the middle of the billing period, the average daily balance should then be close to or even below the previous balance.

If amounts added for new transactions exceed the payment you make, as described above, the average daily balance would then usually exceed the previous balance by an amount close to the difference between the amount for new purchases and your payment. If the creditor's calculation is substantially higher than yours, it may indicate an accounting error.

Remember, though, that this rough estimate can be thrown off if most or all of the amount for new transactions is added to your account before you pay.

If you do not pay the entire balance to avoid finance charges and the creditor does not impose finance charges on amounts added during the current billing cycle, it is more difficult to make a rough estimate of the average daily balance. This is because the calculation for the current cycle is usually based on the balance outstanding at the beginning of the current billing period and the amounts outstanding for new transactions added to the account during the previous billing period.

To estimate the average daily balance you have to look at transactions involving two consecutive billing periods. The average balance should never exceed the sum of the previous balance for the current billing period and the total amount added for new transactions during the previous billing period. Suppose, for example, the balance due at the end of the July 8 billing period is $600. (This would also be the previous, or opening, balance for the next billing period, say the one ending September 8.) If $400 is then added for new transactions during the period ending July 8, and the creditor does *not* impose finance charges during this period, the average balance for the period ending September 8 should not exeed the sum of the $600 previous balance plus the $400 added for new transactions.

How much less than this maximum the average daily balance should be depends on the amount and when you pay the July 8 bill and when the new transactions are added to your account. You could also roughly estimate the average balance in this situation by making the calculation on page 479.

If any of your rough estimates indicate the creditor may have made an accounting error—be it for the finance charge or the average daily balance—claim a billing error. When you do this, simply describe your calculations and ask for a correction. Don't withhold payments based on your own estimates unless it is absolutely clear the creditor is wrong.

CALCULATING A REBATE DUE FOR FINANCE CHARGES WHEN YOU PRE-PAY A CLOSED-END AGREEMENT

The amount due for finance charges under a closed-end credit agreement is often pre-computed for the entire payment period and included in the total balance due. If you prepay the entire balance and are entitled to a rebate of part of the finance charges (see page 461), check your agreement to see if it identifies the formula used for computing a rebate.

The formula most commonly used if repayments are made in a number of *equal* payments is generally referred to as the "rule of 78's" or the "sum of the digits method." Other formulas may be used, but most state laws allow creditors to use the rule of 78's.

This is how it works: The first step for figuring the rebate consists of adding up the number of digits for the payments in a schedule. For example, a schedule calling for fifteen equal monthly payments has fifiteen payments numbering from 1 to 15. Adding up these digits literally means adding $1 + 2 + 3$ and so on for a total of 120. (If you add the digits for a schedule calling for twelve payments, the total is 78, hence the rule of 78's.)

There is a much faster way to figure out the sum of the digits. This is the formula:

$$\frac{N}{2} \times (N + 1) = \text{the sum of the digits}$$

The "N" stands for the number of payments. So if your agreement calls for you to make 15 payments, the "N" stands for 15.

Suppose there are 15 payments and you plug them into the formula. You then get:

$$\frac{15}{2} \times (15 + 1) = 120 \text{ or the sum of the digits for 15 payments}$$
$$7.5 \times 16 = \quad\quad 120$$

The sum of the digits gives you the total number of equal parts into which the finance charge for the entire payment period is divided for the purpose of calculating the rebate. So instead of the finance charge being divided into 15 equal parts based on the number of payments, it is divided into 120 equal parts so there is actually a different amount included for finance charges in each payment. (That is, a different number of equal parts is included for finance charges in each payment made.)

The second step consists of figuring out how many parts of the finance charge remain to be paid upon prepayment. The easy way to do this is to add up the sum of the digits for the *number* of payments that you are paying off ahead of schedule. To get this sum, you use the same formula as before, but now the "N" stands for the number of payments you are prepaying. Suppose, for example, you repaid an entire 15 monthly-payment loan before the due date for the 11th payment. The *number* of payments being repaid ahead of schedule would be 4 (or 15 minus 11) and the "N" would therefore stand for 4.

Thus, the sum of the digits would be:

$$\frac{N}{2} \times (N + 1) = \frac{4}{2} \times (4 + 1) = 2 \times 5 = 10$$

This sum gives you the total number of parts of the finance charge that would be due as a rebate.

The last step is to determine the portion of the total finance charge to be rebated. To figure this amount, simply multiply the rebate fraction by the total finance charge due for the entire loan period.

The rebate fraction is the sum of the digits for the *number* of payments being repaid ahead of schedule *divided by* the sum of the digits for the total *number of* scheduled payments. You then multiply this amount by the total finance charge to get the amount due as a rebate. Here is the formula for making this computation:

$$\frac{\text{(sum for number of payments made early)}}{\text{(sum for number of payments in schedule)}} \text{ (times) (total finance charge)}$$

$$= \$ \text{ amount due as rebate}$$

Suppose, for instance, the total finance charge due for a 15-month loan repaid in 15 equal installments was $225 which you repaid ahead of schedule as in our example. Plugging those numbers into the formula for computing the rebate gives you:

$$\frac{(10)}{(120)} \times (\$225) = (\$18.75), \text{ the amount of your rebate.}$$

So by repaying 4 installments early in a schedule calling for 15 equal payments, you would get back ½ of the total finance charges due for the entire loan period, or—in our example—$18.75 out of the $225.

There are two important points to remember when using these calculations. First, they do *not* work if your payments are not for equal amounts. Nor do they work if the schedule calls for one payment that is much larger than the others; not counting the down payment or any other payments made which were not counted into the amount being financed. You can ignore a slight difference between the last payment and the others, as long as it is no more than a few dollars.

Second, the number of payments that would count as having been completely paid ahead of schedule are normally only those coming due *after* the due date of the next payment coming due when pre-payment occurred. Say, you repay the entire balance one day after the due date of the eleventh payment rather than before its due date as in our example. The twelfth payment would not be counted as having been repaid early and you would be considered to have repaid only 3, rather than 4, payments ahead of schedule.

58 · Fair Credit Billing Act: Special Protections Covering Use of Credit Cards

Some special protections apply to the use of credit cards but not to other types of open-end credit. They are the subject of this chapter and cover the following areas:

- Your right to withhold payment from the card issuer in cases where you have a dispute with a seller about certain kinds of purchases made with a credit card.
- Restrictions on a card issuer's (usually a bank's) right to collect by taking money from an asset account it holds for you.
- Requirements for the prompt reporting and crediting of refunds involving credit card transactions.

YOUR RIGHT TO WITHHOLD PAYMENT FROM CARD ISSUER DURING A DISPUTE WITH A SELLER

Making purchases with a credit card is a very handy way to buy, of course. But until the Fair Credit Billing Act came along, buyers with a valid reason for not paying a seller were usually left with little recourse but to pay the card issuer for amounts charged. This was especially true when the card issuer was a bank, but it could also happen when consumers used a seller's own credit card.

Now, creditors are periodically required to remind you about special rights you have in case of a dispute. They usually do this by including a notice on your periodic statement. In effect, the protections act as defensive legal weapons: if you have legal justification for refusing to pay amounts outstanding, the card issuer cannot collect when the protections available under the act apply. Still, very few consumers seem to be aware of their rights or know how the act can help them. An executive at a major New York bank told me he could not think of a single instance in which a consumer had tried to use these protections. The *Wall Street Journal* recently reported that banks had not gone out of their way to publicize the FCB Act protections and show how they have substantially changed a consumer's rights.

WHEN DO THE PROTECTIONS APPLY?

It's important to note at the outset that the protections apply only in the following circumstances:

1. The purchase itself is made with a credit card, including "no-finance charge" credit cards issued by such companies as American Express.

This requirement therefore *excludes* purchases made with a cash advance obtained with a credit card; with a check which, in turn, accesses an overdraft line of credit tied into your checking account; with a check that directly accesses an open-end credit account; or with debit cards or electronic fund accessing devices that trigger an extension of credit. In other words, using any of the new-fangled payment methods is almost a sure way of losing the protections.

2. The amount charged exceeds $50. (See exceptions under point three below.)

If you pay partly in cash and charge the rest of the amount, the protections apply to the amount charged only if it exceeds $50.

3. The disputed transaction occurs either in your home state or within one hundred miles of your current mailing address except when this geographic limitation does not apply.

In the following circumstances the $50 minimum purchase amount and the geographic limitations do *not* apply; a purchase would be covered by the protections regardless of those limitations.

- The card issuer and the company that honors the card are the same. If you use a Sears credit card to make a purchase at a Sears store, for instance, the purchase would be covered.
- The card issuer and the company that honors the card are linked by common ownership or control. For example, you use a card issued by the XYZ Credit Card Company to buy something from the ABC Sales Company and one of them is owned by the other company, or both are owned by a third company.
- The company that honors the card is a franchised dealer handling the card issuer's products or services. You use a Mobil Oil credit card to buy something from a Mobil station, for instance.
- The card issuer participates in the solicitation or advertising of the products or services which prompt you to buy and you charge the purchase with that card.

WHAT ABOUT MAIL ORDER PURCHASES?

A big question is how the protections apply to mail order purchases made from companies located far from your home state. Does the purchase transaction occur in your home state where you mail the order? Or does it occur in the state where the mail order company is located?

The act does not provide a clear-cut answer; instead it leaves it up to individual state laws. Under contract law, such purchases would usually be considered to have been made in the state where the mail order company is located.

It is possible, however, to argue at least that a transaction occurs in your home state where you mail an order and authorize the company to charge it to your account, especially if you include that as a purchase condition.

This is how you could include such a condition in your order: "By accepting this order and charging the $_____ price to (*identify credit card and account number*) as authorized by the buyer, the seller agrees that, for the purpose of the card holder's rights under the Fair Credit Billing Act, this transaction occurred in the buyer's home state." (See page 000 for how to spell out purchase conditions when ordering.)

The seller may not accept your order under these conditions, of course. If he does you still may not get the protections, but at least it gives you some leverage if things go wrong.

YOUR PROTECTIONS IN A DISPUTE

These are the different ways the act protects you if something goes wrong with a credit card purchase.

Card Issuer Can be Held Responsible for Seller's Failure to Honor the Agreement

The act entitles you to raise all claims and defenses relating to the seller's failure to resolve a dispute against the card issuer. (You cannot, however, hold a card issuer responsible for what are called tort claims, such as product liability claims.) Simply put, this requirement makes the card issuer responsible for the seller's failure to live up to the terms of your contract. And if you wouldn't have to pay the seller, nor would you have to pay the card issuer.

Say, for example, a product doesn't measure up to a warranty under which the seller is accountable, or the seller fails to deliver the product, or otherwise breaks your agreement, you could bring up the same reasons to justify not having to pay the card issuer.

But whether you would no longer owe the money and/or have a claim for money the seller owes you—such as for damages—depends on the rights and remedies you have available for holding the seller accountable, such as your right to reject or revoke acceptance.

A disputed purchase is one for which you have justification to hold the seller accountable.

Your Right to Withhold Amounts Still Due to Card Issuer

The act entitles you to withhold payment of the amount still outstanding at the time you *first* notify the seller or card issuer about the reasons you had for not owing the money. (For this reason always get verification of the date by obtaining a mailing receipt for your notification, or written acknowledgement from the seller.)

Suppose, for example, you charged a $200 purchase but had already repaid $100 when you discovered the product was defective and notified the seller. If you then got involved in a dispute about having the defects corrected, there would be $100 still outstanding for the purchase. The FCB Act would only enable you to hold the card issuer accountable up to that $100 (which you could do by withholding payment of that amount): it would not require the card issuer to refund the $100 you had already repaid. Instead, you would have to get that back from the seller.

The act also specifies how payments and credits are to be applied to the amounts owed to the card issuer. Generally, they are applied to purchases in the order in which charges are entered on the account, so the first item entered is also considered the first one paid. But according to the Act, payments and credits are first applied to late charges due, then to finance charges that have been imposed, and then to any purchases charged.

Although these computations can get very involved, it is usually easy to tell what, if any, portion of the purchase price is still outstanding. Simply add up the total amount outstanding at the time the disputed purchase was posted, plus amounts added for finance and late charges paid by that time. Then add up the total amount you have repaid since then up to the payment made for the billing period before the one during which you first notified the seller and/or card issuer about the dispute. The amount by which the total payments you made exceeds the amount outstanding for other purchases and charges posted to the account before the disputed purchase should then give you a rough estimate of how much was still outstanding for the disputed purchase at the time you first notified the seller or card issuer. If the total amount repaid is less than amounts outstanding for purchases and charges posted before the disputed purchase, the entire amount for the disputed purchase would then still be outstanding.

To keep a card issuer accountable you must, as noted, retain an outstanding balance on your account. Obviously, then, you cannot keep this protection very long if you have an account that requires you to promptly repay the entire balance; or if you use a credit card account that is linked to other accounts which are immediately debited to pay for purchases.

Fancy financial services packages, for instance, often include a credit card along with brokerage accounts and money market funds plus lines of credit. One large brokerage firm is marketing a loan program which extends credit using your home as security, and you can, in effect, tap that credit by making purchases with a credit card. Amounts charged with the credit card, are, however, promptly paid from the line of credit or asset accounts you have as part of the package of services. Since that means, in effect, that your credit card account is paid, it is very unlikely the FCB Act protections would apply, nor are you likely to have those protections under your loan agreement with the brokerage firm.

If you have a credit card account under which purchases are promptly paid out of an asset account, such prompt payment would also almost certainly strip you of the FCB Act protections.

I caution you, therefore, not to use such credit accounts if it is important for you to retain the act's protections. Instead use a credit card account that enables you to delay repaying until you are sure everything is all right with a purchase. Doing this will, of course, trigger finance charges. But that is a price you must pay to cover yourself.

Card Issuer Prohibited from Making Adverse Credit Reports

If you withhold payment, the card issuer may not report the amount in question as delinquent until the dispute is settled (meaning you, the seller and/or card issuer resolve the dispute to your satisfaction), or until a judgment is entered against you (meaning the creditor and/or seller sues and a court decides you actually owe the money). The card issuer can, however, report the amount as being in dispute. He can also take whatever collection action would be normal in the situation, such as demanding payment by sending dunning notices or initiating suit.

But a creditor who closes or restricts your credit card account solely because you withhold payment based on your rights under the FCB Act, risks violating the Equal Credit Opportunity Act. He would be taking adverse action for when you have used your rights in good faith.

YOUR OBLIGATION TO SEEK A SETTLEMENT WITH THE SELLER BEFORE WITHHOLDING PAYMENT

Before you can hold a card issuer accountable and withhold payment, you must first make a good faith attempt to settle the dispute with the seller who honored the card. If it fails you are then entitled to hold the card issuer responsible. To use these rights, you must, therefore, always first try to resolve the problem with the seller.

HOW THE BILLING ERROR PROCEDURE AND YOUR RIGHT TO HOLD A CARD ISSUER ACCOUNTABLE FIT TOGETHER

Some kinds of errors covered by the billing error resolution procedure may also be considered claims or defenses that could be raised against a card issuer. For example, a delivery problem may be both a billing error and a defense for non-payment.

If two rights apply to the same problem, you can assert them separately or both at the same time. There are, however, some differences between the two ways of dealing with disputes.

The billing error procedure applies to any purchase charged to an open-end account *regardless* of where the transaction occurred or of the amount involved; such limitations do apply to the protections covering a dispute about a purchase, however. The billing error resolution procedure sets a time limit by which you must notify a creditor about a billing error; no such time limitations apply for notifying a card issuer when you raise claims and defenses against him.

Your right does expire, though, as soon as you've paid the card issuer for the purchase. You can, however, raise a billing error dispute after you have paid the card issuer for the purchase. It is the time limitation for notifying a creditor about an error which restricts how long you can do this in case of billing errors, and whether you have paid in the case of claims and defenses.

If, however, you notify a creditor about a billing error, you can refuse to pay the disputed amount until the matter is resolved. This *could* mean the outstanding balance for the purchase remains unpaid, so you *may* still raise claims and defenses against the card issuer who denies there is a billing error.

If both your billing error rights and right to raise claims and defenses apply to a transaction, it could be worthwhile to raise a billing error first. If the card issuer denies the error, then raise your claims and defenses. To get maximum leverage out of both rights, raise your claims within the time limit for reasserting a "billing error" (see page 472).

There is a lot of misinformation around about how these two separate protections apply to credit purchases. Don't think, for example, that you lose your right to raise a claim or defense unless you do it within sixty days of receiving the relevant periodic statement. In the same way, don't be misled into thinking the $50 minimum and the geographic restrictions apply to billing errors.

CARD ISSUERS PROHIBITED FROM DEDUCTING PAYMENTS OWED FROM AMOUNTS ON DEPOSIT

If you have funds on deposit at a bank or other financial institution, a favorite collection device if you don't make payments on a loan is simply to deduct what you owe from the funds on deposit in some other account. This is usually called a bank's "right of set-off" and is different from using a deposit account as specific collateral for a loan.

While credit card issuers are now generally prohibited from simply off-setting any debts involving a credit card plan, there are two exceptions.

1. If the card issuer is legally entitled to deduct amounts based on remedies available under your state law to all creditors, such as garnishment of deposited funds, or court orders.

2. If the card issuer has your written authorization to periodically deduct amounts due from a deposit account. If you have given such authorization, a card issuer cannot make deductions for a disputed amount if you specifically request in writing that he not do so.

Regulation Z allows a creditor to include a provision in your agreement which authorizes him to use deposited funds as collateral from which he can deduct money you owe. It is questionable, though, whether he could simply deduct amounts you are entitled to withhold under the FCB Act.

If you are involved in a dispute about whether you owe money involving a credit card purchase, the way to trigger the issuer's potential liability for violating this provision is to request him not to deduct the disputed amount from any deposit accounts.

DEADLINES FOR REPORTING AND CREDITING REFUNDS

The FCB Act sets up certain deadlines if you are due to receive a refund from someone other than a card issuer—a seller, say—which is to be credited to your credit card account. The company giving the credit must send a credit statement to the card issuer within seven business days after it has agreed to the refund. This deadline is triggered on the date the business either *accepts* the return of goods, or says you no longer owe the money for a purchase. (If you obtain a refund, get a *dated* credit statement from the business involved.) The card issuer must then credit your account within three business days after receiving the credit statement.

If you are returning goods by mail, which the seller has agreed to take back for a refund, get a return mailing receipt. Of course, if you are simply returning goods which the seller has not agreed to take back, the date of receipt would not necessarily trigger any deadline for sending a credit statement.

If you are getting the refund from the person who originally billed you for the amount, a failure to reflect the amount on your periodic statement would count as a billing error.

The FCB Act also requires that credit card and cash customers be treated equally when it comes to refunds for returned goods, unless the seller has informed you that credit or cash refunds would not be given for purchases made with credit cards.

59 · Creditor's Liability for Violating the Truth in Lending (Fair Credit Billing) Act

The Truth in Lending Act, including the parts that were separately enacted as the Fair Credit Billing Act, spells out a large number of separate requirements creditors must follow.

A creditor who fails to comply with these requirements becomes liable for violating the act. That means two things. First, that you are entitled to sue the creditor in either state or federal court for failing to comply. And second, if you win your case, the creditor becomes liable to you for the *sum* of the following amounts:

• Any actual damages you suffered as a result, such as the amount of a credit balance that was not refunded to you.

• In the case of an individual suit, a minimum equal to twice the amount of the finance charge involved, with a minimum recovery of $100 and a maximum of $1,000. (This does *not* apply if the creditor only failed to comply with certain credit term disclosure requirements as noted by asterisks on pages 457 to 458 and pages 459 to 461).

• The cost of bringing suit, plus reasonable attorney's fees.

In successful consumer actions, courts have almost routinely awarded these amounts, so it can be very costly for creditors to violate the act. Your actual damages and the minimum amounts recoverable provide your basic bargaining leverage. The chance to recover attorney's fees and costs makes it worthwhile to seek legal advice; and, of course, the threat of legal action gives you further clout for convincing a creditor to settle.

The act also enables consumers to initiate a class action in order to hold a creditor accountable in one suit for the same violation. Such suits can also be very costly for a creditor: the minimum amount awarded is $500,000 or 1 percent of the creditor's net worth—whichever is less.

Generally, a creditor becomes liable for violating the act once he has failed to follow a requirement. There are some instances, though, where the act provides specific corrective action. For example, if a creditor fails to mail a periodic statement within the fourteen-day deadline, he must then take the specific corrective action required—in this case to mail the statement and avoid collecting finance charges. A creditor who takes the required corrective action would not then be violating the Act. But a failure to take the required corrective action would be a violation.

Specific corrective action usually covers billing or accounting practices creditors must follow with open-end accounts.

TIME LIMITATION FOR BRINGING SUIT

Generally speaking, you must sue a creditor within one year of the alleged violation—not one year after you first find out about it, if that timespan is different.

WHEN A CREDITOR MAY NOT BE LIABLE

Sometimes creditors are not liable for violations of the act. This could happen, for instance, if the violation results from a bona fide error; or if the creditor corrects a violation on his own within sixty days (and before you take any action against him); or if, in good faith, he follows rules, regulations or interpretations issued by the Federal Reserve Board which a court later decides do not conform to the law.

There is another exception, too. It applies when your credit agreement is sold to someone else. In this case, the creditor purchasing the agreement usually would not be liable for violations committed by the original creditor unless they were apparent on the original disclosure document. If you discover a violation later, you would probably not be able to hold the new creditor liable. However, if you are entitled to cancel a transaction that is secured by your home, you can use your right to cancel against the original creditor as well as anyone else who purchases the agreement.

FEDERAL ENFORCEMENT AGENCIES

The Truth in Lending (Fair Credit Billing) Acts are enforced by several different federal agencies. The agencies and the creditors they monitor are as follows:

Type of creditor	Enforcement agency and address
Nationally chartered banks (will have "N.A." or "National" in bank's name)	Comptroller of the Currency Deputy Comptroller for Customer and Community Affairs 6th Floor—L'Enfant Plaza Washington, DC 20219
State banks that are members of the Federal Reserve System	Board of Governors of the Federal Reserve System Division of Consumer and Community Affairs 20th and C Streets Washington, DC 20551
Banks that are NOT members of the Federal Reserve System but insured by FDIC (includes such state banks and savings banks)	Federal Deposit Insurance Corporation Office of Consumer Compliance Programs 550 17th Street, N. W. Washington, DC 20429
Savings institutions insured by the FSLIC and members of FHLB System (savings and loan associations)	Federal Home Loan Bank Board Department of Consumer and Civil Rights Washington, DC 20552
Federally chartered credit unions	National Credit Union Administration Office of Consumer Affairs 1776 G Street, N.W. Washington, DC 20456
Air carriers	Civil Aeronautics Board Director, Bureau of Enforcement 1825 Connecticut Street Washington, DC 20428

Federal land banks, federal land bank associations	Farm Credit Administrator 490 L'Enfant Plaza Washington, DC 20578
Retail, department stores, consumer finance companies, all non-bank credit card issuers and any other creditors	Federal Trade Commission Credit Practices Washington, DC 20580

CONTACTING ENFORCEMENT AGENCIES

If you have questions about whether a creditor has complied with the acts, contact the appropriate enforcing agency. Supply *copies* only of all relevant documents and correspondence and ask if the agency thinks the creditor acted in accordance with the law.

It is not the policy of all agencies to provide answers to the public and even if you do hear, it will not necessarily be the last word on the subject. But if you are told that, based on the information supplied, the creditor does not appear to be complying with the law, it will certainly strengthen your position and help you hold a creditor accountable.

The Federal Trade Commission's policy is to inform people whether or not particular practices comply with acts it enforces. Other enforcing agencies may also provide answers to questions, so you have nothing to lose by trying to get this kind of information. (See page 55 for a sample letter.)

STATE CONSUMER CREDIT PROTECTION LAWS

Each state also has its own set of consumer credit laws. They vary considerably from state to state so it is beyond the scope of this book to describe them in detail, but in general this is how they cover the different types of credit.

• *Retail credit agreements.* Every state has one or more laws that govern various kinds of retail credit; usually they are called retail installment sales acts. Some states may have just one law that governs all credit agreements used for selling goods or services; others may have one law for the sale of cars and a separate law for other retail sales; still others may have as many as three separate laws; and some states may have laws that cover certain retail credit sales only. Usually, the state laws set maximum finance charges a seller can charge, and impose other limitations on the terms and conditions included in credit agreements. They are usually enforced by the state attorney general or by a separate agency established for the purpose.

• *Small loan or finance company regulatory loan laws.* Laws that regulate the lending activities of small loan or finance companies usually set the maximum amount chargeable for loans, and limit some of the terms and conditions that can be included in the agreement. These laws are usually enforced by your state's banking department, financial institutions bureau, or an agency that has been set up to regulate various financial institutions.

• *Usury laws.* Usury laws set the maximum interest rates chargeable, unless there are separate laws authorizing creditors to exceed the set rates. Any state that specifically regulates particular types of creditors, or credit, will also authorize creditors to charge more than the maximum set by the state's usury law. Because of exceptions made by these separate laws, your state's usury law (if it has one) is unlikely to apply to most types of consumer credit; nor is it likely to be enforced by a state agency. However, a usury law is still important as a way of getting a creditor to comply with a separate law that regulates consumer credit transactions: that's because if the creditor fails to follow a separate law he would then only be able to charge the lower rate allowed by the usury law.

• *Laws regulating specific types of financial institutions.* Financial institutions that take deposits and make loans (such as banks, credit unions, savings banks, or savings and loan associations) are usually regulated by various state or federal laws depending on how they are chartered. An institution chartered under federal law is usually regulated by the federal agency responsible for enforcing the Truth in Lending Act with respect to that type of creditor. (See page 489.) The state laws under which such institutions are chartered are usually enforced by your state's banking department, financial institutions bureau, or a similarly named agency.

The laws involved often set maximum rates chargeable for consumer credit and may otherwise regulate lending practices. Penalties for creditors who fail to comply vary, depending on the violation and law involved. Generally, those who charge more than the law allows, for instance, are prohibited from collecting any of the finance charge. In some cases, usually involving small loan laws, the creditor may be prohibited from collecting both the principal and interest. In general, if a state law prohibits a creditor from including particular terms and conditions in an agreement, those terms are declared void if they are included. The creditor may also be further penalized for violations.

As a rule, consumers can sue creditors under state laws that specifically regulate consumer credit. This additional leverage makes it worth finding out whether a creditor has complied with the types of laws described above, especially if you are involved in a dispute regarding the purchase transaction itself. You could contact an attorney and ask his advice about whether the creditor has complied with the appropriate laws, or you could contact a state or local consumer protection agency or other agency that is likely to be responsible for enforcing the kind of state laws that could apply. These agencies may furnish brochures explaining the protections that might apply to your transaction. Your local library may also be an excellent information source.

60 · Negotiating Strategy for Disputes Covered by the Truth in Lending (FCB) Act

This chapter traces the initial steps of a negotiating strategy for using the different protections provided by the Truth in Lending (Fair Credit Billing) Act.

The following situations are covered:

- Canceling a credit agreement secured by your home.
- Notifying a creditor about the loss or theft of a credit card.
- Notifying a creditor about a billing error.
- Notifying a creditor about a periodic statement not mailed on time.
- Requesting a refund of a credit balance due you.
- Notifying a card issuer about a dispute involving a purchase made with a credit card.
- Holding a creditor accountable for violations.
- Contacting an enforcement agency about possible violations.

Some of the protections are activated by your initial steps. Others are "self-triggering" in the sense that a creditor's failure to follow a requirement immediately counts as a violation.

A NOTE ABOUT THE SAMPLE LETTERS

The sample letters simply illustrate how to describe a violation: they do not include wording for all the requirements a creditor might violate. To describe the requirement that applies in your particular situation, review chapters that cover the requirements that could apply and adapt the wording used to describe it. The various requirements of the act are covered in Chapters 54 through 59.

The letters do not include wording for all the corrective actions you could insist a creditor take, either. They spell out certain actions that could apply, but again you have to adapt the wording to suit your specific situation. Appropriate corrective actions are based on what the law requires the creditor to do, and what you could be entitled to collect from him for a violation.

It's worth remembering that the amounts you could recover as damages can be set off against amounts that might be due under your agreement. For example, if a violation enables you to recover, say, $1,000 in damages, that amount could be set against a sum you might still owe. This reinforces leverage you could have for settling disputes involving other things that might have gone wrong with a transaction. That is, if a violation entitles you to recover the minimum damages provided by the act, that could give you leverage to convince the seller/creditor to correct something else that went wrong if you waive your claim for damages. A key point to remember, however, is that amounts you could recover as damages usually count as amounts you could claim back from the creditor, not as amounts you would no longer *owe* for a purchase. So don't withhold payment of what might still be outstanding under an agreement when you might be entitled to recover damages based on a violation.

CANCELING AN AGREEMENT SECURED BY YOUR HOME

If you are entitled to cancel a credit agreement that is secured by your home, the creditor must give you a duplicate form explaining your right when you first sign the agreement.

Signing and returning the form within the time period allowed is enough to cancel the agreement and to activate the steps the creditor must take to return any money or property you gave the creditor. If the creditor gave you money or furnished property during the cancellation period, you must offer to return it and send any money back to the address given by the creditor.

Always send a cancellation notice by certified mail, return receipt requested, so you know when the creditor received it and can prove when it was sent. Notice is given when mailed.

The following sample letter can be adapted for canceling an agreement and offering to return money or property a creditor might have given you. Alternative wording covering different circumstances that might apply is given after the letter. I caution you, however, to seek legal advice if the creditor's failure to provide the required cancellation notice or disclosures could entitle you to cancel *after* you have already received and used the money, or any work involved has already been started. It is much trickier to unravel an agreement at that point—even though you may still be entitled to cancel—than in situations in which you owe nothing.

Address and send the letter to the creditor with whom you have a credit agreement when you are entitled to cancel.

100 Witchtree Lane
Anytown, USA 00000

August, 1, 19___

Mr. A. Contractor/A. Lender
ABC Construction Company / ABC Financial Institution
100 Main Street
Anytown, USA 00000

Dear Mr. Contractor/Lender:

I am, as provided by the Truth in Lending Act, canceling the agreement and credit transaction identified on the signed cancellation notice I am enclosing and which had been furnished to me. We entered into the transaction on (July 30, 19___). (NOTE: See alternative opening paragraphs included after this letter for different cancellation situations.)

Please return to me within the twenty days provided by law the $_____ I have already paid in connection with this transaction and the (describe other property you gave creditor/seller) which I furnished you on (_____) and take all necessary steps to terminate this transaction and any resulting security interest in my principal dwelling.

I shall, until then, retain the $_____ that was advanced on (_____) (and/keep the [identify the type of property already delivered] which was delivered on [   ] at the above address) as part of the transaction I have now canceled.

But I am now offering to return that money to you at the address designated as your place of business (and am now offering to return to you at my address, identified above, the property that was delivered to me) once the (ABC Construction Company) carries out its obligations upon receipt of my notice of cancellation as provided by law.

And since I have now canceled this agreement and credit transaction, no amounts are due or owing and any security interest in my principal dwelling which may have arisen from this transaction is now void.

You can contact me at 222-3333 between 9:00 A.M. and 5:00 P.M. and at 333-5555 between 6:00 P.M. and 11:00 P.M. so that we can make any reasonable arrangements for effecting this cancellation.

I appreciate (your help in arranging this transaction and) the steps the company takes to complete the cancellation promptly.

Sincerely,

ALTERNATIVE OPENING PARAGRAPHS FOR DIFFERENT SITUATIONS

(1) "This is to notify you I am, as provided by the Truth in Lending Act, canceling the agreement and credit transaction which we entered into on July 25, 19___, and which is identified on the signed cancellation notice I am enclosing. Although we entered into this transaction on July 25, I did not receive the required "notice of right to cancel" until July 30, so that I am now still canceling the transaction within the three business days available for doing so."

(2) "This is to notify you that I am, as provided by the Truth in Lending Act, canceling the agreement and credit transaction we entered into on July 20, 19___, for (describe the transaction, such as: the $6,850 remodeling job on my house at the above address and the financing of the transaction [OR] a $10,000 loan ((OR) an increase in my credit limit under our agreement of March, 19___) which would be secured by my principal dwelling at the above address.) Although we entered into this transaction on July 20, 19___, I haven't, as of this date, received the required "notice of right to cancel" so that I am now still canceling the transaction within the time available for doing so."

• If you are canceling because you changed your mind but may want to go through with the transaction at some later date, you could tone down the letter by omitting specific references to the law and other phrases that may sound harsh to you, and include wording referring to the possibility of going through with the deal later. Remember, the right to cancel entitles you to get out of a credit transaction after you and the creditor have reached what would otherwise be a binding contract. Naturally, this action is not going to endear you to the creditor, especially if he or she has already spent a lot of time and effort on arranging the transaction. So if you cancel once, you may be unable to get the same deal—or any other deal—from that creditor later. This doesn't mean you should avoid canceling if you have good reason for doing so, though. And the law does not require you to give any reason for changing your mind.

Since the right to cancel applies to credit transactions for which you are putting up your dwelling as security, use the cancellation period to get legal advice. Find out the circumstances under which you could lose the dwelling if you are unable to pay, and how to nail down the work to be done.

Keep in mind, however, that if you made and financed a purchase under a separate agreement but you were only entitled to cancel the agreement under which the purchase was being financed rather than the one under which you made the purchase, you are likely to be breaking the agreement under which you made the purchase if you don't go through with it. This could happen if the creditor who was financing the purchase acquired a security interest in your principal dwelling but the agreement under which you made the purchase did not give the seller that right.

If the creditor returns everything due to you upon cancellation, you must then return any money advanced or property furnished.

RETURNING MONEY OR REAFFIRMING YOUR OFFER TO RETURN PROPERTY

This sample letter can be used when you are returning money and/or reaffirming your offer to return any property that has been furnished to you.

100 Witchtree Lane
Anytown, USA 00000

August 17, 19___

Mr. A. Contractor/A. Lender
ABC Construction Company/ABC Financial Institution
100 Main Street
Anytown, USA 00000

Dear Mr. Contractor/Lender:

Enclosed is my check for the $_____ which had been advanced to me under the agreement and credit transaction of (July 30, 19___) which I canceled on August 1 as provided by the Truth in Lending Act. (I am [also] reaffirming my previous offer to return to you at my residence at the above address the [describe property furnished to you] which had been delivered there in connection with the transaction I have canceled.)

On August 16 I received your refund for the $_____ I had paid you and your notification that you had taken all necessary steps to terminate the security interest taken on my principal dwelling in connection with this transaction.

Please contact me at 222-3333 between 9:00 A.M. and 5:00 P.M. or at 333-5555 between 6:00 P.M. and 11:00 P.M. so that we can make reasonable arrangements for you to pick up the property I have offered to return.

I appreciate the prompt steps the company has taken to effect the cancellation

Sincerely,

NOTIFYING ANOTHER CREDITOR TO WHOM THE AGREEMENT IS ASSIGNED

It is always possible that an agreement and credit transaction you have properly canceled might have been transferred or assigned to another creditor. If that happens, promptly notify the new creditor that the transaction has been canceled and that you don't owe the money. Again I caution you to seek legal advice if you are entitled to cancel some time after the transaction occurred.

Here is a sample letter you can adapt to notify a second creditor that the transaction has been canceled.

100 Witchtree Lane
Anytown, USA 00000

August 15, 19__

XYZ Financing Corporation
100 Moneytree Road
Anytown, USA 00000

Dear Sir:

This is to notify you that, as provided by the Truth in Lending Act, I have canceled the agreement and credit transaction of (July 30, 19__) between myself and (the ABC Construction Company).

On August 14 I received your letter of August 10 informing me that I was to pay to you the $____ scheduled for the repayment of the amount that had been due under that agreement.

But I canceled this transaction on August 1, 19__, by sending the (ABC Construction Company) a copy of the enclosed cancellation letter. The company received the cancellation letter on August 3, as shown by the copy of the return receipt furnished me by the post office.

No amounts are, therefore, due or owing in connection with this canceled transaction, and any security interest in my principal dwelling that may have arisen in connection with this transaction is void.

I therefore request that the (XYZ Financing Corporation) immediately take all necessary and proper steps to reflect the cancellation of this transaction and terminate any security interest in my principal dwelling as provided by the Truth in Lending Act. I also request that you promptly acknowledge that the appropriate steps have been taken.

I will appreciate your giving this matter your immediate attention so that it will be promptly resolved as I have requested.

Sincerely,

Once you have properly canceled a transaction, a creditor who fails to comply with the cancellation procedure becomes liable for violating the act. If the creditor doesn't pick up the property you have offered to return within the twenty-day time period, you would then usually be able to keep it without having to pay for it. Remember, though, that if you cancel but are unable to return property, you would then have to pay for its reasonable value. This isn't likely to happen unless you cancel long after the transaction occurred.

NOTIFYING A CREDITOR ABOUT THE LOSS OR THEFT OF A CREDIT CARD

Promptly notifying the card issuer about the loss or theft of a credit card helps you avoid or minimize the $50 liability you have to pay for unauthorized use.

On pages 416–417 there are sample letters for notifying card issuers about the loss or theft of electronic fund transfer access devices. Simply modify the wording to make clear a credit card is involved in this case, and be sure to refer to the appropriate requirements of the Truth in Lending Act rather than the EFT Act.

If your periodic statement includes amounts resulting from the unauthorized use of credit cards, that would be a billing error the creditor must correct.

NOTIFYING A CREDITOR ABOUT A BILLING ERROR

To preserve your rights under the FCB Act, you must notify the creditor about a billing error within the time limit. (See page 470 for the billing error resolution procedure.) Verbal notification alone will *not* preserve your rights so always follow up with a letter.

The following sample letter includes alternative wording for different situations that might apply. At the end of the letter alternative paragraphs are included to illustrate how to describe different types of billing errors. Insert the appropriate wording at the place indicated in the sample letter. Please see the explanatory footnotes before using wording identified with asterisks.

When you refer to a billing error, identify the transaction exactly as it is described on your statement and include the reference number. Be sure to include copies (*never originals*) of any documentation that helps verify the error. The act doesn't require you to do this, but it makes it easier for the creditor to investigate the matter and harder for him simply to deny there was an error.

100 Witchtree Lane
Anytown, USA 00000

November 1, 19__

(This address must be the one supplied by the creditor for billing error inquiries.)
Charge Accounts Department
XYZ Company
P. O. Box 3000
Anytown, USA 00000

Dear Sir:

This is to notify you of a billing error involving my Master Money Card Account, account number 000-000000-000. The error involves the periodic billing statement dated October 15, 19__ (for the billing period ending October 15, 19__) which was mailed to me on October 25. (The error involves a transaction that first appeared on the periodic billing statement dated October 15/for the billing period ending October 15, which was mailed to me on October 25, 19__ .)

(INSERT DESCRIPTION OF BILLING ERROR HERE. See descriptions included at the end of this letter.)

I am therefore deducting the $_____ disputed amount from the $_____ shown as the balance due for the billing period ending (October 15, 19__), which leaves a balance due of $ _____ for this billing period. I have separately sent you a check for that amount which is then payment in full for the amount due during this billing period. [See NOTE#]

Please correct the billing error by making the appropriate adjustments for my account as provided by the Fair Credit Billing Act. (And if you claim a billing error has not occurred as I have asserted, please furnish the documentary evidence you have for the disputed transaction./Please furnish the clarifying information and documentary evidence you have for verifying this transaction which I cannot identify based on the information furnished.)

Thank you for your cooperation in correcting this billing error.

Sincerely,

ALTERNATIVE PARAGRAPHS FOR DESCRIBING BILLING ERRORS

Insert the appropriate paragraph at the place indicated in the letter above, and modify the wording to suit your own situation.

(1) "This periodic billing statement includes a transaction identified as (include the description appearing on statement), reference number (include as applicable) for $280.95 and which is shown (as having occurred on/as having been posted to the account on) (October 3, 19___). But the billing for this transaction is in error because. . . ."

[Included below are alternative descriptions for various errors]

*(a) ". . . the amount of this transaction actually was $80.95 as shown on the attached copy of the charge slip I signed (as shown on the attached copy of the purchase order I sent to the ABC Mail Order Company which authorized that company to charge my account only for the $80.95 due for this transaction) rather than the $280.95 for which I am being billed. The amount of the error is $200 (and any finance charges that have been imposed on that amount since it was posted to my account are not due or owing)"**

*(b) ". . .** this transaction was not made by anyone authorized to use the account (this transaction was not made with an accepted credit card since all accepted credit cards issued in connection with this account have been in the possession and control of those authorized to use them and this transaction was not made by anyone authorized to use an accepted credit card (OR) this transaction was not made by anyone authorized to use an accepted credit card and occurred after you were notified on October 2, 19___, about the loss or theft of such a card). The amount of the error is the entire $280.95 for which I am being billed (and finance charges that have been imposed on this amount since it was posted to the account are not due or owing)."**

*(c) ". . . this transaction was already included on my periodic billing statement for the billing period ending (September 15, 19___) where it was identified as (include description on that statement), reference number (include as applicable) for $280.95 which is there shown as having occurred on (September 3, 19___) (OR) the same transaction is included on this billing statement as two separate transactions, with the second entry for this transaction being identified as (include description on statement), reference number (include as applicable) for $280.95 and which is shown as having occurred on the same date as the transaction already identified above. The amount of the error is the $280.95 for which I am being billed twice (and any finance charges that have been imposed on that amount since it was posted to the account are not due or owing)."**

*(d) ". . . this transaction actually occurred on October 13, 19___, as shown on the attached copy of the charge slip I signed rather than the October 3 transaction date shown on the periodic statement. The amount of the error is the $280.95 which was posted to the account before the transaction occurred (and any finance charges imposed on the amount before it should have been posted to the account are not due or owing.)"**

(2) "This periodic statement includes a transaction identified as (include description on statement), reference number (include as applicable) for $128.50 and which is shown (as having occurred on/as having been posted to my account on) (date). This transaction is for (identify purchase) which I purchased from the (ABC Company), but which the com-

pany has not delivered as required by our agreement. The company was required to make delivery not later than the October 25, 19___, delivery date (under a destination contract) as shown on the enclosed copy of (my purchase order/the agreement under which I made the purchase). The amount of the billing error is, therefore, the $128.50 charged for the product which has not been delivered as required by the purchase agreement (and any finance charges which have been imposed on that amount since it was posted to the account are not due or owing). I have also notified the company on (October 24, 19___) that I have canceled the purchase because of this breach of contract."***

(3) "This periodic statement includes a transaction identified as (include description appearing on statement), reference number (include as applicable) for $128.50 and which is shown as having occurred on (_____). This transaction is for (identify purchase) which I purchased from the (ABC Company). Although delivery was made on (_____), I have refused to accept the product because it failed to conform to our contract as described in the enclosed copy of my letter of October 24 which I sent to the company to notify it that I was rejecting the delivery.*** The amount of the billing error is, therefore, the $128.50 charged to my account for a product I have refused to accept (and any finance charges that have been imposed on that amount since it was posted to my account are not due or owing.)"*

(4) This periodic statement includes a transaction identified as (include description appearing on statement), reference number (include as applicable) for $52.38 and which is shown as having occurred on October 6, 19___ (but for which the following identifying information is lacking: describe missing information that should have been included). Based on the information furnished, I cannot match (the person identified as the seller/the purchase described/the amount) with any authorized transaction made and therefore need additional clarifying information and any documentary evidence you have showing this was, in fact, an authorized transaction. The amount of the error could, therefore, be the $52.38 charged to my account (and any finance charges imposed on that amount since it was posted to the account may not be due or owing)."*

(5) "This periodic statement fails to reflect a credit for $79.50 which, as shown by the attached copy of my credit memo, was issued to me on (October 6, 19___) by your Riverside Branch store upon my having returned (describe item returned) which I had purchased and charged to this account on (September 28) (OR) for $79.50 which, as shown by the attached copy of my credit memo, was issued to me on September 19 by the (ABC Company) as a credit on my account upon my having returned (describe the item returned) which I had purchased from that company on September 10 with your credit card. The purchase was included on the periodic statement for the billing period ending (October 15, 19___) where it was identified as (include description appearing on statement), reference number (include as applicable). The amount of the error is, therefore, the $79.50 that should have been credited to my account (and any finance charges that have been imposed on that amount since it should have been credited to my account are not due or owing.)"*

(6) "This periodic statement does not properly reflect the $583.50 payment I made on the account with my check number (836) dated (October 1, 19___). The periodic statement credits my account only for a payment of $83.50 which was posted to the account on (October 8). The amount of the error is the $500 that was not properly credited to my account (and

any finance charges imposed on the account as a result of the failure to credit my account properly for the payment made are not due or owing.)"

(7) "This periodic statement does not properly reflect the $583.50 payment I made on the account with my check number (836) dated (October 2, 19___). The periodic statement shows my $583.50 payment (in full) for the amount due for the billing period ending (September 15) was not credited to my account until (October 14) (which was after the [October 10] due date for payment to avoid further finance and late charges). (This resulted in finance charges being imposed on that amount until the date payment was credited to my account and the imposition of a ($5.00) late payment fee./ This resulted in the imposition of $_____ in finance charges and [$5.00] in late payment charges because payment was not made by the due date.) But according to the dated bank endorsement on the check I sent as payment, the check was, in fact, first endorsed by a bank on October 8 so that this payment was received and should have been credited to my account no later than by that date (which was before the due date for payment). The amount of the error is the entire $583.50 payment that was not credited to my account on the date received (and any related finance [and late payment] charges that should not have been imposed had payment been properly credited to my account are not due or owing.)"

(8) "The periodic billing statement for the October billing period normally ending on the 15th of each month was not mailed to my current address (or was delayed or lost in transit since I have not received it as of the 28th of the month by which date your statements usually arrive) (OR) The periodic statement for the billing period ending October 15, 19___ , was not mailed to my current address as identified above but was, instead, mailed to my former address at 600 Pinetree Road, Anytown, USA 00000, even though I had notified you about my change of address on the statement I returned with my payment for the billing period ending (July 15) which was posted to my account on (September 7) so that you had been notified about the change for more than twenty days before the end of the (October 15) billing period. The amount of the error is the $_____ balance due for this billing period (and any related finance or other charges imposed on that amount may not be due or owing.)"

(9)@ "This periodic statement includes a $1,000 accounting error (involving the balance due at the end of the billing period, or otherwise identify the error). According to the statement, the balance due is shown as ($1,582.50). But the opening balance for the account is shown as ($838.50) to which ($431.50) was added for the sum of the itemized transaction identified as having occurred during the billing period plus ($12.50) for finance charges. The total for all amounts due during this billing period was, therefore ($1282.50). Upon deducting the ($700) payment credited to my account on (October 2), the balance due should be ($582.50) rather than the ($1,582.50) shown on the statement. The amount of the error is the ($1,000) not in fact due or owing (and any finance charges imposed on that amount are not in fact due or owing.)"

NOTES ABOUT WORDING USED WITH ASTERISKS

#You could include this wording if you are deducting the disputed amount but paying the remaining balance in full so as to avoid further finance charges. Don't make it a "payment-in-full" check (see page 395) since a creditor is then likely to refuse the check.

@A periodic statement could include any number of accounting errors involving the computation of finance charges, the computation of the average daily balance, the addition of the itemized amounts, etc. These accounting errors usually result from computer or computer-operator foul-ups which a creditor may or may not spot and correct on his own. Identify such errors by describing the computations you used for figuring out the amount of the error. (See Chapter 57 for how to check a creditor's calculations for accuracy.)

*Include the wording about finance and other charges when such charges could have been imposed on the disputed amount. If the creditor admits there was an error, or if those charges were imposed, they must be credited to your account.

**If the billing error involves the unauthorized use of a credit card (see Chapter 55), your maximum liability is $50—that is a defense, or justification, for refusing to pay more if the creditor tries to collect it. There are also situations in which you would have *no* liability. If the amount was extended without the use of a credit card, such as a check overdraft loan, then simply indicate that the transaction wasn't made by anyone authorized to use the account. (See the following section on steps for reasserting a billing error.) Do *not* say all accepted cards have always been in your control unless you are *sure* no accepted cards could have been used for authorizing the transaction.

***Disputes about delivery problems and refusal to accept goods can also be a defense against a creditor. A seller's failure to deliver as required, plus the steps you take to hold him responsible, strengthen your claim that there has been a billing error and can help you raise defenses later if the seller doesn't correct the problem

The wording "under a destination contract" (see page 140) refers to a delivery condition under which a failure to *receive* goods by the delivery date would almost certainly count as a billing error. If you didn't specify that condition in your agreement, the seller would usually be considered to have delivered the goods upon turning them over to the carrier, and no billing error would have occurred if that was done but you failed to receive the goods. Of course, a creditor may completely ignore such fine points and simply treat your failure to receive the goods as a billing error, so always assert such errors. The wording illustrates how you could spell out the relevant information. A creditor could, on the other hand, also get very picky about what the delivery conditions really mean. If you don't set exacting delivery conditions that the seller *must* satisfy, it makes it easier for a creditor to claim that no billing error has occurred.

A creditor who doesn't follow the billing error resolution procedure violates the act and forfeits up to $50 of the disputed amount. If that happens, your follow-up step could be the same as your initial step for holding a creditor accountable for a violation, or you could use a low-keyed warning follow-up step.

REAFFIRMING A BILLING ERROR

If the creditor denies there was a billing error, or says it is different from the one you claim, you can reassert the original error (as described on page 476) as long as you do so within the time limit. This simply helps protect your credit-worthiness, though.

Remember that if you reassert an error and don't pay, a creditor who reports the account as delinquent must also indicate that the amount is in dispute. This helps protect your credit record to some extent because creditors usually do not consider disputed accounts when considering credit worthiness. (If they do, they could be violating the Equal Credit Opportunity Act when the dispute involved your having in good faith used rights you had under the Consumer Credit Protection Act.)

If you reassert an error, and refuse to pay the disputed amount, make it very clear why you don't owe the money. It must relate to why a creditor is not entitled to collect the money under the terms of your agreement, or to legal rights which entitle you to avoid payment. In other words, the matter no longer concerns a simple billing error.

The usual reasons you may not owe the money are as follows:

- The amount involves an unauthorized transaction for which you are not liable.
- The amount is more than the sum you actually charged, either because it was deliberately "raised" or because it has been incorrectly posted to your account. Naturally, written, signed receipts showing the true amount you charged are the best evidence of the correct amount.
- The creditor fails to credit your account for amounts due. (If the problem involves a seller's failure to transmit a credit statement to a card issuer when a refund is due, you would have to assert this failure as a violation of the Fair Credit Billing Act.)
- The creditor overcharges you for finance charges based on the terms of your agreement.
- You are entitled to raise claims and defenses against a card issuer for billing errors that involve delivery problems and/or your refusal to accept goods. In this case, it is usually more practical to assert these claims and defenses against the card issuer rather than to simply reassert a billing error. (See page 482.)

As an alternative to withholding the disputed amount, you might pay and request a refund of the credit balance that could thereby be created when the matter is sorted out. This means you lose the leverage that refusing to pay can give you and it may not work anyway if there is a real dispute about whether you owe the money. (See page 515.) But paying to keep the record straight and then insisting on a refund can help minimize trouble with an account.

The following sample letter illustrates how you could reassert a billing error. It includes alternative wording for different situations and naturally must be modified to suit your situation.

100 Witchtree Lane
Anytown, USA 00000

January 10, 19__

(This address must be the one supplied by the creditor for billing inquiries.)
Charge Accounts Department
XYZ Company
P. O. Box 3000
Anytown, USA 00000

Dear Sir:

This is in response to your letter of (January 3, 19__) in which you asserted that the billing error I notified you about on November 1, 19__, was (not an error/involved a different error from the one I asserted) and (claimed that the $ __ disputed amount/claimed that $ __ of the disputed amount) is now due and payable by (_____).

I am, however, hereby reaffirming that a billing error did in fact occur as I originally asserted in my letter of (November 1, 19___). A copy is enclosed.

As I then explained, the error involved the transaction identified as (describe as identified on statement) on your periodic statement for the billing period ending (October 15, 19___) for my Money Card account, account number 000-000000-000.

Your claim that $____ is now due is incorrect because (describe the error you originally asserted).

And although the documentation you furnished indicates that (the transaction was made by someone using a credit card apparently issued in connection with this account, OR otherwise describe) the transaction occurred after I notified you on (_____) about the loss or theft of a credit card and the signature on the documentation you furnished is not, in fact, the signature of anyone authorized to use the account (OR otherwise describe how the documentation fails to show you really owe the money.)

The $____ you claim as being correct and due under our (Money Card charge) agreement is therefore neither due nor owing under that agreement.

Therefore, I again request that you make the appropriate adjustments in my account by deducting the $____ not, in fact, due or owing and any finance or other charges that have been imposed on that amount, and that you refrain from imposing any finance or other charges on that amount. And as provided by the Fair Credit Billing Act, you are not to take any action to offset this amount against any deposit accounts I have with you. (And I request that you not deduct this amount from the [identify account] out of which I have previously authorized payments to be made for amounts due under my [Money Card agreement].) (OR) if you are going to pay the disputed amount and seek a refund, substitute the following: (But to avoid the account being considered in default while we seek to resolve this matter, I am, at your insistence, making a payment of $____ on my account under protest while reserving all my rights. Since the amount you claim is, however, neither due nor owing, the payment is in excess of amounts due or owing on the account.)

I will appreciate it if you promptly make the appropriate adjustments on my account.

Sincerely,

Note: Paying the disputed amount can sometimes be considered a waiver of your claim. But reserving your rights should minimize the risk. Of course, when you are involved in a dispute about what you owe, both paying and refusing to pay involve some risk.

NOTIFYING A CREDITOR ABOUT A PERIODIC STATEMENT NOT MAILED ON TIME

If a creditor fails to mail a periodic statement on time he may not collect finance or other charges imposed as a result. (See page 468 for mailing requirements.)

The following letter illustrates how to notify a creditor about such a failure and request that he deduct such charges from your account.

200 Witchtree Lane
Anytown, USA 00000

March 10, 19___

(Send to address supplied for billing inquiries.)
Accounting Department
ABC Company
100 Harold Square
Anytown, USA 00000

Dear Sir:

This is to notify you that the $_____ imposed as finance charges (and the $_____ imposed as late charges) on my (Master Money Account, account number 000-000000-000) for the billing period ending (February 28, 19___) resulted from your failure to mail the periodic statement for the billing period ending (January 31) at least fourteen days before the February 28 due date by which such charges were avoidable for that billing period.

The periodic statement for the billing period ending (January 31) was not mailed until (February 12) as indicated by the postmark on the envelope (copy enclosed), which is at least eight days later than the date by which it had to be mailed as provided by the Fair Credit Billing Act.

Although I paid in full (I paid $200 toward) the ($835.60) balance due for the billing period ending (January 31), this payment wasn't credited to my account until (February 25), or seven days after the due date by which the finance (and late) charges were avoidable on the account.

Since the amount imposed for that (those) charge(s) resulted from the failure to mail the periodic statement by the mailing date as required by the Fair Credit Billing Act, the charge(s) is neither due nor owing as provided by that act and Regulation Z.

I therefore request that you make the appropriate adjustments to my account by deducting from the balance the full $_____ imposed for that (those) charge(s), and that you refrain from seeking to collect that amount.

(And since that amount is not, in fact, due or owing, I am deducting it from the $_____ shown as the balance due on the periodic statement for the billing period ending [February 28] and am separately sending my payment for $_____ which is the entire amount due for that billing period. (OR) If you pay the entire balance due, you could say instead: *Although that amount is not, in fact, due or owing, I am separately sending my payment for $_____ shown as the total balance due for the period ending [February 28]. I am, however, doing so only to ensure that my account is promptly credited as paid in full for accounting purposes and to avoid the imposition of further finance charges while the appropriate adjustments are made to the account. This payment does, however, include an excess payment of $_____ which is a credit balance due and owing me.)**

I will appreciate if you will promptly make the appropriate adjustments to my account.

Sincerely,

---

*Note: The alternative wording in this paragraph covers what you could do about charges you don't owe when you are paying the entire balance due.

REQUESTING A REFUND OF A CREDIT BALANCE

The following sample letter includes alternative wording for requesting a refund or insisting a credit balance be credited to your account if the creditor has not done so. (See page 465 for an explanation of the requirement.)

100 Witchtree Lane
Anytown, USA 00000

May 15, 19___

Accounting Department
XYZ Company
100 Orchard Street
Anytown, USA 00000

Dear Sir:

There is now a credit balance due on my (Money Card Account, account number 000-000000-00) (due me under our agreement of April 15, 19___, for the purchase and financing of [identify].)

The credit balance resulted when (describe: see below for alternative wording for various situations).

Please credit the $_____ balance to my account as provided by the Fair Credit Billing Act. (Since no other amounts are now due or owing on my account [under our closed-end credit agreement], please refund the $_____ balance to me at the above address within seven business days of the receipt of this request as provided by the Fair Credit Billing Act.)

I will appreciate your prompt cooperation in this matter.

Sincerely,

ALTERNATIVE WORDING FOR EXPLAINING HOW CREDIT BALANCE OCCURRED

The alternatives include wording you can adapt to cover situations in which you and a creditor settled a dispute about a purchase made under a closed-end credit agreement so that you ended up with a credit balance. (See Chapter 62 for how you could use certain rights to settle disputes in such situations.)

(1) "I made an excess payment on May 1 for the billing period ending (_____). The total amount due for that billing period was ($_____) but I instead paid ($_____) resulting in an excess payment of ($ _____)."

(2) "I paid the entire ($_____) shown as the balance due for the billing period ending (_____) which included ($_____) for the disputed amount resulting from the billing error I described in my letter of (_____). (OR) if you paid finance charges that weren't due, then say: which included ($_____) for finance (and late charges) that were not due and owing for that billing period for the reasons described in my letter of (_____). This resulted in a credit balance of ($_____)."

(3) "I received a credit for ($_____) which was posted to my account on (_____) as shown on your periodic statement for the billing period ending (_____). This resulted in a credit balance of ($_____) now shown on your periodic statement for the billing period ending (_____)."

(4) "I prepaid the entire ($\_\_\_\_) balance due under the agreement of April 15, 19\_, for the purchase and financing of (identify purchase). I prepaid the entire balance on (_____) when I sent you a payment of ($____). This was for the sum of the five payments of ($\_\_\_\_) each still remaining due under the agreement. The credit balance you now hold is, therefore, the rebate of a portion of the ($____) in finance charges that were pre-computed and included in the total balance due, (plus a rebate on the [$____] which had been included for [credit life insurance].)" Note: The last point could apply when you are entitled to a refund of finance, and credit insurance, charges upon prepayment of the total balance due under the agreement.

*(5) "I received a credit of ($\_\_\_\_) for amounts due and owing me under the agreement of (April 15, 19\_) for the purchase and financing of (identify purchase) from the (ABC Company). A copy of the credit statement is attached. Since I have also paid ($____) toward the ($\_\_\_\_) shown as the total balance due under this agreement, the ($____) due and owing me as a credit balance has resulted in an excess payment of ($\_\_\_\_) on the total amount due under the agreement (and the prepayment of the entire balance due). The remaining credit balance you now hold is, therefore, the ($____) excess payment plus a rebate due me on the ($\_\_\_\_) included in the total amount due under the agreement for finance and (credit life insurance) charges. I calculate the rebate should be about ($____) for finance charges (plus what is due for a rebate on credit life insurance charges."

Note: See Chapter 57 for estimating a rebate. If you are unable to estimate the amount due you could say: "The credit balance you now hold in connection with this transaction is the ($____) in excess payment plus the rebate due for finance charges (and credit life insurance) charges."

*(6) "you agreed on (____) that I had rightfully canceled the agreement of April 15, 19_, for the purchase and financing of (identify purchase) from the (ABC Company) and that there was now due me ($\_\_\_\_) as a refund." The credit balance you now hold in connection with this transaction is, therefore, the ($____) due me as a refund."

* Note: These alternatives refer to a credit balance that could be created in connection with a credit transaction only when you and the seller/creditor settle a dispute. The various amounts referred to in the wording above would be disclosed on your Truth in Lending disclosure statement and/or your credit agreement. The amount referred to as the "total balance due" is identified on the disclosure statement as the "total payments." (See page 578 for pinning down what you no longer owe and creating a credit balance for which you could demand a refund under the Fair Credit Billing Act.)

Whether or not you would be entitled to a rebate depends on your state's law governing retail installment credit agreements: most do require such rebates. Such laws usually also require a rebate if the creditor accelerates the remaining payments upon your default. If you are entitled to cancel your agreement, you then would not owe the amount still outstanding. (See Chapter 62.)

The easy way to learn whether you could be entitled to a rebate is to look at your Truth in Lending disclosure statement or your credit agreement. If it indicates you are entitled to a rebate, the creditor would then almost certainly be required to make one under your state's law. If the total balance due includes separate charges for various kinds of credit insurance, such as credit life, accident and health insurance, you might also be due a portion of these charges.

Remember, the Truth in Lending Act does not require a creditor to rebate any portion of the finance charge. It only requires him to refund a credit balance that results from a rebate he is required to make under applicable state law.

NOTIFYING A CARD ISSUER ABOUT A DISPUTE INVOLVING A PURCHASE

Your right to assert any claims and defenses and to withhold from the card issuer amounts you may not owe for a purchase is one of your most important protections under the Fair Credit Billing Act. (See page 482 for an explanation of this right.)

If a credit card purchase you've made is covered by these protections, your first step is to try to settle the dispute with the seller. If he refuses or fails to take care of the problem, then the card issuer is also on the hook based on rights you have to hold the seller accountable.

The practical and legal bargaining leverage provided by these protections is the very real possibility that the card issuer will be unable to collect if you have a valid justification for not owing payment to the seller.

If you raise claims and defenses the card issuer generally has the following options:

- In order to collect the outstanding balance he can insist the seller settle the dispute to your satisfaction. The seller could then correct the problem by giving you a credit or by reaching some other satisfactory settlement with you. The card issuer would then almost certainly go along with it, too.
- He can credit your account for the disputed amount. The card issuer would then almost always get that money back from the seller. However, while you would no longer owe the outstanding amount to the card issuer if he settles up with you this way, you may still be involved in a dispute with the seller about whether you owe him the money.
- He can try to collect the money from you, but in this case you could hold the card issuer responsible for the seller's failure to honor your purchase contract. This, in effect, puts him in the position of having to defend the seller's actions.

In such a situation, the simplest way out for the card issuer is either to get the money back from the seller and credit your account for the disputed amount, or to make it clear to the seller that the dispute had better be settled fast if he doesn't want the card issuer to try to collect it back from him.

Agreements between card issuers and sellers usually contain "charge back" or "recourse" clauses. These normally require that in the case of a dispute the seller pay back the money to the card issuer within ninety days of a purchase being charged. If a dispute arises after the ninety-day period, though, the card issuer may not be able to charge back the amount and could be stuck with the problem. So, if a dispute about a purchase comes up after the normal ninety-day charge-back period, it becomes much more important to furnish the card issuer with information and documentation that backs up your claim. (This charge-back time has nothing to do with whether you can dispute the purchase based on your rights under the Fair Credit Billing Act. It just affects the ease with which you might get the problem solved with the card issuer.)

It's important to remember that if a card issuer clears up your account you still need to reach some settlement with the seller. If you don't, he can sue you for the money. Thus, you must pursue parallel negotiating strategies when you are entitled to withhold payment. In fact, the steps you take to hold a seller accountable would also help you hold the card issuer accountable later.

WHAT HAPPENS IF THE CARD ISSUER AND SELLER ARE THE SAME?

If you used the seller's own credit card to charge the purchase to an open-end account, you could almost always raise all claims and defenses against him based on the remedies available for holding the seller accountable.

Your right to do this would be based on the remedies available under the Uniform Commercial Code, backed up by the Federal Trade Commission's "Preservation of Consumers' Claims and Defenses" Rule. (See page 523.) In situations like this, you could not only hold the seller accountable for an amount still outstanding but you may also be entitled to a refund of payments already made and amounts due you as damages.

In the case of a dispute, you are likely to have these two options:

1. To use the Fair Credit Billing Act protections that apply to purchases made with a credit card both issued and honored by the seller. (In this case, the distance and dollar limitations described on page 482 would not apply.) This is the easiest course if you haven't yet paid anything for the purchase.

If you have already paid something, you might be entitled to a refund. While the FCB Act protections do not enable you to insist on a refund, if you use the protections you could, at the same time, insist on a refund based on your rights under the Code as backed up by the FTC's Rule. The sample letter on page 509 includes wording requesting a refund. Be sure to omit it if the card issuer is someone other than the seller.

2. To assert against the card-issuing seller the remedies available under the Code, as backed up by the FTC's "Holder" Rule with respect to open-end credit agreements, under which you have the seller's credit card so you could hold him accountable for all amounts involved. In effect, the FTC's Rule enables you to combine a demand for a refund with the protections the FCB Act makes available. Since the seller is also the creditor in such situations, the FTC's Rule combined with your remedies under the Code make it easier for you to obtain a refund and to refuse to pay amounts no longer owed.

By using the protections under the Fair Credit Billing Act you limit the card issuer's ability to report the matter to a credit-reporting agency. The FTC's Rule, on the other hand, does *not* specifically impose these limitations. And if you decide to withhold payment based on your rights under the FCB Act, a card issuer or a card-issuing seller who then terminates your account could be violating the Equal Credit Opportunity Act. If you withhold payment based only on your remedies under the Code, as backed up by the FTC Rule, the ECO Act protections would not apply.

If a lot of money is involved, seek legal advice on the most appropriate option in your situation.

RETURNING GOODS FOR WHICH YOU HAVE NOT PAID

A word of caution about situations in which you have not yet paid anything for a product charged. If you are entitled to reject or revoke acceptance of the product because of its failure to conform, you must either return it to the seller or, at least, insist he pick up or make arrangements for shipping back the product. (See Chapter 28.)

The following sample letter can be adapted to notify a credit card-issuer about an unresolved dispute in situations where you could hold him accountable. It includes alternative wording for different situations and must, of course, be adapted to suit your circumstances. It also refers to copies of materials you could furnish to substantiate your claim.

> 200 Witchtree Lane
> Anytown, USA 00000
>
> August 10, 19 ___

Accounting Department
ABC Card Issuer
100 Money Plaza
Anytown, USA 00000

(Send to address supplied for billing inquiries.)

Dear Sir:

This is to inform you about an unresolved dispute involving the purchase of (identify purchase) I made (from your franchised dealer located in: give address) (OR) at your store located in (_____ address _____) (OR) from (identify seller other than card issuer) on (insert date) and charged to my account with your credit card.

My credit card account number is (000-000000-000). The disputed purchase was for ($ _____) and first appeared on my periodic statement for the billing period ending (give date). The transaction was identified on the statement as (indicate how purchase was identified), your reference number (indicate) and was posted to the account on (give date).

I made the purchase in response to a mail solicitation sent by you on (give date) with your periodic statement for the billing period ending (_____). (Although I made the purchase by mail from a company located in [indicate state], my purchase condition and authorization to charge the purchase to my credit card account was conditioned on the seller's agreement that the transaction occurred in my home state as shown on the attached copy of my order.) [Note: Include this wording only if you put this condition in your order, see page 483.]

The matter now involves (briefly describe the problem, such as: the seller's failure to make delivery by the [date] delivery date specified in our agreement (OR) a defect in the product (OR) the product's failure to conform to representations made about it (OR) charges made for unnecessary repair services (OR) charges for unsatisfactory repair services). The matter is more fully described in the enclosed copy of the letter/memo of (date) I furnished (you/the seller).

[See alternative wording for describing your inability to resolve the dispute included at the end of this letter.]

I have now also sustained at least ($_____) in damages due me from (you/the seller) for (describe and indicate amounts due).

Since this matter has not been satisfactorily resolved, (at least $_____ of) the amount outstanding on my account for the disputed transaction as of (date) when I first notified (you/the seller) about this matter is no longer due or owing because of the claims and defenses I can assert against you as provided by the Fair Credit Billing Act.

I therefore request that you promptly credit my account for the amount outstanding for the disputed transaction as of (insert date) (plus any finance and other charges imposed on that amount since then).*

And as I have already informed you by (my letter/memo) of (_____), there is now also due me for the reasons indicated the

*($_____) I have paid you for the purchase (plus amounts I have sustained
as damages). I therefore request that the amount due me as a refund for
payments made be credited to my account (and that you reimburse me
for my damages/in which case I waive my claims for those damages) so
that we can then fully resolve this matter as I have already indicated.*

*(I am, however, still prepared to resolve this matter based on the other
alternatives I have proposed to (you/the seller in my letter/memo of
[insert date]) so that we can still satisfactorily complete this transaction.)*

*But I am reserving my right to raise all claims and defenses arising
from this transaction which relates to the failure to resolve this dispute.*

*(And since, as provided by the Fair Credit Billing Act and Regulation
Z, I am entitled to raise against you claims and defenses arising from this
transaction up to the amount of credit outstanding for the disputed purchase, I shall only pay such amounts as are due under our agreement for
undisputed purchases. But no payments made on my account are to be
applied to the amount that was outstanding for the disputed purchase
except as this matter is satisfactorily resolved [and I am deducting that
amount from the $_____ shown as the balance due on the periodic state-
ment for the billing period ending _____]. I also request that you
not deduct anything for amounts outstanding for the disputed transaction
from the [identify account] out of which I have previously authorized
payments to be made for the amounts due on my [Money card account].
Nor, as provided by the Fair Credit Billing Act, are you to set this amount
off against any accounts I have with you.)***

*I hope that we can resolve this matter as I have proposed. I will appre-
ciate your cooperation so that we can avoid any further dispute about this
purchase and credit transaction.*

Sincerely,

*Note: As an alternative to insisting the card issuer refund finance charges already
imposed on the disputed amount, you could say you are willing to forget about them
if he promptly credits your account for the disputed amount. If you do this, replace
the wording with: "and I waive my claims for a refund of finance or other charges
imposed on that amount if the balance outstanding is promptly credited to my
account."

**Note: This wording indicates you are withholding payment of and deducting
the disputed amount from the balance due. This is a step you may have to take
promptly if you have an account that requires payment in full each month. The card
issuer could then consider the amount to be in dispute, report that fact to a credit-
reporting agency, and even initiate action to collect. The sample wording illustrates
how you could make clear at the outset that you will deduct the disputed amount,
but you could omit this paragraph and delay this step until later.

ALTERNATIVE WORDING FOR DESCRIBING INABILITY TO RESOLVE DISPUTE

Included below are alternative paragraphs you can adapt to describe your inability
to resolve a dispute with the seller and insert in the letter. The Fair Credit Billing
Act doesn't *require* you to say anything about how you have tried to settle the dispute: it only requires you to try to resolve the problem first. If a dispute goes to court,
however, you may have to actually demonstrate how you tried in good faith to settle
with the seller. For this reason, indicating that you have done so lets the card issuer
know that you have fulfilled the act's requirements.

● *"Since I first notified (you/the seller) about this matter on (date), I have tried in good faith to resolve it by (briefly describe your efforts, such as: returning the defective product and requesting a conforming replacement). But the matter has not been satisfactorily resolved because (briefly describe reasons why seller's response was inadequate)."*

● *"Since I first notified (you/the seller) about this matter on (date), I have in good faith proposed that it be resolved as I stated in the enclosed copy of my (letter/memo of [date], I gave/mailed to [you/the seller] when this matter first arose. But I have been unable to resolve it)."*

Note: You could use this alternative if you have already put in writing what you wanted the seller to do.

● *"Since I first notified (you/the seller) about this matter on (date), I have in good faith attempted to resolve it but have been unable to do so because (briefly describe)."* Note: This wording merely indicates to the card issuer you have tried to resolve the dispute as required by the act. If the seller is no longer in business, be sure to indicate that as the reason.

USING YOUR BARGAINING LEVERAGE TO CONVINCE A SELLER TO SETTLE

If the card issuer and the seller are separate, there is one additional negotiating step you could try with the seller.

Prepare the letter you would send to the card issuer, but before mailing it, take it to the store and try once more to settle the dispute. Make it clear that you will send the letter if the seller still refuses to settle.

The preceding sample letter spells out what could happen once the card issuer gets involved in the dispute, but if the seller doesn't get the message, say something like: "Since the Fair Credit Billing Act gives me legal justification for refusing to pay this amount to the card issuer, he is likely to charge the disputed amount back to you. Wouldn't you prefer to resolve this problem now, as I have already suggested, rather than force me to take up the problem with the card issuer."

If the seller still refuses to resolve the dispute, send the letter to the card issuer.

WHAT HAPPENS AFTER YOU NOTIFY A CARD ISSUER ABOUT A DISPUTE?

Once you have mailed your letter to the card issuer your follow-up steps depend on his response. If he credits the disputed amount to your account, he has almost certainly charged back the money to the store. Now you aren't out the money unless the seller sues and wins.

If the dispute involves a problem the seller can correct, or if you may be entitled to pay less than the full amount because, for instance, the seller fails to honor a warranty and you can only deduct the cost of repairs rather than rejecting or revoking acceptance, a card issuer is likely to ask the seller to promptly settle the dispute.

If the card issuer responds in either of these two ways, the store is then likely to contact you to work out a settlement. But don't wait for the seller to contact you. If the card issuer credits the outstanding amount to your account, return to the store and try to work out a settlement. Use whatever steps are appropriate based on the remedies you could use to hold the seller accountable. These steps vary, of course, depending on whether you are entitled to call off the purchase, or are only entitled to deduct amounts for damages.

If the latter situation applies, you could effectively use a "payment-in-full" check for settling the dispute (see page 395). Since this is the fastest and easiest way for the seller to get any money you owe when the amount was charged back to him, it gives you leverage for settling the matter.

If the card issuer doesn't credit your account but indicates you must pay whatever amounts will be due when the matter is satisfactorily resolved, he will usually insist that you confirm the satisfactory settlement in writing. Do *not* sign any such statement until the problem really has been satisfactorily resolved. And make sure it refers *only* to the problem you complained about. Don't go along with wording like this, for instance: "The buyer acknowledges complete satisfaction with the purchase involved in the dispute," or with any wording that remotely indicates that all matters have been taken care of. If you do, and another problem arises, there may be no room for a valid complaint.

If you are asked to sign something, you could adapt the following wording to indicate that your satisfaction depends on the adequacy of the seller's actions.

"The buyer's acknowledgement that (refer to the problem resolved) has now been satisfactorily resolved is conditional on the seller's assurances that (the repairs and adjustments made as of [date] will be adequate to cure the defects (OR) otherwise describe the condition to be satisfied) and this acknowledgement is specifically limited to the matters described."

If the seller and card issuer are the same you will be facing a different situation (see page 508). Any follow-up steps should be taken with either the people responsible for handling disputes involving your credit account, or with someone higher up in the company.

WHAT IF THE CARD ISSUER DEMANDS PAYMENT?

While the right to withhold payment from a credit card issuer, or card-issuing seller, gives you leverage to settle a dispute it does not guarantee the dispute will be promptly settled to your satisfaction. And because the Fair Credit Billing Act does not prevent a card issuer from trying to collect the money, it can result in your being sued for payment.

What good is this protection, then? It prevents a card issuer from ignoring the dispute, and it helps you prevent him from collecting if you don't really owe the money to the seller.

If the card issuer insists that you pay, remember he cannot report your account is delinquent while the matter is unresolved or until a judgment is entered against you. He can report the account as being in dispute, however. A creditor who ignores these requirements violates the Truth in Lending Act (see page 488 for what you could then recover in damages).

To maintain this leverage when the seller insists on payment, you must then at some point take the appropriate steps to withhold payment. See page 515 for the low-keyed warning follow-up steps you could take to make clear you are refusing payment after first notifying the card issuer about the dispute. If the dispute involves a lot of money, seek legal advice before taking them.

HOLDING A CREDITOR ACCOUNTABLE FOR VIOLATIONS

A creditor who fails to comply with the requirements of the Truth in Lending (Fair Credit Billing) Act becomes liable for damages and reasonable court costs, as noted in the previous chapter.

Once a creditor has violated the act you are entitled to sue immediately without having to give any notification of the violation. Obviously, though, it is preferable to try to settle first. The act does not consider it prejudicial if you try to settle and, in fact, a creditor's continuing refusal to comply with requirements is likely to strengthen your position if you eventually sue.

In the case of most violations, you must sue within one year of the date they occurred. If a violation involves your right to rescind a credit transaction secured by your home, you have up to three years to sue. If a creditor is suing you, but has committed a violation in connection with the transaction, you could usually still hold him accountable after the relevant time limit.

You can adapt the following sample letter for holding a creditor accountable by first seeking to settle based on the act's requirements. You must supply the wording to describe the particular violation in question, and to state what you want the creditor to do: the letter only illustrates how to put the information together. When describing the violation, use the information given in Chapter 54. It's best to first describe what the law requires, then show how the creditor failed to comply. The requirements listed also indicate what you can insist the creditor do. If he failed to refund a credit balance on your account, for example, you can insist he do so.

You may also request a creditor to pay amounts recoverable as damages based on the finance charges involved. But remember the larger the amount you insist on, the less likely it is the creditor will pay all you ask. It may still be worthwhile to settle for less than you might be able to recover by suing, however. The choice is yours.

Send the letter to the person or department responsible for handling credit transactions. If the matter involves an open-end transaction, send the letter to the address given for billing inquiries, though this is not compulsory.

200 Witchtree Lane
Anytown, USA 00000

May 20, 19__

Director
Consumer Credit Department
XYZ Financial Institution
100 Finance Plaza
Anytown, USA 00000

Dear Sir:

   This is to inform you of the (XYZ Financial Institution's) failure to comply with the requirements of the Truth in Lending (Fair Credit Billing) Act and Regulation Z with respect to (a transaction involving) the open-end credit (credit card) account I have with you, account number (000-000000-000). (NOTE: If the matter involves a closed-end transaction, then identify it, such as: with respect to the $_____ loan extended under our loan agreement of [date] [OR] with respect to the purchase and financing of the [identify purchase] under our [the] retail installment sales agreement of [date] [between myself] and [identify seller].) (Note: If the violation occurred after you first requested the creditor to take some action which triggers requirements he must then follow, describe what you previously requested. Here is a sample paragraph: I first notified you on [date] about the [$____] credit balance on my account [or otherwise describe what you had done or said, such as: about the billing error involving a transaction on the periodic statement for the billing period ending [_____.])

   Although the Act (requires/prohibits a creditor from) (describe the requirement the creditor was supposed to follow) the (XYZ Financial Institution) instead (describe what the creditor actually did or failed to do).

This has at least resulted in (briefly describe effect of creditor's action, such as: my being misled about the actual terms and conditions of the credit transaction).

I therefore now request that the (XYZ Financial Institution) promptly (state what corrective action you want the company to take). And although your minimum liability could now be $100 (twice the) [$_____] in finance charges imposed in connection with the transaction up to $1,000), I would be prepared to resolve this matter if you will now promptly do what I requested (and pay me [$_____] as compensation for your failure to comply with the Act).

I hope the (XYZ Financial Institution) will now take appropriate steps to comply and that you will contact me promptly so we may fully resolve this matter.

Sincerely,

CONTACTING AN ENFORCEMENT AGENCY ABOUT POSSIBLE VIOLATIONS

If you are not sure if a creditor has complied with the requirements of the Truth in Lending [Fair Credit Billing] Act, send a letter of inquiry to the federal agency responsible for enforcing it against the kind of creditor involved. Furnish copies only of relevant documents and describe any actions you have taken so far. If you have already notified the creditor about the problem in writing, you can simply enclose a copy of that letter.

The FTC has a policy of responding to public inquiries, but not every agency will reply to letters.

200 Witchtree Lane
Anytown, USA 00000

August 10, 19___

Federal Trade Commission
Washington, DC 20580

Dear Sir:

Please inform me whether the (identify creditor) has complied with the relevant requirements of the Truth in Lending Act and Regulation Z with respect to the credit transaction described below, and advise me if there is a reasonable basis for initiating an action to hold the creditor liable for a violation under the act.

The matter involves the creditor's apparent failure to (describe creditor's apparent failure to comply) in connection with a closed-end (open-end) credit transaction. The matter is more fully described in the attached copy of the letter I have already sent the creditor. I am also enclosing copies of all other documents and correspondence relating to this matter. These include (identify copies being sent; be sure to include everything relating to the transaction).

I will appreciate your reviewing this material and advising me. Thank you for your attention.

Sincerely,

61 · Negotiating Strategy Continued: Stages Two and Three

This chapter covers stages two and three of the strategy you could take in the following situations:

- The card issuer won't settle the dispute about a purchase made with a credit card, which usually means the card issuer insists on payment of the amount outstanding for the disputed purchase.
- The creditor simply ignores the violation that occurred.

STAGE TWO: THE LOW-KEYED WARNING

WHEN THE CARD ISSUER REFUSES TO SETTLE A DISPUTE

If the card issuer won't settle and insists you pay the amount due, you have two options: paying to avoid possible legal action, or withholding payment and risking it.

There is one interim negotiating step you could take before actually withholding payment and thereby forcing a showdown. The FCB Act enables you to withhold payment of the amount outstanding for a disputed purchase as of the date you notify the seller and/or card issuer about your justification for doing so. This will usually mean that you do not have to withhold payment of the amount outstanding as of when you notify the seller and/or card issuer but that you could do so later.

But if the card issuer insists on payment of the disputed amount, it is important that you respond by making clear you will withhold payment of the disputed amount if the matter remains unresolved or that you are actually doing so. Otherwise simply continuing to pay could be taken as a sign that you are giving up your chance to withhold payment so that any further payments you make would be applied to the amount outstanding for the disputed purchase.

If you at least notify the card issuer that you will withhold payment when you continue to pay on your account while the dispute is pending, it helps your bargaining position to withhold payment later. In other words, it helps keep the pressure on. Keep in mind, however, that continuing to pay in such situations without specifically indicating you are withholding payment of the disputed amount could result in your losing the chance to withhold payment later. So you have to decide how safe you want to play it.

Once you specifically say you are not paying the disputed amount, you should not then pay any portion of it that remains unpaid.

Whether or not and how soon you must actually withhold payment depends on the type of credit card account you have. If the dispute involves an open-end credit account on which you can stretch out payments and on which you pay finance charges, you must continue to make payments for undisputed purchases added to the account before and after the disputed purchase was posted to it. As long as you pay the minimum amounts called for by the agreement, you are then not actually withholding payment on the account but are simply saying payments you make aren't to be applied to the disputed purchase. The card issuer is then less likely to consider you to be in default and take legal action to collect.

If the dispute involves the type of credit card account that calls for you to pay the entire balance due each billing period (like the travel and entertainment cards issued by companies such as American Express), you would then actually have to withhold payment of the amount in dispute.

It's usually wise to first take the interim negotiating step of telling the card issuer you will withhold payment rather than doing so immediately after the card issuer's refusal or failure to resolve the dispute. Stating that you intend to withhold payment will only be an effective strategy if you actually go through with it, if necessary, of course.

The following sample letter can be adapted for your purposes. Choose only the paragraphs that apply to your situation, of course.

200 Witchtree Lane
Anytown, USA 00000

September 10, 19__

Accounting Department
ABC Card Issuer
100 Money Plaza
Anytown, USA 00000

Dear Sir:

(1) This is in response to your letter of September 3, 19__, in which you informed me that payment for the (identify purchase) I purchased from you (or identify separate seller) would be due on my (Master Card Account, number 000-000000-000) despite the unresolved dispute involving this purchase. I notified you of this dispute by my letter of (date) which more fully explained the matter (copy enclosed). (Since I received no response to my letter of [date], I am again writing you about the unresolved dispute involving the [identify purchase] which I purchased from you [or identify separate seller] and charged to my [Master Card Account] with my credit card, account number 000-000000-000. I am enclosing a copy of that letter which more fully explains this matter.)

(2) Since the dispute about the purchase still has not been satisfactorily resolved by you (the seller), you are, as provided by the Fair Credit Billing Act, subject to all claims and defenses arising from the transaction which relate to the failure to resolve this dispute up to the amount of credit outstanding for this transaction as of (date) when I first notified you (the seller) of reasons why payment for this purchase was neither due nor owing.

(3) I am still prepared to resolve this matter as I proposed in my letter of (date) when I first notified you about it, if you will now promptly do what I requested. (Although I indicated in my letter of [_____] how I was then prepared to resolve this matter, since you failed to do so, I am now prepared to resolve it if you will [indicate what you now want the card issuer to do].)

(4) But if this matter still is not satisfactorily resolved, I am reserving my right to raise against you all claims and defenses arising from the failure to resolve the dispute involving the transaction I have described and to withhold payment of the amount outstanding on my account for the disputed transaction as of the date I first notified you (the seller) about the matter, plus finance or other charges imposed on that amount since then, as provided by the Fair Credit Billing Act.

(5) I do hope, however, that we can, instead, resolve this matter as I

have already proposed so that we may avoid such a dispute with respect to this purchase and credit transaction.

Sincerely,

ALTERNATIVE PARAGRAPHS FOR WITHHOLDING PAYMENT

The following alternative paragraphs can be adapted and substituted for paragraphs (4) and (5) of the above letter if you decide to withhold payment.

(4) "But since this matter still has not been satisfactorily resolved, there is now not due or owing on my account the (at least $____ of the) $____ amount of credit outstanding for the disputed purchase of (date), plus finance or other charges imposed on that amount since then, as provided by the Fair Credit Billing Act. And the continued failure to resolve the dispute would leave me no choice but to raise against you all further claims and defenses arising out of the transaction at least to the fullest extent provided by the Fair Credit Billing Act."

(5) "I am, of course, prepared to pay undisputed amounts as due under our agreement, but no payments I make are to be applied to the amount still outstanding on my account for the disputed purchase except as this matter is satisfactorily resolved. And I am deducting the $____ now no longer due or owing from the $____ shown as the balance due on the periodic statement for the billing period ending ____. My payment of $____ is therefore payment in full of all amounts actually due or owing on my account as of that billing date. And since payments for the disputed amount are not due or owing, I am not now in default under our agreement."

(6) "You also are not to deduct anything for the disputed amount from (identify account) out of which I previously authorized payments to be made for amounts due on my (Money Card account) (or from any other accounts I have with you)."

(7) "I hope, however, that we can still resolve the matter as I have already proposed and that you will promptly contact me about doing so to avoid my having to assert against you all claims and defenses arising from the failure to resolve the dispute involving the transaction I have described."

Once you notify a card issuer about a dispute be sure to keep him informed of any follow-up actions you take with the seller. The following cover letter can be adapted for this purpose.

200 Witchtree Lane
Anytown, USA 00000

September 15, 19__

Accounting Department
ABC Card Issuer
200 Money Plaza
Anytown, USA 00000

Dear Sir:

I am enclosing a copy of my letter/memo of (date) which I sent/gave to (identify seller) and which describes further matters that have arisen in connection with the still unresolved dispute involving the purchase of *(identify purchase)*. I charged this purchase to my account with your credit card, account number 000-000000-000. I first notified you on *(date)* about the unresolved dispute involving the purchase.

(Since I have already indicated in my letter of [_____] that I am, as provided by the Fair Credit Billing Act, raising against you claims and defenses arising from the failure to resolve the dispute), I hope we can now resolve this matter by your promptly crediting my account for the amount outstanding for the disputed purchase as of (date) when I first notified you (the seller) about this matter.

(Alternatively, I am still prepared to resolve this matter if the seller will now promptly do as I have proposed so that we can still satisfactorily complete the transaction.)

But if this matter is not satisfactorily resolved, I am still reserving my right to raise all claims and defenses arising from this transaction which relate to the failure to resolve it.

I will appreciate your prompt cooperation in getting this matter resolved as I have proposed to avoid any further dispute.

Sincerely,

If a card-issuing seller insists payment is due and you decide to pay, rather than withhold payment, adapt the wording of the sample letter included on page 399 for reserving your rights. This may help you retain your chance to sue to get your money back. If the card issuer is not the seller, paying could make it harder for you to sue even though you reserved your rights; you may instead have to get the money back from the seller.

HOLDING A CREDITOR ACCOUNTABLE FOR A VIOLATION

If your initial step for holding a creditor accountable for a violation fails to work, you could send the following low-keyed warning letter. As your final attempt to resolve the matter before considering legal action you could then try the ultimatum step described on page 521.

The sample letter can be adapted to your circumstances. It includes alternative wording for situations in which the creditor claims that no violation actually occurred. You should, of course, consider his claim carefully before you pursue the matter. But if he is clearly wrong, point that out when you respond.

200 Witchtree Lane
Anytown, USA 00000

June 15, 19__

Director
Consumer Credit Department
XYZ Financial Institution
100 Finance Plaza
Anytown, USA 00000

Dear Sir:

This is to notify the (XYZ Financial Institution) about its liability for failing to comply with the requirements of the Truth in Lending (Fair

Credit Billing) Act and Regulation Z with respect to (identify the trans-
action—see page 000 for sample wording). I first notified you about this
matter in my letter of (May 20, 19__) which more fully describes your
failure to comply (copy enclosed).

Although I then requested that the (XYZ Financial Institution)
promptly (restate corrective action you previously requested) (and that it
pay $___ as compensation for its failure to comply with the act), I have
to date received no reply (I was instead informed in your letter of [June
5, 19__] that [summarize what the company claimed]).

(But contrary to the claim of compliance with the act and Regulation
Z, the [XYZ Financial Institution] in fact did [not] [state what the com-
pany did or failed to do].)

I am, however, still prepared to resolve this matter as I have already
proposed if the (XYZ Financial Institution) now promptly satisfies the
requests I made.

I hope we can promptly resolve this matter as I have proposed so that
I will not have to hold you liable for a violation to the fullest extent pro-
vided by the Truth in Lending (Fair Credit Billing) Act.

Sincerely,

STAGE THREE: THE ULTIMATUM

WHEN THE CREDITOR STILL REFUSES TO SETTLE

If the card issuer still refuses to settle and the seller won't resolve the dispute, you
must then decide whether to pay the card issuer and forget about trying to hold him
accountable, or push the dispute to the point of actually withholding payment.

If you withhold payment and the card issuer sues you, you can then formally raise
your claims and defenses to show you don't owe the money. While this is obviously
a drastic move, it may actually result in the card issuer crediting your account for
the disputed amount. That's because his agreement with the seller may allow disputed amounts to be charged back only if the consumer refuses to pay.

When you reach this point you must first repay all undisputed amounts. To make
sure you withhold payment only on the amount of the disputed purchase, plus finance
charges imposed on that amount, as of the date you first notified the seller and/or
card issuer about the problem, make sure you calculate those amounts based on how
payments are applied to your account.

The following sample letter, which informs the card issuer that you are refusing
to pay, can be adapted to your circumstances. It refers to the fact that your account
is paid in full for all other transactions, and includes alternative wording for situations in which you might owe part of the amount outstanding for the disputed
purchase.

The best time for taking this step is when you are making the last payment for
amounts due for other purchases. (You could use the "payment-in-full" check when
making the last payment, but the card issuer could then refuse to accept it.) Briefly
describe previous steps you have taken to resolve the problem. If the seller and card
issuer are the same, request refunds that would be due based on steps you have taken
to hold the seller accountable for failing to honor the sales agreement.

Please note that this sample ultimatum sets the stage either for a settlement or a
lawsuit. It is a last resort move when all other attempts to resolve the problem have
failed and you are determined not to pay an amount you do not owe.

200 Witchtree Lane
Anytown, USA 00000

October 10, 19___

Accounting Department
ABC Card Issuer
100 Money Plaza
Anytown, USA 00000

Dear Sir:

This is to notify you that the dispute about the (identify purchase) I purchased from you (the ABC Company) and charged to my (Money Card) account with your credit card, account number 000-000000-000, has still not been satisfactorily resolved. I first notified you about this matter in my letter of (date) which more fully describes it. I have since notified you by my letter of (include date(s)) about additional matters relating to the failure to resolve the dispute. (Copies of letters enclosed.)

Although I have been trying to resolve this matter with you (and the seller) since the dispute first arose, my attempts have been unsuccessful. I proposed that we resolve this matter by requesting that the $_____ outstanding on my account for the disputed purchase (plus finance charges imposed on that amount) be credited to my account (and indicated I would waive my claims for the crediting of finance charges imposed on the outstanding amount if the disputed amount was promptly credited to my account).* And for the reasons I have already described to you, I also requested that you refund the $_____ I have already paid for the purchase (and that you reimburse me for the $_____ due me for the damages I have described/[OR] and indicated I would waive my claims for damages I sustained if you promptly refunded the amount I have paid for the purchase).** (I also made alternative proposals to you [and the seller] for resolving this matter so that we could still satisfactorily complete the transaction.)

Since these attempts to resolve the matter were unsuccessful (and you insisted that payment for the purchase was due regardless of the dispute I described), I finally informed you on (date) that, as provided by the Fair Credit Billing Act, the $_____ outstanding on the account for the disputed purchase was not due or owing since I was entitled to raise against you the claims and defenses arising from this transaction and that the payments I made were not to be applied to the disputed purchase. And although I again made proposals for resolving this matter, the dispute remains unresolved.

I am, therefore, as provided by the Fair Credit Billing Act deducting from the $_____ balance for the billing period ending (date) (at least) the $_____ outstanding on my account but not due or owing for the disputed purchase, plus the $_____ as finance charges that have been imposed on that amount. I am sending you my check number (687) for $_____ which is for the remaining amount due for other transactions (and for the $ _____ that may be due for the disputed transaction). (And there is now also due from you for the reasons I have already indicated the $_____ I have paid for the disputed purchase plus at least the $_____ I have sustained up to now as damages. I am also only storing the product involved in this matter and now have a security interest in it for the return of pay-

ments on its price as provided by the Uniform Commercial Code but am then prepared to return it as I have already indicated.)****

I am, however, reserving my right to raise all claims and defenses arising from this transaction relating to the failure to resolve dispute.

I hope that we can still resolve this matter by you promptly crediting my account for the amount outstanding but not due or owing for the disputed purchase plus finance charges imposed on that amount (and by you promptly crediting my account for the amounts due me). Please make the appropriate adjustments in my account and promptly notify me so we can finally resolve this matter.

But since no (further) amounts for the disputed purchase are still due or owing on my account, the $____ payment I am sending is payment in full for all amounts due or owing so that I am not in default under our open-end credit agreement. (And as provided by the Fair Credit Billing Act, you are not to off-set against or deduct from my accounts any of the (remaining) amounts not due or owing for the disputed purchase.)*****
[Note: See alternative wording after letter.]

While I hope we can still resolve this matter, your continuing refusal to do so leaves me no choice but to dispute your claims in court and to hold you liable for all amounts I would be entitled to recover as provided by law.

Sincerely,

Notes:

*Use wording about finance charges as appropriate. This would depend on what you had proposed previously.

**The wording about requesting a refund or reimbursement for damages refers to requests you could make of a card-issuing seller.

***The wording applies to a card-issuing seller when you reject and/or revoke acceptance.

****The wording refers primarily to situations in which the only amount you are withholding is an amount you are sure you do not owe.

The following is alternative wording you can adapt for situations in which you withhold the entire amount still outstanding when a failure to resolve the dispute could later entitle you to hold the seller/card issuer accountable for more: "But while at least $ ____of the amount outstanding for the disputed purchase is now not due or owing for the reasons I have already described, if the matter remains unresolved, I shall, to the fullest extent provided by law raise all claims and defenses arising from this transaction relating to the failure to resolve this matter. And, as provided by the Fair Credit Billing Act, you are not to off-set against or deduct from my accounts any of the amounts involving the disputed purchase."

HOLDING A CREDITOR ACCOUNTABLE FOR A VIOLATION

If a creditor violates the requirements of the Truth in Lending (Fair Credit Billing) Act and Regulation Z and continues to refuse to make amends, you could adapt the following sample ultimatum letter. It is addressed to the president of the company, but you could also send it to the person you have dealt with previously.

200 Witchtree Lane
Anytown, USA 00000

July 15, 19___

President
XYZ Financial Institution
100 Finance Plaza
Anytown, USA 00000

Dear Sir:

This is to notify you about the (XYZ Financial Institution's) violation of the Truth in Lending (Fair Credit Billing) Act which occurred with respect to (identify transaction: see page 513 for sample wording).

I first notified your (Consumer Credit Department) about this matter in my letter of (May 20, 19___) which more fully describes the violation that occurred and in which I made my proposals for resolving this matter. When I received no response (When I received a response claiming no violation occurred), I then again brought this matter to your company's attention by my letter of (June 15) and again proposed to resolve this matter by requesting that (restate request previously made).

I am still prepared to resolve this matter as I then proposed if the (XYZ Financial Institution) now promptly complies with my proposal.

But if my request for resolving this matter is not satisfied, I shall then seek to hold the (XYZ Financial Institution) liable for the violation to the fullest extent provided by the Truth in Lending Act. And since $_____ was imposed as a finance charge in connection with this transaction, the minimum liability could now be $_____ . Moreover, my reasonable attorney's fees and costs of bringing suit could also be assessed against you should I be compelled to take legal action.

Sincerely,

62 · The FTC's Preservation of Consumers' Claims and Defenses Rule: Holding a Creditor Accountable for a Purchase

It used to be that if you bought something on credit and the seller sold your agreement to a third party, such as a bank or finance company, you would have to continue payments even if your purchase turned out to be the lemon of the year which could have entitled you to avoid having to pay the money back if you still owed it to the seller.

How could this happen? Very simply. The agreement itself, or the way the credit was extended, cut off your right to refuse payment once the agreement was sold to a third party. If you were entitled to use remedies to hold the seller accountable for breaching the contract, you could have sued the seller, it's true, but suing was generally not worth the money or time involved.

When the Federal Trade Commission adopted the "Preservation of Consumers' Claims and Defenses" Rule, however, it put an end to these practices in the vast majority of cases. The Rule was adopted in November 1975 and went into effect in May 1976. Most states have now also passed laws outlawing these practices in most kinds of credit transactions: in some instances they provide more protection than the FTC Rule. Differences between state laws and the FTC Rule are likely to be important only in unusual situations, though. This FTC Rule will also be referred to as the FTC "Holder" Rule, which is what it is usually called.

WHAT DOES THE RULE COVER?

The FTC Rule only covers goods or services purchased by consumers. It does not apply to commercial transactions or to the purchase of real estate. Two main kinds of credit transactions are covered. First, the rule applies to all credit agreements under which credit is extended in connection with credit sales. This covers purchases made on credit extended by a seller under either an open-end or closed-end credit agreement. The rule does not, however, apply to purchases made with a credit card issued by someone other than the seller (but see Chapter 58 for similar protections that you would have in such cases under the Fair Credit Billing Act). An open-end credit agreement with a seller who issued a credit card that could be used for making purchases on credit would be covered by the rule. The rule also does not apply to any types of transactions exempted from the Truth in Lending Act, the most important being transactions for more than $25,000 that are *not* secured by your dwelling or real property. (See page 454 for other types of transactions that could be excluded because they are exempt under that act.)

Second, the rule covers certain loan arrangements under which a creditor lends money for a purchase: arrangements where the seller engages in a pattern or practice of referring consumers to the creditor who lends you the money, and arrangements where the seller and creditor are affiliated for the purpose of financing sales. Such separate loan arrangements to which the rule applies are known as "purchase money loans," which is how they will be referred to in this book.

The following questions will help you determine if the rule applies to your loan transaction:

- Did the seller help arrange the loan? If so, the rule is likely to apply.
- Did the creditor indicate he would only finance purchases made from a particular seller? If so, the rule is likely to apply.
- Is there anything to indicate the seller and creditor work together to arrange financing? It is harder to pin this down, but look for clues such as the following:

... Similarity of names between the two, which is likely to indicate common ownership.

... Credit forms that have the seller's and creditor's names printed on them. This usually confirms that the two are business affiliates.

... The creditor regularly finances purchases from a particular seller. You could find this out simply by asking the creditor. If so, they are likely to have some arrangement.

... The seller regularly finances sales with a particular creditor. This is something you could ask the seller. If so, they are likely to have some affiliation.

HOW THE FTC RULE WORKS

The rule requires that any credit sales agreement, or purchase money loan agreement include a clause that preserves rights you have for holding a seller accountable.

If the purchase was made on credit extended by a seller, the seller must then include the following clause in bold faced type like that printed below:

NOTICE
ANY HOLDER OF THIS CONSUMER CREDIT CONTRACT IS SUBJECT TO ALL CLAIMS AND DEFENSES WHICH THE DEBTOR COULD ASSERT AGAINST THE SELLER OF GOODS OR SERVICES OBTAINED PURSUANT HERETO OR WITH THE PROCEEDS HEREOF. RECOVERY HEREUNDER BY THE DEBTOR SHALL NOT EXCEED AMOUNTS PAID BY THE DEBTOR HEREUNDER.

If the purchase money loan is provided by a separate lender, the rule requires the *seller* not to accept the proceeds of the loan as payment for the purchase unless the loan agreement includes an almost identically worded clause printed in bold face like that above. The only difference is that a clause used for a purchase money loan would not include the words "pursuant hereto or" which would be included in the clause given above.

The seller himself must see to it that the clause is included by the separate lender. This back-handed method means you must watch out and make sure the clause is actually included when the rule requires it. If the appropriate clause is not included when it should have been, the seller is committing an unfair or deceptive act or practice in violation of the FTC Act. Only the FTC can enforce the act, though; as an individual you can't hold the seller responsible for this particular violation.

If the proper clause is not included, as required by the rule, you may not be covered unless your state law provides similar protection. While it is possible to argue that you are still protected if the purchase is financed as a credit sale, it is difficult, if not impossible, to do so if the purchase is financed with a purchase money loan.

The safest way to avoid trouble is to make sure that any credit agreement you sign includes the appropriate clause when required by the rule. It is especially important that the appropriate clause be included in any promissary note you might be asked to sign in connection with a credit transaction covered by the rule. The required clause then prevents the note from being a negotiable instrument and thus prevent anyone who acquires it from being a holder in due course as explained in Chapter 45.

When the clause is included in the credit agreement, you are protected not because of the FTC Rule but because the rights spelled out by the clause are part of your contract.

Stripped of legalese, the clause means that if you have legal justification for not paying the seller, or you are entitled to get your money back from the seller, these rights hold up in the same way against *anyone else* who holds the credit agreement involved, with one exception. The most money you could get back from a separate creditor would be the amount you had already paid under the credit agreement involved. If you were entitled to recover more than this sum as damages, you would have to get the rest from the seller except to the extent you could offset the excess against what you still owed under the agreement. If, however, you also no longer owed the remaining balance, you would have to get the excess from the seller.

HOW THE RULE PROTECTS YOU

If you are entitled to reject, revoke acceptance, cancel a purchase, or use any other remedies to hold a seller accountable, you can use them whether or not you made the purchase on credit, of course. But the clause required by the FTC Rule allows you to hold a separate creditor accountable in the same way.

[NOTE: If you purchased services on credit, and the person who was supposed to furnish the services fails to perform them as required by your agreement, you could then either hold that person accountable for damages you had or, in case of a very significant failure to honor the agreement, to rescind (cancel) the agreement based on rights under contract law rather than rights under the Uniform Commercial Code. This book does not cover those rights in detail, but in the case of services, your usual recourse would be to recover damages, which would be the loss you sustained because of the failure to perform the services as required. You may also be able to hold a seller accountable under your state's fraud law or deceptive sales practices law or other laws that applied.] If you no longer owe the outstanding amount to the seller because you are entitled to revoke acceptance and cancel, for instance, a separate creditor couldn't collect the money either. And if you are entitled to a refund, you could get the money back from the separate creditor. A separate creditor can no longer say: "Pay me regardless of what went wrong with the purchase; if you have a complaint, take it up with the seller."

Suppose you buy a color TV from Reliable Electronics for $800 under a retail installment contract, for instance. Say you make a $200 down payment and are going to repay the remaining $600, plus $72 in finance charges, in twelve installments of $56 each. Reliable Electronics promptly sells your contract to the Discount Finance Corporation. You make two payments totalling $112 to Discount Finance. Then you discover the set is a lemon, which entitles you to revoke acceptance and cancel. You also suffer $300 in damages because the set is faulty.

Although the set does not work because of its many defects, Reliable Electronics refuses to do anything about it and tells you "that's how it goes." You then tell Reliable Electronics you are revoking acceptance because the value of the set is "substantially impaired." Assuming you are entitled to cancel the purchase—and under these circumstances you almost certainly would be—you would not owe the remaining balance. If either Discount Finance or Reliable Electronics tried to collect by suing, you could then say you don't owe the money. This is called raising your defense to non-payment—a legal justification for not owing money someone is trying to collect. If a court decided you were right, which is likely in such a situation, neither company could collect.

But in this example, you would also be entitled to get back what you had paid for the price of the TV set, plus amounts you could recover as damages. Because, in this particular case, the purchase was made and financed under a credit sales agreement with the seller, any amount you had paid the seller would be included in the amount you could get back from the separate creditor. The amount you could collect from Discount Finance, therefore, would be $312; the $200 down payment, plus the $112 in payments. These amounts would usually cover what you had paid for the price plus finance charges and which, as explained on page 539, you are likely to be able to get back in such situations. Since what you could get back for the price includes everything you have paid, you would have to recover the additional $300 in damages from the seller.

If you financed the purchase with a purchase money loan made by a separate creditor, however, the amount you had paid back to the creditor would usually be the most you could get refunded from him. In other words, any other money paid directly to the seller would have to be refunded by the seller himself. The seller would also be liable for any damages you could be entitled to recover.

Thus the kind of financing arrangement you use can make a big difference in who you can hold accountable—and what for—when things go wrong. From the standpoint of the protections provided, making and financing a purchase under a credit sales agreement with the seller gives you a better deal than a purchase money loan.

MAKING SURE YOUR CREDIT AGREEMENT INCLUDES THE APPROPRIATE CLAUSES

Before signing, always make sure any credit agreement includes the appropriate clause that preserves the claims and defenses arising from the underlying purchase transaction.

It is especially important to do so when you have a purchase money loan. Insist, too, that the agreement identify the seller and the purchase you are financing. Try to get the lender to include a clause like the following, for instance: "Proceeds of this loan are being used for financing the purchase of (identify purchase) from (identify seller being paid) under an agreement dated (_____)."

If a creditor includes the proper clause in the agreement, he should be accomodating enough to include the appropriate identifying information.

If he doesn't want to include such wording, however, but insists on paying you the proceeds of a loan with a check made payable to you and/or the seller, you could include the following notation on the front or back of the check: "Amount of check proceeds from purchase money loan for financing purchase of (identify purchase) from (identify seller) under an agreement dated (_____)." Make a copy of the check before it is cashed.

If the clause is not included when it should be, simply point out what the rule requires and ask a question like:

"Since I am using the loan to finance a purchase from the (_____), isn't this a purchase money loan governed by the FTC's "Preservation of Consumers' Claims and Defenses" Rule?"

If a creditor claims the rule doesn't apply, point to reasons why it should: you were referred by the seller, or the seller arranged the loan, for example.

If the creditor concedes such a point, then ask:

"In that case, doesn't the rule make it an unfair and deceptive practice for the seller to take the proceeds of the loan unless the preservation of claims and defenses clause is included in our loan agreement?

"Why then don't we have this loan agreement written up so that it includes the clause required by the FTC Rule?"

Pursuing the point along these lines will then result either in the creditor using the appropriate clause or refusing to do so. In the latter case, your safest recourse is to say: "I'm sorry, but in that case I don't want the loan." If the lender still won't budge, which means you will be prevented from making the purchase unless you get credit elsewhere, the decision could be tough to make; but remember if you take the loan anyway and something goes wrong with the purchase, you could regret your choice later.

In the case of a purchase money loan, make sure that any agreement you sign with the seller includes wording that specifically entitles you to cancel the purchase for a full refund if you are unable to get the financing. And if possible, pay little or nothing down until then.

The following wording can be adapted for the purpose: "Buyer shall be entitled to cancel this agreement for a full refund of the $_____ down payment made if financing for the remaining balance of the price cannot be arranged by (date) on terms satisfactory to the buyer."

If you have already signed a purchase agreement without a cancellation clause, it puts you under a lot of pressure to go along with whatever financing the seller can arrange, of course.

CANCELING THE PURCHASE

If you cannot get satisfactory financing and want to cancel, as provided by a cancellation clause, request a refund of any amount paid and be sure to get back all copies of the sales agreement and have the original marked "discharged" and signed by the seller.

If the seller refuses to cancel or won't return your down payment, you could adapt the following sample letter:

Certified Mail 1111122222

100 Witchtree Lane
Anytown, USA 00000

June 20, 19 ___

Manager
ABC Sales Company
100 Main Street
Anytown, USA 00000

Dear Sir:

This is to inform you (This is to confirm my verbal notification of [June 19, 19___]) that our agreement of (date) for the sale of (identify product(s)) is canceled as provided by the agreement.

As provided by the agreement, I am entitled to cancel and obtain a full refund of the $ _____ down payment I made on (date) if financing for the (_____) balance of the purchase price could not be arranged by (date) on terms satisfactory to me.

There is now due from you and I request immediate payment of the $_____ I have paid and no payments under this agreement are either due or owing by me. You are also to return to me and indicate that all outstanding instruments are discharged.

I hope the down payment will now immediately be returned to me so I will not have to hold you liable for keeping my money without legal justification.

Sincerely,

If the seller still won't refund your money, you would have to sue to get it back. You could usually do this in small claims court.

HOW YOU LOSE PROTECTIONS SIMPLY BY REFINANCING

If you refinance the balance outstanding on a credit agreement covered by the FTC's Rule, it could result in the loss of your protections. Once you get another loan you use to pay off the outstanding balance on the old agreement, the old agreement terminates and you then owe the money under the new agreement. You could, of course, still hold the seller accountable based on remedies available against him. But such a refinancing arrangement almost always strips you of the protections you had under the first agreement to raise claims and defenses against any subsequent creditor/holder of that agreement. If it was still important for you to preserve those claims and defenses, never let a creditor talk you into such an arrangement however attractive he might make it sound.

FINANCING PURCHASES WITH SEPARATE LOANS NOT COVERED BY FTC RULE

If you finance a purchase with a separate loan that is not covered by the FTC Holder Rule, you would almost always have to pay back the loan regardless of what went wrong with the sales transaction. The seller in such situations will, of course, have almost always been paid in full out of the proceeds of that loan. While you could, of course, still hold the seller accountable based on the remedies you can use against him, you would not have the extra leverage that being entitled to withhold payment could give you when you preserve your right to raise claims and defenses against a creditor holding your credit agreement.

This makes it especially risky for you to finance purchases out of the proceeds of loans made by a separate creditor which are secured by your home or real property. These usually involve what were previously referred to simply as second mortgage loans.

But various types of creditors (such as securities brokers and consumer finance companies) have begun to market this old concept under a new name and have combined it with a fancy package of other financial services through which you can draw on the credit extended under the loan arrangement involved. These new arrangements are usually referred to as "equity loans" on your home and you are usually told it is a way to "unlock" the equity built up in your property so you can use it for financing purchases. But you unlock the equity by putting the property up as collateral so that this new-fangled idea is really nothing more than an old-fashioned second mortgage.

When combined with a fancy package of other services, you can usually tap the credit extended in various ways, such as through a special checking account or even credit cards. Such arrangements then usually result in the amounts involved being immediately paid by the creditor with whom you have the loan arrangement.

The FTC Holder Rule almost certainly does not cover the loan arrangement under which proceeds are advanced to pay for the purchase you made by the methods you can use to tap the credit you have. The creditor with a mortgage on your home has a lot of security to make sure you repay, but you almost certainly do not have any leverage for holding the creditor accountable based on claims and defenses arising from the underlying purchase transaction.

These new-fangled "equity loans" might be an easy way to obtain a large amount of credit. But be aware that this is a very risky way to finance a purchase which could result in a dispute with a seller.

And a word of caution. If you financed a purchase this way, do NOT use the negotiating strategies included in this book for trying to hold a creditor accountable based on the seller's failure to live up to your sales agreement.

63 · A Creditor's Remedies for Default and Liabilities for Improper or Unlawful Collection Action

If the credit extended to you is secured by personal property, the creditor has what is called a "security interest," in that property, which is also called the collateral. The Uniform Commercial Code spells out in detail how a creditor can obtain a security interest, repossess the property if you default on payments, and collect money still owing under your agreement if the value of the property is insufficient to cover the balance outstanding.

(If you get involved in a dispute about a purchase that is secured by real property, such as your home—as opposed to personal property—seek legal advice before trying to hold a seller or creditor, or both, accountable based on claims and defenses you could raise to avoid paying. It is far too risky to try to solve the matter on your own and perhaps jeopardize what may be your most important asset. This is one very good reason why I do not recommend that you make credit purchases secured by your home in the first place.)

A seller/creditor's security interest in personal property must be put in writing and signed by the debtor to count. The terms that spell out the creditor/seller's security interest is usually referred to as the "security agreement," but which is almost always simply a part of the entire credit agreement you sign.

This chapter summarizes a creditor's remedies upon default and the key requirements that apply when a creditor is entitled to repossess personal property. If he engages in wrongful or unlawful conduct when repossessing, or it turns out you are not actually in default when you fail to pay because of a dispute, he could become liable to you.

SUMMARY OF CREDITOR'S REMEDIES

A creditor's remedies when you are in default sometimes depend on the terms and conditions governing your agreement. This right to repossess personal property, however, always depends on the security interest specified in writing and signed by you.

Broadly speaking, if you are in default, a seller/creditor may be able to do the following:

- Sue for the outstanding amount, plus other charges and amounts recoverable as damages. (This is usually the main remedy if the credit extended is *not* secured.)
- Use any remedies available to a seller when a buyer breaks a sales agreement.
- Repossess any collateral securing the debt and, after following the proper procedures, sue for any amount still outstanding because the value of the collateral is not adequate to cover the balance due, plus any recoverable costs and expenses. In this case, a creditor would be trying to get what is called a "deficiency judgment" for the amount by which the collateral is deficient.
- Accelerate all outstanding payments so they become immediately due and payable. A creditor can only do this if your agreement specifically allows him to, but most agreements do have such clauses.

A creditor can also take various steps to collect money that's owed, of course. These could include judicial collection remedies (court sanctioned steps to collect, such as wage garnishment or attachment of property) or some non-judicial remedies (such as wage assignment) if your state's law allows them.

Usually, the creditor would seek to repossess the collateral, of course, and might also sue for a deficiency. This would normally be the fastest way to collect. He could not do this *and* still sue for the entire amount outstanding, however.

Since repossession is usually a creditor's most important remedy, let's look at how he could go about it.

HOW A CREDITOR CAN REPOSSESS COLLATERAL

Generally, there are two ways a creditor can try to repossess collateral.

1. *Self-help repossession.*

Using what is known as "self-help" repossession, a creditor can simply try to take back the property on his own. Generally speaking, he may only do this if he can repossess the property without causing a *breach of the peace.* He may not enter your home to take the property without your permission, for instance, or take property that is outside your home if you protest. If he did so, he would usually be committing a breach of the peace and he could also be liable for other wrongful conduct such as forced entry.

If the collateral is a car, a creditor would not be able to take it forcefully—if it were locked in your garage, for instance, or if it is parked in the street and you were present to protest. But trying to prevent a creditor from using self-help repossession when you are in default can cause problems for you and may, in a few states, result in criminal liability for conversion; that is, refusing to return property which the creditor is rightfully entitled to. However, as explained later, if you have legal justification for not owing the money and are determined to hold a creditor accountable, refusing to return the collateral can give you extra leverage.

2. *Judicial repossession.*

When he uses judicial repossession, a creditor uses court-sanctioned steps to get back the collateral. Each state has its own legal procedures a creditor could use.

Normally, a creditor has to start a legal action to recover the collateral which would then be seized by a sheriff or other authorized official. Before the collateral can be taken, though, you may first be required to be served with a court notice and be entitled to a hearing. You could then take steps to prevent the creditor from actually getting the property until after he establishes in court that he is entitled to it. Legal advice would be necessary at this point.

Forcing a creditor to use judicial methods makes repossession more time-consuming and costly: if he legally is entitled to repossess the property, a creditor can make you pay these additional costs.

WHAT A CREDITOR CAN DO UPON REPOSSESSION

If he does repossess the collateral, a creditor may:

• Properly resell the collateral and return any amount that exceeds what you owe, or sue for deficiency. The Code requires a creditor to notify you that goods will be resold and spells out other requirements he must follow to make a proper resale. As a practical matter, though, these requirements are only important when a creditor tries to sue for a deficiency. You would then need legal advice to hold a creditor accountable for failing to do what the Code requires.

• Treat the repossession as a "strict foreclosure," that is, simply keep the collateral as settlement in full for the remaining debt. In this case, he is required to inform you of the matter in writing and you may insist he resell the collateral instead. The creditor would then have to return any excess money made on the resale. He could also insist you pay for any deficiency. If you do not insist the creditor resell the collateral, he is not required to pay you any excess money that results from a sale; on the other hand, he may not try to collect for any deficiency, either.

If the creditor simply keeps the collateral without notifying you that he is treating it as a strict foreclosure, he would usually be *considered* to have used strict foreclosure in order to prevent him from suing you for a deficiency. If, however, you have already paid 60 percent or more of the debt, he is required to resell the collateral within ninety days unless you specifically tell him otherwise.

A creditor's repossession remedy is a quick and easy way to collect an unpaid debt. That's why creditors want collateral, of course. If you are in default and a creditor wants to repossess, you could ask him to put in writing that he will treat the matter as a strict foreclosure so you won't be responsible for any deficiency. A creditor may be willing to do this if you, in turn, then make it easy for him to pick up the collateral.

CREDITOR'S LIABILITY FOR UNLAWFUL OR WRONGFUL CONDUCT

If a creditor engages in any of the following wrongful or unlawful conduct when repossessing any goods, he could become liable to you (you would, however, need legal help to hold a creditor accountable, but it would usually be worthwhile to get such help if these things happen):

• Entering your house without your permission. He could then become liable for trespassing and other wrongful (tortious) conduct.

• Making threats. This could result in the creditor becoming liable for assault.

• Physical force. This could result in the creditor becoming liable for battery.

• Taking any property which he is not specifically entitled to repossess. This could make the creditor liable for the "conversion" of that property; a legal term for taking or keeping property without actually having legal justification for doing so despite a claim to that effect. A creditor could then owe you for the value of the converted property and could be liable for punitive damages.

• Engaging in collection activities that could amount to intentional infliction of emotional injury and/or invasion of privacy.

In addition to any amounts you could recover as compensation for damages caused by wrongful or unlawful conduct, you could hold a creditor liable for punitive damages if he blatantly disregards your rights. He could also become liable for the statutory penalty spelled out by the Code if he fails to comply with the requirements governing repossession as spelled out by the Code. He would then be liable for any actual loss sustained as a result by the debtor or by any person whose security interest he knew about when he repossessed the goods. (If you specifically tell the seller/creditor about the security interest you have in goods as provided by the Code, you could also be damaged as a person whose security interest he knew about.) His minimum liability would be not less than the sum of the credit service charge, or interest, plus 10 percent of the total amount of the debt in the case of a loan; or the amount of the finance charge, plus 10 percent of the cash price, in the case of a credit sale. If the cash sales price of goods financed was $3,000, for example, and the finance charge for the entire financing period was $630, the minimum penalty would be $630 plus 10 percent of the $3,000, or an additional $300, for a total of $930.

While you can usually hold a creditor financially liable whether or not you are actually in default, your legal position is obviously better if you really don't owe the money and were not in default. A creditor's wrongful conduct in such a situation almost always takes on extra significance since he lacks any justification for what he did.

CREDITOR'S LIABILITY FOR WRONGFUL REPOSSESSION

A creditor could also become liable for wrongfully repossessing and converting goods if you no longer owe the money being secured by the goods, or were not actually in default in the first place.

Suppose, for instance, you rightfully reject or justifiably revoke acceptance and cancel a sale—that would terminate any remaining obligations you have and you would no longer owe anything for the goods involved. The Code enables a creditor to repossess only on default. Once you no longer have any further obligations, any related security interest also terminates.

Moreover, if you have already paid something toward the price of the goods, the Code specifically gives you a security interest in them for that amount (plus any amount you could be entitled to recover as damages for the cost of storing and inspecting the product). This means, in effect, that when you rightfully reject or justifiably revoke acceptance of goods which are in your possession and for which you justifiably have already paid something, you have a security interest in the goods until the money is returned to you and you can hold them until that time. Once you cancel and thereby terminate any remaining obligations, a creditor's security interest also terminates and he would not be entitled to have the goods back until he returns the amount paid. A creditor who tried to take back the goods without returning the amount paid, and for which you have a security interest in the goods would almost certainly be wrongfully repossessing the goods and could be liable for conversion. The amount for which you could then hold him liable would be at least the amount due you as a refund, plus the statutory penalty set by the Code for wrongful repossession.

Similarly, a creditor could be liable for wrongful repossession and conversion if he repossesses property when you are not actually in default. You could, for instance, be paying less than the full amount due because you are entitled to deduct money for damages from the price and still due. (See page 324 for an explanation of how a buyer can deduct damages from the price still due.)

If you want to hold a creditor liable for wrongful repossession and conversion, don't voluntarily return the property in which you have a security interest. The interest lasts only as long as the goods remain in your possession.

HOW TO TRIGGER LIABILITY FOR WRONGFUL REPOSSESSION

The way to trigger the seller's/creditor's liability is to make it clear when you are rejecting and/or revoking acceptance that you are specifically retaining the security interest the Code entitles you to have, and that you are holding the goods until the money you have already paid is refunded.

This informs them you will treat any attempt to repossess as wrongful repossession and conversion.

CREDITOR'S LIABILITY FOR FAILING TO RELEASE CERTAIN SECURITY INTERESTS

A creditor could also become liable if he doesn't properly release a security interest when he is required to do so.

This applies when a creditor has formally filed what is known as a financing statement with a public office which places the security interest on the public record. When the security interest terminates, the Code requires the creditor to file a termination statement with the same office. He is required to do this whether an obligation is terminated because you have repaid the amount in full, or because you no longer actually owe it, and he must do so within thirty days or, if you make a written request, within ten days. If you no longer owe the amount, make a written demand to trigger the creditor's liability.

If he fails to clear the interest, the creditor is liable for $100 plus any other losses you sustain.

HOLDING A CREDITOR ACCOUNTABLE FOR WRONGFUL CONDUCT

To hold a creditor accountable for the types of wrongful conduct described in this chapter you would need the services of an attorney. Nevertheless, a seller/creditor's potential liability gives you bargaining leverage when you use remedies that entitle you to avoid having to pay and to raise claims and defenses against a separate creditor trying to collect.

A creditor's liability for conversion in case of wrongful repossession, for instance, exposes him to a particularly tricky legal liability. It is triggered if he repossesses property without actually having legal justification for doing so. It doesn't matter if he *thinks* he has justification; if a court decides he did not have it, the conversion occurred at the time the property is wrongfully taken.

A creditor's liability for wrongful repossession and other wrongful conduct, therefore, can give you bargaining leverage for settling a dispute about a purchase made on credit under an agreement that enables you to raise claims and defenses against the creditor, or, of course, against a seller who was also a creditor. If he disregards your claims and defenses and you don't owe the money, he would be unable to collect the outstanding amount and you could recover any amounts already paid toward the price, plus any damages you could recover based on what went wrong with the purchase, plus any amounts for which he would be liable based on the wrongful acts he committed. This can make it very risky for a creditor to disregard claims and defenses you are entitled to raise based on what went wrong with the purchase.

64 · Summary of Negotiating Strategy for Raising Claims and Defenses

The key point to remember about raising claims and defenses against a creditor is that they are based on remedies you have for holding a seller accountable. You have two kinds of remedies: those that entitle you to reject and/or revoke acceptance and cancel a purchase, and those that only enable you to recover damages for something that goes wrong with a purchase.

Whether you would have to deal with the seller or creditor or both depends on who receives payments under the agreement involved.

If the purchase was made on credit extended by the seller and you are still making payments to him, you would only have to deal with the seller.

If the purchase was made on credit extended by the seller, but the agreement has been sold to a separate creditor, you should take steps to hold both parties accountable based on the remedies you have for holding the seller accountable. In a situation like this your payment obligation is to the separate creditor, but the seller is primarily responsible for honoring the agreement.

If you financed the purchase with a purchase money loan made by a separate lender under a loan agreement that included the clause required by the FTC's Holder Rule, the situation would be almost identical to the one above and, again, you should take steps to hold both parties accountable based on the remedies you have for holding the seller accountable.

If something goes wrong with a purchase but the seller corrects the problem, it is usually worth keeping a separate creditor/lender informed. Send him copies of the correspondence involved. If you cannot deal with the seller because he is unreachable (he has gone out of business, for instance), then simply deal with the separate creditor/lender as you would with the seller.

LEVERAGE THAT HELPS YOU SETTLE WITH SEPARATE CREDITORS/LENDERS

Separate creditors/lenders who finance consumer credit purchases covered by the FTC Rule are not fools. They don't want to be stuck with agreements on which they may be unable to collect because of claims and defenses you have, any more than you want to be stuck with a defective product. So you can be sure they protect their interests as far as possible.

There are numerous kinds of specific arrangements that help a separate creditor avoid being stuck with worthless paper. But generally they allow him to recover from the seller any money paid to him for the agreement. Such arrangements give you some practical bargaining leverage with both the separate creditor and the seller, therefore.

Often creditors insist on including the specific provisions in the agreement itself which spells out the recourse the creditor has against the seller in case the outstanding amount is uncollectible. These arrangements do not affect what rights you have under the agreement, but they can affect what the separate creditor is likely to do when you raise claims and defenses. Normally such provisions can be found somewhere on the back pages and are usually identified by labeling that includes the word "recourse." The separate creditor is usually referred to as the "assignee," the seller as the "assignor." If the wording indicates the assignee has recourse to get back money from the assignor because of claims and defenses raised by the buyer (or other similar wording) a separate creditor's easiest way out is to insist the seller "buy back" the agreement rather than trying to collect from you. Alternatively, he may join with you to put pressure on the seller to get the problem corrected so he can keep collecting the money. (This is precisely what the rule is designed to do.)

Check the conditions on your agreement carefully. If the wording indicates that the assignee has *no* recourse against the assignor, you may face a much tougher fight with the separate creditor.

If you financed a purchase with a purchase money loan, covered by the FTC rule, the separate lender usually would not have direct recourse for getting the money back from the seller. In this case, the loan and sales agreements are technically completely separate and this can make it more difficult for the separate lender to include in the loan agreement arrangements that could enable him promptly to get back from the seller amounts you could recover from or no longer owed to the separate lender. You would, therefore, be in a much tougher bargaining situation in these circumstances, too. Even if your agreement includes the clause required by the FTC Rule, there are special legal pitfalls you could run into and it is best to seek legal advice when trying to hold a separate lender accountable. However, you do have some leverage and a separate lender is at least likely to have some kind of arrangement for holding the seller accountable in case the money is uncollectable, or he may be willing to put pressure on the seller to correct a problem to avoid being out the money because of claims and defenses you are entitled to raise against him. These arrangements would usually be based on the on-going relationship the lender has with the seller for financing his sales. (If the loan agreement does not include the clause required by the FTC Rule even though it should have, I caution you against trying to raise claims and defenses against the separate lender without legal advice. And if you financed a purchase with a separate loan that is not covered by the FTC Rule, you would almost certainly have to repay regardless of what went wrong with the purchase.)

RISKS YOU TAKE BY ASSERTING CLAIMS AND DEFENSES

While the right to raise claims and defenses against a creditor gives you bargaining leverage, it can also hurt you if you turn out to be wrong and fail to pay.

Simply raising claims and defenses against a creditor and telling him you therefore no longer owe payments may, in itself, trigger collection and/or legal action. And if your credit agreement includes an accelerator clause for insecurity or default, the creditor/seller could insist you repay the entire balance immediately. This move won't help him if you don't actually owe the money, but it could hurt you if it turns out you're wrong.

If you are entitled to use remedies that enable you to avoid payment, it's sometimes possible to play word games that make it clear you are invoking these remedies without saying anything that could justify collection action until you actually don't pay. But you need the help of an attorney to do this effectively since he would use specifics relating to your particular situation. The sample letters included in the next chapter are *not* based on word games. It should be said that word games are unlikely to put off anyone who is prepared to initiate harsh collection action rather than settle the problem. Your most effective protection is likely to be the fact that the creditor risks penalties by acting wrongfully and disregarding any rights you have.

In a word, there simply is no completely safe or foolproof way to raise claims and defenses that could justify not paying the balance outstanding. If you're unwilling to risk collection action or the possibility you may be wrong, it is very difficult to use remedies such as rejecting or revoking acceptance and canceling the purchase. So if you want to play it very safe, seek legal advice before taking the necessary steps to invoke these remedies. Even then, no responsible attorney will tell you that you can assert your rights without taking at least some risks.

An alternative to using such remedies is simply to keep making payments after you notify the seller about the problem, then—if necessary—sue for any damages you could be entitled to recover.

NEGOTIATING ALTERNATIVES AFTER YOU RAISE CLAIMS AND DEFENSES

You may face a number of negotiating alternatives once you raise claims and defenses. Which you use would depend partly on who you have to settle with, how exactly you could settle up, and how the seller and/or creditor responds when you raise your claims and defenses.

TO SETTLE WITH A SEPARATE CREDITOR

To hold a separate creditor accountable along with the seller, you would first have to settle up with the creditor since the amount outstanding is payable to him. If you reach an agreement with the creditor with respect to amounts no longer owing, that would also hold up against the seller so he would be unable to collect that amount. You could then try to recover from the seller any amounts you may still be entitled to but which the creditor refuses to refund or for which you cannot hold him accountable.

If the creditor returns the credit sales agreement to the original seller, however, you would then have to settle the entire dispute with the seller just as you would if he had never sold the agreement in the first place. If a creditor "settles" by telling you, in effect, that you no longer owe payments to him but does not actually terminate the outstanding obligation, don't think the dispute is settled until you have also reached an agreement with the seller. If you can use remedies that entitle you to cancel and the creditor fully resolves the matter by terminating the outstanding obligation and refunding the amount you paid, you would have to return the product. If he settles only with respect to the outstanding payments, you would have to negotiate with the seller for the return of amounts you already paid unless you are determined to get the money back from the creditor when you are entitled to do so. In a situation like this, you would retain your security interest in the product and could hold on to it until you received a refund of amounts paid toward its price.

When a creditor still holds the credit agreement, the only way to settle with the seller is to ask him to refund payments you have already made, plus the entire outstanding balance for the purchase. You could then repay the creditor. Don't do this unless you keep the creditor informed and first get his approval for returning the product to the seller before you have repaid him, or else make arrangements with the seller to return the product only after you have repaid the creditor. A seller may have his own reasons for wanting to settle without your formally bringing the creditor into the dispute. But if you do not raise claims and defenses against the creditor and settle up only with the seller, a creditor who discovers the fact could immediately be entitled to repossess the product in which he had a security interest for the outstanding balance unless you got his approval for returning the product to the seller and repaid the creditor.

TO SETTLE WITH A SEPARATE LENDER WHEN PURCHASE WAS FINANCED WITH PURCHASE MONEY LOAN COVERED BY FTC RULE

If your purchase was financed with a purchase money loan, the sales and loan agreements are two separate contracts. Broadly speaking, you have two basic alternatives in such a situation.

The first is to settle with the seller. You would not then raise claims and defenses against the lender. Since the seller has already been paid, you would, in effect, be dealing with him as a cash customer and would have to try to get back from him all amounts you could recover. At the same time you would have to continue making payments to the creditor, as called for by your loan agreement. (This would also be your *only* option if the loan is *not* covered by the FTC Holder Rule, and this would also be your only safe option if the proper clause was not included in your purchase money loan agreement even though it should have been unless you act on legal advice.)

There are several advantages to this approach: the seller cannot repossess the product or sue since he has already been fully paid; you can hold just one person accountable for everything; and if you are entitled to reject or revoke acceptance, you retain a security interest in the goods until the money you have is refunded. You would, under these remedies, have to return the goods once the seller returns those amounts, but not until then. (Remember to treat the goods as the seller's property when you use these remedies.)

The main disadvantage to using this approach is that you may have to sue to get your money back: this can take a long time and is expensive unless you are able to use small claims court. You also have to keep paying the lender, of course, and if he has a security interest in the goods you must either repay the loan or make other arrangements with him to get the security interest released so you can return the goods to the seller upon receiving a refund. If the lender can be sure the loan balance will be repaid once the seller makes a refund, he would usually cooperate in making the appropriate arrangements.

The second alternative with a purchase money loan would be to raise your claims and defenses against the lender. If you do this, you can only settle up with the lender for any amounts still outstanding under the loan, plus whatever amounts you had already repaid under the loan agreement and would be entitled to recover. You would then have to try to get back from the seller any further amounts you had paid, or could recover as damages.

A key question would usually be when, and to whom, you would have to return the product if you can reject or revoke acceptance and cancel the purchase.

If the separate lender settles so that you no longer owe him the outstanding balance, that would terminate his security interest. You would then have to get back from the seller any amount you had paid, and any damages you could recover. You would still have a security interest in the goods and could hold on to them until the seller returns any portion of the price you were still entitled to recover.

If the separate lender settles up for the entire purchase price, which would be unusual but could happen, you may have to return the product to him rather than the seller. But this could be worked out between you.

If the seller refuses to refund any money due after you have settled up with the separate lender, you would have to sue. Suing the seller could get complicated, however, because of the two separate agreements involved. You cannot, in effect, get a refund from the lender plus no longer owe the rest of the loan *and* also get all your money back from the seller. But, technically speaking, the remedies that would entitle you to settle up this way with the lender would also entitle you to a refund from the seller. If you want to sue in these circumstances, seek legal advice.

If you do settle with the seller after you have reached a settlement with the lender, check what the lender wants to do about being reimbursed from the seller. If the seller refuses to refund amounts still due, the only additional leverage you would have is to sell the product involved. Doing this without strictly following procedures spelled out by the Code would result in a lot of problems, though, so don't even try it without legal advice.

AMOUNTS YOU COULD SETTLE FOR

Whenever you finance a purchase under a closed-end credit agreement, the amount involved usually includes a number of separate items and charges. What you could settle for depends partly on your particular credit arrangement, and partly on the remedies available.

Settling Up When You Are Entitled to Reject or Revoke Acceptance and Cancel

If you are entitled to reject or revoke acceptance and cancel a purchase, you would no longer owe any of the balance outstanding regardless of the different types of charges or fees that may be included in it. Everything would be simple and straightforward as long as only a single purchase was involved.

The question would then be what portion of your payments could you get back, and what additional amounts could you recover as damages. This would depend primarily on whether you had purchased the goods on credit from the seller or used a purchase money loan, and on how different types of charges are debited from payments. You should, as a matter of course, always request a refund of all payments made, but you may not get back the full amount. At a minimum, though, you should receive the portion of the payments that were applied to the price, plus tax.

If you financed the purchase with a purchase money loan, you may be unable to get back any amounts that went for finance charges, credit insurance premiums, or other similar charges. (You may be able to recover them as incidental or consequential damages from the seller, but you would almost always have to sue to do so.)

If, on the other hand, you financed the purchase under a credit sales agreement with the seller, you may be automatically entitled to get back *all* amounts paid. This would depend on how your agreement identifies the "total amount" financed. In many states, the total amount is called the "time-sales price" or the "deferred payment price": the Truth in Lending Act requires that it be identified as the "credit sales price" on the disclosure statement but this wording probably does not matter unless it is also used in your agreement.

The total amount is identified with names such as the time-sales price because of legal doctrines which helped creditors get around usury law ceilings. Now I'll let you in on how that policy could backfire on them. When you are entitled to cancel, the Code allows you to recover "the price." It says nothing about whether "the price" includes only the "cash sales price." So "the price" you paid, and could be entitled to recover, is whatever you paid toward the deferred payment price or time-sale price or other wording used in your credit sales agreement which describes the total amount of the transaction as "the price" paid rather than simply the amount identified as the cash sales price. You could then be entitled to recover everything you had already paid toward, say, the "deferred payment price" which would almost always include the full amount already paid.

If, on the other hand, your credit sales agreement does *not* identify the total amount involved as, say, the time-sales price but refers to it instead as, say, "the time balance," then the amount you could be entitled to recover may only be the actual sales price. You could still insist the creditor or seller refund *all* amounts paid, but, in fact, you may only be able to recover them as incidental or consequential damages.

So, it's always worth checking your agreement to see how the total amount is actually identified. If the phrase involved does *not* include the word "price," it may then be more difficult for you to get a refund of finance or other charges.

When You Are Only Entitled to Recover Damages

If you cannot reject or revoke acceptance and cancel, usually your only remedy would be to recover damages and deduct them from the price still due. You are always entitled to deduct damages when the product was purchased on credit from the seller. Almost certainly you should also be able to do so with a purchase money loan covered by the FTC Rule. Technically speaking, though, in this case you would be deducting the damages from the amount outstanding for the loan rather than the amount still directly outstanding for the price, so you would then have to pay whatever was left over after you deducted your damages. In this situation, it is unlikely you could get a rebate of finance or other charges—unless you might be entitled to do so because the entire balance has been repaid ahead of schedule.

Laws are unclear about whether you could deduct damages from the next payment due, or must spread the amount over the remaining payments. You would either have to work this out with the creditor, or simply tell him what you were going to do.

Settling a Multiple-Purchase Credit Transaction

No matter what remedies you're entitled to use or the type of financing involved, if you have made several purchases under the same credit agreement, the problems involved in settling will usually be very similar. If, for example, you are entitled to cancel one purchase out of several, you could get back what you had paid for it, and have a security interest in the product until the amount was refunded, but you would still owe for the others. So the key question in such situations would be whether you owed anything *after* you had settled up for the disputed purchase.

If you could only hold the seller accountable for damages because the product failed to measure up to your contract, your options would then be the same as in the case of a single-purchase transaction. That is, you could deduct your damages from the price still due.

If you are entitled to cancel only some of several purchases you would no longer owe the amounts still outstanding for them. But usually you would be unable to reduce the amount still outstanding for other purchases simply by deducting the money due back for canceled purchases. You could, of course, request that the creditor do so, by crediting the amounts coming back to you against the balance remaining under the agreement, but if he refuses and you go ahead anyway, you could risk being in default. To avoid the possibility, only withhold amounts actually still outstanding for canceled purchases rather than deducting a refund due you for them. And to be absolutely safe, only withhold the amount that could still be outstanding for the price, not finance or other charges.

If you financed the purchase with a purchase money loan covered by the FTC Rule, you may be unable to recover finance or other charges unless you could recover them as incidental or consequential damages: courts are divided on whether such amounts are recoverable so never assume they are. The same thing could apply if the total amount of a credit sale transaction was *not* identified by wording such as "time-sale price." To be safe, don't deduct such charges even if you are entitled to do so: it's too easy to miscalculate the amount and you could end up being in default if you are unable to settle with the creditor.

Figuring out what portion of the purchase price you haven't paid for canceled purchases can be tricky. At best, you can only make a rough estimate and then ask the creditor to furnish you with an accounting based on it. The Code entitles you to request such an accounting and the creditor must provide it within two weeks. He is not allowed to charge for such an accounting when it is requested only once within a six-month period. Always err on the side of caution in your calculations so you underestimate the amount still outstanding. While this can result in your paying more than is actually owing, it's safer than to miscalculate and end up being in default. You can, however, insist the creditor return any amounts you count as definitely having been paid.

If all your purchases were made at the same time and your agreement calls for repayments in equal installments, you could first roughly estimate the amount still outstanding for the price of all the products by using the finance charge rebate formula described in Chapter 57. This would at least give you a rough estimate as to how much might still be outstanding for the amount financed, but which may include amounts for credit insurance or other charges. To be on the safe side don't count them as no longer owing.

The following shows how you can make a rough estimate of the amount outstanding for the canceled purchases: To calculate the rebate of the finance charge, make the calculation as if pre-payment occurred as of the payment coming due after cancellation. (The number of payments being "pre-paid" would be those coming due after this payment.) Then subtract the rebate from the total still outstanding for the remaining payments. This gives you an estimate of how much could still be outstanding for the amount financed. Then subtract from that estimate the total included in the amount financed for credit insurance and for other fees or charges. This leaves the minimum that would still be outstanding for the actual purchases.

To figure out what portion of the total amount outstanding for all purchases might still be due for the canceled purchases, calculate their purchase price as a percentage of the total price paid. Suppose it was 40 percent. That would then usually be the portion of the total amount outstanding for all purchases which would be outstanding for the cancelled purchases. This calculation assumes, however, that payments were applied to the amounts due for the different purchases in proportion to the price of each purchase. Your agreement may spell out a different method for applying payments, though; such as applying them first toward the repayment of the least costly purchase.

An alternative way of estimating how much of the total monthly payments were applied to different amounts, and what might still be outstanding for the canceled purchases is to first use the finance charge rebate formula to estimate how much went for finance charges. Calculate the rebate as if the entire amount had been repaid when you made the last full monthly payment prior to cancellation. Then subtract the rebate from the total finance charge. This gives you how much of the finance charge you have already repaid. Subtract this amount from the total payments made to get the amount that has been applied to purchases or other charges included in the amount financed. You would then have to calculate how payments made had been applied according to the formula spelled out in your agreement, which would then enable you to estimate how much was still outstanding for the disputed purchases.

It is much trickier to calculate what portion of the outstanding balance you still owe for any canceled purchase when multiple purchases covered by the same closed-end credit agreement are not made at the same time. It would usually depend on whether the purchases were made before or after other purchases that may have been added to the transaction.

At best, you can make a rough estimate only if the disputed purchase was made last and the payments made after it was added were less than its purchase price. To do this, you could count all payments made after the disputed purchase as having been applied to its price. Suppose, for example, you made a purchase for $800 which you were later entitled to cancel after making four payments of $90 each, or a total of $360. The safe way to estimate how much of the $800 is no longer owing would be to count the entire $360 as having been applied to its price, leaving $440 as the amount no longer owing. This would be a gross overestimate in the creditor's favor, however.

Since any estimate involves tricky calculations, it behooves you to seek legal advice before you assert claims and defenses for multiple-purchases made and/or financed under the same closed-end agreement. This is an important reason for not making many different purchases under one closed-end credit agreement.

WAYS THE CREDITOR AND/OR SELLER MAY RESPOND

Once you raise claims and defenses, a creditor and/or seller may respond in one of two ways. A creditor may be willing to settle in ways that either do or do not also resolve the matter with the seller. Or the creditor and/or seller may insist that you owe the money and take legal or other collection action to retrieve it.

If a Creditor is Willing to Settle

If the purchase was made and financed under a credit sales agreement, the easiest way for a creditor to settle is to send the problem back to the seller. He could do this either by making the seller buy back the credit agreement, or by insisting the seller fix the product or replace it.

If the seller buys back the agreement, the dispute would then be between you and the seller. He may settle or he may try to make you pay.

In the case of a purchase money loan covered by the FTC Rule, the lender usually would not be able to make the seller buy back the loan agreement. If the two work closely together when financing purchases, however, the lender may have leverage to make the seller settle with you. He might pressure the seller to refund your money, for instance, so you could, in turn, repay the loan.

If a Creditor or Seller Insists Payment is Due

If the creditor is unwilling to settle and insists you pay the money, you would have two options: back down and pay while perhaps trying to retain your chance to sue, or keep the pressure on by taking additional steps that could help you hold the creditor accountable for taking wrongful action.

If you back down and pay, a creditor would almost certainly refrain from taking legal action. But remember if you do this you also give up your strongest bargaining leverage. (See page 399 for the negotiating steps you could use when taking this approach.)

If you don't want to back down, be prepared for the following collection actions:

- The creditor sues you for the money.
- The creditor tries to repossess the collateral, and sues for additional amounts he might be entitled to recover for expenses and damages. To forestall the first action, take the negotiating steps that could make the creditor/seller liable for wrongful repossession. And if he sues, you could countersue for any amounts you could be entitled to recover.
- The creditor reports you as being delinquent rather than tries to collect. You could attempt to forestall this kind of action by making it clear you will hold him liable for deliberately injuring your reputation or credit standing if he makes any false statements about the transaction. You may also be able to minimize any damage to your credit standing by putting your side of the story into your credit file, as the Fair Credit Reporting Act enables you to do (see Chapter 70).
- The creditor turns your account over to a collection agency. The Fair Debt Collection Practices Act could be of help in this situation.

A WORD ABOUT SEEKING LEGAL ADVICE

Retaining the right to raise claims and defenses can give you very strong practical and legal bargaining leverage. It can also make it much easier and less costly for an attorney to help you settle a dispute. This is because a creditor who wants to collect would usually have to initiate legal action to do so: if you had a reasonable basis for not owing the money, the action would open up a lot of legal strategies that your attorney could pursue in court to make it difficult for a creditor to succeed.

So if it looks like you can use remedies such as rejecting or revoking acceptance and canceling, having an attorney take the appropriate steps could result in a quicker settlement. You could also handle the matter yourself but act on the advice of an attorney to cut down on costs. You could, for instance, prepare a letter asserting your rights, then consult with an attorney before sending it to make sure of your legal position. This would also give you the additional negotiating option of having the attorney step in to reinforce you should the creditor refuse to settle.

The clauses required by the FTC Holder Rule automatically make it easier for you to hold a creditor/seller accountable for things that go wrong with a purchase; they also simplify an attorney's work in helping you assert your rights. This, in turn, often makes it worthwhile to seek legal advice.

SOME GUIDELINES FOR NEGOTIATING WITH A CREDITOR

Your basic negotiating objective should be to make it easier for a creditor to send back a dispute to the seller. In effect, this means you and the creditor should team up to put pressure on the seller. To help get the creditor on your side, suggest a reasonable solution based on the remedies you are entitled to use to hold the seller accountable.

REFERRING TO CREDIT AGREEMENTS

Always identify the agreement in question so the creditor/seller knows exactly what you are talking about. Refer to it in correspondence either in the specific way the agreement itself is labeled, or in the general way the FTC Rule defines credit agreements covered by that rule—that is, as a "consumer credit contract." The sample letters in the next chapter include further information you should provide to identify the specific agreement involved.

SETTING PAYMENT TERMS

There are times when you make a credit purchase when the seller is not required to make delivery or perform services until after you sign the credit agreement. Be sure that any such agreement spells out the delivery conditions or completion dates, and under no circumstances sign anything that says delivery was made or services were completed until it was or they have been.

Generally speaking, your obligation to pay isn't triggered until the seller makes delivery or performs services unless your agreement calls for earlier payment. Watch for wording that says you must start paying *before* delivery, or before services have been fully performed, such as: "Payment is due upon the signing of the agreement." Try to get wording included that says payment won't be due until after delivery or upon the completion of the services you purchase. If you are financing a purchase with a purchase money loan, arrange the sales terms so payment wouldn't be required until delivery has been made, or the services have been performed or spell out a schedule of payments to be made as specific work is completed. If possible, try to hold back the last payment until about thirty days after completion. You should also stipulate that no proceeds of the loan are to be paid out to the seller until you have specifically authorized the lender to do so.

Whether or not you financed a purchase with a purchase money loan or a retail credit sales agreement with the seller, the seller and/or creditor will want written acknowledgement that delivery has been made or services completed—especially when the agreement itself specifies payment won't be due until that time. See page 551 for wording you can adapt to acknowledge delivery. Remember, do not sign anything that says services have been *satisfactorily* performed.

REQUESTING AN ACCOUNTING WHEN DISPUTE INVOLVES ONLY SOME OF PURCHASE MADE

Since it can be tricky to calculate what you may still owe when a dispute involves only some purchases you have made under the same credit contract, make a rough estimate then ask the creditor to furnish you an accounting of what you still owe based on your calculations. The Code requires him to do this for an outstanding amount secured by a security interest in personal property. If he fails to do so after you have indicated what you calculate the amount to be, the Code enables you to hold him accountable for any loss that results, especially if he refuses to give you an exact calculation and tries to hold you accountable for erroneous calculations you may have made. You would need legal advice to do this, but requesting an accounting can at least help you do it.

65 · Negotiating Strategy for Raising Claims and Defenses: Stage One: Opening Skirmishes

Your opening moves for holding a seller accountable based on the remedies available are described in other Chapters.

Your opening moves for raising claims and defenses against a lender/creditor would normally be to notify him that you are holding him accountable along with the seller. This chapter covers steps you can take to notify and hold a separate lender/creditor accountable in the following situations:

- Your agreement is assigned and delivery has not yet been made.
- The seller fails to deliver the product.
- You are canceling a credit purchase within a cancellation period provided by law.
- The product fails to conform to your contract.

WHEN DELIVERY HAS NOT YET BEEN MADE

If you are notified that an agreement under which you made a credit purchase has been sold to a separate creditor, and delivery of the purchase has not yet been made, promptly inform the creditor of the fact. This will automatically strengthen your position to hold him accountable later if the seller fails to make delivery.

If your agreement does not call for payments until after delivery, make that clear. If it does, you will probably have to start making payments until you are entitled to cancel because of the seller's failure to deliver.

Although the purchase of services is governed by general contract law, rather than the Uniform Commercial Code, notifying a separate creditor that services or work have not been performed similarly strengthens your position. The sample letters include alternative wording you could use in this situation.

You can adapt the following sample letter to suit your particular circumstances.

100 Witchtree Lane
Anytown, USA 00000

June 1, 19___

Discount Finance Company
100 Money Plaza
Anytown, USA 00000

Dear Sir:

I am responding to your letter of (date) notifying me that the (consumer credit contract) of (date) under which I purchased and financed (identify purchases) from the (ABC Sales Company) has been assigned to you and that I am to make payments under that agreement to you.

I am hereby notifying you that the product(s) purchased under that agreement (has/have) not yet been delivered by the seller. (I am hereby notifying you that the seller has not yet performed the work/services I purchased under that agreement.)

As provided by that agreement, the product(s) (is/are) to be delivered by (date) (the work/services are to be completed by [date]). And since the agreement provides that payment is due only after delivery (the completion of the work/services to be performed), the (monthly) payment schedule of $____ per month does not commence until then. (Since the first payment in the payment schedule is now apparently due on [date], I shall commence payment.)

I do, of course, expect that a conforming delivery will be made (the services/work will be properly performed) by the seller as required by the agreement so that we can satisfactorily complete this transaction.

Please confirm that payments scheduled under the agreement are to commence only as I have described above and notify me when the initial payment will be due upon a conforming delivery having been made (the proper completion of the services/work to be performed).

Thank you for your cooperation.

Sincerely,

It is possible that taking this step could result in the creditor returning the agreement to the seller: this, in turn, could result in the seller refusing to live up to the agreement. If this happens, it is almost a sure sign you are dealing with a fast-buck operator and you would be better off getting out of the deal as soon as possible rather than trying to hold the seller to it. Even so, you would still have a credit agreement to terminate and, of course, you would want to get back any money you may have already paid the seller.

The quick way to settle in this situation is to ask the seller verbally to call off the deal and to give you a refund of any amount paid. Also ask for the return of any outstanding instruments and insist they be marked "discharged."

If the seller won't settle up quickly, despite telling you he won't go through with the deal, you usually have two options.

The first is to wait until the required delivery date has passed, then take steps to hold the seller accountable for failing to make delivery as required by your agreement. (See page 149 for how to notify the seller about the failure to deliver, and page 382 for canceling the agreement.)

If you cannot afford to wait until the delivery date has passed, or if you purchased services and want to terminate the deal because of the seller's refusal to complete the job, it is best to seek legal advice. Terminating your agreement under these circumstances, especially if it involves services which the seller has already started to perform, can be tricky and this is the only really effective way to protect yourself.

The second option is to immediately ask the seller for assurances that he will make delivery as required. If he fails to give such assurances within thirty days of your request it could entitle you to cancel. This procedure could, however, drag the matter out until after the delivery date passes.

The following sample letter seeks a quick settlement by asking for a refund, but insists the seller complete the deal as required by the agreement if he refuses to return the money. In such circumstances a seller will rarely say in writing that he refuses to go through with an agreement, so you can't simply cancel the agreement and demand your money back until it is clear the seller has broken it. Therefore, the wording proposes that the deal be called off for a full refund only upon the seller's express refusal to complete the terms of your agreement. For all practical purposes, this approach means you would have to wait until the seller fails to deliver as required by your agreement before you could cancel and hold him liable for breaching the contract. It also puts you in the position of having to go through with the deal if the seller insists on completing it. If such a settlement would be unsatisfactory to you either because you want to hold the seller to the deal or you wanted to avoid the possibility of having to complete the deal, seek legal advice.

100 Witchtree Lane
Anytown, USA 00000

July 1, 19___

Mr. J. Slyfox
Manager
ABC Sales Company
100 Downtown Square
Anytown, USA 00000

Dear Mr. Slyfox:

This is in response to my having been verbally informed by you on (June 30, 19___) that you would not (would be unable) to deliver the (identify purchase) which I purchased and financed under our (consumer credit contract) of (date). The reason you gave was (your inability to finance the transaction by the arrangements you normally use: OR describe other reason given).

Although your failure to make delivery as required by our contract will be damaging to me, I am prepared to resolve this matter promptly if you will immediately return to me the $_____ I have already paid. This amount includes the money down payment of $_____ I made on (date) plus the allowance of $_____ for the (identify product) I traded in and turned over to you on (date). You are then also to return to me and indicate in writing that all outstanding instruments are discharged. You are also immediately to take all proper and necessary steps to terminate any security interest arising from this transaction.

If you do not promptly satisfy my proposal for resolving this matter, I will then insist on full and complete performance as required by our contract and therefore expect that a conforming delivery will be made without fail by (indicate seller's delivery obligation).

And since your indicated unwillingness (inability) to make delivery as required by our contract prevents me from relying on your good faith, you are also promptly to furnish me adequate written assurances that a conforming delivery will be made by (date).

(And as provided by our agreement, none of the amounts outstanding under this agreement are payable until after a conforming delivery has been made.)

But since you have already indicated your unwillingness (inability) to make delivery as required by our contract, I hope you will either resolve this matter as I have proposed or that you furnish me the assurances I have requested and make delivery as required by our contract or I will hold you liable to the fullest extent provided by law for breach of contract and you shall have no opportunity to cure a failure to make a conforming delivery.

Sincerely,

WHEN A PURCHASE MONEY LOAN IS INVOLVED

If you have a purchase money loan covered by the FTC Rule, and the proceeds are paid to the seller before he has to make delivery or perform the services involved, the following sample letter shows how you can make it clear to the lender that delivery has not yet been made and strengthen your position. Even if you don't specifically inform the lender, though, you could still hold him accountable if delivery is not made.

100 Witchtree Lane
Anytown, USA 00000

June 1, 19——

Mr. G. Loaner
Manager
Easy Sales Finance Company
500 Finance Plaza
Anytown, USA 00000

Dear Mr. Loaner:

This is to (inform you my verbal notification confirms on [date]) that the/ (identify purchase) I purchased from (identify seller) under an agreement of (date) has not yet been delivered. I am doing so since this purchase was financed with the proceeds of your purchase money loan made under our (consumer credit contract) of (date).

As provided by the agreement with the seller, the product(s) I purchased (is/are) to be delivered by (date) (the services I purchased are to be completed by [date]).

Although the proceeds of the purchase money loan have already been paid to the seller, I, of course, expect that a conforming delivery will be made (the services will be properly performed) as required by the agreement with the seller so that we can satisfactorily complete both the financing and sales transaction involved.

Sincerely,

WHEN THE SELLER FAILS TO DELIVER THE PRODUCT AS REQUIRED

Promptly notify any creditor/lender of a seller's failure to make delivery of goods, as required by your agreement. When you do so initially, either let him know you have arranged an acceptable alternate delivery date with the seller (see page 149 for how to pin down an alternative date with the seller), or that the seller has refused to commit himself to one. In the latter case, give a delivery date that would be acceptable to you.

Remember, your main leverage in this situation is that you could be entitled to cancel: the creditor/lender could then be left holding worthless paper. If your agreement specified a firm delivery date and it was important to you, for instance, you would not have to give the seller another chance. In this case, notify the seller you are canceling and use a low-keyed warning to notify the creditor/lender that the agreement is canceled because of the seller's failure.

The following sample letter includes alternative wording and may be adapted to suit your situation.

100 Witchtree Lane
Anytown, USA 00000

May 1, 19__

Discount Finance Company
100 Money Plaza
Anytown, USA 00000

Dear Sir:

This is to inform you that the (identify purchase) I purchased from (identify seller) has not been delivered as required by my contract. I made and financed this purchase (as one of several purchases) under the (consumer credit contract) of (date) which I was informed has been assigned to you. (I purchased the product [as one of several purchases made] from that company under my contract of [date] and financed it with the proceeds of the purchase money loan made by you under our [consumer credit contract] of [date] and which has already been paid to the seller.)

Although the seller was required to make delivery by (state delivery requirement), delivery has not been made as required.

I notified the seller in writing on (date) about this failure to deliver. I then also informed the seller I was still prepared to complete the transaction as stated in the attached copy of my letter/memo of (date) which more fully describes this matter.

I have accepted (date) as the date by which the seller is now to make delivery (as shown on the attached copy of the seller's written assurances). (Although I indicated I would still be prepared to complete the transaction if the seller assured me that his failure to deliver will be cured by conforming delivery made not later than [indicate acceptable date], the seller refused to do so.)

I now expect that a conforming delivery will be made by the delivery date by which the seller must now do so (but I am not prepared to grant the seller further time for curing the breach). (As I have already informed the seller, I am still prepared to complete this transaction if I am promptly given a definite delivery date of not later than [_____] by which this breach is cured by a conforming delivery.) I am, however, reserving all my rights, and my willingness to grant this additional time is not to be construed as a modification of the agreement.

(I therefore request that the [Discount Finance Company] or the seller promptly confirm a definite delivery date by which this breach will be cured so that we can still satisfactorily complete this transaction.)

And since the [consumer credit contract (of date] provides that payment is due only after delivery, payments under the [monthly] payment schedule do not, therefore, commence until then. [I shall, of course, continue payments as now due for other purchases made] but while reserving all rights with respect to the breach for failure to deliver.)

(Please confirm that payments scheduled under the [consumer credit contract] are to commence only as I have described above and notify me when the initial payment is due after the conforming delivery has been made.)

But if the seller now still fails to cure this breach as I have requested, I shall cancel and you will be subject to all claims and defenses as provided by the (consumer credit contract).

I will, however, appreciate your prompt cooperation in resolving this matter so we can still satisfactorily complete this transaction.

Sincerely,

If the new delivery date isn't met, you may be prepared to give the seller more time. If so, then simply adapt the wording of the above letter when notifying the creditor about any new delivery date. Don't include the wording saying you will not give the seller more time until you are definitely prepared to cancel, of course.

If you purchased other products under the same agreement, or if the lender/creditor has a security interest in personal property other than the product involved in the dispute, it is possible a creditor might try to repossess. Prepare a cancellation letter so you have it available for immediate use in case that happens. (see page 562).

WHEN YOU ARE CANCELING WITHIN A LEGAL CANCELLATION PERIOD

There are times when you are entitled to cancel a transaction within a specific cancellation period provided by law, such as the FTC's "Cooling off Period for Door-to-Door Sales" Rule or the Truth in Lending Act.

If you properly cancel such a purchase but are then notified by a separate creditor that payments are now due and payable to him, immediately inform him that the transaction is canceled and that no payments are therefore owing. And if the seller has not returned a down payment due you, demand payment from the creditor.

The following sample letter can be adapted to suit your circumstances.

Certified Mail #1111122222

100 Witchtree Lane
Anytown, USA 00000

August 1, 19___

Discount Finance Company
100 Money Plaza
Anytown, USA 00000

Dear Sir:

I am responding to your letter of (date) notifying me that the (consumer credit contract) of (date) under which I made and financed the purchase of (identify purchase) from the (ABC Sales Company (and address)) has been assigned to you and that I am to make payments to you.

I am hereby notifying you that I informed the seller on (date) that the transaction was canceled as I was entitled to do under the provisions of (the Truth in Lending Act/the Federal Trade Commission's "Cooling off Period for Door-to-Door Sales" Rule, OR indicate other law that entitles you to cancel). Enclosed is a copy of the cancellation notice I sent and a copy of the mailing receipt showing the notice was sent within the time available for doing so.

Since I have canceled the transaction and the agreement is subject to the FTC's "Preservation of Consumers' Claims and Defenses" Rule, no payments under this agreement are due or owing you.

(And since the seller has still failed to return the $_____ down payment as required, that amount is now due from you.)

I therefore request (payment from you and) that you immediately take all necessary and proper steps to indicate the agreement is discharged, that you terminate any security interest arising with this transaction, and that you return any outstanding instruments to me.

I also insist that you refrain from any further attempts to seek payment and request that you confirm in writing that you will do so.

I will appreciate your cooperation in this matter so we can fully resolve it promptly.

Sincerely,

While the creditor may not comply with all your requests, such as refunding any down payment due from the seller, it is very unlikely that he will request payments from you a second time.

WHEN A PRODUCT FAILS TO CONFORM

If a product is delivered and you discover that it does not measure up to your contract, promptly notify the creditor/lender about steps you are taking to hold the seller accountable.

The following situations are covered in the rest of this chapter:

- You accept a product with the seller's written assurances that it conforms.
- You reject a product on delivery while the seller can still cure the defects.
- You discover defects after delivery which the seller fails to correct.
- The seller does correct defects.

ACCEPTING A PRODUCT WITH A SELLER'S WRITTEN ASSURANCES

If you make a credit purchase, a seller will almost certainly insist that you acknowledge delivery in writing and he may also require written acceptance of the product so he can be sure of being able to collect.

As previously noted, if you buy an expensive or complex product it's worth requesting written assurances that it conforms—even if nothing appears to be wrong with it—especially if the seller insists on written acceptance. This helps strengthen your position to revoke acceptance later if necessary.

The following sample letter can be adapted to notify a creditor/lender that the seller has provided such assurances. But say that you have accepted it only if you have already done so in writing; otherwise say only that you have received the product to avoid putting in writing you accept.

200 Witchtree Lane
Anytown, USA 00000

June 1, 19—

Discount Finance Company
100 Money Plaza
Anytown, USA 00000

Dear Sir:

I am confirming that the (identify product) I purchased from (ABC Sales Company [and address]) was delivered on (_____). I made and financed the purchase under the (consumer credit contract) of (date) which, as you informed me by your letter of (date) has been assigned to you. (I purchased the product from that seller under the contract of [date] and financed it with the proceeds of the purchase money loan you made under our [consumer credit contract] of [_____].)

Although I have indicated that I received (accepted) the product, I am advising you that I have done so only on the seller's assurance that the product fully conforms to the contract as indicated on the enclosed copy of the seller's written assurance.

I am, of course looking forward to full and complete performance under the contract so we can satisfactorily complete this transaction.

Sincerely,

REJECTING GOODS ON DELIVERY WHILE THE SELLER CAN STILL CURE DEFECTS

As explained in Chapter 30, you could face a number of different negotiating situations if you discover defects at the time a product is delivered.

If, however, you said in writing that you accept the goods on delivery, I caution you to seek legal advice before trying to reject them: rejecting goods under these circumstances involves technicalities that are far beyond the scope of this book. This is especially important if the seller/creditor/lender has a security interest in the product.

Your safest course is to treat the problem as you would treat defects in accepted goods. You could then have a chance to revoke acceptance and/or also reject the goods if the defects substantially impair their value. Remember, though, that if you reject goods when you were entitled to do so, the seller could still have an opportunity to cure the defects.

When you buy on credit, you should be more careful about formally rejecting goods than when making a cash purchase. Be more careful, too, about what you hold out for as an adequate cure: if you're wrong about what you can insist the seller do and don't pay you could end up being in default and the creditor/seller, in turn, could repossess. In a cash sale a seller doesn't have that leverage.

If you reject goods but the seller fails to cure the defects within the time allowed, you could be entitled to cancel the sale. That's your main bargaining leverage in such a situation.

If you reject the goods promptly notify the separate creditor/lender. You might first try to resolve how the seller is to cure before notifying the separate creditor/lender; if you do, be sure to notify him as soon as it's clear you and the seller are unable to resolve the matter.

The following sample letter can be adapted for this purpose. Also provide him with a copy of the letter/memo you give the seller.

100 Witchtree Lane
Anytown, USA 00000

June 1, 19___

Discount Finance Company
100 Money Plaza
Anytown, USA 00000

Dear Sir:

I am notifying you that the (identify product) I purchased from (identify seller) did not conform to the contract on delivery and that I have rejected it on *(date)* without taking delivery *(upon having received it on* [*date*]*)*. This product was *(one of several products that were)* sold and financed by that seller under the *(consumer credit contract)* of *(date)* which, as I was informed by your letter of *(date)*, has been assigned to you. *(I purchased the product under my contract with the seller of* [*date*] *and financed it with the proceeds of the purchase money loan you made under our* [*consumer credit contract*] *of* [*date*]*.)*

I rejected the product and have requested the seller to cure the non-conforming delivery as more fully described in the enclosed copy of my memo/letter of *(date)* I furnished the seller. I am now putting you on notice with respect to all matters described which have arisen in connection with this transaction.

The seller has, however, failed to cure the non-conforming delivery as I have requested. *(Although the seller furnished me his assurances that the non-conforming delivery would be cured by* [*describe how defects were to be cured*] *and I consented to keep the product while the seller did so, the defects described in the enclosed copy of my memo of* [*date*] *still have not been satisfactorily cured.)*

Since, as provided by the *(consumer credit contract)* of *(date)*, the *(Discount Finance Company)* is subject to all claims and defenses that I can assert against the seller as a result of the failure to cure the non-conforming delivery, I hope the seller will now promptly carry out his obligation to cure the non-conforming delivery as I have requested so that we can still satisfactorily complete this transaction *(or that we can promptly resolve this matter as I have otherwise proposed in the enclosed letter/memo of* [*date*]*)*.

I therefore request that the *(Discount Finance Company)* promptly contact me so that we can make arrangements for quickly resolving this matter. But if prompt arrangements are not made for curing the non-conforming delivery, I will insist on strict performance and the seller shall have no right to cure beyond the time agreed in the contract for making a conforming delivery.

I am, in the meantime, only storing the product and, as provided by the Uniform Commercial Code, I have a security interest in it for the return of the $_____ I have already paid should the seller's failure to cure the non-conforming delivery compel me to cancel the sale.

And as provided by the Uniform Commercial Code, the balance of the price is now not due or owing for the rejected product. *(I shall, of course, make payments as due for other products I also purchased under the agreement involved. But to indicate that I am, in good faith, seeking to resolve this matter so we can still satisfactorily complete the transaction, I shall commence* [*continue*] *making payments while the seller can still cure the non-conforming delivery. I am, however, doing so only while reserving all my rights.)*

But if, instead of resolving this matter as I have proposed, you or your agents attempt to repossess the goods, the sale is canceled and any repossession will be wrongful and subject you to liability for conversion.

I will, however, appreciate your cooperation in resolving this matter so we can still satisfactorily complete the transaction rather than my having to cancel because of the seller's failure to cure the non-conforming delivery and hold you liable for breach to the fullest extent provided by law.

Sincerely,

YOU DISCOVER DEFECTS AFTER DELIVERY WHICH THE SELLER FAILS TO CORRECT

If the seller refuses or fails to correct defects you discover after delivery, notifying the separate creditor/lender may put pressure on the seller to correct the problem. Assuming the defects do not immediately enable you to reject and/or revoke acceptance, therefore, notifying the creditor should be your initial step. You should also continue to pay while you try to get the defects corrected.

The following sample letter can be adapted to notify the creditor/lender about the problem.

100 Witchtree Lane
Anytown, USA 00000

July 1, 19___

Discount Finance Company
100 Money Plaza
Anytown, USA 00000

Dear Sir:

This is to notify you that the (identify product) I purchased from (identify seller) (still) fails to conform to the contract under which I purchased it. This breach and my proposals for resolving it are more fully described in the enclosed copies of my letters/memos of (dates) I furnished the seller. I am now putting you on notice with respect to all matters described in that correspondence.

I made and financed this purchase under the (consumer credit contract) of (date) with the seller which I have been informed has been assigned to you. (I made this purchase under my contract of [date] with the seller and financed it with the proceeds of the purchase money loan you made under our consumer credit contract of [date].)

Although I requested on (date) that the seller cure the defects (according to the assurances furnished by the seller) (and have already given the seller previous opportunities to cure the defects), the defects have not been satisfactorily corrected (despite the seller's previous assurances that the product would be made to conform). The failure to make the product conform continues to impair its value and is causing me great expense, inconvenience and aggravation since I am being deprived of the use of the product which I need for (describe). The failure to correct the defects would result in my having to incur costs and expenses for (having the defects satisfactorily repaired/obtaining a satisfactory replacement) and has already resulted in my sustaining damages of $_____ for (describe the types and amounts of expenses you had).

Since, as provided by the (consumer credit contract) of (date), the (Discount Finance Company) is subject to all claims and defenses I can assert against the seller, I hope the seller will now promptly carry out his obligation to correct the defects as I have requested so that we can still satisfactorily complete this transaction (or that we promptly resolve this matter as I have otherwise proposed in the enclosed letter/memo of [date]).

I therefore request that the (Discount Finance Company) or the seller promptly contact me so that we can make appropriate arrangements to have the defect(s) quickly and satisfactorily corrected to minimize my damages.

But if the seller does not promptly carry out his obligations to make the product conform to the contract, I shall hold the seller and you liable for breach at least to the fullest extent provided by the Uniform Commercial Code.

I shall, in the meantime, make payments as due but am doing so while reserving all my rights.

I will appreciate your cooperation in resolving this matter so that we can still satisfactorily complete this transaction rather than my having to hold you liable for breach of contract.

Sincerely,

If the defects remain uncorrected, your follow-up steps would depend on whether they substantially impair the product's value and so entitle you to revoke acceptance, or whether you could only recover damages for defects in accepted goods. See the low-keyed warning steps you could use when taking such follow-up actions.

THE SELLER DOES CORRECT DEFECTS

If the seller does correct a defective product, it could still be worth informing the separate creditor/lender about the matter in case later follow-up steps become necessary.

Naturally, use common sense about just how fully you keep the creditor/lender informed—it probably isn't helpful to give him a blow-by-blow account, for instance—and let the seller know what you are doing so it doesn't seem as though you are acting behind his back. Since the seller has corrected the defects, it isn't worth undermining a satisfactory relationship.

The following sample letter can be adapted for this purpose.

100 Witchtree Lane
Anytown, USA 00000

June 15, 19___

Discount Finance Company
100 Money Plaza
Anytown, USA 00000

Dear Sir:

I am informing you about defects I discovered in the (identify product) I purchased from (identify seller). I made and financed this purchase under the (consumer credit contract) of (date) with the seller which I have been informed has been assigned to you. (I made this purchase under my contract of [date] with the seller and financed it with the proceeds of the purchase money loan you made under our [consumer credit contract] of [date].)

The enclosed copy of my letter/memo of (date) to the seller more fully describes the matter. I was told on (date) that the defects have been corrected by the repairs and adjustments completed on (date) (and/I have been assured the following defects will be corrected by [date]: [identify defects seller promised to correct]).

But, as I have also indicated to the seller, the defects I have described are not to be construed as a waiver of any defects that may be revealed by subsequent inspection.

I am informing you about this simply to keep you advised about matters relating to this transaction.

Sincerely,

66 · Negotiating Strategy Continued: Stage Two — The Low-Keyed Warning

This chapter covers stage two of the negotiating strategy to hold a separate creditor/lender accountable. The following situations are covered:

- When defects in a product could enable you to revoke acceptance.
- When you could only deduct damages from the price still due.

THE LOW-KEYED WARNING FOR REVOKING ACCEPTANCE

As explained more fully in Chapter 33, generally you would only be entitled to revoke acceptance when a product's failure to conform to your contract substantially impairs its value.

The sample letter that follows can be adapted to notify a separate creditor/lender that you have taken this step whether you have a credit sales agreement or purchase money loan agreement covered by the FTC Rule. The wording is keyed to the notification you should already have given the seller (see page 269), and a copy of it should be enclosed. The letter also includes wording that warns the separate creditor about trying to repossess the product. It is identified with an asterisk and should be included in the letter or memo you use to notify the seller that you are revoking acceptance.

To maximize your options, you could say you are "rejecting *and/or* revoking acceptance" — especially in a situation where it may not be clear-cut whether you actually accepted the product. It won't hurt to say you are doing both, except in a situation where you've already rejected the product because of defects you found on delivery, then took it because the seller promised to cure the defects only to find he has failed to do so. In this case, you might be entitled to cancel because of the seller's failure to cure the defective delivery rather than having to revoke acceptance. Seek legal advice before you take such a step, though, especially if you have used the product while the seller was trying to cure the defects that entitled you to reject the product. Your right to cancel because of the seller's failure to cure is then no longer that clear cut since you could be considered to have accepted the goods by having taken and used them upon the seller's promise to cure the defects. If you rejected the goods but the seller failed to cure defects that substantially impaired its value, you could not then again reject the goods so your only alternative could then be revoking acceptance.

Whichever option you state—revoking acceptance, or both rejecting and/or revoking acceptance—when both alternatives might still be available to you, be sure you state the same thing in your letters to the seller and the separate creditor.

The sample letter includes alternative wordings for different situations, so adapt it to suit your situation.

Certified Mail 1111122222

100 Witchtree Lane
Anytown, USA 00000

August 15, 19__

Discount Finance Company
100 Money Plaza
Anytown, USA 00000

Dear Sir:

This is to notify you that I have (rejected and/or) revoked acceptance of the (describe product) I purchased from (identify seller). This product was (one of several that were) sold and financed by that seller under the (consumer credit contract of) (date) which has been assigned to you. (This product was [one of several that were sold] under my contract of [date] with the seller and its purchase was financed with the proceeds of the purchase money loan you made under our [consumer credit contract] of [date].)

I (rejected and/or) revoked acceptance of the product for reasons more fully described in the enclosed copies of my letters/memos of (dates) I furnished the seller. I am thereby putting you on notice with respect to all matters described in them. I have in addition previously notified you by my letter of (date) about defects I had discovered earlier and the seller's failure to make satisfactory repairs.

The (Discount Finance Company) is, as provided by the (consumer credit contract) involved in this transaction, subject to all claims and defenses I can assert against the seller. And as provided by the Uniform Commercial Code, the balance remaining for this purchase is no longer due or owing upon my having (rejected and/or revoked acceptance) (and the balance still outstanding under the agreement is therefore reduced at least by that amount). And I now also request a prompt refund of all money paid toward the price, including the $____ down payment I made to the seller, and the $____ for the (identify product) I traded in plus all monthly payments I have made. [NOTE: The wording of the previous sentence covers situations in which you made a single purchase under a credit sales agreement. See alternative wording included after the letter for other situations.]

There is now also due me at least the $____ I have sustained up to now as damages. These are more fully described in the enclosed copy of my letter/memo of (date) to the seller.

And as provided by the Uniform Commercial Code, I have a security interest in the product for the return of all money paid toward its price and shall hold the product until then. (I returned the product to the seller on [date] but you are not to treat its return as a repossession.)

(I am, however, still prepared to complete this transaction if the seller promptly furnishes me a conforming replacement for the defective product.)

I therefore request that you promptly contact me so that we can quickly resolve this matter. (I also request that you furnish me a prompt and complete accounting of the outstanding balance under the agreement upon the proper deduction of amounts no longer due or owing for the product involved in this matter. [I calculate that at least $____ is still outstanding for the product involved, leaving a balance of no more than $____]. I am unable to calculate the balance still outstanding for the product involved and request you to do so and inform me of the balance then remaining.) I further request you promptly credit my account with amounts I have already paid toward (the proceeds of the purchase money loan paid to the seller for) the price of the product involved in this matter.

*I have calculated this amount to be $_____ and which, upon being cred-
ited to my account, would leave an outstanding balance of no more than
$_____ which I am, of course prepared to pay as due [would leave no
balance still outstanding and there would, instead, be a credit balance of
at least $_____ which is to be promptly returned to me]. (I am unable to
calculate this amount and request that you do so and inform me of any
balance still remaining or of amounts then still due me.)*

    ***But if you or your agents attempt to repossess any goods, or if this
matter is not promptly resolved as I have proposed, the sale is canceled
and I shall hold you liable for breach at least to the fullest extent provided by the Uniform Commercial Code. And since there would then be
no outstanding obligation with respect to the canceled sale (and I am not
in default with respect to amounts due for other purchases), any attempt
to repossess will then be wrongful and subject you to liability for conversion. (But if the product I have returned is retained and treated as a
repossession, the sale is canceled and I shall hold you liable for breach
at least to the fullest extent provided by the Uniform Commercial Code.)**

    *I will appreciate your prompt response so that we can quickly resolve
this matter.*

Sincerely,

*Note: Include such warnings whenever you are notifying a seller or creditor that
you are invoking remedies that could enable you to avoid paying any balance outstanding for a purchase.

ALTERNATIVE WORDING FOR DESCRIBING AMOUNT DUE AS REFUND

The following alternative wording can be adapted for describing the amount that
could be due as a refund for payments already made, and for describing how to settle
the outstanding balance.

Purchase Money Loan Used for Financing a Single Purchase

    *"There is now also due from you, and I request a prompt return of, all
money I have repaid for the purchase money loan used for financing the
purchase of the product involved. I calculate this amount as the $_____
I have repaid and which is now a credit balance you are holding for me."*

    While you can request a refund of all payments made, remember the separate
lender may not be required to refund the portion that went for such things as finance
charges and credit insurance premiums.

Multiple Purchases Made Under the Same Credit Sales Agreement

    *"There is now also due me at least the portion of all amounts paid
under this (consumer credit contract) which have been applied to the price
of the product involved in this matter. I calculate this amount to be at
least $_____ which I request be credited to the balance still outstanding
for other purchases made under this agreement. (I am unable to calculate
what this amount would be and request you to do so and then to credit
that amount to the balance still outstanding for other purchases made
under the agreement.)*

    Request an accounting for the remaining balance in such situations.

Multiple Purchases Financed Under the Same Purchase Money Loan Agreement

> *"There is now also due me at least the portion of the repayments I have made under our purchase money loan as have been applied to the amount used for financing the purchase of the product involved in this matter. I calculate this amount to be at least $____ which I request be credited to the balance still outstanding for other purchases financed with the proceeds of this loan. (I am unable to calculate this amount and request you to calculate it and then credit that amount to the balance still outstanding for other purchases financed with the proceeds of the purchase money loan.)*

Request an accounting for the remaining balance in such situations.

THE LOW-KEYED WARNING FOR DEDUCTING DAMAGES

See page 349 for notifying the seller that you are requesting reimbursement for damages that are due for defects in accepted goods. You could then make the same request of the separate creditor/lender to whom you are making payments.

The sample letter includes alternative wording, so adapt it to suit your own circumstances.

> *200 Witchtree Lane*
> *Anytown, USA 00000*
>
> *(Date)*

> *Discount Finance Company*
> *100 Money Plaza*
> *Anytown, USA 00000*

> Dear Sir:

> *This is to notify you that, as more fully described in the enclosed copy of my letter of (date) to the (identify seller), there is now due me at least $ ____ for damages I have sustained because the (identify product) sold by that company failed to conform to the requirements of my contract.*

> *The product was sold and financed under the (consumer credit contract) of (date) with the seller which has been assigned to you. (The product was sold under my contract of [date] with the seller and the purchase was financed with the proceeds of the purchase money loan you made under our [consumer credit contract] of [date].) I also previously notified you about this matter by my letter of (date) when I requested that the seller cure the breach but which the seller failed to do.*

> *Since as provided by the (consumer credit contract) involved in this transaction the (Discount Finance Company) is subject to all claims and defenses I can assert against the seller, I therefore request that you deduct the $____ I have sustained in damages from the balance still outstanding under that contract.*

> *I calculate that upon the proper deduction of the amount due me as damages the balance still outstanding under the (consumer credit contract) involved in this transaction would be $____ . (I calculate that upon the proper deduction of the amount due me as damages, no further amounts are then still due or owing under the consumer credit contract involved in this transaction and there is, instead, due me a credit balance*

of at least $_____ [*plus amounts due me as rebates for finance and other charges upon the prepayment of the total amount financed*].)

I also request that you promptly furnish me a proper and complete accounting of the amount still due upon the proper deduction of the amount due me as damages, and that you provide me your revised payment schedule for the payment of the remaining balance. I am, of course, prepared to pay as due any balance still remaining upon the proper deduction of the amount due me for damages. (*Since no further amounts are due or owing upon the proper deduction of the amount due me for damages, I request that you return to me and indicate in writing that any outstanding instruments are discharged* [*and that, as provided by the Uniform Commercial Code, you file a termination statement within ten days to terminate your security interest if a financing statement covering the product involved has been filed*]. *I also request that you promptly return to me any credit balance you hold with respect to this credit transaction.*)

But if you fail to deduct the amount due me for damages as I have requested so that we may promptly resolve this matter, I shall then, as provided by the Uniform Commercial Code, deduct from the price still due under the contract (from the balance outstanding for the proceeds of the loan used for financing the purchase) the amount due me for damages and that amount is then no longer due or owing. I shall then also hold you liable for any further amount due me for damages to the fullest extent provided by law.

And since I am not in default on any amounts actually due or owing under the consumer credit contract involved in this transaction, any attempt by you or your agents to repossess any goods will be wrongful and subject you to liability for conversion.

Please contact me promptly so we can quickly resolve this matter as I have proposed so that I will not have to hold you liable for breach to the fullest extent provided by law.

Sincerely,

67 · Negotiating Strategy Continued: Stage Three — The Ultimatum for Canceling a Purchase

This chapter covers steps you could take to cancel a purchase after rejecting or revoking acceptance or after the seller has failed to deliver as required. Chapter 68 covers situations in which you are unable to reject and/or revoke acceptance but may deduct damages from the amount still due.

There are two situations in which you could try to cancel. The first is at the time when the seller/creditor tries to repossess the product after you reject and/or revoke acceptance. Canceling would then be a defensive follow-up step for trying to ward off repossession. The second situation would occur if you initiate cancellation on your own after the seller/creditor fails to resolve the matter but before he attempts to repossess after you reject or revoke acceptance or when you cancel because the seller failed to deliver at all. (In non-delivery situations, you would not have the product so, of course, there usually isn't anything to repossess.) Cancelling in these circumstances would, in effect, be an offensive follow-up step. Let's look at these two situations separately.

THE ULTIMATUM FOR CANCELING AT THE TIME REPOSSESSION IS ATTEMPTED

Whenever you reject and/or revoke acceptance, you should be prepared for the possibility that the creditor/seller could try to repossess the product or others in which he has a security interest. Counter this strategy by being prepared to cancel the sale in writing at once. This will, at least, make the project riskier for him.

If the creditor is using self-help, rather than judicially sanctioned methods of repossession, make it clear you are refusing him permission to enter your property or to take the goods. If goods *are* wrongfully repossessed, you would have to seek legal advice. But you would be in a strong position to hold the seller or separate creditor accountable for wrongful repossession and for any other tortious conduct which occurred.

In the case of judicial repossession, you would usually receive a notice that such action is being initiated. *Never* ignore such a notice: immediately notify the seller and creditor by certified mail that you are canceling, and appear in court to contest the action. Contesting a judicial repossession could result in a quick settlement because merely doing so usually entitles you to a hearing about whether the creditor is entitled to repossess. You would almost certainly need legal advice to follow this course, though.

If you cancel and it turns out you are entitled to do so, a creditor/seller who repossesses anyway would almost certainly be liable for wrongful repossession and conversion along with other tortious conduct that occurs. But if you are wrong about being entitled to cancel, you could be in the wrong about refusing to return the goods and could be in default. So it can be risky to use this approach without legal advice. But if you had reasonable grounds for being entitled to cancel, it is also risky for the seller/creditor to ignore rights you could have because of their additional liability for wrongful conduct. That's the leverage this step can give you for reaching a settlement.

Prepare a cancellation letter in advance so it is available for immediate use. If you still owe the money to the seller, rather than a separate creditor, see page 284 for a sample cancellation letter you can adapt to suit your circumstances. The following separate sample letters cover situations in which the purchase was financed by a separate lender with a purchase money loan, and situations in which a credit sales agreement with the seller has been assigned to a separate creditor.

Although the samples include alternative wording you can adapt for situations in which you have made multiple purchases under the same closed-end credit agreement but are only seeking to cancel some of them, I caution you to seek legal advice in these circumstances because of the additional complications that could be involved in settling up.

CANCELING WHEN A PURCHASE MONEY LOAN IS INVOLVED

Adapt the following cancellation letter for use when a purchase money loan is involved and prepare it in advance. Make several copies and have carbon paper handy so the date you put on the original can be copied onto the other first pages. Hand the original to the person trying to repossess for the lender; then send the lender a copy with a short cover note by certified mail, return receipt requested.

Insist the person trying to repossess on behalf of the creditor sign your copy to acknowledge receipt. Make sure he or she understands what's in the letter. Say something like: "You are not to take the property and, as explained in this letter, doing so is wrongful and could result in liability for wrongful repossession and conversion."

The person may claim it isn't any of his business what's in the letter since he doesn't "represent" the creditor and his only job is to repossess the goods. Just make it clear that by trying to repossess for the creditor, the person is acting as the creditor's agent and the creditor's responsibility is based on the notice you are giving him. The key is to convince the person that he had better pay attention to your letter before he does something that could later cause the creditor a lot of trouble. You do that by making clear that the trouble the repossessor can cause the creditor is described in the letter and that if it turns out you are legally right about cancelling, the trouble will be triggered if he goes through with trying to repossess. Then simply ask whether the repossessor really wants to make that decision for the creditor by what he does next.

> 200 Witchtree Lane
> Anytown, USA 00000
>
> (Date—fill in when used)

Discount Finance Company
100 Money Plaza
Anytown, USA 00000

Dear Sir:

I hereby cancel the sale of (identify product) (which was one of several products sold) by the (identify seller) under my contract with the seller of (date), and which I financed with the proceeds of the purchase money loan you made under our (consumer credit contract) of (date).

I am now canceling because I (rejected) (and/or) (revoked acceptance of) the product identified above for reasons more fully described in my letter/memo of (date) I furnished to both you and the seller. Your attempt to repossess now precludes me from relying on you to act in good faith in resolving this matter.

Since the sale described above is now canceled, and since the (Discount Finance Company) is, as provided by the consumer credit contract involved in this matter, subject to all claims and defenses I can assert against the seller, there is now, as provided by the Uniform Commercial Code, no further outstanding obligation under the contract (with respect to the canceled sale and any balance still remaining is reduced at least by the amount no longer due or owing for the canceled sale).

And there is now instead due me the amount I have repaid under the purchase money loan for the sale now canceled. I calculate this amount to be the $____ I have repaid which is now a credit balance you are holding for me and which I request be promptly returned to me. (And there is now instead due me at least the portion of the entire $____ I have repaid as has been applied to the repayment of that portion of the purchase money loan proceeds used for financing the price of the canceled purchase. I calculate this amount to be $____ which is now a credit balance you hold for me. This balance is either to be promptly returned to me or credited to any balance still outstanding for the other purchases that were also financed with this purchase money loan. [OR] I am unable to calculate this amount and request instead that you do so. That amount is then a credit balance you are holding for me which is either to be promptly returned to me or credited to any balance still outstanding for other purchases that were also financed with this purchase money loan.)

There is now also due me at least $____ I have sustained in damages as more fully described below:

(Describe and state amounts you could claim as damages.)

(And so that we can settle accounts with respect to any outstanding balance under the agreement, I request that you promptly furnish me a full and complete accounting of the balance still outstanding when you have properly deducted amounts no longer due or owing for, and have credited to my account amounts now due me for payments made under the agreement toward the price of the canceled sale. I calculate that the amount then still outstanding to be no more than $____ which I am, of course, prepared to pay as due. [I calculate that there would then be no further amounts still due or owing under the agreement (and there is instead due me a credit balance of at least $____ which is to be promptly returned to me.)])

I also reserve the right to hold you liable for damages up to the full amount I have repaid under our agreement.

Since there is now no further outstanding obligation under the contract, the (Discount Finance Company) no longer has a security interest in the goods involved. (Since there is no further outstanding obligation under the contract with respect to the canceled sale, the [Discount Finance Company] no longer has a security interest in the product involved. And since all payments due for any balance remaining under the contract for other purchases are, in fact, paid in full as due, I am not in default and the [Discount Finance Company] has no valid justification for repossessing any goods in which it may have a security interest.)

And as provided by the Uniform Commercial Code, I instead have a security interest in the (identify product) for the return of all moneys paid by me toward its price of $____, part of which was paid with the (portion of the) proceeds of the purchase money loan used for financing (all) the purchase(s) (made with those proceeds). The remainder of the price was *paid with my down-payment of $_____ to the seller plus $_____ for the (identify product) I traded in. I am, therefore, holding the (identify product) in which I have a security interest until the moneys I have repaid you toward the price of the canceled purchase is returned (or properly credited to my account with you); the balance of the purchase money loan no longer due or owing for the canceled purchase is discharged; and the remaining balance of the purchase price paid to the seller is returned to me. (Moreover, I need the return of the amounts due me upon cancellation so I can purchase a satisfactory substitute and thereby minimize my damages.)*

And since there is no further outstanding obligation under contract, you are to return to me and indicate in writing that all outstanding instruments are discharged. And as provided by the Uniform Commercial Code, you are to file a termination statement within ten days to terminate your security interest if a financing statement covering the goods involved has been filed. If you fail to file a termination statement as required, you will be liable under the U.C.C. for $100 plus any losses caused me by your failure. (And since there is no further outstanding obligation under the contract with respect to the canceled sale, you are to indicate that you no longer claim a security interest in the product involved and specify the goods in which you still claim a security interest.)

And if the (Discount Finance Company) now still attempts to repossess any goods in which it no longer has a security interest (and despite my not being in default on any payments actually due or owing under our contract), doing so is wrongful and will subject you to liability for conversion and for any other tortious conduct for which I shall seek to hold you liable to the fullest extent provided by law. Under the Uniform Commercial Code, your liability for wrongful repossession would be at least 10 percent of the amount financed plus the credit service charge. Your liability for conversion could be at least the amount for which I have a security interest in the product and may include punitive damages because of your reckless and deliberate disregard of my rights and your obligations.

I therefore urge you to reconsider your attempt to repossess, and that you instead promptly contact me so we can still quickly resolve this matter as I have proposed, rather than compel me to hold you liable in court for breach of contract and wrongful acts to the fullest extent provided by law.

Sincerely,

Cover Note to the Creditor

The following sample covering note can be adapted for use when you send the lender a copy of the cancellation letter.

Certified Mail #11112222

200 Witchtree Lane
Anytown, USA 00000

(Date)

Discount Finance Company
100 Money Plaza
Anytown, USA 00000

Dear Sir:

Enclosed is a copy of my cancellation letter of (date) which I gave to your employee or agent who wrongfully attempted to repossess goods I hold.

I now again urge that you promptly contact me so we can quickly resolve the matter described in the enclosed letter.

Sincerely,

Notifying the Seller of Your Action

Once you have notified the creditor that the sale is canceled, promptly send the seller a copy of the letter by certified mail, return receipt requested.

The following covering letter can be adapted for notifying the seller.

Certified Mail #11112222

200 Witchtree Lane
Anytown, USA 00000

(Date)

ABC Retailer
100 Hobsons Lane
Anytown, USA 00000

Dear Sir:

I am, by the enclosed copy of my letter of (date) to the (Discount Finance Company), notifying you that the sale of (identify product) (which was one of several products sold) under our contract of (date) is canceled for reasons described in that letter. I am, by the enclosed copy of that letter, also putting you on notice with respect to all matters relating to the transaction that are described in that letter.

And since that sale is now canceled, there is now due from you at least the portion of the $_____ price not paid with the proceeds of the purchase money loan from the (Discount Finance Company) which I used for financing the purchase and which I calculate to be $_____ . This amount includes the down payment of $_____ I made to you on (date) and $_____ for the (identify product) I traded in. I am not, however, hereby waiving any claims for the return of the remaining portion of the price paid with the proceeds of the purchase money loan except as this matter is finally resolved with the (Discount Finance Company).

There is now also due from you and I request the prompt payment of the $_____ I have sustained up to now in damages as more fully described in the enclosed letter.

And as provided by the Uniform Commercial Code, I have a security interest in the (identify product) for the return of all moneys paid by me toward its price, and shall hold the product until the amount no longer due or owing under the contract for the purchase money loan used for financing the payment of the price is discharged and the remaining amounts I have paid toward its price are returned to me (or properly credited to any balance still outstanding on the purchase money loan contract with the [Discount Finance Company]).

I therefore urge that you also contact me so we can promptly resolve this matter.

But if you still refuse to resolve this matter as I have proposed, I shall seek to hold you liable for breach at least to the fullest extent provided by the Uniform Commercial Code (and as provided by the Magnuson-Moss Warranty Act for failing to comply with obligations under a written [and] and implied warranty). That act also makes you liable for my damages and can entitle me to recover my legal expenses, including attorney's fees, should your continuing failure to carry out your obligations compel me to take legal action.

Sincerely,

CANCELING WHEN A CREDIT SALES AGREEMENT IS INVOLVED

You can adapt the following sample letter for use when the purchase was financed under a credit sales agreement which has been assigned to another creditor. Address it to both the seller and the separate creditor and prepare several copies in advance. Have carbon paper handy so you can date them. Hand the original to the person trying to repossess and insist he or she sign your copy to acknowledge receipt. Then send copies to the companies involved. You could also follow-up by sending another copy with a covering note to the company that tried to repossess. Send these letters by certified mail, return receipt requested.

200 Witchtree Lane
Anytown, USA 00000

(insert date when used)

ABC Retailer
100 Hobsons Lane
Anytown, USA 00000

And

Discount Finance Company
100 Money Plaza
Anytown, USA 00000

Dear Sirs:

I hereby cancel the sale of (identify product) (which was one of several products) sold and financed by (identify seller) under the (consumer credit contract of [date]) which has been assigned to the (Discount Finance Company). (I am also notifying you I have now sustained and there is due me at least the amounts for damages more fully described below.)

I am now canceling because I have (rejected) (and/or) (revoked acceptance of) the product identified above for reasons more fully described in my letter/memo of (date) when I also made proposals for resolving this matter. Your attempt to repossess now prevents me from relying on you to act in good faith in resolving this matter.

Since the sale described above is now canceled, and since the (Discount Finance Company) is, as provided by the (consumer credit contract) involved in this matter, also subject to all claims and defenses I can assert against the seller, there is now, as provided by the Uniform Commercial Code, no further outstanding obligation under that contract (with respect to the sale of the product I have canceled and any balance still outstand-

ing under the contract is reduced at least by the amount no longer due or owing for the canceled sale).

And there is now instead due me all moneys I have paid toward the price. I calculate this amount as $_____ which includes the $_____ down payment I made on (date), $_____ for the (identify product) I traded in and all payments I have made. (And there is now instead due me at least the portion of the entire $_____ I have paid which has been applied to the price of the canceled purchase. I calculate this amount to be $_____ and which is now a credit balance you hold. This amount is either to be promptly returned to me or credited to any balance still outstanding for other purchases that were made and financed under this contract./I am unable to calculate this amount and request instead that you properly do so. That amount is then a credit balance you are holding for me which is either to be promptly returned to me or credited to any balance still outstanding for other purchases made and financed under this contract.)

There is now also due me and I request prompt payment for at least the $_____ I have sustained in damages as more fully described below: (Describe and state amounts you could claim as damages.)

(And so that we can settle accounts with respect to any balance still outstanding, I request that you promptly furnish me a full and complete accounting of the outstanding balance upon the proper deduction of amounts no longer due or owing for, and the prompt crediting to my account of amounts now due me for payments made toward the price of the canceled purchase. I calculate that the amount then outstanding to be no more than $_____ which I am, of course, prepared to pay as due. [I calculate there would then be no further amounts still due or owing under the contract (and there is instead due me a credit balance of at least $_____ plus any rebates due for unearned finance and other charges and which is promptly to be returned to me.)]])

Since there is no further outstanding obligation under the contract, neither the (Discount Finance Company) nor the (ABC Retailer) have a security interest in the goods involved. (Since there is no further outstanding obligation under the contract with respect to the cancelled purchase, neither the [Discount Finance Company] nor the [ABC Retailer] have a security interest in the product involved in this matter. And since payments due for any balance remaining under the contract are, in fact, paid in full as due, I am not in default and you have no valid justification for repossessing any goods in which you may have a security interest.)

And as provided by the Uniform Commercial Code, I have a security interest in the (identify product) for the return (or the prompt crediting to my account) of all moneys I have paid under the contract for its price. I am, therefore, holding the product in which I have a security interest until the moneys I have paid toward its price are returned to me (or credited to my account). (Moreover, I need the return of the amounts now due me so I can purchase a satisfactory substitute and thereby minimize my damages.)

And since there is no further outstanding obligation under the contract, any outstanding instruments are to be promptly discharged and returned to me. And as provided by the Uniform Commercial Code, you are to file a termination statement within ten days to terminate your security interest if a financing statement covering the goods involved has been filed. If you fail to file a termination statement as required, you will be liable under the Uniform Commercial Code for $100 plus any losses caused me *by your failure. (And since there is no further outstanding obligation under the contract with respect to the canceled purchase, you are to indicate you no longer have a security interest in the product involved and specify the goods in which you still claim a security interest.)*

And if you or your agents still attempt to repossess the goods in which you no longer have a security interest (and despite my not, in fact, being in default on any payments actually due or owing under the contract) doing so is wrongful and will subject you to liability for conversion and for any other tortious conduct for which I shall seek to hold you liable to the fullest extent provided by law. Under the Uniform Commercial Code, your liability for wrongful repossession would be 10 percent of the cash price plus the finance charge. Your liability for conversion could be at least the amount for which I have a security interest in the product involved in this matter and may include punitive damages for your reckless and deliberate disregard of my rights and your obligations.

I therefore urge you to reconsider your attempt to repossess and that you instead promptly contact me so we can still quickly resolve this matter as I have proposed rather than compel me to hold you liable for breach of contract and wrongful acts to the fullest extent provided by law.

Sincerely,

THE ULTIMATUM FOR CANCELING ON YOUR OWN INITIATIVE

The second situation in which you could cancel is when you have rejected and/or revoked acceptance, or the goods weren't delivered as required by your contract, but you and the seller and/or creditor have failed to resolve the matter. In this situation you would be canceling on your own initiative rather than when the step was forced upon you at the time of repossession.

You could take this step once it becomes clear the matter in dispute won't be settled and you have already started to withhold payment under the agreement. But seek an attorney's advice first, especially if you cannot afford to be wrong, because this step could involve you in legal action.

If the seller/creditor insists you owe the money after you formally reject and/or revoke acceptance and you decide to resolve the matter other than by cancelling and insisting the seller take the product back (such as giving a seller further chances to repair or keeping the product and continuing to pay while getting the defects fixed yourself), you could be giving up your right to use this remedy. The seller and/or creditor might then insist that your only further recourse was to accept the repairs they were prepared to make, for instance, and your only further recourse may be recovering damages for defects in accepted goods.

Only you can decide how important it is to hold the seller/creditor accountable for a failure to live up to the contract.

If you are determined to cancel, notify the seller by adapting the sample cancellation letter on page 284. At the same time notify the separate creditor/lender the sale is canceled by adapting one of the following sample letters, depending on whether a money purchase loan or a credit sales agreement is involved. Enclose a copy of the letter you send the seller.

Again, the sample letters include alternative wording for situations in which you made multiple purchases under the same closed-end credit agreement, but I strongly caution you to seek legal advice before using it because of the additional complications that could be involved in settling up what you owe.

CANCELING WHEN A PURCHASE MONEY LOAN IS INVOLVED

The following sample letter can be adapted for notifying a lender you are canceling a purchase financed with a purchase money loan covered by the FTC Holder Rule.

If you are cancelling because of the seller's failure to deliver goods, then omit the wording that refers to any security interest you have in goods for the return of what you have paid. But retain the wording that refers to any security interest the seller/creditor may have.

Certified Mail #11112222

200 Witchtree Lane
Anytown, USA 00000

(Date)

Discount Finance Company
100 Money Plaza
Anytown, USA 00000

Dear Sir:

I am, by the enclosed copy of my letter of (date) to the (ABC Retailer, and address), notifying you I have canceled the sale of (identify product) (which was one of several products sold) under my contract of (date) with that seller and which I financed with the proceeds of the purchase money loan you made under our (consumer credit contract) of (date). You are, by the enclosed copy of that letter, also notified with respect to all matters relating to this transaction that are described in that letter.

Since the sale is canceled and since the (Discount Finance Company) is, as provided by that consumer credit contract, subject to all claims and defenses I can assert against the seller, there is now, as provided by the Uniform Commercial Code, no further outstanding obligation under that contract (with respect to the sale of the product I have canceled and any balance still remaining is reduced at least by the amount no longer due or owing for the canceled purchase).

There is now instead due me all moneys I have repaid for the purchase money loan used for the financing of the sale now canceled. I calculate this amount to be the $_____ in payments I have made. This amount is now a credit balance you are holding for me and which is to be promptly returned to me. (And there is now instead due me at least the portion of the entire $_____ I have repaid which has been applied to the repayment of that portion of the purchase money loan proceeds used for financing the sale now canceled. This balance is either to be promptly returned to me or credited to any balance still outstanding for other purchases that were also financed with this purchase money loan. [OR] I am unable to calculate this amount and request instead that you do so. That amount is then a credit balance you are holding for me which is either to be promptly returned to me or credited to any balance still outstanding for the other purchases that were also financed with this purchase money loan.)

There is now also due me at least the $_____ I have sustained in damages as described in the enclosed letter.

(And so that we can settle accounts with respect to any remaining balance, I request that you promptly furnish me a full and complete accounting of the balance still outstanding under our contract upon the proper

*deduction of amounts no longer due or owing for, and the prompt cred-
iting to my account of amounts now due me for payments made under
the contract toward the price of the canceled sale. I calculate the amount
still outstanding to be no more than $_____ which I am, of course, pre-
pared to pay as due. (I calculate that there would then be no further
amounts still due or owing under our contract [and there is instead due
me a credit balance of at least $_____ which is to be promptly returned
to me].)*

*I also reserve the right to hold you liable for damages up to the full
amount I have repaid under our contract.*

*Since there is no further outstanding obligation under our contract, the
(Discount Finance Company) no longer has a security interest in the goods
involved. (Since there is no further outstanding obligation under our contract with respect to the canceled sale, the [Discount Finance Company]
no longer has a security interest in the product involved. And since all
payments due for any balance remaining under the contract are, in fact,
paid in full as due, I am not in default.)*

*And as provided by the Uniform Commercial Code, I instead have a
security interest in the (identify product) for the return of all moneys paid
by me toward its price of $_____ , part of which was paid with the (por-
tion of the) proceeds of the purchase money loan used for financing (all)
the purchase(s) (made with those proceeds). The remainder of the price
was paid with my down payment of $_____ to the seller plus $_____ for
the (identify product) I traded in. I am, therefore, holding the (identify
product) in which I have a security interest until the moneys I have repaid
you toward the price of the canceled purchase is returned (or properly
credited to my account with you), the balance of the purchase money loan
no longer due or owing is discharged and the remaining balance of the
price paid to the seller is returned to me. (Moreover, I need the return of
the amounts due me upon cancellation so I can purchase a satisfactory
substitute and thereby minimize my damages.)*

*And since there is no further outstanding obligation under our contract,
you are to discharge and return to me all outstanding instruments. And
as provided by the Uniform Commercial Code, you are to file a termination statement within ten days to terminate your security interest if a
financing statement covering the goods has been filed. If you fail to file a
termination statement as required, you will be liable under the Uniform
Commercial Code for $100 plus any losses I have because of your failure.
(And since there is no further outstanding obligation under our contract
with respect to the sale now canceled, you are to indicate that you no
longer have a security interest in the product involved and to specify the
goods in which you still claim a security interest.)*

*Any attempt by you or your agents to repossess any goods in which you
now no longer have a security interest (and despite the fact that I am not
in default under our contract) will be wrongful and subject you to liability
for conversion and for any other tortious conduct for which I shall seek
to hold you liable to the fullest extent provided by law. Under the Uniform Commercial Code, your liability for wrongful repossession would
be at least 10 percent of the amount financed plus the entire credit service
charge. Your liability for conversion could be at least the amount for
which I have a security interest in the product and may include punitive
damages for your reckless and deliberate disregard of my rights and your
obligations.*

I, therefore, urge that you promptly contact me so that we can still quickly resolve this matter as I have proposed, rather than compel me to hold you liable in court for breach of contract and wrongful acts to the fullest extent provided by law.

Sincerely,

CANCELING WHEN A CREDIT SALES AGREEMENT IS INVOLVED

When you cancel a purchase made and financed with a credit sales agreement that has been assigned to a separate creditor, it is your cancellation letter to the seller that should spell everything out, of course. The following sample letter may be adapted as a covering letter for notifying the separate creditor.

Certified Mail #11112222

200 Witchtree Lane
Anytown, USA 00000

(Date)

Discount Finance Company
100 Money Plaza
Anytown, USA 00000

Dear Sir:

I am, by the enclosed copy of my letter of (date) to the (ABC Retailer), notifying you that I have canceled the sale of (identify product), (which was one of several products) sold and financed under the (consumer credit contract) of (date) with that seller which has been assigned to you. And I am, by the enclosed copy of that letter, putting you on notice with respect to all matters relating to this transaction which are described in that letter.

Since that sale is now canceled and since the (Discount Finance Company) is, as provided by that contract, subject to all claims and defenses I can assert against the seller, please contact me promptly so that we can still quickly resolve this matter as I have proposed rather than compel me to hold you liable in court for the seller's breach to the fullest extent provided by law.

Sincerely,

Remember that once you cancel and stop paying amounts, you could be involved in legal action.

ULTIMATUM IF ATTEMPT IS MADE TO REPOSSESS AFTER CANCELLATION

The following sample letter can be adapted and prepared in advance to warn a creditor against trying to repossess after you have canceled. Since you have already warned the creditor in your cancellation letter, this would be a last attempt to ward off repossession. Attach a copy of the cancellation letter to this letter, and hand them to the person trying to repossess.

This sample letter can be adapted for either a credit sales or purchase money loan transaction.

200 Witchtree Lane
Anytown, USA 00000

[date—insert when used]

Discount Finance Company
100 Money Plaza
Anytown, USA 00000   *(Address as appropriate)*

And

ABC Retailer
100 Hobsons Lane
Anytown, USA 00000

Dear Sirs:

   This is to notify you that if you, or your employees or agents, still attempt to repossess goods in which you do not have a security interest (and despite the fact I am not in default) under the consumer credit contract of (date), for reasons I have already described in my letter of (date), doing so is wrongful and will subject you to liability for conversion and for any other tortious conduct that occurs and for which I shall seek to hold you liable to the fullest extent provided by law.

   Under the Uniform Commercial Code, your liability for wrongful repossession could be at least 10 percent of the amount financed, plus the finance charge involved. Your liability for conversion and other tortious conduct would include all actual damages I sustain and could include punitive damages for your reckless and deliberate disregard of my rights and your contractual obligations and duties under law.

   I, therefore, urge you to reconsider your attempt to repossess and that instead you promptly contact me so that we can still quickly resolve this matter as I have proposed, rather than compel me to hold you liable in court to the fullest extent provided by law for breach of contract, wrongful repossession, conversion, and any other tortious conduct that occurs.

                              Sincerely,

See Chapter 69 for how to pin down any settlement you may reach.

68 · Negotiating Strategy Continued: Stage Three—The Ultimatum for Deducting Damages

This chapter covers the ultimate stage in cases where you are unable to reject or revoke acceptance but are entitled to deduct damages for defects in accepted goods. (See page 324 in Chapter 42 about notifying a seller you are doing so.)

If the creditor has refused to deduct such damages from the balance still outstanding, you can adapt the following sample letter to notify him that you are doing so. Once you take this step, though, you would have to withhold the amount you claim and this could result in legal action. I caution you to seek legal advice before taking this step, therefore, especially if you can't afford to be wrong about the matter.

Certified Mail #11112222

200 Witchtree Lane
Anytown, USA 00000

(Date)

Discount Finance Company
100 Money Plaza
Anytown, USA 00000

Dear Sir:

This is to notify you there is still due me at least the $____ for damages which I described in my letter of (date), a copy of which is enclosed. As more fully described in that letter, this matter involves the (identify product) I purchased and financed under the (consumer credit contract) of (date) with the (ABC Retailer, and address) which has been assigned to you. (As more fully described in that letter, this matter involves the [identify product] I purchased under my contract of [date] with the [ABC Retailer, and address] and which I financed with the proceeds of the purchase money loan you made under our [consumer credit contract] of [date].)

Although I previously requested that either you or the (ABC Retailer) reimburse me for my damages or that you deduct them from the balance remaining under the (consumer credit contract) involved, you failed to do so (or describe other inadequate response).

Since the (Discount Finance Company) is, as provided by the (consumer credit contract) involved in this transaction, subject to all claims and defenses I can assert against the seller, I again urge you to resolve this matter by deducting the $____ due me for damages from the balance remaining under the contract as I have proposed. (And to avoid a dispute about the amount due me for damages, I am prepared to resolve this *matter if you will now deduct at least the $_____ due as damages for [describe the damages for which you definitely want to be reimbursed].)*

But if you still do not promptly confirm that you will resolve this matter as I have proposed, I shall, as provided by the Uniform Commercial Code, then deduct from the $_____ balance still due for the price (still due on the proceeds of the loan paid for the price) (at least) the $_____ now due me for damages. (But since I am now only deducting part of the amount due for damages, I reserve the right to hold you liable for all damages to the fullest extent provided by law.)

I calculate that upon the deduction of the amount due me for damages, the balance still outstanding under the (consumer credit contract) involved in this transaction to be $_____ . (I calculate that upon the deduction of the amount due me as damages, no further amount is still due or owing under the [consumer credit contract] involved in this transaction and there is, instead, due me a credit balance of at least $_____ plus amounts due me as a refund of finance and other charges upon prepayment and which is to be promptly returned to me.)

I also request that you promptly furnish me a proper and complete accounting of the amounts now still outstanding under the contract. I am, of course, prepared to pay as due the remaining balance, but since I need immediate compensation for the damages I have sustained, I am deducting the amounts for those damages from the payments coming due on, and those payments are now not, in fact, due or owing: (give due dates of payments from which you deduct the damages) [OR] (I am deducting $_____ from the $_____ monthly payments due on [give dates of payments from which you deduct damages], leaving a balance of only $_____ then still due for those payments.)

(Since no further amounts are now still due or owing under the consumer credit contract involved in this transaction, I request that you promptly discharge in writing and return to me any outstanding instruments. And as provided by the Uniform Commercial Code, you are to file a termination statement within ten days to terminate security interest if a financing statement covering the goods has been filed. If you fail to file a termination statement as required, you will be liable under the Uniform Commercial Code for $100 plus any losses caused me as a result.)

And since there is no further outstanding obligation under the contract, you have no security interest in the goods involved. (And since the amounts I am deducting for damages I have sustained are now not, in fact, due or owing under our contract, and I have paid as due all amounts actually due, I am not in default.) Any attempt by you or your agents to repossess any goods will, therefore, be wrongful and subject you to liability for conversion and any other tortious conduct that may occur and for which I shall hold you liable to the fullest extent provided by law. Under the Uniform Commercial Code, your liability for wrongful repossession would be 10 percent of the amount financed (the cash sales price) plus the finance charge. Your liability for conversion would be the value of the goods involved and could include punitive damages for your reckless and deliberate disregard of my rights and your obligations under the contract and duties under law.

While I hope we can still satisfactorily resolve this matter, if you and the (ABC Retailer) continue to ignore your obligation to compensate me for my damages as I have proposed, I shall hold you liable for damages at least to the fullest extent provided by the Uniform Commercial Code for breach.

Please contact me promptly so we can still quickly resolve this matter rather than compelling me to hold you liable in court.

Sincerely,

A word of caution about deducting damages from payments coming due. The law is unclear about whether you could deduct the entire damages from the payment coming due immediately after you are entitled to deduct, or whether you would have to make partial deductions from each further payment still due. The safest way, therefore, is to keep making payments in full until you have repaid the full amount except for the damages. This way—if you are right—there would be no further outstanding obligation and this, in turn, would terminate the creditor's security interest.

If you are going to try to deduct damages from payments coming due, indicate you will start doing so in a month or two. This will give you a chance to gauge how the seller/creditor responds and give you more time to consider whether to go through with it if he insists on payment in full.

MAKING PARTIAL DEDUCTIONS

The following sample letter can be adapted to inform the creditor you are making partial deductions for damages from each payment.

200 Witchtree Lane
Anytown, USA 00000

(Date)

Discount Finance Company
100 Money Plaza
Anytown, USA 00000

Dear Sir:

Enclosed is my payment of $_____ due on (date) under the (consumer credit contract) of (date) (for a purchase money loan I obtained from you/ for the purchase and financing of [identify product] from the [ABC Retailer and address] which has been assigned to you).

I am deducting from the $_____ scheduled for this payment $_____ of the $_____ due me for damages for reasons described in my letter of (date) and which then leaves $_____ as still due me for damages. The payment of $_____ I am sending is, therefore, payment in full of the payment scheduled for (date).

Sincerely,

When you send such a payment by check, you could note on the front that it is payment in full, upon the deduction of damages, for the payment scheduled on the due date. If the creditor takes the payment under the terms you spell out, that would usually mean he is in agreement with your proposal. A refusal to do so, on the other hand, is obviously a warning that he is not going along with you and you could be in default when the creditor refuses the check.

Adapt and prepare in advance the sample ultimatum letter included on page 573 in case the seller/creditor tries to repossess. If you still owe money and are deducting damages from payments, then replace the opening paragraph of the letter by adapting the following one:

"This is to notify you that if you, or your employees or agents still attempt to repossess despite the fact that I am not in default under the consumer credit contract of (date) for reasons I have described in my letter of (date) when I notified you I was, as provided by the Uniform Commercial Code, deducting amounts due me as damages, any repossession is wrongful and will subject you to liability for conversion and for any other tortious conduct that occurs and for which I shall seek to hold you liable to the fullest extent provided by law."

The letter you refer to would, of course, be the one you sent to notify the seller/creditor you were deducting your damages from the outstanding balance.

69 · Pinning Down a Settlement

If you get involved in a dispute about a credit transaction, it is important that any settlement you reach be pinned down in writing. It should state either the amount you still owe or the fact that you no longer owe anything.

The following sample wording can be adapted for this purpose. It covers only situations in which a dispute is fully resolved so that, in effect, you give up any additional claims you might have. NEVER try to adapt this wording in a situation where it is still important to keep rights to hold the seller/creditor accountable for additional amounts, even though he is willing to settle up for part of what is due you. Situations like this almost always involve a lot of money and require legal advice.

(DATE)

The *(identify creditor)* of *(address)*, herein called creditor, *(identify seller, if appropriate)* of (_____ address _____) herein called seller, and *(insert your name)* of (_____ your address _____) herein called buyer, agree to resolve as follows the dispute about the sale of *(identify product)*. This sale was made to and financed for the buyer by the seller under the consumer credit contract of *(date)* which has been assigned to and is now held by the creditor. This sale was made to the buyer by the seller under their contract of *(date)* and was financed with a purchase money loan made to the buyer by the creditor under their consumer credit contract of *(date)* now held by the creditor.

1. The creditor *(and seller)* agree(s) the buyer has rightfully rejected *(justifiably revoked acceptance)* of the above product and has canceled the sale. *(The creditor [and seller] agree(s) the buyer has canceled the sale of the above product because of the seller's failure to make delivery as required.)*

2. The creditor *(and seller)* agree(s) that all of the buyer's obligations arising under the consumer credit contract of *(date)* (and the contract with the seller of [date]) are discharged and there is now immediately due and owing to the buyer from the creditor *(seller)* a credit balance of $____ for payments made toward the price and damages. All security interests in and/or liens on the buyer's property arising under these contracts are hereby terminated.

2. *(ALTERNATIVE: The creditor [and seller] agree[s] there is immediately due and owing to the buyer from the creditor [seller] a credit balance of $____ for payments made toward the price of the canceled sale and for damages and the [$____] balance of the price remaining for the canceled sale under the consumer credit contract of [date] is discharged. The creditor shall immediately credit the $____ credit balance toward the $____ balance then remaining under the consumer credit contract of [date] leaving a balance due of [$____] which is to be repaid as follows: [state payment schedule for remaining amount]. The creditor hereby terminates all security interests in or liens on [identify goods] arising under the consumer credit contract of [date]. The payment schedule stated in and security interests or liens arising under the consumer credit contract of [date] are hereby modified as stated herein.)*

3. The creditor *(seller)* accepts the *(identify product returned)* as

returned by the buyer to the seller on (date). (The creditor [seller] and the buyer agree to cooperate to arrange for the prompt return of the [identify product] to the seller at the seller's expense and risk and authorize the buyer to hold the product at the seller's risk until the seller makes arrangements to remove it.)

4. The creditor (seller) agrees to dismiss immediately and with prejudice the suit filed against the buyer on (date) in (describe court).

5. The creditor (and seller) shall not furnish to any person any adverse information about this transaction, which includes any information indicating the buyer was responsible for a breach of any financial obligation arising under the contract(s) involved in this transaction, and shall immediately take all necessary and proper steps to correct any adverse information that has been furnished to any person and specifically to the following person(s) known to the buyer: (_____ identify _____).

Agreed to for (identify company) on (date) by:

_____

(Signature and title)

Agreed to for (identify company) on (date) by:

_____

(Signature and title)

Agreed to by buyer on (date):

_____

(Your signature)

If you are entitled only to reimbursement for damages due for defects in accepted goods, replace paragraph (1) with the following wording to spell out the amount due for damages: "The creditor (and seller) agree(s) the product failed to conform to the contract and the buyer has sustained $_____ as damages now due and owing the buyer."

Then simply adapt as appropriate the remaining wording for spelling out the amount to be credited to any balance remaining under the contract in order to settle what you still owe, or any amount you would be entitled to get back.

70 · The Fair Credit Reporting Act: Protecting the Accuracy of Your Credit File

If you apply for credit, insurance, or a job, the company involved may first make a check on you with a credit reporting agency.

It's almost a certainty that if you have ever used or applied for credit, there is a "file" on you somewhere showing your financial standing, how promptly you pay, whether you have ever been sued, arrested, filed bankruptcy, and so on. And computer technology now makes it easy for the keepers of such files to circulate information.

If it's favorable, the information can be helpful, of course; if it isn't, it can obviously be very damaging. So it's important that information be filed and reported accurately, and only to those who have a legitimate reason for getting it. For this reason, Congress enacted the Fair Credit Reporting Act in 1971. It helps *you* check on the filekeepers and find out whether information that may result in your being turned down for credit, insurance, or employment was obtained from them. The law also helps you protect yourself when you run into problems.

Let's first look at some key terms that help define what the act covers.

A **consumer report** includes information reflecting on an individual's credit-worthiness, character, general reputation or mode of living which is furnished by a consumer reporting agency to help establish an individual's eligibility for credit or insurance used for personal, family, or household purposes or for employment. A report typically includes information about your financial standing, credit history, employment record, or bank accounts. The kind of financial information included in a consumer report is usually referred to as credit information, and a report containing only credit information is normally referred to as a credit report.

An **investigative consumer report** is a special kind of consumer report which includes information about your character, reputation, or mode of living that is obtained by personal interviews with third parties, such as friends or neighbors. There are some special requirements that cover investigative consumer reports in addition to those which cover all consumer reports. (The key point is that any investigative consumer report is also a consumer report.)

The act does not, however, apply to any reports made about you when you are seeking credit or insurance for *business* rather than personal use.

A **consumer reporting agency** is any business that gathers the information contained in consumer reports and sells it to creditors, insurers, or employers. The most common type of consumer reporting agency is usually called a "credit bureau" which furnishes "credit reports" on consumers. But the act also covers companies or investigators who specialize in furnishing reports to insurers or employers.

An individual's *file* consists of all the information about that person that is recorded and retained by a consumer reporting agency.

Let's look now at specific ways the act protects you.

WHO CAN OBTAIN A CONSUMER REPORT?

The law prohibits a consumer reporting agency from furnishing a report unless it is for a legitimate purpose; and obligates it to make sure it gives information only to those who are authorized to obtain it.

A report can be furnished about you if a court orders it; if you specifically provide written authorization; or if the person requesting the information intends to use it for extending credit or providing insurance or employment; or for engaging in a business transaction with the consumer. A report can also be furnished under certain additional circumstances which would rarely involve consumer transactions.

PROHIBITIONS ON REPORTING OBSOLETE INFORMATION

Broadly speaking, a consumer reporting agency is prohibited from reporting "adverse information" that is more than seven years old. Adverse information includes suits or judgments against you, tax liens, arrest records, or other information that could reflect badly on you. If you have declared bankruptcy, however, that fact may be reported for ten years.

These time limits do *not* apply when the credit transaction or insurance policy involved was for $50,000 more; or the employment involved was for a salary of $20,000 or more. The act sets no time limits in these cases.

AN AGENCY'S OBLIGATION TO BE ACCURATE

The act requires an agency to follow procedures that ensure the greatest possible accuracy of the information it reports. An agency is more likely to be held liable to you for disregarding its obligation to ensure the accuracy of information it reports once you notify the agency that the information it is reporting is inaccurate or wrong. That's because up to then, a failure to be accurate will usually be chalked up as a mistake, except in rare situations.

It's a good idea to check your file periodically, especially if you are about to initiate an important credit transaction, or apply for a job. See the next chapter for how to go about it.

DISCLOSURE REQUIREMENTS FOR INVESTIGATIVE REPORTS

Because investigative consumer reports based on interviews with third parties can be fertile sources of incorrect information—not to say downright falsehoods—that may prove very damaging, the act singles them out for special treatment.

Any company or person who asks for an investigative report on you must promptly notify you in writing that one is being prepared. This notice must inform you of your right to know the nature and scope of the investigation. To use this right, you must make a written request for the information within a reasonable time after you were told the report was being prepared. The person requesting the report must, however, only inform you about the kind of investigation to be made rather than the specific information that is obtained.

There is one situation in which you do not have to be told that an investigative report is being prepared: that is, if you are being considered for a job but have not actually applied for it.

WHAT YOU MUST BE TOLD WHEN A BUSINESS TAKES ADVERSE ACTION

A company that turns you down for credit, insurance, or employment, or that charges you more for credit or insurance partly because of information contained in a consumer report, must supply the name and address of the agency that furnished the report. This requirement at least helps you find out, albeit after the fact, if there is something amiss with the information being reported about you.

If a creditor obtained information from someone other than a credit reporting agency, such as another creditor, the act entitles you to find out the nature of that information, too, and the creditor must inform you of your right to do so. You must make a written request for this information within sixty days of learning of the adverse action: the creditor must then supply it within a reasonable time.

WHAT A CONSUMER REPORTING AGENCY MUST DISCLOSE ABOUT INFORMATION IN ITS FILES

Upon your request, a reporting agency must clearly and accurately disclose the following:

- The nature and substance of all the information it has about you in its files, with the exception of medical information. Only two states, California and New York, have laws that require an agency to furnish you a copy of a report itself. In other states, an agency does *not* have to let you see your file, but must tell you what's in it.
- The source of the information. However, an agency does not have to give you the names of persons interviewed in connection with an investigative report, except in the case of a lawsuit.
- The recipients of consumer reports furnished for employment purposes within the previous two years, and the recipients of reports furnished for other purposes within the previous six months.

An agency must provide this information without charge if you request it within thirty days of being notified of adverse action, or of receiving notification from an affiliated debt collection agency that your credit rating has been adversely affected. In other cases, an agency can charge you a reasonable amount for disclosing its information but it must tell you the charge in advance.

CONDITIONS UNDER WHICH DISCLOSURES MUST BE MADE

An agency must make the required disclosures during normal business hours, but you may have to make an appointment. The agency must also allow you to talk to personnel trained to explain the information in your file. If you go to an agency in person, you are entitled to bring another person to sit in on the interview. This is usually a good idea. The other person should have reasonable identification and you may be required to provide written permission for making the disclosures in that person's presence.

You can request that the information be furnished by telephone. But in this case, you may have to submit a prior, written request for a telephone disclosure and properly identify yourself in writing. This requirement prevents snoopers from getting information by using your name. If you ask for such disclosure, first find out what the agency accepts as identification.

PROCEDURES AN AGENCY MUST FOLLOW IF THERE IS A DISPUTE ABOUT ACCURACY

If the information in your file is unfavorable, but complete and accurate, there is nothing you can do about it. If the information is not accurate, though, the act gives you important recourse.

While the act does not define what is considered to be "complete" or "accurate" information, there are commonsense guidelines one can follow. If, for instance, your file indicates you don't pay your bills on time when in fact you do, that's inaccurate information. If the information omits important facts that help explain your side of a story, that's incomplete information. An example would be if you did not pay a bill on time because of a dispute over whether you owed the money, then when the matter was settled the creditor forgot to mention the fact to the credit reporting agency.

If you do not believe the information in your file is accurate or complete, the act entitles you to dispute it by informing the agency of what is wrong with the information in its files. This action triggers a requirement that the agency reinvestigate and record the current status of the information. The agency does not have to do this if it believes your reasons are frivolous or irrelevant; but if it uses this excuse as a dodge it treads on thin ice when you have a reasonable basis for disputing the information.

If, upon reinvestigation, the agency finds the disputed information is either inaccurate or cannot be verified, it must promptly delete it from your file. If reinvestigation does not resolve the dispute, the act entitles you to insert a brief explanation of your side of the matter in your file. (If a consumer reporting agency helps you prepare the explanation, it can limit your statement to one hundred words.) The agency *must* then clearly note in any subsequent consumer report that the information is in dispute and include your statement, or an accurate summary of it, in the report. [The exception is when the agency has reasonable grounds for believing that your statement is frivolous or irrelevant.]

RENOTIFICATION OF RECIPIENTS REQUIRED

If, after reinvestigation, an agency must delete information, or the matter is not resolved and you put a statement in your file, you can request the agency to set the record straight. You can insist that it renotify recipients of reports made for employment purposes within the previous two years, and recipients of reports made for other purposes within the previous six months. You must, however, say which recipients you want renotified.

An agency cannot charge you for doing this if you make your request within thirty days of learning of adverse action taken on the basis of the agency's report or of being notified by an affiliated collection agency that your credit rating has been adversely affected. But an agency cannot charge you for furnishing a corrected report to recipients regardless of when you request it if the agency had to furnish a corrected report because it was required to delete information that was inaccurate or could not be reverified.

In other instances, an agency can make a reasonable charge for renotification but it must tell you the charge in advance. The charge may not be more than the normal fee for a consumer report.

CIVIL LIABILITY FOR NON-COMPLIANCE WITH THE ACT

The act entitles consumers to sue credit reporting agencies or information users who either willfully or negligently violate the requirements of the act. Such suits can turn out to be very costly for those who fail to comply.

Willful noncompliance involves situations in which a failure to comply is deliberate or intentional. Negligent noncompliance usually involves situations in which the failure results more from carelessness than deliberate action.

In either case, if you win a suit you can recover the sum of any actual damages you sustained as a result of the violation, plus the cost of bringing suit and reasonable attorney's fees. The latter gives you real leverage. If the violation was willful, the act also entitles you to recover punitive damages—a fact that gives you a good deal of extra leverage.

The amounts you could recover as actual damages include losses you suffered because you failed to obtain credit, or insurance, or because you failed to get a job as a result of a violation. You may also be able to recover damages for mental anguish and suffering, and for time and expenses spent trying to get the agency involved to comply with the act.

Normally, you must sue within two years of the violation.

One of the most successful such suits was brought against the Credit Bureau of Rochester, Inc. in 1975. In this case, the court noted that the consumer, a Mr. Louis Nitti, "time and again came to the defendant's office (i.e., the Rochester Credit Bureau) and went over the same credit information with the defendant's employees, pointing out errors, all to no purpose. Time and again he tried to have the defendant update and correct its report of him; he pleaded, he lost his temper, all to no avail. Like a character in Kafka, he was totally powerless to move or penetrate the implacable presence brooding, like some stone Moloch, within the Castle."

Mr. Nitti lost his powerlessness, however, when he used the legal weapons provided by the Fair Credit Reporting Act. The court awarded him $10,000 in punitive damages and $8,000 for attorney's fees.

Mr. Nitti's case is just one example of how consumers have been able to make it very costly for reporting agencies to ignore the act.

FEDERAL ENFORCEMENT AGENCIES

The act is also enforced by a number of separate federal agencies although they cannot take action on behalf of individual consumers.

The Federal Trade Commission enforces the act against consumer reporting agencies and everyone else who would be required to comply with the Act except various types of creditors against whom the Act is enforced by other agencies depending on the type of creditor involved. With one exception, the act is enforced against various types of creditors by the same federal agencies that enforce the Truth in Lending act against them (see page 489). The exception is that the FTC enforces the act against securities dealers and brokers rather than the Securities and Exchange Commission.

71 · Negotiating Strategy for Disputes Involving the Fair Credit Reporting Act

The basic aim of your negotiating strategy is to find out what's in your file and therefore being reported to others; to get any inaccurate or incomplete information deleted or corrected; and, if necessary, to have an agency renotify recipients of reports.

STAGE ONE: OPENING SKIRMISHES

If you are turned down for credit, insurance, or employment, promptly arrange an interview with the consumer reporting agency involved. Whoever turns you down is required to provide the name of the agency.

While there are over 2,000 consumer reporting agencies in the country, most only operate locally. When you are simply trying to find out what's in your file you may be able to find the ones in your area by checking the Yellow Pages under "credit bureaus" or "consumer reporting agencies."

However, the bulk of consumer reports used by creditors are distributed by five major consumer reporting agencies that operate nationwide. They are as follows:

TRW Information Services
505 City Parkway West
Orange, California 92688

Trans Union Credit Information Co.
444 N. Michigan Avenue
Chicago, Illinois

Credit Bureau, Inc.
1375 Peachtree Street
Atlanta, Georgia 30309

Chilton Corp.
12606 Greenville Avenue
Dallas, Texas 75243

Pinger System
2505 Fannin
Houston, Texas 77002

These companies have local offices in many major cities.

TIPS FOR SECURING INFORMATION IN YOUR FILE

- If you think a consumer report might have been used, but you aren't given the name of the agency, ask for it, as the Fair Credit Reporting Act entitles you to do.
- In the case of a credit application, the Equal Credit Opportunity Act requires a creditor to tell you the principal reasons for adverse action taken, which makes it easier to find out if a credit report was used. Unfortunately, there are no similar laws requiring employers or insurers to give you such information.

• When you contact an agency, correctly identify your file. Always provide the same information it uses for identification purposes; this could be your full name, social security number, birthdate, or other reference number. This helps prevent file mix-ups. You may have to ask the agency to tell you what identifying information it uses. Check whether the information in your file corresponds to information that has been reported about you.

• Make advance arrangements for a telephone interview and be prepared to take notes, or have someone else listen in on an extension and take notes for you.

• If you plan a personal interview and take someone with you, arrange ahead of time who will ask the questions and who will take notes.

A CHECKLIST TO USE WHEN REVIEWING YOUR FILE

• Get the name of the person you talk to.

• Discover the nature and substance of all the information in your file. Be persistent. Ask questions about whether your file contains specific types of credit information that could or should be there. If an agency fails to disclose information about specific credit you have or have had recently, find out if that creditor regularly reports to the agency; if so, press them about why there is nothing in your file about the account. (It could be a clue the agency has your file confused with someone else's.)

• Find out the names of the businesses, or other sources, that supplied information to the agency.

• Ask for the names of recipients of reports made for employment purposes during the last two years, and recipients of reports made for other purposes during the last six months. Find out the information included in the reports. It could be part of your file, so at least ask for it.

• Later on, check whether the information being reported about you corresponds to information in your file. This may involve cross-checking with recipients. It's always possible that information furnished about you actually came from someone else's file.

CHECKLIST TO USE WHEN THERE IS A REINVESTIGATION

• Find out the results of the reinvestigation and check that your file has been properly corrected if information was inaccurate or could not be verified.

• Ask the agency to renotify anyone who has received inaccurate or incomplete reports. Make sure you are not charged when the agency cannot charge you for renotifications.

• Follow up and make sure recipients you designated have actually been renotified.

• Insist that your version of the facts be inserted in your file if the reinvestigation fails to resolve the dispute.

• Ask the agency to send your statement describing the dispute to previous report recipients when you are entitled to do so.

REQUESTING THE DISCLOSURE OF INFORMATION IN YOUR FILE

You can adapt the following sample letter to request the disclosure of information in your file. If you deliver it personally have someone at the agency sign and date your copy. If you mail it, get a mailing receipt. You can, of course, call first to see if you can obtain the information over the phone. But the agency is likely to insist on a written request.

Usually, agencies have forms for requesting the disclosure of information. Be sure to get a duplicate showing the date, especially if you are responding to adverse action taken on the basis of a report.

> *300 Witchtree Lane*
> *Anytown, USA 00000*
>
> *June 1, 19___*

Anycity Reporting Bureau
500 Main Street
Anytown, USA 00000

Dear Sir:

I request that, as provided by the Fair Credit Reporting Act, you disclose to me (by telephone interview) the:

—nature and substance of all information you have about me in your files;

—the sources of the information; and

—the identity of the recipients of consumer reports furnished by you for employment purposes within the last two years and for other purposes within the last six months.

I am making this request upon having received on (date) a notice from (identify company) informing me that my application for credit was denied (OR otherwise describe adverse action involved) based in part on information contained in a consumer report you furnished (a copy of the company's notice is attached).

(Since the reasons given for the adverse action indicate that the information supplied about me may be inaccurate or incomplete, I request that you promptly make the disclosures so I can review my file and so that all necessary corrections can be promptly made to avoid any further damages to me.)

To help you identify me and my file, my name is (_____), I live at (_____), and my social security number is (_____) (OR include other identifying information, such as code numbers, used in the report).

Since I am requesting that the information be disclosed by a telephone interview, please notify me promptly of when I can call and who I am to talk to to obtain the disclosures I have requested.

Thank you for your prompt cooperation.

> *Sincerely,*

If the company fails to respond, follow up with a phone call and another written request for a telephone interview. Use the same sample letter but revise the wording in the opening paragraph as follows:

> *"Since I have not received a response to my letter of June 1, 19___, I again request that, as provided by the Fair Credit Reporting Act, you disclose to me the ..."*

This time send the letter by certified mail, return receipt requested.

REQUESTING REQUIRED DISCLOSURES ABOUT INVESTIGATIVE REPORTS

If someone requests an investigative consumer report on you, you have a right to know about its nature and scope—except when you are being considered for a job for which you did not apply.

The following sample letter can be adapted to request such information.

300 Witchtree Lane
Anytown, USA 00000

May 10, 19__

Mr. J. Inquirer
Manager
ABC Company
300 Fairview Road
Anytown, USA 00000

Dear Mr. Inquirer:

I received your letter of (date) indicating that you were requesting an investigative consumer report about me in connection with (identify the transaction involved).

I would appreciate it if you would let me know about the nature and scope of this investigation. Naturally, I expect that such a report will fully confirm the information I furnished you.

Thank you for informing me about the report so I may know of possible sources of inaccurate information.

Sincerely,

Obviously, it's a ticklish matter to request a prospective employer to furnish you such information. It's likely to be more worthwhile to ask for the name of the agency involved once you learn you have been turned down. While an employer is required to give you this information if you are turned down partly because of information contained in a report, he may not do so, and you may have to request it. This can, at least, help you find out about and seek to have inaccurate information corrected.

DISPUTING INFORMATION IN YOUR FILE

When you first go to the agency, you could take a written notice with you in case your file contains inaccurate information. Or you could send a letter after you've examined your file. In either case, request a reinvestigation: you could, at the same time, ask the agency to furnish corrected reports to recipients you designate.

If you have information showing the agency's file is inaccurate, be sure to present it. The act doesn't require you to do this, but the more clearly you can verify your side of the matter, the more pressure you can bring to bear. The following sample letter can be adapted to suit your purposes.

300 Witchtree Lane
Anytown, USA 00000

June 3, 19__

Mr. B. Accurate
Manager
Anycity Reporting Bureau
500 Main Street
Anytown, USA 00000

Dear Mr. Accurate:

I am notifying you (This is to confirm I notified [insert name] during the personal [telephone] interview on [date]) that I am disputing the accuracy (and completeness) of the information you have about me in your files as more fully described below. (And your agency has also apparently furnished inaccurate [and incomplete] information about me to [identify report recipients] which was at least partly responsible for my being denied credit [OR describe other adverse action] as indicated in the enclosed copy of the notification I received on [date].)

According to the disclosures made to me on (date) about the information in my files (and about the information furnished to [identify businesses involved] in a consumer report you made), the following item(s) (is/are) inaccurate (or incomplete) for the reasons noted.

[NOTE: Separately describe each item that was inaccurate or incomplete and then furnish the correct or missing information. See examples included after the letter.]

I, therefore, request that you promptly reinvestigate these items and that, upon completing your investigation, you promptly delete all the inaccurate or unverifiable information in my file and note the current status of any information you can verify.

And since incorrect (and incomplete) information about me has been furnished by you at least to the companies identified above, I also request that, upon completing your reinvestigation, you promptly furnish a corrected report to those companies (the companies designated below:) (Identify the companies you want renotified)

I also request that you inform me of the results of your reinvestigation, and that you confirm that the incorrect or unverifiable information has been deleted from my file, and that you have furnished corrected reports to the recipients I have designated, so as to assure the maximum possible accuracy of the information you furnish about me to avoid causing me any further harm.

I do, of course, expect you to promptly take all necessary steps to prevent the further circulation of any inaccurate (and incomplete) information about me.

I would appreciate your prompt response.

Sincerely,

Sample Wording for Describing Incorrect or Incomplete Items

You can adapt the following examples to suit your own particular circumstances. Be sure to describe the information the agency has (or doesn't have) and then state *why* it is inaccurate or incomplete.

●*"The item indicating that I failed to pay the (XYZ Company) as provided by my agreement is inaccurate because, as shown on the enclosed copies of my periodic billing statements for the period involved, I have always paid by the due date."*

• *"The item indicating that I failed to pay the (XYZ Company) for a purchase made on (date) is inaccurate because I, in fact, returned the item on (date) upon rejecting and/or revoking acceptance and canceling the agreement when the product failed to conform to the contract. The matter was resolved so that I did not, in fact, owe the balance claimed as due as shown on the attached copy of the settlement we reached."*

• *"The item indicating that I failed to pay (identify card issuer) for amounts due for a purchase charged to my (identify account) is inaccurate because it fails to indicate the item is in dispute upon my having in good faith exercised my rights under the Consumer Credit Protection Act to withhold payment of amounts not due or owing because of (a billing error) claims and defenses arising out of the transaction."*

• *"The item indicating that I failed to pay as due my account with the (XYZ Company) is incomplete because it fails to note that the late payments during that period resulted from my being unemployed for six months and that I had, in fact, made payments based on alternative arrangements agreed to by the company. And I resumed making payments as due when I got another job on (_____)."*

• *"The item indicating that I was liable with my spouse on the delinquent account with the (XYZ Company) is inaccurate because I was not, in fact, either liable for or authorized to use that account which my spouse, instead, used for business purposes."*

• *"Your file is incomplete because it fails to show an account I had with the (XYZ Company) since (date) and which has, in fact, always been promptly paid." An agency may not be required to report information about all accounts you may have unless the creditor involved regularly reports information to the agency, but you can, at least, request it.)*

If an item of adverse information concerns a dispute arising from your use of rights under any of the laws that are part of the Consumer Credit Protection Act, be sure to include wording such as "upon my having exercised in good faith my rights under the Consumer Credit Protection Act to (and describe what the right was)." Remember, the Equal Credit Opportunity Act prohibits someone from taking adverse action against you because you have, in good faith, used those rights.

VERIFYING THE DELETION OF INACCURATE INFORMATION

If an agency fails to confirm it has actually deleted incorrect information within a reasonable time, follow up by again asking for a disclosure of all the information in your file. Make this request within the thirty-day period during which an agency would have to make such a disclosure without charge. The following sample letter can be adapted for this purpose.

300 Witchtree Lane
Anytown, USA 00000

June 20, 19___

Anycity Reporting Bureau
500 Main Street
Anytown, USA 00000

Dear Sir:

In order to confirm that the inaccurate (and incomplete) information I notified you about on (date) has been properly reinvestigated, its current status noted, and that all incorrect and unverifiable information has, in fact, been deleted as required by the Fair Credit Reporting Act, I request that, as provided by that act, you disclose to me the:

—nature and substance of all information you now have about me in your files;

—the sources of the information; and

—the identity of any recipients of consumer reports furnished by you since (June 1, 19__).

I am making this request to assure the maximum possible accuracy of the information you have about me since, as I already notified you, I had received on (date) a notice from (identify company) that I had been turned down for credit (OR describe other adverse action) based in part on information contained in a consumer report you furnished. (A copy of the company's notice is enclosed.)

Although I disputed the accuracy (and completeness) of information in your files for reasons more fully described in my letter of (_____), and requested that you confirm the steps you have taken to correct the information upon completing your reinvestigation, you have, to date, failed to inform me about the results of your reinvestigation or to confirm that all inaccurate or unverifiable information has, in fact, been deleted and that a corrected report has been furnished to the recipients I designated in my letter of (date).

I, therefore, request the disclosure of the information you now still have in your files and that you confirm that all inaccurate and unverifiable items have, in fact, been deleted and that the recipients I have designated have been furnished a corrected report.

I will appreciate your prompt response.

Sincerely,

REQUESTING AN INVESTIGATION FOR THE SECOND TIME

If you discover that the incorrect information still has not been deleted, you could reassert that the agency reinvestigate, delete the incorrect or unverifiable information, and renotify report recipients.

To do this, adapt the sample letter included on page 589 by making it clear you are requesting a reinvestigation for the second time. The following sample wording can be adapted as appropriate, for instance, and inserted at the beginning of the letter:

"I am notifying you that, as more fully described below, I am again disputing the accuracy (and completeness) of the information you have about me in your files since they still fail to reflect the current status of the information involved, nor have inaccurate and unverifiable items been deleted upon reinvestigation of the items I have already disputed as provided by the Fair Credit Reporting Act."

To emphasize that you are renewing your request, insert words like "again" or "still" at appropriate places; the items you are describing are "still" inaccurate or incomplete, for instance.

Again, follow up to make sure the agency makes the proper corrections. If it still fails to do so, proceed to the low-keyed warning step.

INSERTING A DISPUTE STATEMENT IN YOUR FILE

If you and an agency are unable to resolve a dispute, your main option is to insert a statement in your file. If an item is wrong, you could make a statement to that effect if you don't want to go to the trouble of getting the agency to delete it. But this is obviously less effective than insisting incorrect information be deleted. See the low-keyed warning step you could use to take the latter step.

Inserting a statement telling your side of the story is usually the best you can do in disputes involving the incompleteness of information, however.

The following sample letter can be adapted for situations in which you want to insert a statement in your file.

300 Witchtree Lane
Anytown, USA 00000

July 15, 19___

Anycity Reporting Bureau
500 Main Street
Anytown, USA 00000

Dear Sir:

Although I still dispute the accuracy and completeness of the following item for reasons I have already described in my letter of (date), since we have been unable to resolve the matter upon your reinvestigation, I request that, as provided by the Fair Credit Reporting Act, the (Anycity Reporting Bureau) insert in my file and report the contents of the following statement describing the disputed accuracy (or completeness) of that item.

[Note: Insert dispute statement at this point. See sample wording following the letter.]

I also request that the following recipients of reports you made be notified that I am disputing the accuracy (completeness) of that item:
[Designate the recipients you want notified.]

I again advise you, however, that continuing to report the item as it now appears in your file fails to assure the maximum possible accuracy of the information furnished about me, and I request that you take further steps to reinvestigate the item to ensure you report only factually complete and accurate information about me to avoid causing me any harm.

Sincerely,

SAMPLE STATEMENT DISPUTING ACCURACY OR COMPLETENESS OF INFORMATION

When you make a statement for inclusion in your file, describe the disputed item and state why you believe the information is inaccurate or incomplete.

The following sample wording can be adapted for this purpose: "As a good faith exercise of my rights under the Consumer Credit Protection Act, I dispute the accuracy (completeness) of the item indicating that (describe the information in the file). This item is inaccurate (incomplete) because (state the reasons)."

See the examples on pages 589–590 for describing the reasons involved.

REQUESTING THE ORIGINAL INFORMATION SOURCE TO CORRECT INFORMATION

The Fair Credit Reporting Act does *not* help you hold the original providers of incorrect information to reporting agencies accountable. One way of trying to straighten out such a situation, though, is simply to request the person or company to correct the mistake.

The following sample letter can be adapted for this purpose. Let me caution you, though: If you are determined to hold such an information source accountable under tort law for libel or slander, you must seek legal advice.

300 Witchtree Lane
Anytown, USA 00000

June 10, 19——

Mr. T. Reporter
Manager
Credit Department
XYZ Company
300 Retail Plaza
Anytown, USA 00000

[Or address letter to company official responsible for handling such matters]

Dear Mr. Reporter:

This is to inform you that I learned on (date) that the (XYZ company) has furnished untrue (incomplete) information to (identify recipient) about the actual status of a transaction involving me. The transaction involves (describe the account, agreement or other transaction).

The (XYZ company) has apparently reported that (describe the information furnished about you with respect to the transaction).

But contrary to the information that was furnished, the (XYZ Company) was and should be fully aware that (describe the actual status of the transaction).

The untrue (incomplete) information you furnished has been communicated to others and has damaged me by (my being turned down for credit by [identify company], [OR describe other adverse action that occurred]) partly as a result of the information you furnished.

I, therefore, request that the (XYZ Company) promptly take the appropriate steps to correct the untrue information by providing the (identify the name and address of agency or business), and all others to whom the information was communicated by you, a statement that fully and accurately reflects the actual status of this matter and doing whatever else is appropriate and necessary to avoid my being further harmed by the information you have furnished.

I hope the (XYZ Company) will promptly take the appropriate corrective actions so as to prevent any further harm to me because of the untrue (incomplete) information it has furnished about me. I am not, however, waiving any rights to hold you liable for damages.

Sincerely,

STAGE TWO: THE LOW-KEYED WARNING

You may have to take tougher follow-up action if a reporting agency still fails, or refuses, to delete information, renotify report recipients, or include your dispute statement in reports it furnishes about you. Sometimes you may not find out about the agency's failure until you are again turned down for a credit, insurance, or employment application.

The following sample letter may be adapted for such situations in which a reporting agency still has failed to reinvestigate and delete incorrect information and/or to renotify report recipients.

300 Witchtree Lane
Anytown, USA 00000

August 15, 19___

Mr. B. Accurate
Manager
Anycity Reporting Bureau
500 Main Street
Anytown, USA 00000

Dear Mr. Accurate:

This is to notify you that the (Anycity Reporting Bureau) is failing to comply with the requirements of the Fair Credit Reporting Act upon having been notified about the disputed accuracy (and completeness) of information in your files (and that your failure to comply has resulted in my being further damaged by the inaccurate [and incomplete] information you have continued to report about me).

I initially notified your agency on (date) during a personal (telephone) interview (and by my letter of [date]) that I disputed the accuracy and completeness of the items I then described. I disputed that information after I was informed that I had been denied credit (insurance/employment) by (identify company) partly because of information in a consumer report furnished by you. ([And] Upon having notified your agency on [date] that I was disputing the accuracy [and completeness] of information in your files, I also requested that you furnish a corrected report [furnish a report containing my statement disputing the accuracy (and completeness) of the information in your file] to [Identify business you wanted renotified].)

But despite my already having notified you, the following item(s) in your file are still inaccurate (and incomplete) for the reasons noted:

(Identify the items. See page 589 for sample wording.)

And contrary to the requirements of the Fair Credit Reporting Act, your agency has failed to reinvestigate so as to confirm that the information is, in fact, inaccurate (and incomplete) as I have stated, and to delete from its files and cease reporting information that is inaccurate or cannot be verified. The agency has instead retained the erroneous information without having verified it or noted its current status. ([And] your agency has failed to furnish a corrected report to the report recipients I designated.)

(And I have been further damaged by your failure to comply since I was again denied credit [insurance/employment] by [identify company] partly because of a consumer report furnished by you [which still

*included the incorrect information] as indicated on the enclosed copy of
the notification I received from that company on [date].)*

*Since your agency has now had more than a reasonable time to inves-
tigate and delete the information that is inaccurate or cannot be verified,
and to note the current status of all information in its file ([and] to furnish a corrected report to the recipients I have already designated), your
agency is now to reinvestigate immediately and delete from its file the
inaccurate information I have described (and to furnish a corrected report
to [identify businesses you want renotified].)*

*You are also promptly to inform me of the results of your investigation
and confirm that you have, in fact, deleted from your file the information
that is inaccurate or cannot be verified, and that you have furnished corrected reports to the recipients I have designated.*

*I now expect that your agency will promptly comply with the require-
ments of the Fair Credit Reporting Act so that I will not have to inform
the Federal Trade Commission of your failure to comply and to seek to
hold you liable for violating the Act.*

Sincerely,

The wording of the sample letter indicates you are willing to have the agency
correct your file and/or renotify report recipients rather than trying to hold the
agency liable for violating the Act as you might already be able to do.

If you tell the agency you are willing to resolve the matter in this way, you may
be unable to hold it accountable for violations later if it does what you request. So if
you are determined to take legal action rather than simply having the information
corrected, seek the advice of an attorney.

If an agency's failure to delete inaccurate information caused you considerable
harm, such as a failure to obtain employment, seek prompt legal advice instead of
trying to handle the matter yourself.

If an agency still fails to comply after you take the low-keyed warning follow-up
step, you could notify the FTC. Although it would not take action on your behalf,
the FTC might do so against the reporting agency. (See page 55 for a sample letter
for notifying the Commission about violations of laws it enforces.)

STAGE THREE: THE ULTIMATUM

If, after a reasonable time, a reporting agency still fails to correct the record, you
could try one last negotiating step—an ultimatum. After that, your only effective
recourse would be legal action. In that case, an agency's continuing refusal to correct
the record should considerably strengthen your position to hold it liable for negligently, if not willfully, failing to comply with the act.

Alternatively, if you suffer further damage, seek legal advice at once to see if you
can hold the agency immediately liable for violating the act. Always do this if the
problem involves employment.

The following sample ultimatum can be adapted to suit your particular circumstances. If you deliver it personally have someone sign your copy; otherwise send it
by certified mail, return receipt requested.

300 Witchtree Lane
Anytown, USA 00000

September 15, 19—

Mr. B. Accurate
Manager
Anycity Reporting Bureau
500 Main Street
Anytown, USA 00000

Dear Mr. Accurate:

This is to notify you that the (Anycity Reporting Bureau) is now in violation of the requirements of the Fair Credit Reporting Act upon having been notified about the disputed accuracy (and completeness) of the information in your files about me (and that your failure to comply has resulted in my being further damaged by the inaccurate [and incomplete] information you have continued to report about me).

When I again reviewed the information in my file on (date) upon your failure to confirm that you had, in fact, deleted the inaccurate items I have already notified you about (upon again being informed that I had been denied credit [insurance] by [identify company] partly because of information in a report furnished by you as indicated on the enclosed copy of the notification I received on (date), I discovered that the following inaccurate (and incomplete) items were still in my file and being reported about me although I have already notified you that the following information was inaccurate (and incomplete) for reasons I previously indicated:

(Describe and state why information was inaccurate or incomplete as per your previous letter. See page 589 for sample wording.)

I have (also) discovered that corrected reports have not been furnished to (identify companies) as I have requested.

I first notified your agency on (date) during a personal (telephone) interview that I disputed the accuracy (and completeness) of the information in your files (for reasons I also described in my letter of [date] [copy enclosed]). I also first requested on (date) that you furnish a corrected report (furnish a report containing my statement disputing the accuracy [completeness] of the information in your file) to (identify businesses you wanted notified).

I have since then repeatedly notified your agency about the inaccurate (and incomplete) information you have about me in your files (and have requested that you furnish a corrected report to the recipients I have designated). I also requested that you inform me of the results of your reinvestigation and that you confirm for me that you have, in fact, as required by the Fair Credit Reporting Act, deleted the disputed items you found to be inaccurate or could not verify, or noted the current status of those items. And I further notified you by my letter of (date) that I had been turned down for credit (insurance) partly because of a consumer report furnished by you which then still contained inaccurate information I had already disputed. I have therefore now been denied credit (insurance) on at least (_____) occasions partly because you have continued to report incorrect and incomplete information about me despite the fact I had notified you I was disputing its completeness and accuracy.

Although your agency has now had more than a reasonable period to investigate and delete the disputed items it found to be inaccurate as I stated or which it could not verify as required by the Fair Credit Reporting Act, it has to date still failed to do so and the inaccurate (and incomplete) information remains in my file and continues to be reported about me to my detriment and harm. (Your agency has also had more than enough time to include in my file and report the dispute statement I filed [and] to furnish a corrected report to the recipients I have designated.)

The continued reporting of the inaccurate and incomplete information ([and] The continued failure to furnish corrected reports as I have requested) and your failure to comply with the Fair Credit Reporting Act, has caused me to be denied credit (insurance) and has further caused me at least great inconvenience, mental distress, anxiety and expense.

To avoid causing me any further harm, inconvenience or expense, the (Anycity Reporting Bureau), is immediately to delete from its files and to cease reporting the inaccurate information I have already described and to furnish a corrected report to (identify businesses you want notified), and to confirm to me it has, in fact, done so.

But if your agency now still fails to do so, I shall seek to hold it liable at least to the fullest extent provided by the Fair Credit Reporting Act for non-compliance with the act, under which you could be liable for my damages, plus my reasonable attorney's fees and costs of legal action, and may be liable for punitive damages for willful noncompliance.

Sincerely,

72 · The Fair Debt Collection Practices Act: Protection Against Abusive, Misleading and Unfair Collection Practices

A collection agency is usually the toughest and most persistent adversary you are likely to face.

Collection agencies make their money by taking a cut—usually 50 percent—of what they collect, so they are rarely interested in hearing why you may not owe or be able to pay an amount. And they have developed to a fine art every strategy that is the least likely to get results, from low-pressure to high-pressure tactics that seemingly try to squeeze blood out of a stone.

Until recently most states lacked effective laws for curbing collection practices. Bill collectors, and many other people, often believed tough tactics were justified because they thought debtors were usually deadbeats who were deliberately out to cheat their creditors and hence didn't deserve any consideration from the law when it came time to pay up.

The fact is, though, that studies have repeatedly shown that very few non-payers are so-called deadbeats. The vast majority of people who use credit fully intend to repay, and the reason for default is usually some unforeseen event such as loss of a job or other income, serious illness, marital problems or divorce, or unexpected expenses and credit overextension. And then there are, of course, the consumers who have a valid legal reason for not owing the money for a purchase—the seller has failed to live up to the contract.

The Fair Debt Collection Practices Act became law in 1978. It is designed to stop the use of abusive, misleading, and unfair collection practices. With this act Congress said, in effect, that people who owe money are entitled to decent treatment from those who are trying to collect. The law also provides consumers with legal weapons so they can fight back when a collection agency uses prohibited tactics.

WHAT DOES THE ACT COVER?

The act applies only to attempts to collect debts arising from consumer transactions, such as buying goods or services on credit, or getting a loan to finance such purchases, not to business or agricultural transactions.

Broadly speaking, the act applies primarily to people operating as debt or bill collectors; that is, people who regularly collect money owed to someone else. It does not apply to creditors such as banks and retailers who collect money for themselves. Nor does it apply to attorneys who may collect bills for their clients. If you are in doubt about whether the act applies, ask yourself if the person trying to collect is the one to whom you owe the money. If not, treat him or her as though the act applies.

WHO CAN A BILL COLLECTOR CONTACT ABOUT A DEBT?

A bill collector's stock-in-trade are the contacts he makes to collect on a debt. This usually means contacting the debtor and used to mean contacting anyone else—such as your employer—who might put pressure on you to pay. But now the act sets important restrictions on who a collector can contact and the conditions under which he may do so. Broadly speaking, the only people a collector can communicate with in any way about collecting a bill are:

- You, the consumer (which includes the consumer's spouse; or parents of a minor, someone's guardian, executor or administrator).
- Your attorney.
- A consumer reporting agency to the extent permitted by law.
- The creditor and his attorney.
- The debt collector's own attorney.

This restriction almost completely limits the collector's contacts to those directly involved with the bill. He can no longer communicate with an "outsider," such as your employer, as a way of putting pressure on you to pay. Nor can he communicate with *you* in a way that provides someone else with the knowledge that you are being contacted about a debt.

There are four exceptions to these restrictions.

1. You specifically permit the collector to contact others.
2. In order to find you, the collector has to contact others and does so as per the conditions of the act. (See below.)
3. A court expressly permits the contact.
4. The contact is made to the extent reasonably necessary to implement a post-judgment judicial remedy, such as a wage garnishment to collect money owed *after* the creditor has obtained a judgment.

REQUIREMENTS WHEN A COLLECTOR TRIES TO LOCATE YOU

The act allows debt collectors to contact others in order to locate you, if necessary. The collector can do so to find out where you live, your phone number, or place of employment, for example.

When trying to get this kind of information, a debt collector must comply with the following requirements:

- He must identify himself alone, and not his employer, and state only that he is confirming or correcting location information about you. He may identify his employer only if he is specifically requested to do so by the person he is contacting.
- He must *not* indicate that you owe money.
- He must *not* communicate by postcard, or, when communicating by mail or telegram, reveal in any way that he is collecting a debt. The envelope and the written communication used may not include the name of the debt collection agency, for instance, or any other symbol or wording indicating that the information is being sought in connection with debt collection.
- Once he learns you are represented by an attorney, if that is the case, he must not communicate with anyone else unless the attorney fails to respond to communications within a reasonable time.

These detailed requirements are intended to prevent collectors from using dodges to communicate information about a debt to others. If someone tells you that a collector has been making inquiries about you, therefore, there is a good chance he has violated the requirements. Find out how the person knows about it, and get copies of any written communications the debt collector has used.

REQUIREMENTS WHEN A COLLECTOR CONTACTS YOU PERSONALLY

A debt collector can make reasonable attempts to communicate with you about a bill, of course, but he may not use the following methods:

• Contact you at an unusual time or place or at any time or place the debt collector should know would be inconvenient to the consumer (such as at a neighbor's house). The hours between 8 A.M. and 9 P.M. local time are considered convenient, unless the debt collector knows to the contrary, such as if you work at night.

• Contact you at all once he learns you are being represented by an attorney, unless the attorney consents to the contact or fails to respond to communications within a reasonable time.

• Contact you at work if he knows, or should know, that such communications are prohibited by your employer. You can make this clear by telling the debt collector that such contacts are inconvenient.

• Contact you by telephone without identifying himself in a meaningful way: anonymous calls are out. Failing to do so is considered abusive conduct.

STOPPING A DEBT COLLECTOR FROM COMMUNICATING FURTHER

The Fair Debt Collection Practices Act provides one very potent legal weapon for getting a debt collector off your back. That is the right to insist he cease further communication with you. This simple step prevents him from using any further non-legal recourse for obtaining payment.

To take this step, you must notify the collector in writing either that you refuse to pay the bill, *or* that he is to stop further communication. Upon *receiving* your notification, the collector must stop all further communication with you except to notify you of the following:

• That further communication will be stopped.

• What could happen if you fail or refuse to pay. But he may only tell you about remedies that would normally be used in the situation; he cannot make idle threats.

• That he or the creditor intends to use a specific remedy, such as initiating a lawsuit.

Once you notify a collector to cease further communications, he can then contact you only ONE MORE TIME to tell you one of these three things.

Remember the act only enables you to prevent further communication about a bill; it does not prevent the debt collector or creditor from taking legal action to obtain payment.

WHAT A DEBT COLLECTOR MUST TELL YOU ABOUT A BILL

Within five days of contacting you about a bill, a debt collector must send you the following information in writing (unless you pay before then):

• The amount of the bill.
• The name of the creditor to whom it is owed.
• What to do if you have any questions about who the money is owed to or dispute

any portion of the debt, and how the debt collector will treat the debt if you fail to dispute it.

The notice must also include statements telling you that:

• The debt collector will assume the bill is a valid debt unless you dispute the matter in writing *within thirty days* of receiving the notice. (But your failure to dispute the bill cannot be taken by a court as evidence that you owe the money.)

• If you notify the debt collector within the 30 day period that you dispute any part of the bill, the debt collector will obtain verification of the debt, or a copy of a judgment that has already been obtained, and send it to you.

• If you make a written request within the thirty-day period, the debt collector will furnish the name and address of the original creditor if it is different from the current creditor, and will cease collection efforts until he has done so.

STOPPING FURTHER COLLECTION ATTEMPTS UNTIL VERIFICATION OF A DISPUTED BILL

If a consumer disputes in writing part or all of the bill within the 30 days after receiving the written notice about the bill, the debt collector must then stop further attempts to collect the disputed portion of the debt until after he obtains and mails to the consumer a verification of the debt or a copy of the judgment that has already been obtained.

If the consumer in writing requests within the 30 day period that the debt collector identify the original creditor, the debt collector must also cease trying to collect the bill until after he obtains and mails that information.

A debt collector can, however, resume trying to collect the bill once he obtains and mails the required information.

The act does not specifically spell out what would count as verification, but generally it would be something like a copy of the bill or agreement involved.

YOUR RIGHT TO SAY HOW PAYMENTS ARE TO BE APPLIED TO MULTIPLE DEBTS

If a collector is collecting for more than one debt, the act entitles you to designate which debts are to be paid out of each payment you make. You should make these arrangements in writing.

If you dispute a debt, a debt collector cannot apply any payments you make to that debt.

RESTRICTIONS ON THE LOCALITY IN WHICH YOU CAN BE SUED BY COLLECTORS

A favorite collection device in the past was to use legal technicalities which made it possible to sue a consumer in a court so far from where he lived that for all practical purposes he lost his chance to state his case. And when a consumer didn't contest a suit, the debt collector obtained a "default judgment" which could be enforced through the local court.

The act now prevents debt collectors from using this trick. Instead, it requires that if a debt collector sues a consumer (assuming the debt collector is the person entitled to bring the suit), the debt collector must file (start) the suit in the judicial district where a consumer lives when the suit is brought or where he signed the contract involved. If real property has been used to secure the debt, the suit must be filed in the judicial district where that property is located.

PROHIBITED COLLECTION TACTICS

The act broadly prohibits debt collectors from using certain types of collection tactics and spells out specific tactics that cannot be used. These are the types of and the specific tactics that are illegal under the new law.

HARASSMENT OR ABUSE

A debt collector cannot engage in any conduct that amounts to harassment, oppression or abuse. This includes at least the following tactics:

- Using, or threatening to use, violence or other criminal means to harm you, your property, or reputation.
- Using obscene or profane language.
- Publishing lists of consumers who supposedly don't pay. A debt collector can make a report about a debt to a consumer credit reporting agency, of course.
- Advertising the sale of debts, which, in effect, is a way of publicizing that someone owes money.
- Repeatedly telephoning you, or engaging you in conversation as a means of annoyance. In the past, for instance, a collector might repeatedly call a consumer's number and let the phone ring a long time.
- Making calls without identifying himself properly.

FALSE OR MISLEADING REPRESENTATIONS

It is now illegal for a debt collector to use any false, misleading, or deceptive representations or practices. In the past such tactics often pressured people into paying. Such illegal practices include the following:

Falsifying Credentials or Status
A debt collector cannot:

. . . Falsely imply he represents, is vouched for, or is affiliated with the United States government or any state government.

. . . Falsely imply that he is an attorney, or that communications are being sent by an attorney such as by using an attorney's letterhead, for instance.

. . . Use any false names. A debt collector may only use the real name of the company, business or organization for whom he is employed. If the name reveals the company is in the debt-collection business, however, it cannot be used on an envelope that is sent to you.

. . . Falsely represent that he operates for or is employed by a consumer reporting agency. This might imply that your credit standing will be damaged if you don't pay. However, many credit bureaus do also operate as debt collecting agencies. In such cases, a collector may indicate that he is operating for or is employed by one.

Making Bogus Claims About the Debt or Your Rights
A debt collector cannot:

. . . Misrepresent the character, amount, or legal status of a debt, or the fees that he can lawfully receive for collecting it. He cannot, for example, claim a debt is secured by collateral if it is not; or that you owe more than the actual amount; or that a lawsuit has been filed; or that he can collect a fee from you when that is not the case. There are situations in which an agreement may have provisions allowing a creditor to charge collection fees, but state consumer credit protection laws and/or courts usually limit such fees to around 15 to 20 percent of the debt. But collection fees cannot simply be tacked on by the creditor or debt collector unless your agreement specifically provides for it and such fees are legal under your state law.

... Falsely represent that a debt has been turned over to another creditor who would be entitled to collect regardless of whether you actually owe the money to the original creditor. This is a dodge that might be used if you have a legally valid reason for not paying the orginal creditor/seller but which may not hold up against a separate creditor who bought the debt from the original creditor. This dodge does not work when you retain the right to raise claims and defenses against anyone trying to collect under the agreement involved.

... Falsely represent that the sale or transfer of a debt to another creditor would result in your losing claims and defenses for non-payment, or being subjected to practices prohibited by the act.

Making Bogus Threats or Claims About What Can or Will Be Done to a Consumer for Non-Payment

A debt collector cannot:

... Threaten to take any action that cannot legally be taken or which he doesn't actually intend to take. He cannot, for example, tell you that your car will be repossessed for non-payment if the debt was not secured by your car in the first place.

... Threaten that you will be arrested or imprisoned for failing to pay a debt. There are, however, situations in which you could be subjected to criminal prosecution—if you give someone a bad check, for instance.

... Falsely imply you have committed a crime.

... Threaten to seize, garnish, attach or sell your property or wages *unless* it would actually be legal to do so and he or the creditor really intends to do it.

... Furnish, or threaten to furnish, credit information to a credit reporting agency when he knows, or should know, the information involved is false. This includes failing to report a debt is in dispute.

Using Misleading Communications

A debt collector cannot:

... Send written communications that look like official documents used by a court, or a federal, state, or local government agency. Nor is he allowed to send any written document that creates a false impression as to its source or authorization.

... Represent that papers sent to you are legal forms, such as a summons, in order to make it seem as though legal action is being taken against you.

... Represent that papers sent to you are *not* legal forms when, in fact, they are.

... Fail to clearly disclose in a communication that he is trying to collect a debt, or that information being sought about you will be used for trying to collect a debt (except that a debt collector *cannot* disclose such information when seeking from others location information about a consumer). If, for example, he contacts you to find out where you work, or where you have a bank account, he must tell you that he is trying to obtain the information in order to help collect the bill.

UNFAIR COLLECTION PRACTICES

The act also prohibits debt collectors from using any unfair or unconscionable practices. This includes at least the following:

- Collecting more than the actual amount of the debt, be it in the form of fees, interest, other charges, or expenses that exceed what is actually owed.
- Using postdated checks as a collection device. The act specifically prohibits a collector from accepting a check that is postdated by more than five days unless he

gives you advance written notice that he intends to deposit it. This notice must be sent at least three, but not more than ten, days *before* he will make the deposit. This gives you a chance to stop payment if you don't have the funds to cover the check. (The act also prohibits a collector from depositing a postdated check *before* the date written.)

In the past, a debt collector might trick a consumer into writing a postdated check, then—if the person lacked the funds to cover it—pressure payment by threatening criminal prosecution. Although a person usually cannot be held criminally liable for not having sufficient funds to cover a *postdated* check, the threat of such prosecution gave the debt collector potent leverage.

The best way to protect yourself is *never* to give a debt collector a postdated check, and never to write a currently dated check without having the funds to cover it.

• Tricking you into incurring charges or fees for communications. A collector might get you to accept a collect telephone call or telegram, for example, by falsely identifying himself or the reason for the call. (See page 602.)

• Taking, or threatening to take, your property when there is no present legal right to do so through an enforceable security interest; when there is no real intention to do so; or when the property is legally exempt from repossession.

• Contacting you about a debt by postcard. This is a ploy to embarrass you by letting others know you owe money.

• Putting on an envelope anything other than the debt collector's address. (The name of the business may be included if it does *not* indicate it is in the debt collection business.) This prevents statements such as "overdue bill inside" from being included.

DEBT COLLECTOR'S LIABILITY FOR VIOLATING THE ACT

The law has not yet succeeded in totally stopping debt collectors from using prohibited practices, of course, as numerous actions by the Federal Trade Commission show. For this reason it is important to take immediate steps to stop a debt collector from using illegal tactics.

If a collector violates *any* provision of the act, you can sue and hold him liable for the *sum* of:

• Any actual damages, which would include any money recoverable as compensation for harm caused by the collector's failure to comply, such as the loss of a job because he harassed you at work, and any expenses that resulted from illegal collection attempts or from mental anguish or distress caused by the collector's conduct. These damages could run into thousands of dollars.

• In the case of an individual suit, additional damages of up to $1,000 as allowed by a court. This would, in effect, be punitive damages you could recover on top of actual damages. In the case of a class action brought on behalf of a group of consumers, a debt collector's additional liability could be up to $500,000 or 1 percent of the collector's net worth—whichever is less.

• The cost of the legal action, plus reasonable attorney's fees.

When awarding damages in an individual suit, the act specifically requires a court to consider the type of violation involved, how frequently and persistently the debt collector failed to comply, and the extent to which the violation was intentional.

Because a debt collector can get off the hook if he can demonstrate that a violation was unintentional and resulted from an error, despite procedures he has to prevent errors, the act may not enable you to hold him accountable for every minor violation that occurs. If it becomes clear that a failure to comply is more than a mere slip-up, it's a different matter, of course. Ignoring important requirements can definitely be costly for a debt collector. The U.S. District Court for the Southern District of Florida, for instance, ordered American Collection Systems, Inc. to pay the maximum $1,000 in extra damages when it found the agency violated the act by contacting the debtor personally when it knew the person was represented by an attorney, then further violated the act by concealing the true purpose of its call when it did finally contact the lawyer.

Your chance to recover reasonable attorney's fees helps make it worthwhile to sue to hold a collector accountable. But you must initiate a lawsuit within one year of the violation.

FEDERAL ENFORCEMENT AGENCIES

The Fair Debt Collection Practices Act is enforced primarily by the Federal Trade Commission. But if a bank or other financial institution is involved and acting as a debt collector under the act, the law would then be enforced by the same federal agencies that enforce the Truth-in-Lending Act against such institutions. (See page 489.)

Although enforcement agencies cannot take action on behalf of individual consumers, it can be worthwhile contacting them about violations since they may take action against the debt collector. The FTC can take action on behalf of many consumers who were damaged by a collection agency's failure to comply. Do not, however, expect to get any immediate help from action the FTC might take.

UNLAWFUL USE OF TELEPHONE

Under laws and regulations enforced by the Federal Communications Commission, it is illegal for someone to make anonymous or repeated calls to harass, annoy, or threaten anyone. Moreover, the tariffs filed by the telephone companies with the FCC (and/or state agencies that regulate them) prohibit the use of a telephone for such purposes. Tariffs spell out the terms and conditions under which telephone service is provided.

So, in addition to liability under the Fair Debt Collection Practices Act, a debt collection agency that uses a telephone for making harassing, abusive or threatening calls may also be liable for violating the laws and regulations enforced by the FCC. It also runs the risk of losing telephone service since a phone company may terminate or suspend service to someone who is in violation of the tariff.

73 · Summary of Negotiating Strategy for Dealing With a Debt Collector

The main aim of a negotiating strategy for dealing with a debt collector is to ward off any pressure he might try to generate by using illegal tactics. This means being prepared to apply immediate counter-pressure to make it clear that you will not tolerate any failure to comply with the act's requirements. Your strategy may not necessarily fit into a neat pattern of low to high-pressure steps in this instance, of course. You have to be prepared to use whatever action is appropriate.

Before embarking on a strategy, you must face one basic question: Do you actually owe the money, or are you prepared to dispute the bill? The answer affects the action you take since the creditor has fewer options and less leverage if you have legal justification for not paying.

DEALING WITH BILLS YOU OWE

If you know you owe the money, it's important not to try to evade the issue by making up a tale of woe to win sympathy, or by nitpicking over legal technicalities. Remember, the Fair Debt Collection Practices Act does not help you get out of paying what you owe, nor does it prevent a debt collector from making reasonable efforts to collect, so using technicalities can easily be self-defeating and result in legal action.

And if you're in default because you're having trouble paying, it's seldom worthwhile to bring up new complaints about the purchase—it will just sound as if you're making excuses. This doesn't mean that you can't still raise a valid legal justification for not paying, of course, but it is very difficult to do so successfully at this stage. In these circumstances, take steps to hold the seller accountable, rather than deal with the debt collector, and always seek legal advice first.

The only thing that really helps if you owe the money is to be straightforward about it and demonstrate that you are willing to make a determined effort to pay. Your initial negotiations, therefore, should be to make arrangements for payment. Always be *realistic* about the schedule you set up. Making rosy promises just to get a debt collector off your back is the surest way to trigger the full collection treatment.

I also caution you at the outset that the steps included for dealing with debt collectors are based primarily on the protection available under the Act for warding off illegal tactics rather than the legal protections available to you when you are in default on debts you owe. If you're in default, creditors can use some nasty collection remedies to collect which can cause you a lot of extra financial hardship.

There are laws that can help you protect yourself when you get into financial trouble. Bankruptcy laws can enable you to get rid of debts, for example; other laws can prevent creditors from appropriating certain assets; and certain procedures must be followed when creditors try to seize property. These protections are beyond the scope of this book, but to be used effectively they almost always require the backup of an attorney or a reliable financial counselor.

So my best advice is, if you suddenly find yourself unable to pay *secured* creditors, who have property you own as collateral, seek immediate legal advice or reliable credit counseling help. When the debts involved are *unsecured,* creditors usually have to sue and get a judgment before they can seize any property. In this kind of situation, therefore, you have more leeway in making payment arrangements. The only practical solution is to find out if the creditor will accept reduced payments. If you try to do this with a secured creditor, it can be very risky unless the creditor agrees to a reduced payment schedule in writing and signs to show the original payment terms have been altered.

GETTING HELP WHEN YOU'RE IN FINANCIAL TROUBLE

Once it's apparent that you are headed for financial trouble, try to face it frankly and quickly before things spin out of control. Are you having trouble meeting regular payment obligations? Are you receiving regular dunning notices? Are you being contacted by debt collectors about bills you owe? These are all sure signs you are in financial trouble.

The best thing to do in such situations is to seek reliable financial counseling and/or legal advice rather than try to use the bankruptcy law on your own, or a wage earner plan available under it to repay creditors on a reduced payment schedule. If you get legal help, make sure your lawyer handles everything. If you get counseling aid, never go to a company that charges a percentage of the payments you make to creditors: some charge as much as 35 percent, which would probably leave you worse off than before. Such debt "counseling" or "management" services are illegal in most states.

Many of our larger cities have non-profit counseling agencies that help consumers with credit problems. Look in your telephone directory under "credit counseling," or similar headings, to see if such services are available in your area. If not, you could call or write the Family Services Association of America, 44 East 23rd Street, New York, New York 10010, to find out if they have a local office where you can obtain such help.

If an agency is really non-profit, a counselor should first review your financial situation to see how you can pay your bills. He or she may then also help you arrange payments that are acceptable to creditors and handle them for you. If the agency is really non-profit, it should provide the initial review free. If it also handles payments, this service should be provided for very little or no charge.

If you are involved in a divorce you may get entangled in debt repayment problems while a settlement is pending. Get it straight with your lawyer how outstanding debts will be handled during this time and what your lawyer will do about creditors or debt collectors who demand payment from you. Anything you do on your own about outstanding debts can cause problems in such a situation, so it's usually best to act only on your lawyer's advice.

DISPUTING BILLS

If you have refused payment and the original seller/creditor has turned the matter over to a debt collector, you should try to terminate any confrontation as quickly as possible. The debt collector is in no position to decide whether you owe the money and you might as well make it clear that you are not going to pay and use the leverage the act makes available to get him off your back. Doing this may provoke legal action, of course, but a court is the proper forum for settling the dispute.

KEEPING RECORDS OF COLLECTION PRACTICES

In any confrontation with a debt collector, always keep records that can help you verify the tactics used, and prove—if necessary—that he failed to comply with the act.

KEEP ALL WRITTEN COMMUNICATIONS

Written communications that don't comply with the act are almost always the best evidence to have. So, once a confrontation starts, keep all letters and notices you receive, including mailing envelopes. Try to get copies of any communications about your debt that have been sent to other people, too.

MAKE A RECORD OF ALL PERSONAL COMMUNICATIONS

Make written notes at the time things happen; this can help you verify what occurred. Note the time and place you were contacted and the name of the collector. Write down as accurately as possible the main points of the conversation. Note the names of any other people present who can verify what happened.

TAPE RECORDING CONVERSATIONS

Telling a debt collector that you are recording the conversation is probably the simplest and most effective way to ward off an abusive verbal confrontation. It is definitely intimidating. But it's best to reserve this tactic for occasions when a debt collector is using dirty tricks on you.

A telephone company's tariff requires the use of a beep tone when conversations are being taped. Failing to do this could result in your service being suspended or terminated.

Under federal law it is not illegal to tape your own phone conversation with someone else; but some ten states require you to obtain the other person's permission first. To check your state's law, call your state attorney general's office.

Make it clear to the debt collector before you start that you are going to tape the conversation. Then when you begin taping, state the date and time of the conversation and say something like: "You are aware that, as I have already told you, I am going to tape record this conversation."

Of course, you could decide to tape a conversation without telling the debt collector in order to catch him in a violation. Only do this if you are willing to risk a run-in with the telephone company about a violation of its tariff for failing to use a beep-tone. But don't do this in the states that require you to obtain the other person's permission to tape the conversation because you could then be liable for violating a law.

USE CERTIFIED MAIL

Sometimes protections available under the act are triggered when the debt collector receives a notice from you. In these cases, always use certified mail, return receipt requested.

The act also includes protections that are triggered when a debt collector knew or should have known something, such as the fact that you are represented by an attorney. While the act does *not* require you to send written notification in these cases, doing so and having a record of receipt will help you hold the collector accountable if necessary.

HANDLING PERSONAL CONFRONTATIONS

Personal contact, whether on the phone or face-to-face, is one of the debt collector's main tools.

However unexpected the contact, always try to remain calm during such a confrontation. Stick to the point at issue, such as whether you owe the money, or the arrangements you can make to pay. At the same time, be prepared to fend off any illegal tactics by insisting the collector conduct himself as the act requires. And no matter how abusive he may get, *never* copy such tactics. In the first place, a debt collector is almost certain to be prepared for whatever abusive tactics you might try, and in the second your leverage comes from the act itself not from any abuse you can heap on him.

A personal contact involves more than just what is being said, of course; it is also a test of strength in which the collector tries to get the upper hand by making you feel vulnerable and helpless. He may make a show of force immediately when you insist he identify himself.

Consumer: "Who are you? What do you want?" (You attempt to challenge him.)

Collector: "Are you a smart aleck, or something?" (He turns the challenge back on you.)

Consumer: "I'm serious and I want to know who you are and what this call is about." (Your opening challenge has been turned into a request.)

Collector: "What's the matter with you? You must be really stupid. You know who I am and what I'm calling about." (The collector now humiliates you for asking a seemingly stupid question.)

Consumer: "Would you tell me anyway." (The challenge becomes more a plea for information.)

Collector: "I'm from the Strongarm Collection Agency. Got it. Are you smart enough to write it down? I'll even spell it for you so you can get it right for your lawyer." (Having cowed you into submission, the debt collector "grants" your request while further humiliating you. And your response to the reference to the lawyer will almost certainly tip him off as to whether you have one or are likely to get one. The way you have handled the confrontation also tips the collector off to the fact that you know little or nothing about your rights under the federal law.)

What you have to be prepared to do, of course, is turn such confrontations back on the debt collector by using your rights under the act.

INSIST ON IDENTIFICATION

As soon as it appears likely that a personal contact is about a bill, immediately insist the person identify himself, his employer, and the purpose of the call. A debt collector may first try contacting you to gather personal or financial information that could later help him collect or pressure payment. The sort of questions he asks would be the tip-off.

So, first ask him to identify himself by saying something like:

"Before we go any further, would you please identify yourself, who you work for, and the purpose of the call." (This way you set the terms under which you will talk.)

If he replies by using cute tactics, immediately say something like:

"I don't discuss such matters with anyone unless I know who I am talking to and the reason for the call." (This kind of answer reinforces the terms you originally set for continuing the conversation and puts the collector in the position of having to *comply* with your request.)

You could then counter any further tactics by saying something like:

"You must know that federal law requires you to identify yourself and the purpose of your call if you are collecting a bill. And unless you now comply with the act, this conversation is over." (This ultimatum means the collector has to comply if he wants to continue the conversation.)

Once the person lets you know he is calling about a bill, don't talk further until you are prepared to write things down. You could say something like:

"In that case, you will have to wait until I am ready to write down what we are going to discuss." (Let him cool his heels until you collect yourself and are really prepared to talk. Don't take forever, but take long enough to get paper and pencil in hand. Making the debt collector wait also lets him know that you are not powerless in this situation.)

Once you are ready, don't proceed until you have accurately written down the relevant identifying information. If the collector tries to brow-beat you, respond by saying something like:

"If you want to talk to me about this, then stick to the point so I can consider what you have to say or this conversation is over. We also aren't going to have much more to talk about if you keep ignoring the Fair Debt Collection Practices Act, and I'll be happy to put it in writing for you so there won't be any misunderstanding about it."

Telling a debt collector to stop calling and bothering you is like throwing water off a duck's back. But if you make it clear you will put the request in writing he will know you know enough about the law to force him to stop communicating with you.

INSIST ON A WRITTEN NOTICE OF A DEBT

If the collector's initial contact is by phone, it automatically puts you at a disadvantage for three reasons. First, whether you owe or dispute the bill, an unexpected contact doesn't give you time to consider what to do. Second, if you do owe the money, it may allow the collector to pressure you into making promises to pay that you are unable to keep. And, third, it doesn't verify that the money is being collected for the right creditor or for the correct amount.

So always end the phone call promptly by insisting the collector first furnish you with a written notice of the debt. Even if it is immediately apparent that you owe the money, make it clear you won't pay until you receive the notice.

Here's how you could request a written notice, and make clear how you will deal with the matter if you owe the money.

"I understand what you are calling about and will discuss it with you further after you send me a written notice of the debt. In the meantime, I will plan how I can arrange to pay. We can discuss these arrangements after I've seen the notice and had a chance to verify the amount. So there isn't much point in discussing the matter further at this time because I won't make payments until I have your written notice."

If the collector persists in trying to get immediate payment, or a commitment as to how you will pay, avoid making rosy promises. Say something like:

"I cannot tell you off-the-cuff how I can deal with this. And I don't know you, or if you are authorized to collect, or if the amount is correct. So if you want to discuss this further and work out an arrangement for dealing with the bill, send me the written notice of the debt and I will then discuss it with you."

You could also ask what kind of payments would be acceptable in order to help you plan.

Being assertive while also demonstrating your willingness to deal with a bill, will almost certainly disarm the debt collector and make it clear to him that brow-beating won't work.

Don't simply use the written-notice requirement as a dodge for putting the debt collector off, though. And *never* play games about whether you have received the notice—that will simply convince him you're trying to avoid payment.

If you know you cannot pay, it may be worthwhile to make it clear immediately, rather than say you will try to arrange payment. A creditor could try to take legal action in a case like this, of course. The best way to handle the situation is to seek help.

If it is clear the debt collector is calling about a bill you don't owe, or have disputed with the seller, get that point over at once by saying something like:

"Before we go any further, based on what you are telling me I want to make it clear that you are trying to collect a bill I don't owe because *(and briefly explain why)*."

If the debt collector persists, cut the conversation short by insisting he furnish the written notice. You could say something like:

"If you insist on pursuing this, then furnish me a written notice of the debt and I'll put in writing why I don't owe the money and that you verify the debt. And I don't expect you to keep trying to collect until this is done."

If he still persists, end the conversation by saying something like:

"I've told you what you will have to do if you insist on pursuing this. And until you comply with the Fair Debt Collection Practices Act, this conversation is over. If you like, I'll even put it in writing for you so there won't be any misunderstandings about it."

If the collector contacts you again before you receive the written notice, immediately make it clear you will dispute the bill in writing. Ask for the particulars of the bill and the name and address where you can send your letter.

74 · Negotiating Strategy for Disputes Involving the Fair Debt Collection Practices Act

This chapter covers the following situations:

- Arranging payment.
- Disputing a bill.
- Stopping a collector from contacting you at work.
- Stopping collection efforts after a lawyer or credit counselor has begun to handle your problems.
- Fending off illegal collection tactics.
- Contacting the telephone company about phone harassment.

STAGE ONE: OPENING SKIRMISHES

ARRANGING PAYMENT

If you and a collector settle on a payment schedule, try to have it confirmed in writing. If the collector is reluctant to do this because it could formalize the arrangement into a binding legal commitment, at least try to firm up the arrangements with a confirming letter. Send it with your initial payment.

The following sample letter can be adapted for this purpose. But remember that it also puts in writing further promises to pay a debt on which you are already in default. So only send the letter if you are very sure you can keep the promises.

> 400 Witchtree Lane
> Anytown, USA 00000
>
> October 15, 19___

> Reliable Collectors, Inc.
> 300 Market Street
> Anytown, USA 00000

> Dear Sir:

> This is to confirm the arrangements I made with (name of person) on (date) for the payment of $_____ which (Reliable Collectors, Inc.) is collecting for (insert name of creditor). (Note: If more than one creditor is involved, identify each one and give the amounts owed.)

> This arrangement calls for me to pay you $_____ by the (date) of each month until the $_____ has been repaid.

> Enclosed is my initial payment by my check number _____ for $_____ . (I request you to apply this amount to the bills you are collecting as indicated below: [identify bills and the amount to be applied to each one].)

> I appreciate your willingness to work out the arrangements we have made. I will assume I have stated them correctly unless I hear otherwise.

> Sincerely,

Cover Note

Send each payment with a short cover note indicating what it is for, and how it is to be applied to multiple bills, if necessary..

400 Witchtree Lane
Anytown, USA 00000
November 15, 19___

Reliable Collectors, Inc.
300 Market Street
Anytown, USA 00000

Dear Sir:

Enclosed is my check number _____ for $_____ as payment on the amount due to (identify creditor). The remaining balance on the account is now $_____ .

(Enclosed is my check number _____ for $_____ as payment on the amounts being collected for the following creditors. I request that you apply payment to those bills as indicated below. After payments are applied, the remaining balances should be as shown. [Identify each creditor, the amount to be applied to each bill, and the balance then remaining.])

Thank you for your cooperation.

Sincerely,

Make a note of the payment on the check. If it is a single payment for more than one bill, you could say: "Payment on bills to be applied as noted in letter of (date)."

When you arrange a payment schedule, a debt collector might ask you to provide postdated checks. He may say something like: "To show your good faith and to make payments easy for you, why don't you give us postdated checks for all the payments we have arranged. Just date each check for when the amount is due, and we will deposit it on that date. That will also save you the trouble and expense of mailing each check."

Never fall for a ruse like this. Refuse immediately by telling the collector something like: "I don't issue checks until my account has enough funds to cover them. And why do you want to go to the extra trouble of having to give me advance written notice before you deposit each check?"

DISPUTING A BILL

If you dispute part or all of a bill, you must do so in writing within thirty days of receiving written notification of the debt.

There are several reasons why you may want to dispute a bill. It may not be your bill in the first place, you may dispute the fact that you owe the money, the bill may be for the wrong amount, and so on.

The following sample letter can be adapted to suit your particular situation. If you are disputing only part of the bill, indicate how you will deal with the part that is due. If you can pay this amount, you could use the "payment-in-full" check approach. See page 397 for wording you can adapt and include in this sample letter.

If you don't owe the money at all—say you received unsolicited merchandise, for instance—adapt and include the wording of the letter on page 73.

400 Witchtree Lane
Anytown, USA 00000

October 15, 19___

Reliable Collectors, Inc.
300 Market Street
Anytown, USA 00000

Dear Sir:

This is to notify you that (at least $____ of) the $____ you are seeking to collect for (insert name of creditor) is not, in fact, due or owing. (This is to notify you I am unaware of owing any amounts to [identify creditor named by collector] you identified as the person to whom I allegedly owed $____ as you claimed.) I was initially contacted about this matter by your letter of (date) (when [name of person who called] contacted me by telephone on [date] and on [date] even though I still have not received your written notice of the debt as required by the Fair Debt Collection Practices Act).

(As I already informed [insert name of person] during our telephone conversation, [at least $____ of] the $____ you are seeking to collect is not, in fact, due or owing for the reasons I have already stated to [insert name of creditor/seller] in my letter of [date]. A copy of the letter is enclosed.)

[ALTERNATIVELY, if there are no previous communications relating to the matter, you could say:

"... is not, in fact, due or owing because this bill is for unsolicited merchandise that was mailed to me in violation of the Postal Reorganization Act which also prohibits attempts to collect," or otherwise describe why the money isn't owing.]"

[Note: If appropriate, indicate at this point that you are sending a "payment-in-full" check, or indicate other arrangements for paying the undisputed portion of the debt. See sample wording at end of this letter.]

You are, therefore, to cease all further attempts to collect the amount not, in fact, due or owing until or unless you obtain and mail to me, as provided by the Fair Debt Collection Practices Act, a written verification of the claimed debt. And as also provided by that act, you are, without fail, to refrain from making any untrue statements about this debt to anyone. [ALTERNATIVELY, if you are seeking to arrange payment for the undisputed portion, adapt the following wording:

"I therefore request that you obtain and mail to me, at the above address, written verification of the entire debt as provided by the Fair Debt Collection Practices Act before you seek to collect any portion of the disputed amount stated above." [OR] "Since the creditor you have identified is unknown to me, I request that you obtain and furnish me at the above address the name and address of the original creditor and that you stop trying to collect until then as provided by the Fair Debt Collection Practices Act."]

I hope this matter is now promptly resolved, and I shall insist on full compliance with the Fair Debt Collection Practices Act.

(I will appreciate your cooperation for making arrangements for the

payment of the undisputed amount and for promptly resolving matters relating to the amounts not due or owing.)

Sincerely,

cc: *ABC Retailer**

*If a debt collector is trying to collect an amount you have already disputed, send a copy of your letter to the seller. See cover letter below.

Alternative Wording for Payment Arrangements

You can adapt as appropriate the following wording for payment arrangements for the undisputed portion of the bill.

> *("I do, however, appreciate the arrangements agreed to by [insert name] on [date] for the repayment of the undisputed $_____ of the bill which now calls for me to pay you $_____ by [date] of each month until the undisputed amount is repaid.) ("As I have already indicated to [insert name] on [date], I will appreciate your cooperation in working out arrangements for the repayment of the $_____ that I do not dispute and am prepared to discuss them with you promptly.")*

If you cannot repay the part you owe immediately, it is important to show that you will make an effort to do so, at least.

If you are using a "payment-in-full" check as a way of settling the disputed amount, make it out to the debt collector *and* the seller/creditor. This way both will be required to endorse the check and you can get the original seller/creditor's signature as confirmation of the settlement.

Cover Letter for Original Seller/Creditor

The following sample letter can be adapted as a cover note for the original seller/creditor when you send him a copy of your letter to the debt collector. Simply indicate your willingness to settle the matter as you had already proposed.

400 Witchtree Lane
Anytown, USA 00000

October 15, 19__

ABC Retailer
100 Main Street
Anytown, USA 00000

Dear Sir:

> *Enclosed is a copy of my letter of October 15, 19__, to (Reliable Collectors, Inc.) regarding the purchase of (identify product) I made from you on (_____), under our agreement of (date), and charged to my (Master Money Card account, account number 000-000000-000).*
>
> *Apparently you are still seeking to collect the $_____ , which is not, in fact, due or owing for the reasons I have already described to you on (date) and in my letter of (date) when I previously tried to resolve this matter.*
>
> *I am still prepared to resolve this matter as I last indicated to you in my letter/memo of (date), a copy of which is enclosed.*
>
> *Please contact me promptly so that we can now finally resolve this matter so that I will not have to contest your claims in court and hold you liable to the fullest extent provided by law for the breaches that have occurred.*

Sincerely,

TERMINATING CONTACTS AT WORK

If a collector tries to contact you at work, it's not only embarrassing—it could threaten your employment.

Whether the contact is made by phone or in person, immediately and firmly make it clear that it is inconvenient and/or prohibited by your employer. Having notified the collector of the fact, say you will treat any further contacts at work as a violation of the Fair Debt Collection Practices Act.

The following sample letter can be used to put your objections on record. You could also make it clear that the debt collector is not to contact you at other inconvenient times and places.

400 Witchtree Lane
Anytown, USA 00000

November 10, 19___

Reliable Collectors, Inc.
300 Market Street
Anytown, USA 00000

Dear Sir:

I am confirming that I informed (insert person's name) during our telephone (personal) contact on (date) at my place of employment, that any communication with me by the (Reliable Collectors, Inc.) and its employees or agents in connection with any attempts to collect a bill is inconvenient to me at my place of employment (and is prohibited by my employer).

Since you are now on notice about these facts, (Reliable Collectors, Inc.) and its employees or agents are without fail to cease all further communications with me at my place of employment as provided by the Fair Debt Collection Practices Act.

Your initial communication has been upsetting (and humiliating) to me (and has resulted in a warning from my employer).

Any further communication with me at my place of employment will now be in violation of the Fair Debt Collection Practices Act and would subject (Reliable Collectors, Inc.) to civil liabilities for which I shall seek to hold it accountable to the fullest extent provided by the act.

Sincerely,

STOPPING COLLECTION EFFORTS AFTER YOU GET A LAWYER OR SEEK COUNSELING HELP

With a few exceptions, the act prohibits a debt collector from contacting you once he knows you are represented by a lawyer. The law is not so specific when a credit counselor is involved. Let's look at the two issues separately.

If you have a lawyer who is handling the debt or dispute, and a debt collector contacts you, do *not* discuss the matter at all. Give him your lawyer's name and tell him that any further contacts are to be with your lawyer alone. Inform your attorney about the contact.

It would be worthwhile to notify the collector in writing that you are represented by a lawyer, but discuss this with your lawyer first. The following sample letter may be adapted for this purpose.

400 Witchtree Lane
Anytown, USA 00000

November 10, 19___

Reliable Collectors, Inc.
300 Market Street
Anytown, USA 00000

Dear Sir:

 This confirms that I informed (person's name) during our telephone conversation of (date) (This is to notify you) that I am represented by an attorney with respect to the debt you are seeking to collect for (identify creditor).
 My attorney is (_____name_____) and his office is at (_____address_____).
 Since you are now on notice I am represented by an attorney, (Reliable Collectors, Inc.) and its employees or agents are, without fail, to cease communicating with me about this debt and to communicate instead only with my attorney as provided by the Fair Debt Collection Practices Act.
 Any further communication with me would now be in violation of the Fair Debt Collection Practices Act and subject the (Reliable Collectors, Inc.) to civil liabilities as provided by that act.

Sincerely,

IF YOUR PROBLEMS ARE BEING HANDLED BY A CREDIT COUNSELOR

If a reliable credit counselor is helping you to arrange payments with your creditors, be sure to find out if he or she will help you deal with further communications from debt collectors. If so, politely but firmly cut off any contacts and refer the collector involved to the agency.

While the FDCP Act does *not* specifically prohibit a collector from continuing to contact you if a credit counseling agency is helping you, it does give you the right to tell a collector to stop all further communications with you. Use this leverage to convince a collector to contact the agency instead.

Remember, though, that a creditor or collection agency does not have to deal with a counselor and could, instead use whatever legal remedies are available to make you pay. A secured creditor could, for example, try to repossess the collateral.

You could say something like:

 "Before we discuss this matter any further, I am telling you that (give the names of the counselor and agency) is handling these matters for me and you are to contact him/her about this bill."

If the debt collector persists or gets nasty, say something like:

 "If you refuse to contact the agency that is helping me arrange payments for my bills, this and any further communications from you are over and I'll be happy to put that in writing for you."

The following sample letter can be adapted to request a collector to contact a counseling agency about bills instead of you.

400 Witchtree Lane
Anytown, USA 00000

November 18, 19___

Reliable Collectors,Inc.
300 Market Street
Anytown, USA 00000

Dear Sir:

This is to confirm that I informed (person's name) during our telephone conversation of (date) that (insert name of counselor and identify counseling agency) is helping me arrange payment of the $____ bill you are seeking to collect for (identify creditor) and for other bills I have.

If you wish to discuss the payment of that bill, please contact the agency that is helping me with my financial situation (and you are, therefore, to cease all further communications with me as provided by the Fair Debt Collection Practices Act).

But if you persist in contacting me about this matter, you will leave me no choice but to insist in writing that you cease all further communications with me as provided by the Fair Debt Collection Practices Act.

Sincerely,

You could insist that the debt collector cease all further communications immediately, as provided by the alternative wording. But unless the counseling agency advises otherwise, it is usually worthwhile to leave open possible lines of communication in case something goes wrong with the way the agency is handling your payments.

And remember that forcing a collector to cease further communications does not stave off legal collection action the creditor or collector could take.

FENDING OFF ILLEGAL COLLECTION TACTICS

You are most likely to encounter illegal collection tactics during personal confrontations. A debt collector might, for example, call you repeatedly on the same evening, or threaten to damage your credit standing unless you pay even though you are disputing the bill.

Whenever you encounter illegal tactics, politely but firmly make it clear that you won't tolerate them. You could say something like:

"Stop right there. You must know the Fair Debt Collection Practices Act prohibits you from calling after 9:00 P.M. (OR) making harassing phone calls which is what you are now doing since this is the third time you have called within three hours" (OR) describe whatever violation occurred. "You are not to repeat such tactics or engage in any others that violate the act, and unless you comply with the act this conversation is over. If you persist in ignoring the act, all further communications will be over as well and I'll be happy to put that in writing for you."

If the debt collector refuses to back off, say something like:

"If you keep persisting, I'll also take legal action to hold you liable for violating the act."

A collector might scoff at this, but you could set him straight by saying something like:

"But I won't have to pay to take you to court, the act enables me to recover my attorney's fees from your agency. So you would have to pay what it costs me to enforce the act, plus my damages, and up to an additional $1,000."

If a collector makes phone calls that violate the telephone company tariff, tell him his tactics could result in the suspension of his telephone service. You could say something like:

"You must know you are making harassing and abusive phone calls that are in violation of the phone company's tariff. And unless you immediately stop using the telephone this way, I shall notify the telephone company and insist they take steps to enforce their tariff which could result in the suspension or termination of your phone service."

The following sample letter can be adapted to your situation and used to warn a debt collector about illegal tactics.

400 Witchtree Lane
Anytown, USA 00000

November 10, 19___

Reliable Collectors, Inc.
300 Market Street
Anytown, USA 00000

Dear Sir:

This is to confirm that I cautioned (insert person's name) and (This is to notify) (Reliable Collectors, Inc.) about its failure to comply with the requirements of the Fair Debt Collection Practices Act when I was contacted by phone on (date) (by your letter of [date] about the bill you are seeking to collect for [_____ identify creditor _____].)

Contrary to the requirements of that act, which prohibits (repeated telephone calls to harass, annoy or abuse consumers [OR] otherwise describe illegal tactics involved), I was contacted by (Reliable Collectors, Inc.) three times by telephone between 6:00 and 8:00 P.M. on (date) [OR] otherwise describe what the debt collector did in violation of the act).

(Reliable Collectors, Inc.) and its employees or agents are immediately to cease this practice and refrain from all other communications or practices that fail to comply with the requirements of the Fair Debt Collection Practices Act.

I therefore expect that (Reliable Collectors, Inc.) and its employees or agents will henceforth comply with the requirements of that act so that I will not have to insist in writing that you cease all further communications with me and take legal action to hold you liable as provided by that act for violations that occur.

Sincerely,

If you have made, or are seeking to make, arrangements for payment, you could insert a paragraph to that effect before the last paragraph of the sample letter. The following sample wording can be adapted for this purpose.

"As I indicated to (insert person's name) during our phone conversation of (date), I could at this time pay $_____ by the (date) of each month until the $_____ bill you are collecting for (insert name of creditor) is paid. And I am, of course, prepared to discuss in a reasonable way any other arrangements we can make for the payment of the bill."

Remember, if you are trying to work out arrangements for paying what you owe, don't simply hide behind the act. If you are in default, do what you can to avoid legal action. Tread a fine line between working out arrangements and making it clear you won't tolerate illegal tactics.

CONTACTING THE TELEPHONE COMPANY ABOUT PHONE HARASSMENT

Your phone book usually tells how you can contact the phone company about calls which are prohibited by its tariff. In the New York City area, for instance, the phone company has established an "Annoyance Call Bureau." If there is no special unit in your area, contact the business office.

If calling the appropriate office fails to produce results, you could adapt and send the following sample letter. Address it to the person responsible for handling such matters.

400 Witchtree Lane
Anytown, USA 00000

December 1, 19___

Telephone Company
200 Main Street
Anytown, USA 00000

Dear Sir:

This is to notify you that (Reliable Collectors, Inc.) is continuing to make abusive, harassing and annoying telephone calls to me at (insert your phone number), in violation of the Fair Debt Collection Practices Act and your tariff, despite the fact that I told the company to cease doing so.

These calls occurred as further described below:
[Describe when the calls were made and what happened.]
I, therefore, request that the telephone company take appropriate steps to ensure that (Reliable Collectors, Inc.) immediately cease using your telephone service in violation of your tariff.
Thank you for your prompt cooperation.

Sincerely,

STAGE TWO: THE LOW-KEYED WARNING

If a debt collection agency persists in violating the act, you could try one more low-keyed warning or use an ultimatum to insist that it cease all further communications. Alternatively, if serious violations are involved, seek legal advice.

The following sample low-keyed warning letter can be adapted to suit your situation.

400 Witchtree Lane
Anytown, USA 00000

December 10, 19___

Mr. Able Strongarm
Manager
Reliable Collectors, Inc.
300 Market Street
Anytown, USA 00000

Dear Mr. Strongarm:

This is to notify you about your agency's continuing failure to comply with the requirements of the Fair Debt Collection Practices Act, despite my having previously cautioned it to do so, while seeking to collect amounts for (identify creditor).

I informed your agency (and confirmed) by my letter of (date) that I was not to be contacted at my place of employment ([OR] otherwise describe what you told the agency to stop doing). [*See Note.]

But contrary to the requirements of the Fair Debt Collection Practices Act, which prohibits you from contacting me at my place of employment upon learning that it is inconvenient to me or prohibited by my employer ([OR] otherwise describe practice prohibited by act), I was (again contacted at work on [date] by [insert person's name] despite my having informed you on [date] that such contacts are inconvenient [and prohibited by my employer] [OR] otherwise describe prohibited practice that occurred).

Reliable Collectors, Inc. is, therefore, immediately to refrain from any further communications or practices that fail to comply with the requirements of the Fair Debt Collection Practices Act.

(And your continuing failure to comply has already caused me [my spouse/family] mental anguish, loss of sleep [or otherwise describe harm caused by illegal tactics] [and has resulted in my sustaining damages of at least $_____ for collect telephone calls I was deceived into accepting].)

(You are, therefore, immediately to pay me at least the $_____ as damages for the collect telephone call on [date] which I was deceived into accepting from you when I was told the call was [describe what you were told which led you to accept call], but I am not hereby waiving any other claims I have for damages.)

If (Reliable Collectors, Inc.) and its employees or agents now still fail to comply with the requirements of the Fair Debt Collection Practices Act, I shall notify the Federal Trade Commission about your failure to comply with the act, and shall insist in writing that you cease all further communications with me as provided by the act, and shall seek to hold you liable for all violations to the fullest extent provided by the act.

Sincerely,

[*Note: If a credit counseling agency is helping you to arrange payments but a debt collector continues to use illegal tactics, you could adapt the following wording: "I informed your agency (and confirmed) by my letter of (date) that (identify person working with you and name of agency) was helping me arrange for the payment of the bill you are seeking to collect for (identify creditor) and for other bills I have. I also requested that you contact him (her) about this matter."

ULTIMATUM TO CEASE FURTHER COMMUNICATIONS

Once it is clear that further communications with a debt collector are likely to be fruitless and subject you to continuing abuse, your last potent weapon is to insist that communications cease. Keep in mind, however, that this is a drastic step—especially if you owe the money. It forces the debt collector (and seller/creditor) to either stop collection efforts, or resort to legal remedies.

If you are forced to take this step to get a debt collector off your back, seek the help of an attorney or credit counselor immediately if you have not already done so.

The following sample letter can be adapted to your situation.

Certified letter #11112222

400 Witchtree Lane
Anytown, USA 00000
December 1, 19__

Mr. Able Strongarm
Manager
Reliable Collectors, Inc.
300 Market Street
Anytown, USA 00000

Dear Mr. Strongarm:

As provided by the Fair Debt Collection Practices Act, (Reliable Col-lectors, Inc.) and its employees or agents are hereby directed to cease all further communications regarding the debt(s) your agency has been seek-ing to collect for (identify creditors), except and only to the extent still authorized by the act upon notification to cease further communications.

If (Reliable Collectors, Inc.) and its employees or agents fail to comply, it could be subject to civil liabilities as provided by the Fair Debt Collec-tion Practices Act and I shall seek to hold you liable to the fullest extent provided by that act.

Sincerely,

ULTIMATUM IF YOU DISPUTE THE BILL

The following sample letter can be adapted to insist the debt collector cease com-municating with you about a bill you dispute. While you could also use the previous sample letter for this purpose, it might be worthwhile to again make it clear that you dispute the amount.

If the debt collector has furnished written "verification" which fails to corroborate that you owe the money, or which merely restates the original seller/creditor's claim, reaffirm your reasons for not owing the amount. The act does not require you to do this, but making it clear that you do not intend to pay what you don't owe, could help you convince the creditor to settle. It could also convince him to initiate legal action, though, so be prepared for such a possibility.

If you are disputing only part of the bill, you're usually better off paying the part you owe before insisting the debt collector cease further communications.

Certified Mail #11112222

400 Witchtree Lane
Anytown, USA 00000

November 15, 19__

Mr. Able Strongarm
Manager
Reliable Collectors, Inc.
300 Market Street
Anytown, USA 00000

Dear Mr. Strongarm:

I am again notifying you that the $_____ you are seeking to collect for (identify creditor) is not, in fact, due or owing for the reasons I already described to you in my letter of (date) which I sent after receiving your written notice of this debt on (date).

You have, in the meantime, failed to furnish written verification of the alleged debt as required by the Fair Debt Collection Practices Act, but have instead communicated with me about payment on two further occasions (dates). (Although you furnished what you alleged to be written verification of the debt by your letter of [date], your communication does not, in fact, confirm that the amount claimed is due or owing despite the reasons I gave that the amount was not, in fact, due or owing.)

Since (Reliable Collectors, Inc.) has instead persisted in seeking payment of amounts not, in fact, due or owing, (Reliable Collectors, Inc.) and its employees or agents are, as provided by the Fair Debt Collection Practices Act, hereby directed to cease all further communications regarding this debt except and only to the extent still permitted by the act upon notification to cease further communications.

(Reliable Collectors, Inc.) is also, without fail, to refrain from making any false statements to anyone about this debt as provided by the Fair Debt Collection Practices Act.

If (Reliable Collectors, Inc.) and its employees or agents fail to comply with that act, I shall seek to hold it liable at least to the fullest extent provided by the act. This could result in liability for any actual damages I sustain as a result, additional damages of up to $1,000, plus my reasonable attorney's fees.

Sincerely,

SECTION VIII
SUING IN SMALL CLAIMS COURT

75 · How to Use a Small Claims Court

Sometimes you have to sue in order to win a dispute. Using the regular court system, though, almost always requires the services of an attorney and can be a costly and time consuming business.

When relatively small amounts are involved, it's much easier to use a small claims court where procedures are speedier and less formal. Designed to make it possible for people to take disputes to court on their own without the help of a lawyer, they have been established in almost every state: the exceptions are Arizona, Delaware, Louisiana, Mississippi, South Carolina, Tennessee, Virginia and West Virginia.

Small claims courts are run in different ways in different states. This chapter describes how they operate in general, and some important points to bear in mind if you sue.

AMOUNTS YOU CAN SUE FOR

Broadly speaking, small claims courts can only be used in order to sue someone for *money,* or damages. You cannot get an injunction against someone, for instance, or take other legal action that could not be satisfied by a monetary award. You may also be unable to sue if you are trying to cancel or rescind a contract, despite the fact that your main aim is to get money refunded.

Each state sets a maximum amount for which you can sue in small claims court. It varies from $150 in Texas to $3,000 in Indiana, but the general range is usually $300 to $800.

If your claim is for somewhat more than the maximum, but you want the convenience of a small claims court, it's a question of swings and roundabouts: often it's best to go ahead and simply forget about collecting the full amount. But always be sure to include everything you could be entitled to recover up to the maximum.

LOCATING YOUR STATE'S SMALL CLAIMS COURT

When it comes to bringing a suit, one of the hardest parts may be finding your local small claims court.

There may be a specific listing in your phone book. But more usually a small claims court is just part of a regular court in an area and, depending on the state, that regular court may be called a district, common pleas, municipal or circuit court. Look in the phone book under government listings for "civil courts," or call the local court office and find out what court handles small claims in your area.

STARTING A SUIT

First, find out how your small claims court operates. This sort of information is usually provided by each court in a brochure or pamphlet. If this service is not available in your area, ask the court personnel for information. Find out what forms you will need to proceed; how and when you will be notified of the court date; when you can expect the trial to be held, and so on.

Make sure initially that you can actually sue the person in small claims court. This could depend on whether the person lives or does business in the judicial district in which you are suing, or whether the transaction occurred in the district. Also make sure you have the correct business name of the company involved. A business that is known as Reliable Electronics may actually operate under a different legal name. You must sue a business in its correct legal name. If you are not sure of the name, look for licenses posted on the premises, such as a sales tax license; these are almost always issued in the legal name. The correct name must also be filed with the public records office. Find out from court officers how to locate this information.

Starting a suit usually involves paying a filing fee, stating your claim, and seeing that notice of the suit is served on the person involved. Serving notice is usually called "service of process." This may be done by the court, by specific officers responsible for the task, or by private process servers. Court officers will tell you how it is done in your state, but make sure it *is* done otherwise you will not be able to proceed. You may have to pay an additional fee for this service. All such court fees are recoverable if you win, but be sure to claim them as part of your suit.

It is possible that if you start a suit your opponent may turn around and counter-sue you for money he claims you owe. Naturally, this is something you should consider before you sue and be prepared to counter.

IF YOU REACH A SETTLEMENT

Once you sue, the other person may be prepared to settle. If you reach a settlement, be sure to put it in writing. Make sure you and your opponent sign it and that you get a copy. You may also have to file a copy with the court.

Find out from court personnel what you should do about the case if you settle before the trial. Don't dismiss it however, until you actually receive the money. If a sizeable amount is involved, you may want to get legal advice before signing—especially if your adversary has a lawyer.

PREPARING YOUR CASE

If, on the other hand, the suit goes ahead, get together all the information that helps you demonstrate why you are entitled to your claim—including documents, records, advertising, and any other kind of evidence. Organize this material so you can use it to demonstrate what happened chronologically: start out by showing what the seller promised or was obligated to do based on the agreement, then show what actually happened and how it resulted in the losses you are trying to recover. Be sure to get important dates right.

If you are going to rely on witnesses—and impartial witnesses count for more than a spouse or other relative—be sure to arrange for them to be free on the trial date. You may be able to get a subpoena, a legal document that orders someone to be in court, to help a friendly witness take time off work. It's rarely worthwhile to force a reluctant witness to appear, though, for obvious reasons.

Rehearse what you are going to say and how you will present your case. Small claims courts rarely devote much time to a case—fifteen or twenty minutes is about average—so make sure your presentation is brief and concise and focuses only on what really matters. Be sure that any witnesses are properly prepared and will also be quick and concise.

Don't assert any facts you are not completely sure about and can't back up. Be prepared for likely arguments your opponent may bring up to counter your claim.

Prepare questions to ask him that will help bring out your side of the case: by this time you will know why he has refused to work out a settlement with you and the reasons he is most likely to give to oppose your claim.

Knowing what you are going to say and how you are going to present the facts helps build confidence. Trying to marshall a case on the spur of the moment, on the other hand, is a recipe for disaster.

HOLDING THE TRIAL

You will, of course, be notified of the trial date by the court. Such trials are never scheduled for a particular time so you have to be there when the court opens and wait until your case is called. Failing to be present at the right moment can hurt your case, especially if your opponent is there.

It is possible for either side to request that a trial date be postponed. Courts may grant postponements requested either before the trial date or at the time the trial is scheduled. Small claims courts are usually reluctant to allow parties to use delaying tactics, though, so postponements are kept to a minimum.

Call the court the day beforehand to make sure the trial is still on. If your adversary requests a postponement at the time of the trial, object and make it clear that you are ready to go ahead and that a postponement will be inconvenient and costly; witnesses will have to take further time off from work, there will be additional expenses, and so on. If a postponement is granted, ask the judge to set the next trial date as final so there won't be any further postponements.

If your adversary does not show up at the time your case is called, be sure to request the court to enter a *default judgment* in your favor. Some judges will do this immediately; others may be willing to give the person a chance to present the case later in the day; and some may postpone the trial. If the judge gives your opponent a chance to show up but he fails to appear at all, again request that a default judgment be entered in your favor. Stress the inconvenience and expense of further delay. If such a judgment is entered, it almost always means you have won your claim. It is still possible for the other person to reopen the case, however.

Trials are conducted in various ways. Cases may be heard by "arbitrators," "referees," or judges. Some judges are more formal than others; some take a more active part in questioning the parties and presenting the case than others. Being there before your case is called can help you get a feel for how things are done and adapt your presentation if necessary.

As a general rule, though, a trial in small claims court is in the nature of a "hearing"; it allows both parties to tell their stories. As the plaintiff, the person suing, you present your side of the issue first. Your adversary may then question you or your witnesses. Your opponent then presents his case and you, in turn, may question him. Judges who take an active role in such trials often do the questioning and get involved in the presentation of the case. You are probably better off letting such a judge do the questioning for you, unless you have some very important questions that he fails to ask. Simply ask the judge when you could ask your questions.

Be straightforward and business-like when presenting your case. Don't get argumentative or nasty toward your adversary. And above all, don't try to tell the judge the law. You might refer to or mention a law that could apply to your situation, especially if you have not referred to it in any correspondence with the seller, but be discreet about how you do it.

THE DECISION

A judge may decide the case at the conclusion of the trial. Usually, though, he will postpone giving his decision and you will be notified of it at some future date. At this time you will receive a written judgment which, if you have won, will spell out how much you are legally entitled to collect.

HOW TO APPEAL OR HAVE THE CASE TRANSFERRED

Depending on the state, a person sued in small claims court usually has two options. He may request that the case be removed from small claims court and "transferred to" a regular court, a request that would be automatically accepted. You would then usually need legal advice to proceed. Or, if the case is tried in small claims court, he might be entitled to appeal the decision to a higher court.

In some states, if a decision can be appealed, the case has to be tried all over again in a higher court—in which case you would also need legal advice. In other states, a decision may only be reviewed by a higher court. Again, you may need legal advice in this situation, but the states that follow this procedure make it harder for a defendant to overturn a small claims court decision.

COLLECTING THE MONEY

Once the time for an appeal has run out (find out from the court how long that would be) you become fully entitled to collect the amount awarded. This can present problems if the losing side doesn't pay, of course.

In this case, your first step would be to demand payment of the amount. State law usually entitles you to collect interest on the amount from the date of the judgment; the rate, set by state law, isn't very high but you can add it to whatever is owed. Once the amount is paid, you should notify the court that the judgment has been "satisfied."

If the amount is not paid, you can ask the court personnel what recourse is available to you. They may, or may not, provide it. This is the point where the small claims court system is least helpful to successful plaintiffs. Normally, your main options for collecting are getting what is called a *writ of attachment* on the property of the defendant, and/or a *writ of garnishment* on liquid assets held for the defendant by someone else, usually a bank. The latter may only enable you to freeze the defendant's assets; you may have to get a writ of attachment to entitle you to get the money out of the person's account.

You would have to get these writs from a court, and they would be served by officials whose job it is to serve them. There are additional fees for the use of these judicial collection remedies, but you could usually recover them from your adversary. Be sure to add them to the amount to be collected.

To use either of these collection remedies, you have to find out what assets the other person has and where they are kept, of course, because they must be specifically identified. There are two ways you might be able to locate this information. If you paid the defendant by check, he would almost certainly have deposited it in a bank where he has an account. His endorsement might even indicate the account number. You can use this information to get a writ of garnishment. If the defendant accepted a bank credit card, you could then use these judicial collection remedies to get money from the bank that holds funds coming to the seller for credit card sales made by the seller. Ask your bank to tell you how you might most easily reach such assets.

If you cannot locate the defendant's assets, it is possible to use court procedures to bring him into court in order to require him to reveal them and their whereabouts. Such hearings would be held in regular court, though, so generally you would need legal help to do this.

If you cannot successfully collect what's owed on your own, it may also be best to get legal advice. In the case of a credit purchase, where the amount due you is in the form of a "credit balance," the defendant could be obligated to return it as spelled out by the Truth in Lending Act (See page 465). If he fails to do so, you could be entitled to sue. This, in turn, could enable you to recover your attorney's fees. This additional leverage may be all it takes to convince the other person to return the money due to you.

I · State Deceptive Sales Practices Laws.

This appendix summarizes the state deceptive sales practices laws which allow the individual to sue for violations. The laws of the following states do *not* authorize individual suits and their laws are not included in this appendix: Arkansas, Iowa, Nevada, New York, North Dakota and Oklahoma.

Each state law is enforced by either your state attorney general's office and/or a special state-wide agency that has been specifically authorized to enforce it. About 20 states also allow enforcement by local officials, usually the county prosecutor or district attorney.

The summary for each state includes:

LAW—this refers either to the official name of the law or its unofficial, descriptive name when the word "statute" is used.

PROHIBITION—this identifies the types of acts or practices prohibited by the law. If the prohibition is described as only "itemized practices," the law then prohibits only the types of practices that have been specifically itemized.

RECOVERABLE AMOUNTS—this identifies various amounts a consumer might be entitled to recover. If there is a separate entry for actual and multiple damages (i.e., double or triple damages), the law allows recovery of actual damages which can then be doubled or tripled at either the court's discretion or if the business willfully or knowingly violated the law. You would not, of course, then be entitled to recover actual damages *plus* multiple damages, but only double or triple the amount awarded as actual damages. If only double or triple damages are referred to, the law automatically entitles the winning consumer to recover that many times the actual damages awarded. The summary also indicates whether a law specifically authorizes the recovery of attorney fees and court costs. The specific conditions under which these costs can actually be recovered varies. Most laws allow it as long as the consumer who sues wins his case. Others allow consumers to recover these costs at the court's discretion or if the business willfully or knowingly violated the law. About half of the state laws allow a business to recover such fees from the consumer either if the business wins or if the court finds that the consumer, in effect, sued simply to harass the business. Such requirements are usually meant to discourage consumers from filing frivolous suits.

SPECIAL FEATURE—this identifies notice requirements and provisions for encouraging settlements that are included in some laws. If a consumer rejected a reasonable offer and sued instead, and the amount finally awarded is close to the reasonable offer made, recovery can be limited to the amount of the original reasonable offer.

The summaries included in this appendix do not cover a number of additional provisions that may be included in your state's law. For example, some states have provisions that govern the sending of unsolicited merchandise, that give consumers a cooling off period to cancel door-to-door sales or that declare that violations of other state consumer protection laws automatically count as a violation of the deceptive sales practices law. Most laws specifically authorize a judge to grant consumers additional appropriate redress. Many laws authorize consumers to seek injunctions or to initiate class actions. Keep in mind, therefore, that your state's law may cover more than is described in these summaries.

The time limit (statute of limitations) for filing suit also varies. A few states set a time limit as short as one or two years from the date the violation occurred or the date you first discovered it. It ordinarily would not be worthwhile doing anything about a violation that you discovered after the time limit unless a lot of money was involved. In this case you should seek legal advice.

ALABAMA

LAW: Deceptive Trade Practices Act
PROHIBITION: False, fraudulent, misleading, deceptive, unconscionable practices with itemized list.
RECOVERABLE AMOUNTS: The greater of actual damages or $100; triple damages; attorney's fees and court costs.
SPECIAL FEATURE: Must give business written notice describing prohibited practice and injury caused at least 15 days before filing suit. If business makes written offer to settle within 15 days after receipt of consumer's notice and consumer rejects settlement which was sufficient compensation, consumer cannot recover additional damages or attorney's fees.

ALASKA

LAW: Unfair Trade Practices and Consumer Protection Act
PROHIBITION: Unconscionable practices and only itemized list.
RECOVERABLE AMOUNTS: The greater of actual damages or $200; triple damages; attorney's fees and court costs.

ARIZONA

LAW: Consumer Fraud Act
PROHIBITION: False, fraudulent, misleading or deceptive practices.
RECOVERABLE AMOUNTS: Actual damages; punitive damages, but right to sue and chance to recover punitive damages based on court decisions rather than the Act. (Leading cases: Sellinger v. Freeway Mobile Homes, Inc. and Parks v. Macro-Dynamics, Inc.) Attorney fees not recoverable.

CALIFORNIA

LAW: Consumer Legal Remedies Act
PROHIBITION: Itemized practices.
AMOUNTS RECOVERABLE: Actual damages; punitive damages; attorney fees.
SPECIAL FEATURE: Require written notice of violation 30 days before filing suit and request appropriate redress.

COLORADO:

LAW: Colorado Consumer Protection Act
PROHIBITION: Itemized practices only, but list does not preclude suit based on unfair trade practices actionable under common law.
RECOVERABLE AMOUNTS: Actual damages; attorney fees and court costs.

CONNECTICUT

LAW: Connecticut Unfair Trade Practices Act
PROHIBITION: Unfair or deceptive practices.
RECOVERABLE AMOUNTS: Actual damages; punitive damages; attorney fees and court costs.

DELAWARE

LAW: Consumer Fraud Statute; Deceptive Trade Practices Statute
PROHIBITION: False, fraudulent, misleading or deceptive practices with itemized list.
RECOVERABLE AMOUNTS: Actual damages under Consumer Fraud Statute; triple damages under Deceptive Trade Practices Statute; attorney fees and court costs. (NOTE: The actual damages recoverable under one statute can be tripled under the other statute to the extent violation involves conduct covered by both statutes.)

DISTRICT OF COLUMBIA

LAW: Consumer Protection Procedures Statute
PROHIBITION: Unconscionable practices and only itemized list.
RECOVERABLE AMOUNTS: Actual damages; triple damages; punitive damages; attorney fees.

FLORIDA

LAW: Florida Deceptive and Unfair Trade Practices Act
PROHIBITION: Unfair or deceptive practices.
RECOVERABLE AMOUNTS: Actual damages; attorney fees and court costs.

GEORGIA

LAW: Fair Business Practices Act of 1975
PROHIBITION: Unfair or deceptive practices with itemized list.
RECOVERABLE AMOUNTS: Actual damages; exemplary (punitive) damages up to three times actual damages; attorney fees and court costs.
SPECIAL FEATURE: Require written notice requesting redress at least 30 days before filing suit. If consumer rejects written offer of settlement, recovery can be limited to amount of a reasonable offer.

HAWAII

LAW: Unfair Trade Practices Statute
PROHIBITION: Unfair or deceptive practices.
AMOUNTS RECOVERABLE: The greater of triple damages or $1,000; attorney fees and court costs.

IDAHO

LAW: Idaho Consumer Protection Act
PROHIBITION: False, misleading or deceptive practices with itemized list.
RECOVERABLE AMOUNTS: The greater of actual damages or $500; punitive damages; attorney fees and court costs.

ILLINOIS

LAW: Consumer Fraud and Deceptive Business Practices Act
PROHIBITION: Unfair or deceptive practices with itemized list.
RECOVERABLE AMOUNTS: Actual damages; attorney fees and court costs.

INDIANA

LAW: Deceptive Practices Statute
PROHIBITION: Itemized practices.
RECOVERABLE AMOUNTS: Actual damages; attorney fees.
SPECIAL FEATURE: Must give written notice of prohibited act.

KANSAS

LAW: Kansas Consumer Protection Act
PROHIBITION: Deceptive, unconscionable practices with itemized list.
RECOVERABLE AMOUNTS: The greater of actual damages or a civil penalty of up to $2,000; attorney fees.

KENTUCKY:

LAW: Kentucky Consumer Protection Act
PROHIBITION: Misleading, deceptive, or unfair practices which is defined to mean unconscionable.
AMOUNTS RECOVERABLE: Actual damages; punitive damages are possible but not specifically authorized; attorney fees and court costs.

LOUISIANA

LAW: Unfair Trade Practices and Consumer Protection Law
PROHIBITION: Unfair or deceptive practices.
AMOUNTS RECOVERABLE: Actual damages; triple damages under limited circumstances (i.e., if practice continued after business was put on notice about violation by enforcing agency); attorney fees and court costs.

MAINE

LAW: Unfair Trade Practices Act
PROHIBITION: Unfair or deceptive practices.
AMOUNTS RECOVERABLE: Actual damages; attorney fees and court costs.

MARYLAND

LAW: Consumer Protection Act
PROHIBITION: Unfair or deceptive practices limited to itemized list which includes any other false or misleading practice.
AMOUNTS RECOVERABLE: Actual damages. Attorney fees not recoverable.

MASSACHUSETTS

LAW: Consumer Protection Act
PROHIBITION: Unfair or deceptive practices.
AMOUNTS RECOVERABLE: The greater of actual damages or $25; at least double but up to triple damages; attorney fees and court costs.
SPECIAL FEATURE: Consumer must mail written demand for redress at least 30 days before filing suit. If consumer rejects written settlement offer, recovery can be limited to the amount of a reasonable offer.

MICHIGAN

LAW: Consumer Protection Act
PROHIBITION: Unconscionable practices and only itemized list.
AMOUNTS RECOVERABLE: Greater of actual damages or $250; attorney fees.

MINNESOTA

LAW: Prevention of Consumer Fraud Act
PROHIBITION: False, fraudulent, misleading, deceptive practices.
RECOVERABLE AMOUNTS: Actual damages; attorney fees and court costs.

MISSISSIPPI

LAW: Mississippi Consumer Protection Act
PROHIBITION: Only itemized practices.
RECOVERABLE AMOUNTS: Actual damages; attorney fees.

MISSOURI

LAW: Missouri Merchandising Practices Statute
PROHIBITION: False, fraudulent, misleading, deceptive practices.
RECOVERABLE AMOUNTS: Actual damages; punitive damages; attorney
fees.

MONTANA

LAW: Unfair Trade Practices and Consumer Protection Act
PROHIBITION: Unfair or deceptive practices.
RECOVERABLE AMOUNTS: Greater of actual damages or $200; triple actual
damages; attorney fees.

NEBRASKA

LAW: Consumer Protection Act
PROHIBITION: Unfair or deceptive practices.
RECOVERABLE AMOUNTS: Actual damages, but if they cannot be accurately
measured by ordinary monetary standards, amount can be increased up to $1,000;
attorney fees and court costs.

NEW HAMPSHIRE

LAW: Unfair Trade Practices and Consumer Protection Statute
PROHIBITION: Unfair or deceptive practices with itemized list.
RECOVERY AMOUNTS: Greater of actual damages or $200; at least double or
up to triple damages; attorney fees and court costs.

NEW JERSEY

LAW: Consumer Fraud Act
PROHIBITION: False, fraudulent, misleading, deceptive, or unconscionable
practices.
RECOVERABLE AMOUNTS: Triple actual damages; attorney fees and court
costs.

NEW MEXICO

LAW: Unfair Practices Act
PROHIBITION: Unfair or deceptive practices which are defined as misleading or
deceptive with itemized list.
RECOVERABLE AMOUNTS: Greater of actual damages or $100; attorney fees
and court costs.

NORTH CAROLINA

LAW: Unfair Trade Practices and Consumer Protection Statute
PROHIBITION: Unfair or deceptive practices.
RECOVERABLE AMOUNTS: Actual damages; triple damages; attorney fees.

OHIO

LAW: Ohio Sales Practices Act
PROHIBITION: Unfair or deceptive, unconscionable practices, with itemized list.
RECOVERABLE AMOUNTS: Actual damages; a minimum of $200 or triple damages; attorney fees.
SPECIAL FEATURE: Act specifically provides consumer either seek to recover damages or rescind (void) contract.

OREGON

LAW: Unfair Trade Practices Statute
PROHIBITION: Unfair or deceptive practices with itemized list, but private suit allowed only for willful use of prohibited practice.
RECOVERABLE AMOUNTS: Greater of actual damages or $200; punitive damages; attorney fees and court costs.

PENNSYLVANIA

LAW: Unfair Trade Practices and Protection Law
PROHIBITION: Only itemized practices.
RECOVERABLE AMOUNTS: Greater of actual damages or $100, triple damages; attorney fees.

RHODE ISLAND

LAW: Deceptive Trade Practices Statute
PROHIBITION: Unfair or deceptive practices with itemized list.
RECOVERABLE AMOUNTS: Greater of actual damages or $200; punitive damages; attorney fees and court costs.

SOUTH CAROLINA

LAW: South Carolina Unfair Trade Practices Act
PROHIBITION: Unfair or deceptive practices.
RECOVERABLE AMOUNTS: Actual damages; triple damages; attorney fees and court costs.

SOUTH DAKOTA

LAW: Deceptive Trade Practices and Consumer Protection Act
PROHIBITION: Deceptive practices with itemized list.
RECOVERABLE AMOUNTS: Actual damages. Attorney fees not recoverable.

TENNESSEE

LAW: Tennessee Consumer Protection Act of 1977
PROHIBITION: Unfair or deceptive practices with itemized list.
RECOVERABLE AMOUNTS: Actual damages; triple damages; attorney fees and court costs.
SPECIAL FEATURE: If consumer rejects written reasonable settlement offer, recovery can be limited to amount of that original offer.

TEXAS

LAW: Deceptive Trade Practices - Consumer Protection Act
PROHIBITION: Misleading or deceptive practices but individual suits are
allowed only for violation itemized practices, unconscionable actions plus any
breach of express or implied warranty.
RECOVERABLE AMOUNTS: Double actual damages awarded for amounts not
exceeding $1,000; triple actual damages awarded for amounts exceeding $1,000;
attorney fees and court costs.

UTAH

LAW: Utah Consumer Sales Practices Act
PROHIBITION: Deceptive, unconscionable practices with itemized list.
RECOVERABLE AMOUNTS: Greater of actual damages or $100; attorney
fees.

VERMONT

LAW: Consumer Fraud Act
PROHIBITION: Unfair or deceptive practices.
RECOVERABLE AMOUNTS: Actual damages; triple damages; attorney fees.

VIRGINIA

LAW: Virginia Consumer Protection Act
PROHIBITION: False, fraudulent, misleading, deceptive practices with itemized
list.
RECOVERABLE AMOUNTS: Greater of actual damages or $100; attorney fees
and court costs.

WASHINGTON

LAW: Consumer Protection Act
PROHIBITION: Unfair or deceptive practices.
RECOVERABLE AMOUNTS: Actual damages; triple damages; attorney fees
and court costs.

WEST VIRGINIA

LAW: General Consumer Protection Statute
PROHIBITION: Unfair or deceptive practices with itemized list.
RECOVERABLE AMOUNTS: Greater of actual damages or $200. Attorney
fees not recoverable.

WISCONSIN

LAW: Unfair Practices Statute
PROHIBITION: Unfair practices, but private action allowed only if someone
engaged in types of practices specifically declared unfair by order of the State
Department of Agriculture.
RECOVERABLE AMOUNTS: Double actual damages awarded; attorney fees
and court costs.

WYOMING

LAW: Wyoming Consumer Protection Act
PROHIBITION: Itemized practices, but suits allowed only for what act refers to

RECOVERABLE AMOUNT: Actual damages. Attorney fees not recoverable.

SPECIAL FEATURE: Consumer must give business written notice describing nature of violation and damages sustained. Business then has 15 days to make written offer to cure violation by adjusting or modifying transaction to meet consumer's reasonable satisfaction generated by unlawful practice or to rescind transaction. Consumer can sue if business fails to offer written cure or fails to cure as promised.

II · Finding the Names of Company Officials or the Names of Businesses.

It can sometimes be important to find the name of specific company officials you may want to contact about a problem and the company's address.

The following directories can help you do this and are available in most libraries. Ask your librarian for other directories that can be helpful.

Standard and Poor's *Register of Corporations, Directors and Executives.*

Moody's *Industrial Manual.*

Dun and Bradstreet's *Million Dollar Directory.*

It is very important to identify the exact legal name of any business you sue since any judgment you win binds only the person you specifically named in your suit.

Generally, there are a number of ways you can identify the exact legal name under which someone is doing business in your state.

One way is by the name which appears on the license a business must have to operate and which is required to be posted on the premises. Such licenses will almost always be issued in the full legal name under which the business can operate.

Another way is by checking with your county clerk's or secretary of state's office. People doing business in the county under an assumed name must register the business's full legal name with the county clerk's office. Out-of-state companies doing business in your state or businesses incorporated in your state must file the legal name with the secretary of state's office.

You would usually find a business's full legal name by first looking up the name under which it identifies itself to the public, or by the name of the owner of the business. The actual legal name of a business operated as Camera Discount Shop, for instance, might be Cameras, Inc.

III · Directory of State-wide Consumer Protection Offices.

This directory lists the names and addresses of state consumer protection agencies that you may contact about a wide range of consumer complaints. Most of the offices listed are part of your state attorney general's office, which is the office that is usually responsible for enforcing many of your state's consumer protection laws.

Keep in mind, however, that other state agencies are usually responsible for enforcing specific business licensing laws or regulating specific types of business. Your city or local county government (such as your local prosecutor's office) may also have consumer protection offices that can help you. An easy way to locate such offices is to look up city or county listings in your phone book to see whether a specific consumer protection office has been established by that government.

If you want to address correspondence to the person in charge, call to find out his or her name first.

The U.S. Office of Consumer Affairs publishes the *Consumer's Resource Handbook* which lists the directors of federal, state and local government consumer protection agencies and corporate consumer contacts. You may obtain a free copy by writing "Handbook," Consumer Information Center, Pueblo, Colorado 81009.

STATE, COUNTY, AND CITY GOVERNMENT CONSUMER PROTECTION OFFICES

Listed below are consumer protection offices which are part of state, county, and city governments. Some are located in governors' offices, state attorney generals' offices, or mayors' offices. Check in your state to see which office can help resolve complaints, furnish information or helpful publications, or provide other services. As a general rule, the first place you should go for help with a consumer problem is the local office nearest your home. Since most offices require that complaints be in writing, you might save time by writing, rather than calling, with your initial complaint.

ALABAMA

Director
Consumer Protection Division
Office of Attorney General
560 South McDonough Street
Montgomery, Alabama 36104
(205) 832-5936
800-392-5658 (Alabama only)

ALASKA

Chief
Consumer Protection Section
Office of Attorney General
1049 West Fifth Avenue, Suite 101
Anchorage, Alaska 99501
(907) 279-0428

ARIZONA

Chief Counsel
Financial Fraud Division
Office of Attorney General
207 State Capitol Building
Phoenix, Arizona 85007
(602) 255-5763 (Fraud only)
800-354-8431 (Arizona only)

ARKANSAS

Director
Consumer Protection Division
Office of Attorney General
Justice Building
Little Rock, Arkansas 72201
(501) 371-2341
800-482-8982 (Arkansas only)

CALIFORNIA

State Office
Director
California Department of Consumer
 Affairs
1020 N Street
Sacramento, California 95814
(916) 445-0660 (Complaint assistance)
(916) 445-1254 (Consumer
 information)

Public Inquiry Unit
Office of Attorney General
555 Capitol Mall, Suite 350
Sacramento, California 95814
800-952-5225 (California only)

COLORADO

Antitrust and Consumer Protection
 Enforcement Section
Office of Attorney General
1525 Sherman Street, 2nd Floor
Denver, Colorado 80203
(303) 866-3611

CONNECTICUT

Commissioner
Department of Consumer Protection
State Office Building
165 Capitol Avenue
Hartford, Connecticut 06115
(203) 566-4999
800-842-2649 (Connecticut only)

Assistant Attorney General
Antitrust/Consumer Protection
Office of Attorney General
30 Trinity Street
Hartford, Connecticut 06115
(203) 566-5374

DELAWARE

Director
Delaware Division of Consumer Affairs
Department of Community Affairs and
 Economic Development
820 North French Street, 4th Floor
Wilmington, Delaware 19801
(302) 571-3250

Deputy-in-Charge
Economic Crime and Consumer Rights
 Division
Department of Justice
820 North French Street
Wilmington, Delaware 19801
(302) 571-3849

DISTRICT OF COLUMBIA

Director
D.C. Office of Consumer Protection
1424 K Street, NW, 2nd Floor
Washington, D.C. 20005
(202) 727-1158

FLORIDA

State Offices
Director
Division of Consumer Services
110 Mayo Building
Tallahassee, Florida 32301
(904) 488-2221
800-342-2176 (Florida only)

Consumer Counsel
Consumer Protection Division
Office of Attorney General
State Capitol
Tallahassee, Florida 32301
(904) 488-3266

GEORGIA

Administrator
Governor's Office of Consumer Affairs
205 Butler Street, S.E., Suite 356
Plaza Level East Tower
Atlanta, Georgia 30334
(404) 656-3790
800-282-4900 (Georgia only)

Attorney for Deceptive Practices
Office of Attorney General
228 State Judicial Building
Atlanta, Georgia 30334
(404) 656-3357

HAWAII

Director
Governor's Office of Consumer
  Protection
250 South King Street
P. O. Box 3767
Honolulu, Hawaii, 96812
(800) 548-2560 (Administrative and
  Legal—Hawaii only)
(800) 548-2540 (Complaints—Hawaii
  only)

IDAHO

Chief
Business Regulation Division
Office of Attorney General
State Capitol
Boise, Idaho 83720
(208) 334-2400

ILLINOIS

Special Assistant to the Governor
Governor's Office of Interagency
  Cooperation
160 North LaSalle Street, Suite 2010
Chicago, Illinois 60601
(312) 743-2773

Assistant Attorney General and Chief
Consumer Protection Division
Office of Attorney General
500 South Second Street
Springfield, Illinois 62706
(217) 782-9011

Chief
Consumer Protection Division
Office of Attorney General
228 North LaSalle, Room 1242
Chicago, Illinois 60601
(312) 793-3580

INDIANA

Director
Consumer Protection Division
Office of Attorney General
219 State House
Indianapolis, Indiana 46204
(317) 232-6330 or 6331
800-382-5516 (Indiana only)

IOWA

Assistant Attorney General in Charge
Consumer Protection Division
Office of Attorney General
1300 East Walnut, 2nd Floor
Des Moines, Iowa 50319
(515) 281-5926

William P. Angrick, II
Iowa Citizens' Aide/Ombudsman
515 East 12th Street
Des Moines, Iowa 50319
(515) 281-3592

KANSAS

Deputy Attorney General and Chief
Consumer Protection and Antitrust
  Division
Office of Attorney General
Kansas Judicial Center, 2nd Floor
Topeka, Kansas 66612
(913) 296-3751
800-432-2310 (Kansas only)

KENTUCKY

Assistant Deputy Attorney General
Consumer Protection Division
Office of Attorney General
209 St. Clair Street
Frankfort, Kentucky 40601
(502) 564-2200
800-432-9257 (Kentucky only)

LOUISIANA

Director
State Office of Consumer Protection
2610A Wooddale Boulevard
P.O. Box 44091, Capitol Station
Baton Rouge, Louisiana 70804
(504) 925-4401
800-272-9868 (Louisiana only)

Chief
Consumer Protection Section
Office of Attorney General
1885 Wooddale Boulevard, Suite 1205
Baton Rouge, Louisiana 70806
(504) 925-4181

MAINE

Assistant Attorney General
Consumer Fraud Division
Office of Attorney General
State House Station No. 6
Augusta, Maine 04333
(207) 289-3716

Deputy Superintendent
Bureau of Consumer Protection
Department of Business Regulation
State House Station No. 35
Augusta, Maine 04333
(207) 289-3731

MARYLAND

Chief
Consumer Protection Division
Office of Attorney General
26 South Calvert Street
Baltimore, Maryland 21202
(301) 659-4300

MASSACHUSETTS

Director
Self-Help Consumer Information Office
Executive Office of Consumer Affairs
John W. McCormack Building
One Ashburton Place, Room 1411
Boston, Massachusetts 02108
(617) 727-7780

Chief
Consumer Protection Division
Department of Attorney General
One Ashburton Place, 19th Floor
Boston, Massachusetts 02108
(617) 727-8400

MICHIGAN

Office of Attorney General
690 Law Building
Lansing, Michigan 48913
(517) 373-0573

Executive Director
Michigan Consumers Council
414 Hollister Building
106 West Allegan Street
Lansing, Michigan 48933
(517) 373-0947
800-292-5680 (Michigan only)

MINNESOTA

Special Assistant Attorney General
Consumer Protection Division
Office of Attorney General
Room 200
117 University Avenue
St. Paul, Minnesota 55155
(612) 296-3353

Director
Governor's Office of Consumer Services
128 Metro Square Building
Seventh and Roberts Streets
St. Paul, Minnesota 55101
(612) 296-4512
(612) 296-2331 (Complaints)

MISSISSIPPI

State Offices
Assistant Attorney General and Chief
Consumer Protection Division
Office of Attorney General
P.O. Box 220
Jackson, Mississippi 39205
(601) 961-4244

MISSOURI

Chief Counsel
Trade Offense Division
Office of Attorney General
Supreme Court Building
P.O. Box 899
Jefferson City, Missouri 65102
(314) 751-2616

Director
Missouri Department of Consumer
  Affairs, Regulation and Licensing
P.O. Box 1157
Jefferson City, Missouri 65102
(314) 751-4996

MONTANA

Manager
Consumer Affairs Unit
Department of Commerce
1424 Ninth Avenue
Helena, Montana 59620
(406) 449-3163

NEBRASKA

Assistant Attorney General
Consumer Protection Division
Department of Justice
605 South 14th Street
Lincoln, Nebraska 68509
(402) 471-2682

NEVADA

Deputy Attorney General
Consumer Affairs Division
Office of Attorney General
State Mail Room Complex
Las Vegas, Nevada 89158
(702) 386-5293

Commissioner
Consumer Affairs Division
Department of Commerce
State Mail Room Complex
Las Vegas, Nevada 89158
(702) 386-5293

NEW HAMPSHIRE

Chief
Consumer Protection and Antitrust
  Division
Office of Attorney General
State House Annex
Concord, New Hampshire 03301
(603) 271-3641

NEW JERSEY

Director
Division of Consumer Affairs
Department of Law and Public Safety
1100 Raymond Boulevard, Room 504
Newark, New Jersey 07102
(201) 648-4010

Executive Director
New Jersey Office of Consumer
Protection
1100 Raymond Boulevard, Room 405
Newark, New Jersey 07102
(201) 648-4019

NEW MEXICO

Director
Consumer and Economic Crime
  Division
Office of Attorney General
P.O. Box 1508
Santa Fe, New Mexico 87503
(505) 982-6916

NEW YORK

Chairperson and Executive Director
New York State Consumer Protection
  Board
99 Washington Avenue
Albany, New York 12210
(518) 474-8583

Assistant Attorney General
Consumer Frauds and Protection
  Bureau
Office of Attorney General
State Capitol
Albany, New York 12224
(518) 474-8686

NORTH CAROLINA

State Offices
Special Deputy Attorney General and
  Chief
Consumer Protection Division
Department of Justice Building
P.O. Box 629
Raleigh, North Carolina 27602
(919) 733-7741

NORTH DAKOTA

Consumer Fraud Division
Office of Attorney General
State Capitol Building
Bismarck, North Dakota 58505
(701) 224-3404
800-472-2600 (North Dakota only)

OHIO

Chief
Consumer Frauds and Crimes Section
Office of Attorney General
30 East Broad Street, 15th Floor
Columbus, Ohio 43215
(614) 466-8831 or 4986
1-800-282-0515 (Ohio only)

OKLAHOMA

Director
Department of Complaints,
  Investigation and Mediation
Oklahoma Corporation Commission
Jim Thorpe Building, Room 680
Oklahoma City, Oklahoma 73105
(405) 521-4113

Administrator
Department of Consumer Credit
B82 Jim Thorpe Building
Oklahoma City, Oklahoma 73105
(405) 521-3653

Assistant Attorney General for
  Consumer Protection
Office of Attorney General
112 State Capitol Building
Oklahoma City, Oklahoma 73105-4894
(405) 521-3921

OREGON

State Offices
Chief Counsel
Consumer Protection and Services
  Division
Department of Justice
500 Pacific Building
520 SW Yamhill Street
Portland, Oregon 97204
(503) 229-5522

PENNSYLVANIA

State Offices
Director
Bureau of Consumer Protection
Office of Attorney General
Strawberry Square-15th Floor
Harrisburg, Pennsylvania 17120
(717) 787-9707

RHODE ISLAND

Special Assistant Attorney General and
  Chief
Consumer Protection Unit
Department of Attorney General
72 Pine Street
Providence, Rhode Island 02903
(401) 277-3163

Executive Director
Rhode Island Consumers' Council
365 Broadway
Providence, Rhode Island 02909
(401) 277-2764

SOUTH CAROLINA

Administrator
Department of Consumer Affairs
600 Columbia Building
P.O. Box 5757
Columbia, South Carolina 29250
(803) 758-2040
800-922-1594 (South Carolina only)

Assistant Attorney General
Consumer Fraud and Antitrust Section
Office of Attorney General
P.O. Box 11549
Columbia, South Carolina 29211
(803) 758-3040

SOUTH DAKOTA

Assistant Attorney General
Division of Consumer Protection
Office of Attorney General
Insurance Building
Pierre, South Dakota 57501
(615) 773-4400
800-592-1865 (South Dakota only)

TENNESSEE

Deputy Attorney General
Antitrust and Consumer Protection
  Division
Office of Attorney General
450 James Robertson Parkway
Nashville, Tennessee 37219
(615) 741-2672

TEXAS

Assistant Attorney General
Consumer Protection and Antitrust
  Division
Office of Attorney General
P.O. Box 12548, Capitol Station
Austin, Texas 78711
(512) 475-3288

UTAH

State Offices
Executive Secretary
Division of Consumer Affairs
Utah State Trade Commission
Department of Business Regulation
330 East Fourth South
Salt Lake City, Utah 84111
(801) 533-6441

Assistant Attorney General for
 Consumer Affairs
Office of Attorney General
124 State Capitol
Salt Lake City, Utah 84114
(801) 533-4262

VERMONT

Assistant Attorney General and Chief
 Consumer Protection Division
Office of Attorney General
109 State Street
Montpelier, Vermont 05602
(802) 828-3171
800-642-5149 (Vermont only)

VIRGINIA

State Offices
Assistant Attorney General
Division of Consumer Counsel
Office of Attorney General
11 South 12th Street, Suite 308
Richmond, Virginia 23219
(804) 786-4075

WASHINGTON

Assistant Attorney General and Chief
Consumer Protection and Antitrust
 Division
Office of Attorney General
1366 Dexter Horton Building
Seattle, Washington 98104
(206) 464-7744
800-552-0700 (Washington only)

WEST VIRGINIA

State Offices
Director
Consumer Protection Division
Office of Attorney General
1204 Kanawha Boulevard East
Charleston, West Virginia 25301
(304) 348-8986

WISCONSIN

State Offices
Assistant Attorney General
Office of Consumer Protection
Department of Justice
P.O. Box 7856
Madison, Wisconsin 53707-7856
(608) 266-1852

Division of Trade and Consumer
 Protection
Department of Agriculture, Trade, and
 Consumer Protection
P.O. Box 8911
801 West Badger Road
Madison, Wisconsin 53708
(608) 266-9837
800-362-3020 (Wisconsin only)

WYOMING

State Office
Assistant Attorney General
Office of Attorney General
123 Capitol Building
Cheyenne, Wyoming 82002
(307) 777-7841 or 6286

PUERTO RICO

Department of Consumer Affairs
Minillas Governmental Center
Torre Norte Building
De Diego Avenue, Stop 22
P.O. Box 41059
Santurce, Puerto Rico 00940
(809) 726-6090

VIRGIN ISLANDS

Director
Consumer Service Administration
Golden Rock
Christiansted, St. Croix
U.S. Virgin Islands, 00820
(809) 773-2226

IV · Sample Forms for Credit Transactions Prepared by the Federal Reserve Board.

Installment Loan Sample

Friendly Bank & Trust Co.

700 East Street

Little Creek, USA

Lisa Stone
22-4859-22
300 Maple Avenue
Little Creek, USA

ANNUAL PERCENTAGE RATE	FINANCE CHARGE	Amount Financed	Total of Payments
The cost of your credit as a yearly rate.	The dollar amount the credit will cost you.	The amount of credit provided to you or on your behalf.	The amount you will have paid after you have made all payments as scheduled.
12 %	$ 675.31	$ 5000 –	$ 5675.31

You have the right to receive at this time an itemization of the Amount Financed.

☐ I want an itemization.   ☐ I do not want an itemization.

Your payment schedule will be:

Number of Payments	Amount of Payments	When Payments Are Due
1	$262.03 e	6/1/81
23	$235.36	Monthly beginning 7/1/81

Late Charge: If a payment is late, you will be charged $5 or 10% of the payment, whichever is less.

Prepayment: If you pay off early, you ☒ may   ☐ will not   have to pay a penalty.

Required Deposit: The annual percentage rate does not take into account your required deposit.

See your contract documents for any additional information about nonpayment, default, any required repayment in full before the scheduled date, and prepayment refunds and penalties.

––––––––––

e means an estimate

Refinancing Sample

Everyone's Credit Union

Date: *April 1, 1981*

ANNUAL PERCENTAGE RATE The cost of your credit as a yearly rate.	FINANCE CHARGE The dollar amount the credit will cost you.	Amount Financed The amount of credit provided to you or on your behalf.	Total of Payments The amount you will have paid after you have made all payments as scheduled.
15 %	$1285.06	$5177.73	$6462.79

Your payment schedule will be:

Number of Payments	Amount of Payments	When Payments Are Due
35	$179.53	Monthly starting 5-1-81
1	$179.24	4-1-84

Insurance

Credit life insurance and credit disability insurance are not required to obtain credit, and will not be provided unless you sign and agree to pay the additional cost.

Type	Premium	Signature
Credit Life		I want credit life insurance. _____ Signature
Credit Disability	$177.73	I want credit disability insurance. *Joseph Day* Signature

Security: You are giving a security interest in: ☐ the goods or property being purchased.   ☒ your automobile.

Late Charge: If a payment is late, you will be charged 20% of the interest due with a minimum charge of $.05.

Prepayment: If you pay off early, you will not have to pay a penalty.

See your contract documents for any additional information about nonpayment, default, any required repayment in full before the scheduled date, and prepayment refunds and penalties.

_____
e means an estimate

Itemization of the Amount Financed of $ _5177.73_

$ _1000 –_   Amount given to you directly
$ _3000 –_   Amount paid on your account

Amount paid to others on your behalf
$ _____   to public officials
$ _500 –_   to Coop Credit Union
$ _500_   to Acme Finance Co.
$ _177.73_   to Pan-Galactic Ins. Co.
$ _____   for credit report

$ _____   Prepaid finance charge

Credit Sale Sample

Big Wheel Auto   Alice Green

ANNUAL PERCENTAGE RATE	FINANCE CHARGE	Amount Financed	Total of Payments	Total Sale Price
The cost of your credit as a yearly rate.	The dollar amount the credit will cost you.	The amount of credit provided to you or on your behalf.	The amount you will have paid after you have made all payments as scheduled.	The total cost of your purchase on credit, including your downpayment of $ *1500 –*
14.84 %	$1496.80	$6107.50	$7604.30	$9129.30

You have the right to receive at this time an itemization of the Amount Financed.

☐ I want an itemization.   ☒ I do not want an itemization.

Your payment schedule will be:

Number of Payments	Amount of Payments	When Payments Are Due
36	$211.23	Monthly beginning 6-1-81

Insurance

Credit life insurance and credit disability insurance are not required to obtain credit, and will not be provided unless you sign and agree to pay the additional cost.

Type	Premium	Signature
Credit Life	$120 –	I want credit life insurance. *alice Green* ____ Signature
Credit Disability		I want credit disability insurance. ____ Signature
Credit Life and Disability		I want credit life and disability insurance. ____ Signature

Security: You are giving a security interest in:

☒ the goods being purchased.

☐ _____.

Filing fees $ 12.50   Non-filing insurance $ _____

Late Charge: If a payment is late, you will be charged $10.

Prepayment: If you pay off early, you

☒ may   ☐ will not   have to pay a penalty.

☒ may   ☐ will not   be entitled to a refund of part of the finance charge.

See your contract documents for any additional information about nonpayment, default, any required repayment in full before the scheduled date, and prepayment refunds and penalties.

I have received a copy of this statement.

alice Green _____   5-1-81 _____
Signature   Date

e means an estimate

[Closed end, unsecured/secured credit]

CREDIT APPLICATION

IMPORTANT: Read these Directions before completing this Application.

Check Appropriate Box

☐ If you are applying for individual credit in your own name and are relying on your own income or assets and not the income or assets of another person as the basis for repayment of the credit requested, complete only Sections A and D. If the requested credit is to be secured, also complete the first part of Section C and Section E.

☐ If you are applying for joint credit with another person, complete all Sections except E, providing information in B about the joint applicant. If the requested credit is to be secured, then complete Section E.

☐ If you are applying for individual credit, but are relying on income from alimony, child support, or separate maintenance or on the income or assets of another person as the basis for repayment of the credit requested, complete all Sections except E to the extent possible, providing information in B about the person on whose alimony, support, or maintenance payments or income or assets you are relying. If the requested credit is to be secured, then complete Section E.

Amount Requested   Payment Date Desired   Proceeds of Credit

$...................................   ....   To be Used For ....

SECTION A—INFORMATION REGARDING APPLICANT

Full Name (Last, First, Middle): ....   Birthdate: / /

Present Street Address: ....   Years there: ....

City: .... State: .... Zip: .... Telephone: ....

Social Security No.: .... Driver's License No.: ....

Previous Street Address: ....   Years there: ....

City: .... State: .... Zip: ....

Present Employer: .... Years there: .... Telephone: ....

Position or title: .... Name of supervisor: ....

Employer's Address: ....

Previous Employer: ....   Years there: ....

Previous Employer's Address: ....

Present net salary or commission: $............. per .... No. Dependents: .... Ages: ....

Alimony, child support, or separate maintenance income need not be revealed if you do not wish to have it considered as a basis for repaying this obligation.

Alimony, child support, separate maintenance received under: court order ☐ written agreement ☐ oral understanding ☐

Other income: $............... per .... Source(s) of other income: ....

Is any income listed in this Section likely to be reduced before the credit requested is paid off?

☐ Yes (Explain in detail on separate sheet.)   ☐ No

Have you ever received credit from us? .... When? .... Office ....

Checking Account No.: .... Institution and Branch: ....

Savings Account No.: .... Institution and Branch: ....

Name of nearest relative not living with you: .... Telephone: ....

Relationship: .... Address: ....

SECTION B—INFORMATION REGARDING JOINT APPLICANT OR OTHER PARTY (Use separate sheets if necessary.)

Full Name (Last, First, Middle): ....   Birthdate: / /

Relationship to Applicant (if any): ....

Present Street Address: ....   Years there: ....

City: .... State: .... Zip: .... Telephone: ....

Social Security No.: .... Driver's License No.: ....

Present Employer: .... Years there: .... Telephone: ....

Position or title: .... Name of supervisor: ....

Employer's Address: ....

Previous Employer: ....   Years there: ....

Previous Employer's Address: ....

Present net salary or commission: $............. per .... No. Dependents: .... Ages: ....

Alimony, child support, or separate maintenance income need not be revealed if you do not wish to have it considered as a basis for repaying this obligation.

Alimony, child support, separate maintenance received under: court order ☐ written agreement ☐ oral understanding ☐

Other income: $............... per .... Source(s) of other income: ....

Is any income listed in this Section likely to be reduced before the credit requested is paid off?

☐ Yes (Explain in detail on separate sheet.)   ☐ No

Checking Account No.: .... Institution and Branch: ....

Savings Account No.: .... Institution and Branch: ....

Name of nearest relative not living with Joint Applicant or Other Party: .... Telephone: ....

Relationship: .... Address: ....

SECTION C—MARITAL STATUS
(Do not complete if this is an application for individual unsecured credit.)
Applicant: ☐ Married ☐ Separated ☐ Unmarried (including single, divorced, and widowed)
Other Party: ☐ Married ☐ Separated ☐ Unmarried (including single, divorced, and widowed)

SECTION D—ASSET AND DEBT INFORMATION (If Section B has been completed, this Section should be completed giving information about both the Applicant and Joint Applicant or Other Person. Please mark Applicant-related information with an "A." If Section B was not completed, only give information about the Applicant in this Section.)

ASSETS OWNED (Use separate sheet if necessary.)

Description of Assets	Value	Subject to Debt? Yes/No	Name(s) of Owner(s)
Cash	$		
Automobiles (Make, Model, Year)			
Cash Value of Life Insurance (Issuer, Face Value)			
Real Estate (Location, Date Acquired)			
Marketable Securities (Issuer, Type, No. of Shares)			
Other (List)			
Total Assets	$		

OUTSTANDING DEBTS (Include charge accounts, instalment contracts, credit cards, rent, mortgages, etc. Use separate sheet if necessary.)

Creditor	Type of Debt or Acct. No.	Name in Which Acct. Carried	Original Debt	Present Balance	Monthly Payments	Past Due? Yes/No
1. (Landlord or Mortgage Holder)	☐ Rent Payment ☐ Mortgage		$ (Omit rent)	$ (Omit rent)	$	
2.						
3.						
Total Debts			$	$	$	

(Credit References)

		Date Paid
1.	$	
2.		

Are you a co-maker, endorser, or guarantor on any loan or contract?	Yes ☐ No ☐	If "Yes," for whom?	To whom?
Are there any unsatisfied judgments against you?	Yes ☐ No ☐	Amount $	If "Yes," to whom owed?
Have you been declared bankrupt in the last 14 years?	Yes ☐ No ☐	If "Yes," where?	Year

Other obligations—(E.g., liability to pay alimony, child support, separate maintenance. Use separate sheet if necessary.)

SECTION E—SECURED CREDIT (Complete only if credit is to be secured.) Briefly describe the property to be given as security:
....
....

and list names and addresses of all co-owners of the property:

Name	Address
....	....

If the security is real estate, give the full name of your spouse (if any): ....

Everything that I have stated in this application is correct to the best of my knowledge. I understand that you will retain this application whether or not it is approved. You are authorized to check my credit and employment history and to answer questions about your credit experience with me.

Applicant's Signature	Date	Other Signature (Where Applicable)	Date

Mortgage with Demand Feature Sample

Mortgage Savings and Loan Assoc.

Date: April 15, 1981

Glenn Jones
700 Oak Drive
Little Creek, USA

ANNUAL PERCENTAGE RATE The cost of your credit as a yearly rate.	FINANCE CHARGE The dollar amount the credit will cost you.	Amount Financed The amount of credit provided to you or on your behalf.	Total of Payments The amount you will have paid after you have made all payments as scheduled.
14.85 %	$156,551.54	$44,605.66	$201,157.20

Your payment schedule will be:

Number of Payments	Amount of Payments	When Payments Are Due
360	$558.77	Monthly beginning 6/1/81

This obligation has a demand feature.

You may obtain property insurance from anyone you want that is acceptable to Mortgage Savings and Loan Assoc.. If you get the insurance from Mortgage Savings and Loan Assoc. you will pay $ 150 / year

Security: You are giving a security interest in:

☒ the goods or property being purchased.

☐ _____ .

Late Charge: If a payment is late, you will be charged $ ___NA___ / __5__ % of the payment.

Prepayment: If you pay off early, you may have to pay a penalty.

Assumption: Someone buying your house may, subject to conditions, be allowed to assume the remainder of the mortgage on the original terms.

See your contract documents for any additional information about nonpayment, default, any required repayment in full before the scheduled date, and prepayment refunds and penalties.

---

e means an estimate

Index

WITHDRAWAL